Wow! 1001 Homemade Ground Beef Recipes

(Wow! 1001 Homemade Ground Beef Recipes - Volume 1)

Susan Morris

Content

CHAPTER 3: GROUND BEEF LASAGNA

CHAPTER 4: GROUND BEEF MEATBALL RECIPES 175

CHAPTER 5: GROUND BEEF SLOPPY JOE RECIPES 251

CHAPTER 6: GROUND BEEF DINNER RECIPES..277

11

Chapter 1: Ground Beef Taco Recipes

***

1. Beef & Bean Tacos

Serving: 6 servings. | Prep: 15mins | Cook: 10mins | Ready in:

Ingredients

- 1 pound ground beef
- 1 can (15 ounces) pinto beans, rinsed and drained
- 1 can (14-1/2 ounces) diced tomatoes, undrained
- 1 can (11 ounces) Mexicorn, drained
- 1 can (10-3/4 ounces) condensed nacho cheese soup, undiluted
- 1/4 cup water
- 2 teaspoons chili powder
- 12 taco shells, warmed
- Optional toppings: chopped sweet red pepper, thinly sliced green onions and shredded cheddar cheese

Direction

- Cook beef in a large skillet on medium heat until no longer pink; drain. Stir in the Mexicorn, tomatoes, beans, chili powder, water and soup. Heat to boiling. Lower the heat; and simmer without a cover for 5 minutes.
- Spoon beef mixture into taco shells; serve with optional toppings.

Nutrition Information

- Calories: 407 calories

- Protein: 22g protein.
- Total Fat: 18g fat (6g saturated fat)
- Sodium: 983mg sodium
- Fiber: 6g fiber)
- Total Carbohydrate: 38g carbohydrate (4g sugars
- Cholesterol: 53mg cholesterol

2. Biscuit Topped Taco Casserole

Serving: 6 servings. | Prep: 15mins | Cook: 20mins | Ready in:

Ingredients

- 3 cups leftover taco-seasoned ground beef
- 1 can (16 ounces) kidney beans, rinsed and drained
- 1 cup shredded Monterey Jack cheese
- 2 large eggs, lightly beaten
- 1 cup whole milk
- 1-1/2 cups biscuit/baking mix
- 1 cup (8 ounces) sour cream
- 2 cups shredded lettuce
- 1 medium tomato, diced
- 1 can (2-1/4 ounces) sliced ripe olives, drained

Direction

- Mix beans and taco meat in a big bowl; scoop into a greased 8-in. square baking dish. Drizzle with cheese.
- Mix biscuit mix, milk and eggs in a separate bowl till becoming moistened. Add on top of cheese.
- Bake, while uncovered, at 400 degrees for 20 to 25 minutes or till lightly browned and a knife inserted in the middle comes out clean. Spread along with sour cream. Add olives, tomato, and lettuce on top.

Nutrition Information

- Calories: 611 calories
- Total Carbohydrate: 44g carbohydrate (7g sugars
- Cholesterol: 174mg cholesterol
- Protein: 37g protein.
- Total Fat: 31g fat (15g saturated fat)
- Sodium: 1657mg sodium
- Fiber: 5g fiber)

3. Colorful Tacos

Serving: 10 tacos. | Prep: 20mins | Cook: 15mins |Ready in:

Ingredients

- 1 pound lean ground beef
- 10 flour tortillas (8 inches)
- Seasoned salt
- 4 cups shredded process cheese (Velveeta)
- 1 cup shredded radishes
- 1 large onion, finely chopped
- 1 can (15 ounces) peas, drained and mashed
- 1 can (14-1/2 ounces) diced tomatoes, drained
- Hot pepper sauce to taste

Direction

- Spread beef over half of each tortillas; sprinkle seasoned salt over. Fold the tortillas over the meat; press to seal. Brown tortillas in a greased 10-in. skillet till the meat is not pink anymore, or for 2-3 minutes per side, working in batches. Unfold the tortillas. Arrange tomatoes, peas, onion, radishes and cheese on top; fold up. Serve accompanied with hot pepper sauce.

Nutrition Information

- Calories: 403 calories
- Fiber: 2g fiber)
- Total Carbohydrate: 36g carbohydrate (7g sugars

- Cholesterol: 57mg cholesterol
- Protein: 24g protein.
- Total Fat: 18g fat (9g saturated fat)
- Sodium: 969mg sodium

4. Corny Tacos

Serving: 20 tacos. | Prep: 15mins | Cook: 30mins |Ready in:

Ingredients

- 2 pounds ground beef
- 1 can (8-1/4 ounces) cream-style corn
- 1 can (8 ounces) tomato sauce
- 1 cup milk
- 1 can (6 ounces) ripe olives, drained and chopped
- 1/3 cup cornmeal
- 1/4 teaspoon salt
- Chili powder to taste
- 20 taco shells
- Toppings: shredded cheddar cheese, shredded lettuce, chopped tomatoes

Direction

- Place a large skillet on medium heat; cook in beef till not pink anymore; strain. Put in chili powder, salt, cornmeal, olives, milk, tomato sauce and corn. Remove into an 11x7-in. baking dish coated with grease.
- Bake without a cover at 350° till heated through, or for 30 minutes. In each taco shell, spoon around 1/4 cupful. Serve with any topping of your choice.

Nutrition Information

- Calories: 158 calories
- Sodium: 271mg sodium
- Fiber: 1g fiber)
- Total Carbohydrate: 12g carbohydrate (1g sugars

- Cholesterol: 24mg cholesterol
- Protein: 10g protein.
- Total Fat: 8g fat (3g saturated fat)

---

5. Crispy Beef Tostadas

Serving: 6 servings. | Prep: 35mins | Cook: 20mins | Ready in:

Ingredients

- 3 cups all-purpose flour
- 5 teaspoons baking powder
- 1-1/4 cups milk
- 1 pound ground beef
- 2 garlic cloves, minced
- 1 can (4 ounces) chopped green chilies
- 1 envelope taco seasoning
- 3/4 cup water
- 1 can (16 ounces) refried beans
- Oil for deep-fat frying
- Picante sauce
- Shredded lettuce
- Finely chopped green onions
- Chopped tomatoes
- Shredded cheddar cheese

Direction

- Mix baking powder and flour in a large bowl; put in milk till a soft dough forms. Allow to rest, covered, 1 hour.
- Place a large skillet on medium heat around 30 minutes before serving; cook in beef till not pink anymore; strain. Mix in water, taco seasoning, chilies and garlic; simmer for 10 minutes. Mix in beans; heat through; keep warm.
- Separate the dough into sixths. Roll each portion, on a lightly floured work surface, into a 7-in. circle. Preheat oil in a deep-fat fryer to 375°. Fry tostadas till golden in hot oil, turning once; strain on paper towels. Place tomatoes, onions, lettuce, picante sauce as well as the meat mixture and cheese on top of each.

Nutrition Information

- Calories:
- Sodium:
- Fiber:
- Total Carbohydrate:
- Cholesterol:
- Protein:
- Total Fat:

---

6. Crispy Fried Tacos

Serving: 12 tacos. | Prep: 10mins | Cook: 25mins | Ready in:

Ingredients

- SALSA:
- 1 can (28 ounces) diced tomatoes, undrained
- 1 can (8 ounces) tomato sauce
- 1 can (4 ounces) sliced jalapeno peppers
- 1 small onion, quartered
- 1 teaspoon garlic salt
- TACOS:
- 1 pound ground beef
- 1/2 teaspoon salt
- 12 corn tortillas (6 inches)
- 1/2 cup canola oil
- 1 cup shredded cheddar cheese
- 4 cups shredded lettuce

Direction

- Mix the salsa ingredients together in a blender; pulse with a cover till the salsa attains your desired consistency. Remove into a large bowl; refrigerate with a cover.
- Place a large skillet on medium heat; cook beef till not pink anymore; strain. Sprinkle salt on the meat. Meanwhile, heat oil in another large skillet; fry in tortillas till just crisp, working in batches; strain on paper towels.

- Fill the beef into the tortillas; sprinkle cheese over. Fold in half. Serve accompanied with salsa and lettuce.

Nutrition Information

- Calories: 257 calories
- Total Carbohydrate: 18g carbohydrate (3g sugars
- Cholesterol: 29mg cholesterol
- Protein: 11g protein.
- Total Fat: 16g fat (5g saturated fat)
- Sodium: 546mg sodium
- Fiber: 3g fiber)

7. Deep Dish Beef 'n' Bean Taco Pizza

Serving: 8 servings. | Prep: 15mins | Cook: 15mins | Ready in:

Ingredients

- 3 cups all-purpose flour
- 1/2 cup cornmeal
- 1 teaspoon salt
- 1 package (1/4 ounce) quick-rise yeast
- 2 cups warm water (120° to 130°), divided
- 1 tablespoon honey
- 1 pound ground beef
- 1 envelope taco seasoning
- 1 cup refried beans
- 1/3 cup taco sauce
- 2 cups shredded Colby-Monterey Jack cheese
- OPTIONAL TOPPINGS:
- Shredded lettuce
- Chopped tomatoes
- Crushed tortilla chips
- Sliced ripe olives, drained
- Diced avocado
- Sour cream
- Salsa

Direction

- Heat the oven to 400°F. Mix yeast, salt, cornmeal, and 2-1/2 cups flour together. Mix honey and 1-1/4 cups warm water in another bowl. Add in the dry ingredients slowly. Beat the mixture until it just moistens. Put in remaining flour to make a dough that is soft, but don't knead it. Cover it and let sit for 20 minutes.
- In the meantime, cook the beef over medium heat in a small pan. Stir the beef to crumble until it's not pink anymore; drain grease. Place the remaining water and taco seasoning in the skillet. Keep cooking and stirring until the mixture thickens, 2 minutes.
- Get a greased 13x9 inch pan and press the dough in to fit. Mix the taco sauce and beans, then put a layer over the dough. Put beef mixture and cheese on top. Put on the lower oven rack. Bake it until the cheese is melted and the crust is golden, 15 to 18 minutes. Let it cool for 5 minutes. You can add more toppings when you serve it if you want.

Nutrition Information

- Calories: 469 calories
- Sodium: 1050mg sodium
- Fiber: 3g fiber)
- Total Carbohydrate: 55g carbohydrate (3g sugars
- Cholesterol: 60mg cholesterol
- Protein: 23g protein.
- Total Fat: 16g fat (9g saturated fat)

8. Easy Taco Pie

Serving: 6 | Prep: 15mins | Cook: 35mins |Ready in:

Ingredients

- 1 pound ground beef
- 1 (1.25 ounce) package taco seasoning
- 1 (8 ounce) package refrigerated crescent roll dough

- 1 (14 ounce) can refried beans
- 1 cup sour cream
- 1 cup salsa, drained slightly
- 1 1/2 cups shredded Cheddar cheese

Direction

- Turn the oven to 350°F (175°C) to preheat. Spray cooking spray over a big deep-dish pie pan to coat.
- Place a big frying pan on medium-high heat. Crumble ground beef into tiny pieces and add to the hot frying pan; stir and cook for 7-10 minutes until the beef is not pink anymore and is crumbly. Strain and dispose any excess fat. Use taco seasoning to season the strained beef.
- In the prepared pan, put the chilled dough and press onto the bottom. Spread over the dough with 1 even layer of refried beans. Spread over the refried beans with 1 layer of sour cream. Evenly sprinkle over the sour cream with ground beef, put Cheddar cheese and salsa on top.
- Put in the preheated oven and bake for 25-30 minutes until the crust is brown and the cheese is bubbling and melts.

Nutrition Information

- Calories: 570 calories;
- Total Fat: 35.1
- Sodium: 1418
- Total Carbohydrate: 33.5
- Cholesterol: 98
- Protein: 27.8

9. Eyeball Taco Salad

Serving: 10 servings. | Prep: 45mins | Cook: 25mins | Ready in:

Ingredients

- 2-1/2 pounds lean ground beef (90% lean)
- 1 envelope taco seasoning

- 1 can (8 ounces) tomato sauce
- 3/4 cup water
- 1 package (15-1/2 ounces) nacho-flavored tortilla chips, crushed
- 2 cups shredded Monterey Jack cheese
- 2 cups shredded cheddar cheese
- 4 cups torn iceberg lettuce
- 1 medium red onion, finely chopped
- 10 slices tomato, halved
- 1 cup (8 ounces) sour cream
- 10 pitted ripe olives, halved

Direction

- Preheat the oven to 325 degrees. On medium-high heat, crumble and cook beef for 7-9mins in a six-quart stockpot until the beef is not pink anymore. Mix in water, tomato sauce, and seasoning; boil. Lower heat; simmer for 15mins, uncovered, while occasionally stirring.
- Evenly scatter chips in a greased 15x10x1-in baking pan; dust Monterey Jack cheese on top then top with beef mixture. Add cheddar cheese. Bake for 25-30mins until bubbly.
- Slice into ten 5x3-in pieces; add onion and lettuce on top of each. Make eyeballs by adding olives, sour cream, and tomatoes.

Nutrition Information

- Calories: 569 calories
- Sodium: 962mg sodium
- Fiber: 3g fiber)
- Total Carbohydrate: 35g carbohydrate (4g sugars
- Cholesterol: 99mg cholesterol
- Protein: 32g protein.
- Total Fat: 35g fat (13g saturated fat)

10. Flatbread Tacos With Ranch Sour Cream

Serving: 8 servings. | Prep: 15mins | Cook: 15mins | Ready in:

Ingredients

- 1 cup (8 ounces) sour cream
- 2 teaspoons ranch salad dressing mix
- 1 teaspoon lemon juice
- 1-1/2 pounds ground beef
- 1 can (15 ounces) pinto beans, rinsed and drained
- 1 can (14-1/2 ounces) diced tomatoes, undrained
- 1 envelope taco seasoning
- 1 tablespoon hot pepper sauce
- 1 tube (16.3 ounces) large refrigerated buttermilk biscuits
- Optional toppings: sliced ripe olives and shredded lettuce and cheddar cheese

Direction

- Combine lemon juice, dressing mix and sour cream together in a small bowl; chill till serving.
- Place a large skillet on medium heat; cook in beef till not pink anymore; strain. Put in pepper sauce, taco seasoning, tomatoes and beans; heat through.
- Meanwhile, roll out each biscuit into a 6-in. circle. Place a small non-stick skillet on medium heat; cook each biscuit till golden brown, or for 30-60 seconds per side; keep warm.
- To serve, spread 2 tablespoons of ranch sour cream on each flatbread; place 2/3 cup of the meat mixture on top. Sprinkle with any toppings of your choice.

Nutrition Information

- Calories: 452 calories
- Fiber: 4g fiber)
- Total Carbohydrate: 41g carbohydrate (7g sugars
- Cholesterol: 62mg cholesterol
- Protein: 23g protein.
- Total Fat: 21g fat (10g saturated fat)
- Sodium: 1368mg sodium

11. Greek Tacos

Serving: 12 servings.. | Prep: 10mins | Cook: 20mins | Ready in:

Ingredients

- 1 pound lean ground beef (90% lean)
- 1 can (14-1/2 ounces) diced tomatoes, undrained
- 2 teaspoons Greek seasoning
- 1/2 teaspoon minced garlic
- 1/4 teaspoon pepper
- 2 cups fresh baby spinach
- 1 can (2-1/4 ounces) sliced ripe olives, drained
- 1 package (4-1/2 ounces) taco shells
- 1/2 cup crumbled feta cheese
- 1/4 cup chopped red onion

Direction

- Place a large skillet on medium heat; cook in beef till not pink anymore; strain. Mix in pepper, garlic, Greek seasoning and tomatoes. Boil the mixture. Lower the heat; simmer till thickened, or for 8-10 minutes. Put in olives and spinach; cook while stirring till the spinach is wilted, or for 2-3 minutes.
- Meanwhile, arrange taco shells on an ungreased baking sheet. Bake for 3-5 minutes at 300°, or till heated through. In each shell, spoon around 1/4 cup of the beef mixture. Add onion and feta cheese on top.

Nutrition Information

- Calories: 130 calories
- Sodium: 386mg sodium
- Fiber: 2g fiber)
- Total Carbohydrate: 9g carbohydrate (1g sugars
- Cholesterol: 20mg cholesterol
- Protein: 9g protein. Diabetic Exchanges: 1 lean meat
- Total Fat: 6g fat (2g saturated fat)

12. Haystack Supper

Serving: 2 casseroles (6 servings each). | Prep: 25mins | Cook: 0mins | Ready in:

Ingredients

- 1-3/4 cups crushed saltines (about 40 crackers)
- 2 cups cooked rice
- 3 pounds ground beef
- 1 large onion, chopped
- 1-1/2 cups tomato juice
- 3/4 cup water
- 3 tablespoons taco seasoning
- Seasoned salt, salt and pepper to taste
- 1/2 cup butter, cubed
- 1/2 cup all-purpose flour
- 4 cups milk
- 1 pound process cheese (Velveeta), cubed
- 4 cups shredded lettuce
- 3 cups shredded sharp cheddar cheese
- 3 medium tomatoes, diced
- 1 jar (10 ounces) pimiento-stuffed olives
- 1 package (14-1/2 ounces) tortilla chips

Direction

- Portion the crackers between 2 unoiled baking dishes, about 13x9 inches. Add rice over top of each.
- Cook onion and beef in large skillet until the meat is no longer pink, then drain. Put in seasonings, water and tomato juice; simmer about 15 to 20 mins. Add over rice.
- Melt butter in large saucepan. Stir in the flour until they become smooth. Put in milk gradually. Boil. Cook while stirring until thickened, about 2 mins.
- Lower the heat; mix in the Velveeta cheese until it is melted. Add over the beef mixture. Place the lettuce, the cheddar cheese, the tomatoes, and the olives on top. Enjoy with the chips. Place any leftovers in refrigerator.

Nutrition Information

- Calories: 888 calories
- Total Fat: 55g fat (24g saturated fat)
- Sodium: 1746mg sodium
- Fiber: 3g fiber)
- Total Carbohydrate: 57g carbohydrate (9g sugars
- Cholesterol: 164mg cholesterol
- Protein: 41g protein.

13. Idaho Tacos

Serving: 4 servings. | Prep: 20mins | Cook: 0mins | Ready in:

Ingredients

- 1 pound ground beef
- 1 envelope taco seasoning
- 4 hot baked potatoes
- 1/2 cup shredded cheddar cheese
- 1 cup chopped green onions
- Salsa, optional

Direction

- In a large skillet over medium heat, cook beef until no longer pink; drain. Add taco seasoning; prepare following the instructions on packaging.
- Cut an X in the top of each potato using a sharp knife; fluff pulp with a fork. Have cheese, onions and taco meat to top. If wished, serve with salsa.

Nutrition Information

- Calories: 601 calories
- Sodium: 990mg sodium
- Fiber: 7g fiber)
- Total Carbohydrate: 76g carbohydrate (6g sugars
- Cholesterol: 90mg cholesterol
- Protein: 34g protein.

- Total Fat: 18g fat (9g saturated fat)

Serving: 2 servings. | Prep: 20mins | Cook: 15mins | Ready in:

Ingredients

- 3/4 cup all-purpose flour
- 1/2 teaspoon baking powder
- 1/4 teaspoon salt
- 1/3 cup hot water
- 1/2 pound lean ground beef (90% lean)
- 2 tablespoons taco seasoning
- 1/3 cup water
- Oil for frying
- 2 tablespoons chopped lettuce
- 2 tablespoons chopped tomato
- 2 tablespoons salsa
- 2 tablespoons sour cream

Direction

- Mix salt, baking powder and flour in a small bowl. Mix in hot water and create a soft dough. Cover the dough and leave to sit for 1 hour.
- Over medium heat, cook the beef in small skillet until no pink color remains. Drain beef. Mix in water and taco seasoning. Simmer for 10 minutes while uncovered. Keep the contents warm.
- Separate the dough in half. Roll every portion to form a 4-inch circle onto a lightly floured surface.
- Heat one inch of oil in an electric skillet to 350°. Then fry the bread circles for about 3 to 4 minutes per side in the hot oil or until turned golden. Place on paper towels to drain. Add tomato, lettuce, and meat mixture on top of each. Serve together with sour cream and salsa.

Nutrition Information

- Calories: 407 calories
- Total Carbohydrate: 45g carbohydrate (2g sugars
- Cholesterol: 66mg cholesterol
- Protein: 27g protein.
- Total Fat: 11g fat (5g saturated fat)
- Sodium: 1361mg sodium
- Fiber: 1g fiber)

Serving: 6 servings. | Prep: 10mins | Cook: 20mins | Ready in:

Ingredients

- 1-1/2 pounds extra-lean ground beef (95% lean)
- 1 can (15 ounces) tomato sauce
- 3/4 teaspoon garlic powder
- 1/2 teaspoon salt
- 1/4 teaspoon pepper
- 1/4 teaspoon cayenne pepper
- 12 taco shells, warmed
- Optional toppings: shredded lettuce and cheese, chopped tomatoes, avocado and olives

Direction

- Place a large skillet on medium heat; cook in beef till not pink anymore. Stir in cayenne, pepper, salt, garlic powder and tomato sauce. Boil the mixture. Lower the heat; simmer without a cover for 10 minutes.
- Fill 1/4 cup of the beef mixture in each taco shell. Serve with your favorite toppings.

Nutrition Information

- Calories: 264 calories
- Cholesterol: 65mg cholesterol
- Protein: 25g protein. Diabetic Exchanges: 3 lean meat

- Total Fat: 10g fat (4g saturated fat)
- Sodium: 669mg sodium
- Fiber: 1g fiber)
- Total Carbohydrate: 17g carbohydrate (1g sugars

16. Navajo Tacos

Serving: 6 | Prep: 15mins | Cook: 19mins | Ready in:

Ingredients

- Fry Bread:
- 2 cups all-purpose flour
- 1 teaspoon baking powder
- 1/2 teaspoon salt
- 1 cup warm water
- Chili Mixture:
- 1 pound ground beef
- 1 (15 ounce) can pinto beans, rinsed and drained
- 1 (14.5 ounce) can diced tomatoes, undrained
- 1 (1.25 ounce) package chili seasoning (such as McCormick®)
- vegetable oil (such as Crisco®) for frying

Direction

- In a big bowl, combine salt, baking powder and flour together. Add in the water; mix dough till just blended. Cover using plastic wrap and allow to sit for 15 minutes.
- Over medium heat, heat a big skillet. Put the ground beef; cook and mix for 5 minutes till browned. Allow the grease to drain off. Mix in chili seasoning, diced tomatoes with their juices and pinto beans till well-incorporated. Let simmer for 10 to 15 minutes till chili flavors are blended.
- Slightly oil your hands and pull off a portion of dough approximately the size of a baseball. Pat it with palms forming a circle approximately 4 inches across and half-inch thick. Redo with the rest of dough.

- In a deep fryer or big saucepan, heat 2 to 3 inches of oil. Working in batches, fry dough circles for 2 to 3 minutes each side till cooked completely, puffy and well-browned. Allow to drain on paper towels.
- While still hot, distribute fry bread between serving plates. Scoop chili mixture over.

Nutrition Information

- Calories: 425 calories;
- Cholesterol: 47
- Protein: 21
- Total Fat: 17.7
- Sodium: 1127
- Total Carbohydrate: 44.7

17. One Pan Taco Dinner

Serving: 4 | Prep: 5mins | Cook: | Ready in:

Ingredients

- Nonstick cooking spray
- 1 pound lean ground beef
- 1 (1.25 ounce) package taco seasoning mix
- 2 cups water
- 2 cups Minute® White Rice, uncooked
- 1 cup shredded cheddar cheese
- 2 cups shredded lettuce
- 1 large tomato, chopped

Direction

- Use nonstick cooking spray to coat a large nonstick skillet. Over medium-high heat, cook meat until it is browned. Remove excess fat by draining.
- Stir in water and seasoning mix. Let it boil.
- Add rice; stir well. Drizzle cheese on top; cover. Lower the heat to low; let it simmer for 5 minutes. Add tomato and lettuce on top to serve.

Nutrition Information

- Calories: 583 calories;
- Sodium: 940
- Total Carbohydrate: 54.1
- Cholesterol: 105
- Protein: 33.2
- Total Fat: 24.9

18. Pita Tacos

Serving: 4 tacos. | Prep: 10mins | Cook: 20mins |Ready in:

Ingredients

- 1 pound ground beef
- Salt and pepper to taste
- Oil for frying
- 4 whole pita breads (6 inches)
- 4 cups shredded lettuce
- 2 medium tomatoes, diced
- 1 medium onion, chopped
- Ranch salad dressing

Direction

- Place a large skillet on medium heat; cook beef till not pink anymore; strain. Sprinkle with pepper and salt; set aside.
- Heat 1/4 in. of oil in another skillet. Fry pita breads till golden brown and puffed. Strain on paper towels. Slice each bread in half. Fill with onion, tomatoes, lettuce and the beef mixture. Drizzle salad dressing on top.

Nutrition Information

- Calories:
- Cholesterol:
- Protein:
- Total Fat:
- Sodium:
- Fiber:
- Total Carbohydrate:

19. Seasoned Taco Meat

Serving: 2-1/2 cups. | Prep: 10mins | Cook: 35mins | Ready in:

Ingredients

- 1-1/4 pounds ground beef
- 2 small onions, finely chopped
- 1 cup water
- 2 tablespoons chili powder
- 1-1/4 teaspoons salt
- 1/4 teaspoon garlic powder
- 1/4 teaspoon crushed red pepper flakes
- 1/4 teaspoon ground cumin

Direction

- Place a skillet on medium heat; cook onion and beef till the meat is not pink anymore; strain. Put in seasonings and water. Boil the mixture. Lower the heat; simmer without a cover till the water is absorbed, or for 15 minutes.

Nutrition Information

- Calories: 99 calories
- Sodium: 349mg sodium
- Fiber: 1g fiber)
- Total Carbohydrate: 2g carbohydrate (1g sugars
- Cholesterol: 28mg cholesterol
- Protein: 10g protein.
- Total Fat: 5g fat (2g saturated fat)

20. Taco Bake

Serving: 6 servings. | Prep: 30mins | Cook: 30mins | Ready in:

24

Ingredients

- 1 pound ground beef
- 1 small onion, chopped
- 3/4 cup water
- 1 package (1-1/4 ounces) taco seasoning
- 1 can (15 ounces) tomato sauce
- 1 package (8 ounce) shell macaroni, cooked and drained
- 1 can (4 ounces) chopped green chilies
- 2 cups shredded cheddar cheese, divided

Direction

- In a skillet, brown onion and ground beef over medium heat; let drain. Mix in the tomato sauce, taco seasoning and water; mix. Let boil; decrease heat and simmer for around 20 minutes. Stir in 1 and a half cups of cheese, chilies and macaroni. Pour into a greased baking dish of 1 and a half quart. Use the rest cheese for sprinkling. Bake at 350° for approximately 30 minutes or till heated through.

Nutrition Information

- Calories: 380 calories
- Sodium: 1205mg sodium
- Fiber: 2g fiber)
- Total Carbohydrate: 22g carbohydrate (2g sugars
- Cholesterol: 90mg cholesterol
- Protein: 26g protein.
- Total Fat: 20g fat (12g saturated fat)

21. Taco Burritos

Serving: 8 servings. | Prep: 15mins | Cook: 10mins | Ready in:

Ingredients

- 1-1/2 pounds ground beef or pork
- 1 green pepper, chopped

- 1 medium onion, chopped
- 2 garlic cloves, minced
- 1 envelope taco seasoning
- 1/4 cup water
- 8 flour tortillas
- 1 tablespoon vegetable oil
- Taco toppings of your choice

Direction

- Cook onion, green pepper and meat in a big skillet on medium heat till meat isn't pink; drain. Add water, taco seasoning and garlic; simmer for 2 minutes, uncovered.
- On a microwave-safe plate, put 4 tortillas; microwave for 20 seconds on high. Put 1/2 cup of meat mixture onto each; fold ends and sides over. Put in a greased 13x9-inch baking dish, seam side down. Repeat with leftover filling and tortillas.
- Brush oil on burritos. Bake at 450°, uncovered, till slightly crisp and lightly browned for 9-10 minutes. Serve it with toppings.

Nutrition Information

- Calories:
- Total Fat:
- Sodium:
- Fiber:
- Total Carbohydrate:
- Cholesterol:
- Protein:

22. Taco Crescents

Serving: 8 servings. | Prep: 15mins | Cook: 10mins | Ready in:

Ingredients

- 3/4 pound ground beef
- 1/4 cup chopped onion
- 1 package (1-1/4-ounces) taco seasoning

- 1 can (4-1/4-ounces) chopped ripe olives, drained
- 2 large eggs, lightly beaten
- 1/2 cup shredded cheddar cheese
- 2 tubes (8-ounces) tubes refrigerated crescent rolls

Direction

- Cook onion and beef in a large skillet until the meat is not pink anymore; then drain. Stir in olives and taco seasoning; then put aside to allow to cool. Put in cheese and eggs.
- Unroll the crescent roll dough and form separately into triangles. On a grease-free baking sheet, arrange triangles. Put on each triangle with 2 tbsp. of meat mixture, then roll and form into crescents. Bake at 375 degrees until lightly browned, 10-15 minutes.

Nutrition Information

- Calories: 255 calories
- Fiber: 1g fiber)
- Total Carbohydrate: 17g carbohydrate (3g sugars
- Cholesterol: 81mg cholesterol
- Protein: 13g protein.
- Total Fat: 15g fat (5g saturated fat)
- Sodium: 842mg sodium

23. Taco Joes

Serving: 8 servings. | Prep: 5mins | Cook: 25mins | Ready in:

Ingredients

- 1 pound ground beef
- 1 can (14-1/2 ounces) diced tomatoes, undrained
- 1 teaspoon Worcestershire sauce
- 1 to 2 teaspoons chili powder
- 1 teaspoon garlic salt

- 1/2 teaspoon ground mustard
- 1/2 teaspoon ground cumin
- 1/2 teaspoon sugar
- 8 hamburger buns, split and toasted
- 1 cup shredded cheddar cheese
- 2 cups shredded lettuce

Direction

- Place a skillet on medium heat; cook beef till not pink anymore; strain. Mix in seasonings, Worcestershire and tomatoes. Boil the mixture. Lower the heat; simmer without a cover till thickened, or 15-20 minutes. Spoon onto buns; arrange lettuce and cheese on top.

Nutrition Information

- Calories: 280 calories
- Sodium: 705mg sodium
- Fiber: 2g fiber)
- Total Carbohydrate: 26g carbohydrate (5g sugars
- Cholesterol: 43mg cholesterol
- Protein: 17g protein.
- Total Fat: 11g fat (6g saturated fat)

24. Taco Meat Seasoning

Serving: 8 cups. | Prep: 25mins | Cook: 10mins | Ready in:

Ingredients

- 4 pounds ground beef
- 3 tablespoons chopped onion
- 1 can (14-1/2 ounces) beef broth
- 1 can (8 ounces) tomato sauce
- 1/4 cup chili powder
- 2 tablespoons paprika
- 1 tablespoon beef bouillon granules
- 1 tablespoon ground cumin
- 1 teaspoon chicken bouillon granules
- 1 teaspoon garlic powder

- 1 teaspoon cayenne pepper
- 1/2 teaspoon pepper
- 1/2 teaspoon lime juice
- 1/4 teaspoon onion powder
- 1/4 teaspoon sugar
- 1/4 teaspoon salt
- 1/4 teaspoon garlic salt
- Taco shells or flour tortillas
- Shredded cheese and salsa

Direction

- Cook onion and beef over medium heat in a Dutch oven until the meat is no longer pink, then drain. Mix in next 15 ingredients. Boil. Lower the heat; simmer, covered, for 10 mins.
- Place in the taco shells with salsa and shredded cheese.

Nutrition Information

- Calories: 98 calories
- Cholesterol: 28mg cholesterol
- Protein: 10g protein.
- Total Fat: 5g fat (2g saturated fat)
- Sodium: 263mg sodium
- Fiber: 1g fiber)
- Total Carbohydrate: 2g carbohydrate (0 sugars

25. Taco Plate For Two

Serving: 2 servings. | Prep: 15mins | Cook: 0mins | Ready in:

Ingredients

- 1/2 pound ground beef
- 1/2 cup chopped onion
- 1/3 cup taco sauce
- 1/4 cup chopped green chilies
- 1/4 teaspoon salt
- 1 cup crushed tortilla chips
- 1/2 cup shredded cheddar cheese

Direction

- Cook onion and beef together in a big skillet on medium heat until meat is not pink anymore, then drain. Stir in salt, chilies and taco sauce. Cover and cook on medium low heat until heated through, about 6 to 8 minutes. Scoop over chips and sprinkle over with cheese.

Nutrition Information

- Calories: 501 calories
- Sodium: 956mg sodium
- Fiber: 3g fiber)
- Total Carbohydrate: 29g carbohydrate (5g sugars
- Cholesterol: 105mg cholesterol
- Protein: 32g protein.
- Total Fat: 28g fat (12g saturated fat)

26. Taco Potato Pie

Serving: 4-6 servings. | Prep: 15mins | Cook: 30mins | Ready in:

Ingredients

- 2 cups cold mashed potatoes (prepared with milk and butter)
- 1 envelope taco seasoning, divided
- 1 pound ground beef
- 1/2 cup chopped onion
- 1 can (16 ounces) refried beans
- 1/2 cup barbecue sauce
- 1/4 cup water
- 1 cup shredded lettuce
- 1 medium tomato, seeded and chopped
- 1 cup shredded cheddar cheese
- Sour cream

Direction

- Combine the 2 tablespoons taco seasoning

with potatoes. Press into a 9-in. deep-dish pie plate coated with grease; and put aside.

- Cook onion and beef in a skillet on medium heat until the meat is no longer pink; drain. Stir in the beans, water, leftover taco seasoning and barbecue sauce. Cook while stirring until bubbly and hot. Spoon into potato crust.
- Bake for 30-35 minutes at 350°, until well heated. Put lettuce, tomato, cheese and sour cream on top.

Nutrition Information

- Calories: 407 calories
- Cholesterol: 85mg cholesterol
- Protein: 25g protein.
- Total Fat: 19g fat (10g saturated fat)
- Sodium: 1290mg sodium
- Fiber: 6g fiber)
- Total Carbohydrate: 34g carbohydrate (6g sugars

27. Taco Salad Tacos

Serving: 4 servings. | Prep: 20mins | Cook: 10mins | Ready in:

Ingredients

- 1 pound extra-lean ground beef (95% lean)
- 1 medium onion, chopped
- 1 tablespoon chili powder
- 1 teaspoon garlic powder
- 1 teaspoon reduced-sodium beef bouillon granules
- 1 teaspoon ground cumin
- 1/4 teaspoon salt
- SALAD:
- 3 cups torn romaine
- 1 large tomato, seeded and chopped
- 1 medium sweet orange pepper, chopped
- 3 green onions, chopped
- 8 taco shells, warmed
- 1/2 cup fat-free Catalina salad dressing

- Shredded reduced-fat Colby-Monterey Jack cheese and reduced-fat sour cream, optional

Direction

- Place a large skillet on medium heat; cook in onion and beef till the meat is not pink anymore. Mix in salt, cumin, bouillon, garlic powder and chili powder; take away from the heat.
- Mix green onions, orange pepper, tomato and romaine together in a large bowl. Spoon the beef mixture into taco shells; transfer the salad mixture over. Drizzle dressing on top. Serve with sour cream and cheese if you want.

Nutrition Information

- Calories: 334 calories
- Protein: 26g protein. Diabetic Exchanges: 3 lean meat
- Total Fat: 11g fat (4g saturated fat)
- Sodium: 722mg sodium
- Fiber: 6g fiber)
- Total Carbohydrate: 33g carbohydrate (13g sugars
- Cholesterol: 65mg cholesterol

28. Taco Salad Waffles

Serving: 4 servings. | Prep: 10mins | Cook: 15mins | Ready in:

Ingredients

- 1 pound ground beef
- 1 cup salsa
- 1 can (4 ounces) chopped green chilies
- 1 envelope taco seasoning
- 8 frozen waffles
- Shredded cheddar cheese, shredded lettuce, chopped tomatoes, cubed avocado, salsa and sour cream, optional

Direction

- Place a large skillet on medium heat; cook in beef till not pink anymore; strain. Mix in taco seasoning, chilies and salsa. Boil the mixture; simmer for 5 minutes.
- Meanwhile, following the package directions, toast waffles properly. Serve with the beef mixture and your favorite toppings.

Nutrition Information

- Calories: 0
- Protein: 25 g protein.
- Total Fat: 17 g fat (6 g saturated fat)
- Sodium: 1,676 mg sodium
- Fiber: 2 g fiber
- Total Carbohydrate: 43 g carbohydrate
- Cholesterol: 65 mg cholesterol

29. Taco Skillet

Serving: 4-6 servings. | Prep: 15mins | Cook: 15mins | Ready in:

Ingredients

- 1 pound ground beef
- 1 medium onion, chopped
- 1 can (16 ounces) refried beans
- 1 can (4 ounces) chopped green chilies
- 1/4 to 1/2 teaspoon garlic powder
- 3/4 cup sour cream
- 1/2 to 1 teaspoon ground cumin
- 1/2 to 1 teaspoon chili powder
- 1 medium tomato, seeded and chopped
- 1 can (2-1/4 ounces) sliced ripe olives, drained
- 1 small green pepper, chopped
- 1 cup shredded Mexican cheese blend
- Tortilla chips or taco shells, shredded lettuce and salsa

Direction

- Place a large skillet on medium heat; cook in onion and beef till the meat is not pink

anymore; strain. Mix in garlic powder, chilies and beans; cook till heated through.
- Combine chili powder, cumin and sour cream in a small bowl; spread over the beef mixture. Arrange green pepper, olives and tomato on top. Scatter cheese over. Serve with salsa, lettuce and taco shells or tortilla chips.

Nutrition Information

- Calories: 359 calories
- Protein: 23g protein.
- Total Fat: 20g fat (11g saturated fat)
- Sodium: 598mg sodium
- Fiber: 6g fiber)
- Total Carbohydrate: 19g carbohydrate (5g sugars
- Cholesterol: 80mg cholesterol

30. Taco In A Bowl

Serving: 4 servings. | Prep: 5mins | Cook: 30mins | Ready in:

Ingredients

- 1 pound ground beef
- 1 can (14-1/2 ounces) stewed tomatoes
- 1 envelope taco seasoning
- 3/4 cup water
- 1 can (16 ounces) pork and beans
- Corn chips
- Toppings: shredded lettuce, chopped tomatoes, chopped onions, sliced ripe olives, shredded cheddar cheese, taco sauce

Direction

- Place a skillet on medium heat; cook beef till not pink anymore; strain. Put in water, taco seasoning and tomatoes; stir properly. Put in beans and pork. Boil the mixture. Lower the heat; simmer with a cover for 15 minutes. Arrange corn chips in 4 soup bowls to serve.

Transfer the beef mixture over; top with any toppings of your choice.

Nutrition Information

- Calories:
- Sodium:
- Fiber:
- Total Carbohydrate:
- Cholesterol:
- Protein:
- Total Fat:

31. Tacos Deluxe

Serving: 6-8 servings. | Prep: 25mins | Cook: 10mins | Ready in:

Ingredients

- 1 pound ground beef
- 2 tablespoons chopped onion
- 1 can (15 ounces) tomato sauce
- 1 teaspoon white vinegar
- 1 teaspoon Worcestershire sauce
- 2 to 3 drops hot pepper sauce
- 1 teaspoon sugar
- 1 teaspoon chili powder
- 1/2 teaspoon garlic salt
- 1/4 teaspoon celery salt
- 1/4 teaspoon onion salt
- 1/8 teaspoon ground allspice
- 1/8 teaspoon ground cinnamon
- Dash pepper
- 1/2 cup shredded cheddar cheese
- 6 to 8 taco shells
- Shredded lettuce
- Chopped tomatoes
- SWEET-AND-SOUR DRESSING:
- 1 cup Miracle Whip
- 1/3 cup sugar
- 2 tablespoons white vinegar
- 1/4 teaspoon salt
- 1/2 teaspoon hot pepper sauce

Direction

- Place a large skillet on medium heat; cook onion and beef till not pink anymore; strain. Put in the next 12 ingredients. Simmer without a cover, stirring occasionally, till the liquid is almost reduced completely, or for 10-15 minutes. Allow to cool slightly; mix in cheese.
- Arrange taco shells in a baking pan, open-end up; into each shell, put a scoop of the meat mixture. Bake at 400° till the cheese is melted and the meat is hot, 10-15 minutes.
- Sprinkle tomatoes and lettuce on top of the taco. Mix together the dressing ingredients in a small bowl; drizzle over the tacos.

Nutrition Information

- Calories:
- Sodium:
- Fiber:
- Total Carbohydrate:
- Cholesterol:
- Protein:
- Total Fat:

32. Tacos In A Bowl

Serving: 2 servings. | Prep: 10mins | Cook: 15mins | Ready in:

Ingredients

- 1/2 pound lean ground beef (90% lean)
- 2 tablespoons finely chopped onion
- 3/4 cup canned diced tomatoes, drained
- 2 tablespoons taco seasoning
- 1 cup water
- 1 package (3 ounces) ramen noodles
- 1/4 cup shredded cheddar or Mexican cheese blend
- 1/4 cup crushed tortilla chips, optional

Direction

- Cook the onion and beef in a small skillet on medium heat until the meat is not pink anymore; let drain. Stir in water, taco seasoning, and tomatoes. Boil. Put in the ramen noodles, reserve the seasoning packet for another recipe or discard. Stir and cook until the noodles become tender, 3-5 minutes.
- Put into the serving bowls; if desired, dust with tortilla chips and cheese.

Nutrition Information

- Calories: 435 calories
- Fiber: 2g fiber)
- Total Carbohydrate: 37g carbohydrate (7g sugars
- Cholesterol: 66mg cholesterol
- Protein: 30g protein.
- Total Fat: 18g fat (9g saturated fat)
- Sodium: 922mg sodium

33. Tasty Tacos

Serving: Makes 5 servings, 2 tacos each. | Prep: 15mins | Cook: | Ready in:

Ingredients

- 3/4 cup VELVEETA® Salsa Dip
- 1/2 lb. ground beef , cooked, drained
- 10 TACO BELL® Crunchy Taco Shell s
- 1 cup shredded lettuce
- 3/4 cup chopped tomato

Direction

- Combine cooked meat and VELVEETA salsa dip.
- Scoop into taco shells evenly, then put tomato and lettuce on top evenly.

Nutrition Information

- Calories: 260

- Sodium: 500 mg
- Total Carbohydrate: 19 g
- Cholesterol: 45 mg
- Protein: 14 g
- Sugar: 3 g
- Total Fat: 15 g
- Saturated Fat: 6 g
- Fiber: 2 g

34. Tater Taco Casserole

Serving: 8 servings. | Prep: 20mins | Cook: 30mins | Ready in:

Ingredients

- 2 pounds ground beef
- 1/4 cup chopped onion
- 1 envelope taco seasoning
- 2/3 cup water
- 1 can (11 ounces) whole kernel corn, drained
- 1 can (11 ounces) condensed fiesta nacho cheese soup, undiluted
- 1 package (32 ounces) frozen Tater Tots

Direction

- Cook onion and beef on medium heat in a big skillet till meat is not pink anymore; drain. Mix in water and taco seasoning. Let it simmer, while uncovered, for 5 minutes. Mix in soup and corn.
- Move to a greased 13x9-inch baking dish. Arrange Tater Tots in one layer on the top. Bake, while uncovered, at 350 degrees for 30 to 35 minutes or till potatoes become crispy and golden brown in color.

Nutrition Information

- Calories: 461 calories
- Protein: 25g protein.
- Total Fat: 24g fat (8g saturated fat)
- Sodium: 1307mg sodium

- Fiber: 4g fiber)
- Total Carbohydrate: 40g carbohydrate (3g sugars
- Cholesterol: 60mg cholesterol

- Fiber: 3g fiber)
- Total Carbohydrate: 30g carbohydrate (3g sugars
- Cholesterol: 42mg cholesterol

35. Texas Tacos

Serving: 10 servings. | Prep: 10mins | Cook: 20mins | Ready in:

Ingredients

- 1-1/2 pounds lean ground beef (90% lean)
- 1 medium sweet red pepper, chopped
- 1 small onion, chopped
- 1 can (14-1/2 ounces) diced tomatoes, drained
- 1-1/3 cups frozen corn, thawed
- 1 can (8 ounces) tomato sauce
- 2 tablespoons chili powder
- 1/2 teaspoon salt
- 1 package (8.8 ounces) ready-to-serve brown rice
- 20 taco shells, warmed
- Optional toppings: shredded lettuce, chopped fresh tomatoes and reduced-fat sour cream

Direction

- In the Dutch oven, cook the onion, red pepper and beef on medium heat till the veggies soften and the beef is not pink anymore or for 8 to 10 minutes, crumble beef. Drain off.
- Whisk in the salt, chili powder, tomato sauce, corn and tomatoes; boil. Put in the rice; thoroughly heat. Serve in the taco shells with the desired toppings.

Nutrition Information

- Calories: 294 calories
- Protein: 17g protein. Diabetic Exchanges: 2 starch
- Total Fat: 11g fat (4g saturated fat)
- Sodium: 420mg sodium

36. Walking Tacos

Serving: 5 servings. | Prep: 10mins | Cook: 30mins | Ready in:

Ingredients

- 1 pound ground beef
- 1 envelope reduced-sodium chili seasoning mix
- 1/4 teaspoon pepper
- 1 can (10 ounces) diced tomatoes and green chilies
- 1 can (15 ounces) Ranch Style beans (pinto beans in seasoned tomato sauce)
- 5 packages (1 ounce each) corn chips
- Toppings: shredded cheddar cheese, sour cream and sliced green onions

Direction

- Put beef in a large skillet then cook for about 6-8 minutes over medium heat or until the beef is starting to crumble and turning brown in color then drain excess oil. Add in the beans, chili seasoning mix, tomatoes and pepper then stir until it boils. Lower the heat setting and simmer for about 20-25 minutes more keeping the skillet uncovered while stirring it from time to time, do this until the mixture is thick in consistency.
- Open corn chip bags just before serving. Put the beef mixture and toppings if you want.

Nutrition Information

- Calories: 530 calories
- Protein: 24g protein.
- Total Fat: 28g fat (6g saturated fat)
- Sodium: 1017mg sodium

- Fiber: 6g fiber)
- Total Carbohydrate: 44g carbohydrate (5g sugars
- Cholesterol: 56mg cholesterol

37. Zesty Tacos

Serving: 8 servings. | Prep: 20mins | Cook: 10mins | Ready in:

Ingredients

- 1 pound ground beef
- 1 cup water
- 1 envelope taco seasoning
- 8 taco shells
- 1 can (15-1/2 ounces) black-eyed peas, rinsed and drained
- 1 cup chopped tomatoes
- 1 cup shredded lettuce
- 1 cup shredded cheddar cheese
- 1/2 cup zesty Italian salad dressing

Direction

- Cook beef in a large skillet until no longer pink over medium heat; then drain. Stir taco seasoning and water in. Bring to a boil; lower heat, simmer uncovered until thickened, or for 4-5 minutes.
- In the meantime, prepare taco shells followed the direction of packaging. Add peas into skillet and heat through. Spoon into each shell of taco 1/4 cup of beef mixture. Top with lettuce, cheese and tomatoes. Drizzle with salad dressing.

Nutrition Information

- Calories: 302 calories
- Sodium: 933mg sodium
- Fiber: 2g fiber)
- Total Carbohydrate: 20g carbohydrate (2g sugars

- Cholesterol: 43mg cholesterol
- Protein: 17g protein.
- Total Fat: 17g fat (7g saturated fat)

Chapter 2: Ground Beef Casserole Recipes

***

38. 4 H Corn Special

Serving: 6-8 servings. | Prep: 15mins | Cook: 30mins | Ready in:

Ingredients

- 1 pound ground beef
- 1 small onion, finely chopped
- 1-1/2 cups cooked rice
- 2 cups seeded chopped fresh tomatoes or 1 can (14-1/2 ounces) diced tomatoes, undrained
- 2 cups fresh, frozen or canned sweet corn
- Salt and pepper to taste
- 1 tablespoon Worcestershire sauce
- 1 teaspoon hot pepper sauce
- 1 cup crushed saltines
- 1/4 cup butter, melted

Direction

- Brown onion and beef in a big skillet; drain. Mix in hot pepper sauce, Worcestershire sauce, pepper, salt, corn, tomatoes and rice.
- Add to a greased 13x9-inch baking dish. Mix butter and cracker crumbs; drizzle over top. Bake at 350 degrees for half an hour.

Nutrition Information

- Calories: 256 calories
- Cholesterol: 43mg cholesterol
- Protein: 13g protein.
- Total Fat: 12g fat (6g saturated fat)
- Sodium: 227mg sodium
- Fiber: 2g fiber)
- Total Carbohydrate: 24g carbohydrate (4g sugars

39. Acapulco Delight

Serving: 10 servings. | Prep: 25mins | Cook: 25mins | Ready in:

Ingredients

- 2 pounds ground beef
- 1 envelope (1-1/4 ounces) taco seasoning
- 3/4 cup water
- 1 bottle (15 ounces) mild green taco sauce
- 9 flour tortillas (6 inches)
- 2 cups shredded cheddar cheese
- 1 can (16 ounces) refried beans
- 2 cups sour cream
- 4 green onions, chopped
- 1 can (2-1/4 ounces) sliced ripe olives, drained
- Chopped tomatoes, optional
- Chopped avocados, optional

Direction

- Start preheating oven to 350°F. Take a large skillet on medium heat, crumble and cook beef until it is no longer pink; drain grease. Mix in water and taco seasoning. Put in taco sauce and cook until its texture is slightly thick, 5-10 minutes.
- Take 3 tortillas and cover the bottom of a 13x9-in. pan. Tear tortillas into pieces if necessary. Place half of the meat mixture on top of the tortillas; top with half of cheese. Take another 3 tortillas and layer once again; distribute refried beans. Coat with sour cream and

drizzle with olives and green onions. Take left tortillas and re-layer. Coat with left meat mixture and cheese. For 25-30 minutes, bake. Rest a couple of minutes before serving. Partner with chopped tomatoes and avocadoes if desired.

Nutrition Information

- Calories: 468 calories
- Sodium: 1064mg sodium
- Fiber: 3g fiber)
- Total Carbohydrate: 26g carbohydrate (3g sugars
- Cholesterol: 104mg cholesterol
- Protein: 28g protein.
- Total Fat: 27g fat (14g saturated fat)

40. Au Gratin Taco Bake

Serving: 4-6 servings. | Prep: 15mins | Cook: 01hours10mins | Ready in:

Ingredients

- 1 pound ground beef
- 1 package (4.9 ounces) au gratin potatoes
- 1 can (15-1/4 ounces) whole kernel corn, undrained
- 1 can (14-1/2 ounces) no-salt-added stewed tomatoes, undrained
- 3/4 cup 2% milk
- 1/2 cup water
- 2 tablespoons taco seasoning
- 1 cup shredded cheddar cheese

Direction

- Cook beef on medium heat in a big skillet till meat is not pink anymore; drain. Mix in taco seasoning, water, milk, tomatoes, corn, contents of sauce mix and potatoes. Move into one greased 2-qt. baking dish.
- Keep it covered and baked at 350 degrees for 65 to 70 minutes or till potatoes become soft.

Drizzle with cheese. Bake, while uncovered, till cheese becomes melted or 5 minutes more.

Nutrition Information

- Calories: 373 calories
- Cholesterol: 61mg cholesterol
- Protein: 22g protein.
- Total Fat: 15g fat (8g saturated fat)
- Sodium: 1113mg sodium
- Fiber: 3g fiber)
- Total Carbohydrate: 34g carbohydrate (8g sugars

41. Bacon Cheeseburger Tater Tot Bake

Serving: 12 servings. | Prep: 25mins | Cook: 35mins | Ready in:

Ingredients

- 2 pounds ground beef
- 1 large onion, chopped and divided
- 1 can (15 ounces) tomato sauce
- 1 package (8 ounces) process cheese (Velveeta)
- 1 tablespoon ground mustard
- 1 tablespoon Worcestershire sauce
- 2 cups shredded cheddar cheese
- 12 bacon strips, cooked and crumbled
- 1 package (32 ounces) frozen Tater Tots
- 1 cup grape tomatoes, chopped
- 1/3 cup sliced dill pickles

Direction

- Preheat oven at 400 degrees. Sauté 1 cup of onion and beef in a large skillet put over medium heat for 6-8 minutes or until the onions are soft and the beef is brown and starting to crumble. Drain excess oil. Add in processed cheese, tomato sauce, Worcestershire sauce and mustard and mix for 4-6 minutes until cheese has melted.

- Transfer in a greased 3-1/2-quartz or 13x9-inch baking dish. Top off with bacon and cheddar cheese. Put Tater Tots on top. Put the baking dish uncovered in the preheated oven and bake for 35-40 minutes until it is bubbling. Finish off with a toppings of pickles, remaining onion and tomatoes.

Nutrition Information

- Calories: 479 calories
- Sodium: 1144mg sodium
- Fiber: 3g fiber)
- Total Carbohydrate: 24g carbohydrate (4g sugars
- Cholesterol: 92mg cholesterol
- Protein: 27g protein.
- Total Fat: 31g fat (12g saturated fat)

42. Baked Beans Ole

Serving: 6-8 servings. | Prep: 10mins | Cook: 20mins | Ready in:

Ingredients

- 1/2 pound ground beef
- 1 cup chopped onion
- 2 garlic cloves, minced
- 2 cans (16 ounces each) pork and beans
- 1 cup picante sauce

Direction

- In a frying pan, cook ground beef with garlic and onion till the onion becomes softened and the beef becomes browned; let drain. Whisk in the remaining ingredients. Let it boil; lower heat and simmer while stirring from time to time for 10 minutes.

Nutrition Information

- Calories: 111 calories

- Total Carbohydrate: 14g carbohydrate (5g sugars
- Cholesterol: 14mg cholesterol
- Protein: 8g protein.
- Total Fat: 3g fat (1g saturated fat)
- Sodium: 333mg sodium
- Fiber: 3g fiber)

43. Baked Beef Tacos

Serving: 12 servings. | Prep: 15mins | Cook: 20mins | Ready in:

Ingredients

- 1-1/2 pounds ground beef
- 1 envelope taco seasoning
- 2 cans (10 ounces each) diced tomatoes and green chilies, divided
- 1 can (16 ounces) refried beans
- 2 cups shredded Mexican cheese blend, divided
- 1/4 cup chopped fresh cilantro
- 1 teaspoon hot pepper sauce, optional
- 12 taco shells
- Chopped green onions

Direction

- Preheat oven to 425 degrees. Cook beef on medium heat in a big skillet till meat is not pink anymore or for 6 to 8 minutes, crumble the beef; drain. Mix in 1 can of undrained tomatoes and taco seasoning; heat through.
- At the same time, whisk the rest can of undrained tomatoes, cilantro, half cup of cheese, and beans, if you want, pepper sauce, in a bowl. Spread onto bottom of one greased 13x9-in. baking dish.
- Stand taco shells upright on top of bean mixture. Fill each with 1 tbsp. of cheese and roughly a third cup beef mixture. Bake, while covered, 15 minutes.
- Uncover it; drizzle with the rest of cheese. Bake, while uncovered, 5 to 7 minutes or till

cheese become melted and shells turn browned a bit. Drizzle with green onions.

Nutrition Information

- Calories: 277 calories
- Cholesterol: 52mg cholesterol
- Protein: 17g protein.
- Total Fat: 15g fat (7g saturated fat)
- Sodium: 836mg sodium
- Fiber: 3g fiber)
- Total Carbohydrate: 17g carbohydrate (0 sugars

44. Baked Meal In One Casserole

Serving: 4 servings. | Prep: 15mins | Cook: 50mins | Ready in:

Ingredients

- 1 pound lean ground beef (90% lean)
- 3 medium unpeeled potatoes, thinly sliced
- 1 medium onion, sliced and separated into rings
- 1 cup frozen peas
- 1-1/2 cups sliced mushrooms
- 1-1/2 teaspoons salt, optional
- 1/4 teaspoon pepper
- 1 teaspoon sesame seeds
- 3 tablespoons butter, melted

Direction

- In a skillet, cook beef over medium heat until there is not pink anymore; and then drain. Arrange potatoes in a greased baking dish of 2-quart. Place beef and onion on top. In the center, place peas; and around the peas, arrange mushrooms. Sprinkle with the sesame seeds, pepper and salt; have butter for drizzling.
- Bake while covered at 375° for approximately 50 to 60 minutes until potatoes are soften.

Nutrition Information

- Calories: 391 calories
- Protein: 29g protein. Diabetic Exchanges: 2 starch
- Total Fat: 16g fat (0 saturated fat)
- Sodium: 231mg sodium
- Fiber: 0 fiber)
- Total Carbohydrate: 33g carbohydrate (0 sugars
- Cholesterol: 41mg cholesterol

45. Baked Simple Meatball Stroganoff

Serving: 6 servings. | Prep: 40mins | Cook: 30mins | Ready in:

Ingredients

- 1/3 cup chopped green onions
- 1/4 cup seasoned bread crumbs
- 3 tablespoons grated Parmesan cheese
- 1 pound ground beef
- 1 loaf (1 pound) Italian bread, cut into 1-inch slices
- 1 package (8 ounces) cream cheese, softened
- 1/2 cup mayonnaise
- 1 teaspoon Italian seasoning
- 1/4 teaspoon pepper
- 2 cups shredded part-skim mozzarella cheese
- 3-1/2 cups spaghetti sauce
- 1 cup water
- 2 garlic cloves, minced

Direction

- Combine the Parmesan cheese, breadcrumbs and onions in a big bowl. Let the beef crumbled over mixture and stir thoroughly. Form into 1-inch balls, then arrange on a greased rack in a shallow baking pan. Let bake at 400° for about 15-20 minutes until not pink anymore.

- Meanwhile, in an ungreased 13x9-inch baking dish, line bread in a single layer (all of the bread may not be used). Mix in the pepper, Italian seasoning, mayonnaise and cream cheese; pour over the bread. Top with a half cup of mozzarella.
- Whisk in the garlic, water and spaghetti sauce; put in meatballs. Spread over cheese mixture, then dust with the leftover mozzarella. Bake while uncovered at 350° for about 30 minutes until heated through.

Nutrition Information

- Calories: 641 calories
- Fiber: 3g fiber)
- Total Carbohydrate: 43g carbohydrate (9g sugars
- Cholesterol: 94mg cholesterol
- Protein: 29g protein.
- Total Fat: 39g fat (15g saturated fat)
- Sodium: 1234mg sodium

46. Barbecued Beef And Beans

Serving: 8-10 servings. | Prep: 15mins | Cook: 60mins | Ready in:

Ingredients

- 1 pound ground beef
- 1 medium onion, finely diced
- 1 garlic clove, minced
- 1/2 cup barbecue sauce
- 1/2 cup ketchup
- 1/4 cup molasses
- 1/2 cup packed brown sugar
- 1 jar (32 ounces) northern beans, rinsed and drained
- 1 can (28 ounces) baked beans
- 1 can (16 ounces) red kidney beans
- 1 can (15-3/4 ounces) lima beans, rinsed and drained

- 1 can (15 ounces) garbanzo beans or chickpeas, rinsed and drained
- 1 can (14-1/2 ounces) cut green beans, drained

Direction

- In a skillet, cook garlic, onion and beef over medium heat until beef is not pink anymore. Drain; then in a large greased casserole or roaster, place the beef. Stir in the ketchup, barbecue sauce, brown sugar and molasses. Add all beans and well mix.
- Uncovered while baking at 325° for nearly 30 minutes. Bake while covered for another 30 minutes.

Nutrition Information

- Calories: 433 calories
- Cholesterol: 28mg cholesterol
- Protein: 23g protein.
- Total Fat: 7g fat (2g saturated fat)
- Sodium: 1220mg sodium
- Fiber: 15g fiber)
- Total Carbohydrate: 72g carbohydrate (27g sugars

47. Beef & Tater Bake

Serving: 8 servings. | Prep: 10mins | Cook: 35mins | Ready in:

Ingredients

- 4 cups frozen Tater Tots
- 1 pound ground beef
- 1/4 teaspoon garlic powder
- 1/8 teaspoon pepper
- 1 can (10-3/4 ounces) condensed cream of broccoli soup, undiluted
- 1/3 cup 2% milk
- 1 package (16 ounces) frozen chopped broccoli, thawed
- 1 can (2.8 ounces) French-fried onions, divided

- 1 cup shredded Colby-Monterey Jack cheese, divided
- 1 medium tomato, chopped

Direction

- Preheat oven to 400°. In an ungreased baking dish of 13x9-inch, spread Tater Tots evenly. Uncovered while baking for around 10 minutes.
- In the meantime, in a large skillet over medium heat, cook and crumble beef for nearly 5 to 7 minutes until there is not pink anymore; and then drain. Stir in broccoli, soup, seasonings, milk, 3/4 cup onions, tomato and 1/2 cup cheese; heat through. Then pour over potatoes.
- Covered while baking for another 20 minutes. Have cheese and the remaining onions to sprinkle. Uncovered during bake for approximately 5 to 10 minutes until cheese is melted.

Nutrition Information

- Calories: 400 calories
- Sodium: 805mg sodium
- Fiber: 4g fiber)
- Total Carbohydrate: 29g carbohydrate (3g sugars
- Cholesterol: 50mg cholesterol
- Protein: 17g protein.
- Total Fat: 24g fat (9g saturated fat)

48. Beef 'n' Biscuit Bake

Serving: 6-8 servings. | Prep: 10mins | Cook: 20mins | Ready in:

Ingredients

- 1 pound ground beef
- 1 can (16 ounces) kidney beans, rinsed and drained

- 1 can (15-1/4 ounces) whole kernel corn, drained
- 1 can (10-3/4 ounces) condensed tomato soup, undiluted
- 1/4 cup milk
- 2 tablespoons finely chopped onion
- 1/2 teaspoon chili powder
- 1/4 teaspoon salt
- 1 cup cubed process cheese (Velveeta)
- 1 tube (12 ounces) refrigerated biscuits
- 2 to 3 tablespoons butter, melted
- 1/3 cup yellow cornmeal

Direction

- Set the oven to 375° and start preheating. Cook beef in a saucepan over medium heat until not pink anymore; drain. Put in salt, chilli powder, onion, milk, soup, corn and beans; let it come to a boil. Take it away from the heat; add in cheese and stir until melted. Scoop into a greased baking dish (2-1/2-quart). Bake with no cover for 10 minutes.
- In the meantime, brush butter onto all sides of biscuits; roll in cornmeal. Put atop bubbling meat mixture. Put back to oven and bake for 10-12 minutes or until biscuits are cooked through and lightly browned.

Nutrition Information

- Calories: 439 calories
- Protein: 21g protein.
- Total Fat: 19g fat (8g saturated fat)
- Sodium: 1180mg sodium
- Fiber: 5g fiber)
- Total Carbohydrate: 44g carbohydrate (10g sugars
- Cholesterol: 46mg cholesterol

49. Beef 'n' Noodle Casserole

Serving: 6 servings. | Prep: 15mins | Cook: 30mins | Ready in:

Ingredients

- 1 package (8 ounces) medium noodles
- 1/3 cup sliced green onions
- 1/3 cup chopped green pepper
- 2 tablespoons butter
- 1 pound ground beef
- 1 can (6 ounces) tomato paste
- 1/2 cup sour cream
- 1 cup 4% cottage cheese
- 1 can (8 ounces) tomato sauce

Direction

- Cook noodles following the package instructions; strain.
- Sauté green pepper and onions with butter in a big skillet until soft, about 3 minutes. Add beef and cook until no pink remained. Strain the excess fat.
- Mix sour cream and tomato paste together in a medium-sized bowl, mixing in cottage cheese and noodles. In a 2-quart casserole, layer 1/2 the noodle mixture; put 1/2 the beef mixture on top. Continue doing the same.
- Evenly pour over the top of the casserole with tomato sauce. Bake at 350° until thoroughly heated, about 30-35 minutes.

Nutrition Information

- Calories: 404 calories
- Sodium: 412mg sodium
- Fiber: 3g fiber)
- Total Carbohydrate: 37g carbohydrate (7g sugars
- Cholesterol: 105mg cholesterol
- Protein: 26g protein.
- Total Fat: 16g fat (7g saturated fat)

50. Beef 'n' Rice Bake

Serving: 4-6 servings. | Prep: 15mins | Cook: 30mins | Ready in:

Ingredients

- 1 pound ground beef
- 3 celery ribs, thinly sliced
- 1 medium onion, chopped
- 2 cups cooked rice
- 1/2 cup chopped green pepper
- 1/2 cup chopped sweet red pepper
- 1 jar (4-1/2 ounces) sliced mushrooms, drained
- 1/2 cup soy sauce
- 2 tablespoons butter
- 1 tablespoon brown sugar
- 1 can (3 ounces) chow mein noodles

Direction

- In a large skillet over the medium heat, cook onion, celery and beef till meat is no longer pink; drain. Mix in brown sugar, butter, soy sauce, mushrooms, peppers and rice; heat through.
- Place into a greased baking dish of 2 quarts. Cover up and bake at 350° for 25-30 minutes. Sprinkle chow mein noodles on top. Bake with no cover until the noodles are crisp, about 5-10 more minutes.

Nutrition Information

- Calories: 342 calories
- Sodium: 1488mg sodium
- Fiber: 3g fiber)
- Total Carbohydrate: 31g carbohydrate (5g sugars
- Cholesterol: 47mg cholesterol
- Protein: 20g protein.
- Total Fat: 15g fat (6g saturated fat)

51. Beef 'n' Rice Hot Dish

Serving: 4 servings. | Prep: 15mins | Cook: 10mins | Ready in:

Ingredients

- 1 pound ground beef
- 1 medium onion, chopped
- 1/2 cup chopped green pepper
- 1/2 teaspoon salt
- Pinch pepper
- 1-1/2 cups uncooked instant rice
- 1 can (14-1/2 ounces) stewed tomatoes
- 1 can (8 ounces) tomato sauce
- 1-1/2 cups hot water
- 1 teaspoon prepared mustard

Direction

- Place beef in a large frying pan, cook on medium heat until beef is not pink. Drain the excess grease. Mix in salt, pepper, green pepper, and onion. Over medium heat cook until vegetables are tender stirring constantly. Mix in rest of ingredients and heat to a boil. Cover, decrease heat, and simmer for 10 minutes.

Nutrition Information

- Calories: 376 calories
- Sodium: 833mg sodium
- Fiber: 3g fiber)
- Total Carbohydrate: 45g carbohydrate (9g sugars
- Cholesterol: 56mg cholesterol
- Protein: 25g protein.
- Total Fat: 10g fat (5g saturated fat)

52. Beef Florentine

Serving: 6 | Prep: 20mins | Cook: 25mins | Ready in:

Ingredients

- 2 cups medium egg noodles
- 1 1/2 pounds ground beef
- 2 cloves garlic, chopped
- 1 teaspoon dried oregano

- 1/2 teaspoon salt
- 1/4 teaspoon pepper
- 2 (8 ounce) cans tomato sauce
- 1/2 cup water
- 1 (10 ounce) package frozen chopped spinach, thawed and drained
- 1 (8 ounce) container cottage cheese
- 1/4 cup chopped onion
- 2 tablespoons grated Parmesan cheese
- 8 ounces shredded mozzarella cheese

Direction

- Place a lightly salted water in a big pot and make it boil. Cook in the pasta for 8-10 minutes or until al dente; strain.
- Prepare the oven by preheating to 350°F (175°C).
- Sear ground beef in a skillet over medium heat until equally brown; remove extra fat. Add pepper, salt and oregano to taste. Mix in water and tomato sauce. Separate the skillet from heat and mix in cooked noodles.
- Mix together in a medium-sized bowl the Parmesan cheese, onion, cottage cheese and spinach. In a big casserole dish, spread half of the noodle mixture. Put a layer of all of the spinach mixture then top with the remaining noodle mixture.
- Place in the preheated oven and bake for 15 minutes. Add mozzarella on top and keep on baking for 10 more minutes or until cheese is dissolved.

Nutrition Information

- Calories: 574 calories;
- Cholesterol: 137
- Protein: 37.7
- Total Fat: 39.4
- Sodium: 1110
- Total Carbohydrate: 17.2

53. Beef Noodle Bake

Serving: 6 servings. | Prep: 15mins | Cook: 35mins | Ready in:

Ingredients

- 1-1/2 pounds ground beef
- 1 small onion, chopped
- 2 cans (8 ounces each) tomato sauce
- 1 cup sour cream
- 3 ounces cream cheese, cubed and softened
- 1 teaspoon sugar
- 1/2 to 1 teaspoon garlic salt
- 7 cups uncooked wide egg noodles, cooked and drained
- 1 cup shredded cheddar cheese

Direction

- Cook onion and beef in a large skillet until the meat is no more pink; allow to drain. Remove from the heat; then stir in garlic salt, sugar, cream cheese, sour cream, and tomato sauce.
- In a greased 13x9-in. baking dish, put 1/2 noodles and lay 1/2 of the beef mixture on top. Repeat the layers. Cover and bake until heated through at 350°, for 30-35 minutes. Next, sprinkle with cheese; continue to bake until the cheese is melted, for another 3-5 minutes.

Nutrition Information

- Calories: 559 calories
- Protein: 33g protein.
- Total Fat: 29g fat (17g saturated fat)
- Sodium: 584mg sodium
- Fiber: 2g fiber)
- Total Carbohydrate: 38g carbohydrate (4g sugars
- Cholesterol: 160mg cholesterol

54. Beef Pastitsio

Serving: 6-8 servings. | Prep: 30mins | Cook: 30mins | Ready in:

Ingredients

- 1 pound ground beef
- 1 cup chopped onion
- 1 can (15 ounces) tomato sauce
- 1/2 teaspoon salt
- 1/2 teaspoon dried oregano
- 1/4 teaspoon pepper
- 1 garlic clove, minced
- 2 cups uncooked elbow macaroni
- 1 cup shredded cheddar cheese
- 1 large egg, lightly beaten
- CHEESE SAUCE:
- 3 tablespoons butter, melted
- 3 tablespoons all-purpose flour
- 1-1/2 cups whole milk
- 1 cup shredded cheddar cheese
- 1/2 teaspoon salt

Direction

- Put the onion and beef in a large skillet and cook on medium heat until meat is not pink any more. Strain. Mix in the garlic, pepper, oregano, salt and tomato sauce. Cover and boil gently for 15 minutes.
- In the meantime, cook macaroni based on the package instructions. Strain and rinse.
- Using a large bowl, mix the egg, cheese and macaroni; reserve. Melt the butter in a large saucepan. Mix in flour until it turns smooth; slowly add the milk. Let it boil. Stir and cook for 2 minutes or until it becomes thick. Turn off heat and add in salt and cheese.
- In a 13x9-inch baking dish, scoop half of the macaroni mixture then spread with the meat mixture. Add the remaining macaroni mixture on top. Put cheese mixture over top.
- Place in the oven without cover, and bake for 30 minutes at 350°, or until heated through. Allow to stand for 5-10 minutes prior serving.

Nutrition Information

- Calories: 363 calories
- Sodium: 674mg sodium
- Fiber: 2g fiber)
- Total Carbohydrate: 24g carbohydrate (5g sugars
- Cholesterol: 102mg cholesterol
- Protein: 22g protein.
- Total Fat: 20g fat (12g saturated fat)

55. Beef Potato Casserole

Serving: 4-6 servings. | Prep: 15mins | Cook: 01hours15mins | Ready in:

Ingredients

- 4 medium potatoes, peeled and sliced
- 1 pound ground beef, cooked and drained
- 1 can (10-3/4 ounces) condensed cream of chicken soup, undiluted
- 1 can (10-3/4 ounces) condensed vegetable beef soup, undiluted
- 1/2 teaspoon salt

Direction

- Mix all of the ingredients together in a big bowl. Remove into a 2-quart greased baking dish. Put a cover on and bake at 350° until the potatoes are soft, about 1 1/4-1 1/2 hours.

Nutrition Information

- Calories: 277 calories
- Sodium: 947mg sodium
- Fiber: 3g fiber)
- Total Carbohydrate: 27g carbohydrate (2g sugars
- Cholesterol: 43mg cholesterol
- Protein: 18g protein.
- Total Fat: 11g fat (4g saturated fat)

56. Beef Spinach Hot Dish

Serving: 6-8 servings. | Prep: 30mins | Cook: 20mins | Ready in:

Ingredients

- 1 pound ground beef
- 1 medium onion, chopped
- 2 garlic cloves, minced
- 1 can (4 ounces) mushroom stems and pieces, drained
- 1 teaspoon salt
- 1 teaspoon dried oregano
- 1/4 teaspoon pepper
- 2 packages (10 ounces each) frozen chopped spinach, thawed and squeezed dry
- 1 can (10-3/4 ounces) condensed cream of celery soup, undiluted
- 1 cup (8 ounces) sour cream
- 2 cups shredded part-skim mozzarella cheese, divided

Direction

- Cook onion and beef in a large skillet over medium heat until the beef is no longer pink. Put in garlic; cook for 1 more minute. Drain. Mix in pepper, oregano, salt and mushrooms. Add in sour cream, soup and spinach. Stir in 1/2 the cheese.
- Place into a greased 2-quart baking dish. Bake without covering at 350° for 15 minutes. Sprinkle remaining cheese on top; bake until cheese is melted, about 5 more minutes.

Nutrition Information

- Calories: 269 calories
- Fiber: 2g fiber)
- Total Carbohydrate: 9g carbohydrate (3g sugars
- Cholesterol: 66mg cholesterol
- Protein: 20g protein.
- Total Fat: 16g fat (9g saturated fat)

57. Beef Stuffing Bake

Serving: 6-8 servings. | Prep: 10mins | Cook: 30mins | Ready in:

Ingredients

- 1 pound ground beef
- 1 small onion, chopped
- 1 package (10 ounces) beef- or pork-flavored stuffing mix
- 1 can (10-3/4 ounces) condensed cream of celery soup, undiluted
- 1 can (10-3/4 ounces) condensed cream of mushroom soup, undiluted
- 1 jar (4-1/2 ounces) sliced mushrooms, drained
- 1 cup water
- 1 cup frozen mixed vegetables

Direction

- In a skillet over medium heat, cook onion and beef until meat is no longer pink; drain. Place into ungreased baking dish (13x9 inches).
- Combine vegetables, water, mushrooms, soups and contents of stuffing seasoning packet in a large bowl. Sprinkle stuffing atop the beef mixture; add soup mixture on top.
- Bake with no cover at 350° until heated through, about half an hour.

Nutrition Information

- Calories: 319 calories
- Cholesterol: 31mg cholesterol
- Protein: 16g protein.
- Total Fat: 12g fat (4g saturated fat)
- Sodium: 1239mg sodium
- Fiber: 3g fiber)
- Total Carbohydrate: 35g carbohydrate (6g sugars

58. Beef And Broccoli Casserole

Serving: 6 servings. | Prep: 20mins | Cook: 15mins | Ready in:

Ingredients

- 1 pound ground beef
- 1/2 cup chopped onion
- 1 tablespoon Worcestershire sauce
- 1 teaspoon garlic salt
- 1 teaspoon Italian seasoning
- 1 cup uncooked instant rice
- 1 can (10-3/4 ounces) condensed cream of mushroom soup, undiluted
- 1/2 cup water
- 2 pounds fresh broccoli, chopped or 6 cups frozen chopped broccoli, cooked and drained
- 6 ounces sliced part-skim mozzarella cheese
- Chopped fresh parsley, optional

Direction

- In a skillet, cook onion and beef in oil until meat is no longer pink; drain. Mix in water, soup, rice, Italian seasoning, garlic salt and Worcestershire sauce.
- Arrange cooked broccoli in a baking dish of 11x7 inches; add meat mixture on top. Sprinkle mozzarella cheese on top. Bake with no cover, at 400° for 15-20 minutes. Add parsley on top for extra flavor, if desired.

Nutrition Information

- Calories: 368 calories
- Total Fat: 17g fat (7g saturated fat)
- Sodium: 928mg sodium
- Fiber: 5g fiber)
- Total Carbohydrate: 28g carbohydrate (4g sugars
- Cholesterol: 54mg cholesterol
- Protein: 28g protein.

59. Beef And Mashed Potato Casserole

Serving: 4 servings. | Prep: 25mins | Cook: 20mins | Ready in:

Ingredients

- 1 pound ground beef
- 1 medium onion, chopped
- 2 green onions, sliced
- 1 can (15-1/4 ounces) whole kernel corn, drained
- 1 can (11 ounces) condensed cream of tomato bisque soup, undiluted
- 2 teaspoons minced garlic
- 1/2 teaspoon ground mustard
- 3/4 teaspoon salt
- 1/2 teaspoon pepper
- 1/4 teaspoon dried basil
- 1/4 cup grated Parmesan cheese
- 2-1/2 cups hot mashed potatoes
- 6 slices process cheese

Direction

- In a big skillet over medium heat, cook onion and beef till meat is not pink anymore; let drain. Mix in the basil, pepper, salt, mustard, garlic, soup and corn. Allow to boil. Lessen heat; simmer, covered, for 10-15 minutes. Mix in the Parmesan cheese.
- Spoon the mixture into a greased 13x9-inch baking dish. Cover with cheese slices and mashed potatoes. Bake while uncovered at 350° for around 20-30 minutes or until bubbly.

Nutrition Information

- Calories: 531 calories
- Fiber: 4g fiber)
- Total Carbohydrate: 58g carbohydrate (17g sugars

- Cholesterol: 70mg cholesterol
- Protein: 31g protein.
- Total Fat: 18g fat (8g saturated fat)
- Sodium: 2002mg sodium

60. Beef And Noodle Bake

Serving: 5 | Prep: 30mins | Cook: 30mins | Ready in:

Ingredients

- 1 pound ground beef
- 2 cups elbow macaroni
- 4 cups spaghetti sauce
- 12 ounces processed cheese food (eg. Velveeta), sliced

Direction

- Set oven to 375 degrees F or 190 degrees C and start preheating.
- In a big frying pan, brown beef on medium-high heat; set it aside. Follow directions on package to cook macaroni, drain water and set it aside.
- In a 9x13 pan, make layers of macaroni, beef, tomato sauce, and cheese, repeat layers twice.
- Bake in a 375-degree F or 190-degree C oven until the cheese on top is bubbling, 30 minutes.

Nutrition Information

- Calories: 640 calories;
- Total Carbohydrate: 66.8
- Cholesterol: 87
- Protein: 37.4
- Total Fat: 23.8
- Sodium: 1941

61. Beef And Noodle Casserole

Serving: 4 | Prep: 30mins | Cook: 30mins | Ready in:

Ingredients

- 6 ounces egg noodles
- 1 pound ground beef
- 2 (10.75 ounce) cans condensed tomato soup
- 2 tablespoons Worcestershire sauce
- 2 cloves garlic, minced
- 1/2 pound shredded Cheddar cheese
- 1/4 cup dry sherry
- 1/4 cup grated Parmesan cheese

Direction

- Set an oven to 190°C (375°F) and start preheating.
- Following the package instructions, cook the noodles.
- In a large skillet, brown the ground beef on medium-high heat. Stir in garlic, Worcestershire sauce, and tomato soup, then boil, turn down the heat to low and allow to simmer.
- Stir the cheese and noodles into the simmering sauce once the noodles are finished, until the cheese melts. Add the sherry into the sauce and stir for a minute, arrange in a 2-quart casserole dish and dust to taste with Parmesan cheese.
- In the prepared oven, bake for half an hour.

Nutrition Information

- Calories: 745 calories;
- Total Fat: 38.1
- Sodium: 1540
- Total Carbohydrate: 55.5
- Cholesterol: 169
- Protein: 44.1

62. Beef And Potato Casserole

Serving: 6 servings. | Prep: 15mins | Cook: 25mins | Ready in:

Ingredients

- 4 cups frozen potato rounds
- 1 pound ground beef
- 3 cups frozen chopped broccoli, thawed
- 1 can (10-3/4 ounces) condensed cream of celery soup, undiluted
- 1/3 cup whole milk
- 1 cup shredded cheddar cheese
- 1/4 teaspoon garlic powder
- 1/8 teaspoon pepper

Direction

- Up the sides and on the bottom of a 13x9-inch baking dish, put potato rounds. Bake for 10 minutes at 400°.
- In the meantime, cook beef over medium heat until no pink remains; strain. Put over the potatoes with broccoli and beef. Mix together pepper, garlic powder, 1/2 cup cheddar cheese, milk, and celery soup. Add to the beef mixture.
- Put a cover on and bake for 20 minutes at 400°. Put the leftover cheese on top. Put back into the oven to melt the cheese, about 2-3 minutes.

Nutrition Information

- Calories: 386 calories
- Total Fat: 23g fat (10g saturated fat)
- Sodium: 884mg sodium
- Fiber: 4g fiber)
- Total Carbohydrate: 28g carbohydrate (2g sugars
- Cholesterol: 61mg cholesterol
- Protein: 22g protein.

63. Beef And Potato Nacho Casserole

Serving: 8 servings. | Prep: 20mins | Cook: 01hours15mins |Ready in:

Ingredients

- 2 pounds lean ground beef (90% lean)
- 3/4 cup chopped onion, divided
- 1 envelope taco seasoning
- 1 can (8 ounces) tomato sauce
- 3/4 cup water
- 1 can (4 ounces) chopped green chilies, drained
- 1 can (16 ounces) kidney beans, rinsed and drained
- 1 package (24 ounces) frozen O'Brien potatoes, thawed
- 1 can (10-3/4 ounces) condensed nacho cheese soup, undiluted
- 1/2 cup milk
- 1/4 cup chopped green pepper
- 1 teaspoon Worcestershire sauce
- 1/4 teaspoon sugar
- Paprika

Direction

- Cook 1/2 cup of onion and beef until beef is not pink in a big frying pan with heat on medium. Drain excess grease. Add and stir water, tomato sauce, and taco seasoning. Heat to boiling. Decrease heat and gently boil for 1 minute. Grease a 13x9-in. pan and spread beef mixture in bottom. Put potatoes, green chilies, and beans on top. Mix sugar, remaining onion, milk, Worcestershire sauce, soup, and green pepper in a big bowl. Pour mixture over potatoes. Sprinkle paprika on top. Cover; bake in a 350-degree oven for 1 hour. Remove the cover and bake until light brown, 15 minutes. Let it cool for 10 minutes before serving.

Nutrition Information

- Calories: 365 calories
- Sodium: 1042mg sodium
- Fiber: 6g fiber)
- Total Carbohydrate: 34g carbohydrate (5g sugars
- Cholesterol: 62mg cholesterol
- Protein: 29g protein.

- Total Fat: 11g fat (5g saturated fat)

64. Beef And Wild Rice Casserole

Serving: 6-8 servings. | Prep: 15mins | Cook: 01hours20mins | Ready in:

Ingredients

- 1-1/2 pounds ground beef
- 1 medium onion, chopped
- 1 cup uncooked wild rice, rinsed
- 1 can (10-3/4 ounces) condensed cream of mushroom soup, undiluted
- 1 can (10-3/4 ounces) condensed chicken noodle soup, undiluted
- 2 soup cans water

Direction

- In a skillet, brown ground beef with onion until the onion is soften and the beef is browned; drain. Place in a casserole of 3-quart. Add all the rest ingredients and mix well. Bake while covered at 375° for around 1 hour and 20 minutes, stirring often.

Nutrition Information

- Calories: 279 calories
- Fiber: 2g fiber)
- Total Carbohydrate: 25g carbohydrate (2g sugars
- Cholesterol: 45mg cholesterol
- Protein: 20g protein.
- Total Fat: 10g fat (4g saturated fat)
- Sodium: 612mg sodium

65. Beef, Rice And Chili Casserole

Serving: 6-8 servings. | Prep: 20mins | Cook: 40mins | Ready in:

Ingredients

- 1/2 pound ground beef
- 1 cup chopped celery
- 1/2 cup chopped onion
- 1 small green pepper, chopped
- 1 garlic clove, minced
- 2 cups cooked rice
- 1 can (15-ounce) chili con carne with beans
- 2/3 cup mayonnaise
- Few drops hot pepper sauce
- 1/2 teaspoon salt
- 1 can (14-1/2-ounce) Mexican-style stewed tomatoes
- 1 to 2 cups shredded cheddar cheese
- 4 cups corn chips

Direction

- Cook garlic, green pepper, onion, celery and ground beef in a skillet till meat turns browned and vegetables become softened; drain. Mix in tomatoes, salt, hot pepper sauce, mayonnaise, chili, and rice. Add mixture to one 2-1/2-qt. casserole. Bake at 350 degrees till thoroughly heated or for 35 to 45 minutes. Add corn chips and cheese. Bring back to the oven for 3 - 4 minutes or till cheese is melted. Allow to rest several minutes prior to serving.

Nutrition Information

- Calories:
- Fiber:
- Total Carbohydrate:
- Cholesterol:
- Protein:
- Total Fat:
- Sodium:

66. Beefy Barbecue Macaroni

Serving: 4 servings. | Prep: 15mins | Cook: 0mins | Ready in:

Ingredients

- 3/4 pound ground beef
- 1/2 cup chopped onion
- 3 garlic cloves, minced
- 3-1/2 cups cooked elbow macaroni
- 3/4 cup barbecue sauce
- 1/4 teaspoon pepper
- Dash cayenne pepper
- 1/4 cup whole milk
- 1 tablespoon butter
- 1 cup shredded sharp cheddar cheese
- Additional cheddar cheese, optional

Direction

- Cook garlic, beef, and onion on medium heat in a big frying pan until meat is not pink, 5-6 minutes. As it cooks, break the meat into crumbles; drain excess grease. Add pepper, macaroni, cayenne, and barbecue sauce. In a small pot on medium heat, cook butter and milk until the butter melts. Add the cheese and stir until it melts. Dump over macaroni mixture; carefully mix to coat. If desired, sprinkle with more cheese.

Nutrition Information

- Calories: 456 calories
- Sodium: 647mg sodium
- Fiber: 2g fiber)
- Total Carbohydrate: 39g carbohydrate (9g sugars
- Cholesterol: 81mg cholesterol
- Protein: 28g protein.
- Total Fat: 21g fat (12g saturated fat)

67. Beefy Rice Dinner

Serving: 4-6 servings. | Prep: 20mins | Cook: 10mins | Ready in:

Ingredients

- 1 package (6.8 ounces) beef-flavored rice mix
- 1/2 pound lean ground beef (90% lean)
- 1/3 cup chopped celery
- 1/3 cup chopped green pepper
- 1/8 to 1/4 teaspoon salt
- 1/8 teaspoon pepper
- 1/3 cup shredded cheddar cheese

Direction

- Cook rice following the package instructions. In the meantime, cook green pepper, celery, and beef in a big frying pan until the vegetables are soft and the meat turns brown; strain. Add pepper, salt, and rice.
- Remove into a 2-quart baking dish coated with cooking spray. Sprinkle cheese over. Bake without a cover at 350° until fully heated and the cheese melts, about 10-15 minutes.

Nutrition Information

- Calories:
- Fiber:
- Total Carbohydrate:
- Cholesterol:
- Protein:
- Total Fat:
- Sodium:

68. Biscuit Pizza Bake

Serving: 6-8 servings. | Prep: 15mins | Cook: 30mins | Ready in:

Ingredients

- 1 pound ground beef
- 2 tubes (12 ounces each) refrigerated buttermilk biscuits
- 1 package (3-1/2 ounces) sliced pepperoni
- 1 can (4 ounces) mushroom stems and pieces, drained
- 1 can (15 ounces) pizza sauce

- 1 cup chopped green pepper
- 1/2 cup chopped onion
- 1 cup shredded cheddar cheese
- 1 cup shredded part-skim mozzarella cheese

Direction

- Set oven to 350 degrees and start preheating. In a big skillet on medium heat, cook beef for 6-8 minutes or until not pink anymore, breaking into crumbles. At the same time, cut the biscuits into quarters then put in an oiled 13x9-inch baking dish. Drain beef and arrange over biscuits.
- Layer with onion, green pepper, pizza sauce, mushrooms, and pepperoni. Bake for 15 minutes without cover. Sprinkle cheese over top. Continue to bake for 15-20 minutes or until cheese melts. Let it sit for 5-10 minutes then serve.

Nutrition Information

- Calories: 369 calories
- Protein: 23g protein.
- Total Fat: 19g fat (9g saturated fat)
- Sodium: 968mg sodium
- Fiber: 2g fiber)
- Total Carbohydrate: 27g carbohydrate (3g sugars
- Cholesterol: 64mg cholesterol

69. Broccoli Beef Supper

Serving: 8 servings. | Prep: 15mins | Cook: 35mins | Ready in:

Ingredients

- 4 cups frozen cottage fries
- 1 pound ground beef
- 3 cups frozen chopped broccoli, thawed
- 1 can (2.8 ounces) french-fried onions, divided
- 1 medium tomato, chopped

- 1 can (10-3/4 ounces) condensed cream of celery soup, undiluted
- 1 cup shredded cheddar cheese, divided
- 1/2 cup whole milk
- 1/4 teaspoon garlic powder
- 1/4 teaspoon pepper

Direction

- Line cottage fries on the bottom and sides of a greased baking dish of 13x9 inches. Bake with no cover, at 400° for 10 minutes.
- In the meantime, over medium heat in a large skillet, cook beef till no longer pink; drain. Layer the beef, broccoli, half of the onions and the tomato over fries. Combine pepper, garlic powder, milk, 1/2 cup of cheese and soup in a small bowl; pour over top.
- Cover up and bake at 400° for 20 minutes. Remove the cover; sprinkle with the remaining onions and cheese. Bake until cheese is melted, about 2 more minutes.

Nutrition Information

- Calories: 420 calories
- Sodium: 529mg sodium
- Fiber: 3g fiber)
- Total Carbohydrate: 40g carbohydrate (3g sugars
- Cholesterol: 46mg cholesterol
- Protein: 18g protein.
- Total Fat: 22g fat (9g saturated fat)

70. Bubbly & Golden Mexican Beef Cobbler

Serving: 6 servings. | Prep: 20mins | Cook: 35mins | Ready in:

Ingredients

- 1 pound ground beef
- 1 envelope reduced-sodium taco seasoning

- 3/4 cup water
- 1 jar (16 ounces) salsa
- 1 can (8-3/4 ounces) whole kernel corn, drained
- 2 cups shredded sharp cheddar cheese
- 3-1/3 cups biscuit/baking mix
- 1-1/3 cups 2% milk
- 1/8 teaspoon pepper

Direction

- Put a large skillet over medium heat setting and cook beef for about 6-8 minutes or until brown in color and starting to crumble then drain excess oil. Add in water and taco seasoning into the cooked beef. Cook the mixture bringing it to a boil until the liquid has reduced. Once done, transfer the mixture into an 11x7-inch baking dish and put corn, cheese and salsa on top.
- Put biscuit mix and milk together in a separate large bowl and mix thoroughly then put a couple tablespoonfuls of the mixture over cheese until the baking dish is fully filled. Season with pepper.
- Keep the baking dish uncovered then put into an oven at 350 degrees for about 35-45 minutes or until the topping is bubbling and golden brown in color.

Nutrition Information

- Calories: 646 calories
- Protein: 30g protein.
- Total Fat: 31g fat (14g saturated fat)
- Sodium: 1877mg sodium
- Fiber: 3g fiber)
- Total Carbohydrate: 59g carbohydrate (11g sugars
- Cholesterol: 90mg cholesterol

Ingredients

- 1 lb. lean ground beef
- 1 pkg. (1-1/4 oz.) TACO BELL® Taco Seasoning Mix
- 12 flour tortilla s (6 inch)
- 1 can (16 oz.) TACO BELL® Refried Beans
- 1 cup KRAFT Mexican Style Finely Shredded Cheddar Jack Cheese

Direction

- Cook meat with the seasoning mix according to the package instructions.
- On the base of a 9in pie plate sprayed with cooking spray, put 4 tortillas and overlap them to fully cover the base of the pie plate. Layer with cheese, meat mixture, and layers of half of each beans on top. Repeat the layering and cover it with the rest of the tortillas.
- Bake until cheese melts and meat mixture is heated through, about 30 minutes. Slice into wedges before serving.

Nutrition Information

- Calories: 440
- Sodium: 1270 mg
- Fiber: 5 g
- Sugar: 2 g
- Total Carbohydrate: 44 g
- Cholesterol: 65 mg
- Protein: 28 g
- Saturated Fat: 7 g
- Total Fat: 16 g

72. Cabbage Roll Casserole

Serving: 12 | Prep: 10mins | Cook: 1hours30mins |Ready in:

Ingredients

- 2 pounds ground beef
- 1 cup chopped onion

71. Burrito Bake

Serving: 8 servings | Prep: 15mins | Cook: |Ready in:

- 1 (29 ounce) can tomato sauce
- 3 1/2 pounds chopped cabbage
- 1 cup uncooked white rice
- 1 teaspoon salt
- 2 (14 ounce) cans beef broth

Direction

- Preheat an oven to 175°C/350°F.
- Brown beef in oil in a big skillet on medium high heat till redness goes away. Drain fat.
- Mix salt, rice, cabbage, tomato sauce and onion in a big mixing bowl. Add meat; mix everything together. Put mixture into a 9x13-in. baking dish. Put broth on meat mixture. In preheated oven, bake for 1 hour, covered. Mix. Replace cover. Bake for 30 more minutes.

Nutrition Information

- Calories: 352 calories;
- Sodium: 840
- Total Carbohydrate: 25.5
- Cholesterol: 64
- Protein: 17.1
- Total Fat: 20.6

73. Canadian Meat Pie

Serving: 8 servings. | Prep: 30mins | Cook: 30mins | Ready in:

Ingredients

- 2 cups all-purpose flour
- 1 teaspoon salt
- 2/3 cup plus 2 tablespoons shortening
- 1 egg, beaten
- 2 to 3 tablespoons cold water
- FILLING:
- 3/4 pound ground beef
- 3/4 pound ground pork
- 1 medium onion, chopped
- 1 garlic clove, minced

- 1/4 cup water
- 1 teaspoon salt
- 1/2 teaspoon rubbed sage
- 1/2 teaspoon dried thyme
- 1/4 teaspoon ground allspice
- 1/4 teaspoon pepper
- 1/8 teaspoon ground cloves
- Milk

Direction

- In a big bowl, combine salt and flour. Cut in shortening till the mixture looks coarse crumbs. Put in water and egg; use a fork to lightly toss until it forms a dough ball. Halve the dough; cover with plastic wrap and let cool in the fridge.
- Cook garlic pork, onion, and beef in a big skillet over medium heat until meat is not pink anymore; drain. Mix in seasonings; let heat through.
- Roll out one part of dough on a floured surface. Line a 9-inch pie plate with bottom pastry. Mound filling into the crust. Roll out the leftover dough to fit top of pie. Put over filling. Secure and flute edges. Brush milk over the pastry; cut slits in top.
- Bake at 375° for about 30-35 minutes or until golden brown, loosely covering edges with foil if needed. Allow to stand for about 15 minutes before cutting.

Nutrition Information

- Calories: 480 calories
- Protein: 21g protein.
- Total Fat: 32g fat (9g saturated fat)
- Sodium: 643mg sodium
- Fiber: 1g fiber)
- Total Carbohydrate: 26g carbohydrate (2g sugars
- Cholesterol: 83mg cholesterol

74. Cannelloni

Serving: 8-10 servings. | Prep: 30mins | Cook: 20mins | Ready in:

Ingredients

- FILLING:
- 1 large onion, finely chopped
- 2 tablespoons olive oil
- 1 garlic clove, minced
- 1 package (10 ounces) frozen chopped spinach, thawed and squeezed dry
- 1 pound ground beef
- 1/4 cup grated Parmesan cheese
- 2 tablespoons heavy whipping cream
- 2 large eggs, lightly beaten
- 1/2 teaspoon dried oregano
- 1 teaspoon salt
- 1/4 teaspoon pepper
- 10 lasagna noodles
- 1 can (24 ounces) tomato sauce, divided
- CREAM SAUCE:
- 6 tablespoons butter
- 6 tablespoons all-purpose flour
- 1 cup whole milk
- 1 cup heavy whipping cream
- Salt and pepper to taste
- 1/2 cup grated Parmesan cheese

Direction

- In a large skillet, sauté onion in olive oil until tender. Stir in garlic; cook for approximately 1 minute. Stir in spinach. Cook for around 5 minutes until the spinach starts to stick to the pan and all the water has evaporated, stirring constantly. Place to a large bowl.
- Brown meat in the same skillet; drain and add to the spinach mixture. Mix in the cream, cheese, oregano, eggs, pepper and salt; mix well. Leave aside.
- Cook lasagna noodles following the instruction of the package; drain. Cut in half the width of each noodle; on a large piece of foil, spread noodles out side by side. At one end of noodle, place 1 heaping tablespoon of filling; roll up. With remaining noodles and filling, repeat.
- In a baking dish of 13x9-inch, pour about 1 cup of tomato sauce to the bottom. In the baking dish, place two rolls vertically with seam side down on both sides. Place the rest rolls in four rows of three rolls each; leave aside.
- For making cream sauce, in a heavy saucepan over medium heat, melt butter; mix in flour until smooth; stir in milk and cream gradually. Allow to boil, cook and stir for 1 minute until thickened. Take away from heat; taste with salt and pepper. Spread over lasagna rolls with the cream sauce. Have the rest tomato sauce to cover. Use cheese to sprinkle.
- Bake uncovered at 375° for approximately 20 to 30 minutes until bubbly and hot.

Nutrition Information

- Calories: 443 calories
- Total Carbohydrate: 30g carbohydrate (5g sugars
- Cholesterol: 128mg cholesterol
- Protein: 19g protein.
- Total Fat: 28g fat (15g saturated fat)
- Sodium: 817mg sodium
- Fiber: 3g fiber)

75. Cheeseburger 'n' Fries Casserole

Serving: 6-8 servings. | Prep: 10mins | Cook: 50mins | Ready in:

Ingredients

- 2 pounds lean ground beef (90% lean)
- 1 can (10-3/4 ounces) condensed golden mushroom soup, undiluted
- 1 can (10-3/4 ounces) condensed cheddar cheese soup, undiluted

- 1 package (20 ounces) frozen crinkle-cut french fries

Direction

- Set oven at 350° to preheat. Add beef to a big frying pan, cook over medium heat until it is not pink any longer; drain. Mix in soup. Pour it into a 13x9-inch baking dish coated with cooking spray.
- Lay French fries over top. Bake while uncovered until the fries turn golden brown, about 50 to 55 minutes.

Nutrition Information

- Calories: 352 calories
- Sodium: 668mg sodium
- Fiber: 2g fiber)
- Total Carbohydrate: 25g carbohydrate (1g sugars
- Cholesterol: 62mg cholesterol
- Protein: 25g protein.
- Total Fat: 17g fat (5g saturated fat)

76. Cheeseburger Casserole

Serving: 4 servings. | Prep: 25mins | Cook: 0mins | Ready in:

Ingredients

- 1 pound ground beef
- 1/2 cup chopped onion
- 2 cups water
- 2/3 cup ketchup
- 2 tablespoons prepared mustard
- 1 teaspoon salt
- 1/4 teaspoon pepper
- 2 cups uncooked instant rice
- 2 slices cheddar cheese, cut into 1-inch strips

Direction

- In a frying pan over medium heat, cook the onion and beef until browned; let drain. Put in pepper, salt, mustard, ketchup and water; stir thoroughly. Let it boil. Mix in rice. Cover and take it away from the heat; allow to rest for 5 minutes. Sprinkle with cheese; cover and allow to rest for 3-5 minutes or till cheese becomes melted.

Nutrition Information

- Calories: 469 calories
- Total Carbohydrate: 53g carbohydrate (6g sugars
- Cholesterol: 70mg cholesterol
- Protein: 28g protein.
- Total Fat: 15g fat (8g saturated fat)
- Sodium: 1315mg sodium
- Fiber: 2g fiber)

77. Cheesy Beef 'n' Rice

Serving: 6 servings. | Prep: 30mins | Cook: 50mins | Ready in:

Ingredients

- 1 cup uncooked long grain rice
- 1 garlic clove, minced
- 2 tablespoons butter
- 3 cups water
- 2 medium carrots, shredded
- 2 teaspoons beef bouillon granules
- 1 teaspoon dried parsley flakes
- 1/2 teaspoon dried basil
- 1/2 teaspoon dried minced onion
- 1 pound ground beef, cooked and drained
- 1/2 cup shredded cheddar cheese

Direction

- Sauté garlic and rice in a large saucepan with butter until golden brown. Mix in onion, basil, salt, parsley, bouillon, carrots and water. Let it come to a boil. Lower the heat; cover and let it simmer for 5 minutes. Mix in beef. Place into a greased 9-in square baking dish. Cover and bake at 325° for 45 minutes, stir twice. Remove the cover; sprinkle cheese on top. Continue to bake until cheese is melted, about 5 more minutes.

Nutrition Information

- Calories: 310 calories
- Protein: 18g protein.
- Total Fat: 14g fat (7g saturated fat)
- Sodium: 417mg sodium
- Fiber: 1g fiber)
- Total Carbohydrate: 28g carbohydrate (2g sugars
- Cholesterol: 57mg cholesterol

78. Cheesy Beef Casserole

Serving: 6 servings. | Prep: 20mins | Cook: 30mins | Ready in:

Ingredients

- 4 cups uncooked medium egg noodles
- 1 pound ground beef
- 3/4 cup chopped onion
- 2 cans (8 ounces each) tomato sauce
- 1/2 teaspoon garlic powder
- 1/2 teaspoon salt
- 1/4 teaspoon pepper
- 1 package (8 ounces) cream cheese, softened
- 1 cup (8 ounces) 4% cottage cheese
- 1/2 cup grated Parmesan cheese
- 1/3 cup sliced green onions
- 1/4 cup chopped green pepper
- Additional Parmesan cheese, optional

Direction

- Cook noodles following package instructions. In the meantime, cook onion and beef in a

large skillet over medium heat until meat is no longer pink; drain. Put in pepper, salt, garlic powder and tomato sauce.
- Mix green pepper, onions, Parmesan cheese, cottage cheese and cream cheese together in a large bowl. Drain noodles; put half in a greased 13x9-inch baking dish. Place half of the cheese and meat mixtures on top. Repeat layers. Sprinkle more Parmesan cheese on top if desired.
- Cover and bake at 350° until heated through, about 30-35 minutes.

Nutrition Information

- Calories: 468 calories
- Protein: 30g protein.
- Total Fat: 27g fat (14g saturated fat)
- Sodium: 783mg sodium
- Fiber: 2g fiber)
- Total Carbohydrate: 26g carbohydrate (5g sugars
- Cholesterol: 129mg cholesterol

79. Cheesy Casserole

Serving: 6-8 servings. | Prep: 20mins | Cook: 30mins | Ready in:

Ingredients

- 1 pound ground beef
- 1 can (10-3/4 ounces) condensed tomato soup, undiluted
- 1 teaspoon salt
- 1/8 teaspoon pepper
- 1 cup 4% cottage cheese
- 1 cup sour cream
- 6 to 8 green onions with tops, sliced
- 8 ounces medium noodles, cooked and drained
- 1 cup shredded cheddar cheese

Direction

- Brown beef in a skillet; drain. Add in pepper, salt and soup; allow to simmer for 5 minutes. Discard from the heat.
- Mix noodles, green onions, sour cream and cottage cheese in a large bowl. Layer the noodle mixture alternately with meat sauce in a greased baking dish of 2 quarts.
- Cover up and bake at 350° for 25 minutes. Sprinkle cheese on top; put back to oven and bake till cheese is melted, about 5-10 more minutes.

Nutrition Information

- Calories: 347 calories
- Total Fat: 16g fat (10g saturated fat)
- Sodium: 763mg sodium
- Fiber: 2g fiber)
- Total Carbohydrate: 26g carbohydrate (6g sugars
- Cholesterol: 92mg cholesterol
- Protein: 21g protein.

80. Cheesy Hamburger Supper

Serving: 4 servings. | Prep: 5mins | Cook: 25mins | Ready in:

Ingredients

- 1 pound ground beef
- 1-1/2 cups water
- 1/2 teaspoon poultry seasoning
- 1/4 teaspoon pepper
- 1 envelope brown gravy mix
- 1 medium onion, sliced and separated into rings
- 1 medium carrot, sliced
- 2 medium potatoes, sliced
- 1 cup shredded cheddar cheese

Direction

- In a large skillet over medium heat, cook beef until there is not pink anymore; and then drain. Mix in the water, add pepper and poultry seasoning. Allow to boil. Stir in gravy mix. Cook and stir for around 2 minutes until slightly thickened.
- Place the potatoes, carrot and onion over beef. Lower heat; cover while simmering for approximately 10 to 15 minutes until vegetables are soften. Have cheese for sprinkling. Cover during cook for an addition of 3 to 5 minutes until cheese is melted.

Nutrition Information

- Calories: 412 calories
- Sodium: 796mg sodium
- Fiber: 3g fiber)
- Total Carbohydrate: 30g carbohydrate (6g sugars
- Cholesterol: 86mg cholesterol
- Protein: 30g protein.
- Total Fat: 19g fat (11g saturated fat)

81. Cheesy Pizza Casserole

Serving: 8-10 servings. | Prep: 25mins | Cook: 0mins | Ready in:

Ingredients

- 1 pound ground beef
- 1 package (3-1/2 ounces) sliced pepperoni
- 1 medium onion, chopped
- 1 medium green pepper, chopped
- 1 jar (4-1/2 ounces) sliced mushrooms, drained
- 7 ounces vermicelli, cooked and drained
- 1/3 cup butter, melted
- 1 can (15 ounces) tomato sauce, divided
- 1 cup shredded Swiss cheese
- 4 cups shredded part-skim mozzarella cheese
- 1/2 teaspoon dried oregano
- 1/2 teaspoon dried basil

Direction

- Sauté green pepper, onion, pepperoni, and beef over medium heat in a large skillet until meat is no longer pink; drain. Mix in mushrooms; put to one side.
- Toss vermicelli with butter in an oiled 13x9-inch baking dish, coat by tossing. Add 1 cup of tomato sauce to pasta mixture; spread half of meat mixture over. Combine mozzarella cheese and Swiss cheese; scatter half of cheese mixture over top. Sprinkle with basil and oregano. Arrange the rest of meat and cheese mixture over top. Cover top with the rest of tomato sauce.
- Bake without covering for 25 to 30 minutes at 350°, or until bubbly.

Nutrition Information

- Calories: 422 calories
- Total Carbohydrate: 21g carbohydrate (4g sugars
- Cholesterol: 83mg cholesterol
- Protein: 28g protein.
- Total Fat: 25g fat (14g saturated fat)
- Sodium: 764mg sodium
- Fiber: 2g fiber)

82. Cheesy Potato Beef Bake

Serving: 8 servings. | Prep: 10mins | Cook: 35mins | Ready in:

Ingredients

- 1 pound ground beef
- 2 cans (4 ounces each) mushroom stems and pieces, drained, optional
- 2 packages (5-1/4 ounces each) au gratin potatoes
- 4 cups boiling water
- 1-1/3 cups 2% milk
- 2 teaspoons butter

- 1 teaspoon salt
- 1/2 teaspoon seasoned salt
- 1/2 teaspoon pepper
- 1 cup shredded cheddar cheese

Direction

- In a big frying pan, cook beef over medium heat until no pink remains; strain. Put in a 13x9-inch baking pan coated with cooking spray. Put mushrooms on top.
- Mix potatoes with pepper, seasoned salt, salt, butter, milk, water, contents of sauce mix packets in a small bowl. Add to the mushrooms and beef. Put a cover on and bake at 400° until fully heated, about 30 minutes.
- Sprinkle cheese over. Bake without a cover to melt the cheese, about another 5 minutes. Allow to sit before eating, about 10 minutes.

Nutrition Information

- Calories: 243 calories
- Sodium: 908mg sodium
- Fiber: 1g fiber)
- Total Carbohydrate: 17g carbohydrate (3g sugars
- Cholesterol: 51mg cholesterol
- Protein: 16g protein.
- Total Fat: 12g fat (7g saturated fat)

83. Cheesy Tortilla Bake

Serving: 8 servings. | Prep: 30mins | Cook: 30mins | Ready in:

Ingredients

- TORTILLAS:
- 1 cup all-purpose flour
- 1/2 cup yellow cornmeal
- 1/2 teaspoon salt
- 1-2/3 cups whole milk
- 1 large egg, beaten

- 2 tablespoons butter, melted
- FILLING:
- 1 pound ground beef
- 1/2 cup chopped onion
- 1 garlic clove, minced
- 1 can (10-3/4 ounces) condensed tomato soup, undiluted
- 1/2 cup taco sauce
- 1 teaspoon dried oregano
- 1 can (2-1/4 ounces) sliced ripe olives, drained
- 2 cups shredded cheddar cheese

Direction

- In a bowl, mix salt, cornmeal and flour. Put in butter, egg and milk. Whip till becoming smooth. Position a lightly greased small-sized skillet on medium heat. For each tortilla, add about 3 tbsp. of batter into skillet. Lift and tilt skillet to spread batter. Bring back to the heat source. Cook till browned lightly; flip and brown the other side. Take out to a warm platter; repeat with rest of the batter. Put aside.
- To make filling, cook garlic, onion and ground beef till onion becomes soft and meat turns browned; drain. Mix in olives, oregano, taco sauce and soups.
- At the same time, cover the bottom of a 13x9-in. baking dish with six tortillas, overlapping as necessary. Cover with 1/2 of meat mixture. Add the leftover meat mixture and leftover tortillas on top. Drizzle with cheese.
- Bake at 350 degrees till thoroughly heated or for half an hour. Allow to rest for several minutes prior to serving.

Nutrition Information

- Calories: 389 calories
- Cholesterol: 99mg cholesterol
- Protein: 22g protein.
- Total Fat: 20g fat (11g saturated fat)
- Sodium: 804mg sodium
- Fiber: 2g fiber)
- Total Carbohydrate: 31g carbohydrate (7g sugars

84. Chiles Relleno Casserole

Serving: 6-8 servings. | Prep: 25mins | Cook: 45mins | Ready in:

Ingredients

- 1 pound ground beef
- 1 green pepper, chopped
- 1/2 teaspoon salt
- 1/4 teaspoon pepper
- 1/4 teaspoon dried oregano
- 1/8 teaspoon garlic powder
- 2 cups shredded cheddar cheese
- 2 cups shredded Monterey Jack cheese
- 2 cans (4 ounces each) chopped green chilies
- 4 large eggs, beaten
- 1 cup half-and-half cream
- 1 tablespoon all-purpose flour
- 1 can (8 ounces) tomato sauce
- Additional shredded cheddar cheese, optional

Direction

- Cook beef in a skillet over medium heat until the pink color disappears from meat; drain. Add garlic powder, oregano, pepper, salt and green pepper. Cook until green pepper is softened. Combine Monterey Jack cheese and cheddar cheese; set aside.
- Arrange half each of meat mixture, chilies and cheese in layers in a 2-1/2 quart baking dish; repeat with remaining meat mixture then chilies and cheese.
- In the meantime, combine flour, cream and egg in a bowl; add to cheese layer.
- Bake for 35 minutes at 350°. Remove from oven and pour in tomato sauce until fully covered. Add more cheese on top if desired. Bake for an additional 10 to 15 minutes or until set.

Nutrition Information

- Calories:
- Sodium:
- Fiber:
- Total Carbohydrate:
- Cholesterol:
- Protein:
- Total Fat:

Nutrition Information

- Calories: 521 calories
- Total Carbohydrate: 35g carbohydrate (4g sugars
- Cholesterol: 92mg cholesterol
- Protein: 35g protein.
- Total Fat: 26g fat (9g saturated fat)
- Sodium: 1444mg sodium
- Fiber: 3g fiber)

85. Chili Beef Bake

Serving: 8 servings. | Prep: 15mins | Cook: 30mins | Ready in:

Ingredients

- 2 pounds ground beef
- 1 medium onion, chopped
- 1 garlic clove, minced
- 1 teaspoon chili powder
- 1 teaspoon salt
- 1/4 teaspoon pepper
- 12 flour tortillas (6 inches)
- 2 cans (15 ounces each) pinto beans, rinsed and drained
- 6 slices process cheese (Velveeta)
- 2 cans (10-3/4 ounces each) condensed cream of chicken soup, undiluted
- 1 can (10 ounces) diced tomatoes and green chilies, undrained

Direction

- Brown beef in a skillet, drain. Add garlic and onion; cook until softened. Remove from the heat; add pepper, salt and chili powder.
- In a greased 13x9 inch baking dish, arrange 6 tortillas slightly overlapping. Add half of the meat mixture on top. Arrange beans, remaining meat mixture, cheese and remaining tortillas in layers.
- Combine tomatoes and soup; add to tortillas (the dish will be full) and bake when uncover for 30 minutes at 350° or until heated through and bubbles appear.

86. Chili Casserole

Serving: 6 | Prep: 20mins | Cook: 20mins |Ready in:

Ingredients

- 1 1/2 pounds ground beef
- 1/2 cup chopped onion
- 3 stalks celery, chopped
- 1 (15 ounce) can chili
- 1 (14.5 ounce) can peeled and diced tomatoes with juice
- 1/4 cup taco sauce
- 1 (15 ounce) can corn
- 1 (8 ounce) package egg noodles
- 1/4 cup shredded Cheddar cheese

Direction

- Preheat oven to 350°F (175° C).
- Sauté onion and beef in a big frying pan over medium high heat for about 5-10 minutes or until onion is softened and meat becomes browned; drain the fat. Put in the corn, taco sauce, tomatoes, chili and celery. Let it heat thoroughly, decrease heat to low and let simmer.
- Meanwhile, prepare the noodles as directed in the package. Pour in a 9x13-inch baking dish once cooked. Spread the meat mixture over the noodles, mixing thoroughly. Put cheese atop.
- Bake at 350°F (175°C) for about 20 minutes or until cheese becomes completely bubbly and melted.

Nutrition Information

- Calories: 671 calories;
- Total Fat: 37.7
- Sodium: 843
- Total Carbohydrate: 52.3
- Cholesterol: 145
- Protein: 31.9

87. Chilies Rellenos Casserole

Serving: 6 servings. | Prep: 15mins | Cook: 45mins | Ready in:

Ingredients

- 1 can (7 ounces) whole green chilies
- 1-1/2 cups shredded Colby-Monterey Jack cheese
- 3/4 pound ground beef
- 1/4 cup chopped onion
- 1 cup whole milk
- 4 large eggs
- 1/4 cup all-purpose flour
- 1/4 teaspoon salt
- 1/8 teaspoon pepper

Direction

- Chop chilies and remove seeds; dry over paper towels. Arrange chilies onto the bottom of a greased 2-qt. baking dish. Add cheese on top. Cook onion and beef on medium heat in a skillet till meat is not pink anymore; drain. Scoop on top of the cheese.
- Whip pepper, salt, flour, eggs and milk in a bowl till becoming smooth; add on top of beef mixture. Bake, while uncovered, at 350 degrees for 45 to 50 minutes or until a knife inserted in the middle comes out clean. Allow to rest for 5 minutes prior to serving.

Nutrition Information

- Calories: 321 calories
- Cholesterol: 212mg cholesterol
- Protein: 24g protein.
- Total Fat: 20g fat (11g saturated fat)
- Sodium: 406mg sodium
- Fiber: 0 fiber)
- Total Carbohydrate: 9g carbohydrate (3g sugars

88. Chuck Wagon Mac

Serving: 6-8 servings. | Prep: 20mins | Cook: 15mins | Ready in:

Ingredients

- 1 package (7-1/4 ounces) macaroni and cheese dinner mix
- 1 pound ground beef
- 1/2 cup sliced celery
- 1/4 cup chopped green pepper
- 1/4 cup chopped onion
- 1 can (15-1/4 ounces) whole kernel corn, drained
- 1 can (15 ounces) tomato sauce
- 1/2 teaspoon salt
- 1/4 teaspoon pepper
- Minced fresh parsley

Direction

- Create macaroni and cheese following the package directions; put aside. Cook onion, green pepper, celery and beef in a big skillet on medium heat until meat is not pink; strain. Mix in the leftover macaroni and cheese, pepper, salt, tomato sauce and corn.
- Place in a 13x9-inch baking dish that is greased. Place in the oven and bake for 15-20 minutes or until heated through at 350 degrees Fahrenheit. Decorate with parsley.

Nutrition Information

- Calories:
- Sodium:
- Fiber:
- Total Carbohydrate:
- Cholesterol:
- Protein:
- Total Fat:

89. Church Supper Hot Dish

Serving: 8 servings. | Prep: 40mins | Cook: 30mins | Ready in:

Ingredients

- 1 pound ground beef
- 2 cups sliced peeled potatoes
- 2 cups finely chopped celery
- 3/4 cup finely chopped carrots
- 1/4 cup finely chopped green pepper
- 1/4 cup finely chopped onion
- 2 tablespoons butter
- 1 cup water
- 2 cans (10-3/4 ounces each) condensed cream of mushroom soup, undiluted
- 1 can (5 ounces) chow mein noodles, divided
- 1 cup shredded cheddar cheese

Direction

- Preheat oven to 350°. In a big frying pan over medium heat, cook beef till not pink anymore; let drain and set it aside.
- Sauté onion, green pepper, carrots, celery and potatoes in butter in the same pan for 5 minutes. Put in water; simmer, covered, for 10 minutes or until vegetables becomes softened. Mix in cooked ground beef and soup until blended.
- In a greased shallow 2-quart baking dish, add half of the chow mein noodles. Spread meat mixture over noodles. Bake, covered, for 20 minutes. Top with the leftover noodles and cheese. Bake while uncovered for 10 more minutes or until heated through.

Nutrition Information

- Calories: 339 calories
- Sodium: 537mg sodium
- Fiber: 3g fiber)
- Total Carbohydrate: 25g carbohydrate (2g sugars
- Cholesterol: 53mg cholesterol
- Protein: 16g protein.
- Total Fat: 20g fat (9g saturated fat)

90. Church Supper Spaghetti

Serving: 12 servings. | Prep: 50mins | Cook: 20mins | Ready in:

Ingredients

- 1 pound ground beef
- 1 large onion, chopped
- 1 medium green pepper, chopped
- 1 can (14-1/2 ounces) diced tomatoes, undrained
- 1 cup water
- 2 tablespoons chili powder
- 1 package (10 ounces) frozen corn, thawed
- 1 package (10 ounces) frozen peas, thawed
- 1 can (4 ounces) mushroom stems and pieces, drained
- Salt and pepper to taste
- 12 ounces spaghetti, cooked and drained
- 2 cups shredded cheddar cheese, divided

Direction

- In a large skillet over medium heat, cook green pepper, onion and beef until meat is not pink anymore. Mix in chili powder, water and tomatoes. Cover while simmering for around 30 minutes. Add the peas, corn, mushrooms, pepper and salt. Stir in spaghetti.
- In a greased baking dish of 4-quart size, layer

half of the mixture. Have 1 cup cheese to sprinkle; repeat layers.

- Bake with no cover at 350° for 20 minutes until heated through.

Nutrition Information

- Calories: 290 calories
- Protein: 17g protein.
- Total Fat: 10g fat (6g saturated fat)
- Sodium: 259mg sodium
- Fiber: 4g fiber)
- Total Carbohydrate: 34g carbohydrate (5g sugars
- Cholesterol: 39mg cholesterol

91. Classic Cabbage Rolls

Serving: 4 servings. | Prep: 30mins | Cook: 01hours30mins | Ready in:

Ingredients

- 1 medium head cabbage
- 1-1/2 cups chopped onion, divided
- 1 tablespoon butter
- 2 cans (14-1/2 ounces each) Italian stewed tomatoes
- 4 garlic cloves, minced
- 2 tablespoons brown sugar
- 1-1/2 teaspoons salt, divided
- 1 cup cooked rice
- 1/4 cup ketchup
- 2 tablespoons Worcestershire sauce
- 1/4 teaspoon pepper
- 1 pound lean ground beef (90% lean)
- 1/4 pound Johnsonville® Ground Mild Italian sausage
- 1/2 cup V8 juice, optional

Direction

- Cook cabbage in boiling water in a Dutch oven for 10 minutes, until outer leaves are soft;

drain. Rinse in cold water; drain. Take 8 big outer leaves (refrigerate the remainder cabbage for other use); put aside.

- Sauté 1 cup onion in butter until soft in a big saucepan. Put in 1/2 teaspoon salt, brown sugar, garlic and tomatoes. Simmer for 15 minutes, blending occasionally.
- In the meantime, mix the remaining onion and salt with pepper, Worcestershire sauce, ketchup and rice in a big bowl. Crumble sausage and beef over the mixture and blend well.
- For easier rolling, take thick vein from off the cabbage leaves. Put on each leaf about 1/2 cup meat blend; fold in sides. Begin at an unfolded edge, roll up the leaf to fully enclose filling. Position in a skillet, seam side down. Top the sauce.
- Cover and cook for an hour at medium-low heat. If required, put in V8 juice. Turn heat to low; cook for another 20 minutes or until rolls are heated through and an inserted thermometer into the filling registers 160°

Nutrition Information

- Calories:
- Protein:
- Total Fat:
- Sodium:
- Fiber:
- Total Carbohydrate:
- Cholesterol:

92. Cornbread Taco Bake

Serving: 6 servings. | Prep: 20mins | Cook: 25mins | Ready in:

Ingredients

- 1-1/2 pounds ground beef
- 1 can (15-1/4 ounces) whole kernel corn, drained

- 1 can (8 ounces) tomato sauce
- 1/2 cup water
- 1/2 cup chopped green pepper
- 1 envelope taco seasoning
- 1 package (8-1/2 ounces) cornbread/muffin mix
- 1 can (2.8 ounces) french-fried onions, divided
- 1/3 cup shredded cheddar cheese

Direction

- Cook beef on medium heat in a big skillet till meat is not pink anymore; drain. Mix in taco seasoning, green pepper, water, tomato sauce, and corn. Scoop into one greased 2-qt. baking dish.
- Based on the instruction on package for corn bread, prepare the cornbread. Mix in 1/2 of the onions. Spread on top of beef mixture. Bake, while uncovered, at 400 degrees for 20 minutes.
- Drizzle with leftover onions and cheese. Bake 3 to 5 minutes more or till cheese is melted and a toothpick inserted into corn bread layer comes out clean.

Nutrition Information

- Calories: 0
- Total Carbohydrate: 50 g carbohydrate
- Cholesterol: 91 mg cholesterol
- Protein: 29 g protein.
- Total Fat: 27 g fat (10 g saturated fat)
- Sodium: 1,443 mg sodium
- Fiber: 2 g fiber

93. Cornbread With Black Eyed Peas

Serving: 8-10 servings. | Prep: 15mins | Cook: 40mins | Ready in:

Ingredients

- 1 pound ground beef, browned and drained
- 1 cup cornmeal
- 1/2 cup all-purpose flour
- 3/4 cup cream-style corn
- 1 cup cooked or canned black-eyed peas, drained
- 1 medium onion, chopped
- 1/2 cup canola oil
- 1 cup buttermilk
- 2 large eggs, beaten
- 2 cups shredded cheddar cheese
- 1/2 teaspoon baking soda

Direction

- Mix in all the ingredients in a bowl then transfer to a greased 13x9-inch baking dish. Let it bake for about 40 to 45 minutes at 350°F, or until the bread becomes golden, without the cover.

Nutrition Information

- Calories: 419 calories
- Protein: 21g protein.
- Total Fat: 23g fat (9g saturated fat)
- Sodium: 325mg sodium
- Fiber: 5g fiber)
- Total Carbohydrate: 32g carbohydrate (4g sugars
- Cholesterol: 90mg cholesterol

94. Creamy Beef Casserole

Serving: 8 servings. | Prep: 20mins | Cook: 30mins | Ready in:

Ingredients

- 2 pounds ground beef
- 1 large onion, chopped
- 6 ounces medium egg noodles, cooked and drained

- 1 can (15-1/4 ounces) whole kernel corn, drained
- 1 can (10-3/4 ounces) condensed cream of chicken soup, undiluted
- 1 can (10-3/4 ounces) condensed cream of mushroom soup, undiluted
- 1 cup (8 ounces) sour cream
- 1 can (2 ounces) diced pimientos, drained
- 3/4 teaspoon salt
- 1/4 teaspoon pepper
- 1 cup soft bread crumbs
- 1/4 cup butter, melted

Direction

- In a skillet over the medium heat, cook onion and beef till meat is no longer pink; drain. Put in pepper, salt, pimientos, sour cream, soups, corn and noodles; stir well. Place into a greased baking dish of 3 quarts. Toss butter and bread crumbs together; sprinkle on top of the casserole. Bake with no cover, at 350° until heated through, about half an hour.

Nutrition Information

- Calories: 492 calories
- Sodium: 1107mg sodium
- Fiber: 3g fiber)
- Total Carbohydrate: 32g carbohydrate (6g sugars
- Cholesterol: 115mg cholesterol
- Protein: 27g protein.
- Total Fat: 26g fat (13g saturated fat)

95. Crowned Beef Bake

Serving: 4-6 servings. | Prep: 20mins | Cook: 25mins | Ready in:

Ingredients

- 1 pound ground beef

- 1 can (4 ounces) mushroom stems and pieces, drained
- 1 can (2.8 ounces) french-fried onions, crumbled, divided
- 2 cups frozen mixed vegetables
- 1 can (10-3/4 ounces) condensed cream of celery soup, undiluted
- 1 cup sour cream, divided
- 1 tube (7-1/2 ounces) refrigerated buttermilk biscuits
- 1 large egg, lightly beaten
- 1 teaspoon celery seed
- 1/2 teaspoon salt

Direction

- In a large skillet over medium heat, cook beef until not pink anymore; drain. Place half in a greased 2-quart baking dish. Layer with mushrooms, two-thirds of the onions and all of the vegetables. Pour the remaining beef on top.
- Mix 1/2 cup of sour cream and soup in a large saucepan cook over low heat until heated through. Add over beef. Divide each biscuit into two pieces; place cut side down around the edge of the dish. Scatter the remaining onions in the middle of the casserole.
- Mix the remaining sour cream, salt, celery seed and egg in a small bowl; pour over biscuits. Bake with no cover at 375° until golden brown, about 25-30 minutes.

Nutrition Information

- Calories: 459 calories
- Cholesterol: 101mg cholesterol
- Protein: 22g protein.
- Total Fat: 24g fat (11g saturated fat)
- Sodium: 1153mg sodium
- Fiber: 3g fiber)
- Total Carbohydrate: 37g carbohydrate (4g sugars

96. Crunchy Beef Bake

Serving: 4-6 servings. | Prep: 15mins | Cook: 30mins | Ready in:

Ingredients

- 2 cups uncooked spiral pasta
- 1 pound ground beef
- 3/4 cup chopped green pepper
- 1 garlic clove, minced
- 1 can (14-1/2 ounces) diced tomatoes, undrained
- 1 can (10-3/4 ounces) condensed cream of mushroom soup, undiluted
- 3/4 cup shredded cheddar cheese
- 3/4 teaspoon seasoned salt
- 1 can (2.8 ounces) french-fried onions

Direction

- Cook pasta following package instructions. In the meantime, in a Dutch oven over medium heat, cook garlic, green pepper and beef until green pepper is tender and the beef is no longer pink; drain.
- Drain pasta; put into the beef mixture along with salt, cheese, soup and tomatoes.
- Place into a greased 2-quart baking dish. Cover and bake at 350° for 30-40 minutes. Remove the cover; sprinkle onions on top and return to the oven for 5 more minutes.

Nutrition Information

- Calories: 417 calories
- Total Carbohydrate: 36g carbohydrate (4g sugars
- Cholesterol: 54mg cholesterol
- Protein: 21g protein.
- Total Fat: 20g fat (9g saturated fat)
- Sodium: 884mg sodium
- Fiber: 3g fiber)

97. Dinner In A Bag

Serving: 4 servings. | Prep: 5mins | Cook: 25mins | Ready in:

Ingredients

- 1 pound ground beef
- 2 cans (14-1/2 ounces each) stewed tomatoes
- 1/4 cup dried minced onion
- 1 teaspoon salt
- 1 teaspoon chili powder
- 1/4 to 1/2 teaspoon pepper
- 1/4 teaspoon sugar
- 1 cup uncooked elbow macaroni

Direction

- Cook beef in a large skillet over medium heat until not pink; strain. Put in the sugar, seasonings and tomatoes; make it boil. Lower heat and simmer for 5 minutes.
- Mix in macaroni; cover and gently boil for 15 minutes. Take off cover; gently boil until macaroni is softened and sauce turns thick.

Nutrition Information

- Calories: 289 calories
- Sodium: 858mg sodium
- Fiber: 2g fiber)
- Total Carbohydrate: 25g carbohydrate (8g sugars
- Cholesterol: 56mg cholesterol
- Protein: 24g protein.
- Total Fat: 11g fat (5g saturated fat)

98. Dinner In A Dish

Serving: 12 servings. | Prep: 15mins | Cook: 35mins | Ready in:

Ingredients

- 2 pounds ground beef

- 1 medium onion, chopped
- 2 cans (14-1/2 ounces each) diced tomatoes, undrained
- 3 cups frozen peas
- 2/3 cup ketchup
- 1/4 cup minced fresh parsley
- 2 tablespoons all-purpose flour
- 2 teaspoons beef bouillon granules
- 2 teaspoons dried marjoram
- 1 teaspoon salt
- 1/2 teaspoon pepper
- 6 cups hot mashed potatoes (prepared with milk and butter)
- 2 eggs

Direction

- Cook onion and beef in a big frying pan over medium heat until the beef is not pink anymore; strain. Mix in the next 9 ingredients. Boil it, stir and cook for 2 minutes.
- Add to a non-oiled shallow 3-quart baking dish. Mix together eggs and potatoes. Drop onto beef mixture by 1/2 cupfuls.
- Bake without a cover at 350° until bubbling and the potatoes turns light brown, about 35-40 minutes.

Nutrition Information

- Calories: 302 calories
- Protein: 19g protein.
- Total Fat: 12g fat (6g saturated fat)
- Sodium: 941mg sodium
- Fiber: 5g fiber)
- Total Carbohydrate: 30g carbohydrate (7g sugars
- Cholesterol: 85mg cholesterol

99. Dumpling Company Casserole

Serving: 4-6 servings. | Prep: 30mins | Cook: 20mins | Ready in:

Ingredients

- 2 pounds lean ground beef
- 1/2 cup sour cream
- 3 tablespoons onion soup mix
- 1 large egg, beaten
- 1-1/2 cups soft bread crumbs
- 1/4 cup butter
- 1 can (8 ounces) mushroom stems and pieces, drained
- 1 can (10-3/4 ounces) condensed cream of chicken soup, undiluted
- 1-2/3 cups water
- SAUCE: (optional)
- 1 can (10-3/4 ounces) condensed cream of chicken soup, undiluted
- 1/4 teaspoon poultry seasoning
- 1 teaspoon dried minced onion
- 1/2 cup sour cream
- BUTTER CRUMB DUMPLINGS:
- 2 cups all-purpose flour
- 4 teaspoons baking powder
- 1 tablespoon poppy seed
- 1 teaspoon celery salt
- 1 teaspoon poultry seasoning
- 2 teaspoons dried minced onion
- 1/4 cup vegetable oil
- 3/4 cup plus 2 tablespoons whole milk
- 1/4 cup butter, melted
- 2 cups soft bread crumbs

Direction

- Mix the first five ingredients together in a bowl. Form into 16 balls. Melt butter in a skillet, then brown the meatballs over medium-low heat. Mix in water, soup and mushrooms. Let it simmer for 20 minutes, pouring more water if necessary.
- Turn into a 3-quart baking dish. If extra sauce is desired, mix minced onion, poultry seasoning and the cream of chicken soup together in a small saucepan. Cook until heated through. Take it away from the heat and mix in sour cream; add to meatball mixture.

- To make dumplings: In a bowl, mix onion, poultry seasoning, salt, celery, poppy seed, baking powder and flour together. Stir in milk and oil. Mix breadcrumbs and butter. Spoon heaping tablespoonful of dough into the buttered crumbs; roll to evenly coat. Cover the meatball mixture with dumplings.
- Bake with no cover at 400° until dumplings are golden, about 20-25 minutes.

Nutrition Information

- Calories: 900 calories
- Sodium: 2141mg sodium
- Fiber: 4g fiber)
- Total Carbohydrate: 59g carbohydrate (7g sugars
- Cholesterol: 209mg cholesterol
- Protein: 43g protein.
- Total Fat: 53g fat (23g saturated fat)

100.   Easy Ground Beef Stroganoff

Serving: 6 | Prep: 15mins | Cook: 1hours | Ready in:

Ingredients

- 2 pounds ground beef
- 2 onions, chopped
- 1 clove garlic, minced
- 1 (4.5 ounce) can mushrooms, drained
- 2 teaspoons salt
- 1/4 teaspoon ground black pepper
- 2 cups hot water
- 6 cubes beef bouillon
- 4 tablespoons tomato paste
- 1 1/2 cups water
- 4 tablespoons all-purpose flour

Direction

- On medium-high heat, heat a big pan; sauté mushrooms, ground beef, garlic, and onions

until the onion is golden brown. Sprinkle black pepper and salt.
- Mix in tomato paste, bouillon cubes, and two cups of hot water in the meat mixture. Whisk flour and 1 1/2 cups of cold water together; mix into the pan. Turn to low heat and let it simmer for an hour.

Nutrition Information

- Calories: 524 calories;
- Total Fat: 40.5
- Sodium: 1923
- Total Carbohydrate: 11.3
- Cholesterol: 129
- Protein: 27.6

101.   Easy Taco Casserole

Serving: 6 | Prep: 15mins | Cook: 35mins | Ready in:

Ingredients

- 1 pound ground beef
- 1 cup salsa
- 1/2 cup chopped onion
- 1/2 cup mayonnaise
- 2 tablespoons chili powder
- 1 teaspoon ground cumin
- 2 cups crushed tortilla chips, divided
- 4 ounces shredded Cheddar cheese, divided
- 4 ounces shredded Monterey Jack cheese, divided

Direction

- Preheat oven to 175 degrees C (350 degrees F).
- Cook and stir ground beef on medium high heat in a big skillet for 5-7 minutes till becomes crumbly, equally browned and not pink anymore. Drain and throw away any excess grease. Mix cumin, chili powder, mayonnaise, onion and salsa into the beef. Take out of the heat.

- Spread about 1/2 of the ground beef mixture into the bottom of one 2-quart casserole dish. Spread about 1/2 the tortilla chips in one layer on top of the beef mixture. Layer about 1/2 of each of the Cheddar and Monterey Jack cheeses on top of the tortilla chip layer. Repeat the layers with the rest of the ingredients, ending with Monterey Jack cheese. Use aluminum foil to cover the dish.
- Bake in preheated oven for about half an hour or till the cheese becomes melted in the center.

Nutrition Information

- Calories: 481 calories;
- Sodium: 690
- Total Carbohydrate: 12.2
- Cholesterol: 90
- Protein: 24
- Total Fat: 38

---

102.   Enchilada Beef

Serving: 4 servings. | Prep: 10mins | Cook: 10mins | Ready in:

Ingredients

- 1/2 cup chopped onion
- 1 pound lean ground beef (90% lean)
- 1 cup tomato juice
- 1 can (6 ounces) tomato paste
- 1 can (4 ounces) chopped green chilies, drained
- 2 tablespoons plus 2 teaspoons enchilada sauce mix
- 2 cups shredded Monterey Jack cheese, divided
- 1/2 cup coarsely crushed corn chips
- Additional corn chips, optional

Direction

- In a bowl that's microwave safe, put onions, cover it, and microwave it for 2-3 minutes on

high or until the onions are tender. Crumble up the beef on the onions and mix them well. Cover it up again and cook it for 4-6 minutes on high or until the beef isn't pink anymore and stir it once. Drain it.
- Mix in tomato paste, tomato juice, sauce mix, and green chilies. Spread about half of the beef mix in a microwave-safe dish that's 2 quarts with a cup of cheese on top. Top it off with the rest of the beef mix. Cover it up and microwave it until heated completely through or for 2-3 minutes.
- Sprinkle it with the rest of the cheese and some corn chips that are crushed. Microwave it for another minute or until the cheese melts. Eat this with some extra corn chips if you want.

Nutrition Information

- Calories: 483 calories
- Sodium: 1245mg sodium
- Fiber: 5g fiber)
- Total Carbohydrate: 20g carbohydrate (10g sugars
- Cholesterol: 106mg cholesterol
- Protein: 38g protein.
- Total Fat: 27g fat (14g saturated fat)

---

103.   Enchilada Casserole

Serving: 8 | Prep: 15mins | Cook: 45mins | Ready in:

Ingredients

- 1 (15 ounce) can black beans, rinsed and drained
- 2 cloves garlic, minced
- 1 onion, chopped
- 1 (4 ounce) can diced green chile peppers
- 1 jalapeno pepper, seeded and minced
- 1 (8 ounce) package tempeh, crumbled
- 6 (6 inch) corn tortillas
- 1 (19 ounce) can enchilada sauce

- 1 (6 ounce) can sliced black olives
- 8 ounces shredded Cheddar cheese

Direction

- Preheat oven to 175 degrees C (350 degrees F). Oil one 9x13 inch baking dish a bit.
- Mix tempeh, jalapeno pepper, chile peppers, onion, garlic and beans in a medium-sized bowl. Add enchilada sauce into a shallow bowl.
- Dip 3 tortillas in the enchilada sauce, and add them into the prepped baking dish. Make sure you cover the bottom of the dish as entirely as you can. Add half of the bean mixture over the tortillas, and repeat. Sprinkle the rest of sauce on top of the casserole, and drizzle with shredded cheese and olives.
- Keep it covered, and bake for half an hour. Uncover it, and keep baking for an extra 15 minutes, or till the casserole is bubbling and the cheese is melted.

Nutrition Information

- Calories: 375 calories;
- Cholesterol: 54
- Protein: 17.4
- Total Fat: 24
- Sodium: 709
- Total Carbohydrate: 24.9

104.   Firecracker Casserole

Serving: 10 | Prep: 15mins | Cook: 40mins | Ready in:

Ingredients

- 2 pounds ground beef
- 1 onion, chopped
- 1 (15 ounce) can black beans, drained and rinsed
- 2 tablespoons chili powder
- 1 tablespoon ground cumin

- 1/2 teaspoon salt
- 4 (7 inch) flour tortillas
- 1 (14.5 ounce) can diced tomatoes with green chile peppers
- 1 (10.5 ounce) can cream of mushroom soup
- 1 cup shredded Cheddar cheese

Direction

- Preheat an oven to 175 degrees C (350 degrees F). Grease one 9x13-inch baking dish.
- Heat a large skillet on medium high heat. Cook and stir the ground beef along with the onion in the hot skillet for 7-10 minutes or till browned totally; drain any excess fat. Mix salt, cumin, chili powder and black beans into the beef mixture; cook and stir for roughly 5 minutes or till becoming hot. Add the mixture into the prepped baking dish. Arrange the tortillas on top of the beef mixture.
- In a bowl, stir together cream of mushroom soup, green chile peppers with tomatoes; spread on top of the tortillas. Add the Cheddar cheese on top.
- Bake in the preheated oven for 25-30 minutes or till thoroughly cooked and the cheese becomes melted totally.

Nutrition Information

- Calories: 293 calories;
- Sodium: 701
- Total Carbohydrate: 13
- Cholesterol: 67
- Protein: 20.3
- Total Fat: 17.7

105.   Fold Over Tortilla Bake

Serving: 6 servings. | Prep: 20mins | Cook: 20mins | Ready in:

Ingredients

- 1 pound ground beef

- 1 cup chopped onion
- 2 cans (14-1/2 ounces each) stewed tomatoes
- 1 cup enchilada sauce
- 1 to 2 teaspoons ground cumin
- 1/2 teaspoon salt
- 1/4 teaspoon pepper
- 12 flour or corn tortillas (6 inches)
- 6 ounces cream cheese, softened
- 1 can (4 ounces) chopped green chilies, drained
- 1 cup shredded Monterey Jack cheese
- minced fresh cilantro, optional

Direction

- Cook onion and ground beef in a big skillet till beef is not pink anymore; drain. Mix in seasonings, enchilada sauce and tomatoes. Boil. Lower the heat and simmer, while covered, for 5 minutes. Add 1/2 of the meat sauce into one 13x9-in. baking dish. Put aside.
- Wrap the stack of tortillas in the foil; keep warmed at 350 degrees for 8 to 10 minutes. Spread warm tortillas with cream cheese and add chilies on top. Fold tortillas in half. Arrange folded tortillas on top meat sauce; add leftover sauce on top.
- Keep it covered and baked at 350 degrees for 15 minutes. Drizzle with cheese; bake till cheese becomes melted for 5 minutes more. Add cilantro on top if you want.

Nutrition Information

- Calories: 473 calories
- Total Carbohydrate: 38g carbohydrate (7g sugars
- Cholesterol: 69mg cholesterol
- Protein: 27g protein.
- Total Fat: 25g fat (10g saturated fat)
- Sodium: 1138mg sodium
- Fiber: 2g fiber)

106.   Fourth Of July Bean Casserole

Serving: 12 servings. | Prep: 20mins | Cook: 60mins | Ready in:

Ingredients

- 1/2 pound bacon strips, diced
- 1/2 pound ground beef
- 1 cup chopped onion
- 1 can (28 ounces) pork and beans
- 1 can (16 ounces) kidney beans, rinsed and drained
- 1 can (15-1/4 ounces) lima beans, rinsed and drained
- 1/2 cup barbecue sauce
- 1/2 cup ketchup
- 1/2 cup sugar
- 1/2 cup packed brown sugar
- 2 tablespoons prepared mustard
- 2 tablespoons molasses
- 1 teaspoon salt
- 1/2 teaspoon chili powder

Direction

- Cook onion, beef, and bacon over medium heat in a large skillet until meat is no longer pink; drain off grease.
- Pour mixture into an oiled 2 1/2-quart baking dish. Mix in all of the beans; stir well. Combine the remaining ingredients in a small bowl; mix into bean and beef mixture.
- Bake, covered for 45 minutes at 350°; remove cover, and bake for 15 more minutes.

Nutrition Information

- Calories: 278 calories
- Protein: 12g protein.
- Total Fat: 6g fat (2g saturated fat)
- Sodium: 933mg sodium
- Fiber: 7g fiber)
- Total Carbohydrate: 47g carbohydrate (26g sugars
- Cholesterol: 15mg cholesterol

107. German Skillet Meal

Serving: 6 servings. | Prep: 5mins | Cook: 35mins | Ready in:

Ingredients

- 1 pound ground beef
- 1 cup chopped onion
- 1 cup uncooked long grain rice
- 2 cans (8 ounces each) tomato sauce
- 1 can (16 ounces) sauerkraut, rinsed and well drained
- 1/2 teaspoon caraway seeds
- 1 cup water
- 1/2 teaspoon pepper
- 3/4 teaspoon salt, optional

Direction

- Cook onion and ground beef in a skillet until onion is tender and meat is browned; drain. Mix in pepper, water, caraway seeds, sauerkraut, tomato sauce, rice, and salt if desired. Let it come to a boil. Lower the heat; cover up and allow to simmer until the rice is tender, about 25 minutes.

Nutrition Information

- Calories: 264 calories
- Protein: 17g protein.
- Total Fat: 7g fat (3g saturated fat)
- Sodium: 663mg sodium
- Fiber: 3g fiber)
- Total Carbohydrate: 32g carbohydrate (3g sugars
- Cholesterol: 37mg cholesterol

108. Grandma's Rice Dish

Serving: 4 servings. | Prep: 20mins | Cook: 15mins | Ready in:

Ingredients

- 1 pound ground beef
- 1/3 cup chopped onion
- 1/2 cup chopped green pepper
- 2 cups cooked long grain rice
- 1 can (14-1/2 ounces) diced tomatoes, undrained
- 1 can (11 ounces) whole kernel corn, drained
- 1 can (2-1/4 ounces) sliced ripe olives, drained
- 6 bacon strips, cooked and crumbled
- 2 teaspoons chili powder
- 1 teaspoon garlic powder
- 1/2 teaspoon salt
- 1-1/2 cups shredded cheddar cheese, divided
- 1/2 cup dry bread crumbs
- 1 tablespoon butter, melted

Direction

- Preheat oven to 350 degrees. Cook green pepper, onion and beef on medium heat in a big skillet till meat is not pink anymore; drain.
- Mix in seasonings, bacon, olives, corn, tomatoes and rice; heat through. Mix in one cup of cheese till melted.
- Move to a greased 11x7-in. baking dish. Drizzle with the rest of cheese. Toss bread crumbs with butter; drizzle on top.
- Bake, while uncovered, till cheese becomes melted or for 15 to 20 minutes.

Nutrition Information

- Calories: 719 calories
- Total Carbohydrate: 52g carbohydrate (9g sugars
- Cholesterol: 136mg cholesterol
- Protein: 41g protein.
- Total Fat: 37g fat (18g saturated fat)
- Sodium: 1397mg sodium
- Fiber: 5g fiber)

- Total Carbohydrate: 31g carbohydrate (5g sugars
- Cholesterol: 42mg cholesterol
- Protein: 21g protein.

109. Green Pepper Casserole

Serving: 16 servings. | Prep: 10mins | Cook: 01hours25mins | Ready in:

Ingredients

- 3 pounds ground beef
- 5 small onions, chopped
- 3 cans (10-3/4 ounces each) condensed tomato soup, undiluted
- 1 tablespoon paprika
- 3 medium green peppers, chopped
- 1 can (16 ounces) peas, drained
- 1 can (8 ounces) mushroom stems and pieces, drained
- 1 jar (4 ounces) pimientos, drained
- Salt and pepper to taste
- 1 package (16 ounces) medium pasta shells
- Grated Parmesan cheese

Direction

- Cook onions and beef over in a Dutch oven medium heat till meat is not pink anymore; drain. Put in paprika and soup. Simmer, covered, for 1 hour.
- Mix in the pepper, salt, pimientos, mushrooms, peas and green peppers. Simmer, covered, for 15 minutes or till peppers become softened.
- Meanwhile, cook macaroni as directed in the package; let drain. Put in a big serving bowl; pour meat mixture over. Top with Parmesan cheese.

Nutrition Information

- Calories: 281 calories
- Total Fat: 9g fat (4g saturated fat)
- Sodium: 300mg sodium
- Fiber: 3g fiber)

110. Ground Beef Enchilada Casserole

Serving: 6-8 servings. | Prep: 35mins | Cook: 35mins | Ready in:

Ingredients

- 1 pound ground beef
- 1 large onion, chopped
- 1/4 cup chopped green pepper
- 1 can (14-1/2 ounces) diced tomatoes, drained
- 1 can (10 ounces) enchilada sauce
- 1 can (2-1/4 ounces) sliced ripe olives, drained
- 1 teaspoon salt
- 2 cups shredded cheddar cheese, divided
- 1 cup (8 ounces) 4% cottage cheese
- 1 large egg, beaten
- 1 package (10 ounces) corn tortillas (6 inches), torn into pieces

Direction

- Cook green pepper, onion and beef on medium heat in a skillet till meat is not pink anymore; drain. Mix in salt, olives, enchilada sauce, and tomatoes. Keep it covered and let simmer roughly 20 minutes.
- At the same time, mix egg, cottage cheese, and 1 cup of cheddar cheese. Put aside. Spread 1/3 of the meat mixture into one greased 13x9-in. baking dish. Cover with 1/2 of the tortillas; spread with 1/2 of the cheese mixture. Repeat the layers with the rest ingredients, ending with the meat mixture.
- Bake at 350 degrees for half an hour. Drizzle with the rest of cheddar cheese. Bake till cheese becomes melted or for 3 to 5 minutes. Allow to rest for 5 to 10 minutes prior to serving.

Nutrition Information

- Calories: 352 calories
- Cholesterol: 91mg cholesterol
- Protein: 23g protein.
- Total Fat: 18g fat (9g saturated fat)
- Sodium: 918mg sodium
- Fiber: 4g fiber)
- Total Carbohydrate: 26g carbohydrate (5g sugars

- Bake at 120 degrees C (250 degrees F) till heated through or for 20 minutes.

Nutrition Information

- Calories: 554 calories;
- Total Fat: 26.3
- Sodium: 1155
- Total Carbohydrate: 56.1
- Cholesterol: 108
- Protein: 24.7

---

111.   Hamburger Casserole

Serving: 6 | Prep: 20mins | Cook: 20mins | Ready in:

Ingredients

- 1 pound ground beef
- 1 onion, chopped
- 1 stalk celery, chopped
- 8 ounces egg noodles
- 1 (15 ounce) can chili
- 1 (14.5 ounce) can peeled and diced tomatoes
- 1 (15 ounce) can whole kernel corn, drained
- 1/4 cup salsa
- 1 (1 ounce) package taco seasoning mix

Direction

- Preheat the oven to 120 degrees C (250 degrees F).
- In the big skillet on medium heat, mix celery, onion, and ground beef; sauté till onion softens and meat turns brown or for 10 minutes. Drain off fat and put aside.
- In another saucepan, cook the noodles following the instructions on package. Once cooked, drain off water and whisk in taco seasoning mix, taco sauce, corn, tomatoes, chili, and meat mixture. Stir thoroughly and put the whole mixture into the 10x15-in. baking dish.

---

112.   Hamburger Chilaquiles

Serving: 8 servings. | Prep: 30mins | Cook: 30mins | Ready in:

Ingredients

- 1 pound ground beef
- 1 medium onion, chopped
- 1envelope taco seasoning
- 1 can (4 ounces) chopped green chilies
- 1 can (28 ounces) diced tomatoes, undrained
- 6 ounces tortilla chips
- 4 cups shredded Monterey Jack cheese
- 1/2 cup sour cream
- 1 cup shredded cheddar cheese

Direction

- Cook onion and ground beef in a skillet till onion becomes soft and meat turns browned; drain. Mix in tomatoes, chilies, and taco seasoning. Let it simmer, while uncovered, for 15 minutes.
- Add 1/2 the tortilla chips in a 13x9-in. baking dish. Layer 1/2 of the meat mixture and 1/2 of the Monterey Jack cheese on top of the tortilla chips. Repeat the layers.
- Bake at 350 degrees for 20 minutes. Take out of the oven. Add sour cream dollops on top. Drizzle with cheddar cheese and bake till thoroughly heated or for another 10 minutes.

Nutrition Information

- Calories:
- Protein:
- Total Fat:
- Sodium:
- Fiber:
- Total Carbohydrate:
- Cholesterol:

113.   Hamburger Fry Pan Supper

Serving: 6 servings. | Prep: 10mins | Cook: 25mins | Ready in:

Ingredients

- 1 pound ground beef
- 1 medium onion, chopped
- 2 medium unpeeled red potatoes, julienned
- 2 cups shredded cabbage
- 2 cups thinly sliced celery
- 1/2 cup water
- Salt and pepper to taste

Direction

- Cook onion and beef in a large skillet over medium heat until meat is no longer pink; drain. Put in the remaining ingredients. Cover and let it simmer until vegetables are tender for about 20 minutes, stirring occasionally.

Nutrition Information

- Calories:
- Protein:
- Total Fat:
- Sodium:
- Fiber:
- Total Carbohydrate:
- Cholesterol:

114.   Hamburger Hot Dish

Serving: 8 servings. | Prep: 25mins | Cook: 25mins | Ready in:

Ingredients

- 2 cups uncooked elbow macaroni
- 2 pounds ground beef
- 1 can (28 ounces) diced tomatoes, undrained
- 1 can (15 ounces) tomato sauce
- 1 jar (12 ounces) beef gravy
- 1/2 cup chopped onion
- 1 teaspoon garlic powder

Direction

- Following the package instructions, cook the macaroni. In a big skillet on medium heat, cook the beef until it's not pink anymore. Drain then stir the garlic powder, onion, gravy, tomato sauce and tomatoes in. Strain the macaroni and add it to the beef mixture.
- Move the coated macaroni into a shallow greased 3-qt. baking dish and leave it uncovered. Bake at 350°F until thoroughly heated, about 25 to30 minutes.

Nutrition Information

- Calories: 346 calories
- Protein: 28g protein.
- Total Fat: 15g fat (6g saturated fat)
- Sodium: 748mg sodium
- Fiber: 2g fiber)
- Total Carbohydrate: 24g carbohydrate (5g sugars
- Cholesterol: 77mg cholesterol

115. Hamburger Rice Hot Dish

Serving: 4-6 servings. | Prep: 10mins | Cook: 50mins | Ready in:

Ingredients

- 1 pound ground beef
- 1 can (10-3/4 ounces) condensed cream of chicken soup, undiluted
- 1 cup water
- 1 cup uncooked instant rice
- Minced fresh parsley

Direction

- Over medium heat in a large skillet, cook beef till no longer pink; drain. Mix in the remaining ingredients. Spoon into a baking dish of 1-1/2 quarts.
- Cover up and bake at 325° until rice is tender, about 50-60 minutes.

Nutrition Information

- Calories: 223 calories
- Total Fat: 10g fat (4g saturated fat)
- Sodium: 436mg sodium
- Fiber: 1g fiber)
- Total Carbohydrate: 17g carbohydrate (0 sugars
- Cholesterol: 41mg cholesterol
- Protein: 16g protein.

116. Hamburger Spanish Rice

Serving: 4 servings. | Prep: 5mins | Cook: 30mins | Ready in:

Ingredients

- 1 pound lean ground beef (90% lean)
- 1 medium onion, chopped
- 1/2 green pepper, chopped
- 1 cup uncooked instant rice
- 1 can (15 ounces) tomato sauce
- 3/4 cup hot water
- 1 teaspoon prepared mustard
- 1 teaspoon Worcestershire sauce
- 1 teaspoon salt
- 1 teaspoon sugar

Direction

- Brown rice, green pepper, onion and beef in a big skillet. Mix in the leftover ingredients. Boil. Lower the heat; keep it cover and let simmer till the rice is soft or for 20 - 25 minutes.

Nutrition Information

- Calories: 314 calories
- Fiber: 3g fiber)
- Total Carbohydrate: 29g carbohydrate (4g sugars
- Cholesterol: 71mg cholesterol
- Protein: 26g protein.
- Total Fat: 11g fat (4g saturated fat)
- Sodium: 1169mg sodium

117. Harvest Hamburger Casserole

Serving: 8 servings. | Prep: 20mins | Cook: 01hours15mins | Ready in:

Ingredients

- 1 pound lean ground beef
- 1 cup finely chopped onion
- 1 can (28 ounces) diced tomatoes, undrained
- 1 tablespoon Worcestershire sauce
- 1 teaspoon salt
- 2 cups sliced peeled potatoes
- 1/3 cup all-purpose flour
- 2 cups frozen corn, thawed
- 1-1/2 cups frozen lima beans, thawed
- 1 medium green pepper, julienned

- 1-1/2 cups shredded cheddar cheese

Direction

- Cook beef in a large skillet over medium heat until not pink anymore; drain. Mix in salt, Worcestershire sauce, tomatoes and onion. Place into a greased 3-quart baking dish.
- Layer with potatoes, flour, corn, lima beans and green pepper. Cover and bake at 375° for 45 minutes. Add cheese on top. Bake with no cover until bubbly, about 30 minutes.

Nutrition Information

- Calories: 314 calories
- Total Carbohydrate: 34g carbohydrate (6g sugars
- Cholesterol: 57mg cholesterol
- Protein: 21g protein.
- Total Fat: 11g fat (6g saturated fat)
- Sodium: 662mg sodium
- Fiber: 5g fiber)

118.   Hearty Bean Casserole

Serving: 6-8 servings. | Prep: 20mins | Cook: 45mins | Ready in:

Ingredients

- 1-1/4 pounds ground beef
- 1 large onion, chopped
- 1 large green pepper, diced
- 1 garlic clove, minced
- 1 can (16 ounces) pork and beans, undrained
- 1 can (16 ounces) kidney beans, rinsed and drained
- 1 can (15 ounces) garbanzo beans or chickpeas, rinsed and drained
- 1 cup ketchup
- 3 tablespoons brown sugar
- 3 tablespoons cider vinegar
- 2 tablespoons prepared mustard

- 1 teaspoon salt
- 1/2 teaspoon pepper
- 3 bacon strips, cooked and crumbled

Direction

- In a Dutch oven over medium heat, cook beef till not pink anymore; drain. Put in the garlic, green pepper and onion; cook till softened. Mix in all of the beans.
- Mix pepper, salt, mustard, vinegar, brown sugar, and ketchup together; pour to bean mixture and stir thoroughly. Transfer into a greased 2-1/2-quart baking dish. Put bacon atop. Bake while uncovered at 350° for about 45 minutes or until heated through.

Nutrition Information

- Calories: 337 calories
- Cholesterol: 37mg cholesterol
- Protein: 22g protein.
- Total Fat: 9g fat (3g saturated fat)
- Sodium: 1124mg sodium
- Fiber: 9g fiber)
- Total Carbohydrate: 44g carbohydrate (15g sugars

119.   Hearty Hamburger Casserole

Serving: 4 servings. | Prep: 15mins | Cook: 30mins | Ready in:

Ingredients

- 1 pound ground beef
- 1 can (18.8 ounces) ready-to-serve chunky savory vegetable soup
- 1 package (6 ounces) stuffing mix
- 1/2 cup shredded cheddar cheese

Direction

- Cook ground beef in a frying pan until not pink. Drain excess grease. Follow the directions on the package for making the stuffing. Put half of the stuffing in a sprayed 2-qt. dish. Layer with beef, cheese, and the rest of the stuffing. Do not cover; bake in a 350-degree oven until entirely heated, 30-35 minutes.

Nutrition Information

- Calories:
- Cholesterol:
- Protein:
- Total Fat:
- Sodium:
- Fiber:
- Total Carbohydrate:

120.   Hearty Meat Pie

Serving: 2 pies (6-8 servings each). | Prep: 40mins | Cook: 01hours15mins | Ready in:

Ingredients

- Pastry for two double-crust pies
- 2 cups grated peeled potatoes
- 1-1/4 cups diced celery
- 1 cup grated carrots
- 1/4 cup chopped onion
- 2 tablespoons Worcestershire sauce
- 1 teaspoon salt
- 1/4 teaspoon pepper
- 3/4 pound lean ground beef (90% lean)
- MUSHROOM GRAVY (for each pie):
- 1 can (4 ounces) mushroom stems and pieces
- 2 tablespoons all-purpose flour
- 2 tablespoons canola oil
- 1 teaspoon beef bouillon granules
- 4 drops browning sauce, optional

Direction

- Divide the pastry into 4 parts. Roll out 1 portion on a lightly floured surface to fit a 9-in. pie plate. Combine the next 7 ingredients in a large bowl; crumble the beef over the mixture and mix well. Scoop half into the crust.
- Roll out another part of the pastry to fit the top of the pie; put over the filling and seal the edges. Split vents in the top of the pastry. Repeat the process with the remaining filling and pastry. Cover and chill 1 pie for up to 3 months.
- Bake the second pie for 15 minutes at 375°. Reduce the heat, continue to bake at 350° for 60 minutes. In the meantime, drain the mushrooms, reserve the liquid. Pour water to the liquid to measure 1 cup; put aside.
- Cook flour and mushrooms in oil in a small saucepan until bubbly. Remove from the heat; stir in the reserved mushroom liquid and bouillon. Boil; cook and stir until thickened, for 1 minute. If desired, stir in the browning sauce. Serve the gravy with pie.
- To use the frozen pie: Bake for 70 minutes at 375°. Prepare the gravy as directed; serve with the pie.

Nutrition Information

- Calories: 317 calories
- Protein: 7g protein.
- Total Fat: 17g fat (7g saturated fat)
- Sodium: 464mg sodium
- Fiber: 1g fiber)
- Total Carbohydrate: 33g carbohydrate (3g sugars
- Cholesterol: 23mg cholesterol

121.   Hearty Pork And Beans

Serving: 4-6 servings. | Prep: 15mins | Cook: 15mins | Ready in:

Ingredients

- 1 pound ground beef
- 1 medium tart apple, peeled and diced
- 1 medium onion, chopped
- 1 can (16 ounces) pork and beans
- 4 bacon strips, cooked and diced
- 1/4 cup barbecue sauce
- 1/4 cup molasses
- 1 cup corn chips, coarsely crushed

Direction

- In an ungreased shallow 2-quart. microwave-safe dish, crumble beef; add onion and apple. Microwave, covered, on High for 2-4 minutes while stirring once; let drain. Mix in the pork and beans, molasses, barbecue sauce, and bacon. Cook, covered, on high while stirring once for around 4-6 minutes or till heated through. Allow to rest for 5 minutes. Top with chips just before serving.

Nutrition Information

- Calories:
- Sodium:
- Fiber:
- Total Carbohydrate:
- Cholesterol:
- Protein:
- Total Fat:

122.   Hearty Rice Casserole

Serving: 12-16 servings. | Prep: 10mins | Cook: 60mins | Ready in:

Ingredients

- 1 can (10-3/4 ounces) condensed cream of mushroom soup, undiluted
- 1 can (10-3/4 ounces) condensed creamy onion soup, undiluted
- 1 can (10-3/4 ounces) condensed cream of chicken soup, undiluted

- 1 pound lean ground beef (90% lean)
- 1 pound Jones No Sugar Pork Sausage Roll
- 1 large onion, chopped
- 1 large green pepper, chopped
- 2 celery ribs, chopped
- 1-1/2 cups uncooked long grain rice

Direction

- Mix all ingredients in the greased 4-quart baking dish; stir them well. Keep covered securely and bake at 350 degrees till rice softens or for 60 to 70 minutes.

Nutrition Information

- Calories:
- Sodium:
- Fiber:
- Total Carbohydrate:
- Cholesterol:
- Protein:
- Total Fat:

123.   Hearty Tortilla Casserole

Serving: 2-4 servings. | Prep: 35mins | Cook: 30mins | Ready in:

Ingredients

- 1/2 pound ground beef
- 2 tablespoons taco seasoning
- 1/3 cup water
- 1 small onion, finely chopped
- 1 to 2 Anaheim or Poblano chilies, roasted, peeled and finely chopped or 1 can (4 ounces) chopped green chilies
- 1 jalapeno pepper, seeded and finely chopped
- 1 garlic clove, minced
- 1 tablespoon canola oil
- 1/4 cup heavy whipping cream
- 1/8 teaspoon salt
- 4 flour tortillas (8 inches)

- 1 can (16 ounces) refried beans
- 1 cup shredded Monterey Jack cheese, divided
- 1 cup shredded cheddar cheese, divided
- Sour cream and salsa, optional

Direction

- Cook beef on medium heat in a skillet till meat is not pink anymore. Strain. Pour in water and taco seasoning. Let it simmer, while uncovered, for 5 minutes; take out of the heat and put aside.
- Sauté garlic, jalapeno, and onion in oil in a saucepan roughly 8 minutes or till becoming softened.
- Mix in salt and cream. Keep it covered and let simmer for 5 minutes.
- Spread three tbsp. of sauce in one ungreased 8-in. round or square baking dish. Spread roughly 2 tsp. of sauce over each tortilla; layer with beans, beef mixture and 2 tbsp. of each kind of cheese. Roll up and place seam-side facing downward in baking dish. Add the rest of sauce on top.
- Bake, while uncovered, at 350 degrees for 25 minutes. Drizzle with the rest of cheeses; bake 5 minutes more. Serve along with sour cream and salsa if you want.

Nutrition Information

- Calories: 657 calories
- Total Carbohydrate: 51g carbohydrate (4g sugars
- Cholesterol: 112mg cholesterol
- Protein: 34g protein.
- Total Fat: 35g fat (18g saturated fat)
- Sodium: 1442mg sodium
- Fiber: 7g fiber)

---

124.   Hobo Knapsacks

Serving: 6 servings. | Prep: 15mins | Cook: 50mins | Ready in:

Ingredients

- 2 medium potatoes, peeled and thinly sliced
- 2 large tomatoes, chopped
- 1 large onion, chopped
- 1 package (10 ounces) frozen mixed vegetables, thawed
- 1 can (4 ounces) mushroom stems and pieces, drained
- 1 large egg, beaten
- 1/2 cup tomato juice
- 1/2 cup old-fashioned oats
- 1 tablespoon finely chopped onion
- 1 teaspoon salt
- 1/4 teaspoon pepper
- 1 pound lean ground beef (90% lean)
- Additional salt and pepper, optional

Direction

- Combine mushrooms, mixed vegetables, onion, tomatoes and potatoes in a large bowl; put aside.
- In another large bowl, mix pepper, salt, onion, oats, tomato juice and egg together; crumble beef over the mixture; stir well. Separate the meat mixture into six portions; crumble each portion onto a foil piece of 18x12 inches.
- Place vegetable mixture on top; add in additional pepper and salt for seasoning if desired. Gather the edges of foil together; crimp to seal, creating a packet. Arrange on baking sheets.
- Bake at 350° until a thermometer reads 160° and no more pink color, about 50-60 minutes.

Nutrition Information

- Calories: 252 calories
- Sodium: 603mg sodium
- Fiber: 5g fiber)
- Total Carbohydrate: 27g carbohydrate (7g sugars
- Cholesterol: 82mg cholesterol
- Protein: 20g protein.
- Total Fat: 8g fat (3g saturated fat)

125. Inside Out Stuffed Peppers

Serving: 4-6 servings. | Prep: 15mins | Cook: 01hours05mins | Ready in:

Ingredients

- 1 pound ground beef
- 1/2 cup chopped onion
- 1 can (14-1/2 ounces) stewed tomatoes, cut up
- 1 large green pepper, chopped
- 1/2 cup uncooked long grain rice
- 1/2 cup water
- 2 teaspoons Worcestershire sauce
- 1/2 teaspoon salt
- 1/4 teaspoon pepper
- 1 cup shredded cheddar cheese

Direction

- In a big frying pan over medium heat, cook beef till not pink anymore; let drain. Put to a greased 2-quart casserole. Put in the next eight ingredients.
- Bake, covered, at 350° for 1 hour or until the rice becomes softened. Uncover and dust with cheese; cook for 5 more minutes or until cheese becomes melted.

Nutrition Information

- Calories: 276 calories
- Cholesterol: 57mg cholesterol
- Protein: 19g protein.
- Total Fat: 12g fat (7g saturated fat)
- Sodium: 516mg sodium
- Fiber: 2g fiber)
- Total Carbohydrate: 22g carbohydrate (5g sugars

126. Italian Casserole

Serving: 4 | Prep: 20mins | Cook: 3hours20mins | Ready in:

Ingredients

- 3/4 pound lean ground beef
- 1 onion, chopped
- 1 (28 ounce) can whole peeled tomatoes, chopped
- 1 (6 ounce) can tomato paste
- 1 teaspoon salt
- 1 tablespoon dried parsley
- 1/2 teaspoon garlic salt
- black pepper to taste
- 8 ounces wide egg noodles
- 1 (12 ounce) package process sharp cheddar cheese singles

Direction

- In large skillet, brown onion and ground beef. Mix in tomato paste, tomatoes, parsley, salt, pepper and garlic salt, then simmer over low heat for nearly 3 hours.
- Preheat oven to 350°F (175°C). Boil lightly salted water in a large pot. Add pasta and cook for approximately 8 to 10 minutes or until al dente; drain.
- In a casserole dish of 2-quart, combine meat mixture and noodles. Place cheese slices on top and bake for nearly 15 to 20 minutes until cheese is melted.

Nutrition Information

- Calories: 739 calories;
- Sodium: 2572
- Total Carbohydrate: 62.1
- Cholesterol: 164
- Protein: 41.2
- Total Fat: 39

127. Jumble Lala

Serving: 8-10 servings. | Prep: 15mins | Cook: 01hours20mins |Ready in:

Ingredients

- 1-1/2 pounds ground beef, browned and drained
- 1 medium onion, chopped
- 1 quart tomato juice
- 1 can (10-3/4 ounces) condensed tomato soup, undiluted
- 1 cup uncooked long grain rice
- 1 tablespoon brown sugar
- 1/4 teaspoon dried thyme
- 2 bay leaves
- 1/4 to 1/2 teaspoon curry powder
- 1 teaspoon salt
- 1/2 teaspoon pepper

Direction

- In a big bowl, mix all ingredients. Add to one greased 2-qt. baking dish. Keep it covered and baked at 350 degrees for 80 to 90 minutes or till becomes hot and bubbly.

Nutrition Information

- Calories: 222 calories
- Sodium: 813mg sodium
- Fiber: 1g fiber)
- Total Carbohydrate: 26g carbohydrate (8g sugars
- Cholesterol: 33mg cholesterol
- Protein: 15g protein.
- Total Fat: 6g fat (3g saturated fat)

128. Kids Love It Casserole

Serving: 10-12 servings. | Prep: 35mins | Cook: 30mins | Ready in:

Ingredients

- 1-1/2 pounds ground beef
- 1 cup chopped onion
- 1 garlic clove, minced
- 1 jar (14 ounces) spaghetti sauce
- 1 can (8 ounces) tomato sauce
- 1 can (6 ounces) tomato paste
- 3/4 cup water
- 1 teaspoon Italian seasoning
- 1/2 teaspoon salt
- Dash pepper
- 1 package (7 ounces) small pasta shells, cooked and drained
- 1 package (10 ounces) frozen chopped spinach, thawed and squeezed dry
- 2 large eggs, lightly beaten
- 1 cup shredded sharp cheddar cheese
- 1/2 cup soft bread crumbs
- 1/4 cup grated Parmesan cheese

Direction

- In a large saucepan over medium heat, cook garlic, onion and beef till beef is no longer pink; drain. Put in the next seven ingredients; let it come to a boil. Lower the heat; cover up and allow to simmer for 10 minutes. Mix in bread crumbs, cheese, eggs, spinach and macaroni.
- Place into a greased baking dish of 13x9 inches. Sprinkle Parmesan cheese on top. Cover up and bake at 350° until bubbly, about 30-35 minutes. Allow to sit for 10 minutes before serving.

Nutrition Information

- Calories: 275 calories
- Protein: 19g protein.
- Total Fat: 12g fat (5g saturated fat)
- Sodium: 517mg sodium
- Fiber: 3g fiber)
- Total Carbohydrate: 24g carbohydrate (6g sugars
- Cholesterol: 84mg cholesterol

129.　　　Layered Tortilla Pie

Serving: 4-6 servings. | Prep: 20mins | Cook: 20mins | Ready in:

Ingredients

- 1 pound ground beef
- 1 medium onion, chopped
- 1 can (8 ounces) tomato sauce
- 1 garlic clove, minced
- 1 tablespoon chili powder
- 1/2 teaspoon salt
- 1/4 teaspoon pepper
- 1 can (2-1/4 ounces) sliced ripe olives, drained, optional
- 1 tablespoon butter
- 6 corn tortillas (6 inches)
- 2 cups shredded cheddar cheese
- 1/4 cup water

Direction

- Cook onion and beef in a big skillet till meat is not pink anymore; drain. Put in pepper, salt, chili powder, garlic and tomatoes sauce and, if you want, olives. Boil. Lower the heat; let simmer till becoming thick or for 5 minutes.
- Butter tortillas a bit on one side; add 1 tortilla, buttered side facing downward, in a 2-qt. round casserole. Add a third cup of cheese and roughly half cup of meat mixture on top. Repeat the layers, ending with cheese.
- Add water around the sides of casserole (but don't add on top). Keep it covered and baked at 400 degrees till becoming thoroughly heated or for 20 minutes. Allow to rest for 5 minutes prior to cutting.

Nutrition Information

- Calories: 350 calories
- Total Fat: 20g fat (12g saturated fat)
- Sodium: 722mg sodium
- Fiber: 3g fiber)

- Total Carbohydrate: 19g carbohydrate (2g sugars
- Cholesterol: 82mg cholesterol
- Protein: 24g protein.

130.　　　Makeover Husband's Dinner Delight

Serving: 8 servings. | Prep: 35mins | Cook: 25mins | Ready in:

Ingredients

- 8 ounces uncooked whole wheat egg noodles
- 1-1/2 pounds extra-lean ground beef (95% lean)
- 1 medium onion, chopped
- 1 medium green pepper, chopped
- 1 garlic clove, minced
- 3 cans (8 ounces each) tomato sauce
- 1 tablespoon sugar
- 1/8 teaspoon salt
- 1/8 teaspoon pepper
- 1-1/2 cups (12 ounces) 2% cottage cheese
- 4 ounces reduced-fat cream cheese
- 1/4 cup reduced-fat sour cream
- 3 green onions, chopped
- 1/2 cup shredded sharp cheddar cheese

Direction

- Cook the noodles following the package instructions. In the meantime, cook the garlic, green pepper, onion and beef in a Dutch oven on medium heat, until the vegetables become tender and the meat is not pink anymore; drain.
- Stir in the pepper, salt, sugar and tomato sauce. Drain the noodles and mix it into the sauce. Pour 1/2 of the beef mixture into a cooking spray coated 13x9-inch baking dish.
- Mix together the green onions, sour cream, cream cheese and cottage cheese in a small bowl, then spread it on top of the beef mixture. Put the leftover beef mixture on top.

- Put cover on and let it bake for 20 minutes at 350 degrees. Take off the cover and sprinkle cheddar cheese on top. Let it bake for 5 to 10 minutes more or until the cheese melts.

Nutrition Information

- Calories: 343 calories
- Total Fat: 11g fat (6g saturated fat)
- Sodium: 737mg sodium
- Fiber: 5g fiber)
- Total Carbohydrate: 33g carbohydrate (7g sugars
- Cholesterol: 74mg cholesterol
- Protein: 31g protein. Diabetic Exchanges: 3 lean meat

```
131.        Mashed Potato Beef
                 Casserole
```

Serving: 4-6 servings. | Prep: 30mins | Cook: 25mins | Ready in:

Ingredients

- 2 bacon strips, diced
- 1 pound ground beef
- 1-3/4 cups sliced fresh mushrooms
- 1 large onion, finely chopped
- 1 large carrot, finely chopped
- 1 celery rib, finely chopped
- 2 tablespoons all-purpose flour
- 1 cup beef broth
- 1 tablespoon Worcestershire sauce
- 1 teaspoon dried tarragon
- 1/4 teaspoon pepper
- 3 cups hot mashed potatoes
- 3/4 cup shredded cheddar cheese, divided
- Paprika

Direction

- Cook bacon in a large skillet until crisp; allow to drain, saving 1 teaspoon drippings. Put the

bacon aside. Over medium heat, cook beef in the drippings until no more pink; let drain.
- Toss celery, carrot, onion, and mushrooms in flour; add to the skillet with the broth, pepper, tarragon, and Worcestershire sauce. Bring to a boil. Lower the heat; simmer without cover until the greens are soft, for 15-20 minutes.
- Put in the bacon, then transfer to a greased 2-qt. baking dish. Next, combine 1/2 cup of the cheese and potatoes; spread over the beef mixture. Dust with the remaining cheese and paprika.
- Bake without cover for 20-25 minutes at 350°, or until heated through. Then broil 4 in. from the heat until bubbly, for 5 minutes.

Nutrition Information

- Calories: 381 calories
- Protein: 23g protein.
- Total Fat: 19g fat (9g saturated fat)
- Sodium: 625mg sodium
- Fiber: 1g fiber)
- Total Carbohydrate: 28g carbohydrate (3g sugars
- Cholesterol: 73mg cholesterol

```
132.        Mashed Potato Hot Dish
```

Serving: 4 servings. | Prep: 15mins | Cook: 20mins | Ready in:

Ingredients

- 1 pound ground beef
- 1 can (10-3/4 ounces) condensed cream of chicken soup, undiluted
- 2 cups frozen French-style green beans
- 2 cups hot mashed potatoes (prepared with milk and butter)
- 1/2 cup shredded cheddar cheese

Direction

- Cook beef in a big frying pan over medium heat till not pink anymore; let drain. Blend in beans and soup.
- Put to a greased 2-quart baking dish. Put mashed potatoes on top; dust with cheese. Bake while uncovered at 350° for around 20-25 minutes or until bubbly and cheese becomes melted.

Nutrition Information

- Calories: 431 calories
- Total Fat: 23g fat (12g saturated fat)
- Sodium: 1050mg sodium
- Fiber: 5g fiber)
- Total Carbohydrate: 29g carbohydrate (4g sugars
- Cholesterol: 89mg cholesterol
- Protein: 28g protein.

133. Meat 'n' Pepper Cornbread

Serving: 6 servings. | Prep: 15mins | Cook: 20mins | Ready in:

Ingredients

- 1 pound ground beef
- 1 cup chopped green pepper
- 1 cup chopped onion
- 2 cans (8 ounces each) tomato sauce
- 1-1/2 teaspoons chili powder
- 1/2 teaspoon salt
- 1/4 teaspoon pepper
- 1 cup all-purpose flour
- 3/4 cup cornmeal
- 1/4 cup sugar
- 1 tablespoon baking powder
- 1/2 teaspoon salt
- 1 large egg, beaten
- 1 cup whole milk
- 1/4 cup canola oil

Direction

- Put together green pepper, onion and ground beef in an ovenproof or 10-inch cast-iron pan and cook to brown lightly. Drain and add chili powder, salt, pepper and tomato sauce. Let it simmer for 10 to 15 minutes.
- In a bowl, combine the dry ingredients together. In a separate bowl, mix milk, oil, and egg. Beat together then stir into the dry ingredients. Blend until dry ingredients have moistened then pour over beef mixture.
- Set oven to 400 degrees. Bake mixture in the oven for 20 to 25 minutes until golden. Let it cool briefly then loosen the edges with a knife. Transfer to a serving plate by inverting. This dish can also be served straight from skillet. Cut into wedges then serve.

Nutrition Information

- Calories: 432 calories
- Total Carbohydrate: 46g carbohydrate (13g sugars
- Cholesterol: 87mg cholesterol
- Protein: 22g protein.
- Total Fat: 18g fat (5g saturated fat)
- Sodium: 839mg sodium
- Fiber: 3g fiber)

134. Meat Bun Bake

Serving: 6 servings. | Prep: 20mins | Cook: 20mins | Ready in:

Ingredients

- 1-1/2 pounds ground beef
- 2 cups chopped cabbage
- 1/4 cup chopped onion
- 1/2 teaspoon salt
- 1/4 teaspoon pepper
- 1/2 to 1 cup shredded cheddar cheese
- 1-1/2 cups biscuit/baking mix

- 1 cup 2% milk
- 2 eggs

Direction

- Over medium heat in a large skillet, cook beef till no longer pink; drain. Put in pepper, salt, onion and cabbage; cook over medium heat until the onion and cabbage are tender, about for 15 minutes. Mix in cheese.
- Spoon into a greased baking dish of 13 x 9 inches. Blend eggs, milk and biscuit mix in a large bowl. Pour over beef mixture. Bake with no cover, at 400° until golden brown, about 20-25 minutes.

Nutrition Information

- Calories: 438 calories
- Cholesterol: 162mg cholesterol
- Protein: 31g protein.
- Total Fat: 24g fat (10g saturated fat)
- Sodium: 732mg sodium
- Fiber: 1g fiber)
- Total Carbohydrate: 23g carbohydrate (4g sugars

135.   Meat And Potato Casserole

Serving: 6 servings. | Prep: 10mins | Cook: 50mins | Ready in:

Ingredients

- 4 cups thinly sliced peeled potatoes
- 2 tablespoons butter, melted
- 1/2 teaspoon salt
- 1 pound ground beef
- 1 package (10 ounces) frozen corn
- 1 can (10-3/4 ounces) condensed cream of celery soup, undiluted
- 1/3 cup whole milk
- 1/4 teaspoon garlic powder

- 1/8 teaspoon pepper
- 1 tablespoon chopped onion
- 1 cup shredded cheddar cheese, divided
- Minced fresh parsley, optional

Direction

- With salt and butter, toss potatoes; place in a 13x9-in. greased pan, arranging up the sides and on the bottom. Do not cover; bake in a 400-degree oven until potatoes are just about tender, 25-30 minutes. In the meantime, cook beef in a big frying pan on medium heat until not pink; drain excess grease. Sprinkle corn and beef on top the potatoes. Mix pepper, 1/2 cup cheese, soup, garlic powder, onion, and milk; dump on top of meat mixture. Do not cover; bake in a 400-degree oven until veggies are tender, 20 minutes. Sprinkle on remaining cheese. Bake until cheese melts, 2-3 minutes. If desired, sprinkle on parsley.

Nutrition Information

- Calories: 374 calories
- Fiber: 3g fiber)
- Total Carbohydrate: 31g carbohydrate (3g sugars
- Cholesterol: 71mg cholesterol
- Protein: 22g protein.
- Total Fat: 19g fat (11g saturated fat)
- Sodium: 778mg sodium

136.   Meat And Potato Squares

Serving: 6 servings. | Prep: 15mins | Cook: 30mins | Ready in:

Ingredients

- 1 pound ground beef
- 1 large egg
- 1/4 cup whole milk
- 1 teaspoon salt
- 1 teaspoon prepared mustard

- 1/4 teaspoon pepper
- 1 cup dry bread crumbs
- 1/2 cup chopped onion
- 1 package (16 ounces) frozen shoestring potatoes
- Ketchup, optional

Direction

- In a mixing bowl, combine the first 8 ingredients until well mixed. Put to one side. Arrange 1/2 of the potatoes in a greased 8x8-inch baking dish's bottom. Evenly distribute meat all over the potato layer. Place the rest of potatoes firmly over the top. Bake without covering for 30 minutes at 400°, or until potatoes are lightly browned and meat is cooked through. Slice into squares. Serve right away with ketchup, if desired.

Nutrition Information

- Calories: 327 calories
- Protein: 19g protein.
- Total Fat: 13g fat (5g saturated fat)
- Sodium: 642mg sodium
- Fiber: 3g fiber)
- Total Carbohydrate: 35g carbohydrate (2g sugars
- Cholesterol: 74mg cholesterol

137.   Meatball Hash Brown Bake

Serving: 8 servings. | Prep: 25mins | Cook: 60mins | Ready in:

Ingredients

- 1 can (10-3/4 ounces) condensed cream of chicken soup, undiluted
- 1 large onion, chopped
- 1 cup shredded cheddar cheese
- 1 cup (8 ounces) sour cream

- 1-1/2 teaspoons pepper, divided
- 1 teaspoon salt, divided
- 1 package (30 ounces) frozen shredded hash brown potatoes, thawed and patted dry
- 2 large eggs, lightly beaten
- 3/4 cup crushed saltines (20-25 crackers)
- 6 to 8 garlic cloves, minced
- 1 pound lean ground beef (90% lean)

Direction

- Start preheating the oven to 350°. Combine 1/2 teaspoon salt, 1 teaspoon pepper, and the first 4 ingredients; mix in potatoes. Evenly spread the mixture into a 13x9-inch baking dish coated with cooking spray.
- Mix the leftover salt and pepper, garlic, cracker crumbs, and eggs together in a big bowl. Add beef, gently stir but thoroughly. Form into balls, about 1-inch each ball.
- Brown the meatballs in a big frying pan over medium-high heat. Add to the potato mixture, gently press in.
- Put a cover on and bake for 45 minutes. Remove the cover, bake for 10-15 minutes until the potatoes are soft and the meatballs have fully cooked.

Nutrition Information

- Calories: 387 calories
- Total Carbohydrate: 32g carbohydrate (4g sugars
- Cholesterol: 106mg cholesterol
- Protein: 21g protein.
- Total Fat: 20g fat (9g saturated fat)
- Sodium: 808mg sodium
- Fiber: 3g fiber)

138.   Meatball Stuffed Zucchini

Serving: 8-10 servings. | Prep: 25mins | Cook: 45mins | Ready in:

Ingredients

- 4 to 5 medium zucchini
- 1-1/2 cups soft bread crumbs
- 1 tablespoon minced fresh parsley
- 1/4 cup grated Parmesan cheese
- 1 small onion, chopped
- 1 large egg, lightly beaten
- 1 teaspoon salt
- 1/2 teaspoon pepper
- 1-1/2 pounds lean ground beef
- 1 can (10-3/4 ounces) condensed tomato soup, undiluted
- 1/2 cup water

Direction

- Halve each zucchini lengthwise; remove a thin slice off the bases to have them sit flat. Scoop out the pulp while reserving 1/4-inch shells. Thinly chop pulp.
- Combine the seasonings, egg, onion, Parmesan cheese, parsley, breadcrumbs and pulp in a big bowl. Crumble beef over mixture, then thoroughly combine.
- Fill zucchini shells with meat mixture. Arrange in a 13x9-inch baking dish. Mix water and tomato soup together; spread over zucchini. Bake at 350° for around 45-50 minutes.

Nutrition Information

- Calories: 172 calories
- Total Carbohydrate: 11g carbohydrate (5g sugars
- Cholesterol: 64mg cholesterol
- Protein: 16g protein.
- Total Fat: 7g fat (3g saturated fat)
- Sodium: 528mg sodium
- Fiber: 2g fiber)

139. Meatballs Sausage Dinner

Serving: 6-8 servings. | Prep: 25mins | Cook: 40mins | Ready in:

Ingredients

- 3 cups frozen broccoli florets, thawed
- 2 medium potatoes, peeled and cubed
- 3 medium carrots, sliced
- 1 medium onion, chopped
- 1 pound Johnsonville® Fully Cooked Polish Kielbasa Sausage Rope, halved and cut into 1-inch pieces
- 1/2 pound lean ground beef
- 1 can (14-1/2 ounces) beef broth
- Lemon-pepper seasoning to taste

Direction

- Set oven to 350 degrees and start preheating. Combine onion, carrots, potatoes, and broccoli. Move to an oiled 13x9-inch baking dish. Top with sausage. Form beef into 1-inch balls; place over top. Spread broth over the casserole; sprinkle lemon-pepper seasoning over the surface. Bake for 40 minutes without cover, until meatballs are not pink anymore.

Nutrition Information

- Calories:
- Total Carbohydrate:
- Cholesterol:
- Protein:
- Total Fat:
- Sodium:
- Fiber:

140. Mexican Casserole

Serving: 4 | Prep: 10mins | Cook: 20mins | Ready in:

Ingredients

- 1 (16 ounce) can refried beans
- 3/4 onion, diced
- 5 (10 inch) flour tortillas
- 1 cup salsa
- 2 cups shredded Cheddar or Colby Jack cheese

Direction

- Preheat oven to 190 degrees C (375 degrees F). Spray a 9-inch pie pan using non-stick cooking spray.
- Cook onions and refried beans (to make them tender) in a saucepan over medium high heat for roughly 5 minutes.
- Add one tortilla into the bottom of the greased pan. Spread roughly a third cup of the bean mixture on top of it. Layer several tbsp. of salsa on top of this. Then, add another tortilla on top of the salsa, and add more of the bean mixture. Follow the beans with a large handful of cheese, spreading equally. Repeat the layers, spreading the ingredients equally on top of the tortillas. On the top layer, ensure you use a lot of cheese and salsa!
- Bake for roughly 15-20 minutes or till the cheese becomes melted.

Nutrition Information

- Calories: 651 calories;
- Total Fat: 20.3
- Sodium: 1505
- Total Carbohydrate: 74
- Cholesterol: 68
- Protein: 29.3

141.   Mexican Chip Casserole

Serving: 6 servings. | Prep: 10mins | Cook: 10mins | Ready in:

Ingredients

- 1 pound ground beef
- 1 medium onion, chopped

- 1 garlic clove, minced
- 1 can (10-3/4 ounces) condensed cream of mushroom soup, undiluted
- 1 can (11 ounces) Mexicorn
- 1 can (4 ounces) chopped green chilies
- 1 package (10-1/2 ounces) corn chips
- 1 can (10 ounces) enchilada sauce
- 1 to 2 cups shredded Colby-Monterey Jack cheese

Direction

- Cook garlic, onion, and beef on medium heat in a skillet till meat is not pink anymore and onion is soft; drain. Put in chilies, corn and soup; stir them well.
- In one ungreased shallow 3-qt. baking dish, layer meat mixture, chips and sauce; add cheese on top. Bake, while uncovered, at 350 degrees till thoroughly heated or for 8 to 10 minutes.

Nutrition Information

- Calories: 613 calories
- Cholesterol: 69mg cholesterol
- Protein: 26g protein.
- Total Fat: 36g fat (10g saturated fat)
- Sodium: 1168mg sodium
- Fiber: 5g fiber)
- Total Carbohydrate: 47g carbohydrate (6g sugars

142.   Microwave Pizza Casserole

Serving: 6-8 servings. | Prep: 10mins | Cook: 20mins | Ready in:

Ingredients

- 1 pound ground beef
- 1/2 cup chopped onion
- 1/2 cup chopped green pepper

- 1 can (16 ounces) pizza sauce
- 1 can (4 ounces) sliced mushrooms
- 4 ounces sliced pepperoni
- 1/2 teaspoon salt, optional
- 2 cups uncooked noodles
- 1-1/2 cups water
- 1/2 teaspoon oregano
- 1/2 teaspoon garlic powder
- 1/2 teaspoon basil leaves, crushed
- 3/4 cup shredded mozzarella cheese

Direction

- Microwave the ground beef in a 2-qt. casserole dish for 2 minutes; stir and continue to microwave until done, for 1 1/2 minutes more. Let drain thoroughly. Next, put in the leftover ingredients except for cheese; mix well. Then cook on HIGH for 10-1/2 minutes, during cooking, stir twice. Sprinkle over the casserole with cheese; keep cooking on HIGH for 30 seconds, or until the cheese is melted.

Nutrition Information

- Calories:
- Total Fat:
- Sodium:
- Fiber:
- Total Carbohydrate:
- Cholesterol:
- Protein:

143. Midwest Meatball Casserole

Serving: 6 servings. | Prep: 40mins | Cook: 20mins | Ready in:

Ingredients

- 2 cans (8 ounces each) tomato sauce, divided
- 1 large egg
- 1/4 cup dry bread crumbs

- 1/4 cup chopped onion
- 1 teaspoon salt
- 1 pound lean ground beef (90% lean)
- 1 package (10 ounces) frozen mixed vegetables
- 1/2 teaspoon dried thyme
- 1/8 teaspoon pepper
- 1 package (16 ounces) frozen shredded hash brown potatoes, thawed
- 1 tablespoon butter, melted
- 3 slices process American cheese, cut into 1/2-inch strips

Direction

- Combine egg, 2 tbsp. of tomato sauce, bread crumbs, salt and onion in a large bowl. Crumble beef over mixture and mix well. Form into balls of 1-inch.
- On a greased rack in a shallow baking pan, place meatballs and bake at 375° for approximately 15 to 20 minutes until meatballs are not pink anymore; drain.
- In the meantime, in a large skillet, combine the rest tomato sauce with seasonings and vegetables. Simmer while covered for around 10 to 15 minutes until heated through; mix in meatballs and leave aside.
- In a greased baking dish of 11x7-inch, place potatoes. Brush with butter and bake at 375° for nearly 15 to 20 minutes until lightly browned. Take away from the oven; put meatball mixture on top. Place cheese strips in a lattice pattern on top. Uncovered while baking for an addition of 20 to 25 minutes until cheese is melted and heated through.

Nutrition Information

- Calories: 310 calories
- Protein: 23g protein.
- Total Fat: 12g fat (6g saturated fat)
- Sodium: 884mg sodium
- Fiber: 4g fiber)
- Total Carbohydrate: 27g carbohydrate (4g sugars
- Cholesterol: 97mg cholesterol

144. Mom's Ground Beef Casserole

Serving: 16-18 servings. | Prep: 15mins | Cook: 45mins | Ready in:

Ingredients

- 2 pounds ground beef
- 1 medium green pepper, chopped
- 1 medium onion, chopped
- 9 cups cooked wide egg noodles
- 1 pound process cheese (Velveeta)
- 1 can (15-1/4 ounces) whole kernel corn, drained
- 1 can (11-1/2 ounces) condensed chicken with rice soup, undiluted
- 1 can (10-3/4 ounces) condensed cream of mushroom soup, undiluted
- 1/2 cup milk
- 1 teaspoon salt
- 1/4 teaspoon pepper

Direction

- In a Dutch oven, cook onion, green pepper and beef until the beef is no longer pink; drain. Take away from the heat; mix in the remaining ingredients.
- Place into two greased baking dishes of 2-1/2-qt. Cover up and bake at 350° until bubbly, about 45-50 minutes.

Nutrition Information

- Calories: 304 calories
- Sodium: 782mg sodium
- Fiber: 1g fiber)
- Total Carbohydrate: 22g carbohydrate (4g sugars
- Cholesterol: 70mg cholesterol
- Protein: 19g protein.
- Total Fat: 15g fat (7g saturated fat)

145. Ole Polenta Casserole

Serving: 6 servings. | Prep: 60mins | Cook: 45mins | Ready in:

Ingredients

- 1 cup yellow cornmeal
- 1 teaspoon salt
- 4 cups water, divided
- 1 pound ground beef
- 1 cup chopped onion
- 1/2 cup chopped green pepper
- 2 garlic cloves, minced
- 1 can (14-1/2 ounces) diced tomatoes, undrained
- 1 can (8 ounces) tomato sauce
- 1/2 pound sliced fresh mushrooms
- 1 teaspoon each dried basil, oregano and dill weed
- Dash hot pepper sauce
- 1-1/2 cups shredded part-skim mozzarella cheese
- 1/4 cup grated Parmesan cheese

Direction

- To make polenta, whisk together 1 cup of water, salt and cornmeal in a small bowl until smooth. Bring remaining water to a boil in a large saucepan. Add cornmeal mixture, stirring continuously. Bring to a boil and cook, stirring frequently, for 3 minutes or until mixture is thickened.
- Lower the heat to low and cook, covered, for 15 minutes. Evenly distribute mixture into 2 greased 8 inches square baking dishes. Keep in refrigerator, covered, for about 90 minutes until firm.
- Combine garlic, green pepper, onion and beef in a large skillet and cook over medium heat until the pink color disappears from meat; drain. Stir in hot pepper sauce, herbs, mushrooms, tomato sauce and tomatoes; bring to a boil. Remove cover and lower the heat to simmer for 20 minutes or until thickened.

- Loosen one polenta from dish's bottom and sides. Carefully transfer polenta onto a waxed paper-covered baking sheet; set aside. Drop spoonfuls of half of the meat mixture over remaining polenta. Place half of parmesan cheese and half of mozzarella cheese on top. Arrange saved polenta and remaining meat mixture on top.
- Bake, covered, for 40 minutes at 350° or until heated through. Remove the cover and add remaining cheese on top. Bake for an additional 5 minutes or until cheese is completely melted. Allow to stand for 10 minutes before cutting.

Nutrition Information

- Calories: 345 calories
- Cholesterol: 62mg cholesterol
- Protein: 25g protein.
- Total Fat: 14g fat (7g saturated fat)
- Sodium: 874mg sodium
- Fiber: 4g fiber)
- Total Carbohydrate: 29g carbohydrate (6g sugars

---

146.   Pan Burritos

Serving: 8-10 servings. | Prep: 35mins | Cook: 35mins | Ready in:

Ingredients

- 2 packages (1-1/2 ounces each) enchilada sauce mix
- 3 cups water
- 1 can (12 ounces) tomato paste
- 1 garlic clove, minced
- 1/4 teaspoon pepper
- Salt to taste
- 2 pounds ground beef
- 9 large flour tortillas (9-inch)
- 4 cups shredded cheddar cheese or Mexican cheese blend
- 1 can (16 ounces) refried beans, warmed
- Taco sauce, sour cream, chili peppers, chopped onion and/or guacamole, optional

Direction

- Mix together the first six ingredients in a saucepan. Let it simmer for 15 to 20 minutes.
- Brown the beef in a skillet. Let it drain and mix in 1/3 of the sauce. On the bottom of a 13x9-in. greased baking pan, spread another 1/3 of the sauce.
- Put three tortillas on top of the sauce and tear to fit the bottom of the baking pan. Place half of the meat mixture on the tortillas and drizzle with 1 and a half cup of cheese. Put in another three tortillas. Over the tortillas, spread the refried beans. Put the rest of the meat on top. Drizzle again with 1 and a half cup of cheese. Put in the rest of the tortillas and put the rest of the sauce on top. Drizzle with the remaining cheese.
- Without cover, bake for 35 to 40 minutes at 350°. Allow to rest for 10 minutes and cut. If you want, you can serve it with guacamole (or not), chopped onion, chili peppers, sour cream and taco sauce.

Nutrition Information

- Calories: 578 calories
- Sodium: 1421mg sodium
- Fiber: 11g fiber)
- Total Carbohydrate: 46g carbohydrate (6g sugars
- Cholesterol: 96mg cholesterol
- Protein: 35g protein.
- Total Fat: 25g fat (14g saturated fat)

---

147.   Pizza Mac Casserole

Serving: 6 servings. | Prep: 10mins | Cook: 35mins | Ready in:

Ingredients

- 1 pound ground beef
- 2 cups elbow macaroni, cooked and drained
- 1/2 cup chopped onion
- 1/2 cup chopped green pepper
- 2 jars (14 ounces each) pizza sauce
- 2 cups shredded part-skim mozzarella cheese

Direction

- In a big skillet on medium heat, cook the beef until browned with no hint of pink left. Drain and pour the pizza sauce, green pepper, onion and macaroni in then transfer it into a 2-1/2 quart greased baking dish. Cover it up and bake at 350°F for 20 minutes. Remove the cover to sprinkle cheese in. Continue baking until the cheese melts, another10-15 minutes.

Nutrition Information

- Calories: 308 calories
- Protein: 26g protein.
- Total Fat: 14g fat (7g saturated fat)
- Sodium: 499mg sodium
- Fiber: 2g fiber)
- Total Carbohydrate: 18g carbohydrate (6g sugars
- Cholesterol: 59mg cholesterol

---

148.   Pizza Tot Casserole

Serving: 6-8 servings. | Prep: 10mins | Cook: 30mins | Ready in:

Ingredients

- 1 pound ground beef
- 1 medium green pepper, chopped
- 1 medium onion, chopped
- 1 can (10-3/4 ounces) condensed tomato soup, undiluted
- 1 jar (4-1/2 ounces) sliced mushrooms, drained

- 1 teaspoon Italian seasoning
- 2 cups shredded part-skim mozzarella cheese
- 1 package (32 ounces) frozen Tater Tots

Direction

- Cook pepper, onion, and beef on medium heat in a big frying pan until beef is not pink. Drain excess grease. Add Italian seasoning, mushrooms, and soup. Move to a 13x9-in. greased pan. Top with potatoes and cheese. Do not cover; bake in a 400-degree oven until golden brown, 30-35 minutes.

Nutrition Information

- Calories: 399 calories
- Sodium: 954mg sodium
- Fiber: 4g fiber)
- Total Carbohydrate: 38g carbohydrate (5g sugars
- Cholesterol: 46mg cholesterol
- Protein: 21g protein.
- Total Fat: 21g fat (7g saturated fat)

---

149.   Poor Man's Dinner

Serving: 6 servings. | Prep: 20mins | Cook: 01hours15mins | Ready in:

Ingredients

- 1 pound ground beef
- 1/4 teaspoon pepper
- 1/4 teaspoon garlic powder
- 5 large potatoes, peeled and sliced
- 1 large onion, sliced
- 2 cans (10-3/4 ounces each) condensed cream of mushroom soup, undiluted
- 1/2 cup 2% milk
- Minced fresh parsley

Direction

- Over medium heat in a large skillet, cook beef till no longer pink; drain. Add in garlic powder and pepper for seasoning. Layer the beef, potatoes and onion slices in a shallow baking dish of 2 quarts. Mix milk and soup together; pour over all.
- Cover up and bake at 350° until potatoes are tender, about 1-1/4 hours. Sprinkle with parsley.

Nutrition Information

- Calories: 272 calories
- Cholesterol: 39mg cholesterol
- Protein: 17g protein.
- Total Fat: 9g fat (4g saturated fat)
- Sodium: 410mg sodium
- Fiber: 3g fiber)
- Total Carbohydrate: 30g carbohydrate (4g sugars

150.   Potato Beef Casserole

Serving: 4 servings. | Prep: 20mins | Cook: 01hours10mins | Ready in:

Ingredients

- 1 pound lean ground beef (90% lean)
- 1/2 cup chopped onion
- 1/2 cup chopped celery
- 2 tablespoons chopped celery leaves
- 1 can (10-3/4 ounces) condensed cream of mushroom soup, undiluted
- 1/2 cup milk
- 1 teaspoon Worcestershire sauce
- 1/2 teaspoon pepper
- 4 medium potatoes, peeled and thinly sliced
- 1 teaspoon salt, optional

Direction

- In the skillet, cook celery leaves, celery, onion and beef on medium heat till the veggies

soften and the meat is not pink anymore; drain off. Take out of heat; whisk in the pepper, Worcestershire sauce, milk and soup. Add 1/2 potatoes into the greased 2-quart baking dish; drizzle with half tsp. of the salt if you want. Add 1/2 beef mixture on top.
- Repeat the layers. Keep covered and bake at 400 degrees till potatoes soften or for 70 minutes.

Nutrition Information

- Calories: 353 calories
- Total Carbohydrate: 32g carbohydrate (0 sugars
- Cholesterol: 48mg cholesterol
- Protein: 28g protein. Diabetic Exchanges: 3 meat
- Total Fat: 12g fat (0 saturated fat)
- Sodium: 428mg sodium
- Fiber: 3g fiber)

151.   Potato Pizza Hot Dish

Serving: 8 servings. | Prep: 15mins | Cook: 01hours25mins | Ready in:

Ingredients

- 3 to 4 cups sliced peeled potatoes
- 1 can (11 ounces) condensed cheddar cheese soup, undiluted
- 1/2 cup milk
- 1-1/2 pounds ground beef
- 1 medium onion, chopped
- 1 jar (14 ounces) pizza sauce
- 2 cups shredded part-skim mozzarella cheese

Direction

- In a 13x9-inch baking dish coated with cooking spray, put potatoes. Mix together milk and soup, add to the potatoes.
- Cook onion and beef in a big frying pan over medium heat until the meat is not pink

anymore; strain. Spread onto the soup mixture. Put pizza sauce on the top.

- Put a cover on and bake at 350° until the potatoes are soft, about 80-90 minutes. Sprinkle cheese over, bake until the cheese melts, about another 5 minutes.

Nutrition Information

- Calories: 324 calories
- Total Fat: 16g fat (8g saturated fat)
- Sodium: 702mg sodium
- Fiber: 3g fiber)
- Total Carbohydrate: 21g carbohydrate (6g sugars
- Cholesterol: 65mg cholesterol
- Protein: 26g protein.

152.   Potluck Special

Serving: 6-8 servings. | Prep: 10mins | Cook: 60mins | Ready in:

Ingredients

- 1 pound ground beef
- 1 medium onion, chopped
- 1 can (28 ounces) diced tomatoes, undrained
- 1 can (16 ounces) sauerkraut, rinsed and drained
- 1-1/2 cups cooked rice
- 1 medium green pepper, chopped

Direction

- In a skillet, brown onion and ground beef; drain. Put in the remaining ingredients; place to a baking dish of 2 quarts. Cover up and bake at 350° for 60 minutes.

Nutrition Information

- Calories: 170 calories
- Sodium: 594mg sodium

- Fiber: 3g fiber)
- Total Carbohydrate: 18g carbohydrate (4g sugars
- Cholesterol: 28mg cholesterol
- Protein: 12g protein.
- Total Fat: 5g fat (2g saturated fat)

153.   Quick Tater Tot Bake

Serving: 2-3 servings. | Prep: 15mins | Cook: 30mins | Ready in:

Ingredients

- 3/4 to 1 pound ground beef or turkey
- 1 small onion, chopped
- Salt and pepper to taste
- 1 package (16 ounces) frozen Tater Tot potatoes
- 1 can (10-3/4 ounces) condensed cream of mushroom soup, undiluted
- 2/3 cup 2% milk or water
- 1 cup shredded cheddar cheese

Direction

- Start preheating the oven to 350°. Cook onion and beef in a big skillet over medium heat until the meat is not pink anymore; strain. Use pepper and salt to season.
- Remove into a 2-quart baking dish coated with cooking spray. Put potatoes on top. Mix together milk and soup; add on top of the potatoes. Sprinkle cheese over. Bake without a cover until thoroughly heated, about 30-40 minutes.

Nutrition Information

- Calories: 740 calories
- Sodium: 1634mg sodium
- Fiber: 5g fiber)
- Total Carbohydrate: 52g carbohydrate (6g sugars

- Cholesterol: 127mg cholesterol
- Protein: 38g protein.
- Total Fat: 46g fat (19g saturated fat)

154. Quick Tomato Mac 'n' Beef

Serving: 4 servings. | Prep: 20mins | Cook: 10mins | Ready in:

Ingredients

- 1 pound ground beef
- 1 cup chopped onion
- Salt and pepper to taste
- 1 can (14-1/2 ounces) diced tomatoes with garlic and onion, undrained
- 1 cup water
- 1 cup uncooked elbow macaroni
- 1 cup shredded cheddar cheese
- Sliced green onions and sour cream, optional

Direction

- Cook onion and beef in a big skillet on medium heat until meat is not pink; strain. Add pepper and salt to season. Stir in water and tomatoes; boil. Mix in macaroni.
- Cover then simmer for 10 minutes or until macaroni is soft. Mix in cheese. Decorate with sour cream and onions if wished.

Nutrition Information

- Calories:
- Sodium:
- Fiber:
- Total Carbohydrate:
- Cholesterol:
- Protein:
- Total Fat:

155. Red And Green Casserole

Serving: 4-6 servings. | Prep: 15mins | Cook: 30mins | Ready in:

Ingredients

- 1-1/2 pounds ground beef
- 2 medium onions, chopped
- 1 green pepper, chopped
- 1 sweet red pepper, chopped
- 2 cans (10-3/4 ounces each) condensed tomato soup, undiluted
- 1/4 cup water
- 1 teaspoon sugar
- 1/2 teaspoon chili powder
- Salt and pepper to taste
- 8 ounces wide noodles, cooked and drained
- 1 cup shredded cheddar cheese

Direction

- In a skillet, cook peppers, onions and beef until the vegetables are tender. Drain well. Mix in pepper, salt, chilli powder, sugar, water and soup. Mix in noodles. Place into a greased 13x9-inch baking dish. Sprinkle cheese on top. Bake with no cover at 350° for half an hour.

Nutrition Information

- Calories:
- Sodium:
- Fiber:
- Total Carbohydrate:
- Cholesterol:
- Protein:
- Total Fat:

156. San Jose Tortilla Pie

Serving: 10-12 servings. | Prep: 25mins | Cook: 25mins | Ready in:

Ingredients

- 6 corn tortillas (6 inches)
- Oil for deep-fat frying
- Salt
- 1 pound ground beef
- 1 large onion, chopped
- 1 medium green pepper, chopped
- 1 garlic clove, minced
- 1 tablespoon chili powder
- 1 teaspoon dried oregano
- 1 teaspoon ground cumin
- 2 cups shredded cheddar cheese
- 1 to 2 cans (4 ounces each) chopped green chilies
- 6 large eggs
- 1-1/2 cups whole milk
- 1/2 teaspoon salt
- Sliced ripe olives, optional

Direction

- Cut each tortilla into 8 wedges, sauté in hot oil, few at a time, until crisp. Pat with paper towels to remove excess fat and sprinkle with salt.
- Combine garlic, green pepper, onion and beef in a large skillet, cook over medium heat until vegetables are softened and meat loses its pink color; drain. Stir in cumin, oregano and chili powder.
- Arrange half of tortilla wedges, meat mixture and cheese in layers in a greased 13x9 inch baking dish, evenly place chili on top. Place remaining meat and cheese on top. Arrange remaining tortilla around edge of dish point side up.
- Beat salt, milk and eggs in a small bowl. Evenly distribute on top. Bake when uncover at 375° for 25 to 30 minutes. Place olives on top to garnish if desired.

Nutrition Information

- Calories:
- Total Carbohydrate:
- Cholesterol:
- Protein:
- Total Fat:
- Sodium:
- Fiber:

---

157.   Sauerkraut Hotdish

Serving: 4-6 servings. | Prep: 15mins | Cook: 45mins | Ready in:

Ingredients

- 1 pound ground beef
- 1/4 cup chopped onion
- 1/2 teaspoon salt
- 1/2 teaspoon pepper
- 1 can (32 ounces) sauerkraut, rinsed and well drained
- 2 cups uncooked egg noodles
- 1 can (10-3/4 ounces) condensed cream of celery soup, undiluted
- 1 can (10-3/4 ounces) condensed cream of mushroom soup, undiluted
- 1 cup whole milk
- 1 to 1-1/2 cups shredded cheddar cheese

Direction

- Put the onion and beef in a big frying pan and set heat to medium, cook until beef is not pink. Drain excess grease. Mix in the pepper and salt. Put half of the beef mixture in the bottom of a 13x9-in. pan. Put half of the noodles and sauerkraut on top. Repeat the layers. Mix together milk and soups. Dump on noodles. Cover; bake in a 350-degree oven for 30 minutes. Sprinkle cheese on. Do not cover; bake until heated, 15-20 minutes.

Nutrition Information

- Calories: 367 calories
- Fiber: 5g fiber)
- Total Carbohydrate: 27g carbohydrate (5g sugars

- Cholesterol: 79mg cholesterol
- Protein: 24g protein.
- Total Fat: 19g fat (10g saturated fat)
- Sodium: 2107mg sodium

158. Sauerkraut Beef Bake

Serving: 6 servings. | Prep: 15mins | Cook: 60mins | Ready in:

Ingredients

- 1 pound ground beef
- 1 can (27 ounces) sauerkraut, rinsed and well drained
- 1/2 cup uncooked instant rice
- 1 can (10-3/4 ounces) condensed cream of mushroom soup, undiluted
- 1 soup can water
- 2 tablespoons onion soup mix
- 1 can (4 ounces) mushroom stems and pieces, drained, optional

Direction

- In a skillet over medium heat, cook beef until not pink anymore; drain.
- Combine soup mix, water, soup, rice, sauerkraut and beef together in a greased 2-quart baking dish. If desired, put in mushrooms. Cover and bake at 350° until heated through, about 60 minutes.

Nutrition Information

- Calories:
- Total Carbohydrate:
- Cholesterol:
- Protein:
- Total Fat:
- Sodium:
- Fiber:

159. Scalloped Potatoes And Hamburger

Serving: 6 servings. | Prep: 25mins | Cook: 45mins | Ready in:

Ingredients

- 1 pound ground beef
- 6 medium potatoes, peeled and sliced
- 1 large onion, sliced
- Salt and pepper to taste
- 1 can (10-3/4 ounces) condensed cream of mushroom soup, undiluted
- 1 cup milk
- 1/4 cup chopped green pepper

Direction

- Cook beef in a skillet over medium heat until not pink anymore; drain. Layer 1/2 of the potatoes, onion and beef in a greased baking dish (13x9 inches); season with pepper and salt. Repeat layers. Place green pepper, milk and soup together in a bowl; mix well. Drizzle over top. Cover and bake at 350° for 45 minutes. Remove the cover; bake until potatoes are tender, about 15 more minutes.

Nutrition Information

- Calories:
- Fiber:
- Total Carbohydrate:
- Cholesterol:
- Protein:
- Total Fat:
- Sodium:

160.   Shipwreck

Serving: 6-8 servings. | Prep: 20mins | Cook: 60mins | Ready in:

Ingredients

- 1/2 pound sliced bacon
- 1 pound ground beef
- 1 large onion, chopped
- 1 cup ketchup
- 1/2 cup packed brown sugar
- 1 can (32 ounces) pork and beans

Direction

- In a frying pan, cook bacon until crisp. Transfer on paper towels to drain; crumble and leave it aside. Drain drippings from the pan. Cook the beef until browned; let drain. Put in onion and cook for around 5 minutes until softened. Blend brown sugar and ketchup; mix into beef mixture. Mix in beans and pork and all except for 2 tablespoons of the bacon. Put to an 8-inch square baking dish. Put leftover bacon on top. Bake while uncovered at 350° for 1 hour.

Nutrition Information

- Calories: 328 calories
- Sodium: 915mg sodium
- Fiber: 6g fiber)
- Total Carbohydrate: 43g carbohydrate (24g sugars
- Cholesterol: 36mg cholesterol
- Protein: 19g protein.
- Total Fat: 11g fat (4g saturated fat)

161.   Six Layer Dinner

Serving: 6-8 servings. | Prep: 5mins | Cook: 01hours20mins | Ready in:

Ingredients

- 1-1/2 pounds ground beef
- 2 medium onions, thinly sliced
- 3 medium potatoes, peeled and thinly sliced
- 1 large green pepper, chopped
- 1-1/2 teaspoons salt
- 1/2 teaspoon pepper
- 2 celery ribs, chopped
- 1 can (14-1/2 ounces) stewed tomatoes
- 1/4 teaspoon dried basil

Direction

- In a Dutch oven over medium heat, cook beef till no longer pink; drain. Layer beef with onions, potatoes and green pepper, add pepper and salt into each layer lightly to taste. Add in basil, tomatoes and celery.
- Let it come to a boil. Lower the heat; cover up and let it simmer until vegetables are tender, about 1 hour.

Nutrition Information

- Calories: 233 calories
- Total Fat: 8g fat (3g saturated fat)
- Sodium: 607mg sodium
- Fiber: 3g fiber)
- Total Carbohydrate: 23g carbohydrate (7g sugars
- Cholesterol: 42mg cholesterol
- Protein: 18g protein.

162.   Skillet Casserole

Serving: 4 servings. | Prep: 20mins | Cook: 15mins | Ready in:

Ingredients

- 1 pound ground beef
- 2 medium onions, diced
- 1medium green pepper, diced
- 4 medium potatoes, peeled, cut into 1/2-inch cubes and parboiled

- 2 medium tomatoes, seeded and chopped
- 1 can (10-3/4 ounces) condensed cream of chicken soup, undiluted
- 1/4 cup chili sauce
- 3/4 teaspoon salt
- 1/4 teaspoon pepper
- 1/4 cup grated Parmesan cheese

Direction

- In a large frying pan, cook green pepper, onions and beef over medium heat till meat is not pink anymore; drain. Remove and leave aside. In the same pan, cook ground beef until browned; let drain. Mix in the pepper, salt, chili sauce, soup, tomatoes and potatoes.
- Put to a greased 13x9-inch baking dish. Dust with Parmesan. Bake while uncovered at 350° for 15 minutes or until bubbly.

Nutrition Information

- Calories: 460 calories
- Protein: 28g protein.
- Total Fat: 16g fat (7g saturated fat)
- Sodium: 1432mg sodium
- Fiber: 6g fiber)
- Total Carbohydrate: 50g carbohydrate (13g sugars
- Cholesterol: 66mg cholesterol

163. Sloppy Joe Under A Bun

Serving: 8 servings. | Prep: 15mins | Cook: 25mins | Ready in:

Ingredients

- 1-1/2 pounds ground beef
- 1 can (15-1/2 ounces) sloppy joe sauce
- 2 cups shredded cheddar cheese
- 2 cups biscuit/baking mix
- 2 large eggs, lightly beaten
- 1 cup 2% milk

- 1 tablespoon sesame seeds

Direction

- In a large skillet, cook the beef over medium heat until there is not pink anymore; and then drain. Add in sloppy joe sauce. Place to a lightly greased baking dish of 13x9-inch; have cheese for sprinkling.
- In a large bowl, combine milk, eggs and biscuit mix just until blended. Pour over cheese; use sesame seeds to sprinkle. Uncovered while baking at 400° for nearly 25 minutes until it has the color of golden brown.

Nutrition Information

- Calories: 423 calories
- Protein: 27g protein.
- Total Fat: 23g fat (12g saturated fat)
- Sodium: 961mg sodium
- Fiber: 1g fiber)
- Total Carbohydrate: 26g carbohydrate (6g sugars
- Cholesterol: 129mg cholesterol

164. Sour Cream Beef 'N' Beans

Serving: 4-6 servings. | Prep: 15mins | Cook: 0mins | Ready in:

Ingredients

- 1 pound ground beef
- 1 can (15 ounces) pinto beans, rinsed and drained
- 1 can (15 ounces) enchilada sauce
- 1-1/2 cups shredded cheddar cheese, divided
- 1 can (4 ounces) chopped green chilies, undrained
- 1-1/2 cups crushed corn chips
- 1 tablespoon dried minced onion
- 1 cup (8 ounces) sour cream

- Additional corn chips

Direction

- Crumble beef into an ungreased 2-qt. microwave-safe dish; use waxed paper to cover up. Cook on high till meat is not pink anymore or for 3 to 4 minutes, mixing two times; drain. Mix in onion, crushed corn chips, chilies, one cup cheese, enchilada sauce and beans. Keep it covered and microwave on high till thoroughly heated or for 2 to 2-1/2 min., mixing one time.
- Add the rest of the cheese and sour cream on top. Heat, while uncovered, at 70% power till cheese becomes melted or for 1 to 2 minutes. Serve along with corn chips.

Nutrition Information

- Calories: 523 calories
- Fiber: 6g fiber)
- Total Carbohydrate: 41g carbohydrate (5g sugars
- Cholesterol: 105mg cholesterol
- Protein: 29g protein.
- Total Fat: 27g fat (14g saturated fat)
- Sodium: 745mg sodium

165.   Sour Cream Chili Bake

Serving: 8-10 servings. | Prep: 15mins | Cook: 35mins | Ready in:

Ingredients

- 1 can (15 ounces) pinto beans, rinsed and drained
- 1 pound ground beef
- 1 can (16 ounces) hot chili beans, undrained
- 1 can (10 ounces) enchilada sauce
- 1 can (8 ounces) tomato sauce
- 1 teaspoon chili powder
- 1-1/2 cups shredded cheddar cheese
- 1 tablespoon dried minced onion

- 2 cups corn chips, crushed, divided
- 1 cup sour cream

Direction

- Brown ground beef in a skillet; drain. Mix in 1 cup of corn chips, onion, and 1 cup of cheese, chili powder, tomato sauce, enchilada sauce and beans. Add to one 2-qt. casserole dish. Keep it covered and baked at 375 degrees for half an hour. Take out of the oven and scoop sour cream on top of casserole. Drizzle with one cup of corn chips and the leftover half of cup cheese. Bring back to the oven and bake, while uncovered, till cheese becomes melted or for 2 - 3 minutes.

Nutrition Information

- Calories:
- Total Carbohydrate:
- Cholesterol:
- Protein:
- Total Fat:
- Sodium:
- Fiber:

166.   Southwestern Casserole

Serving: 2 casseroles (6 servings each). | Prep: 15mins | Cook: 40mins | Ready in:

Ingredients

- 2 cups (8 ounces) uncooked elbow macaroni
- 2 pounds ground beef
- 1 large onion, chopped
- 2 garlic cloves, minced
- 2 cans (14-1/2 ounces each) diced tomatoes, undrained
- 1 can (16 ounces) kidney beans, rinsed and drained
- 1 can (6 ounces) tomato paste
- 1 can (4 ounces) chopped green chilies, drained

- 1-1/2 teaspoons salt
- 1 teaspoon chili powder
- 1/2 teaspoon ground cumin
- 1/2 teaspoon pepper
- 2 cups shredded Monterey Jack cheese
- 2 jalapeno peppers, seeded and chopped

Direction

- Based on the instruction on the package, cook macaroni. At the same time, cook onion and beef on medium heat in a big saucepan, crumbling beef, till meat is not pink anymore. Put in garlic; cook for 1 minute more. Drain. Mix in the following 8 ingredients. Boil. Lower the heat; let it simmer, while uncovered, for 10 minutes. Drain macaroni; mix into beef mixture.
- Preheat oven to 375 degrees. Move macaroni mixture into 2 greased 2-qt. baking dishes. Add jalapenos and cheese on top. Keep it covered and baked at 375 degrees for half an hour. Uncover it; bake till bubbly and thoroughly heated for roughly 10 minutes more. Serve one casserole. Cool the second; keep it covered and frozen for the maximum of 3 months.
- To use frozen casserole: Thaw in the fridge 8 hours. Preheat the oven to 375 degrees. Take out of the fridge half an hour prior to baking. Keep it covered and baked, increasing time as needed to heat through and for a thermometer inserted in the middle to reach 165 degrees, 20 to 25 minutes.

Nutrition Information

- Calories: 321 calories
- Cholesterol: 64mg cholesterol
- Protein: 24g protein.
- Total Fat: 15g fat (7g saturated fat)
- Sodium: 673mg sodium
- Fiber: 4g fiber)
- Total Carbohydrate: 23g carbohydrate (5g sugars

Serving: 6 | Prep: 20mins | Cook: 1hours | Ready in:

Ingredients

- 3 pounds spaghetti squash, halved lengthwise and seeded
- 1 tablespoon vegetable oil
- 1 medium onion, chopped
- 1 (8 ounce) can sliced mushrooms
- 1 teaspoon dried basil
- 3/4 cup sour cream
- 1/4 cup freshly grated Parmesan cheese
- 3 slices bread, cubed

Direction

- Preheat an oven to 205°C/400°F.
- On baking sheet, cook squash for 40 minutes till tender in preheated oven. Use fork to shred when slightly cooled; put on lightly oiled casserole dish. Discard shell; don't turn oven off.
- Heat 1 tbsp. oil in skillet on medium heat; mix and cook basil, mushrooms and onions till onions are tender and translucent. Mix sour cream and onion mixture into squash till mixed well. Sprinkle parmesan cheese; use bread cubes to cover.
- In preheated oven, bake for 15 minutes till top is toasted and lightly browned and warmed through.

Nutrition Information

- Calories: 211 calories;
- Total Fat: 10.6
- Sodium: 364
- Total Carbohydrate: 25.9
- Cholesterol: 16
- Protein: 5.9

168.   Spicy Cabbage Casserole

Serving: 8-10 servings. | Prep: 10mins | Cook: 01hours30mins | Ready in:

Ingredients

- 1 small head cabbage, finely chopped
- 1 pound ground beef
- 1 can (10-3/4 ounces) condensed French onion soup, undiluted
- 1 can (14-1/2 ounces) Mexican diced tomatoes, undrained
- 1 cup uncooked long grain rice
- 1 egg, lightly beaten
- 1 large onion, chopped
- 1 medium green pepper, chopped
- 1/2 cup vegetable oil
- 1 tablespoon garlic salt
- 1 tablespoon chili powder
- 1 tablespoon salt
- Dash cayenne pepper

Direction

- Stir all ingredients well in a big bowl. Add to a small-sized covered roasting pan. Bake at 350 degrees for 1-1/2 hours without lifting the lid.

Nutrition Information

- Calories: 321 calories
- Cholesterol: 53mg cholesterol
- Protein: 13g protein.
- Total Fat: 18g fat (4g saturated fat)
- Sodium: 1712mg sodium
- Fiber: 4g fiber)
- Total Carbohydrate: 27g carbohydrate (7g sugars

169.   Spicy Enchilada Casserole

Serving: 2 casseroles (4 servings each). | Prep: 20mins | Cook: 40mins | Ready in:

Ingredients

- 1-1/2 pounds ground beef
- 1 large onion, chopped
- 1 cup water
- 2 to 3 tablespoons chili powder
- 1-1/2 teaspoons salt
- 1/2 teaspoon pepper
- 1/4 teaspoon garlic powder
- 2 cups salsa, divided
- 10 flour tortillas (8 inches), cut into 3/4-inch strips, divided
- 1 cup (8 ounces) sour cream
- 2 cans (15-1/4 ounces each) whole kernel corn, drained
- 4 cups shredded part-skim mozzarella cheese

Direction

- Cook onion and beef on medium heat in a big skillet till meat is not pink anymore; drain. Mix in garlic powder, pepper, salt, chili powder, and water. Boil. Lower the heat; let it simmer, while uncovered, for 10 minutes.
- Add a quarter cup of salsa in each of two greased 8-in. square baking dishes. Add a quarter cup of salsa and a quarter of tortillas on top of each.
- Separate corn, sour cream and meat mixture among the two casseroles. Add cheese, salsa and the rest of the tortillas on top.
- Keep it covered and frozen one casserole for maximum of 1 month. Keep it covered and baked second casserole at 350 degrees for 35 minutes. Uncover it; bake till thoroughly heated or for 5 to 10 minutes more.
- To use frozen casserole: Thaw in fridge for 1 day. Take out of the fridge half an hour prior to baking. Bake following the directions above.

Nutrition Information

- Calories: 592 calories
- Total Carbohydrate: 45g carbohydrate (8g sugars
- Cholesterol: 94mg cholesterol
- Protein: 37g protein.
- Total Fat: 26g fat (13g saturated fat)
- Sodium: 1535mg sodium
- Fiber: 4g fiber)

170. Spinach Beef Bake

Serving: 6-8 servings. | Prep: 10mins | Cook: 45mins | Ready in:

Ingredients

- 1 pound ground beef
- 1 jar (4-1/2 ounces) sliced mushrooms, drained
- 1 medium onion, chopped
- 2 garlic cloves, minced
- 1-1/2 teaspoon dried oregano
- 1-1/4 teaspoon salt
- 1/4 teaspoon pepper
- 2 packages (10 ounces each) frozen chopped spinach, thawed and squeezed dry
- 1 can (10-3/4 ounces) condensed cream of celery soup, undiluted
- 1 cup sour cream
- 1 cup uncooked long grain rice
- 1 cup shredded part-skim mozzarella cheese

Direction

- Brown beef in a frying pan; drain. Add pepper, salt, oregano, garlic, onion and mushrooms. Add rice, sour cream, soup and spinach; combine well.
- Move the mixture to a 2-1/2-quart baking dish coated with cooking spray. Dredge mozzarella cheese over top. Set oven at 350°, bake while covered until the rice gets tender, about 45 to 50 minutes.

Nutrition Information

- Calories: 342 calories
- Protein: 19g protein.
- Total Fat: 17g fat (9g saturated fat)
- Sodium: 835mg sodium
- Fiber: 3g fiber)
- Total Carbohydrate: 27g carbohydrate (3g sugars
- Cholesterol: 69mg cholesterol

171. Spinach Beef Biscuit Bake

Serving: 6 servings. | Prep: 15mins | Cook: 25mins | Ready in:

Ingredients

- 2 tubes (6 ounces each) refrigerated buttermilk biscuits
- 1-1/2 pounds ground beef
- 1/2 cup finely chopped onion
- 2 eggs
- 1 package (10 ounces) frozen chopped spinach, thawed and squeezed dry
- 1 can (4 ounces) mushroom stems and pieces, drained
- 4 ounces crumbled feta cheese
- 1/4 cup grated Parmesan cheese
- 1-1/2 teaspoons garlic powder
- Salt and pepper to taste
- 1 to 2 tablespoons butter, melted

Direction

- Flatten and pack the biscuits on the sides and bottom of an oil 11-in by 7-in baking dish; set it aside.
- On medium heat, cook onion and beef in a pan until the meat is not pink; drain.
- Whisk eggs in a bowl; stir in mushrooms and spinach thoroughly. Mix in beef mixture,

cheeses, pepper, salt, and garlic powder to combine well; scoop to the prepared crust then sprinkle with butter.

- Bake for 25-30 minutes in 375 degrees oven without cover until the crust is pale brown.

Nutrition Information

- Calories: 418 calories
- Sodium: 686mg sodium
- Fiber: 3g fiber)
- Total Carbohydrate: 19g carbohydrate (1g sugars
- Cholesterol: 164mg cholesterol
- Protein: 34g protein.
- Total Fat: 22g fat (10g saturated fat)

172.   Spinach Skillet Bake

Serving: 6 servings. | Prep: 30mins | Cook: 20mins | Ready in:

Ingredients

- 1 pound ground beef
- 1 medium onion, chopped
- 1 package (10 ounces) frozen chopped spinach, thawed and squeezed dry
- 1 can (4 ounces) mushroom stems and pieces, drained
- 1 teaspoon garlic salt
- 1 teaspoon dried basil
- 1/4 cup butter
- 1/4 cup all-purpose flour
- 1/2 teaspoon salt
- 2 cups whole milk
- 1 cup shredded Monterey Jack cheese or part-skim mozzarella cheese
- Biscuits, optional

Direction

- Cook onion and beef in a 10-in. ovenproof skillet or cast-iron over medium heat until

meat is not pink anymore; drain. Mix in basil, garlic salt, mushrooms and spinach. Cover and cook for 5 minutes.

- Melt butter in a saucepan over medium heat. Add in salt and flour until smooth. Slowly pour in milk. Let it come to a boil; cook and stir until thickened, about 2 minutes. Mix in cheese. Pour over meat mixture; stir well. Lower the heat; cook with a cover until heated through. Serve with biscuits, if desired.

Nutrition Information

- Calories: 351 calories
- Sodium: 872mg sodium
- Fiber: 2g fiber)
- Total Carbohydrate: 13g carbohydrate (6g sugars
- Cholesterol: 85mg cholesterol
- Protein: 23g protein.
- Total Fat: 23g fat (13g saturated fat)

173.   Stovetop Hamburger Casserole

Serving: 6 servings. | Prep: 15mins | Cook: 10mins | Ready in:

Ingredients

- 1 package (7 ounces) small pasta shells
- 1-1/2 pounds ground beef
- 1 large onion, chopped
- 3 medium carrots, chopped
- 1 celery rib, chopped
- 3 garlic cloves, minced
- 3 cups cubed cooked red potatoes
- 1 can (15-1/4 ounces) whole kernel corn, drained
- 2 cans (8 ounces each) tomato sauce
- 1-1/2 teaspoons salt
- 1/2 teaspoon pepper
- 1 cup shredded cheddar cheese

Direction

- Cook pasta as directed in the package. Meanwhile, cook onion and beef in a frying pan over medium heat till meat is not pink anymore; let drain. Put in celery and carrots; cook and mix for 5 minutes, or until vegetables become crisp-tender. Put in garlic and cook for 1 minute more.
- Mix in the pepper, salt, tomato sauce, corn and potatoes; let heat through. Let the pasta drain and pour onto the skillet; stir to coat. Top with cheese. Cook while covered until cheese is melted.

Nutrition Information

- Calories: 508 calories
- Cholesterol: 76mg cholesterol
- Protein: 32g protein.
- Total Fat: 17g fat (9g saturated fat)
- Sodium: 1172mg sodium
- Fiber: 5g fiber)
- Total Carbohydrate: 53g carbohydrate (9g sugars

174.   Stuffed Artichokes

Serving: 6 | Prep: 25mins | Cook: 1hours | Ready in:

Ingredients

- 6 whole artichokes
- 3 slices Italian bread, cubed
- 1 clove garlic, minced
- 1/8 cup chopped fresh parsley
- 1/4 cup grated Romano cheese
- 1/2 teaspoon dried oregano
- 5 tablespoons vegetable oil, divided
- salt and pepper to taste

Direction

- Cut the stems and pointed tips of the artichoke leaves; rinse and drain. Hold the base of the artichoke firmly. Bash the top on any hard surface to open.
- Add pepper, salt, bread cubes, 2 tbsp. vegetable oil, garlic, Romano cheese, and parsley in a medium bowl; stir well.
- Stuff half cup of the mixture in every artichoke. Place the stuffed artichokes in a Dutch oven or big saucepan. Pour water until half of the artichokes are covered, add 3 tbsp. oil.
- Boil on high heat. Lower heat and let it simmer for an hour with a cover until the leaves can be easily removed.

Nutrition Information

- Calories: 175 calories;
- Sodium: 149
- Total Carbohydrate: 11.6
- Cholesterol: 5
- Protein: 4
- Total Fat: 13.2

175.   Taco Casserole

Serving: 10 | Prep: 25mins | Cook: 35mins | Ready in:

Ingredients

- 1 pound lean ground beef
- 8 ounces macaroni
- 1/2 cup chopped onion
- 1 (10.75 ounce) can condensed tomato soup
- 1 (14.5 ounce) can diced tomatoes
- 1 (1.25 ounce) package taco seasoning mix
- 2 ounces shredded Cheddar cheese
- 2 ounces shredded Monterey Jack cheese
- 1 cup crushed tortilla chips
- 1/2 cup sour cream (optional)
- 1/4 cup chopped green onions

Direction

- Prepare the oven by preheating to 350°F (175°C).
- Add the pasta in a large pot of boiling water and cook until al dente. Strain. Stir and cook chopped onion and ground beef in a large skillet over medium heat until it turns brown in color. Add in taco seasoning mix, diced tomatoes and tomato soup. Mix in pasta.
- Into a 9x13-inch baking dish, put the beef mixture. Then top with shredded cheese and crumbled taco chips.
- Place in the preheated oven and bake for 30-35 minutes until the cheese is dissolved. Put sour cream and chopped green onions to serve, if wished.

Nutrition Information

- Calories: 334 calories;
- Cholesterol: 50
- Protein: 15.6
- Total Fat: 17
- Sodium: 635
- Total Carbohydrate: 28.2

176. Taco Pie

Serving: 8 | Prep: 20mins | Cook: 10mins | Ready in:

Ingredients

- 1 (8 ounce) package refrigerated crescent rolls
- 1 pound ground beef
- 1 (1 ounce) package taco seasoning mix
- 1 (16 ounce) container sour cream
- 8 ounces shredded Mexican-style cheese blend
- 1 (14 ounce) bag tortilla chips, crushed

Direction

- Preheat oven to 175 degrees C (350 degrees F).
- Lay crescent dough flat onto the bottom of a square cake pan and then following the instructions on the package, bake it.

- At the same time, in a big skillet, brown the ground beef on medium-high heat. Put in the taco seasoning and mix together well. Once dough is done, take out of the oven and add meat mixture over, then layer with sour cream and cheese, and then top off with the crushed nacho chips.
- Bring back to the oven and bake at 175 degrees C (350 degrees F) till cheese is melted or for 10 minutes.

Nutrition Information

- Calories: 687 calories;
- Total Fat: 43.4
- Sodium: 863
- Total Carbohydrate: 50.6
- Cholesterol: 100
- Protein: 24.4

177. Taco Potato Shells

Serving: 6 servings. | Prep: 25mins | Cook: 01hours45mins | Ready in:

Ingredients

- 3 large baking potatoes
- 1 tablespoon butter, melted
- 1 pound ground beef
- 1 can (14-1/2 ounces) diced tomatoes, undrained
- 1 envelope taco seasoning
- 1/2 cup shredded cheddar cheese
- 1/3 cup sour cream
- 2 green onions, sliced

Direction

- Scrub and pierce potatoes. Bake for 1 hour at 375° or until softened. Allow to cool until can be handled easily, cut potatoes in half by the length. Scoop out pulp carefully, leaving a thin shell (place pulp in refrigerator for later use). Coat butter on inside and outside of potato shells and arrange on an ungreased baking sheet cut side up. Bake when uncover for 20 minutes at 375°.

- In the meantime, cook beef in a large skillet over medium heat until the pink color disappears from meat; drain. Add taco seasoning and tomatoes. Bring to a boil; lower the heat to simmer, uncovered, for 20 minutes.
- Place spoonfuls of mixture into shells; add cheese on top. Bake, uncovered, for an additional 5 to 10 minutes or until cheese is completely melted. Add onions and sour cream on top.

Nutrition Information

- Calories: 375 calories
- Fiber: 4g fiber)
- Total Carbohydrate: 42g carbohydrate (6g sugars
- Cholesterol: 61mg cholesterol
- Protein: 20g protein.
- Total Fat: 14g fat (8g saturated fat)
- Sodium: 766mg sodium

178. Taco Salad Casserole

Serving: 4 servings. | Prep: 25mins | Cook: 15mins | Ready in:

Ingredients

- 1 pound ground beef
- 1/4 cup chopped onion
- 1/4 cup chopped green pepper
- 1 envelope taco seasoning
- 1/2 cup water
- 1 cup crushed tortilla chips
- 1 can (16 ounces) refried beans
- 1 cup shredded cheddar cheese
- Toppings: chopped lettuce and tomatoes, sliced ripe olives, sour cream and picante sauce

Direction

- Combine green pepper, onion and beef in a large skillet, cook over medium heat until the pink color disappears from meat; drain. Stir in water and taco seasoning. Cook for about 3 minutes until thickened, remember to stir while cooking. Set aside.
- Arrange chips in a greased 8 inches square baking dish. Stir refried beans in a small bowl and spread on top of chips. Place cheese and beef mixture on top.
- Bake, uncovered, for 15 to 20 minutes at 375° or until heated through. Add olives, tomatoes and lettuce on top. Serve with picante sauce and sour cream.

Nutrition Information

- Calories: 405 calories
- Fiber: 6g fiber)
- Total Carbohydrate: 31g carbohydrate (0 sugars
- Cholesterol: 47mg cholesterol
- Protein: 37g protein.
- Total Fat: 12g fat (0 saturated fat)
- Sodium: 1181mg sodium

179. Taco Twist Bake

Serving: 4 servings. | Prep: 10mins | Cook: 30mins | Ready in:

Ingredients

- 2-1/2 cups cooked Taco-Seasoned Meat
- 2 cans (8 ounces each) tomato sauce
- 1/4 cup chopped green pepper
- 1 package (8 ounces) spiral pasta, cooked and drained
- 1 cup sour cream
- 1 cup shredded cheddar cheese, divided

Direction

- Mix green pepper, tomato sauce, and taco meat in a big saucepan; boil. At the same time, mix sour cream and pasta; add into one greased 8-in. square baking dish. Drizzle with half cup of cheese. Add meat mixture on top.
- Bake, while uncovered, at 325 degrees for 25 minutes. Drizzle with leftover cheese. Bake till cheese becomes melted for 5 to 10 minutes more.

Nutrition Information

- Calories: 721 calories
- Protein: 38g protein.
- Total Fat: 35g fat (17g saturated fat)
- Sodium: 1652mg sodium
- Fiber: 5g fiber)
- Total Carbohydrate: 66g carbohydrate (8g sugars
- Cholesterol: 98mg cholesterol

180.   Tater Tot Casseroles

Serving: 2 casseroles (6 servings each). | Prep: 25mins | Cook: 45mins | Ready in:

Ingredients

- 3/4 pound Johnsonville® Ground Hot Italian sausage
- 3/4 pound lean ground beef (90% lean)
- 1 small onion, chopped
- 2 cans (10-3/4 ounces each) condensed cream of celery soup, undiluted
- 2 cups frozen cut green beans, thawed
- 1 can (15-1/4 ounces) whole kernel corn, drained
- 2 cups shredded Colby-Monterey Jack cheese, divided
- 1/2 cup 2% milk
- 1 teaspoon garlic powder
- 1/4 teaspoon seasoned salt
- 1/4 to 1/2 teaspoon cayenne pepper
- 1 package (32 ounces) frozen Tater Tots

Direction

- In the Dutch oven, cook onion, beef and sausage on medium heat till the meat is not pink anymore; drain off. Put in the cayenne, seasoned salt, garlic powder, milk, 1 cup of the cheese, corn, beans and soup. Move into two greased 11x7-inch baking dishes. Add the Tater Tots on top; drizzle with the rest of the cheese.
- Put cover on and freeze 1 casserole for no more than 3 months. Bake rest of the casserole, with cover, at 350 degrees for 40 minutes. Remove the cover and bake till bubbling or for 5 to 10 minutes more.
- To use the frozen casserole: Thaw it in fridge overnight. Take out of the fridge half an hour prior to baking.
- Put cover on and bake at 350 degrees for 50 minutes. Remove the cover and bake till becoming bubbling or for 5 to 10 minutes more.

Nutrition Information

- Calories: 370 calories
- Protein: 16g protein.
- Total Fat: 22g fat (8g saturated fat)
- Sodium: 1085mg sodium
- Fiber: 3g fiber)
- Total Carbohydrate: 30g carbohydrate (4g sugars
- Cholesterol: 48mg cholesterol

181.   Tater Topped Casserole

Serving: 4-6 servings. | Prep: 15mins | Cook: 45mins | Ready in:

Ingredients

- 1 pound lean ground beef (90% lean)
- 1/2 cup chopped onion
- 1/3 cup sliced celery

- 1/2 teaspoon salt
- 1/4 teaspoon pepper
- 1 can (10-3/4 ounces) condensed cream of celery soup, undiluted
- 1 package (16 ounces) frozen Tater Tots
- 1 cup shredded cheddar cheese

Direction

- Cook the celery, onion and beef in a large skillet until the vegetables become tender and the meat is not pink anymore; let drain. Stir in pepper and salt.
- Place the mixture into a 3-quart baking dish coated with cooking spray. Place with soup. Put the frozen potatoes on top. Bake at 400 degrees until bubbling, 40 minutes. Dust with cheese. Bake until the cheese melts, 5 minutes.

Nutrition Information

- Calories: 353 calories
- Protein: 21g protein.
- Total Fat: 20g fat (8g saturated fat)
- Sodium: 1040mg sodium
- Fiber: 3g fiber)
- Total Carbohydrate: 25g carbohydrate (2g sugars
- Cholesterol: 59mg cholesterol

182.   Tex Mex Casserole

Serving: Makes 6 servings. | Prep: 20mins | Cook: | Ready in:

Ingredients

- 1/2 lb. lean ground beef
- 1 can (15 oz.) black beans, rinsed
- 1 Tbsp. chili powder
- 1 tsp. garlic powder
- 3 tomatoes, chopped
- 2 cups water

- 1/2 cup creamy wheat (enriched farina) hot cereal (1-min., 2-1/2-min. or 10-min. cook time), uncooked
- 1/2 cup KRAFT 2% Milk Shredded Cheddar Cheese
- 1 can (4 oz.) chopped green chiles, undrained
- 1 egg
- 1/2 cup coarsely broken baked tortilla chips

Direction

- 1. In a big skillet, brown the meat; drain. Mix in seasonings and beans; spread on the bottom of an 8-in. square baking dish. Add tomatoes on top.
- 2. In a medium-sized saucepan, boil water. Slowly mix in cereal; cook till becoming thick or for 1 - 3 minutes, mixing continuously. Cool for 5 minutes. Mix in egg, chiles, and cheese; spread on top of meat mixture. Add chips on top.
- 3. Bake till thoroughly heated or for 20 - 25 minutes. Decorate as you want.

Nutrition Information

- Calories: 250
- Total Fat: 7 g
- Sodium: 230 mg
- Sugar: 2 g
- Total Carbohydrate: 30 g
- Protein: 18 g
- Saturated Fat: 2.5 g
- Fiber: 7 g
- Cholesterol: 65 mg

183.   Three Bean Casserole

Serving: 8 | Prep: 15mins | Cook: 25mins | Ready in:

Ingredients

- 1 pound beef frankfurters, sliced
- 1 (15 ounce) can pork and beans

- 1 (15 ounce) can butter beans
- 1 (16 ounce) can chili beans, drained
- 1 small onion, chopped
- 1/2 cup brown sugar
- 1/4 teaspoon dried oregano
- 2 tablespoons distilled white vinegar

Direction

- Set oven to 350 degrees F or 175 degrees C and start preheating.
- Mix chili beans, vinegar, frankfurters, onion, butter beans, pork and beans, oregano, and sugar in a big bowl. After mixing, pour into a 9x13-in. lightly greased pan.
- Do not cover; bake in 350-degree F or 175-degree C oven until bubbling and heated through, 1 hour.

Nutrition Information

- Calories: 364 calories;
- Total Carbohydrate: 38
- Cholesterol: 40
- Protein: 15.6
- Total Fat: 17.9
- Sodium: 1246

184. Tomato Beef And Rice Casserole

Serving: 6 servings. | Prep: 10mins | Cook: 01hours30mins |Ready in:

Ingredients

- 1 pound lean ground beef (90% lean)
- 3 cups canned diced tomatoes, undrained
- 1 medium green pepper, chopped
- 1 cup uncooked long grain rice
- 1 large onion, chopped
- 1 teaspoon chili powder
- 1/2 teaspoon salt
- 1/4 teaspoon pepper

Direction

- Combine all ingredients in a large bowl. Arrange in a greased 2-qt. baking dish. Bake at 400°, covered, for 1-1/2 hours, stirring once or twice. During the last 15 minutes, uncover to get brown.

Nutrition Information

- Calories: 267 calories
- Protein: 18g protein.
- Total Fat: 6g fat (2g saturated fat)
- Sodium: 413mg sodium
- Fiber: 3g fiber)
- Total Carbohydrate: 34g carbohydrate (6g sugars
- Cholesterol: 37mg cholesterol

185. Tortilla Beef Bake

Serving: 6 servings. | Prep: 10mins | Cook: 30mins | Ready in:

Ingredients

- 1-1/2 pounds ground beef
- 1 can (10-3/4 ounces) condensed cream of chicken soup, undiluted
- 2-1/2 cups crushed tortilla chips, divided
- 1 jar (16 ounces) salsa
- 1-1/2 cups shredded cheddar cheese

Direction

- Cook beef on medium heat in a big skillet till meat is not pink anymore; drain. Mix in soup. Drizzle 1-1/2 cups tortilla chips in one greased shallow 2-1/2-qt. baking dish. Add cheese, salsa, and beef mixture.
- Bake, while uncovered, at 350 degrees for 25 to 30 minutes or till becoming bubbly. Drizzle with the rest of the chips. Bake for 3 minutes more or till chips are toasted a bit.

Nutrition Information

- Calories: 464 calories
- Total Carbohydrate: 23g carbohydrate (3g sugars
- Cholesterol: 90mg cholesterol
- Protein: 29g protein.
- Total Fat: 26g fat (12g saturated fat)
- Sodium: 1083mg sodium
- Fiber: 4g fiber)

Nutrition Information

- Calories: 277 calories;
- Cholesterol: 117
- Protein: 15.5
- Total Fat: 16.7
- Sodium: 691
- Total Carbohydrate: 17.6

---

186. Tortilla Casserole

Serving: 12 | Prep: 20mins | Cook: 1hours | Ready in:

Ingredients

- 12 (6 inch) corn tortillas
- 2/3 cup chopped green onions
- 1 (4 ounce) can sliced black olives, drained
- 2 (4 ounce) cans diced green chile peppers, drained
- 1 (4 ounce) jar diced pimento peppers, drained
- 8 ounces Monterey Jack cheese, shredded
- 8 ounces Cheddar cheese, shredded
- 5 eggs
- 2 cups milk
- 1 (8 ounce) jar salsa

Direction

- Grease a 9-inch by 13-inch baking dish lightly. Place four tortillas at the bottom of dish. Add a third each of the chile peppers, green onions, pimento peppers, olives, Cheddar cheese, and Monterey Jack cheese. Repeat for another two layers using the leftover ingredients.
- Whisk salsa, milk, and eggs together in a big bowl; pour on top of the layers. Use a sheet of plastic wrap to cover the dish; place in the refrigerator overnight.
- Take the dish out of the refrigerator then discard the plastic wrap. Preheat the oven to 175°C or 350°Fahrenheit.
- Bake in the oven for 45-60 mins.

---

187. Tortilla Pie

Serving: Makes 4 main-course servings | Prep: 20mins | Cook: 35mins | Ready in:

Ingredients

- 1 (15-oz) can black beans, drained and rinsed
- 1 (10-oz) package frozen corn kernels, thawed
- 1 cup mild tomato salsa
- 1 (8-oz) can tomato sauce
- 6 oz pepper Jack cheese, coarsely grated (2 cups)
- 1/2 cup chopped fresh cilantro
- 2 scallions, thinly sliced
- 1/2 teaspoon ground cumin
- 4 (10-inch) flour tortillas (burrito-size)
- 1 tablespoon olive oil
- Accompaniment: sour cream

Direction

- To make the preparation: Position the oven rack in lower third of oven and preheat oven to 450 degrees F.
- In a big bowl, mix cumin, scallions, cilantro, cheese, tomato sauce, salsa, corn and beans.
- Heat one 12-in. heavy skillet on high heat till smoking. Brush both sides of each tortilla using oil and fry, flipping one time, for roughly 1 minute or till puffed and golden in spots.
- Add one tortilla into a well-oiled 15x10-in. shallow baking pan, and then spread with 1

1/3 cups of filling. Repeat the layers two times, and then add the leftover tortillas on top, pushing lightly to help layers adhere.

- Bake for roughly 12 minutes or till filling is thoroughly heated. Move using a big metal spatula to a platter, then chop the pie into wedges using a serrated knife.

Nutrition Information

- Calories: 679
- Cholesterol: 59 mg(20%)
- Protein: 30 g(60%)
- Total Fat: 29 g(44%)
- Saturated Fat: 14 g(70%)
- Sodium: 1260 mg(53%)
- Fiber: 11 g(46%)
- Total Carbohydrate: 76 g(25%)

188.   Two Meat Macaroni

Serving: 8 servings. | Prep: 15mins | Cook: 01hours30mins | Ready in:

Ingredients

- 1/2 pound ground beef
- 1/2 pound ground pork
- 2 cans (14-1/2 ounces each) diced tomatoes
- 2 cups shredded cheddar cheese
- 2 cups uncooked elbow macaroni
- 1 medium onion, finely chopped
- 1 cup frozen peas, thawed
- 2 cans (2-1/2 ounces each) sliced ripe olives, drained
- 1 jar (2 ounces) diced pimientos, drained
- 1 teaspoon salt
- 1/2 teaspoon paprika
- 1/4 teaspoon celery salt

Direction

- Cook pork and beef in a large skillet over medium heat until not pink anymore; drain. Put in the remaining ingredients.
- Place into a greased 3-quart baking dish. Bake without covering at 350° until the macaroni is tender for about 90 minutes, stirring every 30 minutes.

Nutrition Information

- Calories: 315 calories
- Total Carbohydrate: 22g carbohydrate (5g sugars
- Cholesterol: 63mg cholesterol
- Protein: 20g protein.
- Total Fat: 16g fat (9g saturated fat)
- Sodium: 710mg sodium
- Fiber: 3g fiber)

189.   Unstuffed Peppers

Serving: 6 servings. | Prep: 20mins | Cook: 10mins | Ready in:

Ingredients

- 1 cup uncooked instant rice
- 1 pound ground beef
- 2 medium green peppers, cut into 1-inch pieces
- 1/2 cup chopped onion
- 1 jar (26 ounces) marinara sauce
- 1-1/2 teaspoons salt-free seasoning blend
- 1/2 cup shredded Italian cheese blend
- 1/2 cup seasoned bread crumbs
- 1 tablespoon olive oil

Direction

- Set the oven to 350°, and start preheating. Cook rice following package instructions.
- In the meantime, in a large skillet over the medium-high heat, cook onion, green peppers and beef until meat is no longer pink; drain.

Mix in seasoning blend, marinara sauce and rice. Mix in cheese.

- Place to a greased baking dish of 2 quart. Toss oil and bread crumbs; sprinkle over the top. Bake until topping is golden brown and heated through, about 8-10 minutes.

Nutrition Information

- Calories: 343 calories
- Protein: 20g protein.
- Total Fat: 12g fat (5g saturated fat)
- Sodium: 469mg sodium
- Fiber: 3g fiber)
- Total Carbohydrate: 38g carbohydrate (12g sugars
- Cholesterol: 43mg cholesterol

190. Upside Down Beef Pie

Serving: 6 servings. | Prep: 10mins | Cook: 20mins | Ready in:

Ingredients

- 1 pound ground beef
- 1/2 cup chopped celery
- 1/2 cup chopped onion
- 1/4 cup chopped green pepper
- 1 can (10-3/4 ounces) condensed tomato soup, undiluted
- 1 teaspoon prepared mustard
- 1-1/2 cups biscuit/baking mix
- 1/3 cup water
- 3 slices process American cheese, halved diagonally
- Green pepper rings, optional

Direction

- In a big skillet over medium heat, cook the green pepper, onion, celery and beef until the meat has no hint of pink anymore then drain. Stir the mustard and soup in. Move it into a

greased 9-inch pie plate. In the meantime, combine water and dry baking mix in a big bowl until soft dough is formed. Place it on a lightly floured surface and roll into a 9-inch circle. Put this over the meat mixture. Bake at 425°F until it turns golden brown, about 20 minutes. Leave it to cool for 5 minutes. Loosen the biscuit from the plate by running a knife along the edges then flip it over onto a serving platter. Organize the cheese slices on top of it in a pinwheel pattern. If desired, decorate with green pepper rings.

Nutrition Information

- Calories:
- Cholesterol:
- Protein:
- Total Fat:
- Sodium:
- Fiber:
- Total Carbohydrate:

191. Vegetable Beef Casserole

Serving: 6-8 servings. | Prep: 20mins | Cook: 01hours15mins | Ready in:

Ingredients

- 3 medium potatoes, sliced
- 3 carrots, sliced
- 3 celery ribs, sliced
- 2 cups cut fresh or frozen cut green beans
- 1 medium onion, chopped
- 1 pound lean ground beef (90% lean)
- 1 teaspoon dried thyme
- 1 teaspoon salt
- 1 teaspoon pepper
- 4 medium tomatoes, peeled, seeded and chopped
- 1 cup shredded cheddar cheese

Direction

- Layer half the onion, green beans, celery, carrots and potatoes in a 3-quart casserole. Crumble top of vegetables with half of the uncooked beef. Dust with 1/2 teaspoon each of pepper, salt and thyme. Repeat layers.
- Put tomatoes on top. Cover and bake for 15 minutes at 400°. Lower the heat to 350°; bake for about another hour or until meat is no longer pink and vegetables are soft. Scatter cheese over; cover and allow to stand until cheese melts.

Nutrition Information

- Calories: 243 calories
- Sodium: 452mg sodium
- Fiber: 5g fiber)
- Total Carbohydrate: 25g carbohydrate (7g sugars
- Cholesterol: 43mg cholesterol
- Protein: 17g protein.
- Total Fat: 9g fat (5g saturated fat)

---

192. Western Beef And Corn Casserole

Serving: 6-8 servings. | Prep: 20mins | Cook: 25mins | Ready in:

Ingredients

- FILLING:
- 1 pound ground beef
- 1 can (11 ounces) Mexicorn, drained
- 1 can (8 ounces) tomato sauce
- 1 cup shredded cheddar cheese
- 1/2 cup hickory-flavored sauce
- 1/2 teaspoon salt
- 1/2 teaspoon chili powder
- CRUST:
- 1 cup all-purpose flour
- 1/2 cup yellow cornmeal
- 2 tablespoons sugar
- 1 teaspoon salt

- 1 teaspoon baking powder
- 1 cup shredded cheddar cheese, divided
- 1/4 cup cold butter
- 1/2 cup whole milk
- 1 large egg, lightly beaten

Direction

- Cook beef on medium heat in a big skillet till meat is not pink anymore; drain. Mix in the rest of filling ingredients; put aside.
- To make crust, mix baking powder, salt, sugar, cornmeal and flour in a big bowl. Fold in half cup cheese. Chop in butter till mixture looks like coarse crumbs. Mix in egg and milk.
- Spread crust mixture on the bottom and up the sides of one greased 9-in. square baking dish. Add filling to the crust. Bake, while uncovered, at 400 degrees till becoming bubbly or for 20 to 25 minutes. Drizzle with the rest of cheese; bake till cheese becomes melted or for 5 minutes more.

Nutrition Information

- Calories: 434 calories
- Sodium: 1277mg sodium
- Fiber: 3g fiber)
- Total Carbohydrate: 35g carbohydrate (9g sugars
- Cholesterol: 112mg cholesterol
- Protein: 23g protein.
- Total Fat: 22g fat (13g saturated fat)

---

193. Wild Rice Hot Dish

Serving: 8-12 servings. | Prep: 15mins | Cook: 02hours30mins | Ready in:

Ingredients

- 3 cups boiling water
- 1 cup wild rice
- 1-1/2 pounds ground beef

- 1 medium onion, chopped
- 2 cans (10-3/4 ounces each) condensed cream of chicken soup, undiluted
- 2 cans (4 ounces each) sliced mushrooms, undrained
- 1 can (28 ounces) bean sprouts, drained
- 1 can (10-1/2 ounces) condensed beef broth
- 1-1/3 cups water
- 1/4 cup soy sauce
- 1 bay leaf, crushed
- 1 tablespoon dried parsley flakes
- 1/4 teaspoon each celery salt, onion salt, poultry seasoning, garlic powder, paprika and pepper
- 1/8 teaspoon dried thyme
- 1/2 cup sliced almonds

Direction

- Pour water over rice in a large bowl; allow to stand for 15 minutes. Drain and put aside. Brown onion and ground beef in a skillet. Drain; add to rice along with the remaining ingredients, except for almonds. Place into a 13x9-inch baking dish. Cover and bake at 350° for 2 hours. Add almonds on top; bake with no cover for 30 more minutes.

Nutrition Information

- Calories: 216 calories
- Total Fat: 9g fat (3g saturated fat)
- Sodium: 853mg sodium
- Fiber: 3g fiber)
- Total Carbohydrate: 18g carbohydrate (1g sugars
- Cholesterol: 30mg cholesterol
- Protein: 16g protein.

Ingredients

- 3/4 pound ground beef
- 1 tablespoon butter
- 2 medium zucchini, thinly sliced
- 1/4 pound sliced fresh mushrooms, sliced
- 2 tablespoons sliced green onions
- 1-1/2 teaspoons chili powder
- 1 teaspoon salt
- 1/8 teaspoon garlic powder
- 1-1/2 cups cooked rice
- 1 can (4 ounces) chopped green chilies
- 1/2 cup sour cream
- 1 cup shredded Monterey Jack cheese, divided

Direction

- Cook beef in a large frying pan with heat on medium until not pink. Drain excess grease. Mix in zucchini, onions, butter, and mushrooms. Continue cooking and stir until veggies are soft. Drain any water. Mix in garlic powder, chili powder, and salt. Then put in the chilies, half the cheese, rice, and sour cream. Place in a 2-qt. greased dish. Spread the rest of the cheese on top. Do not cover; bake in a 350-degree oven until cheese is melty, 20-22 minutes.

Nutrition Information

- Calories: 462 calories
- Protein: 29g protein.
- Total Fat: 27g fat (15g saturated fat)
- Sodium: 944mg sodium
- Fiber: 2g fiber)
- Total Carbohydrate: 23g carbohydrate (3g sugars
- Cholesterol: 109mg cholesterol

194.   Zippy Beef Bake

Serving: 4 servings. | Prep: 15mins | Cook: 20mins | Ready in:

195.   Zippy Beef Supper

Serving: 6-8 servings. | Prep: 15mins | Cook: 35mins | Ready in:

Ingredients

- 2 pounds ground beef
- 1 medium onion, chopped
- 1 cup cubed cooked potatoes
- 1 can (11 ounces) condensed nacho cheese soup, undiluted
- 1 can (10-3/4 ounces) condensed cream of onion soup, undiluted
- 1 can (10 ounces) diced tomatoes and green chilies, undrained
- 2 to 3 teaspoons ground cumin
- 1/2 to 1 teaspoon garlic powder
- 3 cups crushed tortilla chips
- 1 cup shredded cheddar cheese

Direction

- Cook onion and beef on medium heat in a big saucepan till meat is not pink anymore; drain. Put in potatoes; cook and stir till becoming heated through. Mix in the garlic powder, cumin, tomatoes and soups.
- Move to a greased 13x9-in. baking dish. Keep it covered and bake at 350 degrees for half an hour. Uncover it; drizzle with tortilla chips and cheese. Bake, while uncovered, till cheese becomes melted or for 5 to 10 minutes longer.

Nutrition Information

- Calories: 589 calories
- Sodium: 1251mg sodium
- Fiber: 4g fiber)
- Total Carbohydrate: 40g carbohydrate (3g sugars
- Cholesterol: 106mg cholesterol
- Protein: 37g protein.
- Total Fat: 31g fat (13g saturated fat)

196.   Zucchini Cheese Casserole

Serving: 6 servings. | Prep: 15mins | Cook: 45mins | Ready in:

Ingredients

- 4 cups shredded unpeeled zucchini (about 3 medium)
- 1/2 teaspoon salt
- 1 cup shredded part-skim mozzarella cheese, divided
- 1 cup shredded cheddar cheese, divided
- 1/2 cup grated Parmesan cheese
- 2 large eggs
- 1 pound ground beef
- 1/2 cup chopped onion
- 1 can (8 ounces) tomato sauce
- 1/4 teaspoon garlic powder
- 1/4 teaspoon dried oregano
- 1 cup chopped green pepper
- 2 cans (4 ounces each) mushroom stems and pieces, drained

Direction

- Put zucchini into a double thickness of cheesecloth; season with salt. Allow to sit for 10 minutes. Gather ends of cheesecloth and squeeze to remove as much liquid as possible.
- Mix eggs, Parmesan cheese, 1/2 cup mozzarella cheese and zucchini together in a bowl. Press into a greased 13x9-inch baking dish. Bake without a cover at 400° until crust is set, about 20 minutes.
- In the meantime, cook onion and beef in a large skillet over medium heat until not pink anymore; drain. Mix in oregano, garlic powder and tomato sauce; let it come to a boil. Spread over crust.
- Scatter mushrooms and green pepper on top; sprinkle with the remaining cheeses. Return to the oven and bake until heated through and cheeses are melted, about 25-35 more minutes.

Nutrition Information

- Calories: 326 calories
- Protein: 29g protein.
- Total Fat: 19g fat (11g saturated fat)
- Sodium: 848mg sodium
- Fiber: 2g fiber)
- Total Carbohydrate: 9g carbohydrate (5g sugars
- Cholesterol: 144mg cholesterol

---

197.   Zucchini Garden Casserole

Serving: 8 servings. | Prep: 20mins | Cook: 01hours15mins |Ready in:

Ingredients

- 4 medium zucchini (about 1-1/2 pounds), sliced
- 1 tablespoon olive oil
- 1 can (28 ounces) diced tomatoes, drained
- 1 cup uncooked instant rice
- 1/4 cup chopped green pepper
- 1/4 cup chopped onion
- 2 tablespoons chopped fresh parsley
- 1 teaspoon salt
- 1/4 teaspoon ground cinnamon
- 1/4 teaspoon ground allspice
- 1/4 teaspoon pepper
- 1-1/2 pounds lean ground beef
- 1 can (8 ounces) tomato sauce
- 1 cup shredded Colby cheese

Direction

- Sauté zucchini in oil in a big frying pan until crisp-tender. In a greased 13x9-inch baking dish, put half of the zucchini. Layer with half of the tomatoes.
- Blend the seasonings, parsley, onion, green pepper, and rice in a big bowl. Crumble the beef over mixture, then stir thoroughly. Whisk

in tomato sauce. Spread over tomato layer. Cover with zucchini and the leftover tomatoes.
- Bake, covered, at 375° for 1 hour or until a thermometer reaches 160°. Uncover, then dust with cheese. Bake for 15 more minutes or until cheese becomes melted.

Nutrition Information

- Calories: 291 calories
- Total Fat: 13g fat (6g saturated fat)
- Sodium: 685mg sodium
- Fiber: 3g fiber)
- Total Carbohydrate: 20g carbohydrate (6g sugars
- Cholesterol: 65mg cholesterol
- Protein: 23g protein.

---

198.   Zucchini Italiano

Serving: 4 servings. | Prep: 25mins | Cook: 30mins | Ready in:

Ingredients

- 4 cups thinly sliced zucchini
- Water
- 1 pound ground beef
- 1 garlic clove, minced
- 1/2 cup chopped onion
- 1 cup cooked rice
- 1 can (8 ounces) tomato sauce
- 1/2 teaspoon dried oregano
- 1/2 teaspoon salt
- 1/4 teaspoon pepper
- 1 large egg, lightly beaten
- 1/2 cup 4% cottage cheese
- 1/2 cup shredded cheddar cheese

Direction

- In the boiling water, cook zucchini until it nearly becomes tender, 2-3 minutes. Then drain thoroughly and put aside.

- Cook onion, garlic, and beef in a large skillet on medium heat until the meat is not pink anymore; then drain. Stir in pepper, salt, oregano, tomato sauce, and rice. Boil. Reduce the heat; bring to a simmer without a cover for 10 minutes.
- Blend cottage cheese and egg in a small bowl. In an 8-inch square baking dish coated with cooking spray, place half of the zucchini slices, slices can overlap each other if necessary. Place the meat mixture over the zucchini; add the cottage cheese mixture on the meat. Put the remaining zucchini slices on top.
- Bake at 350 degrees without a cover until cooked thoroughly, 25 minutes. Dust around the edges with Cheddar cheese; bake until the cheese melts, for 2-3 more minutes.

Nutrition Information

- Calories: 366 calories
- Sodium: 836mg sodium
- Fiber: 2g fiber)
- Total Carbohydrate: 21g carbohydrate (5g sugars
- Cholesterol: 130mg cholesterol
- Protein: 31g protein.
- Total Fat: 17g fat (9g saturated fat)

Chapter 3: Ground Beef Lasagna Recipes

***

199.   Argentine Lasagna

Serving: 12 servings. | Prep: 30mins | Cook: 55mins | Ready in:

Ingredients

- 1 pound ground beef
- 1 large sweet onion, chopped
- 1/2 pound sliced fresh mushrooms
- 1 garlic clove, minced
- 1 can (15 ounces) tomato sauce
- 1 can (6 ounces) tomato paste
- 1/4 teaspoon pepper
- 4 cups shredded part-skim mozzarella cheese, divided
- 1 jar (15 ounces) Alfredo sauce
- 1 carton (15 ounces) ricotta cheese
- 2-1/2 cups frozen peas, thawed
- 1 package (10 ounces) frozen chopped spinach, thawed and squeezed dry
- 1 package (9 ounces) no-cook lasagna noodles
- Fresh basil leaves and grated Parmesan cheese, optional

Direction

- On medium heat, cook garlic, mushrooms, onion, and beef in a Dutch oven until the beef is not pink. Mic in two cups mozzarella cheese, tomato sauce, pepper, and tomato paste; set aside.
- Mix spinach, Alfredo sauce, peas, and ricotta cheese together in a big bowl.
- In a 13-inch by 9-inch greased baking dish, spread a cup of meat sauce. Top with 4 noodles, one and quarter cup meat sauce and 1 1/4 cup spinach mixture. Repeat the process for another 3 times. Add the leftovers mozzarella cheese on top until the pan is full. Bake in 350 degrees F oven, covered, for 45 mins. Remove the cover and bake for another 10 mins until the cheese melts. Let it cool for 10 mins then cut. Sprinkle basil on top and add Parmesan cheese if preferred. Serve.

Nutrition Information

- Calories: 406 calories
- Protein: 28g protein.
- Total Fat: 18g fat (10g saturated fat)
- Sodium: 598mg sodium
- Fiber: 4g fiber)
- Total Carbohydrate: 33g carbohydrate (8g sugars
- Cholesterol: 69mg cholesterol

200.   Aunt May's Lasagna

Serving: 12 servings. | Prep: 60mins | Cook: 35mins | Reudy in:

Ingredients

- 1 pound ground beef
- 1 large onion, chopped
- 2 garlic cloves, minced
- 1 can (28 ounces) stewed tomatoes
- 2 cans (6 ounces each) tomato paste
- 1 teaspoon dried basil
- 1/2 teaspoon dried oregano
- 1/4 teaspoon pepper
- 1 bay leaf
- 9 lasagna noodles
- 1 can (6 ounces) pitted ripe olives, drained and coarsely chopped
- 2 cups shredded part-skim mozzarella cheese
- 1/2 cup grated Parmesan cheese

Direction

- Cook onion and beef over a medium heat using a large pot. Cook until the beef is no longer pink and add garlic. Wait and cook for 60 more seconds before draining it. Mix in tomato paste, oregano, tomatoes, basil, bay leaf and pepper. Once the mixture boils, reduce the heat. Put cover and simmer until thickened for about 40 to 50 minutes.
- Set your oven to 350°F for preheating. Follow the package directions in cooking the noodles. Let it drain and remove the bay leaf from the meat sauce. Add some olives.

- In a greased 13x9-inch baking pan, pour a fourth of the sauce. Lay a third of the mozzarella and Parmesan cheese together with the 3 noodles. Repeat steps to form layers. Top it with the remaining sauce, cheese and noodles.
- Put into the oven and bake, uncovered, for about 35 to 40 minutes until bubbly. Let it rest for 15 minutes before slicing.

Nutrition Information

- Calories: 249 calories
- Protein: 16g protein.
- Total Fat: 10g fat (5g saturated fat)
- Sodium: 412mg sodium
- Fiber: 3g fiber)
- Total Carbohydrate: 25g carbohydrate (7g sugars
- Cholesterol: 36mg cholesterol

201.   Baked Mexican Lasagna

Serving: 6-8 servings. | Prep: 20mins | Cook: 30mins | Ready in:

Ingredients

- 1-1/2 pounds ground beef
- 1-1/2 teaspoons ground cumin
- 1 tablespoon chili powder
- 1/4 teaspoon garlic powder
- 1/4 teaspoon cayenne pepper
- 1 teaspoon salt or to taste
- 1 teaspoon pepper or to taste
- 1 can (14-1/2 ounces) diced tomatoes, drained
- 10 to 12 corn tortillas
- 2 cups (16 ounces) small curd 4% cottage cheese, drained
- 1 cup shredded pepper jack cheese
- 1 large egg
- 1/2 cup shredded cheddar cheese
- 2 cups shredded lettuce
- 1/2 cup chopped tomatoes

- 3 green onions, chopped
- 1/4 cup sliced ripe olives

Direction

- Cook the beef in a big skillet over medium heat until not pink. Drain grease. Add the tomatoes, pepper, cayenne, cumin, chili powder, salt, and garlic powder. Let it cook through. Grease a 9x13 inch baking dish and cover the base and sides with tortillas.
- Spread the beef mixture on the tortillas. Put another layer of tortillas on meat mixture and set aside. Mix the egg, Monterey Jack and cottage cheese. Spread the cheese mixture on top of the tortillas.
- Place it in a 350°F oven for 30 minutes. Take the dish out of the oven; by sprinkling make diagonal rows of olives, lettuce, green onions, tomatoes and cheddar cheese across the middle of the dish.

Nutrition Information

- Calories: 381 calories
- Cholesterol: 101mg cholesterol
- Protein: 30g protein.
- Total Fat: 19g fat (10g saturated fat)
- Sodium: 785mg sodium
- Fiber: 4g fiber)
- Total Carbohydrate: 23g carbohydrate (5g sugars

202. Barbecue Lasagna

Serving: 10 | Prep: 15mins | Cook: 1hours | Ready in:

Ingredients

- 1 (16 ounce) package lasagna noodles
- 2 (18 ounce) containers pulled pork in barbeque sauce
- 1 (16 ounce) package shredded mozzarella cheese

- 1 (16 ounce) package Cheddar cheese, shredded
- 1 (16 ounce) container ricotta cheese
- 1 egg, beaten
- 1/2 teaspoon salt
- 1/4 teaspoon black pepper

Direction

- Let oven warm up to 350°F or 175°C.
- Let boil a big pot of lightly salted water. Once boiling, allow pasta to cook until al dente for about 12 minutes. Discard excess water.
- In a big pot, let the pork in barbeque sauce simmer over medium fire. At a slow simmer, keep warm.
- Mix the cheddar cheese and mozzarella cheese in a bowl. In a separate bowl, blend egg, salt, pepper and ricotta cheese until it becomes smooth.
- In a big deep baking dish, even out barbeque sauce into the bottom. On top of the sauce, arrange noodles until it covers the sauce at the bottom of the baking dish. On top of the noodles, even out pulled pork in barbeque sauce, then layer with mozzarella mixture and ricotta mixture. Duplicate layers then finish it off with ricotta mixture, thin pork layer and with a dash of cheese mixture. Spare a small portion of cheese mixture for later use.
- Let it bake in a warmed up oven for 40 minutes. Garnish lasagna with spared cheese mixture then put back in the oven to bake for another 5 minutes until cheese forms bubbles. Take out of the oven and wait for 15 minutes then serve.

Nutrition Information

- Calories: 710 calories;
- Total Fat: 36.6
- Sodium: 1498
- Total Carbohydrate: 39.9
- Cholesterol: 166
- Protein: 54.2

203.   Beef 'n' Sausage Lasagna

Serving: 12 servings. | Prep: 45mins | Cook: 45mins | Ready in:

Ingredients

- 1 pound ground beef
- 1 pound Johnsonville® Ground Mild Italian sausage
- 1 medium green pepper, chopped
- 1 medium onion, chopped
- 1 jar (26 ounces) spaghetti sauce
- 1 package (8 ounces) cream cheese, cubed
- 1 cup 4% cottage cheese
- 2 large eggs, lightly beaten
- 1 tablespoon minced fresh parsley
- 6 lasagna noodles, cooked and drained
- 2 cups shredded white cheddar cheese
- 3 teaspoons Italian seasoning, divided
- 2 cups shredded part-skim mozzarella cheese

Direction

- On medium heat, cook onion, beef, green pepper, and sausage in a big pan until the meat is not pink; drain. Reserve a cup of spaghetti sauce; pour the remaining sauce with the meat mixture. Let it simmer for 10 mins, uncovered, until the mixture is thick.
- On medium heat, melt cream cheese in a small pot; take off heat. Mix in parsley, eggs, and cottage cheese.
- In a 13-in by 9-inch greased baking dish, pour in meat sauce and add 3 noodles on top. Spread cheddar cheese and 1 1/2tsp Italian seasoning; pour in cream cheese mixture. Add the leftover noodles and saved spaghetti sauce in a layer. Top with mozzarella and leftover Italian seasoning.
- Bake in 350 degrees F oven, covered, for 35 mins. Remove cover and bake for another 10-15 mins or more until the dish is bubbly. Set aside for 15 mins. Serve.

Nutrition Information

- Calories:
- Sodium:
- Fiber:
- Total Carbohydrate:
- Cholesterol:
- Protein:
- Total Fat:

204.   Beef Enchilada Lasagna Casserole

Serving: 12 servings. | Prep: 45mins | Cook: 30mins | Ready in:

Ingredients

- 1-1/2 pounds ground beef
- 1 medium onion, chopped
- 1 garlic clove, minced
- 1 can (14-1/2 ounces) stewed tomatoes, undrained
- 1 can (10 ounces) enchilada sauce
- 1 to 2 teaspoons ground cumin
- 1 large egg, beaten
- 1-1/2 cups 4% cottage cheese
- 3 cups shredded Mexican cheese blend
- 8 flour tortillas (8 inches), cut in half
- 1 cup shredded cheddar cheese

Direction

- Cook beef, garlic and onions in a big pan on medium heat until meat is not pink. Drain grease. Add in tomatoes, cumin and enchilada sauce. Let it boil. Lower the heat and gently boil without lid, 20 minutes.
- Mix cottage cheese and egg in a small bowl, set aside. In a 13 in. x 9 in. greased baking pan, layer 1/3 of meat sauce, 1/2 of tortillas, cottage cheese mixture, cheese blend, and 1/3 of meat sauce. Repeat the layers. Drizzle on cheddar cheese.

- Put cover on. Bake 20 minutes at 350 degrees. Remove the cover and bake for 10 minutes longer until bubbling. Let it sit 15 minutes before slicing.

Nutrition Information

- Calories: 387 calories
- Total Fat: 21g fat (11g saturated fat)
- Sodium: 771mg sodium
- Fiber: 1g fiber)
- Total Carbohydrate: 25g carbohydrate (4g sugars
- Cholesterol: 87mg cholesterol
- Protein: 25g protein.

---

205. Beef Lasagne

Serving: 12 servings. | Prep: 40mins | Cook: 45mins | Ready in:

Ingredients

- 1 pound ground beef
- 2 garlic cloves, minced
- 1-1/2 cups water
- 1 can (15 ounces) tomato sauce
- 1 can (6 ounces) tomato paste
- 1/2 to 1 envelope onion soup mix
- 1 teaspoon dried oregano
- 1/2 teaspoon sugar
- 1/4 teaspoon pepper
- 9 lasagna noodles, cooked and drained
- 2 cups 4% cottage cheese
- 4 cups shredded part-skim mozzarella cheese
- 2 cups grated Parmesan cheese

Direction

- Let beef cook in a big saucepan on medium fire until there is no pink left on the meat. Add garlic and cook in 60 seconds more. Drain. Mix in oregano, pepper, sugar, tomato sauce, paste,

and water well. Boil. Lower heat and place cover then let it simmer for half an hour.
- In a 13x9 inch oiled baking dish, ladle half a cup of meat sauce. Create a layer with 3 noodles, mozzarella, and 1/3 of cottage cheese, parmesan cheese, and meat sauce. Make two more of these layers.
- Let it bake at 350° for 40 minutes until fully heated and bubbles form. Take off cover and let it bake for 5 to 10 minutes more. Wait for 10 minutes then slice.

Nutrition Information

- Calories: 367 calories
- Protein: 27g protein.
- Total Fat: 18g fat (9g saturated fat)
- Sodium: 901mg sodium
- Fiber: 2g fiber)
- Total Carbohydrate: 25g carbohydrate (5g sugars
- Cholesterol: 62mg cholesterol

---

206. Beef And Spinach Lasagna

Serving: 12 servings. | Prep: 40mins | Cook: 40mins | Ready in:

Ingredients

- 1 pound lean ground beef (90% lean)
- 1 medium onion, chopped
- 2 jars (24 ounces each) spaghetti sauce
- 4 garlic cloves, minced
- 1 teaspoon dried basil
- 1 teaspoon dried oregano
- 1 package (10 ounces) frozen chopped spinach, thawed and squeezed dry
- 2 cups ricotta cheese
- 2 cups shredded part-skim mozzarella cheese, divided
- 9 no-cook lasagna noodles

Direction

- Using a large skillet, cook onion and beef on medium heat setting until meat no longer appears rare, then strain. Mix into the pan, garlic, oregano, basil, and pasta sauce. Allow to boil. Then, decrease heat and continue simmering while uncovered for 10 minutes. Mix a cup of mozzarella cheese, ricotta, and spinach evenly in a big bowl. Pour 1-1/2 cups of sauce into a greased 13x9-inch baking tray and distribute evenly on the bottom. Layer as follows; three noodles as the base. Followed by 1-1/2 cups of sauce spread up to the edge of the noodles. Finally, a 1/2 of the spinach mixture above that. Continue layering in this arrangement. Top off with the remaining ingredients of noodles, sauce and mozzarella cheese. Bake while covered for 30 minutes at 375 degrees. Remove cover and continue baking for an additional 10-15 minutes until bubble appears. Let the dish rest for 10 minutes before slicing.

Nutrition Information

- Calories: 281 calories
- Sodium: 702mg sodium
- Fiber: 3g fiber)
- Total Carbohydrate: 26g carbohydrate (11g sugars
- Cholesterol: 50mg cholesterol
- Protein: 20g protein.
- Total Fat: 11g fat (6g saturated fat)

207. Burrito Lasagna

Serving: 12 servings. | Prep: 35mins | Cook: 30mins | Ready in:

Ingredients

- 2 pounds ground beef
- 2 cans (10 ounces each) enchilada sauce
- 1 envelope taco seasoning
- 1 tablespoon ground cumin
- 1 package (8.8 ounces) ready-to-serve Spanish rice
- 12 flour tortillas (8 inches), warmed
- 1 can (15 ounces) refried beans
- 4 cups shredded Mexican cheese blend
- Optional toppings: salsa, sliced avocado, shredded lettuce, taco sauce and/or sour cream

Direction

- Let oven heat up to 350°. Let beef cook on medium fire in a big skillet until brown, then drain. When beef is cooked, heat over cumin, taco seasoning, and enchilada sauce while stirring.
- Follow package instructions to cook rice. Even out 2 tablespoon of beans on each of the tortilla. In a 13x9 inches baking dish grease with oil, even out one cup of meat mixture. On top of it, make a layer of 4 tortillas, 1/3 of the rice, 1/3 of the cheese and 1/3 of the unused meat mixture. Duplicate layers. Finish the leftover tortillas, meat mixture, and rice until the dish is full.
- Let it bake with a cover for 20 minutes. Top with leftover cheese. Take off cover and let it bake for 10 to 15 minutes more until cheese melts. Wait for 10 minutes then serve. You may put toppings that you like.

Nutrition Information

- Calories: 515 calories
- Protein: 29g protein.
- Total Fat: 25g fat (12g saturated fat)
- Sodium: 1325mg sodium
- Fiber: 3g fiber)
- Total Carbohydrate: 44g carbohydrate (1g sugars
- Cholesterol: 83mg cholesterol

208.　　Cannelloni Style Lasagna

Serving: 12 servings. | Prep: 60mins | Cook: 50mins | Ready in:

Ingredients

- 1 tablespoon olive oil
- 1 small onion, finely chopped
- 1/3 cup finely chopped celery
- 1/4 cup finely chopped carrot
- 2 garlic cloves, minced
- 3/4 pound ground beef
- 3/4 pound ground pork
- 1/3 cup white wine or beef stock
- 2/3 cup beef stock
- 1 bay leaf
- 3/4 teaspoon Italian seasoning
- 1/2 teaspoon coarsely ground pepper
- 1/4 teaspoon salt
- 2 jars (15 ounces each) Alfredo sauce, divided
- 2 large egg yolks
- 1 jar (24 ounces) marinara sauce
- 1 package (9 ounces) no-cook lasagna noodles

Direction

- On medium-high heat, heat oil in a Dutch oven; put in carrot, celery, and onion. Cook and stir for 4-6 mins until tender; put in garlic. Cook for another minute.
- Cook in pork and beef for 4-6 mins until the meat is not pink; crumble meat then drain. Pour in wine; boil. Cook for a minute until the liquid nearly evaporates.
- Mix in seasonings and stock; boil. Lower heat, cover, and let it simmer for 15 mins to let the flavors combine; cool for a bit. Discard bay leaf. Mix in egg yolks and a cup of Alfredo sauce.
- Preheat the oven to 350 degrees F. In a 13-inch by 9-inch greased baking dish, pour 3/4 cup marinara sauce and add 4 noodles on top. Spread 3/4 cup Alfredo sauce then two cups meat mixture. Layer 4 noodles, 3/4 cup marinara sauce, then another 4 noodles. Spread 3/4 cup Alfredo sauce and the leftover

meat mixture. Add the leftover noodles and marinara sauce on top. Pour in left Alfredo sauce at the very top.
- Cover and bake for half an hour. Remove cover and bake for another 20-25 mins until the dish is bubbly. Set aside for 15 mins; serve.

Nutrition Information

- Calories: 347 calories
- Fiber: 3g fiber)
- Total Carbohydrate: 27g carbohydrate (5g sugars
- Cholesterol: 88mg cholesterol
- Protein: 18g protein.
- Total Fat: 18g fat (8g saturated fat)
- Sodium: 632mg sodium

209.　　Cheesy Lasagna

Serving: 12 servings. | Prep: 25mins | Cook: 40mins | Ready in:

Ingredients

- 1 pound ground beef
- 1 large onion, chopped
- 1/2 cup chopped green pepper
- 3 cans (6 ounces each) tomato paste
- 3/4 cup water
- 2 tablespoons brown sugar
- 3 to 4 teaspoons dried oregano
- 1 tablespoon cider vinegar
- 1/4 teaspoon garlic powder
- 9 lasagna noodles, cooked and drained
- 2 cups shredded mozzarella cheese
- 2 cups shredded Monterey Jack cheese
- 8 ounces sliced provolone cheese
- 1/4 cup grated Parmesan cheese

Direction

- Sauté onions, beef, and green peppers in a big saucepan over medium heat until beef is not pink; drain grease. Pour garlic powder, water, brown sugar, vinegar, oregano and the tomato paste into the saucepan.

- Pour a cup of the meat sauce in a 9x13-inch greased baking pan. Layer 3 lasagna noodles, another cup of meat sauce, and mozzarella cheese. Repeat the layers 2 more times but substitute Monterey Jack cheese for the mozzarella the first time and Parmesan and provolone the second time.
- Place the uncovered dish in a350°F oven until the cheese melts, 40 to 45 minutes. Let it cool for 10 minutes before slicing. Serve.

Nutrition Information

- Calories: 368 calories
- Total Carbohydrate: 22g carbohydrate (7g sugars
- Cholesterol: 71mg cholesterol
- Protein: 24g protein.
- Total Fat: 20g fat (11g saturated fat)
- Sodium: 398mg sodium
- Fiber: 2g fiber)

210.   Cheesy Shell Lasagna

Serving: 12 servings. | Prep: 25mins | Cook: 45mins | Ready in:

Ingredients

- 1-1/2 pounds lean ground beef (90% lean)
- 2 medium onions, chopped
- 1 garlic clove, minced
- 1 can (14-1/2 ounces) diced tomatoes, undrained
- 1 jar (14 ounces) meatless spaghetti sauce
- 1 can (4 ounces) mushroom stems and pieces, undrained
- 8 ounces uncooked small shell pasta
- 2 cups (16 ounces) reduced-fat sour cream
- 11 slices (8 ounces) reduced-fat provolone cheese

- 1 cup shredded part-skim mozzarella cheese

Direction

- Using a non-stick skillet, cook the onions and beef on medium heat until the meat is no longer pink. Add the garlic in and cook it for another minute. Drain it out and mix in your mushrooms, spaghetti sauce, and tomatoes. Bring it up to a boil then bring the heat down and simmer it for about 20 minutes without a cover.
- While that simmers, cook the pasta by following the directions on the package and drain it.
- Put half of the pasta into a 13x9 inches baking dish without grease. Top the half off with meat sauce, provolone cheese, and sour cream. Repeat this in layers. Sprinkle off the top with mozzarella cheese.
- Cover it up and bake it for 35-40 minutes at 350 degrees. Take out the cover and bake it for another 10 minutes or until the cheese gets a bit brown. Allow it to sit for 10 minutes before slicing and eating.

Nutrition Information

- Calories: 346 calories
- Protein: 27g protein.
- Total Fat: 15g fat (8g saturated fat)
- Sodium: 515mg sodium
- Fiber: 2g fiber)
- Total Carbohydrate: 29g carbohydrate (0 sugars
- Cholesterol: 50mg cholesterol

211.   Christmas Night Lasagna

Serving: 2 casseroles (12 servings each). | Prep: 45mins | Cook: 45mins | Ready in:

Ingredients

- 3 pounds ground beef

- 1 pound Jones No Sugar Pork Sausage Roll sausage
- 1 medium onion, chopped
- 1 medium green pepper, chopped
- 2 jars (28 ounces each) meatless spaghetti sauce
- 1 can (10-3/4 ounces) condensed tomato soup, undiluted
- 1 can (4 ounces) mushroom stems and pieces, undrained
- 2 teaspoons Worcestershire sauce
- 1-1/2 teaspoons Italian seasoning
- 1-1/2 teaspoons salt, divided
- 1-1/2 teaspoons pepper, divided
- 1 teaspoon garlic powder
- 2 eggs, lightly beaten
- 2-1/2 cups (20 ounces) 4% small-curd cottage cheese
- 1 carton (15 ounces) ricotta cheese
- 2 cups shredded Parmesan cheese
- 24 lasagna noodles, cooked and drained
- 12 slices part-skim mozzarella cheese

Direction

- Cook the sausage, beef, green pepper and onion in a Dutch oven or some big skillets on medium heat until meat is not pink; drain the fat. Put in the soup, spaghetti sauce, mushrooms, Italian seasoning, Worcestershire sauce, garlic powder, 1 tsp. salt and 1 tsp. pepper. Let it boil. Lower the heat and simmer half an hour without cover, stir from time to time.
- Mix the cottage cheese, ricotta, left salt, left pepper and eggs in a big bowl.
- Pour 2 cups of meat sauce in each of two 13x9-inch greased baking pan. Layer each pan with 1/3 cup Parmesan, 4 pasta noodles, 1 1/4 cups of cottage cheese mix, and 3 mozzarella slices. Make layers again. Put the remaining pasta, sauce, and Parmesan on top.
- Bake without cover at 350° until bubbling, 45 minutes. Let it sit 15 minutes before slicing.

Nutrition Information

- Calories: 370 calories
- Cholesterol: 77mg cholesterol
- Protein: 27g protein.
- Total Fat: 16g fat (8g saturated fat)
- Sodium: 804mg sodium
- Fiber: 2g fiber)
- Total Carbohydrate: 28g carbohydrate (7g sugars

212. Classic Lasagna

Serving: 10 | Prep: 15mins | Cook: 1hours45mins | Ready in:

Ingredients

- 9 lasagna noodles
- 1 tablespoon olive oil
- 1 pound ground beef
- 1 pound bulk Italian sausage
- 1 (16 ounce) can sliced mushrooms, drained
- 1 teaspoon garlic salt
- 1 teaspoon dried oregano
- 1/2 teaspoon dried thyme
- 1/4 teaspoon dried basil
- 4 (15 ounce) cans tomato sauce
- salt and pepper to taste
- 1 (15 ounce) container ricotta cheese
- 3 eggs, beaten
- 1/3 cup grated Parmesan cheese
- 1 pound shredded mozzarella cheese

Direction

- Turn oven to 175°C (350°F).
- Boil slightly salted water in a big pot. Place lasagna pasta and olive oil in the pot until al dente, about 8-10 minutes. Drain water.
- Cook sausage and ground beef in a big pot on medium heat. Add in the garlic salt, mushrooms, oregano, thyme, tomato sauce and basil. Season with pepper and salt. Let it simmer 30 minutes.
- Combine eggs, parmesan cheese and ricotta cheese in a bowl.

- Cover bottom of 13in.x9in. pan with a thin layer of meat sauce. Place a layer of three noodles. Pour 1/4 of ricotta cheese mixture over. Layer with 1/3 of mozzarella cheese and 1/3 of meat sauce. Repeat layers twice; put a 1/4 pound mozzarella cheese on top.
- Bake in oven for 1 1/2 hours. Let it set for 10-15 minutes then serve.

Nutrition Information

- Calories: 647 calories;
- Sodium: 2012
- Total Carbohydrate: 31.2
- Cholesterol: 174
- Protein: 38.8
- Total Fat: 41.4

---

213. Contest Winning Tex Mex Lasagna

Serving: 12 servings. | Prep: 20mins | Cook: 45mins | Ready in:

Ingredients

- 1 pound lean ground beef (90% lean)
- 1 can (16 ounces) refried black beans
- 1 can (15 ounces) black beans, rinsed and drained
- 1/2 cup frozen corn, thawed
- 1 jalapeno pepper, seeded and chopped
- 1 envelope taco seasoning
- 1 can (15 ounces) tomato sauce, divided
- 2-1/2 cups salsa
- 12 no-cook lasagna noodles
- 1-1/2 cups shredded reduced-fat Monterey Jack cheese or Mexican cheese blend
- 1-1/2 cups shredded reduced-fat cheddar cheese
- 1 cup (8 ounces) fat-free sour cream
- 1 medium ripe avocado, peeled and cubed
- 4 green onions, thinly sliced

Direction

- On medium heat, cook beef in a big non-stick pan until the meat is not pink; drain. Mix in 3/4 cup tomato sauce, beans, taco seasoning, corn, and jalapeno.
- Mix the leftover tomato sauce and salsa together. Using cooking spray, grease a 13-inch by 9-inch baking dish; pour in quarter cup of the salsa mixture. Lay 4 noodles, slightly overlapping on top. Spread 1/2 of the meat sauce, a cup of salsa mixture, and half cup each of Monterey Jack and cheddar cheese; repeat process. Add leftover noodles, salsa mixture, and cheeses on top.
- Bake in a 350 degrees F oven, covered, for 45-50 mins until the cheese melts and bubbly on the edges. Set aside for 10 mins then cut. Add onions, avocado, and sour cream. Serve.

Nutrition Information

- Calories: 381 calories
- Total Fat: 13g fat (7g saturated fat)
- Sodium: 1170mg sodium
- Fiber: 5g fiber)
- Total Carbohydrate: 39g carbohydrate (6g sugars
- Cholesterol: 47mg cholesterol
- Protein: 25g protein.

---

214. Corn Tortilla Lasagna

Serving: 10-12 servings. | Prep: 20mins | Cook: 30mins | Ready in:

Ingredients

- 1-1/2 pounds ground beef
- 1/3 cup chopped onion
- 1/2 teaspoon minced garlic
- 1 jar (16 ounces) picante sauce
- 1 package (10 ounces) frozen chopped spinach, thawed and squeezed dry

- 2 medium tomatoes, seeded and chopped
- 1 large sweet red pepper, chopped
- 1 can (8 ounces) tomato sauce
- 1 tablespoon lime juice
- 12 corn tortillas
- 3/4 cup shredded Monterey Jack cheese
- 2 cups (16 ounces) sour cream
- Additional picante sauce, optional

Direction

- Sauté onion, garlic and beef in a big skillet over medium heat until beef is brown, drain excess oil. Mix in the tomatoes, tomato sauce, red pepper, lime juice, picante sauce and spinach.
- In a greased 13x9-inch baking dish, put 6 tortillas at the bottom. Put a layer of 1/4 cup of cheese, 1/2 of the meat mixture and remaining tortillas on top. Put in the sour cream evenly on top. Finish off with a layer of the remaining meat mixture and cheese.
- Put in the uncovered baking dish in the preheated oven at 350°F and bake for 30 to 40 minutes or until cooked through. Allow it to cool down for 10 minutes. Serve it with extra picante sauce but this is optional.

Nutrition Information

- Calories: 287 calories
- Fiber: 3g fiber)
- Total Carbohydrate: 20g carbohydrate (4g sugars
- Cholesterol: 61mg cholesterol
- Protein: 16g protein.
- Total Fat: 15g fat (8g saturated fat)
- Sodium: 408mg sodium

215.   Cream Cheese And Swiss Lasagna

Serving: 12 servings. | Prep: 40mins | Cook: 55mins | Ready in:

Ingredients

- 1-1/2 pounds lean ground beef (90% lean)
- 1 pound Johnsonville® Ground Mild Italian sausage
- 1 medium onion, finely chopped
- 3 garlic cloves, minced
- 2 cans (15 ounces each) tomato sauce
- 1 can (14-1/2 ounces) Italian diced tomatoes, undrained
- 1 can (6 ounces) tomato paste
- 2 teaspoons dried oregano
- 1 teaspoon dried basil
- 1 teaspoon Italian seasoning
- 1/2 teaspoon sugar
- 1/2 teaspoon salt
- 1/4 teaspoon pepper
- 9 no-cook lasagna noodles
- 12 ounces cream cheese, softened
- 2 cups shredded part-skim mozzarella cheese, divided
- 2 cups shredded Parmesan cheese
- 2 cups shredded Swiss cheese

Direction

- Cook the sausage, onion and beef in a Dutch oven on medium heat until meat is not pink. Put in garlic; cook 1 more minute and drain. Add in the tomatoes, tomato sauce, tomato paste, basil, oregano, Italian seasoning, pepper, sugar and salt. Let it boil. Lower the heat and let it simmer, without lid, 30 minutes.
- Grease 13x 9-inch baking tray, pour in 1 cup sauce. Layer with 3 pasta noodles, 1/3 of cream cheese by teaspoonfuls, 1/2 cup of mozzarella, 2/3 cup Parmesan, 2/3 cup Swiss cheese, and 1/3 of remaining sauce. Repeat the layers twice more (pan should be filled). Put the pan on a cookie sheet.
- Cover pan and bake at 350°, 45 minutes. Drizzle with left mozzarella. Return to the oven without cover, 10 to 15 minutes longer until bubbling and cheese melts. Let it sit for 15 minutes before slicing.

Nutrition Information

- Calories: 522 calories
- Protein: 35g protein.
- Total Fat: 31g fat (17g saturated fat)
- Sodium: 1196mg sodium
- Fiber: 3g fiber)
- Total Carbohydrate: 24g carbohydrate (8g sugars
- Cholesterol: 118mg cholesterol

---

216.   Creamy Beef Lasagna

Serving: 12 servings. | Prep: 20mins | Cook: 45mins | Ready in:

Ingredients

- 1-1/2 pounds ground beef
- 2 cans (15 ounces each) tomato sauce
- 1/4 cup chopped onion
- 2 teaspoons sugar
- 2 teaspoons salt
- 2 teaspoons Worcestershire sauce
- 1/2 teaspoon garlic salt
- 2 packages (8 ounces each) cream cheese, softened
- 1 cup sour cream
- 1/4 cup milk
- 18 lasagna noodles, cooked and drained
- 1 cup shredded cheddar cheese
- Minced fresh parsley, optional

Direction

- Cook beef until not pink on medium heat in a frying pan. Drain excess grease. Mix in sugar, garlic salt, onion, Worcestershire sauce, tomato sauce, and salt. Beat milk, cream cheese, and sour cream until smooth in a different bowl. Take a 13x9-in. greased pan and add a fourth of the meat sauce. Layer with six noodles and a third of cream cheese mixture. Starting with meat sauce, repeat the layers twice. Put remaining meat sauce on top.

Cover; bake in a 350-degree oven for 40 minutes. Remove cover and sprinkle on cheddar cheese. Bake until cheese melts, 5 minutes. Let it cool for 15 minutes before cutting. Sprinkle parsley on top.

Nutrition Information

- Calories: 403 calories
- Cholesterol: 82mg cholesterol
- Protein: 21g protein.
- Total Fat: 20g fat (11g saturated fat)
- Sodium: 795mg sodium
- Fiber: 2g fiber)
- Total Carbohydrate: 33g carbohydrate (4g sugars

---

217.   Creamy Lasagna Casserole

Serving: 2 casseroles (4-6 servings each). | Prep: 30mins | Cook: 25mins | Ready in:

Ingredients

- 2 pounds ground beef
- 1 can (29 ounces) tomato sauce
- 1 teaspoon salt
- 1/2 teaspoon pepper
- 1/2 teaspoon garlic powder
- 6 ounces cream cheese, softened
- 2 cups (16 ounces) sour cream
- 2 cups shredded cheddar cheese, divided
- 4 green onions, chopped
- 12 to 14 lasagna noodles, cooked and drained

Direction

- Put beef in a Dutch oven then cook over medium heat until brown then drain excess oil. Mix in garlic powder, salt, pepper and tomato sauce. Let it boil. Lower the heat then simmer the uncovered mixture for 15 minutes.

- Whisk cream cheese in a large bowl until the consistency is smooth. Put in onions, sour cream and 1 cup of cheddar cheese then mix thoroughly.
- In two greased 8-inch square baking dishes, put 1/2 cup of meat sauce evenly. Put in 2-3 noodles into each baking dish, trim the excess part if it doesn't fit. Put 1/2 cup of cream cheese mixture then 2/3 cup of meat sauce on top of the noodles. Do the layering process twice in both baking dishes. Put 1/2 cup of cheddar cheese on top of each dish.
- Cover one casserole and keep in the freezer for up to 1 month. Put the other casserole dish uncovered in an oven at 350 degrees and bake for 25 to 30 minutes or until the sauce is bubbling and everything is cooked through. Let it cool down a bit for about 15 minutes before slicing.
- Once you are ready to eat the frozen casserole: transfer the casserole mixture into the fridge and let it thaw for 18 hours. Before baking, remove the casserole from the fridge and let it sit for 30 minutes. Put the thawed casserole uncovered in the oven at 350 degrees and bake for 40 to 50 minutes or until heated through.

Nutrition Information

- Calories:
- Cholesterol:
- Protein:
- Total Fat:
- Sodium:
- Fiber:
- Total Carbohydrate:

218.   Donna Lasagna

Serving: 12 servings. | Prep: 40mins | Cook: 60mins | Ready in:

Ingredients

- 1 pound lean ground beef (90% lean)
- 8 ounces Johnsonville® Ground Mild or Hot Italian sausage
- 1 can (15 ounces) tomato puree
- 2 cans (6 ounces each) tomato paste
- 3 tablespoons dried parsley flakes, divided
- 2 tablespoons sugar
- 1 tablespoon dried basil
- 1-1/2 teaspoons salt, divided
- 1 garlic clove, minced
- 2 large eggs, lightly beaten
- 3 cups (24 ounces) cream-style cottage cheese
- 1/2 cup grated Parmesan cheese
- 1/2 teaspoon pepper
- 9 lasagna noodles, cooked and drained
- 4 cups shredded part-skim mozzarella cheese

Direction

- Put sausage and beef in a Dutch oven and cook over medium heat until not pink then drain excess oil. Mix in sugar, garlic, basil, tomato paste, tomato puree, 1 teaspoon of salt and 1 tablespoon of parsley. Let it boil. Lower the heat then remove the cover and let it simmer for 30 minutes.
- Mix Parmesan cheese, eggs, pepper, cottage cheese, salt and remaining parsley together in a big bowl.
- In a 13x9-inch greased baking dish, pour 1/2 cup of meat mixture evenly on bottom. Layer in 3 lasagna noodles, 1/3 of the cheese mixture, 1-1/3 cups of mozzarella cheese, and 1/3 of the remaining meat sauce. Do the whole layering process 2 more times.
- Put it in the preheated oven at 350°F and bake for an hour or until the thermometer registers 160°F. Before slicing, let it cool down for about 15 minutes.

Nutrition Information

- Calories: 377 calories
- Total Fat: 18g fat (10g saturated fat)
- Sodium: 925mg sodium
- Fiber: 2g fiber)

- Total Carbohydrate: 24g carbohydrate (7g sugars
- Cholesterol: 102mg cholesterol
- Protein: 29g protein.

219.   Easy Mexican Lasagna

Serving: 12 servings. | Prep: 15mins | Cook: 01hours35mins | Ready in:

Ingredients

- 1 pound lean ground beef (90% lean)
- 1 can (16 ounces) refried beans
- 2 teaspoons dried oregano
- 1 teaspoon ground cumin
- 3/4 teaspoon garlic powder
- 12 uncooked lasagna noodles
- 2-1/2 cups water
- 2-1/2 cups picante sauce or salsa
- 2 cups sour cream
- 3/4 cup finely sliced green onions
- 1 can (2-1/4 ounces) sliced ripe olives, drained
- 1 cup shredded Monterey Jack cheese

Direction

- Mix oregano, garlic powder, beef, cumin and beans. In a 13x9-inch baking pan, arrange the 4 uncooked lasagna and spread 1/2 of the beef mixture over it. Layer it with 4 more noodles and again, spread the other half of the beef mixture. End by covering it with the remaining noodles. Mix first the picante sauce and water before pouring it all over the layers.
- Seal it securely with foil and let it bake at 350°F for one and a half hours. Be sure it's already tender before spooning onions, olives and sour cream over the casserole. Sprinkle cheese on top and bake it, uncovered, for about 5 minutes and until the cheese is completely melted.

Nutrition Information

- Calories: 325 calories
- Protein: 17g protein.
- Total Fat: 14g fat (8g saturated fat)
- Sodium: 473mg sodium
- Fiber: 3g fiber)
- Total Carbohydrate: 30g carbohydrate (5g sugars
- Cholesterol: 57mg cholesterol

220.   Easy Skillet Lasagna

Serving: 8 servings. | Prep: 5mins | Cook: 01hours10mins | Ready in:

Ingredients

- 2 pounds ground beef
- 1 envelope spaghetti sauce mix, divided
- 2 cups 4% cottage cheese
- 3 cups uncooked wide egg noodles
- 1 tablespoon dried parsley flakes
- 1 teaspoon salt
- 1 teaspoon dried basil
- 1 teaspoon Italian seasoning
- 1 can (14-1/2 ounces) stewed tomatoes
- 1 cup spaghetti sauce with meat
- 1 cup water
- 2 cups shredded mozzarella cheese

Direction

- At medium heat settings, cook beef in a skillet until well done, and then strain. Scatter 1/2 of the pasta sauce mix. Scoop cottage cheese and place on the meat. Add the noodles on top. Scatter salt, Italian seasoning, basil, pasta sauce mix, and parsley on top. Add pasta sauce mix and tomatoes. Top off with pasta sauce, water, and tomatoes. Boil. Decrease heat settings, cover the dish and allow to simmer for 35 minutes, or until noodles have tenderized. Scatter with mozzarella cheese. Replace cover and allow to simmer for another 5 minutes or until cheese has fully melted.

Nutrition Information

- Calories:
- Total Carbohydrate:
- Cholesterol:
- Protein:
- Total Fat:
- Sodium:
- Fiber:

---

221.   Easy Zucchini Lasagna

Serving: 6 servings. | Prep: 25mins | Cook: 40mins | Ready in:

Ingredients

- 1 pound ground beef
- 1/2 cup chopped onion
- 2 jars (24 ounces, one 14 ounces) spaghetti sauce
- 1 can (15 ounces) crushed tomatoes
- 1 teaspoon dried basil
- 1 teaspoon dried oregano
- 1 teaspoon fennel seed, crushed
- 1 teaspoon minced garlic
- 9 no-cook lasagna noodles
- 2 cups sliced zucchini
- 1 cup ricotta cheese
- 1 carton shredded Asiago cheese

Direction

- Cook the beef with the onions in a big skillet on medium heat until beef is not pink. Drain grease. Mix the spaghetti sauce, garlic, basil, oregano, fennel, and tomatoes with the cooked beef. Cover with a lid when the sauce boils. Lower the heat and let it simmer for 10 minutes.
- In a greased 13x9 inch baking dish, layer 1-1/2 cups of the cooked meat sauce then put 3 lasagna noodles on top. Put on 1-1/2 cups meat sauce on top and spread to the noodle's edges. On top put half the zucchini and a half

cup of each ricotta and Asiago cheese. Repeat the layers. On the top put left noodles, the sauce, and the Asiago cheese.
- Cover with a lid and bake at 375°F for half an hour. Remove the lid and bake for another 10-15 minutes or until bubbling. Let it rest for 5 minutes before cutting. Serve.

Nutrition Information

- Calories: 485 calories
- Sodium: 1088mg sodium
- Fiber: 6g fiber)
- Total Carbohydrate: 49g carbohydrate (18g sugars
- Cholesterol: 75mg cholesterol
- Protein: 33g protein.
- Total Fat: 18g fat (10g saturated fat)

---

222.   Egg Noodle Lasagna

Serving: 12-16 servings. | Prep: 20mins | Cook: 04hours00mins | Ready in:

Ingredients

- 6-1/2 cups uncooked wide egg noodles
- 3 tablespoons butter
- 1-1/2 pounds ground beef
- 2-1/4 cups spaghetti sauce
- 6 ounces process cheese (Velveeta), cubed
- 3 cups shredded mozzarella cheese

Direction

- Follow package instructions to cook the lasagna noodles; then drain. Put in melted butter and mix well until the noodles are coated.
- Put beef in a big skillet and cook over medium heat until not pink; then drain excess oil. In an ungreased 5-quart slow cooker, put 1/4 of spaghetti sauce evenly on bottom. Add in 1/3 of noodles, 1/3 of the beef, 1/3 of remaining

spaghetti sauce, and 1/3 of the cheeses. Do the whole layering process 2 more times.

- On low heat setting, cook the lasagna in covered slow cooker 4 hours or until the cheese melts and the lasagna is cooked through.

Nutrition Information

- Calories: 266 calories
- Sodium: 432mg sodium
- Fiber: 1g fiber)
- Total Carbohydrate: 16g carbohydrate (3g sugars
- Cholesterol: 65mg cholesterol
- Protein: 17g protein.
- Total Fat: 15g fat (8g saturated fat)

223.   Enchilada Lasagna

Serving: 8 | Prep: 20mins | Cook: 1hours15mins |Ready in:

Ingredients

- 1 tablespoon vegetable oil
- 1 onion, chopped
- 3 cloves garlic, chopped
- 1 1/4 pounds ground turkey
- 1 (28 ounce) can enchilada sauce
- 1 (14.5 ounce) can diced tomatoes with lime juice and cilantro
- 1 (16 ounce) package small-curd cottage cheese
- 1 egg
- 1 tablespoon ground cumin
- 5 (6 inch) corn tortillas, halved
- 2 cups shredded Mexican cheese blend
- cooking spray
- 1 green onion, diced

Direction

- Put oil in a big pot and heat over medium heat setting. Sauté and stir garlic and onion for

about 5 minutes or until the onion becomes translucent. Add in ground turkey and cook for 5 minutes or until meat is not pink. Drain excess oil.

- Mix diced tomatoes and enchilada sauce into the turkey mixture. Let it simmer for about 20 minutes until the flavors have fully blended. Remove the pot from heat.
- Preheat the oven at 375°F (190°C).
- In a small bowl, combine egg, cumin and cottage cheese.
- In an 8-inch pan, put 1/3 of turkey sauce evenly on bottom. Top the turkey sauce with 1/2 of corn tortillas. Put 1/2 of the cottage cheese mixture evenly on top of the corn tortillas. Top with 1/3 of Mexican cheese. Do the whole layering process again finishing with the remaining turkey sauce and Mexican cheese at the very top.
- Cover the baking dish with greased aluminum foil.
- Put in heated oven and bake for about 30 minutes or until bubbling. Remove the foil cover and continue baking for about 15 minutes or until the cheese on top is brown. Let it cool down for 15 minutes then serve while still warm. Top with green onion.

Nutrition Information

- Calories: 428 calories;
- Total Carbohydrate: 22.1
- Cholesterol: 120
- Protein: 31
- Total Fat: 24.1
- Sodium: 930

224.   Favorite Mexican Lasagna

Serving: 12 servings. | Prep: 25mins | Cook: 40mins | Ready in:

Ingredients

- 1-1/4 pounds ground beef
- 1 medium onion, chopped
- 4 garlic cloves, minced
- 2 cups salsa
- 1 can (16 ounces) refried beans
- 1 can (15 ounces) black beans, rinsed and drained
- 1 can (10 ounces) enchilada sauce
- 1 can (4 ounces) chopped green chilies
- 1 envelope taco seasoning
- 1/4 teaspoon pepper
- 6 flour tortillas (10 inches)
- 3 cups shredded Mexican cheese blend, divided
- 2 cups crushed tortilla chips
- Sliced ripe olives, guacamole, chopped tomatoes and sour cream, optional

Direction

- On medium heat, cook onion and beef in a big pan until the meat is not pink; put in garlic. Cook for another minute then drain. Mix in pepper, salsa, taco seasoning, beans, chilies, and enchilada sauce. Heat the mixture through.
- In a 13-inch by 9-inch greased baking dish, pour in a cup of meat mixture then lay 2 tortillas on top. Spread 1/3 of the left meat mixture and a cup of cheese. Repeat process, ending with the leftover tortillas and meat mixture on top.
- Bake in a 375 degrees F oven, covered, for half an hour. Remove cover and top with leftover cheese and tortilla chips.
- Bake for another 10-15 mins until the cheese melts. Set aside for 10 mins. Serve with sour cream, olives, tomatoes, and guacamole if preferred.

Nutrition Information

- Calories: 448 calories
- Sodium: 1240mg sodium
- Fiber: 8g fiber)

- Total Carbohydrate: 43g carbohydrate (3g sugars
- Cholesterol: 57mg cholesterol
- Protein: 22g protein.
- Total Fat: 19g fat (9g saturated fat)

225.   Fiesta Lasagna

Serving: 12 servings. | Prep: 25mins | Cook: 01hours10mins | Ready in:

Ingredients

- 1 pound ground beef
- 1/4 cup chopped onion
- 1 can (16 ounces) refried beans
- 1 can (16 ounces) mild chili beans, undrained
- 1 can (14-1/2 ounces) Mexican stewed tomatoes, drained
- 1 cup salsa
- 1 can (4 ounces) chopped green chilies
- 1 envelope reduced-sodium taco seasoning
- 1 teaspoon dried oregano
- 1 teaspoon ground cumin
- 1/4 teaspoon garlic powder
- 1-1/4 cups shredded Monterey Jack cheese
- 1-1/4 cups shredded part-skim mozzarella cheese
- 3/4 cup 4% cottage cheese
- 1-1/4 cups sour cream, divided
- 9 lasagna noodles, cooked, rinsed and drained

Direction

- Use a Dutch oven in cooking beef and onion until meat is no longer pink. Cook at medium heat. Drain. Add in the beans, salsa, tomatoes, chilies and seasonings.
- Mix Monterey jack and mozzarella cheese in a large bowl. Reserve 1 cup. Add the cottage cheese and 3/4 cup sour cream into the remaining cheese mixture.
- Place 1 cup meat sauce into a greased 13x9in. baking pan. Layer 3 pasta, 1/3 of the cottage

cheese mixture and the meat sauce. Repeat the layer two times (pan will be full).

- Turn oven to 350 degree F and bake with cover for an hour. Remove cover, pour remaining sour cream. Drizzle with the reserved cheeses. Bake 10-12 minutes longer until cheeses melt. Let it set for 10 min. before serving.

Nutrition Information

- Calories: 373 calories
- Cholesterol: 63mg cholesterol
- Protein: 22g protein.
- Total Fat: 16g fat (9g saturated fat)
- Sodium: 838mg sodium
- Fiber: 5g fiber)
- Total Carbohydrate: 34g carbohydrate (6g sugars

---

226.   Fiesta Surprise

Serving: 8-10 servings. | Prep: 25mins | Cook: 45mins | Ready in:

Ingredients

- 1-1/2 pounds ground beef
- 1 medium onion, chopped
- 1 envelope taco seasoning
- 1 cup water
- 1/2 cup taco sauce
- 10 corn tortillas (6 inches)
- 2 packages (10 ounces each) frozen chopped spinach, thawed and partially drained
- 3 cups shredded Monterey Jack cheese
- 1/2 cup chopped fully cooked ham
- 1 cup sour cream

Direction

- Sauté onion and beef in a skillet over medium heat until beef is not pink. Drain grease. Pour water and the taco seasoning in the beef. Put a lid on and let it simmer for 10 minutes. In a 9x13-inch baking pan, spread 1/4 cup of taco sauce. Use sauce to coat both sides of 5 tortillas. Lay the tortillas overlapping in the bottom of pan.
- Add and stir a package of spinach into beef mixture. Spread the beef mixture on top of tortillas and add half of cheese. Use the remaining tortillas, overlapping if necessary, to cover. Spread on remaining taco sauce. Arrange pieces of ham on top and spread on sour cream. Cover the top with the remaining spinach and cheese.
- Bake in a 350°F oven until it is cooked through, 45 minutes. Remove the dish from the oven and let it cool for 5-10 minutes. Serve.

Nutrition Information

- Calories:
- Protein:
- Total Fat:
- Sodium:
- Fiber:
- Total Carbohydrate:
- Cholesterol:

---

227.   Four Cheese Lasagna

Serving: 12 servings | Prep: 20mins | Cook: | Ready in:

Ingredients

- 1 lb. extra-lean ground beef
- 1 onion, chopped
- 1 pkg. (8 oz.) PHILADELPHIA Neufchatel Cheese, softened
- 1 cup BREAKSTONE'S or KNUDSEN 2% Milkfat Low Fat Cottage Cheese
- 1 pkg. (8 oz.) KRAFT Shredded Low-Moisture Part-Skim Mozzarella Cheese, divided
- 1/2 cup KRAFT Grated Parmesan Cheese, divided
- 1 egg, beaten

- 1 jar (24 oz.) OLIVO by CLASSICO Traditional Pasta Sauce
- 1 can (14.5 oz.) diced tomatoes, drained
- 1/2 tsp. dried oregano leaves
- 12 lasagna noodles, cooked

Direction

- In a big skillet, put in the onions and meat and let it cook until the meat turns brown in color. While the onions and meat are cooking, combine 1 1/2 cups of mozzarella, Neufchatel, egg, cottage cheese and 1/4 cup of Parmesan together; mix until everything is well-combined.
- Drain the cooked meat and put it back into the skillet. Mix in the tomatoes, oregano and pasta sauce and let it simmer for 5 minutes. Remove the skillet away from the heat. In a 13x9-inch baking dish, with a spoon, spread an even layer of 1 cup of the meat sauce at the bottom, then put layers of 3 lasagna noodles, 1 cup of the cheese mixture and 1 cup of the meat sauce on top. Do the whole layering process again 2 times. Finish it off with the remaining noodles, meat sauce, mozzarella and Parmesan on top; cover the baking dish.
- Put it in a preheated oven and let it bake for 50 minutes until the lasagna is well-heated, remove the cover from the baking dish after 40 minutes. Before serving, allow the baked lasagna to rest for 10 minutes prior to slicing it.

Nutrition Information

- Calories: 300
- Total Fat: 13 g
- Fiber: 2 g
- Saturated Fat: 7 g
- Sodium: 650 mg
- Sugar: 5 g
- Total Carbohydrate: 23 g
- Cholesterol: 70 mg
- Protein: 22 g

228. Garden Style Beef Lasagna

Serving: 6-8 servings. | Prep: 25mins | Cook: 30mins | Ready in:

Ingredients

- 1-1/2 pounds lean ground beef (90% lean)
- 3/4 cup chopped onion
- 1 teaspoon minced garlic
- 1-1/2 cups garden-style pasta sauce
- 1 can (15 ounces) tomato sauce
- 2 tablespoons dried parsley flakes, divided
- 1 teaspoon dried oregano
- 2 cups 4% cottage cheese
- 1/2 cup grated Parmesan cheese, divided
- 1 large egg
- 1 teaspoon dried basil
- 6 no-cook lasagna noodles
- 2 cups shredded part-skim mozzarella cheese, divided

Direction

- Break the beef in to small pieces and place it in a microwaveable container. Add and mix well garlic and onion. Put a lid on and microwave for 3 minutes on high setting. Stir and microwave it for another 2-3 minutes until the meat is not pink. Add 1 tablespoon of parsley, oregano, pasta sauce, and tomato sauce. Put the lid back on and cook in the microwave for another 2 minutes until everything is properly heated. Let it rest.
- Beat the egg, remaining parsley, basil, cottage cheese, and 1/4 cup of Parmesan cheese in a separate bowl. In a greased 7 by 11-inch microwaveable dish, pour 1-1/3 cups of meat sauce.
- Lay 3 noodles on top of the meat sauce. Add a cup of cheese mixture and half a cup of mozzarella cheese. Repeat the layers, ending with the remaining meat sauce on top.
- Loosely cover. Cook in the microwave until

the noodles are tender, 15-18 minutes at 50% power. Sprinkle the remaining cheese on top.

- Cook again in the microwave without cover until the cheese melts, 5 minutes. Cool for 15 minutes and serve.

Nutrition Information

- Calories: 408 calories
- Protein: 35g protein.
- Total Fat: 19g fat (9g saturated fat)
- Sodium: 873mg sodium
- Fiber: 3g fiber)
- Total Carbohydrate: 24g carbohydrate (8g sugars
- Cholesterol: 119mg cholesterol

229. Ground Beef Spinach Alfredo Lasagna

Serving: 8 servings. | Prep: 20mins | Cook: 04hours00mins | Ready in:

Ingredients

- 1 pound ground beef
- 1 medium onion, chopped
- 2 garlic cloves, minced
- 1 jar (24 ounces) spaghetti sauce
- 1 carton (15 ounces) ricotta cheese
- 1/2 cup grated Parmesan cheese
- 2 tablespoons minced fresh parsley
- 1/2 teaspoon pepper
- 1 package (8 ounces) no-cook lasagna noodles
- 8 cups shredded part-skim mozzarella cheese
- 1 package (10 ounces) frozen chopped spinach, thawed and squeezed dry
- 1 jar (15 ounces) Alfredo sauce

Direction

- Put onion, garlic and beef in a big frying pan and sauté for 6 to 8 minutes over medium heat until the beef is cooked through the middle

and crumbling then drain excess oil. Mix in the spaghetti sauce.

- Combine parsley, pepper, Parmesan cheese and ricotta cheese in a small bowl. In an ungreased 5-quartz or 6-quartz slow cooker, put 1 cup of meat mixture evenly on the bottom. Put in a layer of 4 lasagna noodles (breaking it if need be in order to fit), 1 cup of meat mixture, 1/2 of the ricotta mixture and 2 cups of mozzarella cheese.
- For the next layer, put 4 lasagna noodles, Alfredo sauce, spinach and 2 cups of mozzarella cheese. Continue with layers of 4 lasagna noodles, 1 cup of meat mixture, the remaining ricotta mixture and 2 cups of mozzarella cheese. Finish off with any remaining lasagna noodles, remaining meat mixture and mozzarella cheese.
- Cover the slow cooker and cook on low heat for 4-5 hours or until noodles are soft.

Nutrition Information

- Calories: 757 calories
- Sodium: 1362mg sodium
- Fiber: 4g fiber)
- Total Carbohydrate: 43g carbohydrate (13g sugars
- Cholesterol: 143mg cholesterol
- Protein: 55g protein.
- Total Fat: 40g fat (23g saturated fat)

230. Hearty Lasagna

Serving: 12 servings. | Prep: 01hours45mins | Cook: 45mins | Ready in:

Ingredients

- 1-1/2 pounds ground beef
- 1 medium onion, chopped
- 1 garlic clove, minced
- 3 tablespoons olive oil

- 1 can (28 ounces) Italian diced tomatoes, undrained
- 1 can (8 ounces) tomato sauce
- 1 can (6 ounces) tomato paste
- 1 teaspoon dried oregano
- 1 teaspoon sugar
- 1 teaspoon salt
- 1/4 teaspoon pepper
- 2 carrots, halved
- 2 celery ribs, halved
- 12 ounces lasagna noodles
- 1 carton (15 ounces) ricotta cheese
- 2 cups shredded part-skim mozzarella cheese
- 1/2 cup grated Parmesan cheese

Direction

- Cook garlic, onion, and beef in oil using a large skillet, until the onion is tenderized, and the meat turns brown. Strain. Add tomato paste, tomato sauce, tomatoes, oregano, salt, pepper, and sugar and mix evenly. Add in celery and carrots into the sauce. Simmer without covering for 1-1/2 hours, periodically stirring the sauce. In the meantime, follow package instructions to prepare the lasagna noodles. Strain and run under cold water. Dispose celery and carrots. Grease a 13x9-inch baking tray and layer as follows; 1/3 of noodles, 1/3 of meat sauce, 1/3 ricotta cheese, 1/3 mozzarella cheese, and 1/3 Parmesan cheese. Repeat the arrangement again. Cover with excess noodles and meat sauce. Cut a piece of aluminum foil into a heart and place at the center of the sauce. Distribute remainder of ricotta around the heart. Scatter remaining Parmesan and mozzarella. Bake while uncovered for 45 minutes at 350 degrees. Dispose the heart-shaped foil. Let the dish sit for 10-15 minutes before slicing.

Nutrition Information

- Calories: 391 calories
- Protein: 25g protein.
- Total Fat: 16g fat (8g saturated fat)
- Sodium: 790mg sodium

- Fiber: 3g fiber)
- Total Carbohydrate: 36g carbohydrate (12g sugars
- Cholesterol: 56mg cholesterol

231.   Hearty Mexican Lasagna

Serving: 72 servings. | Prep: 40mins | Cook: 45mins | Ready in:

Ingredients

- 18 pounds ground beef
- 3 cups chopped onion
- 18 envelopes taco seasoning
- 6 cans (15 ounces each) tomato sauce
- 6 cans (14-1/2 ounces each) diced tomatoes, undrained
- 32 to 40 flour tortillas (10 inches), cut into 2-inch strips
- 4-1/2 pounds shredded cheddar cheese, divided

Direction

- Sauté onion and beef in multiple Dutch ovens over medium heat until beef is not pink; drain grease. Pour the tomato sauce, taco seasoning, and tomatoes in to the meat. Wait for it to boil. Lower the heat, cover with a lid, and let it simmer for another 10 minutes.
- Spread 2 cups of sauce on each of the six, 13x9 inch baking dishes. Place a single layer of tortilla strips on top of the sauce and add a cup cheese. Do the same process in each dish for two more layers. Evenly distribute the remaining meat sauce between the dishes. Every pan should have about 7 cups of sauce in total. Place the remaining tortillas on the top layer.
- Cover the dishes. Place them in the 350°F oven until bubbling, 40 minutes. Remove the cover and add the remaining cheese on top. Bake for another 5-10 minutes or until the cheese melts.

Nutrition Information

- Calories: 420 calories
- Cholesterol: 85mg cholesterol
- Protein: 30g protein.
- Total Fat: 21g fat (11g saturated fat)
- Sodium: 1262mg sodium
- Fiber: 3g fiber)
- Total Carbohydrate: 23g carbohydrate (1g sugars

232. Hearty Potato Lasagna

Serving: 10-12 servings. | Prep: 20mins | Cook: 01hours25mins |Ready in:

Ingredients

- 1-1/2 pounds ground beef
- 1 medium onion, chopped
- 4 cups spaghetti sauce
- 1 teaspoon dried basil
- 1 teaspoon dried oregano
- 1 teaspoon sugar
- 1/2 teaspoon salt
- 1/4 teaspoon pepper
- 1/3 cup water
- 1 can (4 ounces) mushroom pieces and stems, drained
- 5 medium potatoes, peeled and thinly sliced
- 2 cups shredded part-skim mozzarella cheese

Direction

- Cook ground beef with onions in a skillet until browning occurs, then strain. Mix spaghetti sauce, water, mushrooms, and seasonings into the skillet and combine until even. In a baking tray measuring 13x9-in, pour 1/2 of the sauce. Top the sauce with potatoes. Use foil to cover the tray tightly. Bake for an hour and 15 minutes, at 350 degrees, or until potatoes are soft. Scatter mozzarella cheese, and continue baking for an additional 10 minutes, or until the cheese has fully melted.

Nutrition Information

- Calories: 301 calories
- Fiber: 3g fiber)
- Total Carbohydrate: 25g carbohydrate (8g sugars
- Cholesterol: 48mg cholesterol
- Protein: 21g protein.
- Total Fat: 13g fat (6g saturated fat)
- Sodium: 722mg sodium

233. Hearty Slow Cooker Lasagna

Serving: 8 servings. | Prep: 25mins | Cook: 04hours00mins |Ready in:

Ingredients

- 1 pound ground beef
- 1 tablespoon olive oil
- 1/2 cup chopped onion
- 1/2 cup chopped zucchini
- 1/2 cup chopped carrot
- 1 jar (24 ounces) marinara sauce
- 2 teaspoons Italian seasoning
- 1/2 teaspoon crushed red pepper flakes, optional
- 2 cartons (15 ounces each) part-skim ricotta cheese
- 1 cup grated Parmesan cheese
- 4 large eggs
- 1/2 cup loosely packed basil leaves, chopped
- 12 no-cook lasagna noodles
- 3 cups shredded part-skim mozzarella cheese
- Quartered grape tomatoes and additional chopped fresh basil, optional

Direction

- Using strips of durable foil cut it by 25x3 inches into crisscross until they look like wheel rods. Settle these cut strips on the bottom and up sides of the 5 qt. slow cooker. Use cooking spray to coat the strips.

- Let the beef cook until there's no visible pink on medium heat for 6 to8 minutes. Drain excess water and set-side.
- Heat the same pot with oil on medium high fire. Cook and stir onion, zucchini, and carrot for 2 to 3 minutes. If it becomes tender, stir marinara sauce, Italian seasoning and beef mixture; crushed red pepper can also be added if you want. Mix parmesan egg, ricotta, and basil in a big bowl.
- At the bottom of the slow cooker, spread half cup meat sauce. Arrange 4 noodles on top of it, break if necessarily to fit. Level with 1 to 2/3 cups cheese mixture, one cup mozzarella cheese, and 1 to one and a half cups meat mixture. Do this process twice to form layers. Place cover and let it cook on low heat for four hours. Once noodles are tender, let it stand for half an hour. You may garnish it with additional basil and grape tomatoes if you want.

Nutrition Information

- Calories: 631 calories
- Protein: 43g protein.
- Total Fat: 32g fat (15g saturated fat)
- Sodium: 1074mg sodium
- Fiber: 3g fiber)
- Total Carbohydrate: 40g carbohydrate (8g sugars
- Cholesterol: 199mg cholesterol

234. Hearty Zucchini Lasagna

Serving: 4-6 servings. | Prep: 40mins | Cook: 40mins | Ready in:

Ingredients

- 1 pound ground beef
- 1 medium onion, chopped

- 1 can (15 ounces) tomato sauce
- 1/2 teaspoon salt
- 1/2 teaspoon dried oregano
- 1/4 teaspoon dried basil
- Dash pepper
- 4 medium zucchini, cut lengthwise into 1/4-inch strips
- 2 tablespoons all-purpose flour
- 1 cup 4% cottage cheese
- 1 large egg
- 1 cup shredded part-skim mozzarella cheese
- 1/2 cup grated Parmesan cheese

Direction

- Sauté the onion and beef in a pan over medium heat. Cook until the beef is not pink. Drain grease. Add salt, pepper, tomato sauce, basil, and oregano to the mix. Let it boil. Turn down the heat and let it simmer while uncovered for about 10 minutes. Stir it from time to time.
- Grease a 7x11-inch baking dish. Arrange half of the zucchini in the bottom and add 1 tablespoon flour. Beat the egg and cottage cheese in a separate bowl and thoroughly. Spread the mixture over zucchini and add half of the meat sauce. Top with the remaining zucchini and flour. Spread mozzarella cheese and the left meat mixture. Use Parmesan cheese to top everything.
- For 40 minutes, bake the dish without cover in a 375°F oven until cooked through. Set aside for another 5-10 minutes to cool. Slice and serve.

Nutrition Information

- Calories: 334 calories
- Cholesterol: 110mg cholesterol
- Protein: 31g protein.
- Total Fat: 17g fat (8g saturated fat)
- Sodium: 919mg sodium
- Fiber: 3g fiber)
- Total Carbohydrate: 14g carbohydrate (7g sugars

235. Homemade Mexican Lasagna

Serving: 10 servings. | Prep: 20mins | Cook: 45mins | Ready in:

Ingredients

- 2 pounds ground beef
- 1/2 cup chopped onion
- 1 jar (24 ounces) picante sauce
- 1 can (16 ounces) chili beans, undrained or 1 can (15 ounces) pinto beans, rinsed and drained
- 1 teaspoon salt
- 1/2 teaspoon pepper
- 2 cups 4% cottage cheese
- 1 large egg, beaten
- 2 cups shredded Monterey Jack cheese
- 12 corn tortillas (6 inches)
- 1 cup shredded cheddar cheese
- 1/2 cup thinly sliced green onions, optional
- 1/2 cup sour cream, optional

Direction

- Let beef and onion cook over medium fire in a big skillet, wait until beef becomes brown and onion becomes tender; drain excess fat. Mix in beans, pepper, salt and picante sauce then put aside.
- Blend in egg and cottage cheese in a small bowl. In a 13x9-inch baking dish (you can also use two 8-inch square baking dish), even out 1/3 of meat mixture. On top of it, even out half cottage cheese mixture, half Monterey Jack cheese and six tortillas; if needed break tortillas to cover entire cheese. Duplicate layers and finish with meat. Dash with cheddar cheese.
- Let it bake at 350° for 45-50 minutes. Wait for a few minutes then serve. You may serve it with embellished green onions or sour cream.

Nutrition Information

- Calories: 455 calories
- Cholesterol: 108mg cholesterol
- Protein: 34g protein.
- Total Fat: 22g fat (12g saturated fat)
- Sodium: 1122mg sodium
- Fiber: 4g fiber)
- Total Carbohydrate: 31g carbohydrate (5g sugars

236. Lasagna Corn Carne

Serving: 12 servings. | Prep: 30mins | Cook: 45mins | Ready in:

Ingredients

- 1 pound ground beef
- 1 jar (16 ounces) salsa
- 1 can (16 ounces) kidney beans, rinsed and drained
- 1 can (14-3/4 ounces) cream-style corn
- 1 large onion, chopped
- 1 medium green pepper, chopped
- 1 celery rib, chopped
- 3 garlic cloves, minced
- 1 tablespoon minced fresh basil or 1 teaspoon dried basil
- 1 teaspoon salt
- 1 teaspoon chili powder
- 12 lasagna noodles, cooked and drained
- 2 cups shredded part-skim mozzarella cheese
- 1/2 cup grated Parmesan cheese

Direction

- Using a large skillet, cook beef in medium heat until no longer pink. Drain and put in the salsa, vegetables, beans, garlic and seasonings. Let it boil. Lower the heat and cover. Gently boil for 15 minutes.
- Place 1/4 meat sauce in a 13x9 greased baking pan. Put 4 noodles on top. Repeat the layer once. Put 1/2 of the remaining sauce. Drizzle

1/2 of the cheeses. Put the remaining pasta, sauce and cheeses.

- Cover and let it bake at 350° F for half an hour. Do not cover; let it bake 15- 20 min. Longer or until heated through. Let it set for 15 min. before slicing.

Nutrition Information

- Calories: 313 calories
- Fiber: 5g fiber)
- Total Carbohydrate: 35g carbohydrate (5g sugars
- Cholesterol: 42mg cholesterol
- Protein: 19g protein.
- Total Fat: 10g fat (5g saturated fat)
- Sodium: 690mg sodium

237. Lasagna Deliziosa

Serving: 12 servings. | Prep: 45mins | Cook: 50mins | Ready in:

Ingredients

- 9 uncooked lasagna noodles
- 1 package (19-1/2 ounces) Italian turkey sausage links, casings removed
- 1/2 pound lean ground beef (90% lean)
- 1 large onion, chopped
- 2 garlic cloves, minced
- 1 can (28 ounces) diced tomatoes, undrained
- 1 can (12 ounces) tomato paste
- 1/4 cup water
- 2 teaspoons sugar
- 1 teaspoon dried basil
- 1/2 teaspoon fennel seed
- 1/4 teaspoon pepper
- 1 large egg, lightly beaten
- 1 carton (15 ounces) reduced-fat ricotta cheese
- 1 tablespoon minced fresh parsley
- 1/2 teaspoon salt
- 2 cups shredded part-skim mozzarella cheese
- 3/4 cup grated Parmesan cheese

Direction

- Follow package instructions to cook the lasagna noodles. While waiting for the noodles to cook, sauté onion, sausage and beef in a Dutch oven over medium heat or until meat is not pink. Put in garlic and cook for 1 more minute. Drain excess oil from the beef mixture.
- Put in water, tomatoes, tomato paste, pepper, sugar, fennel and basil into the beef mixture and mix. Let it boil. Lower the heat and let the covered meat sauce simmer while occasionally stirring once for 15-20 minutes.
- In the meantime, preheat the oven at 375°F. Combine ricotta cheese, salt, parsley and egg in a small bowl. Drain the noodles and use cold water to rinse. In a greased 13x9-inch baking dish, put 1 cup of meat sauce evenly on bottom. Layer with 3 noodles, 2 cups of meat sauce, 2/3 cup of ricotta cheese mixture, 2/3 cup of mozzarella, and 1/4 cup of Parmesan. Do the whole layering process 2 times more.
- Put the covered baking dish in the preheated oven and bake for 40 minutes. Remove the cover and continue to bake for 10 to 15 more minutes or until the sauce is bubbling. Before slicing, allow the lasagna to cool down for 10 minutes.

Nutrition Information

- Calories: 323 calories
- Protein: 25g protein. Diabetic Exchanges: 3 lean meat
- Total Fat: 12g fat (5g saturated fat)
- Sodium: 701mg sodium
- Fiber: 4g fiber)
- Total Carbohydrate: 28g carbohydrate (11g sugars
- Cholesterol: 79mg cholesterol

238. Lasagna Pizza Roll Ups

Serving: 8 servings. | Prep: 30mins | Cook: 30mins | Ready in:

Ingredients

- 8 uncoooked lasagna noodles
- 1/2 pound ground beef or turkey
- 1 small onion, chopped
- 3/4 teaspoon garlic salt
- 1/4 teaspoon crushed red pepper flakes
- 1 jar (24 ounces) spaghetti sauce with mushrooms, divided
- 2 cups shredded mozzarella cheese, divided

Direction

- Follow noodle packing instructions for cooking. Discard excess water and then wash with cold water. Let onion and beef cook in a big skillet over a medium fire until meat turns to brown; discard excess fat. Dash with pepper flakes and garlic salt. Take off from heat; mix half cup spaghetti sauce. Mix in one and half cups cheese until well combined.
- Ladle one cup spaghetti sauce into an 11x7-inch baking dish. Ladle about 1/4 cup meat mixture into the middle of each noodle then roll up. In a baking dish, place roll up noodle with seam side down. Ladle leftover spaghetti sauce over roll-ups evenly.
- Place cover and let it bake at 375°F for half an hour to 35 minutes until heated fully. Take off cover and dash excess cheese. Wait for 5 minutes until cheese is melted.

Nutrition Information

- Calories: 262 calories
- Fiber: 2g fiber)
- Total Carbohydrate: 30g carbohydrate (8g sugars
- Cholesterol: 36mg cholesterol
- Protein: 15g protein.
- Total Fat: 10g fat (5g saturated fat)
- Sodium: 759mg sodium

239. Lasagna Roll Ups

Serving: 12 | Prep: 30mins | Cook: 30mins | Ready in:

Ingredients

- 1 (16 ounce) package uncooked lasagna noodles
- 1 pound mozzarella cheese, shredded
- 1 (15 ounce) container ricotta cheese
- 1 pound firm tofu
- 1 (10 ounce) package frozen chopped spinach - thawed, drained and squeezed dry
- 2 cups grated Parmesan cheese
- 1 (28 ounce) jar pasta sauce

Direction

- Let water in a big pot with a little bit of salt boil. Put the lasagna noodles in the boiling salted water and cook for 5-8 minutes until al dente, drain the noodles and rinse in cold water.
- Combine tofu, frozen spinach, 1 cup of Parmesan cheese, grated cheese and ricotta cheese in a big mixing bowl.
- Put a noodle in a clean surface. Put a layer of cheese mixture and a thin layer of sauce evenly on the noodle. Roll up the noodle and put it in a 13x9-inch pan, seam side down. Do this with the remaining noodles. Put the remaining sauce and Parmesan cheese all over the top.
- Put in the preheated oven at 350°F (175°C) and bake for 30 minutes until the sauce is boiling and hot.

Nutrition Information

- Calories: 455 calories;
- Total Carbohydrate: 42.2
- Cholesterol: 48
- Protein: 31.3

- Total Fat: 18.7
- Sodium: 775

240. Lasagna Rolls

Serving: 6 | Prep: | Cook: 45mins | Ready in:

Ingredients

- 12 whole-wheat lasagna noodles
- 1 tablespoon extra-virgin olive oil
- 3 cloves garlic, minced
- 1 14-ounce package extra-firm water-packed tofu, drained, rinsed and crumbled
- 3 cups chopped spinach
- ½ cup shredded Parmesan cheese
- 2 tablespoons finely chopped Kalamata olives
- ¼ teaspoon crushed red pepper
- ¼ teaspoon salt
- 1 25-ounce jar marinara sauce, preferably lower-sodium, divided
- ½ cup shredded part-skim mozzarella cheese

Direction

- Boil water in a large pot and cook the noodles by following the directions at the back of the package. Rinse and drain then put it back to the pot with cold water, covered. Set aside until ready to use.
- On a large nonstick pan, warm oil over medium heat. Cook and stir the garlic for 20 seconds until the aromatic. Put in spinach and tofu and cook for about 3-4 minutes until the spinach is wilted and the mixture is heated enough; stir frequently. Place it in a bowl and add some olives, salt, 2/3 cup of marinara sauce, Parmesan and the smashed red pepper.
- Clean the pan first and on the bottom, place a cup of the remaining marinara sauce. Spread the noodle on surface and fill it with 1/4 cup of tofu filling. Roll it up to make a lasagna roll and bring it in the pan, positioning it seam-side down. Repeat same steps to make lots of rolls. (The rolled tofu will be placed tightly on

the dish.) Pour all the marinara sauce left on top of the rolls.
- Over a high heat, bring the covered pan to a simmer then reduce the heat to medium and let it simmer again for 3 minutes. Drizzle some mozzarella cheese on top; continue cooking with cover for 60 to 120 seconds until the rolls are warmed enough and the cheese has already melted. Start serving it while still hot.

Nutrition Information

- Calories: 338 calories;
- Total Fat: 11
- Sodium: 444
- Cholesterol: 11
- Saturated Fat: 3
- Fiber: 6
- Total Carbohydrate: 45
- Sugar: 6
- Protein: 19

241. Lasagna Toss

Serving: 8 | Prep: 15mins | Cook: 25mins | Ready in:

Ingredients

- 2 cups uncooked penne pasta
- 1 pound ground Italian sausage
- 1 (26 ounce) jar garlic and onion spaghetti sauce (such as Ragu® Robusto® Sauteed Onion & Garlic Pasta Sauce)
- 1 cup cottage cheese
- 2 cups shredded mozzarella cheese, divided

Direction

- Let oven heat to 350°F or 175°C, then put oil in a 2.5 quart baking dish.
- Boil a big pot with water with a pinch of salt. In the same pot, cook pasta for 8 to 10 minutes until al dente then drain water.

- In a big skillet, cook the Italian sausage on medium heat for 8 to 10 minutes until it turns brown, with constant stirring. Discard fat from the meat then transfer the spaghetti sauce and cooked pasta into the skillet, mix it well. Once the sauce and pasta is well combined, let the mixture boil.
- Halve the hot pasta and sausage mixture then transfer half of it in a baking dish. Layer it with the cottage cheese evenly, half the mozzarella cheese and top it over. Layer the other half of the pasta mixture again on top of the cottage cheese and top the other half of the mozzarella cheese.
- Let it bake in a heated oven for 25 minutes until casserole becomes hot, the cheese dissolves, and becomes bubbly. Let it cool for 5 minutes then serve.

Nutrition Information

- Calories: 386 calories;
- Sodium: 1135
- Total Carbohydrate: 29.6
- Cholesterol: 46
- Protein: 22.1
- Total Fat: 19.3

242.   Lasagna With Two Sauces

Serving: 15 servings. | Prep: 45mins | Cook: 60mins | Ready in:

Ingredients

- 1-1/2 pounds each ground beef and ground pork
- 1 cup finely chopped onion
- 4 garlic cloves, minced
- 1 teaspoon dried oregano
- 2 tablespoons olive oil
- 1 cup dry red wine or beef broth
- 4 cans (15 ounces each) tomato sauce

- 1/2 teaspoon salt
- 1/4 teaspoon pepper
- Dash paprika
- 15 uncooked lasagna noodles
- CREAM CHEESE SAUCE:
- 1/2 cup butter
- 1 cup all-purpose flour
- 4 cups milk
- 1 package (8 ounces) cream cheese, softened
- 1/4 teaspoon each salt and ground nutmeg
- 1/8 teaspoon pepper
- 1-1/2 cups (6 ounces each) grated Parmesan cheese

Direction

- Use a big skillet to cook onion, meat, oregano and garlic in oil until meat is not pink; drain excess fat. Add in broth or wine. Softly boil with the lid on until wine is almost evaporated. Put the seasonings and tomato sauce in; let it boil, turn heat down. Softly boil for 3 hours without the lid, stir every now and then.
- Cook lasagna pasta as stated in package instructions; drain the pasta. Melt butter in a big pot and add in flour, stir and cook 6-8 minutes until slightly brown. Slowly add in milk, continue stirring until smooth. Put the seasonings and cream cheese in, stir and cook on low heat until thick and smooth.
- Grease a 13x9 inch baking tray and put in one cup meat sauce. Layer the tray with 5 lasagna noodles, 1/3 of cream cheese sauce, 1/3 of meat sauce, and half cup Parmesan cheese. Do layering again and finish with remaining lasagna noodles, cream cheese sauce, meat sauce, and Parmesan. (Tray will be filled.) Put cover on and bake at 350°, 45 minutes. Remove cover and bake 15 minutes longer. Before slicing, let it sit for 20 minutes.

Nutrition Information

- Calories: 517 calories
- Total Fat: 32g fat (15g saturated fat)
- Sodium: 1069mg sodium

- Fiber: 2g fiber)
- Total Carbohydrate: 30g carbohydrate (0 sugars
- Cholesterol: 107mg cholesterol
- Protein: 27g protein.

243. Lasagna With White Sauce

Serving: 10-12 servings. | Prep: 40mins | Cook: 40mins | Ready in:

Ingredients

- 1 pound ground beef
- 1 large onion, chopped
- 1 can (14-1/2 ounces) diced tomatoes, undrained
- 2 tablespoons tomato paste
- 1 teaspoon beef bouillon granules
- 1-1/2 teaspoons Italian seasoning
- 1 teaspoon salt
- 1/2 teaspoon pepper
- 1/4 teaspoon cayenne pepper
- WHITE SAUCE:
- 2 tablespoons butter
- 3 tablespoons all-purpose flour
- 1 teaspoon salt
- 1/4 teaspoon pepper
- 2 cups 2% milk
- 1-1/4 cups shredded mozzarella cheese, divided
- 10 to 12 uncooked lasagna noodles

Direction

- Put onion and beef in a Dutch oven and cook over medium heat until the meat is not pink; then drain excess oil. Mix in the bouillon, seasonings, tomatoes and tomato paste. Cover the Dutch oven and cook for about 20 minutes over medium-low heat while occasionally stirring.
- While the meat sauce is cooking, melt butter in a big pan then mix in the salt, pepper and

flour until fully combined. Slowly put in the milk. Let it boil and cook for 1 minute or until sauce is thick in consistency. Remove the pan from heat then add 1/2 of cheese and mix; put aside.
- In an ungreased 13x9-inch pan, put in 1/2 of meat sauce on bottom. Layer on 1/2 of the lasagna noodles and the remaining meat sauce. Put the remaining lasagna noodles on top. Put the white sauce evenly on top of the noodles. Finish with the remaining cheese on top.
- Put the covered baking dish in the preheated oven at 400°F and bake for 40 minutes or until bubbling and the noodles are soft.

Nutrition Information

- Calories: 232 calories
- Protein: 14g protein.
- Total Fat: 10g fat (5g saturated fat)
- Sodium: 639mg sodium
- Fiber: 1g fiber)
- Total Carbohydrate: 22g carbohydrate (5g sugars
- Cholesterol: 38mg cholesterol

244. Lazy Lasagna

Serving: Makes 8 servings. | Prep: 10mins | Cook: | Ready in:

Ingredients

- 1 container (24 oz.) BREAKSTONE'S or KNUDSEN 2% Milkfat Low Fat Cottage Cheese
- 1/2 cup cholesterol-free egg product
- 2 cups KRAFT Shredded Low-Moisture Part-Skim Mozzarella Cheese, divided
- 1 jar (24 oz.) OLIVO by CLASSICO Traditional Pasta Sauce
- 2 cups frozen BOCA Veggie Ground Crumbles

- 2 cups rotini pasta, uncooked

Direction

- Combine the egg product, 1 cup of mozzarella cheese and cottage cheese then give it a stir. Mix the crumbles and sauce together and put half of the crumble-sauce mixture evenly at the bottom of a greased 13x9-inch baking pan using a cooking spray.
- Place layers of pasta and half of the cottage cheese mixture over the sauce layer at the bottom, then put in a layer of the remaining sauce and cottage cheese mixture on top. Drizzle with the remaining mozzarella then cover the baking pan.
- Put it in an oven and let it bake for 1 hour or till heated through (about160°F). Remove the cover from the baking pan after 30 minutes of the baking process. Before serving, allow the baked lasagna to rest for 10 minutes prior to slicing it.

Nutrition Information

- Calories: 320
- Protein: 29 g
- Saturated Fat: 3.5 g
- Sodium: 940 mg
- Fiber: 4 g
- Total Carbohydrate: 30 g
- Total Fat: 8 g
- Sugar: 5 g
- Cholesterol: 30 mg

---

245. Lighter Lasagna Corn Carne

Serving: 12 servings. | Prep: 30mins | Cook: 45mins | Ready in:

Ingredients

- 1 pound lean ground beef (90% lean)

- 1 jar (16 ounces) salsa
- 1 can (16 ounces) kidney beans, rinsed and drained
- 1 can (14-3/4 ounces) cream-style corn
- 1 large onion, chopped
- 1 medium green pepper, chopped
- 1 celery rib, chopped
- 3 garlic cloves, minced
- 1 tablespoon minced fresh basil or 1 teaspoon dried basil
- 1 teaspoon salt
- 1 teaspoon chili powder
- 12 lasagna noodles, cooked, rinsed and drained
- 2 cups shredded part-skim mozzarella cheese
- 1/2 cup grated Parmesan cheese

Direction

- Cook beef until not pink on medium heat. Drain excess fat. Mix in the salsa, vegetables, beans, garlic and seasonings. Let it boil. Put heat to low and cover. Gently boil 15 minutes.
- Place 1/4 meat sauce in a greased 13 in. x 9 in. baking pan. Put four pieces of pasta on top and repeat the layering one time. Top with 1/2 of remaining sauce. Drizzle on 1/2 of cheeses. Top with left, pasta noodles, sauce, and the cheeses.
- Cover and let it bake for 30 minutes at 350 degrees. Remove the cover. Bake for 15 to 20 minutes until cooked completely. Let sit 15 minutes before slicing.

Nutrition Information

- Calories: 292 calories
- Cholesterol: 37mg cholesterol
- Protein: 20g protein. Diabetic Exchanges: 2-1/2 starch
- Total Fat: 8g fat (4g saturated fat)
- Sodium: 674mg sodium
- Fiber: 4g fiber)
- Total Carbohydrate: 36g carbohydrate (5g sugars

246. Make Once, Eat Twice Lasagna

Serving: 2 lasagnas (12 servings each). | Prep: 35mins | Cook: 55mins | Ready in:

Ingredients

- 18 lasagna noodles
- 3 pounds ground beef
- 3 jars (26 ounces each) spaghetti sauce
- 2 large eggs, lightly beaten
- 1-1/2 pounds ricotta cheese
- 6 cups shredded part-skim mozzarella cheese, divided
- 1 tablespoon dried parsley flakes
- 1 teaspoon salt
- 1/2 teaspoon pepper
- 1 cup grated Parmesan cheese

Direction

- Follow the packet directions in cooking the noodles. Set a Dutch oven over medium heat and cook beef until brown. Drain the beef; mix in the spaghetti sauce and set aside. Mix 4 1/2 cups of mozzarella cheese, salt and pepper, eggs, parsley, and ricotta cheese in a large bowl.
- Drain the cooked noodles. Prepare two greased 13x9-inch baking pans. At the bottom of each pan, layer a cup of meat sauce, three pieces of noodles, a cup of the made ricotta mixture, and a cup and a half of meat sauce. Repeat the layers two times; then top with Parmesan cheese and remaining mozzarella cheese. Cover one of the lasagna pans and freeze for up to 3 months. Bake the leftover covered pan in a preheated oven at 375°F for 45 minutes. Remove aluminum foil and bake until the top becomes bubbly or for 10 minutes longer. Leave to cool for 10 minutes before serving.

Nutrition Information

- Calories: 365 calories
- Sodium: 820mg sodium
- Fiber: 2g fiber)
- Total Carbohydrate: 25g carbohydrate (9g sugars
- Cholesterol: 78mg cholesterol
- Protein: 27g protein.
- Total Fat: 17g fat (8g saturated fat)

247. Make Ahead Lasagna

Serving: 12 servings. | Prep: 35mins | Cook: 55mins | Ready in:

Ingredients

- 1 pound ground beef
- 1 pound Johnsonville® Ground Hot Italian sausage
- 2 cups marinara sauce
- 1 can (15 ounces) pizza sauce
- 2 large eggs, lightly beaten
- 1 carton (15 ounces) whole-milk ricotta cheese
- 1/2 cup grated Parmesan cheese
- 1 tablespoon dried parsley flakes
- 1/2 teaspoon pepper
- 12 no-cook lasagna noodles
- 4 cups shredded part-skim mozzarella cheese

Direction

- On medium heat, cook sausage and beef in a big pan until the meat is not pink; crumble and drain. Mix in pizza and marinara sauces. Combine pepper, eggs, parsley, Parmesan cheese, and ricotta cheese in a bowl.
- In a 13-inch by 9-inch greased baking dish, pour in a cup of meat sauce and top with 4 noodles. Add 1/2 of the ricotta mixture, a cup of meat sauce, and a cup of mozzarella cheese; repeat process. Layer leftover noodles, meat sauce, and mozzarella on top. Let it chill in the refrigerator, covered, for eight hours to overnight.

- Preheat the oven to 375 degrees F. Meanwhile, take the lasagna out of the refrigerator. Bake for 45 mins, covered. Remove cover and bake for another 10-15 mins until the cheese melts. Set aside 10 mins then cut.

Nutrition Information

- Calories: 462 calories
- Sodium: 931mg sodium
- Fiber: 2g fiber)
- Total Carbohydrate: 26g carbohydrate (7g sugars
- Cholesterol: 117mg cholesterol
- Protein: 30g protein.
- Total Fat: 27g fat (12g saturated fat)

248.   Makeover Beef & Sausage Lasagna

Serving: 12 servings. | Prep: 45mins | Cook: 45mins | Ready in:

Ingredients

- 3/4 pound lean ground beef (90% lean)
- 3/4 pound Italian turkey sausage links, casings removed
- 1 medium onion, chopped
- 1 medium green pepper, chopped
- 1 jar (26 ounces) spaghetti sauce
- 1 package (8 ounces) reduced-fat cream cheese, cubed
- 1 cup 1% cottage cheese
- 1 large egg, lightly beaten
- 1 tablespoon minced fresh parsley
- 6 whole wheat lasagna noodles, cooked and drained
- 1 cup shredded reduced-fat Italian cheese blend
- 3 teaspoons Italian seasoning, divided
- 1 cup shredded part-skim mozzarella cheese

Direction

- On medium heat, cook green pepper, beef, onion, and sausage in a big pan until the meat is not pink; drain. Reserve a cup of spaghetti sauce and mix the left sauce with the meat mixture; boil. Lower heat and let it simmer for 8-10 mins, uncovered, until the mixture is thick.
- On medium heat, melt cream cheese in a small pot; take off heat. Mix in parsley, egg, and cottage cheese.
- Using cooking spray, grease a 13-inch by 9-inch baking dish; pour in meat sauce. Layer 3 noodles, Italian cheese blend, and 1 1/2 tsp. Italian seasoning. Add cream cheese mixture, left noodles, and saved spaghetti sauce. Spread mozzarella and left Italian seasoning on top.
- Bake in a 350 degrees F oven, covered, for 35 mins. Remove cover and bake for another 10-15 mins until the dish is bubbly. Set aside for 15 mins then cut.

Nutrition Information

- Calories: 298 calories
- Cholesterol: 78mg cholesterol
- Protein: 23g protein. Diabetic Exchanges: 3 lean meat
- Total Fat: 15g fat (7g saturated fat)
- Sodium: 772mg sodium
- Fiber: 3g fiber)
- Total Carbohydrate: 17g carbohydrate (7g sugars

249.   Makeover Lasagna With Two Sauces

Serving: 15 servings. | Prep: 45mins | Cook: 60mins | Ready in:

Ingredients

- 1 pound lean ground beef (90% lean)
- 1/2 pound lean ground pork

- 1 cup finely chopped onion
- 4 garlic cloves, minced
- 1 cup dry red wine or beef broth
- 4 cans (15 ounces each) tomato sauce
- 2 teaspoons sugar
- 1 teaspoon dried oregano
- 1/4 teaspoon pepper
- Dash paprika
- 2/3 cup bulgur
- 2 cups boiling water
- 12 uncooked lasagna noodles
- CREAM CHEESE SAUCE:
- 1/4 cup butter
- 1 cup all-purpose flour
- 4 cups fat-free milk
- 1 package (8 ounces) reduced-fat cream cheese, cubed
- 1/4 teaspoon each salt and ground nutmeg
- 1/8 teaspoon pepper
- 1 cup shredded Parmesan cheese

Direction

- Use a large non-stick skillet, mix garlic and onion and cook meat until no longer pink. Drain. Add in the broth and wine. Remove cover; gently boil until the wine has almost completely reduced. Place seasonings and tomato sauce. Let it boil. Lower down the heat; simmer without cover for 3 hours. Stir from time to time. Put Bulgur in a bowl. Put boiling water and let it set for an hour. Drain and set aside. Cook the lasagna pasta, refer to package instructions. Strain the pasta. Use a saucepan and heat butter until golden brown in medium heat; for about 4 minutes. Take out from the heat. In a bowl, mix until smooth the flour and milk and add into the butter. Let it boil, cook and stir for 2 minutes. Lower the heat; add seasonings and cream cheese. Cook and stir until smooth. Stir bulgur into meat sauce.
- Use a 13x9in. baking pan and spray with cooking spray. Place 1 cup meat sauce, arrange and layer 4 pasta, 1/3 cream cheese and meat sauces, 1/3 cup parmesan cheese. Repeat layers. Top with remaining noodles, sauces and Parmesan cheese

- (Dish will be full). Bake with cover at 350 degrees F, for 45 minutes. Remove the cover and bake 15 minutes. Let it set for 20 minutes before slicing.

Nutrition Information

- Calories: 334 calories
- Cholesterol: 50mg cholesterol
- Protein: 20g protein. Diabetic Exchanges: 2 starch
- Total Fat: 13g fat (7g saturated fat)
- Sodium: 926mg sodium
- Fiber: 3g fiber)
- Total Carbohydrate: 33g carbohydrate (0 sugars

---

250.   Meaty Chili Lasagna

Serving: 12 servings. | Prep: 20mins | Cook: 45mins | Ready in:

Ingredients

- 12 uncooked lasagna noodles
- 1-1/2 pounds ground beef
- 1 medium onion, chopped
- 1 medium green pepper, chopped
- 2 to 3 jalapeno peppers, seeded and chopped
- 1 to 2 tablespoons chili powder
- 1 garlic clove, minced
- 1 can (10-3/4 ounces) condensed cream of mushroom soup, undiluted
- 1 cup frozen corn
- 1 can (8 ounces) tomato sauce
- 3 tablespoons tomato paste
- 1 can (2-1/4 ounces) sliced ripe olives, drained
- 4 cups shredded cheddar cheese

Direction

- Cook noodles, refer to package instructions. Meanwhile, mix the onion, beef, peppers and chili powder in a large skillet. Add garlic and cook a minute longer. Drain. Put the corn, soup, tomato paste, tomato sauce and olives. Simmer until heated through.

- Strain pasta. Put half cup meat sauce in a greased 13x9 in. baking pan. Layer 4 pasta, 1/2 of the remaining sauce and 1/3 cheese. Do layer again. Put the remaining pasta and cheese on top.
- Cover and bake for 350° F for 30 min. without cover. Bake for about 15 minutes more until cheese are melted. Let set for 15 min. before slicing.

Nutrition Information

- Calories: 405 calories
- Total Fat: 21g fat (12g saturated fat)
- Sodium: 597mg sodium
- Fiber: 3g fiber)
- Total Carbohydrate: 29g carbohydrate (4g sugars
- Cholesterol: 82mg cholesterol
- Protein: 25g protein.

251. Mexi Corn Lasagna

Serving: 12 servings. | Prep: 30mins | Cook: 40mins | Ready in:

Ingredients

- 1 pound ground beef
- 2 cups fresh corn
- 1 can (15 ounces) tomato sauce
- 1 cup picante sauce
- 1 tablespoon chili powder
- 1-1/2 teaspoons ground cumin
- 10 flour tortillas (7 inch)
- 2 cups (16 ounces) 4% cottage cheese
- 2 eggs, lightly beaten
- 1/4 cup grated Parmesan cheese
- 1 teaspoon dried oregano
- 1/2 teaspoon garlic salt
- 1 cup shredded cheddar cheese

Direction

- Let ground beef cook in a skillet until brown. Discard liquid then add picante sauce, tomato sauce, corn, cumin, and chili powder. Let it boil. Lower heat then place cover and let it simmer for five minutes.
- In a 13x9 inch baking pan, grease the bottom and sides with oil, then place half of the tortillas. Ladle meat mixture on top of the tortillas. Then mix eggs, cottage cheese, garlic salt, parmesan, and oregano then top it on the meat mixture. Level the other half of tortillas on top of the mixture. Use foil to cover.
- Let it bake for half an hour at 375°. Top with cheese then put back to the oven until cheese melts for 10 minutes.

Nutrition Information

- Calories: 330 calories
- Sodium: 793mg sodium
- Fiber: 1g fiber)
- Total Carbohydrate: 32g carbohydrate (4g sugars
- Cholesterol: 80mg cholesterol
- Protein: 21g protein.
- Total Fat: 13g fat (6g saturated fat)

252. Mexican Lasagna

Serving: 12 | Prep: 30mins | Cook: 1hours30mins | Ready in:

Ingredients

- 1 pound extra-lean ground beef
- 1 (16 ounce) can refried beans
- 2 teaspoons dried oregano
- 1 teaspoon ground cumin
- 3/4 teaspoon garlic powder
- 12 dry lasagna noodles
- 2 1/2 cups water
- 2 1/2 cups salsa

- 2 cups sour cream
- 3/4 cup chopped green onions
- 1 (2 ounce) can sliced black olives
- 1 cup shredded Pepper Jack cheese

Direction

- Put a skillet on medium-high heat and cook ground beef until browned evenly. Drain grease. Mix refried beans, cooked beef, oregano, cumin, and garlic powder in a bowl.
- Put 4 uncooked pasta in the bottom of a 13 in x 9 in baking pan. Pour 1/2 of beef mixture on top of the pasta. Layer with 4 more uncooked pasta, the remaining 1/2 of beef mixture, and the remaining pasta. Mix salsa and water in a bowl and pour on top.
- Use foil to tightly cover and bake in oven at 175°C (350°F). Cook for 1 1/2 hours until pasta is soft.
- Mix green onions, sour cream, and olives in a bowl. Scoop over lasagna and put shredded cheese on top. Put it back in oven and bake for 5-10 min. until cheese melts.

Nutrition Information

- Calories: 559 calories;
- Total Fat: 19.1
- Sodium: 604
- Total Carbohydrate: 72.3
- Cholesterol: 60
- Protein: 25.6

253.   Mexican Lasagne

Serving: 12 servings. | Prep: 30mins | Cook: 40mins | Ready in:

Ingredients

- 1 pound lean ground beef (90% lean)
- 2 cups fresh or frozen corn
- 2 cans (8 ounces each) no-salt-added tomato sauce

- 1 cup picante sauce
- 1 tablespoon chili powder
- 1-1/2 teaspoons ground cumin
- 10 flour tortillas (8 inches)
- 2 cups 1% cottage cheese
- 1/2 cup egg substitute
- 2 tablespoons grated Parmesan cheese
- 1 teaspoon dried oregano
- 1/2 teaspoon garlic powder
- 1 cup shredded reduced-fat cheddar cheese

Direction

- Cook ground beef in a pan until brown; drain. Put in cumin, corn, chili powder, tomato sauce, and picante sauce; boil. Lower heat and let it simmer, covered, for 5 mins. At the bottom and sides of a 13-inch by 9-inch greased baking pan, arrange 1/2 of the tortillas and add meat mixture on top.
- Mix garlic powder, cottage cheese, oregano, egg substitute, and Parmesan cheese together; spread the mixture on top of the meat mixture. Add the leftover tortillas on top; use a sheet of foil to cover. Bake in a 375 degrees F oven for half an hour. Add cheese on top then bake for another 10 mins until the cheese melts.

Nutrition Information

- Calories: 294 calories
- Sodium: 635mg sodium
- Fiber: 1g fiber)
- Total Carbohydrate: 33g carbohydrate (0 sugars
- Cholesterol: 20mg cholesterol
- Protein: 22g protein. Diabetic Exchanges: 2-1/2 lean meat
- Total Fat: 8g fat (0 saturated fat)

254.   Microwave Lasagna

Serving: 8 servings. | Prep: 15mins | Cook: 25mins | Ready in:

Ingredients

- 1 pound ground beef
- 1 jar (26 ounces) spaghetti sauce
- 1/2 teaspoon dried basil
- 1/4 teaspoon garlic powder
- 2 cups 1% cottage cheese
- 1 tablespoon minced fresh parsley
- 1 large egg, beaten
- 1/4 teaspoon pepper
- 6 uncooked lasagna noodles
- 2 cups shredded mozzarella cheese, divided
- 1/2 cup water

Direction

- Place beef in a microwaveable dish, set microwave on maximum and cook beef for 3 minutes then stir. Let beef cook for 2 minutes more until pink color is gone. Discard excess fat. Mix in garlic powder, spaghetti sauce and basil. Place cover and cook in the microwave for 2 minutes until cooked through. Put aside. Mix in egg, parsley, pepper and cottage cheese in a bowl.
- In an 11x7-inch microwaveable dish greased with oil, even out half cup meat sauce. Arrange 3 noodles on top of the sauce with half of the cottage cheese, half of the excess meat sauce, and one cup mozzarella cheese. Arrange leftover noodles, cottage cheese and meat sauce in another layer. Dispense water on the rim of the casserole on tiny sides of the dish.
- Wrap it with plastic covering. Set microwave on a maximum for 20 minutes until noodles becomes tender. Dash with leftover cheese. Place a cover and warm until cheese has dissolved for 2 minutes. Wait for 10 minutes then cut.

Nutrition Information

- Calories: 324 calories
- Fiber: 2g fiber)
- Total Carbohydrate: 25g carbohydrate (9g sugars

- Cholesterol: 78mg cholesterol
- Protein: 27g protein.
- Total Fat: 13g fat (7g saturated fat)
- Sodium: 785mg sodium

255.   Mom's Lasagna

Serving: | Prep: 20mins | Cook: 1hours | Ready in:

Ingredients

- 1.5 pounds Ground beef
- 1 can Crushed Tomatos
- 1 teaspoon Salt
- 1 teaspoon Organo
- 1 teaspoon Pepper
- 16 ounces Mozzarella Cheese
- 1 package Lasagna Noodles
- 16 ounce Cottage Cheese

Direction

- Cook beef until browning occurs, then add some seasoning, and allow to simmer for 20 minutes.
- Cook the noodles.
- Layer as follows; noodles, followed by mozzarella, cottage cheese, and meat sauce.
- Place inside oven and bake at 350 degrees for 30 minutes.

256.   No Noodle Lasagna

Serving: 6 servings. | Prep: 20mins | Cook: 25mins | Ready in:

Ingredients

- 1-1/2 pounds ground beef
- 1/2 cup chopped onion
- 1 can (6 ounces) tomato paste
- 1 tablespoon dried parsley flakes
- 1/2 teaspoon dried basil

- 1/2 teaspoon dried oregano
- 1/2 teaspoon salt
- 1/2 teaspoon pepper
- Dash garlic salt
- 1 large egg
- 1-1/2 cups (12 ounces) 4% cottage cheese
- 1/4 cup grated Parmesan cheese
- 2 tubes (8 ounces each) refrigerated crescent rolls
- 8 slices part-skim mozzarella cheese
- 1 tablespoon milk
- 1 tablespoon sesame seeds

Direction

- Put onion and beef in a large skillet and sauté over medium heat until the beef is brown in color then drain excess oil. Add in the seasonings and tomato paste into the sautéed beef. Mix cottage cheese, Parmesan cheese and egg together in a separate small bowl.
- Unroll the crescent dough in each tube into a 15x10-inch rectangle and put between wax papers. On a greased 15x10x1-inch baking pan, put one crescent dough rectangle. Put in half of the meat mixture evenly on top of the crescent dough leaving about an inch along the edges untouched, sprinkle half of the cheese mixture on top. Layer the remaining half of the meat and cheese mixture on top.
- Add in mozzarella cheese. Slowly cover the top with the second crescent dough rectangle then press down the edges to seal. Spread milk on top using a brush then put sesame seeds. Put in the baking pan uncovered in the oven at 350 degrees and bake for 25-30 minutes or until it is golden brown.

Nutrition Information

- Calories: 560 calories
- Sodium: 1025mg sodium
- Fiber: 2g fiber)
- Total Carbohydrate: 26g carbohydrate (10g sugars
- Cholesterol: 136mg cholesterol
- Protein: 40g protein.

- Total Fat: 32g fat (14g saturated fat)

257. One Skillet Lasagna

Serving: 6 servings. | Prep: 15mins | Cook: 15mins | Ready in:

Ingredients

- 3/4 pound ground beef
- 2 garlic cloves, minced
- 1 can (14-1/2 ounces) diced tomatoes with basil, oregano and garlic, undrained
- 2 jars (14 ounces each) spaghetti sauce
- 2/3 cup condensed cream of onion soup, undiluted
- 2 large eggs, lightly beaten
- 1-1/4 cups 1% cottage cheese
- 3/4 teaspoon Italian seasoning
- 9 no-cook lasagna noodles
- 1/2 cup shredded Colby-Monterey Jack cheese
- 1/2 cup shredded part-skim mozzarella cheese

Direction

- Cook beef and garlic in medium heat using a large skillet. Cook until meat is no longer pink; drain. Add in spaghetti sauce and tomatoes, heat through. Transfer to a large bowl.
- Mix soup, cottage cheese, eggs and Italian seasoning in a small bowl.
- Put 1 cup of meat sauce back to the skillet and spread evenly. Put a layer of a cup of cottage cheese mixture, half of the pasta (break if needed to fit), and 1 1/2 cups meat sauce.
- Repeat layers of cottage cheese mixture, meat sauce and noodles. Put on top the remaining meat sauce and let boil. Put to low heat and let it simmer with cover for 15-17 minutes until pasta are tender.
- Take out from the heat, drizzle with shredded cheeses. Cover and let it set for 2 minutes until it melts.

Nutrition Information

- Calories: 478 calories
- Protein: 31g protein.
- Total Fat: 20g fat (8g saturated fat)
- Sodium: 1552mg sodium
- Fiber: 4g fiber)
- Total Carbohydrate: 43g carbohydrate (15g sugars
- Cholesterol: 128mg cholesterol

---

258. Pancake Lasagna

Serving: 8 servings | Prep: 15mins | Cook: | Ready in:

Ingredients

- 8 egg s
- 1/4 cup BREAKSTONE'S or KNUDSEN Sour Cream
- 1/2 tsp. ground black pepper
- 1 pkg. (8 oz.) KRAFT Shredded Mild Cheddar Cheese with a TOUCH OF PHILADELPHIA , divided
- 8 frozen pancakes (4 inch)
- 1/2 cup maple-flavored or pancake syrup
- 6 slices cooked OSCAR MAYER Bacon , crumbled

Direction

- In a medium-sized bowl, beat the eggs until it is well-mixed. Add in the pepper, 1/2 cup of cheese and sour cream then give it a mix then place in a big non-stick skillet. Let the mixture cook for 3-4 minutes over medium heat setting while stirring it from time to time until the eggs have begun to set. (There's no need to let the eggs set completely.)
- Use a cooking spray to grease an 8-inch square baking dish; put 1 layer of 4 pieces of pancakes at the bottom of the baking dish then pour in 1/4 cup of syrup evenly on top. Place layers of half of the following over the pancake layer: eggs, bacon and remaining cheese. Do the

whole layering process again then cover the baking dish once done.
- Put it in a preheated oven and let it bake for 25-30 minutes or until it is thoroughly heated.

Nutrition Information

- Calories: 360
- Sugar: 15 g
- Cholesterol: 235 mg
- Protein: 16 g
- Sodium: 540 mg
- Fiber: 1 g
- Saturated Fat: 10 g
- Total Carbohydrate: 29 g
- Total Fat: 20 g

---

259. Pasticho (Venezuelan Lasagna)

Serving: 20 servings. | Prep: 01hours50mins | Cook: 35mins | Ready in:

Ingredients

- 1 pound ground beef
- 1 pound ground pork
- 1 large Spanish onion, finely chopped
- 1 celery rib, finely chopped
- 1 small carrot, shredded
- 3 tablespoons olive oil
- 4 garlic cloves, minced
- 2 cans (28 ounces each) whole tomatoes with basil, undrained
- 1 can (29 ounces) tomato puree
- 1 bay leaf
- 1 teaspoon salt
- MUSHROOM SAUCE:
- 2-1/4 cups sliced baby portobello mushrooms
- 1/3 cup butter, cubed
- 1 tablespoon olive oil
- 6 cups heavy whipping cream
- 1/2 teaspoon salt

- 1/4 teaspoon pepper
- 1-1/4 cups shredded Parmesan cheese
- LAYERS:
- 3 packages (9 ounces each) no-cook lasagna noodles
- 7 cups shredded part-skim mozzarella cheese
- 2 cups shredded Parmesan cheese

Direction

- On medium heat, cook carrot, beef, celery, onion, and pork in a Dutch oven until the meat is not pink; put in garlic. Cook for another minute then drain. Mix in salt, tomatoes, bay leaf, and tomato puree; boil. Lower heat and let it simmer for an hour without cover.
- Put in oil and butter in a Dutch oven; sauté mushrooms until tender. Put in pepper, salt, and cream; boil. Cook and stir in Parmesan cheese for 20-15 mins until the mixture is thick.
- Remove bay leaf from the sauce. In a greased four-quart baking dish, pour in 1 1/4 cup meat sauce and add 6 noodles on top. Put on 1 3/4 cup meat sauce, a cup of mozzarella cheese, and 6 noodles. Spread 1 1/4 cup mushroom sauce, 1/3 cup Parmesan cheese, and half cup mozzarella cheese. Repeat the process for another 3 layers. Add the leftover noodles, meat and mushroom sauce, mozzarella, and Parmesan on the very top until full.
- Bake in 400 degrees F oven, covered, for 20 mins. Remove cover and bake for another 15-20 mins until bubbly and golden. Set aside for 10 mins then cut.

Nutrition Information

- Calories: 721 calories
- Protein: 31g protein.
- Total Fat: 49g fat (27g saturated fat)
- Sodium: 813mg sodium
- Fiber: 3g fiber)
- Total Carbohydrate: 40g carbohydrate (6g sugars
- Cholesterol: 167mg cholesterol

---

260.   Pepperoni Lasagna

Serving: 12 servings. | Prep: 60mins | Cook: 45mins | Ready in:

Ingredients

- 1-1/2 pounds ground beef
- 1 small onion, chopped
- 2-1/2 cups water
- 1 can (8 ounces) tomato sauce
- 1 can (6 ounces) tomato paste
- 1 teaspoon beef bouillon granules
- 1 tablespoon dried parsley flakes
- 2 teaspoons Italian seasoning
- 1 teaspoon salt
- 1/4 teaspoon garlic salt
- 2 large eggs
- 1-1/2 cups 4% small-curd cottage cheese
- 1/2 cup sour cream
- 8 lasagna noodles, cooked and drained
- 1 package (3-1/2 ounces) sliced pepperoni
- 2 cups shredded part-skim mozzarella cheese
- 1/2 cup grated Parmesan cheese

Direction

- Cook beef and onion in a skillet on medium heat until it is not pink. Drain grease. Put in the tomato sauce, tomato paste, water, bouillon and seasonings; let it boil. Put down to low heat and let it simmer without cover for half an hour.
- Use a small bowl to mix in cottage cheese, sour cream and eggs. Place 1/2 cup of meat sauce in a 13 in. x 9 in. greased baking pan. Layer on 4 pasta, cottage cheese mixture and pepperoni. Put the remaining pasta and meat sauce on top. Drizzle on parmesan and mozzarella cheeses.
- Put a cover on and bake 35 minutes at 350 degrees. Remove the cover; bake 10 minutes more until cooked completely. Let it sit 15 minutes before slicing.

Nutrition Information

- Calories: 356 calories
- Fiber: 2g fiber)
- Total Carbohydrate: 19g carbohydrate (6g sugars
- Cholesterol: 106mg cholesterol
- Protein: 26g protein.
- Total Fat: 19g fat (9g saturated fat)
- Sodium: 838mg sodium

---

261.   Petite Lasagna

Serving: 2 servings. | Prep: 30mins | Cook: 30mins | Ready in:

Ingredients

- 5 lasagna noodles
- 1/2 pound ground beef
- 1/4 cup each chopped onion, green pepper and fresh mushrooms
- 1 jar (14 ounces) meatless spaghetti sauce
- 1 large egg, beaten
- 3/4 cup ricotta cheese
- 2 tablespoons grated Parmesan cheese
- 2 tablespoons minced fresh parsley
- 1-1/2 teaspoons Italian seasoning
- 1 cup shredded mozzarella cheese

Direction

- Follow the directions on the packet to cook lasagna noodles. As the noodles cook, set big large saucepan on medium heat, and stir in mushrooms, onions, beef, and green pepper. Cook until the beef is browned, then drain. Pour in the spaghetti sauce. Allow the mixture to cook, while stirring occasionally, for 5 minutes. Combine parsley, egg, Italian seasoning, ricotta cheese, and Parmesan cheese in a small bowl; set aside. Drain the noodles.
- At the bottom of an 8x4-inch greased loaf pan, spread a quarter cup of meat sauce. Top sauce with 2 pieces of noodles. The noodles may be

trimmed to fit the pan. Layer with a third of cheese mixture and a third of meat sauce; add 1/3 cup of mozzarella cheese. Repeat the layers twice then top with leftover noodle trimmings. Cook in the preheated oven at 350°F until well heated through and the cheese has melted (about 30 to 35 minutes). Rest for 5 minutes then cut.

Nutrition Information

- Calories: 856 calories
- Total Carbohydrate: 74g carbohydrate (23g sugars
- Cholesterol: 247mg cholesterol
- Protein: 59g protein.
- Total Fat: 36g fat (20g saturated fat)
- Sodium: 1400mg sodium
- Fiber: 6g fiber)

---

262.   Pizza Lasagna

Serving: 12 | Prep: 20mins | Cook: 48mins | Ready in:

Ingredients

- 1 (8 ounce) package lasagna noodles
- 6 Cajun-style sausage links, casings removed
- 2 (24 ounce) jars marinara sauce
- 1 (7 ounce) package sliced pepperoni
- 1 (8 ounce) package sliced fresh mushrooms
- 1 onion, sliced
- 1 large green bell pepper, chopped
- 2 (2.25 ounce) cans sliced black olives
- 2 (8 ounce) packages shredded pizza cheese blend

Direction

- Preheat oven to 175° C (350°F). Put light salt in water using a large pot and let it boil. Cook lasagna pasta in the boiling water, stir from time to time until tender yet firm to the bite for 8 minutes Drain.

- Put a large skillet to medium-high heat. Cook sausage in the hot skillet, break into bite size pieces until brown; about 5 -7 min.
- Pour layer of sauce in the bottom of a 9x13 inch baking dish. Place lasagna pasta side by side. Pour more sauce. Ladle more sauce on top. Add pepperoni on the noodles and put sausage on top of pepperoni. Make a layer of mushrooms, onion, green bell pepper, black olives, and cheese blend on top. Continue to layer until all ingredients are used.
- Bake in the preheated oven until heated completely and bubbling about 35 min.

Nutrition Information

- Calories: 409 calories;
- Cholesterol: 50
- Protein: 17.9
- Total Fat: 23.1
- Sodium: 1153
- Total Carbohydrate: 33.2

263.   Potato Beef Lasagna

Serving: 8 servings. | Prep: 20mins | Cook: 01hours10mins |Ready in:

Ingredients

- 1 pound lean ground beef
- 1/2 pound Johnsonville® Ground Mild Italian sausage
- 1 can (19 ounces) ready-to-serve tomato-basil soup
- 1 can (14-1/2 ounces) Italian diced tomatoes, undrained
- 1 package (20 ounces) refrigerated sliced potatoes
- 1 medium onion, thinly sliced
- 1 cup shredded part-skim mozzarella cheese
- 1-1/2 cups shredded Gruyere or Swiss cheese
- 3 tablespoons minced fresh parsley

Direction

- Let sausage and beef cook on medium fire in a big skillet. When beef is cooked with no pink color; drain the excess water. Add tomatoes and soup, stir. Put aside.
- Halve potatoes and onions and place into a 13x9 inches greased baking dish. Make the other half into layers. Use meat mixture and mozzarella cheese as topping.
- Place cover and let it bake for an hour at 350°. Remover the cover and top with Gruyere cheese. Let it bake for 10 to 15 minutes more. When cheese melts and potatoes become tender, wait for 10 minutes then serve. Top with parsley.

Nutrition Information

- Calories: 372 calories
- Total Fat: 17g fat (8g saturated fat)
- Sodium: 765mg sodium
- Fiber: 2g fiber)
- Total Carbohydrate: 26g carbohydrate (7g sugars
- Cholesterol: 71mg cholesterol
- Protein: 27g protein.

264.   Potluck Lasagna

Serving: 12-15 servings. | Prep: 30mins | Cook: 55mins | Ready in:

Ingredients

- 1 pound ground beef
- 1 can (14-1/2 ounces) Italian stewed tomatoes, cut up
- 1 can (6 ounces) tomato paste
- 1 tablespoon minced fresh parsley
- 1/2 teaspoon minced garlic
- 2 large eggs
- 1-1/2 cups 4% cottage cheese
- 1-1/2 cups ricotta cheese

- 1 cup grated Parmesan cheese
- 1 teaspoon salt
- 1 teaspoon pepper
- 6 lasagna noodles, cooked and drained
- 2 cups shredded part-skim mozzarella cheese

Direction

- Cook beef in a large skillet over medium heat until its color is not anymore pink. Let it drain before adding the parsley, tomato paste, garlic and tomatoes. Take it away from the heat.
- Whisk the ricotta cheese, cottage cheese, Parmesan cheese, pepper, eggs, and the salt in a large bowl. Prepare a greased 13x9-inch baking dish then layer the 3 noodles, 1/2 of the cottage cheese mixture, a cup of mozzarella cheese and 1/2 of the meat sauce. Follow again the same steps to make another layer.
- You can cover and store it in the freezer for 3 months. Also, you can bake it already for 30 minutes, still covered at a temperature of 375°F. Remove its cover and bake it again for 25-30 minutes and until the thermometer reads a temperature of 160°F. Set it aside for 10 minutes before cutting to serve.
- If ever you stored the lasagna in the freezer, thaw it first in the refrigerator overnight before following the same steps for baking.

Nutrition Information

- Calories: 238 calories
- Protein: 19g protein.
- Total Fat: 12g fat (7g saturated fat)
- Sodium: 552mg sodium
- Fiber: 1g fiber)
- Total Carbohydrate: 15g carbohydrate (6g sugars
- Cholesterol: 74mg cholesterol

---

265.   Power Lasagna

Serving: 8 servings. | Prep: 30mins | Cook: 40mins | Ready in:

Ingredients

- 9 whole wheat lasagna noodles
- 1 pound lean ground beef (90% lean)
- 1 medium zucchini, finely chopped
- 1 medium onion, finely chopped
- 1 medium green pepper, finely chopped
- 3 garlic cloves, minced
- 1 jar (24 ounces) meatless pasta sauce
- 1 can (14-1/2 ounces) no-salt-added diced tomatoes, drained
- 1/2 cup loosely packed basil leaves, chopped
- 2 tablespoons ground flaxseed
- 5 teaspoons Italian seasoning
- 1/4 teaspoon pepper
- 1 carton (15 ounces) fat-free ricotta cheese
- 1 package (10 ounces) frozen chopped spinach, thawed and squeezed dry
- 1 large egg, lightly beaten
- 2 tablespoons white balsamic vinegar
- 2 cups shredded part-skim mozzarella cheese
- 1/4 cup grated Parmesan cheese

Direction

- Let oven heat up to 350°. Follow noodles package instructions for the noodles. Let beef cook in a 6-quart stockpot on medium fire, add onion, zucchini, and green onion, wait until beef is cooked well with no pink in it then break into crumbles. Mix garlic in and cook for 60 seconds more. Drain.
- Add pasta sauce, basil, diced tomatoes, Italian seasoning, pepper, and flax cook while stirring. Drain noodles then wash in cold water.
- Blend in a small bowl egg, spinach, vinegar, and ricotta cheese. In a 13x9 inches baking dish grease with cooking spray, take one cup of meat mixture and then spread. On top of it, even out 3 noodles, 1 and 1/4 cups ricotta cheese mixture, 2/3 cup mozzarella cheese,

and 2 cups of meat mixture. Duplicate layers. Finish with leftover noodles, mozzarella cheese, and meat mixture. Top with Parmesan cheese.

- Let it bake with a cover for half an hour. Take off cover and let it bake for another 10 to 15 minutes until cheese melts. Wait for 10 minutes then serve.

Nutrition Information

- Calories: 392 calories
- Total Carbohydrate: 39g carbohydrate (13g sugars
- Cholesterol: 89mg cholesterol
- Protein: 32g protein. Diabetic Exchanges: 3 lean meat
- Total Fat: 12g fat (5g saturated fat)
- Sodium: 691mg sodium
- Fiber: 8g fiber)

266.   Quick 'n' Easy Lasagna

Serving: 6-8 servings. | Prep: 25mins | Cook: 35mins | Ready in:

Ingredients

- 16 lasagna noodles
- 2 pounds ground beef
- 1 jar (28 ounces) spaghetti sauce
- 1 pound process cheese (Velveeta), cubed

Direction

- Make the lasagna noodles as specified on the box directions. On medium heat, cook the beef in a big skillet until it is not pink. Drain grease. Mix in the spaghetti sauce and cook through. Rinse the noodles and drain.
- Spread about 1/3 of the cooked meat sauce in a greased 13x9 inch baking dish. Top with half of the lasagna noodles and cheese. Repeat the layering process. Add any remaining sauce on top of the dish.

- Cover the baking dish. Set the timer for 35 minutes and bake at 350°F or until bubbling.

Nutrition Information

- Calories: 625 calories
- Cholesterol: 94mg cholesterol
- Protein: 40g protein.
- Total Fat: 28g fat (14g saturated fat)
- Sodium: 1248mg sodium
- Fiber: 3g fiber)
- Total Carbohydrate: 51g carbohydrate (13g sugars

267.   Ravioli Lasagna

Serving: 6 | Prep: 10mins | Cook: 50mins | Ready in:

Ingredients

- 2 cups ricotta cheese
- 1 (10 ounce) package frozen chopped spinach - thawed, drained and squeezed dry
- 1 1/2 cups grated Romano cheese
- 2 eggs
- salt and pepper to taste
- 1/4 cup spaghetti sauce
- 1 (25 ounce) package frozen cheese ravioli
- 1/2 cup spaghetti sauce
- 1/2 cup grated Romano cheese

Direction

- Let oven warm up to 375° F or to 190°C. In an 8x8 baking dish, spray it with cooking oil then set aside.
- In a bowl, mix in together eggs, pepper, salt, spinach, ricotta cheese, and 1 1/2 cups Romano cheese.
- At the bottom of the baking dish, arrange a single layer the lasagna and level it with 1/4 cup of spaghetti sauce and place chilled raviolis. Level about one cup ricotta mixture on top of the ravioli. Make three more layers

with chilled raviolis on top. Place half cup spaghetti sauce spreading it on top and then top leftover half a cup of Romano cheese. Use aluminum foil to cover the dish.

- Let it bake in a warm up oven for 40 minutes. When the casserole forms bubbles, take off the aluminum foil and let it bake for 10 minutes more until cheese turns brown. Allow it to cool for 10 minutes then serve.

Nutrition Information

- Calories: 496 calories;
- Total Carbohydrate: 45.2
- Cholesterol: 150
- Protein: 30.2
- Total Fat: 22
- Sodium: 922

268.   Saucy Skillet Lasagna

Serving: 8 servings. | Prep: 5mins | Cook: 25mins | Ready in:

Ingredients

- 1 pound ground beef
- 1 can (14-1/2 ounces) diced tomatoes, undrained
- 2 large eggs, lightly beaten
- 1-1/2 cups ricotta cheese
- 4 cups marinara sauce
- 1 package (9 ounces) no-cook lasagna noodles
- 1 cup shredded part-skim mozzarella cheese, optional

Direction

- Using a large skillet, cook beef in medium heat for 6 to 8 minutes until no longer pink, smash into smaller crumbles; let it drain. Place in a large bowl and add in tomatoes. In a small bowl, mix ricotta cheese and eggs. Put 1 cup of the meat mixture back in a skillet, spread out evenly. Place in a layer 1 cup ricotta mixture,

half of the pasta (cut to fit), 1 1/2 cups marinara sauce. Repeat the layers and put the remaining marinara sauce on top.

- Let it boil and lower down the heat, let it simmer with cover for 15-17 min. Until pasta are soft. Take out from the heat. Can be sprinkled with mozzarella cheese if desired. Let it set for 2 min. until cheese melts.

Nutrition Information

- Calories: 430 calories
- Protein: 27g protein.
- Total Fat: 18g fat (8g saturated fat)
- Sodium: 750mg sodium
- Fiber: 4g fiber)
- Total Carbohydrate: 41g carbohydrate (11g sugars
- Cholesterol: 108mg cholesterol

269.   Shortcut Lasagna

Serving: 12 | Prep: 15mins | Cook: 45mins | Ready in:

Ingredients

- 1 pound ground beef
- 2 teaspoons minced garlic
- 1 (26 ounce) jar spaghetti sauce
- 1/2 cup water
- 1 (12 ounce) container cottage cheese
- 1 egg, lightly beaten
- 1 1/2 teaspoons ground black pepper
- 8 lasagna noodles
- 1 (10 ounce) package frozen chopped spinach, thawed and drained
- 1 (8 ounce) package shredded mozzarella cheese
- 1/2 cup grated Parmesan cheese

Direction

- In a 2-quart microwaveable bowl, put in garlic and crumbled beef. Put in the microwave set on high setting and heat for about 6 minutes until beef is not pink. Mix then drain excess oil from the beef. Mix in the water and spaghetti sauce.

- In a separate bowl, mix black pepper, cottage cheese and eggs together.
- In a 9x13-inch pan, put 1/2 cup of the meat sauce evenly on the bottom. Put a layer of noodles and cottage cheese mixture on top of the meat sauce. Top with 1/2 the spinach, 1/2 the meat sauce, and 1/2 of the mozzarella cheese. Do the whole layering process again with remaining ingredients.
- Use a durable plastic wrap to cover the baking dish then put in the microwave set on high heat and heat for 8 minutes. Lower the microwave setting to medium and continue to heat for 30-32 minutes or until the cheese melts and the noodles are soft, occasionally turn the baking dish. Put Parmesan cheese on top and let the lasagna cool down for 15 minutes, slice then serve while still warm.

Nutrition Information

- Calories: 282 calories;
- Cholesterol: 57
- Protein: 20.3
- Total Fat: 12.1
- Sodium: 576
- Total Carbohydrate: 22.8

270.   Simple Mexican Lasagna

Serving: 9 servings. | Prep: 15mins | Cook: 60mins | Ready in:

Ingredients

- 1 pound lean ground beef (90% lean)
- 1 can (16 ounces) fat-free refried beans
- 2 teaspoons dried oregano
- 1 teaspoon ground cumin
- 3/4 teaspoon garlic powder

- 9 uncooked lasagna noodles
- 1 jar (16 ounces) salsa
- 2 cups water
- 2 cups reduced-fat sour cream
- 1 can (2-1/4 ounces) sliced ripe olives, drained
- 1 cup shredded reduced-fat Mexican cheese blend
- 1/2 cup thinly sliced green onions

Direction

- Using a non-stick skillet. Cook beef in medium heat until no longer pink. Drain. Mix in oregano, refried beans, cumin and garlic powder. Heat thoroughly.
- In a 13x9 in. baking pan, coat with cooking spray. Place 3 pasta, cover with half of the meat mixture. Repeat the layers. Top with the last pasta. Mix water and salsa; pour over the pasta.
- Cover and let it bake at 350 degrees F for an hour to 70 minutes until pasta is soft. Pour sour cream, spread and drizzle with olives, onions and cheese.

Nutrition Information

- Calories: 355 calories
- Total Carbohydrate: 35g carbohydrate (7g sugars
- Cholesterol: 51mg cholesterol
- Protein: 24g protein. Diabetic Exchanges: 2 starch
- Total Fat: 12g fat (7g saturated fat)
- Sodium: 655mg sodium
- Fiber: 6g fiber)

271.   Skillet Bow Tie Lasagna

Serving: 4 servings. | Prep: 5mins | Cook: 35mins | Ready in:

Ingredients

- 1 pound ground beef

- 1 small onion, chopped
- 1 garlic clove, minced
- 1 can (14-1/2 ounces) diced tomatoes, undrained
- 1-1/2 cups water
- 1 can (6 ounces) tomato paste
- 1 tablespoon dried parsley flakes
- 2 teaspoons dried oregano
- 1 teaspoon salt
- 2-1/2 cups uncooked bow tie pasta
- 3/4 cup 4% cottage cheese
- 1/4 cup grated Parmesan cheese

Direction

- Put onion, garlic and beef in a big frying pan and sauté until the beef is brown in color, drain excess oil. Mix in the water, tomatoes, tomato paste, salt, parsley and oregano. Add in the pasta and let it boil. Lower the heat and let it simmer with the lid cover on for 20 to 25 minutes or until the pasta is soft, stir once.
- Mix all the cheese ingredients in a small bowl and put dollops of the cheese mixture on top of the pasta. Cover and cook for 5 more minutes.

Nutrition Information

- Calories:
- Sodium:
- Fiber:
- Total Carbohydrate:
- Cholesterol:
- Protein:
- Total Fat:

272.   Skillet Lasagna

Serving: 6-8 servings. | Prep: 25mins | Cook: 40mins | Ready in:

Ingredients

- 1-1/2 pounds lean ground beef (90% lean)
- 1 small onion, chopped
- 1 medium green pepper, chopped
- 1 jar (24 ounces) spaghetti sauce with mushrooms
- 1 teaspoon dried oregano
- 1 teaspoon dried basil
- 6 lasagna noodles, cooked and rinsed
- 3 cups shredded mozzarella cheese
- 1/2 cup grated Parmesan cheese

Direction

- Use a Dutch oven to cook beef, pepper and onion until brown. Drain excess fat. Add in spaghetti sauce, basil and oregano. Let it simmer without cover, 10-15 minutes.
- In a 10-inch pan, place 1/4 cup of meat sauce. Arrange 3 pasta noodles on top, cut to fit if necessary. Continue layering with 1/2 remaining sauce and 1/2 mozzarella and parmesan cheeses.
- Place the remaining pasta noodles, meat sauce and parmesan cheese on top.
- Put cover on and cook over medium heat 3 minutes. Turn to low heat and let it cook 35 minutes. Drizzle on remaining mozzarella and let it sit 10 minutes with cover slightly ajar.

Nutrition Information

- Calories: 395 calories
- Cholesterol: 78mg cholesterol
- Protein: 31g protein.
- Total Fat: 18g fat (9g saturated fat)
- Sodium: 842mg sodium
- Fiber: 3g fiber)
- Total Carbohydrate: 29g carbohydrate (10g sugars

273. Slow Cooker Cheesy White Lasagna

Serving: 8 servings. | Prep: 30mins | Cook: 03hours00mins | Ready in:

Ingredients

- 1 pound ground chicken or beef
- 2 teaspoons canola oil
- 1-3/4 cups sliced fresh mushrooms
- 1 medium onion, chopped
- 2 medium carrots, chopped
- 2 garlic cloves, minced
- 2 teaspoons Italian seasoning
- 3/4 teaspoon salt
- 1/2 teaspoon pepper
- 1/2 cup white wine or chicken broth
- 1 cup half-and-half cream
- 4 ounces cream cheese, softened
- 1 cup shredded white cheddar cheese
- 1 cup shredded Gouda cheese
- 1 large egg, beaten
- 1-1/2 cups (12 ounces) 2% cottage cheese
- 1/4 cup minced fresh basil or 4 teaspoons dried basil
- 9 no-cook lasagna noodles
- 4 cups shredded part-skim mozzarella cheese
- Additional minced fresh basil, optional

Direction

- Take a durable foil and fold it into two 18 inches square then fold into thirds. In a 6-qt. slow cooker, intersect strips on the bottom and up its side. Spray the strips with cooking oil.
- Let the chicken cook on medium heat for 6 to 8 minutes. When the chicken is no longer pink break it into crumbles. Drain if there's excess water. Put chicken aside.
- Using the same pot, warm oil on medium fire. Put onions, carrots, and mushrooms in the pot then stir and let it cook for 6-8 minutes. Once it become tender, add then Italian seasoning, pepper, and salt; cook for a minute more. Now add wine and stir. Let the wine boil for 4 to 5 minutes until level is halved. Afterwards, stir

the Gouda cheese, cheddar, cream, and cream cheese. Put chicken back into the pot. Mix basil, egg, and cottage cheese in a big bowl.

- In the slow cooker, take 1 cup of the meat mixture and spread. On top of it, place three noodles (you may break it if it won't fit), add one cup of the meat mixture, one cup mozzarella cheese, and half a cup of cottage cheese. Duplicate this process twice to form layers. Use leftover cheese and meat mixture as a topping. Let noodles cook and place cover on low heat for 3 to 4 hours. When noodles are tender, take out of slow cooker and wait for 30 minutes to cool. Top with additional basil if desired.

Nutrition Information

- Calories: 603 calories
- Total Fat: 35g fat (19g saturated fat)
- Sodium: 1086mg sodium
- Fiber: 2g fiber)
- Total Carbohydrate: 28g carbohydrate (7g sugars
- Cholesterol: 165mg cholesterol
- Protein: 40g protein.

274. Slow Cooker Sausage Lasagna

Serving: 8 servings. | Prep: 40mins | Cook: 04hours00mins | Ready in:

Ingredients

- 1 pound ground beef
- 1 pound ground mild Italian sausage
- 1 medium onion, finely chopped
- 1 garlic clove, minced
- 1 jar (24 ounces) spaghetti sauce
- 1 can (14-1/2 ounces) diced tomatoes in sauce, undrained
- 1/2 cup water
- 1 teaspoon dried basil

- 1 teaspoon dried oregano
- 1 carton (15 ounces) whole-milk ricotta cheese
- 2 large eggs, lightly beaten
- 1/2 cup grated Parmesan cheese
- 9 uncooked lasagna noodles
- 4 cups shredded part-skim mozzarella cheese
- Minced fresh basil, optional

Direction

- Use heavy-duty foil as lining along the sides of an oval 6-qt slow cooker, using cooking spray to coat the foil. Cook onion, sausage, garlic, and beef at medium heat settings in a Dutch oven for 8-10 minutes until the meat no longer appears rare, then crush the sausage and beef into crumbles, and strain. Mix tomatoes, water, herbs, and pasta sauce while stirring and allow to heat. Combine Parmesan cheese, eggs, and ricotta cheese in a small bowl. Pour 1-1/2 cups of meat sauce into bottom of prepped slow cooker and spread evenly. Layer as follows; three noodles (break to fit if necessary), 3/4 cup of ricotta mix, 1 cup of mozzarella cheese, and 2 cups of meat sauce. Continue layering steps for two more times. Scatter remainder of mozzarella cheese. Cook while covered on low heat settings until noodles are tenderized or for 3 1/2 - 4 hours. Switch off the slow cooker, and remove the insert. Leave it to one side for 15 minutes. If preferred, scatter fresh basil on top.

Nutrition Information

- Calories: 667 calories
- Fiber: 4g fiber)
- Total Carbohydrate: 41g carbohydrate (14g sugars
- Cholesterol: 164mg cholesterol
- Protein: 42g protein.
- Total Fat: 37g fat (17g saturated fat)
- Sodium: 1310mg sodium

275.   Slow Cooked Lasagna

Serving: 6 servings. | Prep: 45mins | Cook: 04hours15mins | Ready in:

Ingredients

- 1 pound ground beef
- 1 medium green pepper, chopped
- 1 medium onion, chopped
- 1 jar (24 ounces) herb and garlic pasta sauce
- 4 cups shredded part-skim mozzarella cheese
- 1 carton (15 ounces) ricotta cheese
- 1 tablespoon Italian seasoning
- 1/2 teaspoon garlic powder
- 1/2 teaspoon salt
- 1/4 teaspoon pepper
- 4 no-cook lasagna noodles
- 2 tablespoons shredded Parmesan cheese

Direction

- Sauté onion, green pepper and beef in a large pan over moderate heat. Cook until the meat is not anymore pink and then let it drain. Heat and mix in the pasta sauce. Get a large bowl and mix the Italian seasonings together with the other ingredients like salt, garlic powder, mozzarella cheese, pepper and ricotta cheese.
- In an oval 3-quart slow cooker, pour in a cup of the meat sauce. Divide 1 lasagna noodle into 3 pieces. Cover 1 1/3 noodle over the sauce. You can cut or break the noodles if you want just to fit in. Spread 2/3 cup of the meat mixture and 1 1/3 cup of cheese mixture all over its top. Make same steps twice in order to form layers. End it by spreading the remaining sauce on its top.
- Let it cook, covered, on low heat for 4 to 5 hours just until the noodles are soft. Top some Parmesan cheese and return to cooking, covered, for 15 minutes more. Before cutting into pieces, let it rest first for 10 minutes.

Nutrition Information

- Calories: 608 calories

- Sodium: 1174mg sodium
- Fiber: 4g fiber)
- Total Carbohydrate: 33g carbohydrate (17g sugars
- Cholesterol: 136mg cholesterol
- Protein: 47g protein.
- Total Fat: 32g fat (17g saturated fat)

276. Sneaky Lasagna

Serving: 10-12 servings. | Prep: 25mins | Cook: 55mins | Ready in:

Ingredients

- 2 pounds ground beef
- 1 package (16 ounces) frozen California-blend vegetables
- 2 large eggs, beaten
- 3 cups (24 ounces) 2% cottage cheese
- 2 jars (26 ounces each) spaghetti sauce
- 12 no-cook lasagna noodles
- 2 cups shredded part-skim mozzarella cheese

Direction

- On medium heat, cook beef in a Dutch oven until the meat is not pink. Prepare the veggies following the package instructions; drain. Chop the vegetables finely and move to a bowl. Mix in cottage cheese and eggs; set the mixture aside.
- Drain the beef. Mix the spaghetti sauce with the beef. In a 13-inch by 9-inch greased baking dish, pour in two cups of meat mixture and add 4 noodles on top. Slather 1/2 of the veggie mixture on the edges of the noodles. Spread two cup meat mixture and a cup of mozzarella on top. Layer 4 noodles, left veggie mixture, and two cups of meat mixture. Finish with the leftover noodles, meat mixture, and mozzarella on top.
- Bake in a 375 degrees F oven, covered, for 50mins until its temperature reaches 160 degrees F. Remove cover and bake for another

5-10 mins until the cheese melts and the dish is bubbly. Set aside for 15 mins then cut.

Nutrition Information

- Calories:
- Total Fat:
- Sodium:
- Fiber:
- Total Carbohydrate:
- Cholesterol:
- Protein:

277. Southwestern Lasagna

Serving: 12 | Prep: 1hours | Cook: 1hours45mins | Ready in:

Ingredients

- 4 cups canned crushed tomatoes
- 1 (7 ounce) can diced green chiles
- 1 (4 ounce) can diced jalapeno peppers
- 1 onion, diced
- 3 cloves garlic, minced
- 10 sprigs fresh cilantro, chopped
- 2 tablespoons ground cumin
- 2 pounds chorizo sausage
- 1 (32 ounce) container ricotta cheese
- 4 eggs, lightly beaten
- 1 (16 ounce) package Mexican style shredded four cheese blend
- 1 (8 ounce) package no-cook lasagna noodles

Direction

- Cook the green chiles, tomatoes, jalapenos, onion, cumin, garlic and cilantro in a big saucepan on medium heat until the mixture boils. Turn the heat to low and gently boil, 45-60 minutes until the onion is tender.
- Warm a big skillet on medium-high heat; add in chorizo. Mix and cook until the chorizo is

browned evenly and crumbly. Drain the fat and remove any excess grease.

- Heat an oven to 175°C (350° F). Whisk together the eggs and ricotta cheese. Set the mixture aside.
- To prepare, pour third of tomato sauce in the base of a 9x13-in. baking pan. Layer with sausage, half of remaining sauce, 1/2 of grated cheese, pasta running lengthwise, ricotta cheese mixture, and another layer of pasta. Finish with left tomato sauce and grated cheese. Use foil to cover: to avoid sticking, do not let the foil touch the cheese or coat it with cooking spray.
- Bake in the oven for half an hour. Discard the foil; bake 15-30 minutes or until the top is brown.

Nutrition Information

- Calories: 718 calories;
- Sodium: 1767
- Total Carbohydrate: 30.1
- Cholesterol: 186
- Protein: 41.5
- Total Fat: 49.7

```
278.     Spicy Lasagna Skillet
                  Dinner
```

Serving: 6 servings. | Prep: 15mins | Cook: 15mins | Ready in:

Ingredients

- 1 package (6.4 ounces) lasagna dinner mix
- 1 pound lean ground beef (90% lean)
- 1 large onion, chopped
- 1 medium green pepper, chopped
- 1 garlic clove, minced
- 1 jar (14 ounces) meatless spaghetti sauce
- 1/2 cup chunky salsa
- 1 teaspoon garlic powder
- 1 teaspoon Italian seasoning

- 1/2 teaspoon dried thyme
- 1/2 teaspoon ground cumin
- 1/4 teaspoon salt
- 1/4 teaspoon crushed red pepper flakes
- 1 cup shredded mozzarella and provolone cheese blend

Direction

- Pour water to cover 3/4 of a big saucepan and boil. Add pasta from lasagne dinner, cook while uncovered until tender, about 10 to 12 minutes.
- In the meantime, add garlic, green pepper, onion and beef to a big frying pan, cook over medium heat until the vegetables get tender and beef is not pink any longer, about 6 to 8 minutes, crumbling the beef; and drain.
- Mix in the contents of seasoning packet from the lasagna dinner, seasonings, salsa and spaghetti sauce. Boil the mixture. Lower the heat, simmer while uncovered for 5 minutes. Take away from the heat.
- Drain the pasta. Add it to the tomato mixture and mix to coat. Dredge the cheese on top, cover and let rest until the cheese melts. If you want to freeze: freeze the cheese and cooled pasta mixture in different freezer containers. When using, defrost in fridge partly overnight. Heat through in a frying pan, stirring periodically and adding some water if needed. Take away from the heat. Dredge cheese over top, cover and let rest until the cheese melts.

Nutrition Information

- Calories: 319 calories
- Total Fat: 11g fat (5g saturated fat)
- Sodium: 1403mg sodium
- Fiber: 3g fiber)
- Total Carbohydrate: 31g carbohydrate (7g sugars
- Cholesterol: 60mg cholesterol
- Protein: 24g protein.

279. Swiss Cheese Lasagna

Serving: 12 servings. | Prep: 60mins | Cook: 40mins
| Ready in:

Ingredients

- 1 pound ground beef
- 1 large onion, chopped
- 1 garlic clove, minced
- 3 cups water
- 1 can (12 ounces) tomato paste
- 2 teaspoons salt
- 1/2 to 1 teaspoon dried rosemary, crushed
- 1/4 teaspoon pepper
- 1 package (8 ounces) lasagna noodles
- 8 ounces sliced Swiss cheese
- 1-1/2 cups (12 ounces each) 4% cottage cheese
- 1/2 cup shredded part-skim mozzarella cheese

Direction

- Cook the beef, garlic and onion on moderate heat in a big skillet until meat is not pink; drain the fat. Add in the tomato paste, water, salt, pepper and rosemary. Let it boil. Lower the heat and let simmer for half an hour, without cover.
- Cook lasagna pasta following package instructions; drain the pasta. Grease a 13x 9-inch baking tray. Layer with 1/3 of meat sauce, lasagna pasta, and Swiss. Make the layers again. Place cottage cheese and left Swiss cheese, lasagna pasta and sauce on top. Drizzle on mozzarella.
- Bake at 350°, covered for half an hour. Take off cover and bake 10 to 15 minutes more until bubbling. Let it sit 10 minutes. Serve.

Nutrition Information

- Calories: 275 calories
- Sodium: 596mg sodium
- Fiber: 3g fiber)
- Total Carbohydrate: 23g carbohydrate (7g sugars
- Cholesterol: 48mg cholesterol

- Protein: 20g protein.
- Total Fat: 11g fat (7g saturated fat)

280. Taco Lasagna

Serving: 9 | Prep: 10mins | Cook: 10mins | Ready in:

Ingredients

- 11 ounces lasagna noodles
- 1 pound lean ground beef
- 24 ounces tomato sauce
- 1/2 cup water
- 1 (1 ounce) package taco seasoning mix
- 8 cups shredded Cheddar cheese
- 1/2 cup crushed tortilla chips

Direction

- In a pot, prepare salt water and bring to a boil. Cook pasta for 8 to 10 minutes, or until it becomes al dente; once cooked, drain water.
- In a skillet, cook beef over medium heat, until brown; drain. Add water, tomato sauce, and taco seasoning. Reduce heat and continue to cook for 5 minutes.
- Using a 9 x 13 baking dish, arrange ingredients as the following: noodles on the bottom layer, then meat mixture, then cheese; repeat this sequence twice more. Make sure it has 3 layers.
- Cover dish using plastic wrap and put inside microwave; cook for 10 minutes. Once done, remove from microwave, peel off cover, and let cool for 5 minutes.
- Top with tortilla chips before serving.

Nutrition Information

- Calories: 709 calories;
- Total Fat: 45.4
- Sodium: 1304
- Total Carbohydrate: 35.8
- Cholesterol: 143

- Protein: 39.3

- Sodium: 1310 mg
- Fiber: 4 g
- Saturated Fat: 7 g
- Protein: 20 g

281.   Tex Mex Lasagna

Serving: Makes 8 servings. | Prep: 10mins | Cook: | Ready in:

Ingredients

- 1 lb. ground beef
- 2 jars (16 oz. each) TACO BELL® Thick & Chunky Salsa
- 1 can (15 oz.) whole kernel corn , drained
- 12 corn tortilla s (6 inch)
- 1 pkg. (8 oz.) VELVEETA Shredded Pasteurized Prepared Cheese Product

Direction

- Preheat the oven to 375°F. In a big skillet, put in the meat and let it cook until it turns brown in color, then drain off any excess oil. Add in the corn and salsa then mix well.
- In a 12x8-inch baking dish, spread 1 cup of the prepared meat mixture with a spoon. Place a layer of half of the following over the meat layer: tortillas, remaining meat mixture and Velveeta; do the whole layering process again. Use a foil to cover the baking dish once the layering process is done.
- Put it in the preheated oven and let it bake for 20 minutes. Remove the cover from the baking dish. Keep baking the lasagna for 5 more minutes or until the mixture is thoroughly heated and the Velveeta has fully melted. If you want, you may top with Knudsen or Breakstone's sour cream before serving.

Nutrition Information

- Calories: 350
- Sugar: 7 g
- Total Carbohydrate: 35 g
- Cholesterol: 60 mg
- Total Fat: 15 g

282.   Three Cheese Lasagna

Serving: 2 casseroles (4 servings each). | Prep: 25mins | Cook: 15mins | Ready in:

Ingredients

- 2 pounds ground beef
- 1/2 cup chopped onion
- 1 package (6.4 ounces) lasagna dinner mix
- 2-1/4 cups hot water
- 2 cans (14-1/2 ounces each) diced tomatoes, undrained
- 1 package (10 ounces) frozen chopped spinach, thawed and squeezed dry
- 1 cup sliced fresh mushrooms
- 1/2 cup chopped green onions
- 1 cup 4% cottage cheese
- 1/4 cup grated Parmesan cheese
- 1-1/2 cups shredded part-skim mozzarella cheese

Direction

- Oven must be preheated to 350°F. In medium heat, cook the onion and beef for about 10-12 minutes or until the meat is not pink anymore in a large skillet then drain. Blend in water, tomatoes, mushrooms, onions, spinach, pasta from dinner mix and contents of seasoning mix and let it boil.
- Lessen the heat and then cover and simmer the skillet for about 10 to 13 minutes or until pasta softens. After that, blend in Parmesan and cottage cheese.
- In a two greased 8-inch square baking dishes, transfer the contents of large skillet and drizzle with mozzarella cheese. You can store one casserole for up to three months, just keep it frozen and covered.

- Bake the remaining casserole, covered, for 15 to 20 minutes until the cheese is melted and the casserole is bubbly.
- In using frozen casserole: Thirty minutes before baking, remove from freezer (don't defrost). At 350°F, let it bake, don't remove the cover, for 60 minutes. Then remove the cover and bake again until heated through for another 15 to 20 minutes.

Nutrition Information

- Calories: 384 calories
- Protein: 34g protein.
- Total Fat: 16g fat (8g saturated fat)
- Sodium: 1012mg sodium
- Fiber: 4g fiber)
- Total Carbohydrate: 27g carbohydrate (9g sugars
- Cholesterol: 76mg cholesterol

---

283. Tomato French Bread Lasagna

Serving: 10 servings. | Prep: 30mins | Cook: 40mins | Ready in:

Ingredients

- 1 pound ground beef
- 1/3 cup chopped onion
- 1/3 cup chopped celery
- 2 garlic cloves, minced
- 14 slices French bread (1/2 inch thick)
- 4 large tomatoes, sliced 1/2 inch thick
- 1 teaspoon dried basil
- 1 teaspoon dried parsley flakes
- 1 teaspoon dried oregano
- 1 teaspoon dried rosemary, crushed
- 1 teaspoon garlic powder
- 3/4 teaspoon salt
- 1/2 teaspoon pepper
- 2 teaspoons olive oil, divided
- 3 tablespoons butter

- 3 tablespoons all-purpose flour
- 1-1/2 cups whole milk
- 1/3 cup grated Parmesan cheese
- 2 cups shredded mozzarella cheese

Direction

- Let beef, celery, garlic and onion cook over medium fire in a skillet, wait until beef is no longer pink, then discard excess fat and put aside. Let bread to toast, then arrange 10 slices at the bottom of a 13x9-inch baking dish without grease. Level it with half tomatoes and half of the meat mixture.
- Mix the seasonings. Halve the seasoning and dash over tomatoes. Sprinkle with one teaspoon oil. Crush leftover bread and top it over. Duplicate layers.
- Dissolve butter in a saucepan over medium fire, stir in flour until it becomes smooth. Slowly mix in milk and let it boil with steady stirring. Allow it to cook for two minutes until it becomes thick and bubbly. Take off from the heat then mix parmesan. Transfer over casserole. Add mozzarella as topping. Let it bake without cover at 350°F for 40 to 45 minutes until cheese turns golden brown and bubbly.

Nutrition Information

- Calories: 280 calories
- Protein: 17g protein.
- Total Fat: 16g fat (8g saturated fat)
- Sodium: 500mg sodium
- Fiber: 2g fiber)
- Total Carbohydrate: 17g carbohydrate (4g sugars
- Cholesterol: 56mg cholesterol

---

284. Tortilla Lasagna

Serving: 8 servings. | Prep: 25mins | Cook: 50mins | Ready in:

Ingredients

- 1 pound ground beef
- 1 cup water
- 1 envelope taco seasoning
- 1/2 teaspoon garlic powder
- 1/4 teaspoon cayenne pepper
- 1-1/2 cups (12 ounces) sour cream
- 1-1/2 teaspoons chili powder
- 2 cups shredded Monterey Jack cheese
- 2 cups shredded cheddar cheese
- 1 tablespoon cornmeal
- 10 flour tortillas (6 inches)
- 1 cup salsa
- 1 small onion, sliced

Direction

- On medium heat, cook beef in a big pan until the meat is not pink; drain. Mix in cayenne, water, garlic powder, and taco seasoning; boil. Lower heat and let it simmer for 10mins without cover.
- Mix chili powder and sour cream together in a small bowl. Mix the cheeses together in a big bowl; put aside. In a 13-inch by 9-inch baking dish, sprinkle cornmeal.
- Place 5 overlapping tortillas in the base of the dish; pour in half cup salsa. Spread 1/2 of the meat blend, onion, and sour cream blend on top. Top with 1 1/2 cup cheese mixture. Repeat process.
- Bake in a 375 degrees F oven, uncovered, for 40 mins. Add the left cheese mixture. Bake for another 10 mins until the cheese melts. Set aside for 10 mins then cut.

Nutrition Information

- Calories: 568 calories
- Protein: 29g protein.
- Total Fat: 36g fat (21g saturated fat)
- Sodium: 1180mg sodium
- Fiber: 0 fiber)
- Total Carbohydrate: 27g carbohydrate (4g sugars
- Cholesterol: 125mg cholesterol

---

285. Traditional Lasagna

Serving: 12 servings. | Prep: 30mins | Cook: 01hours10mins | Ready in:

Ingredients

- 1 pound ground beef
- 3/4 pound Jones No Sugar Pork Sausage Roll sausage
- 3 cans (8 ounces each) tomato sauce
- 2 cans (6 ounces each) tomato paste
- 2 garlic cloves, minced
- 2 teaspoons sugar
- 1 teaspoon Italian seasoning
- 1/2 to 1 teaspoon salt
- 1/4 to 1/2 teaspoon pepper
- 3 large eggs
- 3 tablespoons minced fresh parsley
- 3 cups 4% small-curd cottage cheese
- 1 carton (8 ounces) ricotta cheese
- 1/2 cup grated Parmesan cheese
- 9 lasagna noodles, cooked and drained
- 6 slices provolone cheese (about 6 ounces)
- 3 cups shredded part-skim mozzarella cheese, divided

Direction

- Cook and grind the sausage and beef in a large pan over medium heat. Cook until it is no longer pink before draining the fats. Mix in the next 7 ingredients and bring it to boil. Then let it simmer in a low heat for 60 minutes. Make sure that it is uncovered so that you can stir it from time to time. You can put salt and pepper according to your taste.
- Slowly whisk the eggs in a large bowl and mix in some parsley, together with the cheeses - cottage, ricotta and Parmesan.
- Set your oven to preheat at 375°F. Prepare an ungreased 13x9 baking pan and lay there a cup of meat sauce. Make a layer of these following ingredients: 3 noodles, provolone

cheese, 2 cups of cottage cheese mixture, and a cup of mozzarella. Layer it again with 3 noodles, 2 cups of meat sauce, remaining cottage cheese mixture and another cup of mozzarella. End the layers by putting the remaining noodles together with the meat sauce and mozzarella. Layer until the pan is all full.

- Put a cover and let it bake for 50 minutes. Uncover it afterwards so that you can bake it until all the parts are warm enough for 20 minutes. Set aside for 15 minutes before cutting it. Serve.

Nutrition Information

- Calories: 503 calories
- Total Carbohydrate: 30g carbohydrate (9g sugars
- Cholesterol: 136mg cholesterol
- Protein: 36g protein.
- Total Fat: 27g fat (13g saturated fat)
- Sodium: 1208mg sodium
- Fiber: 2g fiber)

---

286.   Turkey Ravioli Lasagna

Serving: 12 servings. | Prep: 30mins | Cook: 35mins | Ready in:

Ingredients

- 1 pound ground turkey
- 1/2 teaspoon garlic powder
- Salt and pepper to taste
- 1 cup grated carrots
- 1 cup sliced fresh mushrooms
- 1 tablespoon olive oil
- 3-1/2 cups spaghetti sauce
- 1 package (25 ounces) frozen cheese ravioli, cooked and drained
- 3 cups shredded part-skim mozzarella cheese
- 1/2 cup grated Parmesan cheese
- Minced fresh parsley, optional

Direction

- Cook the turkey in a large pan over moderate heat. Cook until it is no longer pink and then drain. Add in some salt, pepper and garlic powder then set aside for later use.
- Sauté the mushrooms and carrots in a large skillet with oil until already soft. Add the spaghetti sauce in the pan; stir. Grease your 13x9-inch baking pan and lay half cup of the sauce. Arrange 1/2 of the ravioli, spaghetti sauce mixture, turkey, and cheeses to form layers twice. You can top it with parsley if you want.
- Let it bake covered for 25-30 minutes at a temperature of 375°F until bubbling. Remove the cover and bake it again for another 10 more minutes. Let it rest for 15 minutes before serving it.

Nutrition Information

- Calories:
- Protein:
- Total Fat:
- Sodium:
- Fiber:
- Total Carbohydrate:
- Cholesterol:

---

287.   Two Squash Lasagna

Serving: 8-10 servings. | Prep: 25mins | Cook: 50mins | Ready in:

Ingredients

- 1 pound ground beef
- 1 small onion, chopped
- 1 can (28 ounces) spaghetti sauce
- 1/2 teaspoon fennel seed, crushed
- 1 teaspoon salt
- 1/2 teaspoon pepper

- 2 cups shredded part-skim mozzarella cheese, divided
- 2 cups (16 ounces) small-curd cottage cheese or ricotta cheese
- 2 large eggs, beaten
- 2 medium zucchini, sliced lengthwise into 1/2-inch strips
- 4 tablespoons all-purpose flour
- 1 small unpeeled yellow squash, shredded
- 1/4 cup grated Parmesan cheese

Direction

- First, cook beef and onion in a large pan over a medium heat (cook until the beef is no longer pink). When done, make sure to drain before mixing the fennel seed, pepper, salt and the spaghetti sauce. Let it rest.
- Blend ricotta or cottage cheese, eggs, and a cup of mozzarella cheese in a small bowl. Grease a 13x9-inch baking pan, then add half of the zucchini into it. Mix in 1/2 of flour and put 1/2 of the meat sauce and 1/2 of the cheese mixture on top. Repeat steps and layers for the zucchini, flour, meat sauce and cheese mixture. Mix all what's left of mozzarella with the yellow squash and set it over the cheese mixture. Drizzle the layers with some Parmesan cheese.
- Lastly, bake it at 375°F for about 50 minutes until the zucchini is already soft. Be reminded to leave it for 10 minutes before serving.

Nutrition Information

- Calories: 286 calories
- Protein: 24g protein.
- Total Fat: 14g fat (7g saturated fat)
- Sodium: 972mg sodium
- Fiber: 2g fiber)
- Total Carbohydrate: 15g carbohydrate (9g sugars
- Cholesterol: 91mg cholesterol

288. Weekday Lasagna

Serving: 9 servings. | Prep: 35mins | Cook: 60mins | Ready in:

Ingredients

- 1 pound lean ground beef (90% lean)
- 1 small onion, chopped
- 1 can (28 ounces) crushed tomatoes
- 1-3/4 cups water
- 1 can (6 ounces) tomato paste
- 1 envelope spaghetti sauce mix
- 1 large egg, lightly beaten
- 2 cups fat-free cottage cheese
- 2 tablespoons grated Parmesan cheese
- 6 uncooked lasagna noodles
- 1 cup shredded part-skim mozzarella cheese

Direction

- Cook onion and beef on medium heat in a big pot until meat is not pink; drain excess grease. Mix in spaghetti sauce mix, water, tomatoes, and tomato paste. Heat to a boil. Cover, decrease heat, simmer, and stir occasionally for 15-20 minutes.
- Mix Parmesan, egg, and cottage cheese in a small bowl. Spread 2 cups of meat sauce in a greased 13x9-in. pan. Layer three noodles, half the cottage cheese mixture, and half the remaining meat. Repeat the layers.
- Cover; bake in a 350-degree oven until thermometer says 160 degrees, 50 minutes. Remove cover; sprinkle on mozzarella. Bake until bubbling and cheese melts, 10-15 minutes. Let it cool for 15 minutes before slicing.

Nutrition Information

- Calories: 280 calories
- Total Carbohydrate: 29g carbohydrate (6g sugars
- Cholesterol: 65mg cholesterol
- Protein: 25g protein. Diabetic Exchanges: 3 lean meat

- Total Fat: 7g fat (3g saturated fat)
- Sodium: 804mg sodium
- Fiber: 4g fiber)

289. Where's The Squash Lasagna

Serving: 12 servings. | Prep: 40mins | Cook: 60mins | Ready in:

Ingredients

- 1 pound ground beef
- 2 large zucchini (about 1 pound), shredded
- 3/4 cup chopped onion
- 2 garlic cloves, minced
- 1 can (14-1/2 ounces) stewed tomatoes
- 2 cups water
- 1 can (12 ounces) tomato paste
- 1 tablespoon minced fresh parsley
- 1-1/2 teaspoons salt
- 1 teaspoon sugar
- 1/2 teaspoon dried oregano
- 1/2 teaspoon pepper
- 9 lasagna noodles, cooked, rinsed and drained
- 1 carton (15 ounces) ricotta cheese
- 2 cups shredded part-skim mozzarella cheese
- 1 cup grated Parmesan cheese

Direction

- Cook the beef, onion, and zucchini in a pan on medium heat until meat is not pink. Put in garlic and cook one minute more. Drain excess grease.
- Mix tomatoes, with lid on, in an electric blender or food processor until smooth. Add to beef mixture. Pour in the tomato paste, water, seasonings and parsley. Let it boil. Turn heat down and let simmer without the lid for half an hour, stirring every now and then.
- Slightly grease a 13x 9-inch baking tray, pour in 1 cup meat sauce. Layer with 3 pastas, 1/3 of meat sauce, 1/2 of ricotta cheese, 1/3 of Parmesan and mozzarella cheeses. Make the

layers again. Finish with the remaining pasta, meat sauce, and the cheeses.
- Cover the tray and bake 45 minutes at 350°. Remove cover and bake 15 minutes more until bubbling. Let it sit for 15 minutes before slicing.

Nutrition Information

- Calories: 309 calories
- Cholesterol: 53mg cholesterol
- Protein: 21g protein.
- Total Fat: 13g fat (8g saturated fat)
- Sodium: 642mg sodium
- Fiber: 3g fiber)
- Total Carbohydrate: 27g carbohydrate (10g sugars

290. White Sauce Lasagna

Serving: 14-16 servings. | Prep: 25mins | Cook: 30mins | Ready in:

Ingredients

- 1 pound ground beef
- 1 cup finely chopped celery
- 1 cup finely chopped onion
- 1 garlic clove, minced
- 1 cup half-and-half cream
- 3 ounces cream cheese, cubed
- 2 teaspoons dried basil
- 1 teaspoon dried oregano
- 1/2 teaspoon Italian seasoning
- 1/2 teaspoon salt
- 1/2 teaspoon pepper
- 2 cups shredded cheddar cheese
- 7 ounces shredded Gouda cheese
- 2 cups (16 ounces) 4% cottage cheese
- 1 large egg, lightly beaten
- 8 ounces lasagna noodles, cooked and drained
- 12 ounces sliced or 3 cups shredded part-skim mozzarella cheese
- Minced fresh parsley

Direction

- Onions, beef, and celery are cooked in a large skillet at medium heat until the meat is no longer rare. Garlic is then added. It is cooked for another minute or until the garlic tenderized. Add in cream cheese, basil, Italian seasoning, oregano, cream, salt and pepper to stir evenly over low heat settings. Slowly mix Gouda cheese and cheddar into the mixture until cheese has melted; lift from heat. Prepare a mix of egg and farmer cheese to leave to one side. Grease a 13x9-in baking tray and line with half of the lasagna noodles. Cover with one half of the meat sauce, one half of the cottage cheese mixture, and one half of the mozzarella mixture. Continue the layering until the ingredients are finished. Leave the tray uncovered while baking for 30-35 minutes at 375 degrees. Scatter parsley on top. Set aside to cool 10 minutes before serving.

Nutrition Information

- Calories: 329 calories
- Sodium: 526mg sodium
- Fiber: 1g fiber)
- Total Carbohydrate: 15g carbohydrate (3g sugars
- Cholesterol: 87mg cholesterol
- Protein: 24g protein.
- Total Fat: 19g fat (12g saturated fat)

------

291.   Ziti Lasagna

Serving: 3 servings. | Prep: 15mins | Cook: 20mins | Ready in:

Ingredients

- 2 cups uncooked ziti or small tube pasta
- 1/2 pound lean ground beef
- 1/4 cup chopped onion
- 1/4 cup chopped green pepper

- 1 can (8 ounces) tomato sauce
- 1/2 teaspoon Italian seasoning
- 1/4 teaspoon garlic powder
- Dash pepper
- 3/4 cup ricotta cheese
- 1 cup shredded part-skim mozzarella cheese

Direction

- Cook ziti following package instructions. Stir the onion, green pepper and beef in a pan on medium heat until meat is not pink; drain the excess grease. Add in the Italian seasoning, tomato sauce, pepper and garlic powder. Stir and cook until cooked completely, 3 minutes.
- Drain the pasta. Pour 1/2 of meat sauce in a 1-quart pan sprayed with cooking spray. Layer with half each of ziti, ricotta cheese, and mozzarella. Make the layers again. Bake without cover at 350° until baked thoroughly, 20 to 25 minutes. Let it sit 5 minutes then serve.

Nutrition Information

- Calories: 437 calories
- Sodium: 613mg sodium
- Fiber: 2g fiber)
- Total Carbohydrate: 38g carbohydrate (8g sugars
- Cholesterol: 83mg cholesterol
- Protein: 35g protein.
- Total Fat: 15g fat (8g saturated fat)

------

292.   Zucchini Beef Lasagna

Serving: 12 servings. | Prep: 50mins | Cook: 30mins | Ready in:

Ingredients

- 1 pound lean ground beef (90% lean)
- 2 garlic cloves, minced
- 2 cans (8 ounces each) no-salt-added tomato sauce

- 1/2 cup water
- 1 can (6 ounces) tomato paste
- 2 bay leaves
- 1 teaspoon minced fresh parsley
- 1 teaspoon Italian seasoning
- 1 package (16 ounces) lasagna noodles, cooked, rinsed and drained
- 1 cup (8 ounces) fat-free cottage cheese
- 1 small zucchini, sliced and cooked
- 1 cup (8 ounces) reduced-fat sour cream

Direction

- Prepare a large pan and cook on a moderate heat the beef and garlic until the beef is not anymore pinkish. Let it drain before mixing in water, bay leaves, tomato sauce, tomato paste, Italian seasoning and parsley. Let it boil before reducing the heat. Simmer while it's uncovered for about 30-40 minutes.
- Remove the bay leaves. Prepare a 13x9-inch baking pan and coat it with a cooking spray. Lay in the pan half cup of the meat sauce. Fit five noodles on the pan (cut it if necessary). Place cottage cheese and cover the layer with zucchini, five noodles, and half of the meat sauce. Cover again with sour cream and five noodles. Top the layers with the remaining meat sauce and noodles.
- At the temperature of 350°F, bake it, uncovered, for about 30-35 minutes until heated enough. Set aside for 15 minutes before cutting and serving.

Nutrition Information

- Calories: 187 calories
- Sodium: 270mg sodium
- Fiber: 2g fiber)
- Total Carbohydrate: 19g carbohydrate (0 sugars
- Cholesterol: 21mg cholesterol
- Protein: 14g protein. Diabetic Exchanges: 1 starch
- Total Fat: 8g fat (0 saturated fat)

Chapter 4: Ground Beef Meatball Recipes

***

┌─────────────────────────────┐
│ **293.**   **All Day Meatballs** │
└─────────────────────────────┘

Serving: 6 servings. | Prep: 25mins | Cook: 06hours00mins | Ready in:

Ingredients

- 1 cup milk
- 3/4 cup quick-cooking oats
- 3 tablespoons finely chopped onion
- 1-1/2 teaspoons salt
- 1-1/2 pounds ground beef
- 1 cup ketchup
- 1/2 cup water
- 3 tablespoons cider vinegar
- 2 tablespoons sugar

Direction

- In a large bowl, combine the first four ingredients. Crumble beef over mixture and mix well. Form into balls, 1-inch each. In a 5-quart slow cooker, place those balls.
- In a small bowl, combine the water, ketchup, sugar and vinegar. Pour mixture over meatballs. Cook while covered on low mode for approximately 6 to 8 hours until meat is no longer pink.

Nutrition Information

- Calories: 346 calories
- Protein: 26g protein.
- Total Fat: 16g fat (6g saturated fat)

- Sodium: 1139mg sodium
- Fiber: 2g fiber)
- Total Carbohydrate: 24g carbohydrate (11g sugars
- Cholesterol: 81mg cholesterol

294.   Apple Meatballs

Serving: 72 meatballs. | Prep: 45mins | Cook: 30mins | Ready in:

Ingredients

- 1 egg
- 2 tablespoons butter, melted
- 1/4 cup crushed seasoned stuffing
- 1 envelope onion soup mix
- 2-1/2 pounds lean ground beef
- SAUCE:
- 2 bottles (18 ounces each) barbecue sauce
- 1 jar (12 ounces) apple jelly
- 1 can (8 ounces) tomato sauce

Direction

- Combine the first four ingredients in a large bowl. Crumble beef over the mixture; mix properly. Form into 1-in. balls.
- Brown the meatballs in a large skillet; drain. Place on a greased 3-qt. baking dish. Combine the sauce ingredients in a large saucepan; allow to boil. Lower the heat; simmer for 10 minutes. Pour over the meatballs.
- Bake with a cover at 325° till the meat is not pink anymore or 30 minutes.

Nutrition Information

- Calories: 304 calories
- Total Fat: 12g fat (5g saturated fat)
- Sodium: 450mg sodium
- Fiber: 0 fiber)
- Total Carbohydrate: 26g carbohydrate (21g sugars

- Cholesterol: 97mg cholesterol
- Protein: 23g protein.

295.   Apricot Meatballs

Serving: 4 servings. | Prep: 30mins | Cook: 30mins | Ready in:

Ingredients

- 1 egg
- 1 cup soft bread crumbs
- 1/4 cup chopped onion
- 1 teaspoon salt
- 1 pound ground beef
- 1/2 cup apricot preserves
- 1/4 cup barbecue sauce

Direction

- Mix the first 4 ingredients in a bowl. Crumble the beef over the blend and stir well. Form into balls of 1 inch. Brown meatballs in several batches in a skillet; drain. Move to a greased baking dish of 2-quart. Mix in preserves and barbecue sauce; pour over meatballs. Cover and bake for 30 minutes at 350°, until the meat is not pink anymore.

Nutrition Information

- Calories: 353 calories
- Sodium: 803mg sodium
- Fiber: 1g fiber)
- Total Carbohydrate: 29g carbohydrate (27g sugars
- Cholesterol: 128mg cholesterol
- Protein: 25g protein.
- Total Fat: 16g fat (6g saturated fat)

296.   Autumn Meatballs

Serving: 20 meatballs. | Prep: 15mins | Cook: 60mins | Ready in:

Ingredients

- 2 eggs
- 1 cup dry bread crumbs
- 1 cup shredded peeled tart apple
- 1/4 cup shredded cheddar cheese
- 1 garlic clove, minced
- 1 teaspoon salt
- 1/4 teaspoon pepper
- 1/4 teaspoon ground nutmeg
- 1 pound lean ground beef
- 1-3/4 cups tomato juice
- 3/4 cup ketchup
- 1/2 cup chopped celery
- 1/2 teaspoon Worcestershire sauce

Direction

- Combine the first eight ingredients in a bowl. Crumble beef over mixture and mix well. Form into balls of 1 and a half inch in size. In a greased baking dish of 2-quart in size, place those balls. Combine the ketchup, tomato juice, Worcestershire sauce and celery; pour over meatballs. Bake while covering and at 350° for 1 hour or until meat is not pink anymore.

Nutrition Information

- Calories: 427 calories
- Protein: 31g protein.
- Total Fat: 15g fat (6g saturated fat)
- Sodium: 1884mg sodium
- Fiber: 3g fiber)
- Total Carbohydrate: 42g carbohydrate (13g sugars
- Cholesterol: 183mg cholesterol

297.   BBQ Sauce Meatballs

Serving: 2 dozen. | Prep: 20mins | Cook: 07hours00mins | Ready in:

Ingredients

- 1 large egg, beaten
- 1/2 cup shredded Colby-Monterey Jack cheese
- 1/4 cup seasoned bread crumbs
- 1/4 cup finely chopped onion
- 2 pounds ground beef
- SAUCE:
- 2 cups ketchup
- 2 tablespoons prepared mustard
- 1 tablespoon brown sugar
- 1 tablespoon cider vinegar
- 1 tablespoon lemon juice
- 1 tablespoon soy sauce

Direction

- Mix the onion, bread crumbs, cheese, and egg in a large bowl. Crumble beef over the mixture and stir well. Form into 1 to 1/2-inch balls. Put to a 3-qt slow cooker.
- Mix the sauce ingredients in a small bowl; put over meatballs. Cook for 7 to 8 hours on low, covered, or until meat is no longer pink.

Nutrition Information

- Calories: 109 calories
- Total Fat: 5g fat (2g saturated fat)
- Sodium: 363mg sodium
- Fiber: 0 fiber)
- Total Carbohydrate: 7g carbohydrate (6g sugars
- Cholesterol: 33mg cholesterol
- Protein: 8g protein.

Serving: 3 dozen. | Prep: 25mins | Cook: 10mins | Ready in:

Ingredients

- 1 large egg
- 1 envelope onion soup mix
- 1 pound ground beef
- 2 tablespoons all-purpose flour
- 2 tablespoons 2% milk
- 1 cup shredded cheddar cheese
- 4 bacon strips, cooked and crumbled
- COATING:
- 2 large eggs
- 1 cup crushed saltines (about 30 crackers)
- 5 tablespoons canola oil

Direction

- In a large bowl, combine soup mix and egg together. Crumble beef over mixture then stir well. Divide into 36 portions; put aside. In a different big bowl, combine milk and flour till smooth. Add bacon and cheese; stir properly.
- Form cheese mixture into 36 balls. Shape around each cheese ball with one beef portion. Beat the eggs in a shallow bowl. In another bowl, add cracker crumbs. Dip meatballs into egg, and coat with crumbs.
- In a large skillet over medium heat, cook meatballs for 10-12 minutes in oil, or till the meat is no longer pink and coating becomes golden brown.

Nutrition Information

- Calories: 222 calories
- Total Carbohydrate: 7g carbohydrate (1g sugars
- Cholesterol: 90mg cholesterol
- Protein: 13g protein.
- Total Fat: 16g fat (5g saturated fat)
- Sodium: 396mg sodium
- Fiber: 0 fiber)

Serving: 60 meatballs. | Prep: 25mins | Cook: 30mins | Ready in:

Ingredients

- 10 bacon strips, diced
- 2 eggs
- 1/3 cup tomato paste
- 1-1/2 cups soft bread crumbs
- 1/3 cup minced fresh parsley
- 2 tablespoons chopped slivered almonds
- 1 tablespoon dried oregano
- 1 tablespoon salt
- 1-1/2 teaspoons pepper
- 2 pounds ground beef
- 1 pound fresh mushrooms, sliced
- 1 medium onion, chopped
- 2 cans (10-3/4 ounces each) condensed cream of mushroom soup, undiluted
- 1 can (10-1/2 ounces) beef consomme

Direction

- Cook bacon in a big skillet. Use a slotted spoon to transfer bacon onto paper towels; drain. Keep drippings in the skillet.
- In a big bowl, combine bacon, pepper, salt, oregano, almonds, parsley, crumbs, tomato paste and eggs. Crumble beef and add to the mixture, combine well.
- Form into 1-inch balls. In drippings, brown meatballs. Take meatballs out using a slotted spoon. Drain, keeping one tablespoon drippings. Sauté onion and mushrooms in the drippings.
- Mix together consommé and soup, mix into mushroom mixture until combined. Bring meatballs back to the pan. Heat to a boil then lower the heat. Let simmer 10 minutes without cover, until meat is not pink anymore.

Nutrition Information

- Calories: 459 calories
- Cholesterol: 131mg cholesterol
- Protein: 29g protein.
- Total Fat: 31g fat (12g saturated fat)
- Sodium: 1754mg sodium
- Fiber: 3g fiber)
- Total Carbohydrate: 16g carbohydrate (5g sugars

300.   Bacon Wrapped Meatballs

Serving: 4 dozen. | Prep: 35mins | Cook: 15mins | Ready in:

Ingredients

- 2 eggs, lightly beaten
- 2 tablespoons milk
- 3/4 cup shredded Parmesan cheese
- 1/4 cup seasoned bread crumbs
- 1/2 teaspoon salt
- 1/4 teaspoon pepper
- 1 pound lean ground beef (90% lean)
- 24 bacon strips, cut in half widthwise

Direction

- Combine the milk, eggs, cheese, pepper, bread crumbs, and salt in a big bowl. Crumble the beef on the mixture and stir it well. Form into 1-in. balls.
- Place the bacon in a big skillet and let it cook over medium heat until partly cooked yet not crisp. Transfer to paper towels to remove excess fat and drain. Wrap a piece of bacon around every meatball; seal using a wooden toothpick.
- Arrange the meatballs on an oiled rack in a shallow baking pan. Let it bake for 8 minutes at 375°. Turn to the other side; continuously bake for additional 3-5 minutes or until the bacon is crisp and the meat is no longer pink.

Nutrition Information

- Calories: 42 calories
- Cholesterol: 19mg cholesterol
- Protein: 4g protein. Diabetic Exchanges: 1/2 lean meat
- Total Fat: 3g fat (1g saturated fat)
- Sodium: 135mg sodium
- Fiber: 0 fiber)
- Total Carbohydrate: 1g carbohydrate (0 sugars

301.   Baked Cranberry Meatballs

Serving: 4-1/2 dozen. | Prep: 30mins | Cook: 01hours20mins | Ready in:

Ingredients

- 1 cup dry bread crumbs
- 1 envelope onion soup mix
- 2 pounds lean ground beef (90% lean)
- 2 large eggs, lightly beaten
- SAUCE:
- 1 can (14 ounces) sauerkraut, rinsed and well drained
- 1 can (14 ounces) whole-berry cranberry sauce
- 1 bottle (12 ounces) chili sauce
- 1-1/4 cups water
- 1 cup packed brown sugar

Direction

- Start preheating the oven to 350°. Mix soup mix and bread crumbs in large bowl. Put in beaten eggs and beef; mix thoroughly and lightly. Form into 1-inch balls. Place in an oiled baking dish, about 13x9-inches.
- Combine the sauce ingredients in large saucepan; just bring to a boil over the medium heat, dissolving the sugar by stirring. Add over the uncooked meatballs.

- Bake, covered, for 60 mins. Uncover; bake until sauce has thickened and meatballs have been cooked through, about 20-30 mins more.

Nutrition Information

- Calories: 72 calories
- Fiber: 0 fiber)
- Total Carbohydrate: 11g carbohydrate (7g sugars
- Cholesterol: 17mg cholesterol
- Protein: 4g protein.
- Total Fat: 2g fat (1g saturated fat)
- Sodium: 225mg sodium

---

302.   Barbecue Meatballs

Serving: Makes 36 servings. | Prep: 20mins | Cook: | Ready in:

Ingredients

- 1-1/2 lb. ground turkey
- 1 cup quick-cooking oats
- 1 can (5 oz.) evaporated milk
- 1 egg , beaten
- 1/4 cup finely chopped onion s
- 1/2 tsp. freshly ground black pepper
- 1/2 tsp. ground red pepper (cayenne)
- 1 bottle (18 oz.) KRAFT Original Barbecue Sauce

Direction

- 1. Combine all the ingredients but not barbecue sauce; form into 36 (1-inch) meatballs.
- 2. Put in a 13x9-inch pan coated with cooking spray; pour barbecue sauce on top.
- 3. Bake for 40 to 45 minutes or until meatballs are done (160 degrees F).

Nutrition Information

- Calories: 60
- Protein: 4 g
- Total Fat: 2 g
- Sodium: 200 mg
- Cholesterol: 20 mg
- Saturated Fat: 0.5 g
- Fiber: 0 g
- Sugar: 4 g
- Total Carbohydrate: 7 g

---

303.   Barbecued Party Starters

Serving: 16 servings (1/3 cup each). | Prep: 30mins | Cook: 02hours15mins | Ready in:

Ingredients

- 1 pound ground beef
- 1/4 cup finely chopped onion
- 1 package (16 ounces) miniature hot dogs, drained
- 1 jar (12 ounces) apricot preserves
- 1 cup barbecue sauce
- 1 can (20 ounces) pineapple chunks, drained

Direction

- Combine beef and onion in a large bowl, mixing gently yet thoroughly. Form into 1-in. balls. In a large skillet, cook meatballs in two batches over medium heat until cooked through, flipping occasionally.
- Transfer meatballs to a 3-qt. slow cooker with a slotted spoon. Put in hot dogs; mix in barbecue sauce and preserves. Cook with a cover, on high until heated through, about 2-3 hours.
- Mix in pineapple; cook with a cover, 15-20 more minutes until heat through.

Nutrition Information

- Calories:
- Sodium:

180

- Fiber:
- Total Carbohydrate:
- Cholesterol:
- Protein:
- Total Fat:

---

304. Bavarian Meatballs

Serving: 2 servings. | Prep: 15mins | Cook: 25mins | Ready in:

Ingredients

- 2 tablespoons chopped onion
- 1 teaspoon butter
- 3/4 cup soft bread crumbs
- 1 tablespoon milk
- 1/2 teaspoon prepared mustard
- 1/2 teaspoon salt
- Dash pepper
- 1/2 pound ground beef
- 1 can (4 ounces) mushroom stems and pieces, undrained
- 2 gingersnaps, coarsely crushed
- 2 tablespoons water
- 1 tablespoon brown sugar
- 1/2 teaspoon beef bouillon granules

Direction

- Sauté onion in butter in a big skillet until soften. Turn the mixture to a big bowl, then put in pepper, salt, mustard, milk and bread crumbs. Break up beef over the mixture and combine well. Form into 6 meatballs and put into a greased 1-quart baking dish.
- Heat the oven to 350 degrees. Mix bouillon, brown sugar, water, gingersnap crumbs and mushrooms in a small saucepan. Cook and stir on low heat until thicken, about 2 to 3 minutes.
- Drizzle over meatballs, then cover and bake until meat is not pink anymore, about 25 minutes

Nutrition Information

- Calories: 364 calories
- Protein: 26g protein.
- Total Fat: 17g fat (7g saturated fat)
- Sodium: 1225mg sodium
- Fiber: 2g fiber)
- Total Carbohydrate: 24g carbohydrate (11g sugars
- Cholesterol: 82mg cholesterol

---

305. Beef Stroganoff Meatballs

Serving: 6 servings. | Prep: 30mins | Cook: 15mins | Ready in:

Ingredients

- 1 egg
- 1/4 cup milk
- 1/4 cup finely chopped onion
- 2 teaspoons Worcestershire sauce
- 1-1/2 cups soft bread crumbs
- 1 teaspoon salt
- 1/4 teaspoon pepper
- 1-1/2 pounds ground beef
- SAUCE:
- 1-1/2 cups sliced fresh mushrooms
- 1/2 cup chopped onion
- 1/4 cup butter
- 4 tablespoons all-purpose flour, divided
- 1/4 teaspoon salt
- 1-1/2 cups beef broth
- 1 cup (8 ounces) sour cream
- Hot cooked noodles
- Paprika, optional

Direction

- Combine Worcestershire sauce, onion, milk, and egg in a big bowl. Mix in pepper, salt, and bread crumbs. Add in beef, combine well. Form into 1 1/4 -inch balls. Put meatballs in an oiled rack set in a shallow baking pan. Bake at

350 degrees without cover till the meat is not pink anymore, about 15-20 minutes; drain.

- In a big saucepan, in butter, sauté onion and mushrooms until tender. Mix in salt and 3 tablespoons flour until combined. Slowly pour in broth. Heat to a boil on medium heat. Stir and cook 2 minutes until thickened.
- Mix the rest of flour with sour cream until smooth; mix into the mushroom mixture. Put in meatballs. Allow to simmer without cover for 4-5 minutes, mixing from time to time, until heated through. Arrange over noodles to serve. If wanted, sprinkle paprika over top.

Nutrition Information

- Calories: 455 calories
- Total Fat: 30g fat (16g saturated fat)
- Sodium: 944mg sodium
- Fiber: 1g fiber)
- Total Carbohydrate: 15g carbohydrate (4g sugars
- Cholesterol: 159mg cholesterol
- Protein: 28g protein.

306.   Beef And Sauerkraut Dinner

Serving: 6-8 servings. | Prep: 20mins | Cook: 15mins | Ready in:

Ingredients

- 1-1/2 pounds ground beef
- 1 egg, lightly beaten
- 1-1/2 cups soft rye bread crumbs
- 1/3 cup milk
- 1/4 cup chopped onion
- 1 tablespoon cider vinegar
- 1-1/2 teaspoons caraway seeds
- 1 teaspoon salt
- 1 tablespoon canola oil
- 2 cans (15 ounces each) sliced potatoes, drained

- 2 cans (14 ounces each) sauerkraut, undrained
- 2 tablespoons minced fresh parsley
- 1/4 cup each mayonnaise and horseradish, optional

Direction

- In a bowl, combine egg, beef, milk, crumbs, vinegar, onion, salt and caraway; mix well. Form into balls of 1 and a half inch in size.
- In a Dutch oven over medium heat, brown meatballs in oil; drain. Stir in the sauerkraut and potatoes, then mix well. Allow to boil. Decrease the heat; simmer while covering for 15 to 20 minutes or until heated through. Use parsley to sprinkle.
- If you want to have a sauce, combine horseradish and mayonnaise; serve along the side.

Nutrition Information

- Calories: 250 calories
- Protein: 20g protein.
- Total Fat: 14g fat (5g saturated fat)
- Sodium: 850mg sodium
- Fiber: 3g fiber)
- Total Carbohydrate: 12g carbohydrate (2g sugars
- Cholesterol: 84mg cholesterol

307.   Beefy Mushroom Meatballs

Serving: 6-8 servings. | Prep: 15mins | Cook: 40mins | Ready in:

Ingredients

- 2 slices bread, torn
- 2 tablespoons milk
- 1 egg, lightly beaten
- 3 tablespoons finely chopped onion
- 1/2 teaspoon salt

- 1/4 teaspoon pepper
- 1-1/2 pounds ground beef
- 1 tablespoon butter
- 2 tablespoons all-purpose flour
- 1 can (10-1/2 ounces) beef consomme
- 2 cans (4 ounces each) mushroom stems and pieces, drained
- 1 tablespoon dried parsley flakes
- 1 teaspoon Worcestershire sauce
- 1 teaspoon beef bouillon granules
- 1/2 cup sour cream
- Hot cooked noodles, optional
- Minced fresh parsley

Direction

- Mix together milk and bread in a big bowl. Put in egg, salt, onion, and pepper. Over the mixture, crumble meat and properly mix.
- Form into 1-in. balls. On medium heat, cook meatballs in small batches in a big pan until browned and not pink. Place on paper towels to drain.
- Melt butter in a large saucepan. Mix in flour until smooth; add consommé little by little. Boil. Thicken by cooking and stirring for about 2 minutes. Lessen the heat and put in the parsley, mushrooms, bouillon, Worcestershire sauce, and meatballs. Leave uncovered and cook for 30 minutes; stir from time to time.
- Take off heat and mix in sour cream. Serve alongside noodles if preferred. Take parsley and sprinkle on top.

Nutrition Information

- Calories: 227 calories
- Total Carbohydrate: 7g carbohydrate (2g sugars
- Cholesterol: 82mg cholesterol
- Protein: 19g protein.
- Total Fat: 13g fat (6g saturated fat)
- Sodium: 735mg sodium
- Fiber: 1g fiber)

308.   Best Spaghetti And Meatballs

Serving: 16 servings. | Prep: 30mins | Cook: 02hours00mins | Ready in:

Ingredients

- 2 tablespoons olive oil
- 1-1/2 cups chopped onions
- 3 garlic cloves, minced
- 2 cans (12 ounces each) tomato paste
- 3 cups water
- 1 can (29 ounces) tomato sauce
- 1/3 cup minced fresh parsley
- 1 tablespoon dried basil
- 2 teaspoons salt
- 1/2 teaspoon pepper
- MEATBALLS:
- 4 large eggs, lightly beaten
- 2 cups soft bread cubes (cut into 1/4-inch pieces)
- 1-1/2 cups whole milk
- 1 cup grated Parmesan cheese
- 3 garlic cloves, minced
- 2 teaspoons salt
- 1/2 teaspoon pepper
- 3 pounds ground beef
- 2 tablespoons canola oil
- 2 pounds spaghetti, cooked

Direction

- Heat the olive oil in a Dutch oven on medium heat. Put in onions and sauté until they are softened. Put in garlic and cook for 1 more minute. Add in the tomato paste and cook for 3-5 minutes. Put in the next 6 ingredients. Boil. Turn down the heat; put a cover on and bring to a simmer for 50 minutes.
- Mix the first 7 meatballs ingredients. Put in beef and combine lightly yet thoroughly. Form 1 1/2-inch balls.
- Heat the canola oil in a large skillet on medium heat. Drop the meatballs; working in

batches, brown them until meatballs are not pink anymore. Drain. Add into the sauce and boil. Turn down the heat; put on a cover and bring to a simmer, stirring from time to time, for an hour until the flavors are combined. Serve alongside hot cooked spaghetti.

Nutrition Information

- Calories: 519 calories
- Total Carbohydrate: 59g carbohydrate (8g sugars
- Cholesterol: 106mg cholesterol
- Protein: 30g protein.
- Total Fat: 18g fat (6g saturated fat)
- Sodium: 1043mg sodium
- Fiber: 4g fiber)

309.   Blue Plate Beef Patties

Serving: 4 servings. | Prep: 10mins | Cook: 10mins | Ready in:

Ingredients

- 1 egg
- 2 green onions with tops, sliced
- 1/4 cup seasoned bread crumbs
- 1 tablespoon prepared mustard
- 1-1/2 pounds ground beef
- 1 jar (12 ounces) beef gravy
- 1/2 cup water
- 2 to 3 teaspoons prepared horseradish
- 1/2 pound fresh mushrooms, sliced

Direction

- In a bowl, beat the egg; mix in mustard, bread crumbs and onions. Add beef and mix well. Form into four patties of half an inch thickness.
- In an ungreased skillet, cook patties for 4 to 5 minutes on each side or until meat is not pink anymore; drain.

- Combine horseradish, water and gravy in a small bowl; add mushrooms. Pour over patties. Cook without a cover for 5 minutes or until mushrooms are softened and heated through.

Nutrition Information

- Calories: 438 calories
- Cholesterol: 170mg cholesterol
- Protein: 41g protein.
- Total Fat: 24g fat (9g saturated fat)
- Sodium: 825mg sodium
- Fiber: 1g fiber)
- Total Carbohydrate: 14g carbohydrate (2g sugars

310.   Cheese Meatballs

Serving: about 4 dozen. | Prep: 20mins | Cook: 15mins | Ready in:

Ingredients

- 3 cups (12 ounces) finely shredded cheddar cheese
- 1 cup biscuit/baking mix
- 1/2 teaspoon salt
- 1/4 teaspoon pepper
- 1/4 teaspoon garlic powder
- 1 pound lean ground beef (90% lean)

Direction

- Combine the first 5 ingredients in a large bowl. Crumble the beef over the mixture and mix well. Next, roll into 1-in. balls. On a greased rack in a shallow baking pan, place these meatballs.
- Bake for 12-15 minutes at 400°, or until the meat is no more pink; drain.

Nutrition Information

- Calories: 148 calories
- Cholesterol: 36mg cholesterol
- Protein: 10g protein.
- Total Fat: 9g fat (6g saturated fat)
- Sodium: 314mg sodium
- Fiber: 0 fiber)
- Total Carbohydrate: 5g carbohydrate (0 sugars

- Total Fat: 6g fat (3g saturated fat)
- Sodium: 313mg sodium
- Fiber: 0 fiber)
- Total Carbohydrate: 10g carbohydrate (1g sugars
- Cholesterol: 53mg cholesterol

311.   Cheeseburger Bites

Serving: 2 dozen. | Prep: 20mins | Cook: 5mins | Ready in:

Ingredients

- 1 large egg yolk, beaten
- 1/2 pound lean ground beef
- 2 tablespoons grated onion
- 1/2 teaspoon salt
- Dash pepper
- 6 slices bread
- 24 cubes cheddar cheese (1/2-inch cubes)

Direction

- Combine ground beef with pepper, salt, onion, and egg yolk in a bowl. Form mixture into 24 balls by teaspoonfuls. Remove crusts off bread; flatten and cut into rounds, about 1 1/2 inches. Arrange meatballs on meat rounds; make a depression in each ball and fill with a cheese cube, making sure that meat mixture covers the bread completely.
- Arrange on a baking sheet. Broil in the preheated oven about 6 inches from the heat source until meat is no longer pink, for 3 to 5 minutes. Garnish with ketchup, mustard, sliced dill pickles or sliced green onions if desired.

Nutrition Information

- Calories: 135 calories
- Protein: 9g protein.

312.   Classic Swedish Meatballs

Serving: 3-1/2 dozen. | Prep: 15mins | Cook: 20mins | Ready in:

Ingredients

- 1-2/3 cups evaporated milk, divided
- 2/3 cup chopped onion
- 1/4 cup fine dry bread crumbs
- 1/2 teaspoon salt
- 1/2 teaspoon allspice
- Dash pepper
- 1 pound lean ground beef (90% lean)
- 2 teaspoons butter
- 2 teaspoons beef bouillon granules
- 1 cup boiling water
- 1/2 cup cold water
- 2 tablespoons all-purpose flour
- 1 tablespoon lemon juice
- Canned lingonberries, optional

Direction

- Mix 2/3 cup evaporated milk with the next 5 ingredients together. Add in beef and mix lightly.
- Refrigerate until chilled.
- Form meat mixture into 1-inch balls using your wet hands. Heat butter over medium heat in a large skillet. Cook meatballs in melted butter, working in batches, until browned. Stir bouillon in boiling water until dissolved. Stream over meatballs; bring everything to a boil; simmer, covered, for 15 minutes.

- In the meantime, combine flour and cold water. Take meatballs out of the skillet; ladle off fat, saving cooking juices. Add the rest of evaporated milk and flour mixture to pan juices; cook without covering over low heat until sauce is thickened, stirring while cooking.
- Place meatballs back into the skillet. Whisk in lemon juice. Top with lingonberries (if using).

Nutrition Information

- Calories: 36 calories
- Sodium: 87mg sodium
- Fiber: 0 fiber)
- Total Carbohydrate: 2g carbohydrate (1g sugars
- Cholesterol: 10mg cholesterol
- Protein: 3g protein.
- Total Fat: 2g fat (1g saturated fat)

---

313. Cranberry Appetizer Meatballs

Serving: about 7 dozen. | Prep: 25mins | Cook: 10mins | Ready in:

Ingredients

- 2 large eggs, lightly beaten
- 1 cup dry bread crumbs
- 1/3 cup minced fresh parsley
- 1/3 cup ketchup
- 2 tablespoons finely chopped onion
- 2 tablespoons soy sauce
- 2 garlic cloves, minced
- 1/2 teaspoon salt
- 1/4 teaspoon pepper
- 2 pounds ground beef
- CRANBERRY SAUCE:
- 1 can (14 ounces) whole-berry cranberry sauce
- 1 bottle (12 ounces) chili sauce
- 1 tablespoon brown sugar
- 1 tablespoon prepared mustard

- 1 tablespoon lemon juice
- 2 garlic cloves, minced

Direction

- Set an oven to 400 degrees and start preheating. Blend the first 9 ingredients. Put the crumbled beef over the mixture and combine thoroughly. Form into 1-inch balls.
- In a shallow baking pan, arrange the meatballs on a rack. Bake for 15 minutes until they are not pink anymore. Place into a 3-quart chafing dish or slow cooker.
- At the same time, blend all the sauce ingredients in a large saucepan; bring to a simmer and stir from time to time for 10 minutes. Spread over the meatballs. Then serve them warm.

Nutrition Information

- Calories: 39 calories
- Sodium: 124mg sodium
- Fiber: 0 fiber)
- Total Carbohydrate: 4g carbohydrate (2g sugars
- Cholesterol: 11mg cholesterol
- Protein: 2g protein.
- Total Fat: 1g fat (1g saturated fat)

---

314. Cranberry Kraut Meatballs

Serving: 6 servings. | Prep: 10mins | Cook: 01hours30mins | Ready in:

Ingredients

- 1 envelope onion soup mix
- 1 cup dry bread crumbs
- 2-1/2 pounds ground beef
- 1 can (14 ounces) whole-berry cranberry sauce
- 1 can (14 ounces) sauerkraut, rinsed and drained

- 1-1/3 cups water
- 1 bottle (12 ounces) chili sauce
- 3/4 cup packed brown sugar
- Hot mashed potatoes

Direction

- In a large bowl, combine the bread crumbs and soup mix; crumble beef over mixture and mix well. Form into 18 meatballs. In an ungreased baking dish of 13x9-inch, place those balls.
- In a large saucepan, combine the sauerkraut, cranberry sauce, water, brown sugar and chili sauce. Allow to boil. Pour mixture over meatballs.
- Uncover and bake at 350° for 1 and a half hours until meat is no longer pink. Serve with mashed potatoes.

Nutrition Information

- Calories: 727 calories
- Total Fat: 24g fat (9g saturated fat)
- Sodium: 1888mg sodium
- Fiber: 3g fiber)
- Total Carbohydrate: 87g carbohydrate (56g sugars
- Cholesterol: 125mg cholesterol
- Protein: 41g protein.

315.   Creamy Herbed Meatballs

Serving: 16 meatballs. | Prep: 15mins | Cook: 35mins | Ready in:

Ingredients

- 1 egg
- 1/4 cup dry bread crumbs
- 1/4 cup finely chopped onion
- 1 tablespoon dried basil
- 1/2 teaspoon salt

- 1/2 teaspoon pepper
- 1 pound ground beef
- 1 can (10-3/4 ounces) condensed cream of mushroom soup, undiluted
- 1/2 cup water
- 2 tablespoons minced fresh parsley

Direction

- Combine the initial 6 ingredients in a big bowl. Crumble beef and add to the mixture; combine well. Form into 1 1/2 -inch balls.
- In a big skillet, in batches, cook meatballs till a thermometer shows 160° and all sides are browned; drain. Mix in the rest of ingredients. Put on cover and simmer, mixing from time to time, until heated through, about 20 minutes.

Nutrition Information

- Calories: 291 calories
- Fiber: 1g fiber)
- Total Carbohydrate: 13g carbohydrate (2g sugars
- Cholesterol: 112mg cholesterol
- Protein: 24g protein.
- Total Fat: 16g fat (6g saturated fat)
- Sodium: 980mg sodium

316.   Crispy Meatballs

Serving: 16 meatballs. | Prep: 15mins | Cook: 30mins | Ready in:

Ingredients

- 1 egg
- 1/4 cup ketchup
- 1 cup crisp rice cereal
- 1 tablespoon brown sugar
- 1 tablespoon finely chopped onion
- 1 teaspoon salt
- 1/2 teaspoon ground mustard
- 1/4 teaspoon pepper

- 1/8 teaspoon ground nutmeg
- 1 pound ground beef

Direction

- In a large bowl, combine the first nine ingredients. Crumble beef over mixture and mix well. Form into balls of 1 and a half inch in size. On a greased rack in a shallow pan, place meatballs. Bake without a cover at 400° for 30 minutes or until the meat is not pink anymore.

Nutrition Information

- Calories: 298 calories
- Fiber: 0 fiber)
- Total Carbohydrate: 14g carbohydrate (6g sugars
- Cholesterol: 128mg cholesterol
- Protein: 25g protein.
- Total Fat: 15g fat (6g saturated fat)
- Sodium: 903mg sodium

317.   Easy Cranberry Meatballs

Serving: 5 dozen. | Prep: 30mins | Cook: 10mins |Ready in:

Ingredients

- 1 pound ground beef
- 1 pound ground pork
- 2 eggs, lightly beaten
- 1 cup crushed saltines (about 15 crackers)
- 1 medium onion, finely chopped
- 2 teaspoons salt
- 1/4 teaspoon pepper
- 2 cans (16 ounces each) whole-berry cranberry sauce
- 2 cans (10-3/4 ounces each) condensed tomato soup, undiluted
- 1 teaspoon prepared mustard

Direction

- Blend the first 7 ingredients in a bowl. Form into 1-inch meatballs. In a shallow baking pan, arrange the meatballs on a rack that's greased. Bake at 400 degrees until a thermometer registers 160 degrees or 15 minutes, then drain.
- At the same time, in a large saucepan, blend mustard, soup, and cranberry sauce. Boil. Turn down the heat; drop the meatballs. Uncover and bring to a simmer for 10 minutes.

Nutrition Information

- Calories: 158 calories
- Total Fat: 7g fat (3g saturated fat)
- Sodium: 401mg sodium
- Fiber: 1g fiber)
- Total Carbohydrate: 14g carbohydrate (7g sugars
- Cholesterol: 51mg cholesterol
- Protein: 10g protein.

318.   Easy Spaghetti And Meatballs

Serving: 4 servings | Prep: 35mins | Cook: |Ready in:

Ingredients

- 1/2 lb. spaghetti, uncooked
- 1 lb. extra-lean ground beef
- 1/2 cup KRAFT Shredded Parmesan Cheese, divided
- 1/4 cup dry bread crumbs
- 1   egg
- 2 cloves garlic, minced
- 1 Tbsp. oil
- 2 cups OLIVO by CLASSICO Traditional Pasta Sauce

Direction

- 1. Follow directions on package to cook spaghetti, omit the salt. In the meantime, mix bread crumbs, garlic, meat, egg, and 1/4 cup Parmesan. Form into 20 balls.

- 2. In a big frying pan, heat oil over medium-high heat. Add the meatballs; stir occasionally and cook until evenly brown, 5-7 minutes. Mix in pasta sauce and cover. Simmer over medium-low heat until meatballs are done, 15 minutes. Stir occasionally.
- 3. Drain water from spaghetti. Eat topped with remaining Parmesan cheese and sauce mixture.

Nutrition Information

- Calories: 530
- Sodium: 660 mg
- Total Carbohydrate: 54 g
- Total Fat: 17 g
- Fiber: 4 g
- Sugar: 8 g
- Cholesterol: 130 mg
- Protein: 38 g
- Saturated Fat: 5 g

319. Favorite Cranberry Meatballs

Serving: 4 main-dish servings. | Prep: 30mins | Cook: 10mins | Ready in:

Ingredients

- 1 pound lean ground beef (90% lean)
- 1 large egg, lightly beaten
- 1/2 cup crushed saltines
- 1/2 small onion, diced
- 1 teaspoon salt
- 1/2 teaspoon pepper
- 1 can (14 ounces) whole-berry cranberry sauce
- 1 can (10-3/4 ounces) condensed tomato soup, undiluted
- Cooked rice or noodles

Direction

- Mix the first six ingredients together in a bowl. Form into 1-1/2-inch balls. Lay the balls on the cooking-spray-coated shallow baking tray. Set oven at 400° and bake for 20 minutes.
- In the meantime, mix the tomato soup with the cranberry sauce. Heat through. Add meatballs, simmer for 10 minutes. Serve with noodles or rice. It can be served as an appetizer.

Nutrition Information

- Calories: 458 calories
- Sodium: 1423mg sodium
- Fiber: 3g fiber)
- Total Carbohydrate: 63g carbohydrate (37g sugars
- Cholesterol: 112mg cholesterol
- Protein: 26g protein.
- Total Fat: 12g fat (4g saturated fat)

320. Fiesta Meatballs

Serving: 4 servings. | Prep: 25mins | Cook: 30mins | Ready in:

Ingredients

- 1 egg
- 1-1/2 teaspoons Worcestershire sauce
- 1/4 cup finely chopped onion
- 1/4 cup finely chopped celery
- 2-1/2 teaspoons garlic salt, divided
- 1/4 teaspoon pepper
- 1 pound ground beef
- 1 cup soft bread crumbs
- 1 tablespoon cornstarch
- 1 cup beef broth
- 1 can (14-1/2 ounces) stewed tomatoes
- 2 cups sliced zucchini
- 1 teaspoon dried oregano
- 1/2 teaspoon sugar
- 1/2 teaspoon dried basil

Direction

- Combine pepper, 1 1/2 teaspoons of garlic salt, celery, onion, Worcestershire sauce and egg together in a large bowl. Include in beef; stir properly. Sprinkle with bread crumbs; stir just till well combined. Form into 2-in. balls. Place on a greased rack in a shallow baking pan. Bake without a cover at 375° till the meat is not pink anymore, or for 20 minutes.
- Meanwhile, combine broth with cornstarch till smooth in a saucepan. Mix in the remaining garlic salt, basil, sugar, oregano, zucchini and stewed tomatoes. Allow to boil; cook while stirring till thickened, or for 2 minutes.
- Drain the meatballs; pour the tomato mixture on top. Bake till heated through, or for 10 more minutes.

Nutrition Information

- Calories: 333 calories
- Sodium: 1683mg sodium
- Fiber: 2g fiber)
- Total Carbohydrate: 20g carbohydrate (8g sugars
- Cholesterol: 128mg cholesterol
- Protein: 27g protein.
- Total Fat: 16g fat (6g saturated fat)

---

321. Garden's Plenty Meatballs

Serving: 8 servings. | Prep: 20mins | Cook: 45mins | Ready in:

Ingredients

- 1 egg
- 1 cup unsweetened applesauce
- 1 cup soft bread crumbs
- 2 teaspoons salt
- 1/4 teaspoon ground allspice
- 1/4 teaspoon pepper
- 2 pounds ground beef
- 1/2 cup all-purpose flour

- 3 tablespoons vegetable oil
- 1 can (28 ounces) diced tomatoes, undrained
- 1 cup sliced carrots
- 1 small green pepper, chopped
- 1 small onion, sliced

Direction

- Mix the first six ingredients in a large bowl. Crumble beef over the mixture; mix thoroughly. Form into 1 1/2-inch meatballs. Roll in flour. Brown meatballs in oil in a large skillet; strain. Move to a greased 3-quart baking dish. Mix onion, pepper, carrots and tomatoes. Pour the mixture over meatballs. Bake with a cover at 350° till the meat is no longer pink, 45 minutes.

Nutrition Information

- Calories: 320 calories
- Total Carbohydrate: 20g carbohydrate (8g sugars
- Cholesterol: 82mg cholesterol
- Protein: 23g protein.
- Total Fat: 16g fat (5g saturated fat)
- Sodium: 836mg sodium
- Fiber: 3g fiber)

---

322. German Meatballs With Gingersnap Gravy

Serving: 4 servings. | Prep: 20mins | Cook: 25mins | Ready in:

Ingredients

- 1 large egg, beaten
- 3/4 cup soft bread crumbs
- 1-3/4 cups water, divided
- 1/4 cup chopped onion
- 1/2 teaspoon salt
- Dash pepper
- 1 pound lean ground beef (90% lean)

- 2 beef bouillon cubes
- 1/3 cup packed brown sugar
- 1/4 cup raisins
- 2-1/2 teaspoons lemon juice
- 1/2 cup coarsely crushed gingersnaps (about 10 cookies)
- Cooked noodles

Direction

- Combine the bread crumbs, egg, onion, 1/4 cup water, pepper and salt; crumble beef over mixture and mix well. Form into balls of 2 and a half inches in size.
- In a large skillet, boil the rest of water. Add brown sugar, bouillon, raisins, gingersnaps and lemon juice. Stir until combined thoroughly. Add meatballs to the skillet. Simmering without a cover for 20 minutes or until meat is not pink anymore. Stir occasionally. Have noodles to serve with.

Nutrition Information

- Calories: 387 calories
- Sodium: 985mg sodium
- Fiber: 1g fiber)
- Total Carbohydrate: 44g carbohydrate (31g sugars
- Cholesterol: 109mg cholesterol
- Protein: 26g protein.
- Total Fat: 12g fat (4g saturated fat)

323.   Glazed Meatballs

Serving: about 3-1/2 dozen. | Prep: 30mins | Cook: 15mins | Ready in:

Ingredients

- 2 eggs, lightly beaten
- 2/3 cup milk
- 1 tablespoon prepared horseradish
- 1-1/4 cups soft bread crumbs

- 1-1/2 pounds ground beef
- 1 cup water
- 1/2 cup chili sauce
- 1/2 cup ketchup
- 1/4 cup maple syrup
- 1/4 cup reduced-sodium soy sauce
- 1-1/2 teaspoons ground allspice
- 1/2 teaspoon ground mustard

Direction

- Combine bread crumbs, horseradish, milk and eggs in a large bowl. Crumble the beef over the mixture, then mix well. Form into 1-1/2-inch balls.
- In shallow baking pan, put meatballs on an oiled rack. Bake at 375° until cooked through, about 15 to 20 mins; drain.
- Combine remaining ingredients in large saucepan. Boil. Put in meatballs. Lower the heat and simmer, covered, stirring occasionally, until heated through, about 15 mins.

Nutrition Information

- Calories: 141 calories
- Sodium: 568mg sodium
- Fiber: 0 fiber)
- Total Carbohydrate: 11g carbohydrate (7g sugars
- Cholesterol: 56mg cholesterol
- Protein: 11g protein.
- Total Fat: 6g fat (2g saturated fat)

324.   Grandma's Swedish Meatballs

Serving: 12 | Prep: 10mins | Cook: 25mins | Ready in:

Ingredients

- 1 pound ground beef
- 1/2 cup bread crumbs

- 1 large egg
- 2 tablespoons grated onion
- 1/8 teaspoon ground black pepper
- 1/8 teaspoon ground nutmeg
- salt to taste

Direction

- Preheat oven to 400 °F (200 °C).
- In a bowl, mix bread crumbs, ground beef, onion, egg, black pepper, salt, and nutmeg together; form into small balls. On a baking sheet, arrange those balls.
- In the preheated oven, bake for 10 minutes. Flip meatballs and continue baking for 12 to 15 minutes until cooked through. An inserted instant-read thermometer into the center should measure at least 160 °F (70 °C).

Nutrition Information

- Calories: 100 calories;
- Protein: 7.4
- Total Fat: 6.1
- Sodium: 73
- Total Carbohydrate: 3.5
- Cholesterol: 39

---

325. Great Grandma's Italian Meatballs

Serving: 8 servings. | Prep: 30mins | Cook: 20mins | Ready in:

Ingredients

- 2 teaspoons olive oil
- 1 medium onion, chopped
- 3 garlic cloves, minced
- 3/4 cup seasoned bread crumbs
- 1/2 cup grated Parmesan cheese
- 2 large eggs, lightly beaten
- 1 teaspoon each dried basil, oregano and parsley flakes

- 3/4 teaspoon salt
- 1 pound lean ground turkey
- 1 pound lean ground beef (90% lean)
- Hot cooked pasta and pasta sauce, optional

Direction

- Start preheating the oven to 375°. Heat oil in a small skillet over medium-high heat. Put in onion; stir and cook until soft, about 3-4 minutes. Add garlic then cook for another 1 minute. Cool briefly.
- Mix onion mixture, seasonings, eggs, cheese, and bread crumbs together in a big bowl. Add beef and turkey, stirring gently but well. Form into balls, about 1-1/2-inch each ball.
- On a greased rack set over a 15x10x1-inch baking pan, put the meatballs. Bake until thoroughly cooked and turning light brown, about 18-22 minutes. Enjoy with pasta sauce and pasta if you want.

Nutrition Information

- Calories: 271 calories
- Protein: 27g protein. Diabetic Exchanges: 4 lean meat
- Total Fat: 13g fat (5g saturated fat)
- Sodium: 569mg sodium
- Fiber: 1g fiber)
- Total Carbohydrate: 10g carbohydrate (1g sugars
- Cholesterol: 125mg cholesterol

---

326. Ham Balls

Serving: 8 | Prep: | Cook: | Ready in:

Ingredients

- 1 1/4 pounds ground smoked ham
- 1 pound ground pork
- 1 pound lean ground beef
- 1 cup milk

- 2 eggs
- 1 1/2 cups graham cracker crumbs
- 1 (10.75 ounce) can tomato soup
- 1/4 cup cider vinegar
- 1 cup packed brown sugar
- 1 teaspoon mustard powder

Direction

- Set oven at 175°C (350°F) to preheat.
- Mix the ground beef, sausage or pork and ham together in a big bowl. Mix in the graham cracker crumbs, eggs and milk. Shape into 2-inch balls and lay them on a 9x13-inch baking dish.
- In a different medium bowl, mix the mustard powder, brown sugar, vinegar and soup together well and pour on top of the meatballs.
- Put the balls into the preheated oven, bake at 350° until the inside temperature of the meatballs reach 73°C (160°F), about 60 minutes.

Nutrition Information

- Calories: 646 calories;
- Total Carbohydrate: 46.1
- Cholesterol: 173
- Protein: 39.6
- Total Fat: 33
- Sodium: 1388

---

327.   Hobo Meatball Stew

Serving: 4 servings. | Prep: 25mins | Cook: 06hours00mins |Ready in:

Ingredients

- 1 pound lean ground beef (90% lean)
- 1-1/2 teaspoons salt or salt-free seasoning blend, divided
- 1/2 teaspoon pepper, divided

- 4 medium potatoes, peeled and cut into chunks
- 4 medium carrots, cut into chunks
- 1 large onion, cut into chunks
- 1/2 cup water
- 1/2 cup ketchup
- 1-1/2 teaspoons cider vinegar
- 1/2 teaspoon dried basil

Direction

- Mix 1/4 teaspoon pepper, 1 teaspoon salt and the beef in a bowl. Form into 1-in balls. Place a frying pan over medium heat, cook in meatballs on all sides until browned; drain off oil.
- Put onion, carrots and potatoes into a 3-qt. slow cooker; put meatballs on top. Stir together pepper, remaining salt, basil, vinegar, ketchup and water together; spoon over meatballs.
- Cook on low with a cover for 6 to 8 hours or till the vegetables are tender.

Nutrition Information

- Calories: 402 calories
- Protein: 26g protein. Diabetic Exchanges: 3 starch
- Total Fat: 14g fat (6g saturated fat)
- Sodium: 1324mg sodium
- Fiber: 5g fiber)
- Total Carbohydrate: 43g carbohydrate (11g sugars
- Cholesterol: 75mg cholesterol

---

328.   Hoisin Meatballs

Serving: about 2 dozen. | Prep: 15mins | Cook: 02hours30mins |Ready in:

Ingredients

- 1 cup dry red wine or beef broth

- 3 tablespoons hoisin sauce
- 2 tablespoons soy sauce
- 1 large egg
- 4 green onions, chopped
- 1/4 cup finely chopped onion
- 1/4 cup minced fresh cilantro
- 2 garlic cloves, minced
- 1/2 teaspoon salt
- 1/2 teaspoon pepper
- 1 pound ground beef
- 1 pound ground pork
- Sesame seeds

Direction

- Start preheating the broiler. Beat the soy sauce, hoisin sauce, and wine together in a 3-quart slow cooker. Put a cover on and cook on high for half an hour. At the same time, blend the next 7 ingredients. Put in pork and beef; combine lightly yet thoroughly. Form them into 1 1/2-inch meatballs; in a broiler pan, arrange them on a rack. Broil 3-4 inches away from the heat for 3-4 minutes until they are browned.
- Drop the meatballs into the slow cooker. Put a cover on, cook and stir halfway through on low for 2-3 hours until the meatballs are cooked thoroughly. Dust with the sesame seeds. Freeze option: Put the cooled meatball mixture in the freezer containers to freeze. Put in the fridge overnight to thaw partially to use. Put a cover on, microwave on high and stir gently halfway through for approximately 8 minutes until heated thoroughly.

Nutrition Information

- Calories: 73 calories
- Total Fat: 5g fat (2g saturated fat)
- Sodium: 156mg sodium
- Fiber: 0 fiber)
- Total Carbohydrate: 1g carbohydrate (1g sugars
- Cholesterol: 28mg cholesterol
- Protein: 6g protein.

329. Holiday Appetizer Meatballs

Serving: about 3 dozen. | Prep: 15mins | Cook: 50mins | Ready in:

Ingredients

- 1 egg, lightly beaten
- 1/2 cup soft bread crumbs
- 1/4 cup 2% milk
- 1/3 cup finely chopped onion
- 1 teaspoon salt
- 1/2 teaspoon Worcestershire sauce
- 1 pound ground beef
- SAUCE:
- 1/2 cup ketchup
- 1/2 cup chopped onion
- 1/3 cup sugar
- 1/3 cup vinegar
- 1 tablespoon Worcestershire sauce
- 1/8 teaspoon pepper

Direction

- Mix the first 6 ingredients in a small bowl. Break the beef into crumbles over the mixture, combine thoroughly. Form into 1-inch meatballs.
- Brown the meatballs in a large skillet over medium heat; drain the meatballs. Arrange them in a 2 1/2-quart baking dish. Mix the sauce ingredients. Spread onto the meatballs. Without the cover, bake at 350 degrees until the meatballs are not pink anymore, 50-60 minutes.

Nutrition Information

- Calories: 84 calories
- Total Carbohydrate: 7g carbohydrate (5g sugars
- Cholesterol: 29mg cholesterol

- Protein: 6g protein.
- Total Fat: 4g fat (1g saturated fat)
- Sodium: 245mg sodium
- Fiber: 0 fiber)

330. Homemade Spaghetti And Meatballs

Serving: 8-10 servings. | Prep: 20mins | Cook: 03hours00mins | Ready in:

Ingredients

- SAUCE:
- 2 cans (10-3/4 ounces each) condensed tomato soup, undiluted
- 2-2/3 cups water
- 1 can (12 ounces) tomato paste
- 1 jar (4-1/2 ounces) sliced mushrooms, undrained
- 1 medium onion, chopped
- 3 tablespoons Worcestershire sauce
- 3 tablespoons chili powder
- 1 teaspoon salt
- 1/2 teaspoon cayenne pepper
- 2 garlic cloves, minced
- Pinch pepper
- MEATBALLS:
- 2 large eggs, beaten
- 1/4 cup chopped onion
- 1 teaspoon garlic salt
- 1/3 teaspoon pepper
- 2 pounds ground beef
- Hot cooked spaghetti

Direction

- Mix together all the sauce ingredients in a big Dutch oven or you can also use a kettle. Make it to a simmer for 2 hours, without placing any cover. Combine the onion, eggs, pepper and garlic salt in a bowl; crumble the beef on top of the mixture and mix thoroughly. Form into small meatballs; fry in a skillet, a few at a time until browned. Transfer the meatballs on the

sauce and make it to a simmer for an hour. Serve alongside spaghetti.

Nutrition Information

- Calories: 266 calories
- Sodium: 807mg sodium
- Fiber: 4g fiber)
- Total Carbohydrate: 17g carbohydrate (9g sugars
- Cholesterol: 103mg cholesterol
- Protein: 22g protein.
- Total Fat: 13g fat (5g saturated fat)

331. Honey Garlic Meatballs

Serving: 10-12 servings. | Prep: 5mins | Cook: 25mins | Ready in:

Ingredients

- 2 pounds ground beef
- 1 cup dry bread crumbs
- 2 large eggs
- 1 teaspoon salt
- 1 tablespoon butter
- 6 garlic cloves, minced
- 3/4 cup ketchup
- 1/2 cup honey
- 1/4 cup soy sauce
- Cooked rice

Direction

- Mix the salt, eggs, breadcrumbs and ground beef; combine them well. Form into 48 balls, roughly 1.5 inch diameter. Add the meatballs onto the greased rack in the shallow baking pan. Bake at 500 degrees for 12 to 15 minutes, flip frequently; drain off. Melt butter in the big skillet; sauté the garlic till becoming soft. Mix the soy sauce, honey, and ketchup; put into the skillet. Boil. Lower the heat and let simmer, keep covered, roughly 5 minutes. Put in the meatballs. Let simmer, while uncovered, till meatballs become glazed a bit and sauce becomes thick. Serve on the rice.

Nutrition Information

- Calories:
- Total Fat:
- Sodium:
- Fiber:
- Total Carbohydrate:
- Cholesterol:
- Protein:

---

332.   Horseradish Meatballs

Serving: 3 dozen. | Prep: 30mins | Cook: 35mins | Ready in:

Ingredients

- 2 large eggs
- 1/2 cup dry bread crumbs
- 1/4 cup chopped green onions
- 1 tablespoon prepared horseradish
- 1/2 teaspoon salt
- 1/4 teaspoon pepper
- 1-1/2 pounds lean ground beef (90% lean)
- 1/2 pound ground pork or turkey
- SAUCE:
- 1 small onion, finely chopped
- 1/2 cup water
- 1/2 cup chili sauce
- 1/2 cup ketchup
- 1/4 cup packed brown sugar
- 1/4 cup cider vinegar
- 1 tablespoon Worcestershire sauce
- 1 tablespoon prepared horseradish
- 1 garlic clove, minced
- 1 teaspoon ground mustard
- 1/4 teaspoon hot pepper sauce

Direction

- Preheat an oven to 350°. Mix initial 6 ingredients. Add pork and beef; lightly yet thoroughly mix. Form to 1 1/2-in. balls. Put on greased rack in 15x10x1-in. pan. Bake for 35-40 minutes till thermometer reads 160° or 165° for ground turkey (if used).
- Meanwhile, boil sauce ingredients in big saucepan, frequently mixing. Lower heat. Simmer for 10 minutes, uncovered. Mix meatballs in gently.

Nutrition Information

- Calories:
- Protein:
- Total Fat:
- Sodium:
- Fiber:
- Total Carbohydrate:
- Cholesterol:

---

333.   Hot Tamale Meatballs

Serving: 8-10 servings. | Prep: 20mins | Cook: 45mins | Ready in:

Ingredients

- 4 cups tomato juice, divided
- 3/4 cup cornmeal
- 2 tablespoons ground cumin, divided
- 2 tablespoons chili powder, divided
- 3/4 teaspoon salt, divided
- 2 garlic cloves, minced
- 1/4 to 1/2 teaspoon cayenne pepper
- 1/2 pound lean ground beef (90% lean)
- 1/2 pound Jones No Sugar Pork Sausage Roll

Direction

- In a small bowl, mix cayenne, garlic, 1/4 teaspoon of salt, 1 tablespoon of chili powder, 1 tablespoon of cumin, cornmeal, and 1/3 cup of tomato juice. Put in sausage and beef; combine well. Form into 1 1/4 -inch balls.

- In a Dutch oven, mix salt, chili powder, cumin, and the leftover tomato juice; heat to a boil. Add meatballs; simmer, covered, in 45 minutes, or until a thermometer shows 160°.

Nutrition Information

- Calories:
- Cholesterol:
- Protein:
- Total Fat:
- Sodium:
- Fiber:
- Total Carbohydrate:

---

334.   Inside Out Brussels Sprouts

Serving: 8-10 servings. | Prep: 15mins | Cook: 01hours15mins | Ready in:

Ingredients

- 2 pounds ground beef
- 1-1/2 cups uncooked instant rice
- 1 medium onion, chopped
- 2 large eggs, lightly beaten
- 1-1/2 teaspoons garlic salt
- 1/2 teaspoon pepper
- 1 package (10 ounces) frozen brussels sprouts
- 2 cans (15 ounces each) tomato sauce
- 1 cup water
- 1 teaspoon dried thyme

Direction

- Mix together the initial 6 ingredients in a big bowl; combine well. Form meatballs by shaping a scant 1/4 cupful around every frozen brussels sprout.
- Put on an unoiled 15x10x1-inch baking dish. Mix together thyme, water, and tomato sauce;

spread over meatballs. Put on cover and bake 1 1/4 hours at 350 degrees till meatballs have been cooked through.

Nutrition Information

- Calories: 276 calories
- Total Fat: 12g fat (5g saturated fat)
- Sodium: 527mg sodium
- Fiber: 2g fiber)
- Total Carbohydrate: 18g carbohydrate (2g sugars
- Cholesterol: 103mg cholesterol
- Protein: 22g protein.

---

335.   Iowa Ham Balls Main Dish

Serving: 8 servings. | Prep: 15mins | Cook: 60mins | Ready in:

Ingredients

- 2 pound ground ham
- 2 pounds ground beef
- 2 cups graham cracker crumbs
- 2 large eggs
- 1-1/2 cups milk
- SAUCE:
- 2 cans (10-3/4 ounces each) tomato soup, undiluted
- 3/4 cup white vinegar
- 2-1/4 cups brown sugar
- 2 teaspoons ground mustard

Direction

- Mix milk, eggs, and crumbs in a large bowl. Break beef and ham into crumbles over mixture. Form meat mixture, 1/2 cup each time, into balls individually and arrange in a 13x9-inch baking dish.
- Blend the sauce ingredients and transfer over

balls. Bake, without covering, at 350° in 1 hour, or until a thermometer shows 160°.

Nutrition Information

- Calories: 897 calories
- Fiber: 1g fiber)
- Total Carbohydrate: 84g carbohydrate (70g sugars
- Cholesterol: 198mg cholesterol
- Protein: 49g protein.
- Total Fat: 40g fat (15g saturated fat)
- Sodium: 1924mg sodium

---

336. Italian Meatball Mix

Serving: 16 meatballs per batch. | Prep: 15mins | Cook: 20mins |Ready in:

Ingredients

- 2-1/2 cups dry bread crumbs
- 2/3 cup dried minced onion
- 2/3 cup grated Parmesan cheese
- 1/3 cup dried parsley flakes
- 1 tablespoon garlic powder
- 1 tablespoon garlic salt
- ADDITIONAL INGREDIENTS (for each batch):
- 1 egg, lightly beaten
- 1 pound ground beef

Direction

- Blend the first 6 ingredients in a big bowl. Store for up to 2 months in the refrigerator. Yield: 4 batches (around total of 4 cups).
- To prepare meatballs: Mix 1 cup meatball mix and egg in a big bowl. Crumble beef over the blend and stir well. Form into balls of 1-1/2 inch.
- Brown meatballs in a skillet; drain. Move to a baking dish of 13 x 9-inch. Bake for 20 to 25

minutes at 400°, until meat is not pink anymore.

Nutrition Information

- Calories: 83 calories
- Total Fat: 4g fat (2g saturated fat)
- Sodium: 155mg sodium
- Fiber: 0 fiber)
- Total Carbohydrate: 4g carbohydrate (1g sugars
- Cholesterol: 33mg cholesterol
- Protein: 7g protein.

---

337. Italian Spaghetti 'n' Meatballs

Serving: 4 servings. | Prep: 20mins | Cook: 30mins | Ready in:

Ingredients

- 1 cup chopped onion
- 1 tablespoon canola oil
- 1 can (28 ounces) stewed tomatoes
- 2 cans (6 ounces each) tomato paste
- 1 tablespoon sugar
- 1 teaspoon salt
- 1/2 teaspoon dried basil
- 1/4 teaspoon dried oregano
- 1/8 teaspoon dried marjoram
- 1/8 teaspoon paprika
- Dash pepper
- 2 eggs
- 1 garlic clove, minced
- 2 teaspoons dried parsley flakes
- 1 pound lean ground beef
- 1 cup grated Parmesan cheese
- 1/2 cup dry bread crumbs
- Hot cooked spaghetti

Direction

- In a Dutch oven, in oil, sauté onion until tender. Mix in seasonings, sugar, tomato paste, and tomatoes; heat to a boil.
- At the same time, whisk parsley, garlic, and eggs in a big bowl. Crumble beef and add to the mixture, blend nicely. Sprinkle with bread crumbs and cheese; combine gently.
- Form into 1 1/2 -inch balls. Put into the sauce; decrease heat. Put on cover and simmer till meat is not pink anymore, about 30 minutes. Serve sauce and meatballs with spaghetti.

Nutrition Information

- Calories: 510 calories
- Fiber: 5g fiber)
- Total Carbohydrate: 42g carbohydrate (23g sugars
- Cholesterol: 191mg cholesterol
- Protein: 38g protein.
- Total Fat: 22g fat (9g saturated fat)
- Sodium: 1552mg sodium

338.   Italian Spaghetti And Meatballs

Serving: 6 servings. | Prep: 30mins | Cook: 01hours30mins | Ready in:

Ingredients

- 2 cans (28 ounces each) diced tomatoes, undrained
- 1 can (12 ounces) tomato paste
- 1-1/2 cups water, divided
- 3 tablespoons grated onion
- 1 tablespoon sugar
- 1-1/2 teaspoons dried oregano
- 1 bay leaf
- 1-1/4 teaspoons salt, divided
- 1 teaspoon minced garlic, divided
- 3/4 teaspoon pepper, divided
- 6 slices day-old bread, torn into pieces
- 2 large eggs, lightly beaten

- 1/2 cup grated Parmesan cheese
- 2 tablespoons minced fresh parsley
- 1 pound ground beef
- Hot cooked spaghetti
- Additional Parmesan cheese, optional

Direction

- Mix 1/2 teaspoon each of pepper, garlic, and salt, bay leaf, oregano, sugar, onion, 1 cup water, tomato paste, and tomatoes together in a Dutch oven. Boil it. Lower the heat and simmer without a cover for 1 1/4 hours.
- In the meantime, put bread in the leftover water to soak. Extract the excess liquid. Mix the leftover pepper, garlic, and salt, parsley, Parmesan cheese, eggs and bread together in a big bowl. Crumble over the mixture with beef and stir thoroughly. Form into 36 meatballs, about 1-1/2-inch each meatball.
- In a rack set over a shallow baking pan, put the meatballs. Bake without a cover at 400° until the meat is not pink anymore, about 20 minutes; strain. Remove to the spaghetti sauce. Simmer without a cover, whisking sometimes, until thoroughly heated. Remove the bay leaf. Enjoy with spaghetti. Put more Parmesan on top if you want.

Nutrition Information

- Calories: 373 calories
- Protein: 26g protein.
- Total Fat: 13g fat (5g saturated fat)
- Sodium: 1201mg sodium
- Fiber: 7g fiber)
- Total Carbohydrate: 39g carbohydrate (17g sugars
- Cholesterol: 123mg cholesterol

339.   Meal On A Stick

Serving: 8 servings. | Prep: 25mins | Cook: 10mins | Ready in:

Ingredients

- 8 small red potatoes
- 2 eggs, lightly beaten
- 2 teaspoons Worcestershire sauce
- 1-1/4 cups seasoned bread crumbs
- 1 teaspoon curry powder
- 1-1/2 pounds ground beef
- 24 pimiento-stuffed olives
- 8 plum tomatoes, halved
- 2 medium green peppers, cut into quarters
- 8 large fresh mushrooms
- 1/4 cup barbecue sauce

Direction

- Scour and prick potatoes; put on a microwavable plate. Microwave on high with no cover, for 3 to 5 minutes or till lightly soft.
- In the meantime, mix curry powder, breadcrumbs, Worcestershire sauce and eggs in a big bowl. Break up the beef on top of the mixture and combine thoroughly. Distribute into 2 dozen portions; form every portion surrounding an olive.
- Alternately thread vegetables and meatballs on 8 soaked wooden or metal skewers. Let kabobs grill with cover, over moderate-hot heat for 5 minutes per side, brushing with barbecue sauce from time to time, till meatballs are not pink anymore, flipping one time.

Nutrition Information

- Calories: 351 calories
- Fiber: 3g fiber)
- Total Carbohydrate: 29g carbohydrate (5g sugars
- Cholesterol: 110mg cholesterol
- Protein: 23g protein.
- Total Fat: 16g fat (5g saturated fat)
- Sodium: 742mg sodium

340.   Meatball Cabbage Rolls

Serving: 4 servings. | Prep: 25mins | Cook: 08hours00mins | Ready in:

Ingredients

- 1 large head cabbage
- 1 can (8 ounces) no-salt-added tomato sauce
- 1 small onion, chopped
- 1/3 cup uncooked long grain rice
- 2 tablespoons chili powder
- 1/4 teaspoon garlic powder
- 1/8 teaspoon salt
- 1 pound lean ground beef (90% lean)
- 1 can (15 ounces) tomato sauce

Direction

- In the Dutch oven, cook the cabbage in the boiling water just till leaves fall off the head. Put aside 12 big leaves for rolls. Store the rest of the cabbage for other use. Chop out thick vein from bottom of each reserved leaf, shaping one V-shaped cut.
- In the big bowl, mix the salt, garlic powder, chili powder, rice, onion and no-salt-added tomato sauce. Break up the beef on the mixture; stir well. Form into 12 balls. Put one meatball onto each cabbage leaf; overlap the cut ends of the leaf. Fold in the sides, starting from the cut end. Roll them up entirely to enclose the meatball. Secure using the toothpicks.
- Remove into the 5-quart slow cooker. Put the rest of the tomato sauce on top of the cabbage rolls. Put a cover on and cook on low heat till the cabbage softens and the meat is not pink anymore or for 8 hours. Get rid of the toothpicks.

Nutrition Information

- Calories: 323 calories
- Fiber: 7g fiber)
- Total Carbohydrate: 31g carbohydrate (8g sugars

- Cholesterol: 71mg cholesterol
- Protein: 28g protein. Diabetic Exchanges: 3 lean meat
- Total Fat: 11g fat (4g saturated fat)
- Sodium: 762mg sodium

341.   Meatball Chili With Dumplings

Serving: 6 servings. | Prep: 20mins | Cook: 50mins | Ready in:

Ingredients

- 1 large egg, beaten
- 3/4 cup finely chopped onion, divided
- 1/4 cup dry bread crumbs or rolled oats
- 5 teaspoons beef bouillon granules, divided
- 3 teaspoons chili powder, divided
- 1 pound ground beef
- 3 tablespoons all-purpose flour
- 1 tablespoon canola oil
- 1 can (28 ounces) diced tomatoes, undrained
- 1 garlic clove, minced
- 1/2 teaspoon ground cumin
- 1 can (16 ounces) kidney beans, rinsed and drained
- CORNMEAL DUMPLINGS:
- 1-1/2 cups biscuit/baking mix
- 1/2 cup yellow cornmeal
- 2/3 cup whole milk
- Minced chives, optional

Direction

- In a large bowl, combine 1/4 cup onion, egg, 1 teaspoon chili powder, 3 teaspoons bouillon and bread crumbs; crumble beef over mixture and well mix. Form into twelve meatballs, each 1 and 1/2 inches. Roll in flour.
- Heat oil in a cast-iron of 12 inches or other ovenproof skillet to brown meatballs. Place on paper towels for draining. In the meantime, combine the garlic, tomatoes, and cumin with the bouillon, remaining onion, and chili

powder in a large saucepan. Add meatballs. Cook covered for about 20 minutes over low heat. Stir in beans.
- Combine dumpling components. Drop on chili by spoonfuls; cook uncovered on low mode for 10 minutes. Cook while covered for an addition of 10-12 minutes or until a toothpick pinned in dumpling comes out clean. Sprinkle with minced chives (if desired).

Nutrition Information

- Calories: 475 calories
- Protein: 26g protein.
- Total Fat: 16g fat (6g saturated fat)
- Sodium: 1523mg sodium
- Fiber: 7g fiber)
- Total Carbohydrate: 56g carbohydrate (8g sugars
- Cholesterol: 76mg cholesterol

342.   Meatball Garden Stew

Serving: 6 servings. | Prep: 25mins | Cook: 40mins | Ready in:

Ingredients

- 1 pound lean ground beef
- 4 tablespoons all-purpose flour, divided
- 1 teaspoon salt
- Dash pepper
- 1 large egg
- 1/4 cup whole milk
- 1/4 cup chopped onion
- 1 tablespoon butter
- 1 garlic clove, minced
- 1 can (14-1/2 ounces) beef broth
- 2/3 cup water
- 1/2 teaspoon dried thyme
- 6 medium potatoes, peeled and quartered
- 6 medium carrots, halved lengthwise and crosswise
- 6 green onions, chopped

- 1 package (10 ounces) frozen peas, thawed

Direction

- In a medium bowl, blend onion, milk, egg, pepper, salt, 2 tablespoons of flour and beef. Shape into 1-inch balls.
- In the Dutch oven or big skillet, melt butter. Sauté garlic for about 1 minute. Brown meatballs evenly on all sides. Transfer to the side. Blend the drippings and the remaining flour together. Add thyme, water and broth. Let mixture boil. Cook and mix for another 1-2 minutes, until condensed.
- Add onions, carrots, and potatoes then stir with sauce and meatballs. Simmer while covered for 30-35 minutes, up to the vegetables turn softened. Add peas, then cook for 5 minutes more.

Nutrition Information

- Calories: 370 calories
- Cholesterol: 88mg cholesterol
- Protein: 23g protein.
- Total Fat: 10g fat (4g saturated fat)
- Sodium: 790mg sodium
- Fiber: 7g fiber)
- Total Carbohydrate: 48g carbohydrate (11g sugars

---

343.   Meatball Pie

Serving: 6 servings. | Prep: 50mins | Cook: 45mins | Ready in:

Ingredients

- 1 pound ground beef
- 3/4 cup soft bread crumbs
- 1/4 cup chopped onion
- 2 tablespoons minced fresh parsley
- 1 teaspoon salt
- 1/2 teaspoon dried marjoram
- 1/8 teaspoon pepper
- 1/4 cup milk
- 1 large egg, lightly beaten
- 1 can (14-1/2 ounces) stewed tomatoes
- 1 tablespoon cornstarch
- 2 teaspoons beef bouillon granules
- 1 cup frozen peas
- 1 cup sliced carrots, cooked
- CRUST:
- 2-2/3 cups all-purpose flour
- 1/2 teaspoon salt
- 1 cup shortening
- 7 to 8 tablespoons ice water
- Half-and-half cream

Direction

- Mix the first 9 ingredients together in a big bowl (the mixture should be tender). Separate into 4 portions, forming each portion into 12 small meatballs. Working in batches, in a big skillet, brown the meatballs; strain and put aside.
- Strain the tomatoes, saving the liquid. Mix the liquid with cornstarch, adding to the skillet. Add bouillon and tomatoes; boil it over medium heat, whisking continually. Mix in carrots and peas. Take away from heat and put aside.
- Start preheating the oven to 400°. To prepare the crust, mix salt with flour in a big bowl. Cut in shortening until the mixture looks like coarse crumbs. Add water, 1 tablespoon each time; use a fork to gently stir. Remove onto a surface lightly scattered with flour. Lightly knead to make a dough. (The mixture will be crumbly in the beginning, but it will come together and make a dough when you knead it). Split the dough into 2 portions.
- Between 2 pieces of waxed paper lightly scattered with flour, roll each portion of the dough to a 1/8-inch thick circle. Discard the top piece of the waxed paper from 1 pastry circle, flipping onto a 9-inch deep-dish pie plate. Discard the leftover waxed paper. Snip the pastry to even with the rim. Put in the meatballs, spooning over the top with the tomato mixture.

202

- Discard the top piece of the waxed paper from the leftover pastry circle, flipping onto the pie. Discard the leftover waxed paper. Snip, seal, and flute the edge. Cut vents in the top, brushing cream over.
- Bake for 45-50 minutes until the crust turns golden brown. Use a foil to loosely cover the edges during the final 10 minutes if necessary to avoid over-browning. Allow to sit before slicing, about 10 minutes.

Nutrition Information

- Calories: 735 calories
- Fiber: 4g fiber)
- Total Carbohydrate: 58g carbohydrate (8g sugars
- Cholesterol: 87mg cholesterol
- Protein: 25g protein.
- Total Fat: 43g fat (12g saturated fat)
- Sodium: 1094mg sodium

---

344. Meatball Potato Supper

Serving: 6-8 servings. | Prep: 30mins | Cook: 60mins | Ready in:

Ingredients

- 2 eggs
- 1/2 cup dry bread crumbs
- 1 envelope onion soup mix
- 1-1/2 pounds lean ground beef (90% lean)
- 2 tablespoons all-purpose flour
- 6 medium potatoes, peeled and thinly sliced
- 1 can (10-3/4 ounces) condensed cream of celery soup, undiluted
- 1 cup 2% milk
- Paprika, optional

Direction

- Mix soup mix, bread crumbs, and eggs together in a big bowl. Crumble over the

mixture with beef and stir thoroughly. Form into balls, about 1-inch each ball. Working in small batches, brown the meatballs in a big frying pan over medium heat; strain. Sprinkle flour over, lightly roll to blend.
- In a 2 1/2-quart greased baking dish, put 1/2 of the potatoes. Put the leftover potatoes and the meatballs on top. Mix together milk and soup in a small bowl until combined, add to the potatoes. If wanted, sprinkle paprika over.
- Put a cover on and bake at 350° until the potatoes are soft, about 60-65 minutes.

Nutrition Information

- Calories: 361 calories
- Protein: 24g protein.
- Total Fat: 11g fat (4g saturated fat)
- Sodium: 739mg sodium
- Fiber: 3g fiber)
- Total Carbohydrate: 42g carbohydrate (5g sugars
- Cholesterol: 100mg cholesterol

---

345. Meatball Rigatoni Alfredo

Serving: 6 servings. | Prep: 01hours15mins | Cook: 20mins | Ready in:

Ingredients

- 1 large egg, lightly beaten
- 3/4 cup seasoned bread crumbs
- 1/3 cup water
- 1/4 cup grated Parmesan cheese
- 4-1/2 teaspoons each minced fresh thyme, oregano and basil or 1-1/2 teaspoons each dried thyme, oregano and basil
- 1-1/2 teaspoons pepper
- 1/2 teaspoon salt
- 1-1/2 pounds ground beef
- 1 tablespoon canola oil
- 1 small onion, chopped
- 3 garlic cloves, minced

- 1/3 cup dry red wine or beef broth
- 1 can (28 ounces) crushed tomatoes
- 1 tablespoon minced fresh parsley
- 12 ounces uncooked rigatoni or large tube pasta
- ALFREDO TOPPING:
- 1/4 cup butter, cubed
- 2 tablespoons all-purpose flour
- 2 cups half-and-half cream
- 1 cup grated Parmesan cheese, divided
- 1 teaspoon minced fresh thyme or 1/4 teaspoon dried thyme
- 1 teaspoon minced fresh oregano or 1/4 teaspoon dried oregano

Direction

- Mix together seasonings, cheese, water, bread crumbs and egg in a large bowl. Crumble beef over mixture and combine well. Form into 1-1/2-in. balls. Brown meatballs in oil in batches in a Dutch oven; take them out and keep warm.
- Drain, and reserve 1 tablespoon of drippings. Sauté onion in drippings until it becomes tender. Add garlic; and cook for 1 more minute. Add wine, cook while stirring for 3 minutes.
- Transfer meatballs back to pan; stir in parsley and tomatoes. Bring to a boil. Lower the heat; simmer with a cover until meat is no longer pink, about 25-30 minutes.
- At the meantime, Set the oven to 400° and start preheating. Cook rigatoni as directed on the package.
- Melt butter in a small saucepan. Stir in flour until smooth; add cream gradually. Bring to a boil; cook while stirring until thickened, about 1-2 minutes. Take away from the heat. Stir in 3/4 cup Parmesan cheese.
- Drain rigatoni and transfer to a large bowl. Add sauce and meatballs, stir to coat. Place in a greased 13x9-in. baking dish.
- Pour Alfredo sauce on top; drizzle with oregano, remaining Parmesan cheese, and thyme. Bake without a cover until bubbly, about 20-25 minutes.

Nutrition Information

- Calories: 849 calories
- Protein: 47g protein.
- Total Fat: 41g fat (20g saturated fat)
- Sodium: 1027mg sodium
- Fiber: 6g fiber)
- Total Carbohydrate: 69g carbohydrate (6g sugars
- Cholesterol: 196mg cholesterol

```
346.        Meatball Skillet Meal
```

Serving: 6 servings. | Prep: 30mins | Cook: 0mins | Ready in:

Ingredients

- 1/2 cup finely chopped fresh mushrooms
- 1/3 cup quick-cooking oats
- 2 tablespoons finely chopped green pepper
- 2 tablespoons finely chopped onion
- 2 tablespoon dried parsley flakes
- 1 teaspoon dried basil
- 1 teaspoon dried oregano
- 1/2 teaspoon dried thyme
- 1/2 teaspoon salt
- 1/4 teaspoon pepper
- 1 pound ground beef
- 4 medium carrots, sliced
- 1 small zucchini, sliced
- 1 can (14-1/2 ounces) diced tomatoes, undrained
- 4 cups hot cooked rice

Direction

- Mix the first 10 ingredients together in a big bowl then crumble beef over it. Mix thoroughly then use the mixture to form balls around 1-1/4 inches.
- In a big skillet on medium heat, cook the meatballs until they are not pink anymore.

Drain then add the zucchini and carrots in, leaving it uncovered. Cook until the vegetables are tender, about 5 minutes. Stir the tomatoes in and heat thoroughly. Serve the meatballs and vegetables with rice.

Nutrition Information

- Calories: 312 calories
- Total Carbohydrate: 42g carbohydrate (6g sugars
- Cholesterol: 37mg cholesterol
- Protein: 18g protein.
- Total Fat: 8g fat (3g saturated fat)
- Sodium: 352mg sodium
- Fiber: 4g fiber)

347.   Meatball Stew

Serving: 8-10 servings. | Prep: 15mins | Cook: 45mins | Ready in:

Ingredients

- 1 large egg, lightly beaten
- 1 cup soft bread crumbs
- 1/4 cup finely chopped onion
- 1 teaspoon salt
- 1/2 teaspoon dried marjoram
- 1/4 teaspoon dried thyme
- 1-1/2 pounds lean ground beef (90% lean)
- 2 tablespoons canola oil
- 2 cans (10-3/4 ounces each) condensed tomato soup, undiluted
- 2 cans (10-1/2 ounces each) condensed beef broth, undiluted
- 4 medium potatoes, peeled and diced
- 4 medium carrots, diced
- 1 jar (16 ounces) whole onions, drained
- 1/4 cup minced fresh parsley

Direction

- In a large bowl, combine the bread crumbs, egg, salt, chopped onion, thyme and marjoram. Crumble beef over the top and mix well. Form into 24 meatballs. In a Dutch oven, heat oil. Brown meatballs in batches; drain.
- Stir in the broth, soup, potatoes, whole onions and carrots. Allow to boil; decrease the heat and simmer for 30 minutes or until the meat is not pink anymore. Garnish with parsley.

Nutrition Information

- Calories: 248 calories
- Protein: 17g protein.
- Total Fat: 9g fat (3g saturated fat)
- Sodium: 895mg sodium
- Fiber: 3g fiber)
- Total Carbohydrate: 24g carbohydrate (7g sugars
- Cholesterol: 55mg cholesterol

348.   Meatball Stroganoff With Noodles

Serving: 6 servings. | Prep: 40mins | Cook: 15mins | Ready in:

Ingredients

- 2 cups all-purpose flour
- 1 teaspoon salt
- 3 egg yolks
- 1 egg
- 6 tablespoons water
- MEATBALLS:
- 1 egg, lightly beaten
- 2 tablespoons ketchup
- 1/4 cup quick-cooking oats
- 1 tablespoon finely chopped onion
- 1/2 teaspoon salt
- 1 pound ground beef
- SAUCE:
- 2 cans (10-3/4 ounces each) condensed cream of mushroom soup, undiluted

- 1 cup (8 ounces) sour cream
- 1 cup milk
- 1 tablespoon paprika
- 2 quarts water
- 1 teaspoon salt
- 1 tablespoon butter
- 1 tablespoon minced parsley

Direction

- In a large bowl, mix salt and flour. In the center, make a well. Whisk water, egg and egg yolks; pour into the well. Mix together to form a dough. Turn the dough onto a floured surface; knead 8 to 10 times. Separate into thirds; roll out each as thin as possible. Allow to stand till partially dried, 20 minutes. Cut into 1/4-inch strips; then into 2-inch pieces; set aside.
- In another large bowl, mix salt, onion, oats, ketchup and egg. Crumble beef over the mixture; mix thoroughly. Form into 1 1/2 balls.
- In a shallow baking pan, arrange meatballs on a greased rack. Bake without a cover at 400° till no longer pink, 10-15 minutes; strain.
- In a large saucepan, mix paprika, milk, sour cream and soup; heat through. Put in meatballs; cook with a cover while stirring often till heated through.
- In another saucepan, bring water and salt to a boil; put in noodles. Cook till noodles are tender, 12-15 minutes; strain. Toss with parsley and butter. Serve with meatballs.

Nutrition Information

- Calories: 504 calories
- Total Carbohydrate: 44g carbohydrate (5g sugars
- Cholesterol: 252mg cholesterol
- Protein: 25g protein.
- Total Fat: 24g fat (12g saturated fat)
- Sodium: 1533mg sodium
- Fiber: 2g fiber)

---

349. Meatball And Sausage Bites

Serving: about 40 servings. | Prep: 20mins | Cook: 40mins |Ready in:

Ingredients

- 2 eggs
- 1 small onion, finely chopped
- 1 cup dry bread crumbs
- 1/2 teaspoon garlic salt
- 1/2 teaspoon pepper
- 2 pounds ground beef
- 2 packages (1 pound each) miniature smoked sausages
- 2 cans (20 ounces each) pineapple chunks, drained
- 1 jar (10 ounces) pimiento-stuffed olives, drained
- 1 cup packed brown sugar
- 2 bottles (20 ounces each) barbecue sauce

Direction

- Mix the first five ingredients in a large bowl. Break beef into pieces over the mixture and combine well. Form into 1-inch balls. Put meatballs on a rack that is greased, in a shallow baking pan.
- Bake for 15 minutes at 350 degrees, uncovered or until not pink anymore; strain. Place meatballs to two shallow 3-qt. baking dishes using a slotted spoon. Add olives, pineapple, and sausages to each; toss cautiously to combine.
- Mix barbecue sauce and brown sugar; put half over each casserole. Bake for 25 minutes at 350 degrees, uncovered or until heated through.

Nutrition Information

- Calories: 141 calories
- Sodium: 414mg sodium
- Fiber: 0 fiber)

- Total Carbohydrate: 11g carbohydrate (9g sugars
- Cholesterol: 33mg cholesterol
- Protein: 7g protein.
- Total Fat: 8g fat (2g saturated fat)

350.   Meatballs And Beans

Serving: 4-6 servings. | Prep: 10mins | Cook: 20mins | Ready in:

Ingredients

- 2/3 cup soft bread crumbs
- 1/2 cup evaporated milk
- 1 teaspoon salt
- 1/4 teaspoon pepper
- 1 pound lean ground beef
- 1 small onion, divided
- 1 can (16 ounces) baked beans, undrained
- 2 to 3 tablespoons ketchup
- 1 tablespoon brown sugar
- 1/4 to 1/2 teaspoon ground mustard

Direction

- Mix pepper, salt, milk, and bread crumbs. Break beef into crumbles over mixture and combine well. Form into 1 1/2-inch balls.
- Cook onion and meatballs in a large skillet until meatballs are browned; drain. Put in mustard, brown sugar, ketchup, and beans. Heat to a boil. Lower the heat; simmer, covered, for 20 to 25 minutes, or until meatballs are not pink anymore.

Nutrition Information

- Calories: 254 calories
- Protein: 20g protein.
- Total Fat: 9g fat (4g saturated fat)
- Sodium: 847mg sodium
- Fiber: 5g fiber)

- Total Carbohydrate: 24g carbohydrate (11g sugars
- Cholesterol: 58mg cholesterol

351.   Meatballs And Gravy

Serving: 6 servings. | Prep: 15mins | Cook: 25mins | Ready in:

Ingredients

- 1 egg
- 1/2 cup milk
- 1 tablespoon cornstarch
- 1 medium onion, finely chopped
- 1 teaspoon salt
- Dash pepper
- 1/4 teaspoon ground nutmeg
- 1/4 teaspoon ground allspice
- 1/4 teaspoon ground ginger
- 1-1/2 pounds lean ground beef (90% lean)
- 3 to 4 tablespoons butter
- GRAVY:
- 1 tablespoon butter
- 2 tablespoons all-purpose flour
- 1 cup beef broth
- 1/2 cup milk or half-and-half cream
- Salt and pepper to taste
- Minced fresh parsley, optional

Direction

- Beat ginger, allspice, nutmeg, pepper, salt, onion, cornstarch, milk and egg in a big bowl. Put in the beef; mix well. Form 1- 1/2 -inch meatballs. (In case the mixture is very soft, frequently rinse your hands with cold water for easier shaping). Brown the meatballs with butter over medium heat in a big skillet, half at once, for approximately 10 minutes or until there is no pink meat left. Place the meatballs on paper towels to drain, keep 1 tablespoon of drippings in the skillet.
- To make gravy, put butter into the drippings. Stir in flour. Pour in milk and broth. Boil, cook

while stirring for 2 minutes or until the mixture is thickened. Add pepper and salt for seasoning. Put the meatballs back to the skillet, heat them through on low. If needed, garnish with parsley.

Nutrition Information

- Calories: 302 calories
- Total Fat: 18g fat (9g saturated fat)
- Sodium: 712mg sodium
- Fiber: 1g fiber)
- Total Carbohydrate: 8g carbohydrate (4g sugars
- Cholesterol: 117mg cholesterol
- Protein: 25g protein.

352.　　Meatballs In Barbecue Sauce

Serving: about 4 dozen. | Prep: 20mins | Cook: 30mins | Ready in:

Ingredients

- 1 large egg, lightly beaten
- 1 can (5 ounces) evaporated milk
- 1 cup quick-cooking oats
- 1/2 cup finely chopped onion
- 1 teaspoon salt
- 1 teaspoon chili powder
- 1/4 teaspoon garlic powder
- 1/4 teaspoon pepper
- 1-1/2 pounds ground beef
- SAUCE:
- 1 cup ketchup
- 3/4 cup packed brown sugar
- 1/4 cup chopped onion
- 1/2 teaspoon Liquid Smoke, optional
- 1/4 teaspoon garlic powder

Direction

- Combine the initial 8 ingredients in a big bowl. Crumble beef and add to the mixture; combine nicely. Form into 1-inch balls.
- Arrange meatballs on an oiled rack set in a shallow baking pan. Bake at 350 degrees without cover until meat is not pink anymore, about 18-20 minutes. Drain.
- At the same time, in a saucepan, mix together sauce ingredients. Heat to a boil. Lower the heat and simmer, mixing often, about 2 minutes. Spread over meatballs then bake for 10 to 12 more minutes.

Nutrition Information

- Calories: 474 calories
- Protein: 28g protein.
- Total Fat: 18g fat (7g saturated fat)
- Sodium: 973mg sodium
- Fiber: 2g fiber)
- Total Carbohydrate: 51g carbohydrate (35g sugars
- Cholesterol: 119mg cholesterol

353.　　Meatballs In Dill Cream Sauce

Serving: 4 main-dish servings. | Prep: 20mins | Cook: 20mins | Ready in:

Ingredients

- 8 ounces lean ground beef (90% lean)
- 8 ounces lean ground pork
- 1 small onion, finely chopped
- 1/2 teaspoon salt
- 1/2 teaspoon pepper
- 1/4 teaspoon dried thyme
- 1/4 teaspoon dried marjoram
- 1/4 teaspoon ground nutmeg
- 1-1/2 cups fresh bread crumbs
- 1/2 cup water
- SAUCE:
- 2 tablespoons butter

- 2 tablespoons all-purpose flour
- 1-1/2 cups beef broth
- 2 tablespoons snipped fresh dill or 1 teaspoon dill weed
- 1/2 cup half-and-half cream
- Cooked buttered wide egg noodles, optional

Direction

- Mix the water, crumbs, seasonings, onion, pork and beef in a bowl. Form into 1-1/4-inch balls and lay on a cooking-spray-coated rack in a shallow baking tray. Set oven at 400°, bake until a thermometer reaches 160°, about 20 minutes then drain.
- In the meantime, to make the sauce, add butter to a big frying pan and melt. Mix in flour until smooth. Add the broth and boil. Stir and cook until the mixture gets thick, about 2 minutes. Add the meatballs and dill. Lower to low heat, simmer while uncovered for 15 minutes.
- Mix in cream. Stir and cook until the mixture gets thick, about 15 minutes. If preferred, serve with noodles or as an appetizer.

Nutrition Information

- Calories: 370 calories
- Sodium: 833mg sodium
- Fiber: 1g fiber)
- Total Carbohydrate: 15g carbohydrate (3g sugars
- Cholesterol: 96mg cholesterol
- Protein: 25g protein.
- Total Fat: 22g fat (11g saturated fat)

---

354. Meatballs In Honey Buffalo Sauce

Serving: about 2-1/2 dozen. | Prep: 45mins | Cook: 02hours00mins | Ready in:

Ingredients

- 2 large eggs, lightly beaten
- 15 Ritz crackers, crushed
- 1/2 medium onion, finely chopped
- 1/4 cup 2% milk
- 4 teaspoons brown sugar
- 1/2 teaspoon garlic powder
- 1/2 teaspoon ground chipotle pepper
- 1/4 teaspoon smoked paprika
- 1/4 teaspoon salt
- 1/8 teaspoon pepper
- 1/2 pound ground beef
- 1/2 pound ground pork
- 1/2 pound ground veal
- SAUCE:
- 1/2 cup honey
- 1/4 cup Buffalo wing sauce
- 1/4 cup packed brown sugar
- 2 tablespoons orange marmalade
- 2 tablespoons apricot spreadable fruit
- 2 tablespoons reduced-sodium soy sauce
- 1/4 teaspoon crushed red pepper flakes
- Hot cooked rice or pasta
- Sliced celery, optional

Direction

- Preheat the oven to 400 degrees. Mix the initial 10 ingredients. Put in the meat; stir gently but completely. Form the meat mixture into 1.5-inch balls; bake on the greased rack in the 15x10x1-inch baking pan that is lined with the foil, for 12 to 15 minutes or till turning brown a bit. At the same time, in the small-sized saucepan on medium heat, stir the sauce ingredients together till the brown sugar dissolves.
- Move the meatballs into the 3-quart slow cooker; pour in the sauce. Cook, while covered, over low heat for roughly 2 hours or till the meatballs become thoroughly cooked. Serve along with the pasta or hot cooked rice and, if you want, the sliced celery.
- Freeze option: Freeze the sauce and cooled meatballs in the freezer containers. To use, partly thaw in the fridge overnight. Thoroughly heat in the covered sauce pan, whisking lightly and pouring in a bit of

water/broth if needed. Serve following the instructions.

Nutrition Information

- Calories: 258 calories
- Sodium: 459mg sodium
- Fiber: 0 fiber)
- Total Carbohydrate: 30g carbohydrate (26g sugars
- Cholesterol: 81mg cholesterol
- Protein: 14g protein.
- Total Fat: 10g fat (3g saturated fat)

355.   Meatballs In Potato Cups

Serving: 4 servings. | Prep: 25mins | Cook: 35mins | Ready in:

Ingredients

- 2 cups leftover mashed potatoes
- 1 large egg
- 1/2 small onion, finely chopped
- 1 celery rib, finely chopped
- 2/3 pound lean ground beef
- 1/2 cup quick-cooking oats
- 1/3 cup nonfat dry milk powder
- 1/2 teaspoon salt
- 1/4 teaspoon pepper
- BOUILLON GRAVY:
- 1 tablespoon butter
- 2 tablespoons all-purpose flour
- 1 cup water
- 1 teaspoon beef bouillon granules
- 1/2 teaspoon browning sauce, optional

Direction

- Combine egg with potatoes in a bowl. Put eight mounds of the potato mixture onto a greased 15x10x1-in. baking pan with an ice cream scoop.

- Mix pepper, salt, milk, oats, beef, celery and onion; form into eight meatballs. In each potato "cup", halfway press one meatball. Bake at 350° till the potatoes and meat are well browned, or for 35-40 minutes.
- Meanwhile, melt butter in a small saucepan for gravy; take away from the heat. Whisk in flour. Mix in bouillon and water. Include in browning sauce if you want. Cook while stirring till thickened and smooth. Place gravy over the potato cups with a spoon; pass any remaining gravy.

Nutrition Information

- Calories: 203 calories
- Protein: 7g protein.
- Total Fat: 6g fat (3g saturated fat)
- Sodium: 819mg sodium
- Fiber: 1g fiber)
- Total Carbohydrate: 30g carbohydrate (1g sugars
- Cholesterol: 63mg cholesterol

356.   Meatballs In Sweet Clove Sauce

Serving: 6 servings. | Prep: 20mins | Cook: 55mins | Ready in:

Ingredients

- 4 slices dry bread, diced
- 1/4 cup lemon juice
- 1 egg
- 1 small onion, diced
- 1 teaspoon seasoned salt
- 1-1/2 pounds ground beef
- SAUCE:
- 1 cup tomato juice
- 1/2 cup chili sauce
- 1/2 cup packed brown sugar
- 1 teaspoon ground mustard
- 1/4 teaspoon ground cloves

Direction

- Soak bread in lemon juice for 2 minutes in a bowl. Put in salt, onion and egg; mix in beef. Form into 1 1/2 – inch balls; arrange meatballs on a greased rack in a shallow baking pan. Bake without a cover at 350°, about 25 minutes; strain. Mix sauce ingredients; pour the sauce over the meatballs. Bake for 30 more minutes, till hot and bubbly.

Nutrition Information

- Calories:
- Fiber:
- Total Carbohydrate:
- Cholesterol:
- Protein:
- Total Fat:
- Sodium:

357. Meatballs With Cream Sauce

Serving: 6 servings. | Prep: 15mins | Cook: 20mins | Ready in:

Ingredients

- 1 egg, lightly beaten
- 1/4 cup 2% milk
- 2 tablespoons ketchup
- 1 teaspoon Worcestershire sauce
- 3/4 cup quick-cooking oats
- 1/4 cup finely chopped onion
- 1/4 cup minced fresh parsley
- 1 teaspoon salt
- 1/4 teaspoon pepper
- 1-1/2 pounds lean ground beef (90% lean)
- 3 tablespoons all-purpose flour
- CREAM SAUCE:
- 2 tablespoons butter
- 2 tablespoons all-purpose flour
- 1/4 teaspoon dried thyme

- Salt and pepper to taste
- 1 can (14 ounces) chicken broth
- 2/3 cup heavy whipping cream
- 2 tablespoons minced fresh parsley

Direction

- In a large bowl, combine the milk, egg, Worcestershire sauce, ketchup, onion, oats, parsley, pepper and salt. Crumble beef over mixture and mix well. Form into balls of 1 and a half inch in size. Roll in flour to coat, shaking off excess.
- On greased racks in shallow baking pans, place meatballs. Bake without a cover at 400° for 10 minutes. Turn meatballs; bake for an addition of 12 to 15 minutes or until meat is not pink anymore.
- In the meantime, for making sauce, melt butter over medium heat in a saucepan. Mix in the thyme, flour, pepper and salt until smooth. Add cream and broth gradually. Allow to boil; cook and stir for 2 minutes or until thickened.
- Place meatballs on paper towels for draining; Remove to a serving dish. Use sauce for serving; sprinkle with parsley.

Nutrition Information

- Calories: 389 calories
- Cholesterol: 139mg cholesterol
- Protein: 27g protein.
- Total Fat: 24g fat (12g saturated fat)
- Sodium: 874mg sodium
- Fiber: 1g fiber)
- Total Carbohydrate: 16g carbohydrate (3g sugars

358. Meatballs With Mushroom Sauce

Serving: 30 meatballs. | Prep: 20mins | Cook: 30mins | Ready in:

Ingredients

- 1/4 cup evaporated milk
- 1/4 cup dry bread crumbs
- 1/2 teaspoon salt
- 1/4 teaspoon pepper
- 1-1/2 pounds ground beef
- SAUCE:
- 1 can (10-3/4 ounces) condensed cream of mushroom soup, undiluted
- 2/3 cup evaporated milk
- 2/3 cup water

Direction

- Combine the initial 4 ingredients in a big bowl. Crumble meat and add to the mixture, combine nicely. Form into 1 1/2 -inch balls. Brown meatballs in a big oven-proof skillet; drain. Mix sauce ingredients together; spread over meatballs. Bake at 350 degrees without cover until meat is not pink anymore, about 30 minutes.

Nutrition Information

- Calories: 285 calories
- Sodium: 703mg sodium
- Fiber: 1g fiber)
- Total Carbohydrate: 11g carbohydrate (4g sugars
- Cholesterol: 70mg cholesterol
- Protein: 24g protein.
- Total Fat: 15g fat (7g saturated fat)

---

359.   Meatballs With Pepper Sauce

Serving: 60 meatballs. | Prep: 25mins | Cook: 01hours15mins | Ready in:

Ingredients

- 1 cup evaporated milk
- 1 tablespoon Worcestershire sauce

- 1 envelope onion soup mix
- 2 pounds ground beef
- SAUCE:
- 1/2 pound sliced fresh mushrooms
- 1-1/2 cups ketchup
- 3/4 cup packed brown sugar
- 3/4 cup water
- 1/2 cup chopped green pepper
- 1/2 cup chopped sweet red pepper
- 2 tablespoons chopped onion
- 1 tablespoon Worcestershire sauce

Direction

- In the big bowl, mix soup mix, Worcestershire sauce, and milk. Break up the beef on top of mixture and stir well. Form into 1-inch balls.
- Put the meatballs onto the rack in the shallow baking pan. Broil 4 to 6 inches away from heat till turning brown or for 5 to 8 minutes. In the Dutch oven, mix the sauce ingredients. Boil. Lower the heat; put in the meatballs. Let simmer, while uncovered, till meat is not pink anymore or for 60 minutes.

Nutrition Information

- Calories: 329 calories
- Fiber: 1g fiber)
- Total Carbohydrate: 33g carbohydrate (23g sugars
- Cholesterol: 68mg cholesterol
- Protein: 21g protein.
- Total Fat: 13g fat (6g saturated fat)
- Sodium: 782mg sodium

---

360.   Meatballs With Rice

Serving: 6-8 servings. | Prep: 15mins | Cook: 01hours20mins | Ready in:

Ingredients

- 1 pound ground beef

- 1/2 cup rolled oats
- 1-1/2 teaspoons salt, divided
- 1/2 teaspoon pepper
- 1/2 teaspoon celery salt
- 1 teaspoon dried parsley flakes
- 2 cans (10-3/4 ounces each) condensed cream of asparagus soup, undiluted
- 2 cups water
- 1 cup uncooked rice
- 1-1/2 cups sliced celery
- 1 large onion, chopped
- 1 can (4 ounces) mushroom stems and pieces, drained

Direction

- In a bowl, combine the oats, beef, pepper, half a teaspoon of salt, parsley and celery salt. Form by tablespoonful into meatballs. On a greased rack in a shallow baking pan, place meatballs. Bake at 400° for 18 to 20 minutes or until it has browned in color.
- In the meantime, combine celery, rice, mushrooms, onion, soup, the remaining salt and water. Remove meatballs to a greased casserole of 3-quart in size; pour soup mixture over. Bake while covering at 350° for 1 hour or until rice is tender and liquid is absorbed.

Nutrition Information

- Calories: 250 calories
- Fiber: 2g fiber)
- Total Carbohydrate: 28g carbohydrate (3g sugars
- Cholesterol: 39mg cholesterol
- Protein: 15g protein.
- Total Fat: 9g fat (3g saturated fat)
- Sodium: 866mg sodium

361.   Meatballs With Spaetzle

Serving: 4 servings. | Prep: 10mins | Cook: 50mins | Ready in:

Ingredients

- 1 egg
- 1/4 cup milk
- 1/4 cup dry bread crumbs
- 1 tablespoon dried parsley flakes
- 1/2 teaspoon salt
- 1/4 teaspoon poultry seasoning
- Dash pepper
- 1 pound ground beef
- 1 can (10-1/2 ounces) condensed beef broth, undiluted
- 1 can (4 ounces) mushroom stems and pieces, drained
- 1 medium onion, chopped
- 1 tablespoon all-purpose flour
- 1 teaspoon caraway seeds
- 1 cup (8 ounces) sour cream
- HOMEMADE SPAETZLE:
- 2 cups all-purpose flour
- 1 teaspoon salt
- 2 eggs, lightly beaten
- 1 cup milk
- 2 quarts water or beef broth

Direction

- In a bowl, blend the first seven ingredients together. Break the beef into crumbles over the mixture and stir well. Roll into balls of 1 and a half inch in size.
- In a skillet, brown meatballs; drain. Add onion, mushrooms and broth. Allow to boil. Decrease the heat; simmer while covering for 30 minutes. Combine the sour cream, caraway seeds and flour until smooth; mix into meatball mixture. Cook over low heat for approximately 10 minutes until heated through and thickened.
- In the meantime, in a bowl, combine the salt, flour, milk and eggs. Allow to rest for 5 minutes. In a large saucepan, set broth or water to a rapid boil. In a colander or spaetzle press, place spaetzle batter. Holding over the boiling liquid, press the batter through holds of colander. Cook and stir for 5 minutes or

until soften; drain. Serve over spaetzle with meatballs and sauce.

Nutrition Information

- Calories: 692 calories
- Protein: 40g protein.
- Total Fat: 28g fat (14g saturated fat)
- Sodium: 1811mg sodium
- Fiber: 3g fiber)
- Total Carbohydrate: 65g carbohydrate (10g sugars
- Cholesterol: 264mg cholesterol

362.   Microwave Meatball Stew

Serving: 4-6 servings. | Prep: 15mins | Cook: 10mins | Ready in:

Ingredients

- 1 egg, lightly beaten
- 1/2 cup dry bread crumbs
- 1/2 cup finely chopped onion
- 2 tablespoons onion soup mix
- 1 pound ground beef
- 1 can (15 ounces) whole potatoes, drained and quartered
- 1-1/4 cups frozen sliced carrots
- 1-1/4 cups frozen peas
- 1 can (10-3/4 ounces) condensed cream of mushroom soup, undiluted
- 1 can (10-1/2 ounces) condensed beef broth, undiluted
- 1/2 teaspoon dried savory
- 1/4 teaspoon dried thyme
- 2 tablespoons cornstarch
- 2 tablespoons water
- 1/4 teaspoon browning sauce, optional

Direction

- Combine soup mix, onion, crumbs, and egg in a large bowl. Break beef apart and sprinkle

over the mixture; stir well. Form the mixture into 1 1/2-inch balls.
- Transfer the balls to a microwaveable baking dish. Microwave, covered for 3 to 4 minutes on high power. Turn meatballs over and cook in microwave for 3 to 4 more minutes; drain.
- Combine the next 7 ingredients in a large bowl; ladle over meatballs. Cook, covered at 50% power until meat is no longer pink, or for 8 to 10 minutes. Combine water, cornstarch, and browning sauce (if using) until no lumps remain; slowly mix into the stew. Microwave, covered for 1 to 2 minutes on high power, stirring from time to time, or until bubbly and thickened.

Nutrition Information

- Calories: 333 calories
- Protein: 22g protein.
- Total Fat: 14g fat (5g saturated fat)
- Sodium: 1274mg sodium
- Fiber: 5g fiber)
- Total Carbohydrate: 29g carbohydrate (5g sugars
- Cholesterol: 88mg cholesterol

363.   Minted Meatballs

Serving: 40 meatballs. | Prep: 15mins | Cook: 20mins | Ready in:

Ingredients

- 4 slices bread
- 1/2 cup water
- 1 egg, beaten
- 1 medium onion, finely chopped
- 1/2 cup minced fresh parsley
- 1 garlic clove, minced
- 2 teaspoons dried mint flakes
- 1 teaspoon salt
- 1/8 teaspoon pepper
- 1 pound ground beef

- 1 cup all-purpose flour
- 1/2 cup vegetable oil

Direction

- Plunge the bread into water, squeeze to remove excess water. Break the bread into crumbs in a big bowl. Mix in the pepper, salt, mint, garlic, parsley, onion and egg. Break the beef into crumbs then mix well into the mixture. Form into 1-inch balls. Roll into flour. Add meatballs to oil in a big frying pan, cook over medium heat until it is not pink any longer, about 15 minutes.

Nutrition Information

- Calories:
- Cholesterol:
- Protein:
- Total Fat:
- Sodium:
- Fiber:
- Total Carbohydrate:

364.   Mom's Meatballs

Serving: 7 dozen. | Prep: 15mins | Cook: 10mins |Ready in:

Ingredients

- 1-1/2 cups chopped onion
- 1/3 cup ketchup
- 3 tablespoons lemon juice
- 1 tablespoon Worcestershire sauce
- 3/4 cup crushed saltines (about 24 crackers)
- 3 pounds ground beef

Direction

- Mix crackers, Worcestershire sauce, lemon juice, ketchup, and onion in a big bowl. Crumble beef and add to the mixture; combine nicely. Form into 1-inch balls.

- Arrange meatballs over an oiled rack set in a shallow baking pan. Bake at 400 degrees without cover, about 10 minutes until meat is not pink anymore. Drain. Immediately serve meatballs or keep in the fridge or freeze for other uses.

Nutrition Information

- Calories: 36 calories
- Sodium: 28mg sodium
- Fiber: 0 fiber)
- Total Carbohydrate: 1g carbohydrate (0 sugars
- Cholesterol: 11mg cholesterol
- Protein: 3g protein.
- Total Fat: 2g fat (1g saturated fat)

365.   Monterey Jack Meatballs

Serving: 20 meatballs. | Prep: 20mins | Cook: 20mins | Ready in:

Ingredients

- 1 egg
- 1/2 cup milk
- 1 cup soft bread crumbs
- 2 tablespoons dried minced onion
- 1/2 teaspoon salt
- 1/8 teaspoon pepper
- 1 pound lean ground beef (90% lean)
- 1 block (4 ounces) Monterey Jack cheese, cut into 20 cubes
- 2 tablespoons canola oil
- 1 jar (14 ounces) spaghetti sauce
- 1/2 cup shredded Monterey Jack cheese

Direction

- Mix the first six ingredients together in a large bowl. Crumble beef over the mixture; mix properly. Separate into 20 portions; roll each around a cheese cube.

- Brown the meatballs in a large skillet with oil; strain. Include in spaghetti sauce. Allow to boil. Lower the heat; simmer with a cover till the meat is not pink anymore, or for 10 minutes. Sprinkle with cheese.

Nutrition Information

- Calories: 436 calories
- Cholesterol: 126mg cholesterol
- Protein: 30g protein.
- Total Fat: 28g fat (11g saturated fat)
- Sodium: 954mg sodium
- Fiber: 2g fiber)
- Total Carbohydrate: 15g carbohydrate (8g sugars

366.   Nacho Meatballs

Serving: 30 meatballs. | Prep: 25mins | Cook: 01hours30mins | Ready in:

Ingredients

- 2 eggs
- 1/2 cup ketchup
- 1 large onion, chopped
- 2/3 cup crushed saltines
- 1/2 cup mashed potato flakes
- 1/2 teaspoon garlic powder
- 1/4 teaspoon pepper
- 2 pounds lean ground beef
- 1 can (11 ounces) condensed nacho cheese soup, undiluted
- 1 can (10-3/4 ounces) condensed cream of mushroom soup, undiluted
- 1-1/3 cups water
- 1 can (2.8 ounces) french-fried onions

Direction

- In a large bowl, combine the first seven ingredients. Crumble beef over mixture and mix well. Form into balls, 1 1/2-inch each. On

a greased rack in a shallow baking pan, place meatballs.
- Uncover and bake at 350° for about 1 hour, turning once; drain. Combine water and soups; pour mixture over meatballs. Use onions for sprinkling. Bake for an additional 30 minutes until meat is no longer pink.

Nutrition Information

- Calories: 389 calories
- Total Fat: 20g fat (7g saturated fat)
- Sodium: 924mg sodium
- Fiber: 2g fiber)
- Total Carbohydrate: 24g carbohydrate (4g sugars
- Cholesterol: 129mg cholesterol
- Protein: 27g protein.

367.   No Fuss Meatballs

Serving: 6 servings. | Prep: 15mins | Cook: 30mins | Ready in:

Ingredients

- 1 egg
- 1/4 cup milk
- 1/4 cup finely chopped onion
- 3/4 cup seasoned bread crumbs
- 1/2 teaspoon salt
- Dash pepper
- 1-1/2 pounds lean ground beef
- 1-1/3 cups ketchup
- 2 cups ginger ale
- Hot cooked rice

Direction

- In a bowl, stir the first six ingredients together. Put in beef; mix properly. Roll into 1-1/4-in. balls. In a big saucepan or Dutch oven, boil ginger ale and ketchup over medium heat. Lower heat. Add meatballs; simmer, covered, for 30 minutes till meat has no pink left. Serve on top of rice.

Nutrition Information

- Calories: 332 calories
- Total Carbohydrate: 33g carbohydrate (14g sugars
- Cholesterol: 106mg cholesterol
- Protein: 26g protein.
- Total Fat: 11g fat (4g saturated fat)
- Sodium: 1115mg sodium
- Fiber: 1g fiber)

368.   Norwegian Meatballs

Serving: about 16 servings. | Prep: 30mins | Cook: 20mins | Ready in:

Ingredients

- 2 large eggs, lightly beaten
- 1 cup whole milk
- 1 cup dry bread crumbs
- 1/2 cup finely chopped onion
- 2 teaspoons salt
- 2 teaspoons sugar
- 1/2 teaspoon each ground ginger, nutmeg and allspice
- 1/4 teaspoon pepper
- 2 pounds extra-lean ground beef (95% lean)
- 1 pound ground pork
- GRAVY:
- 2 tablespoons finely chopped onion
- 3 tablespoons butter
- 5 tablespoons all-purpose flour
- 4 cups beef broth
- 1/2 cup heavy whipping cream
- Dash cayenne pepper
- Dash white pepper

Direction

- Combine seasonings, onion, bread crumbs, milk, and eggs in a big bowl. Let sit till crumbs have absorbed milk. Put in meat and mix until nicely combined. Form into 1-inch meatballs.
- Arrange meatballs on an oiled rack set in a shallow baking pan. Bake for 18 minutes until browned or a thermometer shows 160° then drain. Put aside.
- For gravy, in a big skillet, in butter, sauté onion until tender. Mix in flour; brown slightly. Slowly pour in broth, stir and cook until thickened and smooth. Mix in white pepper, cayenne, and cream. Kindly mix in meatballs and heat through yet not boiling.

Nutrition Information

- Calories: 255 calories
- Protein: 19g protein.
- Total Fat: 15g fat (7g saturated fat)
- Sodium: 638mg sodium
- Fiber: 0 fiber)
- Total Carbohydrate: 9g carbohydrate (2g sugars
- Cholesterol: 98mg cholesterol

369.   One Pot Unstuffed Cabbage

Serving: 6-8 servings. | Prep: 15mins | Cook: 01hours20mins | Ready in:

Ingredients

- TOMATO SAUCE:
- 1 large onion, chopped
- 1 medium head cabbage, coarsely chopped (about 8 cups)
- 1 can (28 ounces) diced tomatoes, undrained
- 1 can (8 ounces) tomato sauce
- 1 cup water
- 1/4 cup lemon juice
- 1/3 cup raisins
- MEATBALLS:

- 1/2 cup uncooked long grain rice
- 1 teaspoon Worcestershire sauce
- 1/2 teaspoon salt
- 1/4 teaspoon pepper
- 1 pound lean ground beef (90% lean)

Direction

- Mix sauce ingredients in a large skillet. Bring to boil; lower the heat; simmer.
- Meanwhile, mix pepper, salt, Worcestershire sauce and rice in a large bowl. Crumble beef over the rice mixture; mix well. Form into 36 balls, about 1 1/4 in. in diameter. Put into the simmering sauce.
- Simmer with a cover till the cabbage is tender, 45 minutes. Cook without a cover till the sauce is thickened, 15 more minutes.

Nutrition Information

- Calories: 210 calories
- Sodium: 524mg sodium
- Fiber: 4g fiber)
- Total Carbohydrate: 28g carbohydrate (11g sugars
- Cholesterol: 28mg cholesterol
- Protein: 15g protein.
- Total Fat: 5g fat (2g saturated fat)

370. Onion Meatball Stew

Serving: 4 servings. | Prep: 20mins | Cook: 25mins | Ready in:

Ingredients

- 1 egg, lightly beaten
- 1/2 cup soft bread crumbs
- 1 garlic clove, minced
- 1/2 teaspoon salt
- 1/2 teaspoon dried savory
- 1 pound ground beef
- 1 tablespoon vegetable oil

- 1 can (10-1/2 ounces) condensed French onion soup, undiluted
- 2/3 cup water
- 3 medium carrots, cut into 3/4-inch chunks
- 2 medium potatoes, peeled and cut into 1-inch chunks
- 1 medium onion, cut into thin wedges
- 1 tablespoon minced fresh parsley

Direction

- In a big bowl, mix savory, salt, garlic, bread crumbs, and egg together. Crumble beef over the combination and stir properly. Form into 1 - 1/4-inch balls.
- In a large frying pan over medium heat, cook meatballs in oil until browned; then drain. Stir in onion, potatoes, carrots, water and soup. Let it boil. Lessen heat, simmer while covered for 25-30 minutes, until vegetables are softened. Dust with parsley.

Nutrition Information

- Calories: 381 calories
- Protein: 26g protein.
- Total Fat: 17g fat (5g saturated fat)
- Sodium: 1015mg sodium
- Fiber: 4g fiber)
- Total Carbohydrate: 32g carbohydrate (10g sugars
- Cholesterol: 112mg cholesterol

371. Oven Meatball Stew

Serving: 6 servings. | Prep: 25mins | Cook: 60mins | Ready in:

Ingredients

- 1 egg
- 1/3 cup milk
- 1/4 cup cornmeal
- 2 tablespoons finely chopped onion

- 2 tablespoons finely chopped green pepper
- 1-1/2 teaspoons ground mustard
- 1 teaspoon salt
- 1 teaspoon chili powder
- 1 pound lean ground beef
- 2 to 3 tablespoons olive oil
- 1/4 cup all-purpose flour
- 2-1/2 cups tomato juice
- 12 pearl onions, peeled
- 3 medium potatoes, peeled and quartered
- 6 medium carrots, cut into 3-inch pieces

Direction

- Mix the first 8 ingredients together in a big bowl. Then you crumble the beef into the mixture and stir thoroughly. Form into 12 meatballs.
- Brown meatballs with oil in a Dutch oven. Take it out using a slotted spoon and put aside. Stir flour into drippings until the mixture is smooth. Slowly stir in tomato juice and boil it. Cook while stirring until thickened, about 2 minutes.
- Put the meatballs back in the pan. Add vegetables, mix lightly. Bake with a cover at 350° until the vegetables are soft and the meat is not pink anymore, about 1 hour.

Nutrition Information

- Calories: 341 calories
- Sodium: 838mg sodium
- Fiber: 5g fiber)
- Total Carbohydrate: 38g carbohydrate (11g sugars
- Cholesterol: 83mg cholesterol
- Protein: 20g protein.
- Total Fat: 13g fat (4g saturated fat)

372.   Oven Porcupines

Serving: 4 servings. | Prep: 20mins | Cook: 01hours15mins | Ready in:

Ingredients

- 1 pound lean ground beef
- 1/2 cup uncooked long grain rice
- 1/2 cup water
- 1/3 cup chopped onion
- 1 teaspoon salt
- 1/2 teaspoon pepper
- 1/4 teaspoon garlic powder
- 1 can (15 ounces) tomato sauce
- 1 cup hot water
- 2 teaspoons Worcestershire sauce

Direction

- In a bowl, stir the first seven ingredients; form into 12 balls. In an ungreased 8-inch square baking dish, position the meatballs. Whisk the rest of ingredients; put over meatballs.
- Use foil to cover then bake at 350° for 1 hour. Bake, uncovered, for 15 more minutes.

Nutrition Information

- Calories: 291 calories
- Total Carbohydrate: 26g carbohydrate (3g sugars
- Cholesterol: 69mg cholesterol
- Protein: 25g protein.
- Total Fat: 9g fat (4g saturated fat)
- Sodium: 1157mg sodium
- Fiber: 1g fiber)

373.   Party Appetizer Meatballs

Serving: 8 dozen. | Prep: 15mins | Cook: 40mins | Ready in:

Ingredients

- 2 pounds lean ground beef
- 2 large eggs, lightly beaten
- 1 cup shredded part-skim mozzarella cheese
- 1/2 cup dry bread crumbs
- 1/4 cup finely chopped onion

- 2 tablespoons grated Parmesan cheese
- 1 tablespoon ketchup
- 2 teaspoons Worcestershire sauce
- 1 teaspoon Italian seasoning
- 1 teaspoon dried basil
- 1 teaspoon salt
- 1/4 teaspoon pepper
- SAUCE:
- 1 bottle (14 ounces) hot or regular ketchup
- 2 tablespoons cornstarch
- 1 jar (12 ounces) apple jelly
- 1 jar (12 ounces) currant jelly

Direction

- Combine the first 12 ingredients in a bowl. Roll into 1-in. balls. In a shallow baking pan, arrange the meatballs on a greased rack.
- Bake for 10-15 minutes at 350°; drain. In a roasting pan, combine cornstarch and ketchup. Stir in jellies, put in the meatballs. Cover and continue to bake for another 30 minutes.

Nutrition Information

- Calories: 133 calories
- Sodium: 271mg sodium
- Fiber: 0 fiber)
- Total Carbohydrate: 19g carbohydrate (16g sugars
- Cholesterol: 34mg cholesterol
- Protein: 7g protein.
- Total Fat: 3g fat (2g saturated fat)

---

374.   Party Meatballs

Serving: 8 | Prep: | Cook: | Ready in:

Ingredients

- 1 cup MUSSELMAN'S® Apple Butter, divided
- 1 tablespoon butter
- 1/2 cup grated red onion
- 1 pound pork sausage

- 1 pound ground beef
- 2 cups panko bread crumbs
- 1/4 cup sour cream
- 2 eggs
- 2 teaspoons salt
- 1 teaspoon black pepper
- 1 teaspoon allspice
- 1/2 cup beef broth
- 2 tablespoons honey
- Cayenne pepper

Direction

- Set an oven to 400°F and start preheating, use foil to line a large-rimmed baking sheet.
- In a skillet arranged on medium heat, let the butter melt. Put in the grated onions and sauté until softened, 3-4 minutes once the butter is melted.
- Combine the allspice, pepper, salt, eggs, sour cream, 1/2 cup of apple butter, panko, ground beef, and sausage in a large bowl. When it cools, put the onion. Mix it properly with your hands until blended evenly.
- Measure out the meatballs into 1-ounce portions. Roll to form tight balls and arrange them close together on the baking sheet without touching. You should roll 40-45 meatballs.
- Bake them for 15 minutes. At the same time, combine 1-2 dashes of cayenne pepper, honey, and beef broth with the remaining 1/2 cup of apple butter. Beat them thoroughly.
- Take the meatballs out from the oven after 15 minutes. Place the sauce over the top to cover each meatball, then return to the oven for 5-7 minutes.
- Lightly shake the baking sheet to loosen meatballs when cooked thoroughly, then serve warm.

Nutrition Information

- Calories: 457 calories;
- Total Fat: 25.5
- Sodium: 1325

- Total Carbohydrate: 41.8
- Cholesterol: 120
- Protein: 21.7

375.   Passover Meatballs

Serving: 6 dozen. | Prep: 30mins | Cook: 50mins |Ready in:

Ingredients

- 2 eggs, lightly beaten
- 1 cup water, divided
- 1-1/2 cups finely chopped onion, divided
- 1/2 cup matzo meal
- 1 teaspoon salt
- 1/4 teaspoon pepper
- 2 pounds ground beef
- 1 can (8 ounces) tomato sauce
- 1 cup sugar
- 1/2 cup lemon juice

Direction

- Combine the eggs, pepper, salt, matzo meal, 1/2 cup onion, and 1/2 cup water in a large bowl. Crumble the beef over the mixture and blend well. Roll into 1-in. balls.
- Combine the remaining water and onion, lemon juice, sugar, and tomato sauce in a Dutch oven. Add meatballs and boil. Reduce the heat; simmer, covered, until the meat is no longer pink, for 45 minutes. Use a slotted spoon to serve with.

Nutrition Information

- Calories: 74 calories
- Protein: 5g protein.
- Total Fat: 3g fat (1g saturated fat)
- Sodium: 115mg sodium
- Fiber: 0 fiber)
- Total Carbohydrate: 8g carbohydrate (6g sugars

- Cholesterol: 24mg cholesterol

376.   Pasta Meatball Stew

Serving: 6-8 servings. | Prep: 35mins | Cook: 45mins | Ready in:

Ingredients

- 1 egg, lightly beaten
- 1/4 cup dry bread crumbs
- 1/4 cup milk
- 1/2 teaspoon ground mustard
- 1/2 teaspoon salt
- 1/2 teaspoon pepper
- 1 pound ground beef
- 1 tablespoon canola oil
- SAUCE:
- 1 cup chopped onion
- 2 garlic cloves, minced
- 1 tablespoon canola oil
- 2 tablespoons all-purpose flour
- 1-1/2 cups beef broth
- 1 can (14-1/2 ounces) diced tomatoes, undrained
- 2 tablespoons tomato paste
- 1 bay leaf
- 3/4 teaspoon dried thyme
- 1/2 teaspoon salt
- 1-1/2 cups sliced carrots
- 1-1/2 cups chopped zucchini
- 1 cup chopped green pepper
- 1 cup chopped sweet red pepper
- 1 tablespoon minced fresh parsley
- 2 cups cooked pasta

Direction

- Mix pepper, salt, mustard, milk, crumbs, and egg together in a big bowl. Add beef and crumble it into the mixture. Form into balls, about 1 inch each. In a Dutch oven, brown meatballs in oil over medium heat; strain and put aside.

- Sauté garlic and onion in oil in the same pan until the onion is soft. Mix in flour. Slowly pour in the broth, whisking continuously; boil it. Cook while stirring until thickened, about 1-2 minutes. Mix in salt, thyme, bay leaf, paste, and tomatoes. Add carrots and meatballs; boil it. Lower the heat, simmer with a cover for 30 minutes.
- Add peppers and zucchini; boil it. Lower the heat, simmer with a cover until the vegetables are soft, about 10-15 minutes. Add pasta and parsley, thoroughly heat. Discard the bay leaf.

Nutrition Information

- Calories: 274 calories
- Sodium: 596mg sodium
- Fiber: 4g fiber)
- Total Carbohydrate: 25g carbohydrate (8g sugars
- Cholesterol: 65mg cholesterol
- Protein: 17g protein.
- Total Fat: 12g fat (4g saturated fat)

---

377. Peppered Meatballs

Serving: 1-1/2 dozen. | Prep: 35mins | Cook: 02hours00mins |Ready in:

Ingredients

- 1/2 cup sour cream
- 2 teaspoons grated Parmesan or Romano cheese
- 2 to 3 teaspoons pepper
- 1 teaspoon salt
- 1 teaspoon dry bread crumbs
- 1/2 teaspoon garlic powder
- 1-1/2 pounds ground beef
- SAUCE:
- 1 can (10-3/4 ounces) condensed cream of mushroom soup, undiluted
- 1 cup (8 ounces) sour cream
- 2 teaspoons dill weed

- 1/2 teaspoon sugar
- 1/2 teaspoon pepper
- 1/4 teaspoon garlic powder

Direction

- Combine cheese and sour cream in a large bowl. Add garlic powder, bread crumbs, salt, and pepper. Crumble the meat over the mixture and mix well. Roll into 1-in. balls.
- In a shallow baking pan, place the meatballs on a greased rack. Bake at 350° until no more pink, for 20-25 minutes; drain.
- Transfer the meatballs to a 1-1/2-qt. slow cooker. Mix the sauce ingredients, then pour over the meatballs. Cook on high, covered, until heated through, for 2-3 hours.

Nutrition Information

- Calories: 259 calories
- Fiber: 0 fiber)
- Total Carbohydrate: 5g carbohydrate (2g sugars
- Cholesterol: 77mg cholesterol
- Protein: 17g protein.
- Total Fat: 18g fat (9g saturated fat)
- Sodium: 565mg sodium

---

378. Pineapple Appetizer Meatballs

Serving: 2 dozen. | Prep: 15mins | Cook: 15mins |Ready in:

Ingredients

- 1 can (8 ounces) crushed pineapple
- 1 egg
- 1/4 cup dry bread crumbs
- 1/8 teaspoon pepper
- 1/2 pound Jones No Sugar Pork Sausage Roll sausage
- 1/2 pound ground beef

- GLAZE:
- 1/4 cup packed brown sugar
- 1/4 cup ketchup
- 1/4 cup white vinegar
- 1/4 cup water
- 2 tablespoons Dijon-mayonnaise blend

Direction

- Drain pineapple, keeping the juice. In a large bowl, place 2 tablespoons juice and pineapple (put the leftover juice aside for glaze). Add the breadcrumbs, egg and pepper into pineapple. Crumble beef and sausage over mixture and thoroughly mix. Form into 1-in. balls.
- Arrange meatballs on a greased rack placed in a shallow baking pan. Bake without a cover for 12 to 15 minutes at 450°, until a thermometer reaches 160°.
- In the meantime, combine the reserved pineapple juice and glaze ingredients in a large skillet. Add in meatballs. Heat to boiling over medium heat. Lower the heat; cook for 5 to 10 minutes while stirring, until well heated.

Nutrition Information

- Calories:
- Protein:
- Total Fat:
- Sodium:
- Fiber:
- Total Carbohydrate:
- Cholesterol:

---

379.   Piquant Meatballs

Serving: 4 dozen. | Prep: 20mins | Cook: 40mins | Ready in:

Ingredients

- 1 can (14 ounces) jellied cranberry sauce
- 1 bottle (12 ounces) chili sauce

- 1 tablespoon lemon juice
- 2 eggs, lightly beaten
- 1 cup crushed cornflakes
- 1/3 cup ketchup
- 1/3 cup dried parsley flakes
- 3 tablespoons soy sauce
- 2 tablespoons dried minced onion
- 3/4 teaspoon salt
- 1/2 teaspoon pepper
- 1/4 teaspoon garlic powder
- 2 pounds lean ground beef (90% lean)

Direction

- Mix lemon juice, chili sauce, and cranberry sauce in a saucepan. Bring to a boil over medium heat; stir and cook until smooth. Put aside.
- Mix the next nine ingredients in a bowl; put in the beef and stir well. Form into 1-inch balls. Transfer to a greased 13x9-inch baking dish. Pour sauce over meatballs.
- Bake without a cover for 40 to 50 minutes at 350 degrees or until the sauce is bubbly meatballs are not pink.

Nutrition Information

- Calories: 183 calories
- Protein: 13g protein.
- Total Fat: 5g fat (2g saturated fat)
- Sodium: 722mg sodium
- Fiber: 1g fiber)
- Total Carbohydrate: 22g carbohydrate (12g sugars
- Cholesterol: 54mg cholesterol

---

380.   Pizza Meatballs

Serving: 12 | Prep: 25mins | Cook: | Ready in:

Ingredients

- Nonstick cooking spray

- 1 cup fresh cremini or button mushrooms, finely chopped
- ½ cup finely chopped green sweet pepper
- ½ cup finely chopped onion
- 2 cloves garlic, minced
- ¾ cup soft whole wheat bread crumbs (about 1 slice)
- 1 egg white, lightly beaten
- 1½ teaspoons dried Italian seasoning, crushed
- ⅛ teaspoon black pepper
- 8 ounces uncooked bulk turkey sausage
- 8 ounces ground turkey breast
- 1 cup shredded reduced-fat Italian blend cheeses (4 ounces)
- 1½ cups purchased low-sodium pasta sauce

Direction

- Set an oven to 350°F and start preheating. Use cooking spray to grease a large non-stick skillet; heat the skillet on medium heat. Put in onion, green pepper, and mushrooms. Cook and regularly stir until the vegetables become tender, for 5-8 minutes. Add in garlic and stir, then put aside.
- Blend black pepper, Italian seasoning, egg white, and breadcrumbs in a large bowl. Add in the mushroom mixture and stir. Put in cheese, turkey breast, and turkey sausage. Combine thoroughly.
- Use foil to line a 15x10x1-inch baking pan. Use cooking spray to grease the foil; put aside. Form the meat mixture into 24 meatballs with a diameter of 1 1/2-inch using wet hands, then place the meatballs in the lined pan. Bake until done, about 160 degrees F, for 20 minutes.
- At the same time, heat the pasta sauce on medium heat and stir from time to time in a small saucepan. Serve it together with meatballs.

Nutrition Information

- Calories: 122 calories;
- Saturated Fat: 2
- Fiber: 1
- Total Carbohydrate: 8
- Cholesterol: 29
- Sugar: 4
- Protein: 12
- Total Fat: 4
- Sodium: 225

381.   Poached Meatballs In Lemon Sauce

Serving: 4 servings. | Prep: 15mins | Cook: 20mins | Ready in:

Ingredients

- 1/2 cup seasoned bread crumbs
- 1 large egg, beaten
- 1/2 teaspoon salt
- 1 teaspoon grated lemon zest
- 1 pound ground beef
- 2-1/4 cups water, divided
- 2 teaspoons beef bouillon granules
- 2 teaspoons cornstarch
- 2 tablespoons lemon juice
- 2 large egg yolks
- Cooked rice

Direction

- Combine lemon zest, salt, egg, and bread crumbs in a bowl. Put in ground beef and combine well. Form into twelve 1 1/2 -inch-diameter meatballs; put aside.
- Heat 2 cups of water to a boil in a saucepan; add in bouillon, mix to dissolve. Kindly place meatballs into the broth. Lower the heat and simmer till meatballs are not pink anymore, about 10 minutes; transfer to a warm bowl.
- Mix remaining water and cornstarch together; mix into broth. Put in lemon juice; stir and cook until thick. Into egg yolks, mix a small portion of broth; combine nicely. Bring back to the saucepan, heat through. Spread sauce over meatballs and serve.

Nutrition Information

- Calories: 291 calories
- Protein: 25g protein.
- Total Fat: 15g fat (6g saturated fat)
- Sodium: 1036mg sodium
- Fiber: 1g fiber)
- Total Carbohydrate: 13g carbohydrate (1g sugars
- Cholesterol: 215mg cholesterol

---

382.   Polynesian Meatballs

Serving: 6 | Prep: | Cook: | Ready in:

Ingredients

- 2 cups Minute® Brown Rice, uncooked
- 1 (20 ounce) can crushed pineapple, divided
- 1 (20 ounce) package ground turkey or chicken
- 3/4 cup green onions, thinly sliced, divided
- 1/2 cup teriyaki sauce, divided
- 1 egg, lightly beaten
- 1 teaspoon ground ginger
- 1/2 teaspoon ground nutmeg
- 2 tablespoons orange marmalade

Direction

- Preheat an oven to 175 °C or 350 °F. Prepare the rice following packaging instructions.
- For the meatballs, drain half cup of crushed pineapple. Set aside the rest of pineapple and juice for the sauce.
- In a big bowl, mix together nutmeg, ginger, egg, quarter cup teriyaki sauce, half cup green onions, half cup pineapple, cooked rice and ground chicken or turkey. Combine thoroughly.
- Spoon the mixture and gently roll into preferred size of meatball, suggested approximately the size of a golf ball; put the meatballs on baking sheet lined with aluminum foil with sides. Bake for 25 minutes to half an hour or till meatballs are done.

- While baking the meatballs, prepare sauce, in a medium saucepan, mix together orange marmalade, the leftover 1/4 cup teriyaki sauce and the rest of pineapple and juice; heat to boiling. Lower the heat and let it simmer for 3 to 4 minutes without a cover. Mix in the leftover quarter cup of green onions.
- Put sauce on top of cooked meatballs.

Nutrition Information

- Calories: 352 calories;
- Total Fat: 9.7
- Sodium: 1033
- Total Carbohydrate: 46.8
- Cholesterol: 102
- Protein: 21.5

---

383.   Popeye's Favorite Meatballs

Serving: 8 servings. | Prep: 15mins | Cook: 10mins | Ready in:

Ingredients

- 1/4 cup egg substitute
- 1 tablespoon water
- 1 cup (8 ounces) 1% cottage cheese
- 1/4 cup dry bread crumbs
- 2 tablespoons dried minced onion
- 1/2 teaspoon garlic powder
- 1 package (10 ounces) frozen chopped spinach, thawed and well drained
- 1-1/2 pounds lean ground beef

Direction

- Combine the initial 6 ingredients in a bowl. Put in beef and spinach; combine well. Form into 1-inch balls and arrange on an unoiled baking tray. Broil 4 to 6 inches from heat, about 8 minutes. Turn, broil for 3 to 5 more minutes until meat is not pink anymore.

Nutrition Information

- Calories: 176 calories
- Total Fat: 9g fat (0 saturated fat)
- Sodium: 198mg sodium
- Fiber: 0 fiber)
- Total Carbohydrate: 6g carbohydrate (0 sugars
- Cholesterol: 44mg cholesterol
- Protein: 18g protein. Diabetic Exchanges: 2 meat

---

384. Porcupine Meatballs

Serving: Makes 4 servings | Prep: 30mins | Cook: 2.5hours | Ready in:

Ingredients

- 1 pound uncooked shrimp, peeled, deveined, and tails removed
- 2 tablespoons finely chopped scallions
- 2 teaspoons soy sauce
- 1/2 teaspoon grated fresh ginger
- 1/2 cup short-grain rice (such as arborio), soaked in 2 cups very hot water for 2 hours
- Cabbage or lettuce leaves
- Ponzu sauce (available at Asian specialty stores) or more soy sauce

Direction

- Pulse 1/2 shrimp in food processor till finely chopped.
- Add rest; pulse several additional times; 1/2 mixture will stay roughly chopped, rest will be used as binding paste.
- Put in bowl; add ginger, soy sauce and scallions. Mix till combined well using your hands.
- Drain rice; spread on plate. Shape shrimp mixture to 1 1/2-inhes balls; Roll every ball in rice.

- Line leaves on steamer basket; add meatballs. Steam for 8-9 minutes till shrimp is pink and rice is cooked. Serve with soy sauce or ponzu.

---

385. Potluck Meatballs

Serving: 2-1/2 dozen. | Prep: 25mins | Cook: 35mins | Ready in:

Ingredients

- 1 egg, lightly beaten
- 2/3 cup soft bread crumbs
- 1/2 cup grated onion
- 1 teaspoon salt
- 1/2 teaspoon ground allspice
- 1/4 teaspoon pepper
- 1 pound ground beef
- 1 tablespoon cornstarch
- 1 can (10-1/2 ounces) condensed beef consomme, undiluted

Direction

- Mix the first six ingredients in a large bowl; break beef into pieces over mixture and stir well. Form into 1-1/4-inch balls. Brown meatballs in batches in a large skillet; drain.
- Bring to a 1-1/2-qt baking dish that is greased. Mix consomme and cornstarch until smooth; add into the skillet. Bring to a boil, whisking to loosen browned bits from the pan. Boil for 2 minutes or until thickened.
- Pour over the meatballs. Bake for 35 to 40 minutes at 350 degrees, uncovered, or until not pink anymore.

Nutrition Information

- Calories: 117 calories
- Total Fat: 6g fat (2g saturated fat)
- Sodium: 477mg sodium
- Fiber: 0 fiber)
- Total Carbohydrate: 4g carbohydrate (1g sugars

- Cholesterol: 53mg cholesterol
- Protein: 11g protein.

---

386.   Reuben Meatballs

Serving: 5 servings. | Prep: 15mins | Cook: 60mins | Ready in:

Ingredients

- 1 egg
- 1 small onion, finely chopped
- 2/3 cup soft bread crumbs
- 1/4 cup minced fresh parsley
- 1/2 teaspoon salt
- 1/2 teaspoon pepper
- 1 cup cooked rice
- 1-1/2 pounds lean ground beef
- 2 cups sauerkraut, rinsed and well drained
- 1 to 2 teaspoons caraway seeds
- 1 can (10-3/4 ounces) condensed cream of mushroom soup, undiluted
- 1/2 cup Thousand Island salad dressing
- 1/4 cup shredded Swiss cheese
- Rye bread, optional

Direction

- In a bowl, mix pepper, salt, parsley, bread crumbs, onion and egg. Mix in rice. Crumble beef over the mixture; mix thoroughly. Form into 15 balls. Arrange meatballs on a greased rack in a shallow baking pan. Bake without a cover at 350° till browned, about 15-20 minutes; strain.
- Move meatballs into an ungreased 13x9-inch baking dish. Add sauerkraut over meatballs; top with caraway seeds. Mix salad dressing and soup; spread over the top.
- Bake with a cover for 35-45 minutes, till the meat is no longer pink. Take the cover away; top with Swiss cheese. Bake for 10 more minutes or till the cheese is melted. If wanted, serve with rye bread.

Nutrition Information

- Calories: 455 calories
- Sodium: 1408mg sodium
- Fiber: 3g fiber)
- Total Carbohydrate: 25g carbohydrate (6g sugars
- Cholesterol: 141mg cholesterol
- Protein: 32g protein.
- Total Fat: 25g fat (8g saturated fat)

---

387.   Reunion Meatballs

Serving: 20 | Prep: 15mins | Cook: 10mins | Ready in:

Ingredients

- 2 eggs
- 1 envelope onion soup mix
- 1/2 cup seasoned bread crumbs
- 2 tablespoons chopped fresh parsley
- 1 1/2 pounds lean ground beef
- 1 (16 ounce) can whole berry cranberry sauce
- 3/4 cup ketchup
- 1/2 cup beef broth
- 3 tablespoons brown sugar
- 3 tablespoons finely chopped onion
- 2 teaspoons cider vinegar

Direction

- In a large bowl, mix together soup mix, eggs, parsley, and bread crumbs. Crumble beef into the mixture, and mix well; form 1-inch balls from the mixture.
- In a microwave-safe plate, place 12 to 14 beef balls, then cover with waxed paper. Place in the microwave and heat for 3 to 4 minutes on high power, or until they're no longer pink in color. Transfer meatballs to paper towels to drain excess oil. Repeat the procedure with the rest of the meatballs.
- In a microwave-safe dish, mix together cranberry sauce, beef broth, brown sugar, ketchup, vinegar, and onion. Put waxed paper

on top and cook in the microwave for 3 to 4 minutes on high power. Serve meatballs with sauce.

Nutrition Information

- Calories: 137 calories;
- Sodium: 330
- Total Carbohydrate: 15.7
- Cholesterol: 41
- Protein: 7.9
- Total Fat: 4.9

---

388.   Rice Mix Meatballs

Serving: 8-10 servings. | Prep: 15mins | Cook: 30mins | Ready in:

Ingredients

- 1 package (6.8 ounces) beef-flavored rice mix
- 1 egg, lightly beaten
- 1 pound ground beef
- 2-1/2 cups boiling water
- 2 tablespoons cornstarch
- 3 tablespoons cold water

Direction

- Put the rice seasoning packet aside. Mix egg and rice in a big bowl. Crumble beef over bowl and stir well. Make into 1-in. balls. Brown meatballs on all sides in a big frying pan on medium heat. In the meantime, mix the seasoning packer with boiling water in a small bowl. Mix into frying pan. Cover; simmer until rice is tender, 30 minutes. Mix cold water and cornstarch until smooth; add to frying pan. Heat to a boil. Stirring constantly, cook until thick, 2 minutes.

Nutrition Information

- Calories:

- Fiber:
- Total Carbohydrate:
- Cholesterol:
- Protein:
- Total Fat:
- Sodium:

---

389.   Saucy Microwave Meatballs

Serving: 4 servings. | Prep: 15mins | Cook: 15mins | Ready in:

Ingredients

- 1 egg
- 1/4 cup finely chopped onion
- 1 teaspoon salt
- 1 pound ground beef
- 1 can (8 ounces) tomato sauce
- 1/3 cup packed brown sugar
- 3 tablespoons lemon juice
- 1/8 teaspoon garlic salt
- Hot cooked spaghetti

Direction

- Combine salt, onion, and egg in a big bowl. Crumble beef and add to the mixture; mix nicely. Form into 1-1/2-inch balls
- Arrange 1/2 of meatballs into a microwave-safe 2-quart dish. Put on cover and microwave for 2-2 1/2 minutes, until meatballs are not pink anymore and firm. Drain. Repeat with the rest of meatballs.
- In a microwave-safe bowl, mix together garlic salt, lemon juice, brown sugar, and tomato sauce. Cook on high without cover, mixing every 15 seconds, until sugar has been dissolved, about 1/2 to 1 minute. Arrange over meatballs. Put on cover, microwave for 3-4 minutes at 50% power, until heated through. Serve along with spaghetti.

Nutrition Information

- Calories: 330 calories
- Protein: 25g protein.
- Total Fat: 15g fat (6g saturated fat)
- Sodium: 984mg sodium
- Fiber: 1g fiber)
- Total Carbohydrate: 23g carbohydrate (20g sugars
- Cholesterol: 128mg cholesterol

Nutrition Information

- Calories: 363 calories
- Fiber: 1g fiber)
- Total Carbohydrate: 11g carbohydrate (3g sugars
- Cholesterol: 133mg cholesterol
- Protein: 26g protein.
- Total Fat: 23g fat (8g saturated fat)
- Sodium: 644mg sodium

---

390.   Savory Meatballs

Serving: 8 servings. | Prep: 25mins | Cook: 45mins | Ready in:

Ingredients

- 2 large eggs, lightly beaten
- 1 medium onion, chopped
- 2 teaspoons ground mustard
- 1 teaspoon salt
- 1/2 teaspoon pepper
- 1/2 teaspoon poultry seasoning
- 1/3 cup cornmeal
- 3/4 cup whole milk
- 2 pounds ground beef
- 3 tablespoons vegetable oil
- 2 cans (10-3/4 ounces each) condensed cream of mushroom soup, undiluted
- 1-1/2 cups water

Direction

- In a large bowl, mix the first eight ingredients. Crumble beef over the mixture; mix thoroughly. Form into 2-inch balls. Place a large skillet on medium-high heat; brown meatballs in batches in oil.
- Arrange on a 2-qt baking dish. Mix water and soup; pour over the meatballs. Bake without a cover at 350° till a thermometer reads 160° when inserted in the meatballs, 45-50 minutes.

---

391.   Savory Sweet And Sour Meatballs

Serving: 8 servings. | Prep: 25mins | Cook: 25mins | Ready in:

Ingredients

- 1 can (20 ounces) unsweetened pineapple chunks
- 1 egg
- 1 cup soft bread crumbs
- 1 garlic clove, minced
- 1 teaspoon salt
- 1/4 teaspoon pepper
- 1-1/2 pounds lean ground beef (90% lean)
- 1 teaspoons canola oil
- 2 large green peppers
- 1 cup chicken broth
- 1/2 cup sugar
- 3 tablespoons cornstarch
- 1/2 cup cider vinegar
- 3 tablespoons reduced-sodium soy sauce
- 6 cups hot cooked rice

Direction

- Drain pineapple, saving 1/2 cup of juice (discarding the leftover juice or reserve for another time). Put pineapple and juice aside. In a large bowl, blend pepper, salt, garlic, bread crumbs, and egg. Break beef into crumbles over mixture and combine well. Form into 40 meatballs.

- Brown meatballs in oil in a nonstick skillet; drain. Slice green peppers into chunks. Put in reserved pineapple, pepper, and broth to meatballs. Heat to a boil. Lower the heat; simmer, without covering, for 5 to 7 minutes.
- In the meantime, in a large bowl, mix cornstarch and sugar. Blend in reserved pineapple juice, soy sauce, and vinegar until smooth. Pour in the meatball mixture. Heat to a boil; cook and stir in 2 minutes, or until thickened. Use with rice.

Nutrition Information

- Calories: 456 calories
- Cholesterol: 58mg cholesterol
- Protein: 23g protein.
- Total Fat: 10g fat (3g saturated fat)
- Sodium: 755mg sodium
- Fiber: 2g fiber)
- Total Carbohydrate: 66g carbohydrate (0 sugars

---

392.   Simple Meatball Stew

Serving: 8 servings. | Prep: 30mins | Cook: 30mins | Ready in:

Ingredients

- 1 egg, beaten
- 1 cup soft bread crumbs
- 1/4 cup finely chopped onion
- 1 teaspoon salt
- 1 teaspoon dried marjoram
- 1/2 teaspoon dried thyme
- 1-1/2 pounds ground beef
- 2 tablespoons canola oil
- 2 cans (14-1/2 ounces each) beef broth
- 2 cans (10-3/4 ounces each) condensed golden mushroom soup, undiluted
- 4 medium potatoes, peeled and quartered
- 4 medium carrots, cut into chunks
- 1 jar (16 ounces) whole pearl onions, drained

- 1/4 cup minced fresh parsley

Direction

- Mix thyme, marjoram, salt, chopped onion, bread crumbs, and egg together in a bowl. Add beef and stir thoroughly. Form into 48 meatballs.
- Put meatballs in a Dutch oven with oil to brown; strain. Add pearl onions, carrots, potatoes, soup, and broth; boil it. Lower the heat, simmer until the vegetables are soft, about 30 minutes. Use parsley to sprinkle on top.

Nutrition Information

- Calories: 374 calories
- Fiber: 4g fiber)
- Total Carbohydrate: 35g carbohydrate (7g sugars
- Cholesterol: 85mg cholesterol
- Protein: 23g protein.
- Total Fat: 16g fat (5g saturated fat)
- Sodium: 858mg sodium

---

393.   Slow Cooker Spaghetti & Meatballs

Serving: 12 servings (about 3-1/2 quarts sauce). | Prep: 50mins | Cook: 05hours00mins | Ready in:

Ingredients

- 1 cup seasoned bread crumbs
- 2 tablespoons grated Parmesan and Romano cheese blend
- 1 teaspoon pepper
- 1/2 teaspoon salt
- 2 large eggs, lightly beaten
- 2 pounds ground beef
- SAUCE:
- 1 large onion, finely chopped
- 1 medium green pepper, finely chopped

- 3 cans (15 ounces each) tomato sauce
- 2 cans (14-1/2 ounces each) diced tomatoes, undrained
- 1 can (6 ounces) tomato paste
- 6 garlic cloves, minced
- 2 bay leaves
- 1 teaspoon each dried basil, oregano and parsley flakes
- 1 teaspoon salt
- 1/2 teaspoon pepper
- 1/4 teaspoon crushed red pepper flakes
- Hot cooked spaghetti

Direction

- Combine salt, pepper, cheese, and breadcrumbs in a large bowl; add in eggs and stir. Put in the beef; combine lightly and thoroughly. Form into 1 1/2 inch balls. Work in batches, brown the meatballs in a large skillet on medium heat; let drain.
- In a 6-quart slow cooker, arrange the first 5 sauce ingredients; stir in the seasonings and garlic. Drop in the meatballs and carefully stir to coat. Put a cover on and cook on low heat until the meatballs are heated thoroughly, for 5-6 hours.
- Take the bay leaves out. Serve along with spaghetti.

Nutrition Information

- Calories: 250 calories
- Fiber: 4g fiber)
- Total Carbohydrate: 20g carbohydrate (7g sugars
- Cholesterol: 79mg cholesterol
- Protein: 20g protein.
- Total Fat: 11g fat (4g saturated fat)
- Sodium: 1116mg sodium

394. Slow Cooker Sweet Sour Meatballs

Serving: 2 servings. | Prep: 10mins | Cook: 05hours00mins | Ready in:

Ingredients

- 16 frozen fully cooked homestyle meatballs (1/2 ounce each) , thawed
- 1/2 cup sugar
- 2 tablespoons plus 2 teaspoons cornstarch
- 1/3 cup white vinegar
- 1 tablespoon reduced-sodium soy sauce
- 1/2 medium green pepper, cut into 1-inch pieces
- 1 can (8 ounces) pineapple chunks, undrained
- Hot cooked rice, optional

Direction

- Put the meatballs in a 1 1/2-quart slow cooker. Combine soy sauce, sugar, vinegar, and cornstarch in a small bowl; pour all over the meatballs then put in green pepper. Cook for 4 1/2hrs on low while covered until the pepper is tender-crisp.
- Mix in pineapple, cover then cook for another half hour. If desired, serve over rice.

Nutrition Information

- Calories: 794 calories
- Sodium: 582mg sodium
- Fiber: 2g fiber)
- Total Carbohydrate: 94g carbohydrate (63g sugars
- Cholesterol: 186mg cholesterol
- Protein: 39g protein.
- Total Fat: 29g fat (10g saturated fat)

395. Slow Cooked Spaghetti And Meatball Soup

Serving: 20 servings (about 4-1/2 quarts). | Prep: 20mins | Cook: 05hours00mins | Ready in:

Ingredients

- 1 cup finely chopped onion, divided
- 1 teaspoon salt
- 1/2 teaspoon pepper
- 3 pounds ground beef
- 1 can (46 ounces) tomato juice
- 1 can (28 ounces) diced tomatoes, drained
- 1 can (15 ounces) tomato sauce
- 2 celery ribs, chopped
- 3 bay leaves
- 2 garlic cloves, minced
- 2 teaspoons Italian seasoning
- Hot cooked spaghetti, cut into bite-size pieces

Direction

- Mix pepper, 1/2 cup onion, and salt in a big bowl. Crumble beef over the bowl and stir well. Make into 1-in. balls. On medium heat, brown remaining onion and meatballs in a big frying pan. Move to a 6-qt. slow cooker; add bay leaves, tomato sauce, Italian seasoning, tomato juice, celery, garlic, and tomatoes. Cover; set to low and cook until cooked through, 5-6 hours. Discard the bay leaves. Eat with spaghetti.

Nutrition Information

- Calories: 135 calories
- Fiber: 1g fiber)
- Total Carbohydrate: 7g carbohydrate (4g sugars
- Cholesterol: 33mg cholesterol
- Protein: 13g protein.
- Total Fat: 6g fat (3g saturated fat)
- Sodium: 550mg sodium

396. Smothered Meatballs

Serving: 5 | Prep: 30mins | Cook: 1hours | Ready in:

Ingredients

- 2 pounds lean ground beef
- 1/3 cup finely chopped green bell pepper
- 1/3 cup finely chopped onion
- 2 eggs
- 1 1/2 cups Italian-style dry bread crumbs
- 1/2 teaspoon salt
- 1/4 teaspoon ground black pepper
- 2 (10.75 ounce) cans condensed golden mushroom soup
- 1 cup sliced fresh mushrooms
- 1 cup sour cream
- 1/2 cup milk
- 2 tablespoons browning sauce
- salt to taste
- ground black pepper to taste

Direction

- Start preheating the oven at 375°F (190°C).
- Mix pepper, salt, seasoned bread crumbs, eggs, onion, green pepper, and ground beef in a big mixing bowl. Combine completely.
- Form the meat mixture into large meatballs, approximately 2-inches in diameter. Arrange around 1-inch apart on a large, shallow baking sheet. Bake in a prepared oven in 30 minutes. While baking the meatballs, make the sauce.
- In a 9x13-inch baking dish, blend pepper, salt, browning sauce, milk, sour cream, mushrooms, and soup to taste. Mix well.
- When baking is done, take them out from the baking sheet and arrange them into the soup mixture. Blend in the meatballs to coat. Bring back to the preheated oven and bake for 20 to 30 minutes, or until the sauce starts to bubble.

Nutrition Information

- Calories: 849 calories;
- Sodium: 1920
- Total Carbohydrate: 40.6

- Cholesterol: 238
- Protein: 44.5
- Total Fat: 55.1

---

397. Snappy Cocktail Meatballs

Serving: About 5 dozen. | Prep: 15mins | Cook: 15mins | Ready in:

Ingredients

- 2 large eggs, lightly beaten
- 1-1/4 cups soft bread crumbs
- 1 teaspoon salt
- 1/2 teaspoon garlic salt
- 1/2 teaspoon onion powder
- 1/2 teaspoon pepper
- 2 pounds lean ground beef (90% lean)
- SAUCE:
- 1 can (28 ounces) diced tomatoes, undrained
- 1/2 cup packed brown sugar
- 1/4 cup vinegar
- 1/2 teaspoon salt
- 1 teaspoon grated onion
- 10 gingersnaps, finely crushed

Direction

- Mix the first 6 ingredients together in a large bowl. Crumble beef over mixture and stir to combine.
- Form beef mixture into balls about 1 1/4 inches in diameter. Arrange meatballs on a greased rack in a shallow baking sheet. Bake for 15 minutes at 450°. Transfer to paper towels to drain.
- In the meantime, prepare sauce. In a large saucepan, combine onion, salt, vinegar, brown sugar, and tomatoes. Boil mixture. Mix in gingersnaps; keep boiling until sauce is clear and thick. Lower heat to a simmer; add in meatballs. Cook until thoroughly heated.

Nutrition Information

- Calories: 126 calories
- Sodium: 370mg sodium
- Fiber: 0 fiber)
- Total Carbohydrate: 11g carbohydrate (8g sugars
- Cholesterol: 44mg cholesterol
- Protein: 10g protein.
- Total Fat: 4g fat (2g saturated fat)

---

398. Spaghetti Con Carne

Serving: 4-6 servings. | Prep: 5mins | Cook: 35mins | Ready in:

Ingredients

- SAUCE:
- 1 teaspoon vegetable oil
- 1 garlic clove, minced
- 1 small onion, chopped
- 3 cups tomato juice
- 1 to 2 tablespoons chili powder
- 1 teaspoon salt
- MEATBALLS:
- 1 pound ground beef
- 1 large egg, beaten
- 1 garlic clove, minced
- 1 small onion, minced
- 1/4 cup yellow cornmeal
- 1 teaspoon salt
- 1/2 teaspoon pepper
- 1/2 teaspoon dried oregano
- 1 tablespoon vegetable oil
- Cooked spaghetti

Direction

- Heat oil in a large saucepan for sauce. Sauté onion and garlic; include in salt, chili powder and tomato juice. Keep simmering for 10 minutes. Combine the first eight meatball ingredients in a bowl. Roll into 3/4-in. balls. Brown the meatballs on all sides in a skillet with hot oil. Place the meatballs into the sauce. Simmer with a cover till the meatballs are cooked through, or for 10 minutes. Serve over spaghetti.

Nutrition Information

- Calories: 244 calories
- Protein: 18g protein.
- Total Fat: 14g fat (4g saturated fat)
- Sodium: 1286mg sodium
- Fiber: 2g fiber)
- Total Carbohydrate: 13g carbohydrate (6g sugars
- Cholesterol: 86mg cholesterol

399.   Spaghetti Meatball Bake

Serving: 10 servings. | Prep: 45mins | Cook: 30mins | Ready in:

Ingredients

- 1-1/2 cups dry bread crumbs, divided
- 3 large eggs, lightly beaten
- 1-1/2 cups cooked spaghetti (3 ounces uncooked), coarsely chopped
- 2 garlic cloves, minced
- 2 teaspoons dried basil
- 3/4 teaspoon salt
- 1 teaspoon dried oregano
- 1 teaspoon pepper
- 2 pounds ground beef
- SAUCE:
- 2 jars (24 ounces each) meatless pasta sauce
- 1 small onion, finely chopped
- 2 garlic cloves, minced
- 2 teaspoons dried basil
- 1 teaspoon dried oregano
- 2 cups shredded part-skim mozzarella cheese

Direction

- Preheat oven to 375°. In a shallow bowl, place 1 cup of bread crumbs. In a large bowl, combine chopped spaghetti, eggs, garlic, the rest of bread crumbs and seasonings. Add beef; lightly mix but thoroughly. Form into balls, 1 1/2- inch each.
- Roll meatballs in bread crumbs; transfer to a greased 13x9-inch baking dish. Bake for approximately 15 to 20 minutes until cooked through.
- In a large saucepan, combine onion, pasta sauce, seasonings and garlic; boil over medium heat, stirring occasionally. Pour mixture over meatballs; dust cheese over. Bake for an additional 15 to 20 minutes until cheese is browned lightly.

Nutrition Information

- Calories: 390 calories
- Protein: 29g protein.
- Total Fat: 17g fat (7g saturated fat)
- Sodium: 1074mg sodium
- Fiber: 3g fiber)
- Total Carbohydrate: 29g carbohydrate (10g sugars
- Cholesterol: 124mg cholesterol

400.   Spaghetti Meatballs

Serving: 30 meatballs. | Prep: 20mins | Cook: 0mins | Ready in:

Ingredients

- 1 pound lean ground beef
- 1 envelope spaghetti sauce mix

Direction

- In a bowl, combine sauce mix and beef. Form into balls of 1-inch in size. Transfer into a shallow microwave-safe dish of 2-quart in size. Microwave while covering on high mode for 2 minutes. Rotate a quarter turn. Microwave for an addition of 1 minute or until meat is not pink anymore; drain.

Nutrition Information

- Calories:
- Sodium:
- Fiber:
- Total Carbohydrate:
- Cholesterol:
- Protein:
- Total Fat:

401.   Spaghetti And Meatballs

Serving: Makes 6 main-course servings | Prep: 1hours30mins | Cook: 2hours45mins | Ready in:

Ingredients

- 2 28-ounce cans whole peeled tomatoes in juice, drained, juice reserved, tomatoes finely chopped
- 1/2 cup (1 stick) unsalted butter
- 2 medium onions, peeled, halved through root end
- 1/2 teaspoon (or more) salt
- 1 cup fresh breadcrumbs made from crustless French or country-style bread
- 1/3 cup whole milk
- 8 ounces ground beef (15% fat)
- 8 ounces ground pork
- 1 cup finely ground (not grated) Parmesan cheese
- 1/3 cup finely chopped Italian parsley
- 1 teaspoon salt
- 1/4 teaspoon freshly ground black pepper
- 2 large eggs
- 2 large garlic cloves, pressed
- 1 pound spaghetti
- Freshly grated Parmesan cheese (for serving)

Direction

- Sauté: Simmer salt, onions, butter and tomatoes and juice in big wide pot on medium heat. Lower heat; simmer for 45 minutes, with no cover, occasionally mixing. Discard onions. Briefly process sauce to break up any big tomato pieces with immersion blender; texture should be even yet not fully smooth. Season with freshly ground black pepper and extra salt; take off heat.
- Meatballs: Mix milk and breadcrumbs till evenly moist in small bowl; stand for 10 minutes.
- Break up pork and beef to small chunks in big bowl; add pepper, salt, parsley and 1 cup ground parmesan.
- Whisk eggs in small bowl to blend; whisk garlic in then add to meat mixture.
- Squeeze milk from breadcrumbs with hands; reserve milk. Put breadcrumbs in meat mixture; gently and quickly mix meat mixture with hands till all ingredients are combined evenly; don't overmix. Chill mixture for a minimum of 15-60 minutes.
- Use some reserved milk from breadcrumbs to moisten hands; between palms, roll meat mixture to golf ball size balls, moistening hands with milk occasionally as needed and putting meatballs in sauce in pot in 1 layer; simmer.
- Lower heat to medium low and cover; simmer for 15-20 minutes till meatballs are cooked through. You can make this 2 days ahead; slightly cool. Chill till cold, with no cover; cover then keep chilled. Reheat before proceeding.
- Cook spaghetti in big pot with boiling salted water till just tender yet firm to chew, occasionally mixing; drain.
- Put meatballs on platter with slotted spoon. Put pasta in sauce in pot; toss to coat then divide pasta to 6 plates. Put meatballs on each serving; sprinkle freshly grated parmesan cheese on meatballs and serve.

Nutrition Information

- Calories: 849
- Protein: 37 g(75%)
- Total Fat: 41 g(63%)
- Saturated Fat: 20 g(100%)
- Sodium: 1264 mg(53%)
- Fiber: 9 g(36%)
- Total Carbohydrate: 84 g(28%)
- Cholesterol: 171 mg(57%)

402.   Spiced Meatballs

Serving: 16 meatballs. | Prep: 20mins | Cook: 50mins | Ready in:

Ingredients

- 1/2 cup cooked rice
- 2 tablespoons finely chopped green pepper
- 1 tablespoon finely chopped onion
- 1 garlic clove, minced
- 1 teaspoon salt
- 1/4 teaspoon celery salt
- 1 pound lean ground beef (90% lean)
- 2 cups tomato juice
- 2 tablespoons sugar
- 1 tablespoon Worcestershire sauce
- 4 whole cloves
- 1/2 teaspoon ground cinnamon

Direction

- Mix the first six ingredients together in a bowl. Crumble beef over the mixture; mix properly. Roll into 1 1/2-in. balls. Combine cinnamon, cloves, Worcestershire sauce, sugar and tomato juice together in a skillet. Allow to boil. Lower the heat; include in the meatballs.
- Simmer with a cover while stirring occasionally till the meat is not pink anymore, or for 50 minutes. Discard the cloves. Serve.

Nutrition Information

- Calories:

- Sodium:
- Fiber:
- Total Carbohydrate:
- Cholesterol:
- Protein:
- Total Fat:

403.   Spicy Party Meatballs

Serving: 8-10 servings. | Prep: 20mins | Cook: 15mins | Ready in:

Ingredients

- 1-1/2 pounds ground beef
- 1-1/2 cups soft bread crumbs
- 1/2 medium onion, chopped
- 1/3 cup whole milk
- 1/4 cup chopped fresh parsley
- 1/2 teaspoon pepper
- 1 large egg, beaten
- 1 pound Mexican or plain process cheese (Velveeta), cubed
- 1 can (4 ounces) chopped green chilies
- 1 package (1-1/4 ounces) taco seasoning

Direction

- Combine the first 7 ingredients in a bowl. Form into 1/2-inch balls. In a skillet, cook over medium-high heat until browned, about 2-3 mins; drain.
- Combine taco seasoning, green chilies and cheese in a saucepan; stir until cheese is melted and blended well. Put in meatballs and simmer, covered, until heated through.

Nutrition Information

- Calories:
- Protein:
- Total Fat:
- Sodium:
- Fiber:

- Total Carbohydrate:
- Cholesterol:

- Total Fat: 15g fat (6g saturated fat)
- Sodium: 1047mg sodium
- Fiber: 2g fiber)
- Total Carbohydrate: 25g carbohydrate (16g sugars

---

404. Spicy Sweet And Sour Meatballs

Serving: 25 meatballs. | Prep: 20mins | Cook: 25mins | Ready in:

Ingredients

- 1 egg
- 1/2 cup water
- 1 cup finely chopped water chestnuts
- 1/2 cup soft bread crumbs
- 2 tablespoons prepared horseradish
- 1 pound ground beef
- SAUCE:
- 1/4 cup sugar
- 1 tablespoon cornstarch
- 1/2 cup water
- 1/4 cup cider vinegar
- 1/4 cup soy sauce
- 1 small onion, finely chopped

Direction

- Combine the first five ingredients together in a large bowl. Crumble beef over the mixture; mix properly. Roll into 1-in. balls. Arrange in a greased rack in a shallow baking pan. Bake without a cover at 350° till the meat is not pink anymore, or for 25 minutes. Meanwhile, mix the first five sauce ingredients together in a saucepan till smooth; include in onion. Allow to boil; cook while stirring till thickened, or for 2 minutes. Drain the meatballs; transfer the sauce on top.

Nutrition Information

- Calories: 351 calories
- Cholesterol: 128mg cholesterol
- Protein: 27g protein.

---

405. Stroganoff Meatballs

Serving: 4 servings. | Prep: 20mins | Cook: 15mins | Ready in:

Ingredients

- 1 large egg
- 1/2 cup dry bread crumbs
- 1/4 cup milk
- 1 tablespoon dried minced onion
- 1 tablespoon dried parsley flakes
- 1/4 teaspoon garlic salt
- 1/4 teaspoon pepper
- 1 pound ground beef
- SAUCE:
- 1 can (10-3/4 ounces) condensed cream of mushroom soup, undiluted
- 1/2 cup sour cream
- 2 tablespoons chili sauce
- 1/4 teaspoon dried oregano
- 1/4 teaspoon pepper
- 1/8 teaspoon garlic salt

Direction

- In a large bowl, whisk the egg; put in the next six ingredients. Put in the beef; mix thoroughly. Form into 1-inch balls; arrange on a greased rack in a shallow baking pan. Bake without a cover at 450° till no longer pink, 12-15 minutes. Strain on paper towels; in a serving dish, arrange meatballs; keep warm. In a medium saucepan, mix all of the sauce ingredients; cook while stirring till well combined and heated through. Scoop over the meatballs.

Nutrition Information

- Calories: 392 calories
- Total Fat: 21g fat (10g saturated fat)
- Sodium: 1050mg sodium
- Fiber: 1g fiber)
- Total Carbohydrate: 21g carbohydrate (5g sugars
- Cholesterol: 134mg cholesterol
- Protein: 26g protein.

---

406.   Stuffing Meatballs

Serving: 6 servings. | Prep: 15mins | Cook: 15mins | Ready in:

Ingredients

- 1-1/2 pounds ground beef
- 2/3 cup crushed seasoned stuffing
- 1 tablespoon vegetable oil
- 1 jar (26 ounces) meatless spaghetti sauce

Direction

- In a bowl, stir stuffing mix and beef. Form into 1-inch balls. Place a large skillet on medium heat; brown meatballs in small batches in oil; strain. Take all meatballs back to the pan; put in spaghetti sauce. Bring the mixture to a boil. Turn the heat down; simmer with a cover till the meat is no longer pink, about 6-8 minutes.

Nutrition Information

- Calories: 317 calories
- Cholesterol: 75mg cholesterol
- Protein: 25g protein.
- Total Fat: 16g fat (6g saturated fat)
- Sodium: 683mg sodium
- Fiber: 2g fiber)
- Total Carbohydrate: 16g carbohydrate (8g sugars

---

407.   Surprise Meatball Skewers

Serving: 6 servings. | Prep: 30mins | Cook: 20mins | Ready in:

Ingredients

- 1/3 cup honey
- 3 tablespoons Dijon mustard
- 2 tablespoons finely chopped onion
- 2 tablespoons apple juice
- Dash cayenne pepper
- 1 egg
- 1/4 cup dry bread crumbs
- 1 tablespoon minced fresh parsley
- 1 teaspoon Italian seasoning
- 1/4 teaspoon salt
- Pepper to taste
- 1 pound ground beef
- 1 block (1-1/2 ounces) Monterey Jack cheese, cut into 12 cubes
- 12 small mushrooms, stems removed
- 1 medium green pepper, cut into pieces
- 1 medium sweet yellow or red pepper, cut into pieces
- 1 medium onion, cut into wedges

Direction

- Mix the first five ingredients together in a saucepan and let it boil. Reduce the heat and simmer without lid for 5-7 minutes or until the onions are soft and the sauce reduces to a slightly thickened consistency. Remove from heat and set aside for basting. Take a large bowl and stir together the egg, parsley, bread crumbs, salt, pepper, and Italian seasoning. Add in the beef and mix well. Make 12 portions. Take a mushroom cap and put in a cheese cube, then take a portion of beef and form a meatball around the mushroom. Alternately skewer meatballs, onion wedges, and peppers on six metal or pre-soaked wooden skewers. Cook on an open grill over medium heat for 3 minutes per side. Cook for another 10-12 minutes, turning occasionally, until meat juices are clear. Baste meatballs at the last 2 minutes of grilling time.

Nutrition Information

- Calories: 302 calories
- Protein: 20g protein.
- Total Fat: 13g fat (5g saturated fat)
- Sodium: 417mg sodium
- Fiber: 2g fiber)
- Total Carbohydrate: 27g carbohydrate (18g sugars
- Cholesterol: 93mg cholesterol

408.   Swedish Dill Meatballs

Serving: 10-12 servings. | Prep: 20mins | Cook: 60mins | Ready in:

Ingredients

- 2 large eggs, beaten
- 1/2 cup whole milk
- 1 cup dry bread crumbs
- 2 teaspoons salt
- 1/2 teaspoon pepper
- 1-1/2 teaspoons dill weed
- 1/4 teaspoon ground allspice
- 1/4 teaspoon ground nutmeg
- 1 cup chopped onion
- 2 tablespoons butter
- 2 pounds ground beef
- 1/2 pound ground pork
- SAUCE:
- 1/4 cup butter
- 1/2 cup all-purpose flour
- 2 cans (14-1/2 ounces each) beef broth
- 1 pint heavy whipping cream
- 1/2 teaspoon dill weed
- 1/2 teaspoon salt
- 1/4 teaspoon pepper
- Fresh dill sprigs, optional

Direction

- Preheat oven to 350°. In a large bowl, combine milk, eggs, seasonings and bread crumbs; put aside. In a skillet, sauté onion in butter until softened; add to egg mixture. Add ground pork and beef; mix well. Cover and allow to cool for 1 hour in refrigerator.
- Preheat oven to 350°. Shape meat mixture into balls, about 1-1/4-inch to 1-1/2-inch each. On a greased rack in a shallow baking pan, place meatballs. Uncovered and bake for nearly 20 to 25 minutes until a thermometer reads 160°. Take out of oven and place in a baking dish of 3-quart.
- For making sauce, in a saucepan, melt butter; mix in flour to form a smooth paste. Stir in broth gradually; allow to boil, stirring constantly. Lower heat; blend in dill, cream, pepper and salt. If you want a thicker sauce, continue cooking for an addition of 10 to 15 minutes, stirring occasionally. Pour sauce over meatballs.
- Uncover and bake for around 40 to 45 minutes until bubbly and heated through. Use fresh dill to garnish if wished.

Nutrition Information

- Calories: 457 calories
- Total Carbohydrate: 14g carbohydrate (3g sugars
- Cholesterol: 169mg cholesterol
- Protein: 23g protein.
- Total Fat: 34g fat (18g saturated fat)
- Sodium: 824mg sodium
- Fiber: 1g fiber)

409.   Swedish Meatballs

Serving: 5 | Prep: | Cook: 50mins | Ready in:

Ingredients

- ½ cup finely chopped onion
- ¼ cup dry whole-wheat breadcrumbs (see Tip)
- ¾ teaspoon salt, divided
- ½ teaspoon freshly ground pepper
- ¼ teaspoon freshly grated nutmeg
- ¼ teaspoon ground cardamom (optional)
- 8 ounces ground turkey breast
- 8 ounces ground pork
- 1 tablespoon extra-virgin olive oil
- 1 pound button mushrooms, sliced
- 1 14-ounce can reduced-sodium chicken broth
- ¼ cup all-purpose flour
- ½ cup reduced-fat sour cream
- ¼ cup finely chopped flat-leaf parsley
- 1 tablespoon lingonberry or seedless raspberry jam

Direction

- In a big bowl, mix together nutmeg, pepper, 1/4 teaspoon salt, bread crumbs, onion, and cardamom if wanted. Add pork and turkey; kindly stir to combine (don't overmix). Form 20 meatballs, a scant 2 tablespoons of mixture for each.
- In a big nonstick skillet, heat oil on medium heat. Put in meatballs, cook until mostly cooked, turning from time to time and decreasing heat when the pan is too hot, about 10-12 minutes. Remove to a plate.
- Place mushrooms in the pan and rise to medium-high heat. Cook for 8-10 minutes, mixing from time to time, till their liquid is released and evaporated.
- In a bowl, beat flour and broth, pour in the pan with the meatballs. Heat to a simmer, cook for 2 minutes till sauce is thickened and meatballs has just been cooked through. Take away from heat. Into the sauce, put remaining 1/2 teaspoon salt, jam, parsley, and sour cream; nicely mix until combined.

Nutrition Information

- Calories: 255 calories;
- Fiber: 2

- Total Carbohydrate: 16
- Protein: 24
- Cholesterol: 62
- Sugar: 5
- Total Fat: 11
- Saturated Fat: 4
- Sodium: 636

410.   Sweet 'n' Saucy Meatballs

Serving: 4-6 servings. | Prep: 15mins | Cook: 40mins | Ready in:

Ingredients

- 1 egg
- 1/2 cup quick-cooking oats
- 1 pound lean ground beef (90% lean)
- 1-1/2 cups water
- 1-1/4 cups ketchup
- 1 cup sugar

Direction

- In a large bowl, combine oats and egg. Crumble beef over mixture and mix well. Form into balls of 1 and a half inch in size.
- In a lightly greased baking dish of 11x7-inch in size, place the meatballs. Combine sugar, ketchup and water; pour mixture over meatballs. Bake without a cover at 350° for 40 to 50 minutes or until meat is not pink anymore.

Nutrition Information

- Calories: 334 calories
- Fiber: 1g fiber)
- Total Carbohydrate: 51g carbohydrate (38g sugars
- Cholesterol: 82mg cholesterol
- Protein: 17g protein.
- Total Fat: 7g fat (3g saturated fat)
- Sodium: 637mg sodium

- Total Fat: 6g fat (2g saturated fat)
- Sodium: 432mg sodium
- Fiber: 0 fiber)
- Total Carbohydrate: 15g carbohydrate (11g sugars
- Cholesterol: 41mg cholesterol

411. Sweet 'n' Soy Snack Meatballs

Serving: 5 dozen. | Prep: 25mins | Cook: 20mins |Ready in:

Ingredients

- 1 egg
- 1/4 cup finely chopped onion
- 1 tablespoon ketchup
- 1-1/2 teaspoons salt
- 1/2 teaspoon pepper
- 1/2 teaspoon seasoned salt
- 1/2 teaspoon Worcestershire sauce
- 2 pounds ground beef
- 3/4 cup dry bread crumbs
- SAUCE:
- 2 tablespoons plus 1-1/2 teaspoons cornstarch
- 1 cup orange marmalade
- 3 to 4 tablespoons soy sauce
- 2 tablespoons lemon juice
- 2 garlic cloves, minced

Direction

- Combine first 7 ingredients in large bowl. Crumble the beef over the mixture. Then sprinkle bread crumbs over and gently mix. Form into 1-inch balls.
- In shallow baking pan, put meatballs on an oiled rack. Bake, uncovered, for 20-25 mins at 350°, until the meat is no longer pink; then drain.
- In the meantime, combine sauce ingredients in small saucepan. Boil; cook while stirring until thickened, about 2 mins. Arrange meatballs onto the serving dish; enjoy with the sauce.

Nutrition Information

- Calories: 156 calories
- Protein: 10g protein.

412. Sweet And Sour Meatballs With Pineapple

Serving: about 3 dozen. | Prep: 20mins | Cook: 20mins | Ready in:

Ingredients

- 1 egg
- 1 medium onion, finely chopped
- 1 tablespoon cornstarch
- 1/2 teaspoon salt
- 1/2 teaspoon pepper
- 1 pound lean ground beef (90% lean)
- 2 tablespoons canola oil
- SAUCE:
- 1 can (20 ounces) pineapple chunks, undrained
- 2 medium green peppers, julienned
- 1/2 cup sugar
- 3 tablespoons cider vinegar
- 1 tablespoon canola oil
- 1 tablespoon soy sauce
- 3 tablespoons cornstarch
- 1/3 cup cold water

Direction

- Mix the first five ingredients in a large bowl. Crumble beef over the mixture; mix thoroughly. Form into 1-inch balls.
- In a large skillet, brown the meatballs in oil while turning often. Use a slotted spoon to take them out; set aside; strain.
- Add soy sauce, oil, vinegar, sugar, green peppers and pineapple into the skillet. Simmer with a cover for 5 minutes, till tender. Take the meatballs back into the skillet; simmer till the meat is no longer pink.

- Mix water and cornstarch till smooth. Stir into the skillet. Bring it to a boil; cook while stirring for 2 minutes, till thickened.

Nutrition Information

- Calories: 328 calories
- Fiber: 2g fiber)
- Total Carbohydrate: 36g carbohydrate (27g sugars
- Cholesterol: 72mg cholesterol
- Protein: 17g protein.
- Total Fat: 13g fat (3g saturated fat)
- Sodium: 416mg sodium

---

413.   Sweet And Tangy Meatballs

Serving: 6 servings. | Prep: 15mins | Cook: 25mins | Ready in:

Ingredients

- 1/4 cup egg substitute
- 2 tablespoons fat-free milk
- 1 cup seasoned bread crumbs
- 2 tablespoons chopped onion
- 1/8 teaspoon pepper
- 1 pound lean ground beef (90% lean)
- 1 tablespoon cornstarch
- 3/4 cup unsweetened pineapple juice
- 1/2 cup barbecue sauce
- 1/4 cup water
- 1 cup whole-berry cranberry sauce
- 6 unsweetened pineapple slices
- 6 green pepper rings
- Hot cooked rice

Direction

- In a large bowl, combine milk and egg substitute. Stir in the pepper, onion and crumbs. Add beef and mix well. Form into 36 1-inch balls.

- In a large skillet, use cooking spray to coat; brown meatballs; drain if necessary. Combine the pineapple juice, cornstarch, water and barbecue sauce until smooth; mix in cranberry sauce.
- Pour mixture over meatballs. Allow to boil; cook and stir for nearly 2 minutes until thickened. Lower heat; put pineapple and green pepper to top.
- Simmer while covered for approximately 10 minutes until meatballs are no longer pink. Serve along with rice.

Nutrition Information

- Calories: 338 calories
- Protein: 19g protein.
- Total Fat: 8g fat (3g saturated fat)
- Sodium: 556mg sodium
- Fiber: 2g fiber)
- Total Carbohydrate: 48g carbohydrate (25g sugars
- Cholesterol: 47mg cholesterol

---

414.   Sweet And Sour Meatballs

Serving: Makes about 25 | Prep: | Cook: | Ready in:

Ingredients

- 1 pound lean ground beef
- 1/2 cup plain dry breadcrumbs
- 1/4 cup minced celery
- 1/4 cup minced fresh parsley
- 1 large egg
- 1/2 teaspoon ground black pepper
- 1 1-ounce package dry onion soup mix
- 1 12-ounce bottle home-style chili sauce
- 3/4 cup water
- 1/2 cup golden raisins
- 1/2 cup tarragon vinegar
- 2 tablespoons sugar

Direction

- In a medium bowl, combine 1/2 teaspoon pepper, egg, parsley, celery, breadcrumbs and ground beef. Put in 1 1/2 tablespoons soup mix, mix nicely. With moistened hands, shape mixture into balls, 1 inch in diameter for each then arrange them on sheet of foil.
- In a heavy and big pot, combine remaining soup mix, sugar, vinegar, raisins, 3/4 cup water and chili sauce. Heat to a simmer on medium-low heat. Into the sauce, place meatballs. Put cover on the pot and allow to simmer for 30 minutes, mixing from time to time, until sauce is thickened and meatballs are cooked through.

Nutrition Information

- Calories: 75
- Fiber: 1 g(5%)
- Total Carbohydrate: 8 g(3%)
- Cholesterol: 19 mg(6%)
- Protein: 5 g(9%)
- Total Fat: 2 g(3%)
- Saturated Fat: 1 g(4%)
- Sodium: 306 mg(13%)

```
415.        Sweet And Sour Meatballs
                     Appetizer
```

Serving: 3-4 dozen. | Prep: 15mins | Cook: 20mins | Ready in:

Ingredients

- 2 cups soft bread crumbs
- 1/2 cup milk
- 1/2 cup lean ground beef
- 1/2 pound Jones No Sugar Pork Sausage Roll sausage
- 1 can (8 ounces) whole water chestnuts, finely chopped and drained
- 1 tablespoon soy sauce
- 1/2 teaspoon garlic powder
- 1/4 teaspoon onion salt

- Prepared sweet-and-sour sauce, optional

Direction

- In a small bowl, combine milk and bread crumbs; put aside. In the meantime, combine sausage, ground beef with onion salt, garlic powder, soy sauce, and water chestnuts. Put beef mixture into the bread crumb mixture and mix until well combined. Shape mixture into meatballs of 1 1/2 inches in diameter. Arrange meatballs on an oiled rack in a shallow baking pan.
- Bake for 20 minutes at 350° until a thermometer registers 160°; drain well. If desired, serve meatballs with sweet-and-sour sauce.

Nutrition Information

- Calories:
- Cholesterol:
- Protein:
- Total Fat:
- Sodium:
- Fiber:
- Total Carbohydrate:

```
416.        Taco Meatball Ring
```

Serving: 16 servings. | Prep: 30mins | Cook: 15mins | Ready in:

Ingredients

- 2 cups shredded cheddar cheese, divided
- 2 tablespoons water
- 2 to 4 tablespoons taco seasoning
- 1/2 pound ground beef
- 2 tubes (8 ounces each) refrigerated crescent rolls
- 1/2 medium head iceberg lettuce, shredded
- 1 medium tomato, chopped
- 4 green onions, sliced

- 1/2 cup sliced ripe olives
- 2 jalapeno peppers, sliced
- Sour cream and salsa, optional

Direction

- Mix taco seasoning, water and 1 cup cheese in a big bowl. Crumble beef above mixture. Mix well. Form to 16 balls.
- On a greased rack inside a shallow baking pan, put meatballs. Bake at 400 degrees, uncovered, or until meat isn't pink anymore for 12 minutes. Drain the meatballs on top of paper towels. Lower heat to 375 degrees.
- On a greased 15-inch pizza pan, put crescent rolls. Create a ring, face pointed ends on the pan's outer edge, with the wide ends overlapping.
- On each roll, put a meatball. Fold point on meatball. Tucker under the roll's wide end, you should see the meatball. Repeat process. Bake until rolls are golden brown or for 15-20 minutes.
- Put on a serving platter. Use sour cream and salsa (optional), leftover cheese, jalapenos, olives, onions, tomato and lettuce in the middle of the ring.

Nutrition Information

- Calories: 203 calories
- Sodium: 457mg sodium
- Fiber: 1g fiber)
- Total Carbohydrate: 14g carbohydrate (3g sugars
- Cholesterol: 24mg cholesterol
- Protein: 8g protein.
- Total Fat: 12g fat (5g saturated fat)

417. Taco Meatballs

Serving: 3-1/2 dozen. | Prep: 45mins | Cook: 15mins | Ready in:

Ingredients

- 1 cup biscuit/baking mix
- 1 envelope taco seasoning
- 1 cup shredded cheddar cheese
- 1/2 cup water
- 1 pound lean ground beef (90% lean)
- Salsa and taco sauce

Direction

- Mix the first 4 ingredients together in a big bowl. Crumble the beef over the mixture and combine well. Form into balls with 1 inch size.
- On a greased rack in a shallow baking pan, position meat balls. Bake at 350° without a cover until balls are not pink anymore, for 15 to 20 minutes. Drain, then serve together with taco sauce and salsa.

Nutrition Information

- Calories: 120 calories
- Total Fat: 6g fat (3g saturated fat)
- Sodium: 407mg sodium
- Fiber: 0 fiber)
- Total Carbohydrate: 8g carbohydrate (0 sugars
- Cholesterol: 24mg cholesterol
- Protein: 9g protein.

418. Tangy Baked Meatballs

Serving: 7 to 7-1/2 dozen. | Prep: 30mins | Cook: 01hours35mins | Ready in:

Ingredients

- 2 cups cubed rye bread
- 2 cups milk
- 3 eggs
- 1 envelope onion soup mix
- 2 teaspoons salt
- 1-1/2 teaspoons dried thyme
- 1/2 teaspoon pepper
- 1/4 teaspoon ground nutmeg

- 5 pounds ground beef
- 2 pounds Jones No Sugar Pork Sausage Roll sausage
- 1 bottle (40 ounces) ketchup
- 2 cups crab apple or apple jelly, melted
- 4 teaspoons browning sauce, optional

Direction

- Combine milk and the bread cubes; allow to stand for 5 minutes. Add the next six ingredients; mix well. Crumble meat into bread mixture; stir just until blended. Form into balls of 1 and a half inches in size.
- On four greased racks in four shallow baking pans, place meatballs. Bake without a cover at 350° for 45 minutes; drain.
- In the meantime, combine jelly, ketchup, and browning sauce (if you want); spoon over meatballs. Lower the heat to 325°; bake while covering for an addition of 50 to 60 minutes or until a thermometer reads 160°.

Nutrition Information

- Calories: 329 calories
- Protein: 19g protein.
- Total Fat: 16g fat (6g saturated fat)
- Sodium: 880mg sodium
- Fiber: 1g fiber)
- Total Carbohydrate: 27g carbohydrate (18g sugars
- Cholesterol: 85mg cholesterol

419.   Tangy Meatballs

Serving: 12 servings. | Prep: 50mins | Cook: 20mins | Ready in:

Ingredients

- 2 large eggs
- 2 cups quick-cooking or rolled oats
- 1 can (12 ounces) evaporated milk

- 1 cup chopped onion
- 2 teaspoons salt
- 1/2 teaspoon pepper
- 1/2 teaspoon garlic powder
- 3 pounds lean ground beef (90% lean)
- SAUCE:
- 2 cups ketchup
- 1-1/2 cups packed brown sugar
- 1/2 cup chopped onion
- 1 to 2 teaspoons liquid smoke
- 1/2 teaspoon garlic powder

Direction

- Whisk eggs in a big bowl. Add garlic powder, pepper, salt, onion, milk, and oats. Add ground beef, stirring thoroughly. Form into balls, about 1 1/2 each ball. On racks coated with cooking spray in shallow baking pans, put the meatballs. Bake without a cover for 30 minutes at 375°; strain.
- In one of the pans, put all the meatballs. Boil all the sauce ingredients in a saucepan. Add onto the meatballs. Put back into the oven and bake without a cover until the meatballs have been done, about 20 minutes.

Nutrition Information

- Calories: 423 calories
- Cholesterol: 100mg cholesterol
- Protein: 27g protein.
- Total Fat: 12g fat (5g saturated fat)
- Sodium: 991mg sodium
- Fiber: 2g fiber)
- Total Carbohydrate: 51g carbohydrate (35g sugars

420.   Tangy Meatballs Over Noodles

Serving: 8 servings (40 meatballs). | Prep: 25mins | Cook: 50mins | Ready in:

Ingredients

- 1 egg, lightly beaten
- 1/3 cup milk
- 1/4 cup seasoned bread crumbs
- 1 tablespoon dried minced onion
- 1 teaspoon salt
- 1-1/2 pounds ground beef
- 2 cans (14-3/4 ounces each) beef gravy
- 1/2 cup packed brown sugar
- 1/4 cup cider vinegar
- 3/4 teaspoon ground ginger
- 1/4 teaspoon ground cloves
- 1 package (12 ounces) egg noodles

Direction

- Mix the first five ingredients in a big bowl and crumble beef over it, mixing thoroughly. Form the mixture into balls around 1-1/2 inches. In a shallow pan, place the greased rack with meatballs on it. Bake them without any cover on at 350°F, about 20 minutes. Drain.
- Use a slotted spoon to move the meatballs into a 2-1/2 quart greased baking dish. Mix cloves, ginger, vinegar, brown sugar and gravy together then pour the entire thing over meatballs. Cover it. Continue baking for an additional 30 minutes until the meat isn't pink anymore. As the meatballs are baking, follow the package instructions to cook the noodles. Drain it and eat with meatballs. Serve.

Nutrition Information

- Calories: 435 calories
- Protein: 26g protein.
- Total Fat: 14g fat (5g saturated fat)
- Sodium: 747mg sodium
- Fiber: 1g fiber)
- Total Carbohydrate: 51g carbohydrate (16g sugars
- Cholesterol: 127mg cholesterol

421.   Tender Tangy Meatballs

Serving: 10 servings. | Prep: 25mins | Cook: 30mins | Ready in:

Ingredients

- 3 slices white bread, torn into small pieces
- 1 cup milk
- 1 medium onion, finely chopped
- 1 tablespoon mustard seed
- 2 teaspoons seasoned salt
- 2 garlic cloves, minced
- 1 egg, beaten
- Salt and pepper to taste
- 2-1/2 pounds ground beef
- 1/2 pound Jones No Sugar Pork Sausage Roll sausage
- 3 tablespoons canola oil
- 2 bottles (10 ounces each) chili sauce
- 1 jar (8 ounces) grape jelly
- 1-1/2 cups beef broth

Direction

- Mix milk and bread in a large mixing bowl. Squeeze bread to remove extra milk and throw out the milk. Mix in mustard seed, pepper, egg, onion, garlic, salt, and seasoned salt. Add crumbled sausage and beef on top and combine well. Make 1-1/2-in. balls with mixture. Place oil in a large frying pan and brown the meatballs. Drain excess grease. Using a Dutch oven or large pot, mix together jelly, beef broth, and chili sauce and gradually heat to a boil. Add in the browned meatballs and boil until thermometer says 160 degrees, 30-45 minutes.

Nutrition Information

- Calories: 442 calories
- Protein: 27g protein.
- Total Fat: 24g fat (8g saturated fat)
- Sodium: 1017mg sodium
- Fiber: 1g fiber)

- Total Carbohydrate: 29g carbohydrate (21g sugars
- Cholesterol: 108mg cholesterol

422. Teriyaki Meatballs

Serving: 4 servings | Prep: 15mins | Cook: | Ready in:

Ingredients

- For the Meatballs:
- 16 ounces lean ground turkey
- 1/2 cup panko bread crumbs
- 1/4 cup finely chopped green onion
- 1 large egg
- 1 teaspoon freshly grated ginger or 1/4 teaspoon ground ginger
- 1 garlic clove, pressed
- 2 teaspoons sesame oil
- Reynolds Wrap® Aluminum Foil
- For the Teriyaki Sauce:
- 1/4 cup light brown sugar , lightly packed
- 2 tablespoons hoisin sauce
- 1 tablespoon soy sauce
- 1/2 tablespoon sesame oil
- 1 medium garlic clove, pressed
- 1/2 teaspoon fresh ginger or 1/8 teaspoon ground ginger
- Optional Garnish:
- sesame seed s and green onion

Direction

- 1. 1. Use Reynolds® Aluminum Foil to cover inside a 17x12-in. rimmed baking sheet. Set the oven at 400°F and start preheating.
- 2. 2. In a large bowl, mix sesame oil, garlic, ginger, egg, green onion, bread crumbs and turkey. Blend by hands or by a spoon just till well combined.
- 3.3. Shape in 1 1/4-inch to 1 1/2-inch meatballs; bake at 400°F till tender and juices run clear or a meat thermometer reads 170°F, about 10-12 minutes.

- 4.4. Meanwhile, in a small saucepan, simmer the sauce ingredients while stirring often till slightly thickened, 3-5 minutes.
- 5. 5. Move the warm meatballs into a mixing bowl, drizzle the meatballs with warm sauce; toss to mix.

423. Tiny Taco Meatballs

Serving: 14-16 servings. | Prep: 15mins | Cook: 15mins | Ready in:

Ingredients

- 2 eggs
- 1 medium onion, finely chopped
- 1 envelope taco seasoning
- 1/2 teaspoon salt
- 1/4 teaspoon pepper
- 2 pounds ground beef
- Taco sauce, optional

Direction

- Mix the first 5 ingredients together in a bowl. Add beef, stir thoroughly. Form into balls, about 1-inch each ball. On a rack coated with cooking spray set over a shallow baking pan, put the meatballs.
- Bake at 400° until the meat is not pink anymore, about 14-18 minutes. Enjoy with taco sauce if you want.

Nutrition Information

- Calories: 131 calories
- Protein: 12g protein.
- Total Fat: 8g fat (3g saturated fat)
- Sodium: 309mg sodium
- Fiber: 0 fiber)
- Total Carbohydrate: 3g carbohydrate (1g sugars
- Cholesterol: 64mg cholesterol

Serving: 6-8 servings. | Prep: 15mins | Cook: 01hours30mins | Ready in:

Ingredients

- 4 slices bread, torn into small pieces
- 1/2 cup whole milk
- 1 large egg, beaten
- 1 pound lean ground beef
- 2 celery ribs, chopped
- 1/4 cup chopped onion
- 1/4 cup uncooked instant rice
- 1 teaspoon salt
- 1/4 teaspoon pepper
- 2 cups tomato sauce

Direction

- Soak bread in milk in a large bowl. Put in pepper, salt, rice, onion, celery, beef and egg; mix thoroughly.
- Form into eight balls; arrange in a greased 2 1/2-qt. baking dish. Add tomato sauce over meatballs. Bake at 350° for 1 1/2 hours.

Nutrition Information

- Calories:
- Protein:
- Total Fat:
- Sodium:
- Fiber:
- Total Carbohydrate:
- Cholesterol:

Serving: 6 servings. | Prep: 30mins | Cook: 25mins | Ready in:

Ingredients

- 4 cups water
- 2 medium peeled potatoes, cut into 1-inch cubes
- 2 medium carrots, cut into 3/4-inch chunks
- 1 large onion, cut into eighths
- 2 tablespoons beef bouillon granules
- 1 bay leaf
- 1 teaspoon dried thyme
- 1 teaspoon dried basil
- 1/2 teaspoon salt
- 1/2 teaspoon pepper
- 1/2 cup seasoned dry bread crumbs
- 1 egg, lightly beaten
- 1 teaspoon Worcestershire sauce
- 1 pound ground beef
- 2 medium sweet potatoes, peeled and cut into 1-inch cubes
- 2 medium parsnips, peeled and cut into 3/4-inch slices
- 1 cup frozen peas
- 1/3 cup all-purpose flour
- 1/2 cup cold water
- 1/4 teaspoon browning sauce, optional

Direction

- Bring water in a big soup kettle or Dutch oven to a boil. Add seasonings, onion, carrots, and potatoes; bring to another boil. Lower heat; simmer, covered for 10 minutes.
- In the meantime, combine Worcestershire sauce, egg, and bread crumbs in a small bowl. Break beef into small pieces over the mixture and stir well to combine.
- Form mixture into 1-inch balls. Put the meatballs into the Dutch oven along with parsnips and sweet potatoes. Bring to a boil. Lower heat; simmer, covered until vegetables are tender, or for 15 minutes.
- Remove bay leaf. Mix in peas. Combine cold water, flour, and browning sauce (if using) until no lumps remain; slowly mix into the stew. Bring to a boil; cook, stirring often until thickened, or for 2 minutes.

Nutrition Information

- Calories:
- Cholesterol:
- Protein:
- Total Fat:
- Sodium:
- Fiber:
- Total Carbohydrate:

- Calories: 343 calories
- Sodium: 1923mg sodium
- Fiber: 4g fiber)
- Total Carbohydrate: 22g carbohydrate (4g sugars
- Cholesterol: 112mg cholesterol
- Protein: 27g protein.
- Total Fat: 16g fat (6g saturated fat)

426. Veggie Meatball Medley

Serving: 4 servings. | Prep: 15mins | Cook: 30mins | Ready in:

Ingredients

- 1 egg
- 1/4 cup dry bread crumbs
- 1/2 teaspoon salt
- 1/4 teaspoon pepper
- 1 pound ground beef
- 2 cups frozen stir-fry vegetable blend
- 1 medium onion, chopped
- 1 can (10-3/4 ounces) condensed cream of mushroom soup, undiluted
- 1/4 cup soy sauce
- 1/4 teaspoon garlic powder
- Hot cooked rice

Direction

- Mix the first four ingredients together in a large bowl. Crumble beef over the mixture; mix properly. Form into 1 1/2-in. balls. Cook onion, vegetables and the meatballs in a large nonstick skillet till the meatballs are well browned; strain.
- Mix in garlic powder, soy sauce and the soup. Allow to boil. Lower the heat; simmer without a cover while stirring occasionally till the meat is not pink anymore, or for 20 minutes. Serve over rice.

Nutrition Information

427. Veggie Meatball Stew

Serving: 8 servings. | Prep: 20mins | Cook: 01hours05mins | Ready in:

Ingredients

- 1 can (8 ounces) tomato sauce, divided
- 1 egg
- 1 medium onion, finely chopped
- 1/2 cup dry bread crumbs
- 1/2 teaspoon salt
- 1/4 teaspoon pepper
- 1/8 teaspoon ground allspice
- 1 pound ground beef
- 3 cups water
- 3 medium potatoes, peeled and quartered
- 6 medium carrots, sliced
- 1 package (10 ounces) frozen peas
- 1/2 cup chopped green pepper
- 1 envelope onion soup mix

Direction

- Combine allspice, pepper, salt, bread crumbs, onion, egg, and 1/4 cup tomato sauce in a bowl. Crush beef into small pieces over the mixture and stir to combine. Form the mixture into 1-inch balls. Cook meatballs in a large saucepan until browned; drain. Add the remaining tomato sauce, soup mix, green pepper, peas, carrots, potatoes, and water; bring to a boil. Lower heat; simmer, covered until vegetables are tender and meat is no longer pink, or about 45 minutes.

Nutrition Information

- Calories:
- Sodium:
- Fiber:
- Total Carbohydrate:
- Cholesterol:
- Protein:
- Total Fat:

---

428. Yummy Sweet 'n' Sour Meatballs

Serving: 4-6 servings. | Prep: 20mins | Cook: 20mins | Ready in:

Ingredients

- 1 large egg, beaten
- 1/4 cup whole milk
- 1/2 cup dry bread crumbs
- 2 tablespoons finely chopped onion
- 3/4 teaspoon salt
- 1/2 teaspoon Worcestershire sauce
- 1 pound lean ground beef (90% lean)
- SAUCE:
- 1/2 cup packed brown sugar
- 2 tablespoons cornstarch
- 1 can (20 ounces) unsweetened pineapple chunks, undrained
- 1/3 cup cider vinegar
- 1 tablespoon soy sauce
- 1 medium green pepper, cut into bite-size pieces

Direction

- Mix the first six ingredients in a big bowl. Crumble ground beef over bowl and stir well. Take a little at a time and make into 1-1/2-in. balls. Brown meatballs on every side in a frying pan. Make sure to turn them often. Remove the meatballs, set aside, and drain excess fat. To make the sauce, put cornstarch and brown sugar in the frying pan. Mix in soy

sauce, pineapple, and vinegar until combined. Heat to a boil. Stirring constantly, cook until thick, 2 minutes. Add the green pepper and decrease heat. Put the cover on and gently boil until soft. Put the meatballs back into the pan and cook through.

Nutrition Information

- Calories: 296 calories
- Cholesterol: 74mg cholesterol
- Protein: 17g protein.
- Total Fat: 7g fat (3g saturated fat)
- Sodium: 610mg sodium
- Fiber: 1g fiber)
- Total Carbohydrate: 39g carbohydrate (29g sugars

---

429. Zesty Meatballs

Serving: 6 servings. | Prep: 15mins | Cook: 15mins | Ready in:

Ingredients

- 1/3 cup finely chopped onion
- 2 egg whites, lightly beaten
- 1/4 cup fat-free milk
- 2 teaspoons prepared mustard
- 1/2 teaspoon salt
- 3/4 cup graham cracker crumbs
- 3/4 pound lean ground beef (90% lean)
- 3/4 pound lean ground turkey
- BARBECUE SAUCE:
- 1/2 cup packed brown sugar
- 3 tablespoons cornstarch
- 1/2 cup cider vinegar
- 1/2 cup ketchup
- 1/2 cup molasses
- 1/4 cup orange juice concentrate
- 2 tablespoons Dijon mustard
- 2 tablespoons reduced-sodium soy sauce
- 1/4 teaspoon hot pepper sauce
- 6 cups hot cooked yolk-free noodles

Direction

- In a small microwave-safe bowl, put onion. Put a cover on and microwave on high until soft, about 1 1/2 minutes. Mix onion, cracker crumbs, salt, mustard, milk, and egg whites together in a big bowl. Crumble over the mixture with turkey and beef and stir thoroughly.
- Form into balls, about 1 1/4-inch each ball. On a greased rack set over a shallow baking pan, put the meatballs. Bake at 375° until the meat is not pink anymore, about 15-18 minutes; strain.
- In the meantime, mix together cornstarch and brown sugar in a big saucepan. Mix in vinegar until smooth. Add hot pepper sauce, soy sauce, mustard, orange juice concentrate, molasses, and ketchup. Boil it; stir and cook until thickened, about 2 minutes. Add the meatballs then thoroughly heat. Enjoy with noodles.

Nutrition Information

- Calories: 672 calories
- Protein: 34g protein. Diabetic Exchanges: 7 starch
- Total Fat: 13g fat (4g saturated fat)
- Sodium: 1050mg sodium
- Fiber: 4g fiber)
- Total Carbohydrate: 105g carbohydrate (0 sugars
- Cholesterol: 66mg cholesterol

Chapter 5: Ground Beef Sloppy Joe Recipes

***

---

430. All American Barbecue Sandwiches

Serving: 18 servings. | Prep: 5mins | Cook: 20mins | Ready in:

Ingredients

- 4-1/2 pounds ground beef
- 1-1/2 cups chopped onions
- 2-1/4 cups ketchup
- 3 tablespoons prepared mustard
- 3 tablespoons Worcestershire sauce
- 2 tablespoons vinegar
- 2 tablespoons sugar
- 1 tablespoon salt
- 1 tablespoon pepper
- 18 hamburger buns, split

Direction

- Cook onions and beef in a Dutch oven till the onion turns tender and the meat is not pink anymore; strain. Mix in pepper, salt, sugar, vinegar, Worcestershire sauce, mustard and ketchup. Heat through. Serve on buns.

Nutrition Information

- Calories: 391 calories
- Fiber: 2g fiber)
- Total Carbohydrate: 33g carbohydrate (9g sugars
- Cholesterol: 75mg cholesterol
- Protein: 27g protein.
- Total Fat: 16g fat (6g saturated fat)
- Sodium: 1100mg sodium

---

431. Baked Sloppy Joes

Serving: 4 servings. | Prep: 40mins | Cook: 15mins | Ready in:

Ingredients

- 1 pound ground beef
- 1/4 cup chopped green pepper
- 1 tablespoon chopped onion
- 1 can (8 ounces) tomato sauce
- 1/2 cup ketchup
- 2 tablespoons grated Parmesan cheese
- 3/4 teaspoon garlic powder, divided
- 1/2 teaspoon fennel seed, crushed
- 1/4 teaspoon dried oregano
- 3 tablespoons butter, melted
- 1/2 teaspoon paprika
- 4 kaiser rolls, split
- 4 slices mozzarella cheese

Direction

- Cook onion, green pepper and beef over medium heat in a skillet until meat is not pink anymore; drain off excess liquid. Stir in the oregano, fennel seed, half a teaspoon of garlic powder, Parmesan cheese, ketchup and tomato sauce. Cook until boiling. Lower heat; uncover and simmer for 20 minutes. Mix the rest of garlic powder, paprika and butter in a bowl; combine well. Brush mixture over cut sides of rolls. On roll bottoms, spread meat mixture; add mozzarella cheese on top. Replace roll tops. Use heavy-duty foil to wrap each. Place on a baking sheet. At 350°, bake for 15 minutes or until cheese has been melted.

Nutrition Information

- Calories:
- Sodium:
- Fiber:
- Total Carbohydrate:
- Cholesterol:
- Protein:
- Total Fat:

432.   Barbecue Sliders

Serving: 8 servings. | Prep: 15mins | Cook: 10mins | Ready in:

Ingredients

- 1 pound ground beef
- 1 pound Jones No Sugar Pork Sausage Roll sausage
- 1 cup barbecue sauce, divided
- 16 Hawaiian sweet rolls, split
- Optional toppings: lettuce leaves, sliced plum tomatoes and red onion

Direction

- Combine sausage and beef completely in a big bowl. Form into 16 half inch thick patties.
- Cook patties on grill covered with lid, over medium heat or broil 4 to 5 inches away from the heat. Cook 3 to 4 minutes per side or until an instant-read thermometer shows 160°. 2 minutes from being done, baste patties with fourth cup sauce. Serve with the last barbecue sauce on rolls; pour on top if you like. Freezing option: Transfer patties on a baking sheet lined with plastic wrap; wrap the patties and store in the freezer until hard. Take from pan and place in a big closable plastic bag; put back to freezer. To use, grill frozen patties following the direction, lengthen time if needed.

Nutrition Information

- Calories: 499 calories
- Fiber: 2g fiber)
- Total Carbohydrate: 47g carbohydrate (23g sugars
- Cholesterol: 96mg cholesterol
- Protein: 24g protein.
- Total Fat: 24g fat (9g saturated fat)
- Sodium: 885mg sodium

433. Barbecue Glazed Sweet Onion Burgers

Serving: 8 servings. | Prep: 60mins | Cook: 10mins | Ready in:

Ingredients

- 1 large sweet onion, cut into 1/2-inch pieces
- 2 tablespoons plus 2/3 cup canola oil, divided
- 1-1/2 teaspoons salt, divided
- 1/2 teaspoon pepper
- 8 tablespoons barbecue seasoning, divided
- 1/4 cup packed brown sugar
- 2 pounds ground beef
- 8 hamburger buns, split
- Optional toppings: lettuce leaves and sliced cheddar cheese and dill pickles

Direction

- Preheat the oven to 350 degrees F. Mix onion, 2tbsp oil, and half teaspoon each of pepper and salt; layer onions in a 15-in. x 10-in. x 1-in. baking pan. Roast onions for 25-30mins until golden, mix one time; move to a big bowl. Mix in 2tbsp barbeque seasoning; completely cool.
- Combine the remaining barbeque seasoning, salt, oil, and brown sugar in a small bowl until incorporated. Transfer 1/2 of the mixture to a separate bowl; save for brushing burgers as they cook.
- Thoroughly but lightly mix in beef to the onion mixture; form into 8 half-inch thick patties. Slather the remaining paste mixture on each side of the patties.
- Grease the grill rack with a paper towel moistened with cooking oil and long-handled tongs. On medium heat, grill burgers while covered or broil four inches from heat for 4-6mins per side until an inserted thermometer registers 160 degrees F. Slather the reserved paste mixture all over the burgers on the final 3mins of cooking. Serve burgers on buns with your preferred toppings.

Nutrition Information

- Calories:
- Total Carbohydrate:
- Cholesterol:
- Protein:
- Total Fat:
- Sodium:
- Fiber:

434. Barbecued Burgers

Serving: 6 servings. | Prep: 25mins | Cook: 15mins | Ready in:

Ingredients

- SAUCE:
- 1 cup ketchup
- 1/2 cup packed brown sugar
- 1/3 cup sugar
- 1/4 cup honey
- 1/4 cup molasses
- 2 teaspoons prepared mustard
- 1-1/2 teaspoons Worcestershire sauce
- 1/4 teaspoon salt
- 1/4 teaspoon liquid smoke
- 1/8 teaspoon pepper
- BURGERS:
- 1 large egg, lightly beaten
- 1/3 cup quick-cooking oats
- 1/4 teaspoon onion salt
- 1/4 teaspoon garlic salt
- 1/4 teaspoon pepper
- 1/8 teaspoon salt
- 1-1/2 pounds ground beef
- 6 hamburger buns, split
- Toppings of your choice

Direction

- Mix together the first 10 ingredients in a small saucepan. Heat until it boils. Take it away from the heat. Reserve 1 cup of barbecue sauce to add to burgers to serve.
- Mix together salt, pepper, garlic salt, onion salt, 1/4 cup of the remaining barbecue sauce,

oats and egg in a large bowl. Add crumbled beef to the mixture and stir well to combine. Form into 6 patties.

- Put them on grill grate over medium heat with cover until a thermometer reaches 160 degrees, about 6 to 8 minutes per side; use 1/2 cup barbecue sauce to baste in the last 5 minutes. Put onto buns; top with any toppings you want and add reserved barbecue sauce to serve.

Nutrition Information

- Calories: 626 calories
- Protein: 30g protein.
- Total Fat: 19g fat (7g saturated fat)
- Sodium: 1146mg sodium
- Fiber: 2g fiber)
- Total Carbohydrate: 86g carbohydrate (56g sugars
- Cholesterol: 121mg cholesterol

435. Barbecued Hamburgers

Serving: 12 servings. | Prep: 20mins | Cook: 40mins | Ready in:

Ingredients

- 1/2 cup crushed saltines (about 15 crackers)
- 1 cup milk
- 1 teaspoon salt
- 1/4 teaspoon pepper
- 2 pounds ground beef
- 1-1/2 cups ketchup
- 1 large onion, chopped
- 1/3 cup Worcestershire sauce
- 3 tablespoons sugar
- 3 tablespoons cider vinegar
- 12 hamburger buns, split

Direction

- Mix pepper, salt, milk and saltines together in a large bowl. Crumble beef over the mixture; stir properly. Form into 12 patties. Place a large skillet on medium heat; brown the patties on both sides, working in batches. Arrange in a large roasting pan.
- Mix together vinegar, sugar, Worcestershire sauce, onion and ketchup; transfer over the patties. Bake with a cover at 350° till a thermometer reads 160°, or for 40-45 minutes. Serve on buns.

Nutrition Information

- Calories: 318 calories
- Cholesterol: 40mg cholesterol
- Protein: 19g protein.
- Total Fat: 10g fat (4g saturated fat)
- Sodium: 960mg sodium
- Fiber: 2g fiber)
- Total Carbohydrate: 38g carbohydrate (12g sugars

436. Beef & Veggie Sloppy Joes

Serving: 10 servings. | Prep: 35mins | Cook: 05hours00mins | Ready in:

Ingredients

- 4 medium carrots, shredded
- 1 medium yellow summer squash, shredded
- 1 medium zucchini, shredded
- 1 medium sweet red pepper, finely chopped
- 2 medium tomatoes, seeded and chopped
- 1 small red onion, finely chopped
- 1/2 cup ketchup
- 3 tablespoons minced fresh basil or 3 teaspoons dried basil
- 3 tablespoons molasses
- 2 tablespoons cider vinegar
- 2 garlic cloves, minced
- 1/2 teaspoon salt

- 1/2 teaspoon pepper
- 2 pounds lean ground beef (90% lean)
- 10 whole wheat hamburger buns, split

Direction

- Mix the first thirteen ingredients in a 5-6-quart slow cooker. Cook beef in a big skillet over medium heat until no pink remains, crumbling into pieces, about 8-10 minutes. Strain; remove the beef to the slow cooker. Toss to blend.
- Cover and cook on low until the vegetables are soft and fully heated, about 5-6 hours. On buns, put the beef mixture, using a slotted spoon, and enjoy.

Nutrition Information

- Calories: 316 calories
- Total Carbohydrate: 36g carbohydrate (15g sugars
- Cholesterol: 57mg cholesterol
- Protein: 22g protein. Diabetic Exchanges: 2 starch
- Total Fat: 10g fat (3g saturated fat)
- Sodium: 565mg sodium
- Fiber: 5g fiber)

437.   Bulgur Barbecue

Serving: 12 servings. | Prep: 25mins | Cook: 50mins | Ready in:

Ingredients

- 2-3/4 cups water, divided
- 2/3 cup bulgur
- 1-1/2 pounds lean ground beef (90% lean)
- 1-1/2 cups chopped celery
- 1 large onion, chopped
- 1 can (8 ounces) tomato sauce
- 1/2 cup packed brown sugar
- 1/2 cup ketchup
- 1 tablespoon white vinegar

- 1/2 teaspoon prepared mustard
- 1/4 teaspoon salt
- 1/4 teaspoon pepper
- 12 hamburger buns, split

Direction

- Boil 2 cups of water in a saucepan. Mix in bulgur, then lower the heat. Put on a cover and, simmer for 15 minutes. Take away from the heat, then drain and squeeze it dry; put aside.
- Cook the onion, celery and beef over medium heat in a big nonstick frying pan, until the meat has no pink color, then drain. Add the leftover water, pepper, salt, mustard, vinegar, ketchup, brown sugar and tomato sauce, then mix in the reserved bulgur.
- Move to a 2-quart baking dish. Put on a cover and bake for 50-60 minutes at 350 degrees until heated through, then serve on buns.

Nutrition Information

- Calories: 289 calories
- Protein: 17g protein. Diabetic Exchanges: 2-1/2 starch
- Total Fat: 7g fat (2g saturated fat)
- Sodium: 521mg sodium
- Fiber: 5g fiber)
- Total Carbohydrate: 41g carbohydrate (0 sugars
- Cholesterol: 21mg cholesterol

438.   Cabbage Sloppy Joes

Serving: 8 servings. | Prep: 25mins | Cook: 10mins | Ready in:

Ingredients

- 1 pound ground beef
- 1-1/2 cups finely shredded cabbage
- 1 medium onion, chopped
- 1 celery rib, chopped

- 1/4 cup chopped green pepper
- 1 cup ketchup
- 3 tablespoons brown sugar
- 2 tablespoons lemon juice
- 1 tablespoon white vinegar
- 1 tablespoon Worcestershire sauce
- 1 tablespoon prepared mustard
- 1 teaspoon salt
- Dash pepper
- 8 sandwich rolls, split

Direction

- Cook together green pepper, celery, onion, cabbage and beef in a big skillet on moderate heat until meat is not pink anymore, then drain. Stir in pepper, salt, mustard, Worcestershire sauce, vinegar, lemon juice, brown sugar and ketchup. Place a cover and simmer until cabbage is soft, about 10 minutes. Scoop on each roll with 1/2 cup of the beef mixture.

Nutrition Information

- Calories: 365 calories
- Protein: 18g protein.
- Total Fat: 10g fat (5g saturated fat)
- Sodium: 1085mg sodium
- Fiber: 3g fiber)
- Total Carbohydrate: 52g carbohydrate (16g sugars
- Cholesterol: 28mg cholesterol

439.   Cheese Topped Sloppy Joes

Serving: 6 servings. | Prep: 10mins | Cook: 15mins | Ready in:

Ingredients

- 1 pound ground beef
- 2 celery ribs, chopped

- 1 tablespoon chopped onion
- 1 tablespoon all-purpose flour
- 1 tablespoon brown sugar
- 1/2 teaspoon ground mustard
- 3/4 cup ketchup
- 6 hamburger buns, split
- 6 slices Swiss cheese

Direction

- Place a large skillet on medium heat; cook in onion, celery and beef till the meat is not pink anymore; strain. Mix in ketchup, mustard, brown sugar and flour.
- Boil the mixture. Lower the heat; simmer without a cover, stirring occasionally, 10 minutes. Serve accompanied with cheese on buns.

Nutrition Information

- Calories: 376 calories
- Total Carbohydrate: 33g carbohydrate (13g sugars
- Cholesterol: 62mg cholesterol
- Protein: 24g protein.
- Total Fat: 16g fat (9g saturated fat)
- Sodium: 693mg sodium
- Fiber: 1g fiber)

440.   Chipotle Chili Sloppy Joes

Serving: 6 servings. | Prep: 15mins | Cook: 20mins | Ready in:

Ingredients

- 1 pound lean ground beef (90% lean)
- 1 cup finely chopped sweet onion
- 1/2 cup finely chopped green pepper
- 1 jalapeno pepper, seeded and finely chopped, optional
- 1/2 cup chili sauce
- 1/2 cup water

- 1 to 2 chipotle peppers in adobo sauce, finely chopped
- 1 tablespoon packed brown sugar
- 1 teaspoon yellow mustard
- 6 kaiser rolls or hamburger buns, split
- 2 tablespoons butter, softened
- Pickle slices, optional

Direction

- Preheat the broiler. Place a large skillet on medium heat; cook green pepper, onion, beef and jalapeno if you want till the beef is not pink anymore, while breaking up the beef into crumbles or for 5 to 7 minutes; strain.
- Mix in mustard, brown sugar, chipotle peppers, water and chili sauce; boil the mixture. Simmer without a cover till thickened slightly, or for 8-10 minutes, stirring occasionally.
- Use butter to spread the cut sides of rolls lightly; arrange with butter-sided up, on a baking sheet. Broil 3-4 in. from the heat source for around 30 seconds, or till toasted lightly. Fill with pickles if you like and the beef mixture. Freeze option: Place the cooled meat mixture into freezer containers and freeze. Before using, place in the refrigerator to thaw partially for overnight. In a saucepan, heat through while stirring occasionally; put in a little water if needed.

Nutrition Information

- Calories: 313 calories
- Total Fat: 12g fat (5g saturated fat)
- Sodium: 615mg sodium
- Fiber: 2g fiber)
- Total Carbohydrate: 32g carbohydrate (11g sugars
- Cholesterol: 57mg cholesterol
- Protein: 19g protein. Diabetic Exchanges: 2 starch

441. Church Supper Sloppy Joes

Serving: 50 servings. | Prep: 10mins | Cook: 30mins | Ready in:

Ingredients

- 7 pounds lean ground beef (90% lean)
- 1-1/2 cups chopped onion
- 1-1/2 cups chopped celery
- 1/2 cup packed brown sugar
- 2 tablespoons prepared mustard
- 6 cups tomato sauce
- 1/2 cup white vinegar
- 2 to 3 teaspoons minced garlic
- Salt and pepper to taste
- 1-1/2 cups shredded sharp cheddar cheese
- Hamburger buns

Direction

- Cook celery, onion and beef in a several large skillet till the beef is not pink anymore; strain. Put in pepper, salt, garlic, vinegar, tomato sauce and brown sugar. Mix in cheese; cook till the cheese is melted. Serve on buns.

Nutrition Information

- Calories: 125 calories
- Protein: 13g protein.
- Total Fat: 6g fat (3g saturated fat)
- Sodium: 207mg sodium
- Fiber: 0 fiber)
- Total Carbohydrate: 4g carbohydrate (3g sugars
- Cholesterol: 35mg cholesterol

442. Classic Homemade Sloppy Joes

Serving: 8 servings. | Prep: 15mins | Cook: 60mins | Ready in:

Ingredients

- 1 pound ground beef
- 1/2 cup chopped green pepper
- 1 can (14-1/2 ounces) diced tomatoes, undrained
- 1 can (8 ounces) tomato sauce
- 1/2 cup tomato paste
- 1 tablespoon Worcestershire sauce
- 1-1/2 teaspoons sugar
- 1 teaspoon celery salt or celery seed
- 1 teaspoon onion salt or onion powder
- 1/2 teaspoon paprika
- 1/8 to 1/4 teaspoon cayenne pepper
- 1-1/2 bay leaves
- 8 hamburger buns, split

Direction

- Cook green pepper and beef together in a Dutch oven on moderate heat until beef is not pink anymore, then drain. Stir in seasonings, tomato paste, tomato sauce and tomatoes, then bring the mixture to a boil. Lower heat and cook with a cover on low heat for a half hour.
- Take off the cover and cook until thicken, about 30 to 40 minutes more. Get rid of bay leaves and serve each bun with 1/2 cup of the meat mixture.

Nutrition Information

- Calories: 248 calories
- Total Carbohydrate: 30g carbohydrate (9g sugars
- Cholesterol: 28mg cholesterol
- Protein: 16g protein.
- Total Fat: 7g fat (3g saturated fat)
- Sodium: 884mg sodium
- Fiber: 3g fiber)

443. Cranberry Sloppy Joes

Serving: 8 servings. | Prep: 10mins | Cook: 30mins | Ready in:

Ingredients

- 1 pound ground beef
- 1 cup chopped celery
- 1 cup chopped onion
- 1 can (10-3/4 ounces) condensed tomato soup, undiluted
- 1 can (8 ounces) jellied cranberry sauce
- 1/2 teaspoon salt
- 1/4 teaspoon chili powder
- Dash hot pepper sauce
- Hamburger buns, split and toasted

Direction

- Cook onion, celery and beef in a skillet till the vegetables become tender and the meat is browned. Strain. Mix in hot pepper sauce, chili powder, salt, cranberry sauce and soup. Simmer without a cover, stirring occasionally, around 30 minutes. Spoon into buns.

Nutrition Information

- Calories: 164 calories
- Protein: 11g protein.
- Total Fat: 5g fat (2g saturated fat)
- Sodium: 430mg sodium
- Fiber: 2g fiber)
- Total Carbohydrate: 18g carbohydrate (11g sugars
- Cholesterol: 28mg cholesterol

444. Easy Sloppy Joes

Serving: 14 servings. | Prep: 10mins | Cook: 10mins | Ready in:

Ingredients

- 3 pounds ground beef
- 3 cups ketchup
- 2/3 cup sweet pickle relish
- 1 envelope onion soup mix
- 14 hamburger buns, split

Direction

- Place a Dutch oven on medium heat; cook beef till not pink anymore; strain. Combine in soup mix, relish and ketchup; heat through. Allow the mixture to cool before putting into a freezer container, or serve on buns immediately. Freeze with a cover for up to 3 months.
- For using the frozen sloppy joes, place the beef mixture in the refrigerator to thaw; put into a saucepan; heat through. Serve on buns.

Nutrition Information

- Calories: 344 calories
- Total Fat: 11g fat (4g saturated fat)
- Sodium: 1193mg sodium
- Fiber: 1g fiber)
- Total Carbohydrate: 40g carbohydrate (18g sugars
- Cholesterol: 48mg cholesterol
- Protein: 21g protein.

445. Family Favorite Barbecues

Serving: 16 servings. | Prep: 5mins | Cook: 40mins | Ready in:

Ingredients

- 3 pounds ground beef
- 3-1/2 cups tomato juice
- 1-1/2 cups cooked long grain rice
- 1 tablespoon prepared mustard
- 2 teaspoons salt
- 1-1/2 teaspoons chili powder

- 1 teaspoon pepper
- 16 hamburger buns, split

Direction

- Place a Dutch oven or a large saucepan on medium heat; cook in beef till not pink anymore; strain. Mix in seasonings, mustard, rice and tomato juice; stir properly. Simmer with a cover for 25 minutes. Scoop onto the buns.

Nutrition Information

- Calories: 286 calories
- Protein: 20g protein.
- Total Fat: 10g fat (4g saturated fat)
- Sodium: 797mg sodium
- Fiber: 2g fiber)
- Total Carbohydrate: 28g carbohydrate (5g sugars
- Cholesterol: 42mg cholesterol

446. Family Pleasing Sloppy Joe Sandwiches

Serving: 8 servings. | Prep: 10mins | Cook: 45mins | Ready in:

Ingredients

- 2 pounds ground beef
- 1 large onion, chopped
- 1-1/4 cups ketchup
- 1/2 cup water
- 1 tablespoon brown sugar
- 1 tablespoon white vinegar
- 1/2 teaspoon salt
- 1/2 teaspoon ground mustard
- 1/2 teaspoon chili powder
- 1/4 teaspoon ground allspice
- 8 sandwich buns, split

Direction

- Cook onion and beef in a Dutch oven on medium heat until meat is no longer pink; drain. Stir in the allspice, chili powder, mustard, salt, vinegar, brown sugar, water and ketchup. Heat to boiling. Lower the heat; and simmer without a cover for 35-40 minutes, until well heated.
- Spoon about 1/2 cup meat mixture onto each bun.

Nutrition Information

- Calories: 441 calories
- Sodium: 1016mg sodium
- Fiber: 3g fiber)
- Total Carbohydrate: 49g carbohydrate (12g sugars
- Cholesterol: 56mg cholesterol
- Protein: 28g protein.
- Total Fat: 15g fat (7g saturated fat)

447.   Favorite Sloppy Joes

Serving: 12 servings. | Prep: 10mins | Cook: 20mins | Ready in:

Ingredients

- 2 pounds ground beef
- 1/2 cup chopped onion
- 3/4 cup chili sauce
- 1/2 cup water
- 1/4 cup prepared mustard
- 2 teaspoons chili powder
- 12 hamburger buns, split
- 12 slices cheddar cheese

Direction

- Cook onion and beef in a big skillet until the beef is browned. Drain. Put in chili powder, mustard, water, and chili sauce. Allow to simmer 20 minutes without cover, mixing occasionally. With a spoon, transfer 1/2 cup into each bun; place a cheese slice on top.

Nutrition Information

- Calories: 392 calories
- Sodium: 737mg sodium
- Fiber: 1g fiber)
- Total Carbohydrate: 28g carbohydrate (7g sugars
- Cholesterol: 77mg cholesterol
- Protein: 25g protein.
- Total Fat: 20g fat (9g saturated fat)

448.   Flavorful Sloppy Joes

Serving: 2 servings. | Prep: 5mins | Cook: 20mins | Ready in:

Ingredients

- 1/2 pound lean ground beef (90% lean)
- 2 tablespoons chopped onion
- 2 tablespoons chopped green pepper
- 1/2 cup ketchup
- 1-1/2 teaspoons brown sugar
- 1-1/2 teaspoons prepared mustard
- 1-1/2 teaspoons Worcestershire sauce
- 2 hamburger buns, split

Direction

- Cook the green pepper, onion and beef in a small frying pan on medium heat until it has no visible pink color, then drain.
- Stir in Worcestershire sauce, mustard, brown sugar and ketchup, then boil. Lower the heat and let it simmer for 5 minutes without cover. Serve it on buns.

Nutrition Information

- Calories: 379 calories
- Protein: 27g protein. Diabetic Exchanges: 3 lean meat
- Total Fat: 11g fat (4g saturated fat)

- Sodium: 1112mg sodium
- Fiber: 2g fiber)
- Total Carbohydrate: 44g carbohydrate (14g sugars
- Cholesterol: 56mg cholesterol

449.　　Grandma's Sloppy Joes

Serving: 4 | Prep: 10mins | Cook: 45mins | Ready in:

Ingredients

- 1 pound ground beef
- 1 cup chopped onion
- 1 cup chopped green bell pepper
- 1 tablespoon brown sugar
- 1 tablespoon vinegar
- 1 cup ketchup
- 2 tablespoons prepared mustard
- 1/2 teaspoon ground cloves
- 1 teaspoon salt
- 4 hamburger buns, split

Direction

- Mix green pepper, onion, and ground beef in a large skillet on medium heat. Cook until the meat is browned, the drain all the excess grease. Stir in mustard, ketchup, vinegar, and brown sugar, flavor with salt and cloves. Bring to a simmer on low heat for half an hour. Place on hamburger buns and serve.

Nutrition Information

- Calories: 429 calories;
- Total Fat: 16.2
- Sodium: 1648
- Total Carbohydrate: 47
- Cholesterol: 69
- Protein: 24.9

450.　　Gumbo Sloppy Joes

Serving: 6-7 servings. | Prep: 5mins | Cook: 20mins | Ready in:

Ingredients

- 1 pound ground beef
- 1/3 cup chopped onion
- 1 can (10-3/4 ounces) condensed chicken gumbo soup, undiluted
- 3/4 cup ketchup
- 1-1/2 teaspoons prepared mustard
- 6 to 7 hamburger buns, split

Direction

- In a large pan, cook onion and beef over medium heat until meat is no longer pink. Drain. Mix in the soup, mustard, ketchup and let it boil. Uncover it and reduce heat to simmer for 10 to 15 minutes or until mixture reaches desired thickness. Put on buns and serve.

Nutrition Information

- Calories: 258 calories
- Protein: 16g protein.
- Total Fat: 8g fat (3g saturated fat)
- Sodium: 908mg sodium
- Fiber: 2g fiber)
- Total Carbohydrate: 29g carbohydrate (7g sugars
- Cholesterol: 35mg cholesterol

451.　　Homemade Sloppy Joes

Serving: 6 | Prep: 15mins | Cook: 55mins | Ready in:

Ingredients

- 1 1/2 pounds extra lean ground beef
- 1/2 onion, diced
- 2 cloves garlic, minced

- 1 green pepper, diced
- 1 cup water
- 3/4 cup ketchup
- 1 dash Worcestershire sauce
- 2 tablespoons brown sugar
- 1 teaspoon Dijon mustard
- 1 1/2 teaspoons salt, or to taste
- 1/2 teaspoon ground black pepper
- 1 cup water
- cayenne pepper to taste (optional)

Direction

- In a big skillet, put in the onion and ground beef. Set the heat setting to medium heat and let the mixture cook for about 10 minutes while continuously stirring it until the ground beef turned brown in color and are formed into small crumbles.
- Add in the green bell pepper and the garlic and mix everything together; let the mixture cook for 2-3 minutes while stirring it until it becomes soft. Pour in 1 cup of water and give it a mix, scrape any browned flavor bits off the bottom of the skillet and let it dissolve in the mixture.
- Add in the brown sugar, black pepper, ketchup, salt, Worcestershire sauce and Dijon mustard and mix well. Pour in another 1 cup of water and allow the mixture to get back to a simmer. Lower the heat setting to low heat and let the mixture simmer for about 40 minutes while stirring it from time to time until the mixture becomes thick in consistency and the cooking liquid has evaporated. Add in black pepper, cayenne pepper and salt to taste.

Nutrition Information

- Calories: 251 calories;
- Sodium: 1002
- Total Carbohydrate: 14.4
- Cholesterol: 69
- Protein: 21.5
- Total Fat: 11.9

452. Italian Sausage Sloppy Joes

Serving: 8 servings. | Prep: 20mins | Cook: 04hours00mins | Ready in:

Ingredients

- 1 pound Johnsonville® Ground Mild Italian sausage
- 1 medium sweet red pepper, chopped
- 1 medium onion, chopped
- 1-1/2 pounds lean ground beef (90% lean)
- 2 cans (8 ounces each) no-salt-added tomato sauce
- 1 can (6 ounces) tomato paste
- 1 teaspoon garlic powder
- 1 teaspoon liquid smoke, optional
- 16 slices smoked mozzarella cheese (about 3/4 pound)
- 8 hoagie buns, split and toasted
- Pickled hot cherry peppers, optional

Direction

- Crumble and cook sausage with onion and red pepper in a big frying pan over medium-high heat for 5-7 minutes, or until no sign of pink remains. Remove to a 3- or 4-quart slow cooker.
- Crumble and cook beef in the same pan over medium-high heat for 5-7 minutes, or until no sign of pink remains. Add the beef to the slow cooker by a slotted spoon. Mix in garlic powder, tomato paste, tomato sauce, and liquid smoke (if you like). Cover and cook on low for 4-5 hours, or until the flavors combine.
- For serving, on bun bottoms, put cheese; put the meat mixture and peppers (if you like) on top. Close the sandwiches. If you want to freeze: In freezer containers, put the cooled meat mixture to freeze. Preparation for using, partially thaw overnight in the fridge. Thoroughly heat in a saucepan, whisking sometimes and adding a small amount of water if needed.

Nutrition Information

- Calories: 661 calories
- Fiber: 3g fiber)
- Total Carbohydrate: 46g carbohydrate (9g sugars
- Cholesterol: 121mg cholesterol
- Protein: 42g protein.
- Total Fat: 35g fat (14g saturated fat)
- Sodium: 1231mg sodium

453.   Make Ahead Sloppy Joes

Serving: 14-16 servings. | Prep: 30mins | Cook: 0mins | Ready in:

Ingredients

- 1 pound Jones No Sugar Pork Sausage Roll sausage
- 1 pound ground beef
- 1 medium onion, chopped
- 14 to 16 sandwich buns, split
- 2 cans (8 ounces each) tomato sauce
- 2 tablespoons prepared mustard
- 1 teaspoon dried parsley flakes
- 1 teaspoon garlic powder
- 1 teaspoon salt
- 1/4 teaspoon pepper
- 1/4 teaspoon dried oregano

Direction

- Place a large skillet on medium heat; cook in onion, beef and sausage till the meat is not pink anymore; strain. Separate the centers from the bottoms and tops of each bun. Tear removed bread into small pieces; put into the skillet. Set the buns aside.
- Combine the remaining ingredients into the sausage mixture. On the bottom of each bun, spoon around 1/3 cupful; replace the tops. Use heavy-duty foil to wrap individually.

- Bake at 350° till heated through, or for 20 minutes, or freeze for up to 3 months.
- To use the frozen sandwiches, bake at 350° till heated through, or for 35 minutes.

Nutrition Information

- Calories: 294 calories
- Sodium: 672mg sodium
- Fiber: 2g fiber)
- Total Carbohydrate: 33g carbohydrate (6g sugars
- Cholesterol: 24mg cholesterol
- Protein: 14g protein.
- Total Fat: 12g fat (5g saturated fat)

454.   Ozark Sloppy Joes

Serving: 8 servings. | Prep: 10mins | Cook: 15mins | Ready in:

Ingredients

- 1-1/2 pounds ground beef
- 1 medium green pepper, chopped
- 1 small onion, chopped
- 2 teaspoons sugar
- 1-1/2 teaspoons all-purpose flour
- 1-1/2 teaspoons Italian seasoning
- 1/2 teaspoon chili powder
- 1/4 teaspoon salt
- 1/4 teaspoon garlic powder
- 1/8 teaspoon cayenne pepper
- 1 can (8 ounces) tomato sauce
- 1-1/2 teaspoons Worcestershire sauce
- 8 hamburger buns, split

Direction

- Cook the onion, green pepper and beef in a large skillet on medium heat until the meat is no longer pink; drain.
- Stir in the Worcestershire sauce, tomato sauce, seasonings, flour and sugar. Simmer with a

cover for 10-15 minutes while stirring occasionally. Spoon 1/2 cup over each bun.

Nutrition Information

- Calories: 274 calories
- Total Fat: 10g fat (4g saturated fat)
- Sodium: 479mg sodium
- Fiber: 2g fiber)
- Total Carbohydrate: 26g carbohydrate (5g sugars
- Cholesterol: 42mg cholesterol
- Protein: 20g protein. Diabetic Exchanges: 2 lean meat

455. Ozarks Sloppy Joes

Serving: 8 servings. | Prep: 10mins | Cook: 15mins | Ready in:

Ingredients

- 1-1/2 pounds lean ground beef (90% lean)
- 1 medium green pepper, chopped
- 1 small onion, chopped
- 2 teaspoons sugar
- 1-1/2 teaspoons all-purpose flour
- 1-1/2 teaspoons Italian seasoning
- 1/2 teaspoon chili powder
- 1/4 teaspoon salt
- 1/4 teaspoon garlic powder
- 1/8 teaspoon cayenne pepper
- 1 can (8 ounces) tomato sauce
- 1-1/2 teaspoons Worcestershire sauce
- 8 hamburger buns, split

Direction

- Place a large skillet on medium heat; cook in onion, green pepper and beef till the meat is not pink anymore; strain.
- Mix in Worcestershire sauce, tomato sauce, seasonings, flour and sugar. Simmer with a

cover, stirring occasionally, 10-15 minutes. Spoon 1/2 cup onto each bun.

Nutrition Information

- Calories: 268 calories
- Sodium: 478mg sodium
- Fiber: 2g fiber)
- Total Carbohydrate: 26g carbohydrate (5g sugars
- Cholesterol: 42mg cholesterol
- Protein: 21g protein. Diabetic Exchanges: 2 starch
- Total Fat: 8g fat (3g saturated fat)

456. Pumpkin Sloppy Joes

Serving: 8 servings. | Prep: 15mins | Cook: 15mins | Ready in:

Ingredients

- 1 pound ground beef
- 1/2 cup chopped onion
- 1 garlic clove, minced
- 1 cup canned pumpkin
- 1 can (8 ounces) tomato sauce
- 2 tablespoons brown sugar
- 2 tablespoons prepared mustard
- 2 teaspoons chili powder
- 1/2 teaspoon salt
- American and mozzarella cheese slices
- 8 hamburger buns, split

Direction

- Cook together garlic, onion and beef in a big skillet on moderate heat until beef is not pink anymore, then drain. Stir in salt, chili powder, mustard, brown sugar, tomato sauce and pumpkin, then bring the mixture to a boil. Lower heat and simmer without a cover about 10 minutes.

- In the meantime, use a pumpkin-shaped cookie cutter to cut American cheese slices. Cut mozzarella cheese into shapes such as half-circles, triangles, etc. to create pumpkin faces. Scoop onto buns with the meat mixture and put a pumpkin on top of each bun.

Nutrition Information

- Calories: 250 calories
- Protein: 15g protein.
- Total Fat: 8g fat (3g saturated fat)
- Sodium: 607mg sodium
- Fiber: 3g fiber)
- Total Carbohydrate: 30g carbohydrate (9g sugars
- Cholesterol: 28mg cholesterol

457.   Pumpkin Sloppy Joes For 2

Serving: 2 servings. | Prep: 15mins | Cook: 15mins | Ready in:

Ingredients

- 1/2 pound lean ground beef (90% lean)
- 3 tablespoons finely chopped onion
- 1/4 cup ketchup
- 2 tablespoons tomato juice
- 1/4 teaspoon chili powder
- Dash each ground cloves and nutmeg
- Dash pepper
- 2/3 cup canned pumpkin
- 2 hamburger buns, split

Direction

- Place a large skillet on medium heat; cook in onion and beef till the meat is not pink anymore; strain.
- Put in pepper, nutmeg, cloves, chili powder, tomato juice and ketchup. Boil the mixture. Mix in pumpkin. Lower the heat; simmer with

a cover to let all flavors blend well, 15-20 minutes. Serve on buns.

Nutrition Information

- Calories: 350 calories
- Total Fat: 11g fat (4g saturated fat)
- Sodium: 730mg sodium
- Fiber: 3g fiber)
- Total Carbohydrate: 36g carbohydrate (11g sugars
- Cholesterol: 56mg cholesterol
- Protein: 27g protein. Diabetic Exchanges: 3 lean meat

458.   Quick Tangy Sloppy Joes

Serving: 6 servings. | Prep: 5mins | Cook: 15mins | Ready in:

Ingredients

- 1 pound ground beef
- 1 cup finely chopped onion
- 3/4 cup finely chopped sweet red or green pepper
- 1/4 cup finely chopped celery
- 1/2 cup ketchup
- 1 tablespoon white vinegar
- 2 teaspoons chili powder
- 1-1/2 teaspoons Worcestershire sauce
- 1 teaspoon sugar
- 1 teaspoon salt
- 6 hamburger buns, split

Direction

- Place a large skillet on medium heat; cook celery, red pepper, onion and beef together till the vegetables are crisp-tender and the meat is not pink anymore; strain.
- Combine salt, sugar, Worcestershire sauce, chili powder, vinegar and ketchup together in a small bowl; mix into the beef mixture.

Simmer without a cover, stirring occasionally, 10 minutes. Serve on buns.

Nutrition Information

- Calories: 314 calories
- Total Fat: 12g fat (4g saturated fat)
- Sodium: 935mg sodium
- Fiber: 3g fiber)
- Total Carbohydrate: 32g carbohydrate (8g sugars
- Cholesterol: 50mg cholesterol
- Protein: 20g protein.

459. Salsa Sloppy Joes

Serving: 16-20 servings. | Prep: 30mins | Cook: 0mins | Ready in:

Ingredients

- 3 pounds ground beef
- 1 cup chopped onion
- 1 jar (16 ounces) salsa
- 1 can (15 ounces) sloppy joe sauce
- 16 to 20 hamburger buns, split

Direction

- Cook onion and beef together in a big skillet on moderate heat until beef is not pink anymore, then drain. Stir in sloppy joe sauce and salsa, then bring to a boil. Lower heat and simmer, with cover, about 20 minutes. Scoop onto each bun with 1/2 cup of the beef mixture.

Nutrition Information

- Calories: 225 calories
- Sodium: 470mg sodium
- Fiber: 2g fiber)
- Total Carbohydrate: 21g carbohydrate (5g sugars

- Cholesterol: 33mg cholesterol
- Protein: 15g protein.
- Total Fat: 8g fat (3g saturated fat)

460. Sensational Sloppy Joes

Serving: 5 servings. | Prep: 5mins | Cook: 25mins | Ready in:

Ingredients

- 1 pound ground beef
- 1/2 cup chopped onion
- 1/2 cup condensed tomato soup, undiluted
- 1/2 cup ketchup
- 3 tablespoons grape jelly
- 1 tablespoon brown sugar
- 1 tablespoon cider vinegar
- 1 tablespoon prepared mustard
- 1/2 teaspoon salt
- 1/2 teaspoon celery seed
- 5 hamburger buns, split

Direction

- Place a large skillet on medium heat; cook onion and beef till the meat is not pink anymore; strain. Mix in celery seed, salt, mustard, vinegar, brown sugar, jelly, ketchup and soup. Boil the mixture. Lower the heat; simmer without a cover till heated through, or 10 minutes. Serve on buns.

Nutrition Information

- Calories: 330 calories
- Total Carbohydrate: 40g carbohydrate (18g sugars
- Cholesterol: 44mg cholesterol
- Protein: 20g protein.
- Total Fat: 10g fat (4g saturated fat)
- Sodium: 955mg sodium
- Fiber: 2g fiber)

461. Simple Sloppy Joes

Serving: 12 servings. | Prep: 5mins | Cook: 35mins | Ready in:

Ingredients

- 2 pounds ground beef
- 1 large onion, chopped
- 2 garlic cloves, minced
- 1 can (8 ounces) tomato sauce
- 1 can (6 ounces) tomato paste
- 1/2 cup ketchup
- 1/3 cup packed brown sugar
- 3 tablespoons soy sauce
- 12 hamburger buns, split and toasted

Direction

- Cook the garlic, onion and beef in a large skillet over medium heat until meat is not pink anymore; drain. Stir in soy sauce, brown sugar, ketchup and tomato paste and sauce.
- Cook until boiling. Lower heat; simmer with cover, stirring occasionally, for 15-20 minutes. Onto each bun, scoop about half a cup meat mixture.

Nutrition Information

- Calories: 300 calories
- Protein: 19g protein.
- Total Fat: 9g fat (4g saturated fat)
- Sodium: 740mg sodium
- Fiber: 3g fiber)
- Total Carbohydrate: 35g carbohydrate (13g sugars
- Cholesterol: 37mg cholesterol

462. Sloppy Cheesesteaks

Serving: 6 servings. | Prep: 15mins | Cook: 5mins | Ready in:

Ingredients

- 1 pound ground beef
- 1 medium green pepper, chopped
- 1 medium onion, chopped
- 1 teaspoon garlic powder
- 1/2 teaspoon salt
- 1/2 teaspoon pepper
- 6 French rolls
- 6 slices provolone cheese
- Mayonnaise, optional

Direction

- Start preheating the broiler. Cook and crumble the beef with onion and pepper in a large skillet on medium-high heat for 5-7 minutes until the meat is not pink anymore; then drain. Add in seasonings and stir.
- Slice the rolls in two horizontally. On a baking sheet, arrange the bottoms; then broil 3-4 inches from the heat source for half a minute until they are toasted. Put the beef mixture and then cheese on top. Broil for 45-60 seconds until the cheese melts.
- On a baking sheet, arrange the roll tops; then broil 3-4 inches from the heat source for half a minute until they are toasted. Spread with mayonnaise if desired. Then close the sandwiches. Freeze option: Put the cooled beef mixture into the freezer containers to freeze. Put in the fridge overnight to thaw partially to use. Put a cover on and place into a microwave-safe dish to microwave on high heat, stirring from time to time, until heated through. Prepare the sandwiches as instructed.

Nutrition Information

- Calories: 417 calories
- Protein: 27g protein.
- Total Fat: 19g fat (9g saturated fat)
- Sodium: 798mg sodium
- Fiber: 2g fiber)
- Total Carbohydrate: 34g carbohydrate (2g sugars
- Cholesterol: 66mg cholesterol

463. Sloppy Joe Burgers

Serving: 6 servings. | Prep: 20mins | Cook: 0mins | Ready in:

Ingredients

- 1 pound ground beef
- 2 tablespoons all-purpose flour
- 1 can (10-1/2 ounces) condensed French onion soup, undiluted
- 1/4 teaspoon Worcestershire sauce
- 6 hamburger buns, split and toasted

Direction

- Brown the beef in a big skillet then drain. Stir in Worcestershire sauce, soup and flour until combined, then bring to a boil. Cook and stir on moderate heat until thickened, about 2 minutes. Serve on buns.

Nutrition Information

- Calories: 278 calories
- Total Fat: 10g fat (4g saturated fat)
- Sodium: 679mg sodium
- Fiber: 2g fiber)
- Total Carbohydrate: 28g carbohydrate (5g sugars
- Cholesterol: 39mg cholesterol
- Protein: 18g protein.

464. Sloppy Joe Sandwich

Serving: 100 servings. | Prep: 5mins | Cook: 01hours05mins | Ready in:

Ingredients

- 20 pounds lean ground beef (90% lean)
- 3 cups chopped onions
- 1/4 cup Worcestershire sauce
- 3-1/2 cups packed brown sugar
- 1 cup prepared mustard
- 2 tablespoons chili powder
- 1 gallon ketchup
- Salt and pepper to taste
- Hamburger buns

Direction

- Place several large kettles on medium heat; cook in beef till not pink anymore; strain. Put in the next 7 ingredients. Simmer with a cover, stirring occasionally, till heated through and thickened, or for 1 hour. Serve on buns.

Nutrition Information

- Calories: 197 calories
- Protein: 18g protein.
- Total Fat: 7g fat (3g saturated fat)
- Sodium: 551mg sodium
- Fiber: 1g fiber)
- Total Carbohydrate: 16g carbohydrate (9g sugars
- Cholesterol: 44mg cholesterol

465. Sloppy Joe Sandwiches

Serving: 2 | Prep: 5mins | Cook: 40mins | Ready in:

Ingredients

- 1/2 pound ground beef
- 1/2 onion, chopped
- 1/2 cup ketchup
- 2 tablespoons water
- 1 tablespoon brown sugar
- 1 teaspoon Worcestershire sauce
- 1 teaspoon prepared mustard
- 1 teaspoon white vinegar
- 1 teaspoon chili powder
- 1/4 teaspoon garlic powder
- 1/4 teaspoon onion powder

- 1/4 teaspoon salt
- 2 hamburger buns, split

Direction

- Take a big frying pan and heat it over medium high heat. Stir fry onion and ground beef for about 10 minutes until beef becomes crumbly, no longer pink and evenly brown. Remove excess grease. Mix in salt, onion powder, garlic powder, chili powder, vinegar, mustard, Worcestershire sauce, brown sugar, water and ketchup.
- Boil beef mixture over high heat. Lower the heat to low and let it simmer, covered, for 30-40 minutes until the sauce becomes thick. Put on buns and serve.

Nutrition Information

- Calories: 467 calories;
- Total Fat: 20.3
- Sodium: 1339
- Total Carbohydrate: 47.8
- Cholesterol: 69
- Protein: 24

466.   Sloppy Joes Sandwiches

Serving: 4 servings. | Prep: 5mins | Cook: 35mins | Ready in:

Ingredients

- 1 pound ground beef
- 1 cup ketchup
- 1/4 cup water
- 2 tablespoons brown sugar
- 2 teaspoons Worcestershire sauce
- 2 teaspoons prepared mustard
- 1/2 teaspoon garlic powder
- 1/2 teaspoon onion powder
- 1/2 teaspoon salt
- 4 hamburger buns, split

Direction

- Cook beef in a big saucepan on moderate heat until it is not pink anymore, then drain. Stir in salt, onion powder, garlic powder, mustard, Worcestershire sauce, brown sugar, water and ketchup, then bring the mixture to a boil. Lower heat and simmer with a cover about 30 to 40 minutes. Serve beef mixture on buns.

Nutrition Information

- Calories: 439 calories
- Fiber: 2g fiber)
- Total Carbohydrate: 46g carbohydrate (17g sugars
- Cholesterol: 75mg cholesterol
- Protein: 27g protein.
- Total Fat: 16g fat (6g saturated fat)
- Sodium: 1360mg sodium

467.   Sloppy Joes For 100

Serving: 100 servings (12 quarts). | Prep: 60mins | Cook: 03hours00mins | Ready in:

Ingredients

- 20 pounds ground beef
- 4 large onions, chopped
- 4 large green peppers, chopped
- 4 cups chopped celery
- 1 cup packed brown sugar
- 1 cup spicy brown mustard
- 4 cups ketchup
- 2 cans (12 ounces each) tomato paste
- 4 cans (15 ounces each) tomato sauce
- 6 to 8 cups water
- 1 cup vinegar
- 2/3 cup Worcestershire sauce
- 100 hamburger buns

Direction

- Brown celery, peppers, onions and beef in a large Dutch oven, working in batches, till the meat is browned. Using a slotted spoon, transfer to a large roaster; put in the next 8 ingredients. Simmer with a cover for 3-4 hours. Serve on buns.

Nutrition Information

- Calories: 295 calories
- Sodium: 491mg sodium
- Fiber: 2g fiber)
- Total Carbohydrate: 29g carbohydrate (8g sugars
- Cholesterol: 44mg cholesterol
- Protein: 20g protein.
- Total Fat: 10g fat (4g saturated fat)

468.   Sloppy Joes For 8 Dozen

Serving: 96 servings. | Prep: 20mins | Cook: 01hours30mins | Ready in:

Ingredients

- 15 pounds ground beef
- 6 medium onions, chopped
- 1 gallon ketchup
- 3/4 cup Worcestershire sauce
- 1/2 cup packed brown sugar
- 1/2 cup prepared yellow mustard
- 1/4 cup white vinegar
- 1 tablespoon chili powder
- 96 hamburger buns, split

Direction

- In 2 stockpots, cook while stirring onions and beef over medium heat until the meat is no longer pink, then drain.
- Mix in chili powder, vinegar, mustard, brown sugar, Worcestershire sauce and ketchup. Boil. Lower the heat and simmer, uncovered, for 60

mins to let the flavors blend. Spoon onto each bun about one third cup.

Nutrition Information

- Calories: 281 calories
- Total Carbohydrate: 34g carbohydrate (15g sugars
- Cholesterol: 35mg cholesterol
- Protein: 17g protein. Diabetic Exchanges: 2 starch
- Total Fat: 8g fat (3g saturated fat)
- Sodium: 796mg sodium
- Fiber: 1g fiber)

469.   Slow Cooker Sloppy Joes

Serving: 8 servings. | Prep: 20mins | Cook: 03hours00mins | Ready in:

Ingredients

- 1-1/2 pounds ground beef
- 2 celery ribs, chopped
- 1 small onion, chopped
- 1 bottle (12 ounces) chili sauce
- 2 tablespoons brown sugar
- 2 tablespoons sweet pickle relish
- 1 tablespoon Worcestershire sauce
- 1 teaspoon salt
- 1/8 teaspoon pepper
- 8 hamburger buns, split

Direction

- Cook onion, celery, and beef in a big skillet over medium-high heat until the beef is not pink anymore, about 8-10 minutes, crumbling the beef into pieces; drain. Transfer to a 3-quart slow cooker.
- Mix in pepper, salt, Worcestershire sauce, pickle relish, brown sugar, and chili sauce. Put the lid on and cook on low until fully heated and the flavors combine, about 3-4 hours. On

bun bottoms, put the meat mixture. Return the tops.

Nutrition Information

- Calories: 324 calories
- Sodium: 1313mg sodium
- Fiber: 1g fiber)
- Total Carbohydrate: 40g carbohydrate (16g sugars
- Cholesterol: 42mg cholesterol
- Protein: 19g protein.
- Total Fat: 10g fat (4g saturated fat)

470.   Slow Cooked Sloppy Joes

Serving: 12 servings. | Prep: 15mins | Cook: 04hours00mins | Ready in:

Ingredients

- 2 pounds ground beef
- 1 cup chopped green pepper
- 2/3 cup chopped onion
- 2 cups ketchup
- 2 envelopes sloppy joe mix
- 2 tablespoons brown sugar
- 1 teaspoon prepared mustard
- 12 hamburger buns, split

Direction

- Cook onion, pepper and beef in a big skillet over medium heat till the meat is not pink anymore; then drain. Stir in mustard, brown sugar, sloppy joe mix and ketchup.
- Put into a 3-quart slow cooker. Cook, covered, on low until the flavors blend, about 4 to 5 hours. Spoon a half cup onto per bun.

Nutrition Information

- Calories: 337 calories
- Sodium: 1251mg sodium

- Fiber: 1g fiber)
- Total Carbohydrate: 47g carbohydrate (23g sugars
- Cholesterol: 37mg cholesterol
- Protein: 18g protein.
- Total Fat: 9g fat (4g saturated fat)

471.   Southern Barbecue Beef

Serving: 2 servings. | Prep: 10mins | Cook: 15mins | Ready in:

Ingredients

- 1/2 pound lean ground beef (90% lean)
- 1/2 cup chopped onion
- 1/2 cup chopped green pepper
- 1/3 cup ketchup
- 4-1/2 teaspoons cider vinegar
- 1 tablespoon brown sugar
- 1 tablespoon prepared mustard
- 2 kaiser rolls, split
- 1/2 cup creamy deli coleslaw

Direction

- Place a non-stick skillet on medium heat; cook in green pepper, onion and beef till the meat if not pink anymore, or for 4-5 minutes; strain.
- Mix in mustard, brown sugar, vinegar and ketchup. Boil the mixture. Lower the heat; simmer without a cover till thickened, or for 5-7 minutes. Spoon onto roll bottoms; place coleslaw on top. Replace the roll tops.

Nutrition Information

- Calories: 519 calories
- Fiber: 4g fiber)
- Total Carbohydrate: 61g carbohydrate (23g sugars
- Cholesterol: 63mg cholesterol
- Protein: 30g protein.
- Total Fat: 17g fat (5g saturated fat)

- Sodium: 1051mg sodium

472. Speedy Sloppy Joes

Serving: 6-8 servings. | Prep: 0mins | Cook: 20mins | Ready in:

Ingredients

- 1 pound ground beef
- 1 can (10-3/4 ounces) condensed tomato soup, undiluted
- 2 tablespoons sweet pickle relish
- 2 tablespoons ketchup
- 2 tablespoons barbecue sauce
- 6 to 8 onion rolls or hamburger buns, split

Direction

- Cook beef in a big skillet over medium heat until not pink anymore; drain. Add the barbecue sauce, ketchup, relish and soup; simmer with a cover for 10 minutes. Serve on buns.

Nutrition Information

- Calories: 262 calories
- Sodium: 582mg sodium
- Fiber: 2g fiber)
- Total Carbohydrate: 28g carbohydrate (7g sugars
- Cholesterol: 38mg cholesterol
- Protein: 16g protein.
- Total Fat: 9g fat (4g saturated fat)

473. Steak Sauce Sloppy Joes

Serving: 15 servings. | Prep: 15mins | Cook: 30mins | Ready in:

Ingredients

- 3 pounds ground beef
- 4 medium onions, chopped
- 2 celery ribs, chopped
- 1 garlic clove, minced
- 1 can (28 ounces) diced tomatoes, undrained
- 1/4 cup Worcestershire sauce
- 1/4 cup A.1. steak sauce
- 2 tablespoons chili powder
- 2 tablespoons paprika
- 1/4 teaspoon pepper
- 15 hamburger buns, split

Direction

- Cook together celery, onions and beef in a Dutch oven on moderate heat until meat is not pink anymore. Put in garlic and cook for one more minute, then drain.
- Stir in pepper, paprika, chili powder, steak sauce, Worcestershire sauce and tomatoes, then bring the mixture to a boil. Lower heat and simmer without a cover until heated through and thicken, about 20 minutes. Serve the beef mixture on buns.

Nutrition Information

- Calories: 302 calories
- Protein: 21g protein. Diabetic Exchanges: 3 lean meat
- Total Fat: 10g fat (4g saturated fat)
- Sodium: 469mg sodium
- Fiber: 3g fiber)
- Total Carbohydrate: 30g carbohydrate (8g sugars
- Cholesterol: 44mg cholesterol

474. Stuffed Barbecue Burgers

Serving: 4 servings. | Prep: 10mins | Cook: 20mins | Ready in:

Ingredients

- 2 pounds ground beef
- 1 cup shredded cheddar or cheese of your choice
- 1/3 cup finely chopped green pepper
- 1/3 cup finely chopped tomato
- 3 fresh mushrooms, finely chopped
- 2 green onions, finely chopped
- 1/2 cup barbecue sauce
- 1 tablespoon sugar
- 4 hamburger buns, split

Direction

- Form beef into 8 patties. Mix together onions, mushrooms, tomato, green pepper, and cheese in a big bowl. Put vegetable mixture on top of half of the patties. Use the rest of patties to cover; seal edges by pressing firmly.
- Grill over medium heat with a cover or broil 4 inches from heat, 3 minutes per side. Brush barbecue sauce over and sprinkle sugar on top. Grill with a cover or broil 5-6 more minutes per side till juices run clear and a thermometer shows 160°, basting from time to time. Place onto buns to serve.

Nutrition Information

- Calories: 714 calories
- Sodium: 777mg sodium
- Fiber: 2g fiber)
- Total Carbohydrate: 32g carbohydrate (11g sugars
- Cholesterol: 180mg cholesterol
- Protein: 56g protein.
- Total Fat: 39g fat (18g saturated fat)

475.   Sweet Barbecue Sandwiches

Serving: 10 servings. | Prep: 5mins | Cook: 30mins | Ready in:

Ingredients

- 2 pounds ground beef
- 1 medium onion, chopped
- 1 can (10-3/4 ounces) condensed tomato soup, undiluted
- 1 can (8 ounces) tomato sauce
- 2 tablespoons Worcestershire sauce
- 2 teaspoons molasses
- 1 teaspoon salt
- 1 teaspoon ground cinnamon
- 1 teaspoon ground mustard
- 1/2 teaspoon chili powder
- 1/2 teaspoon pepper
- 1/4 teaspoon ground cloves
- 10 hamburger buns, split

Direction

- Place a large skillet on medium heat; cook in onion and beef till the meat is not pink anymore; strain. Mix in seasonings, molasses, Worcestershire sauce, tomato sauce and soup; stir properly. Simmer with a cover for 20 minutes. Serve on buns.

Nutrition Information

- Calories: 305 calories
- Cholesterol: 44mg cholesterol
- Protein: 21g protein.
- Total Fat: 10g fat (4g saturated fat)
- Sodium: 856mg sodium
- Fiber: 2g fiber)
- Total Carbohydrate: 31g carbohydrate (8g sugars

476.   Tangy Barbecue Beef Sandwiches

Serving: 6 servings. | Prep: 10mins | Cook: 20mins | Ready in:

Ingredients

- 1-1/2 pounds lean ground beef (90% lean)

- 2 celery ribs, sliced
- 1 large onion, chopped
- 1 can (8 ounces) tomato sauce
- 1/4 cup ketchup
- 2 tablespoons brown sugar
- 2 tablespoons barbecue sauce
- 1 tablespoon prepared mustard
- 1 tablespoon Worcestershire sauce
- 6 hamburger buns, split

Direction

- Cook the onion, celery and beef in a big nonstick frying pan on medium heat, until the meat has no visible pink color, then drain.
- Stir in the Worcestershire sauce, mustard, barbecue sauce, brown sugar, ketchup and tomato sauce, then boil. Lower the heat and let it simmer for 10 to 15 minutes without cover, to enable the flavors to combine. Spoon 3/4 cup onto each of the buns.

Nutrition Information

- Calories: 348 calories
- Total Fat: 11g fat (4g saturated fat)
- Sodium: 719mg sodium
- Fiber: 2g fiber)
- Total Carbohydrate: 35g carbohydrate (12g sugars
- Cholesterol: 56mg cholesterol
- Protein: 27g protein. Diabetic Exchanges: 3 lean meat

477.   Tangy Barbecue Burgers

Serving: 4 servings. | Prep: 20mins | Cook: 10mins | Ready in:

Ingredients

- 1 cup sauerkraut, rinsed and well drained
- 1/3 cup whole-berry cranberry sauce
- 1/4 cup barbecue sauce

- 2 tablespoons brown sugar
- 1 egg
- 1/4 cup water
- 1 envelope onion soup mix
- 1 pound ground beef
- 4 hamburger buns, split and toasted

Direction

- Mix brown sugar, barbecue sauce, cranberry sauce, and sauerkraut together in a large saucepan. Allow to simmer for 15 minutes, occasionally stirring.
- In the meantime, beat egg; put in soup mix and water. Allow to rest for 5 minutes. Crumble beef and add into mixture; toss just till mixed. Shape into 4 patties.
- Grill for 5-6 minutes, uncovered, over medium-hot heat till meat is not pink anymore. Lay burgers on buns and pair with the warm sauce for serving.

Nutrition Information

- Calories: 460 calories
- Sodium: 1298mg sodium
- Fiber: 3g fiber)
- Total Carbohydrate: 45g carbohydrate (18g sugars
- Cholesterol: 128mg cholesterol
- Protein: 29g protein.
- Total Fat: 18g fat (6g saturated fat)

478.   Tangy Barbecued Beef Sandwiches

Serving: 6 servings. | Prep: 10mins | Cook: 15mins | Ready in:

Ingredients

- 1-1/2 pounds ground beef
- 1 large onion, chopped
- 3/4 cup ketchup

- 2 tablespoons brown sugar
- 2 tablespoons water
- 2 tablespoons Worcestershire sauce
- 2 tablespoons prepared mustard
- 2 teaspoons white vinegar
- 1/4 teaspoon salt
- 6 hamburger buns, split

Direction

- Place a Dutch oven on medium heat; cook onion and beef till beef is not pink anymore, or for 6-8 minutes while breaking up the beef into crumbles; strain. Mix in salt, vinegar, mustard, Worcestershire sauce, water, brown sugar and ketchup; heat through. Serve on buns. Freeze option: Put the cooled beef mixture into freezer containers. Before using, place in the refrigerator to thaw partially overnight. Microwave with a cover in a microwave-safe dish, on high, stirring gently and put in a little broth or water if needed, till heated through.

Nutrition Information

- Calories: 387 calories
- Sodium: 864mg sodium
- Fiber: 2g fiber)
- Total Carbohydrate: 37g carbohydrate (17g sugars
- Cholesterol: 70mg cholesterol
- Protein: 25g protein.
- Total Fat: 15g fat (5g saturated fat)

479.   Tangy Sloppy Joes

Serving: 6 servings. | Prep: 15mins | Cook: 15mins | Ready in:

Ingredients

- 1 pound ground beef
- 1/2 cup chopped celery
- 1/3 cup chopped onion

- 2 tablespoons chopped green pepper
- 1 cup ketchup
- 1/2 cup chili sauce
- 1 tablespoon sugar
- 1 tablespoon brown sugar
- 1 tablespoon cider vinegar
- 2 teaspoons ground mustard
- 1/4 teaspoon salt
- 1/8 teaspoon pepper
- 6 hamburger buns, split

Direction

- Cook green pepper, onion, celery and beef in a big skillet on moderate heat until vegetables are soft and meat is not pink anymore, then drain.
- Stir in pepper, salt, mustard, vinegar, sugars, chili sauce and ketchup, then bring to a boil. Lower heat and simmer about 15 minutes without a cover. Serve on buns.

Nutrition Information

- Calories: 331 calories
- Sodium: 1180mg sodium
- Fiber: 2g fiber)
- Total Carbohydrate: 44g carbohydrate (17g sugars
- Cholesterol: 37mg cholesterol
- Protein: 18g protein.
- Total Fat: 9g fat (4g saturated fat)

480.   Tasty Sloppy Joes

Serving: 10 servings. | Prep: 15mins | Cook: 45mins | Ready in:

Ingredients

- 1-1/2 pounds lean ground beef (90% lean)
- 1 cup milk
- 3/4 cup quick-cooking oats
- 1 medium onion, chopped

- 1 tablespoon Worcestershire sauce
- 1-1/2 teaspoons salt
- 1/4 teaspoon pepper
- 1 cup ketchup
- 1/2 cup water
- 3 tablespoons white vinegar
- 2 tablespoons sugar
- 10 sandwich buns, split

Direction

- Place a large skillet on medium heat; cook in pepper, salt, Worcestershire sauce, onion, oats, milk and beef till the meat is not pink anymore. Remove into an ungreased 8-in. square baking dish. Mix together sugar, vinegar, water and ketchup; transfer over the meat mixture. Bake without a cover at 350°, stirring every 15 minutes, for 45 minutes. Into each bun, spoon around 1/2 cup.

Nutrition Information

- Calories: 391 calories
- Sodium: 1058mg sodium
- Fiber: 3g fiber)
- Total Carbohydrate: 51g carbohydrate (13g sugars
- Cholesterol: 37mg cholesterol
- Protein: 23g protein.
- Total Fat: 11g fat (5g saturated fat)

---

481. Tex Mex Sloppy Joes

Serving: 6 | Prep: 10mins | Cook: | Ready in:

Ingredients

- 2 teaspoons vegetable oil
- 2 medium onions, chopped
- 1 medium green sweet pepper, chopped
- ½ cup fresh or frozen whole kernel corn
- 2 large cloves garlic, minced

- 1 fresh jalapeño chile pepper, seeded (if desired) and finely chopped (see Tip)
- 1 pound uncooked ground chicken breast or turkey breast
- 1 teaspoon chili powder
- 1 teaspoon ground cumin
- 1 teaspoon dried oregano, crushed
- ¾ cup ketchup
- 4 teaspoons Worcestershire sauce
- 6 whole grain sandwich-style rolls
- Dill pickle slices (optional)

Direction

- Over medium-high heat, heat oil in a very large nonstick skillet and then add jalapeño pepper, garlic, corn, sweet pepper and onion. Let cook while stirring sometimes for about 4 to 5 minutes or until the onion becomes tender. Mix in oregano, cumin, chili powder, and turkey or chicken. Cook for about 5 to 6 minutes or until the turkey or chicken is no longer pink. Mix in Worcestershire sauce and ketchup and then heat through.
- Distribute the mixture between rolls. Top with slices of pickle if desired.

Nutrition Information

- Calories: 280 calories;
- Saturated Fat: 1
- Total Carbohydrate: 35
- Sugar: 9
- Sodium: 644
- Fiber: 4
- Cholesterol: 44
- Protein: 23
- Total Fat: 6

Chapter 6: Ground Beef Dinner Recipes

***

Serving: 2 servings. | Prep: 15mins | Cook: 50mins | Ready in:

482.   **Au Gratin Beef Bake**

Serving: 6 servings. | Prep: 20mins | Cook: 45mins | Ready in:

Ingredients

- 1 pound ground beef
- 1 large onion, chopped
- 2 celery ribs, chopped
- 1/2 cup chopped green pepper
- 1 package (5-1/4 ounces) au gratin potatoes
- 1 can (10-3/4 ounces) condensed tomato soup, undiluted
- 1 teaspoon Worcestershire sauce
- 1-3/4 cups water
- 2/3 cup milk

Direction

- In a large skillet, cook the onion, beef, green pepper and celery until vegetables are soften and meat is not pink anymore; and then drain. In a greased baking dish of 2 and a half quart, combine potatoes with contents of sauce mix, beef mixture, Worcestershire sauce and soup. Pour in milk and water. Bake, uncovered at 400° for around 45 to 50 minutes until potatoes are tender.

Nutrition Information

- Calories: 307 calories
- Total Carbohydrate: 31g carbohydrate (8g sugars
- Cholesterol: 54mg cholesterol
- Protein: 19g protein.
- Total Fat: 11g fat (4g saturated fat)
- Sodium: 858mg sodium
- Fiber: 3g fiber)

Ingredients

- 1/2 pound ground beef
- 1 small onion, chopped
- 1/4 cup chopped celery
- 2-1/4 cups tomato juice
- 1/2 cup water
- 1/4 cup medium pearl barley
- 1 to 1-1/2 teaspoons chili powder
- 1/2 teaspoon salt
- 1/4 teaspoon pepper

Direction

- Cook celery, onion, and beef in a large saucepan on medium heat until the meat is no longer pink, then drain. Stir in pepper, salt, chili powder, barley, water, and tomato juice, then allow to boil. Lower the heat and simmer, covered, for 50 - 60 minutes or until the barley becomes tender.

Nutrition Information

- Calories: 332 calories
- Sodium: 1681mg sodium
- Fiber: 6g fiber)
- Total Carbohydrate: 35g carbohydrate (12g sugars
- Cholesterol: 56mg cholesterol
- Protein: 25g protein.
- Total Fat: 11g fat (5g saturated fat)

484.   **Beef & Rice Stuffed Cabbage Rolls**

Serving: 6 servings. | Prep: 20mins | Cook: 06hours00mins | Ready in:

Ingredients

- 12 cabbage leaves
- 1 cup cooked brown rice
- 1/4 cup finely chopped onion
- 1 large egg, lightly beaten
- 1/4 cup fat-free milk
- 1/2 teaspoon salt
- 1/4 teaspoon pepper
- 1 pound lean ground beef (90% lean)
- SAUCE:
- 1 can (8 ounces) tomato sauce
- 1 tablespoon brown sugar
- 1 tablespoon lemon juice
- 1 teaspoon Worcestershire sauce

Direction

- In boiling water, cook cabbage in batches until crisp-tender, about 3-5 minutes. Strain; cool a little bit. Cut the thick vein from the bottom of each cabbage leaf, creating a V-shaped cut.
- Mix pepper, salt, milk, egg, onion, and rice together in a big bowl. Add the beef; stir gently but well. On each cabbage leaf, put approximately 1/4 cup beef mixture. Overlap the cut edges of leaf by gathering them together; fold over the filling. Fold in the sides and roll up.
- In a 4- or 5-quart slow cooker, put 6 rolls with the seam-side down. Combine the sauce ingredients in a bowl; pour half of sauce mixture over the cabbage rolls. Put the rest of the rolls and sauce on top. Cover and cook on low until the cabbage is soft and a thermometer displays 160° when you insert it into the beef, about 6-8 hours.

Nutrition Information

- Calories: 204 calories
- Protein: 18g protein. Diabetic Exchanges: 2 lean meat
- Total Fat: 7g fat (3g saturated fat)
- Sodium: 446mg sodium
- Fiber: 2g fiber)

- Total Carbohydrate: 16g carbohydrate (5g sugars
- Cholesterol: 83mg cholesterol

485.   Beef And Corn Casserole

Serving: 8-10 servings. | Prep: 20mins | Cook: 60mins | Ready in:

Ingredients

- 1 package (10 ounces) fine egg noodles
- 1 pound ground beef
- 1 medium onion, chopped
- 1 can (15-1/4 ounces) whole kernel corn, drained
- 1 can (10-3/4 ounces) condensed tomato soup, undiluted
- 1 cup water
- 1 cup diced process cheese (Velveeta)
- 1/2 medium green pepper, chopped
- 1 medium carrot, thinly sliced
- 1 teaspoon salt
- 1/2 teaspoon pepper

Direction

- Follow package instructions to cook noodles; drain. Cook beef and onion in a big skillet on medium heat, until meat is not pink anymore; drain. Add in the rest of ingredients and noodles.
- Move to an oiled 13x9-inch baking dish. Put on cover and bake for 30 minutes at 325 degrees. Remove cover and bake for 30-35 minutes more or until bubbly.

Nutrition Information

- Calories: 295 calories
- Sodium: 698mg sodium
- Fiber: 3g fiber)
- Total Carbohydrate: 33g carbohydrate (7g sugars

- Cholesterol: 64mg cholesterol
- Protein: 17g protein.
- Total Fat: 10g fat (4g saturated fat)

486. Campfire Stew

Serving: 4 servings. | Prep: 5mins | Cook: 15mins | Ready in:

Ingredients

- 1 pound ground beef
- 1 can (15 ounces) mixed vegetables, drained
- 1 can (10-3/4 ounces) condensed tomato soup, undiluted
- 1 can (10-1/2 ounces) condensed vegetable beef soup, undiluted
- 1/4 cup water
- 1/4 teaspoon garlic powder
- 1/4 teaspoon onion powder
- 1/4 teaspoon salt
- 1/8 teaspoon pepper

Direction

- Cook beef until not pink in a big pot on medium heat; drain excess grease. Mix in the rest of the ingredients. Heat to a boil. Cover, decrease heat, and simmer until cooked through, 8-10 minutes.

Nutrition Information

- Calories: 353 calories
- Sodium: 1428mg sodium
- Fiber: 4g fiber)
- Total Carbohydrate: 24g carbohydrate (9g sugars
- Cholesterol: 78mg cholesterol
- Protein: 29g protein.
- Total Fat: 15g fat (6g saturated fat)

487. Cheese 'n' Pasta In A Pot

Serving: 8-10 servings. | Prep: 40mins | Cook: 30mins | Ready in:

Ingredients

- 2 pounds ground beef
- 1 large onion, chopped
- 1 garlic clove, minced
- 1 jar (14 ounces) spaghetti sauce
- 1 can (14-1/2 ounces) stewed tomatoes
- 1 can (4 ounces) mushroom stems and pieces, drained
- 8 ounces uncooked medium pasta shells
- 2 cups sour cream, divided
- 6 ounces sliced provolone cheese
- 6 ounces sliced part-skim mozzarella cheese

Direction

- Cook garlic, onion, and beef on medium heat in a large skillet until not pink anymore; let drain. Stir in mushrooms, tomatoes, and spaghetti sauce. Boil. Turn down the heat; uncover and bring to a simmer for 20 minutes.
- At the same time, following the package instructions, cook the pasta; then drain and wash under cold water. Place half of the shells into an ovenproof Dutch oven. Arrange with half of the meat mixture. Place a cup of sour cream; put provolone cheese on top. Place with the sour cream, the meat mixture, and the remaining pasta; put mozzarella cheese on top.
- Put a cover on and bake at 350 degrees until cooked thoroughly and bubbling, 30-40 minutes.

Nutrition Information

- Calories: 439 calories
- Protein: 27g protein.
- Total Fat: 23g fat (13g saturated fat)
- Sodium: 564mg sodium
- Fiber: 2g fiber)

- Total Carbohydrate: 27g carbohydrate (8g sugars
- Cholesterol: 91mg cholesterol

488. Cheeseburger Skillet Dinner

Serving: 6 servings. | Prep: 10mins | Cook: 15mins | Ready in:

Ingredients

- 1 package (7-1/4 ounces) macaroni and cheese
- 1 pound ground turkey or beef
- 1/2 cup chopped onion
- 1 package (16 ounces) frozen mixed vegetables
- 1/3 cup ketchup
- 1/4 cup water
- 1/2 teaspoon prepared mustard
- 1/4 teaspoon garlic powder
- 3/4 cup shredded cheddar cheese
- Salt and pepper to taste

Direction

- Cook macaroni and cheese based on the package directions.
- In the meantime, brown the beef or turkey with the onion in a big skillet then strain. Mix in the garlic powder, mustard, water, ketchup and vegetables. Cook for about 10 minutes until the vegetables are crisp-tender. Stir in cheddar cheese until dissolved. Stir in the macaroni and cheese. Add pepper and salt to taste.

Nutrition Information

- Calories: 436 calories
- Total Fat: 20g fat (10g saturated fat)
- Sodium: 679mg sodium
- Fiber: 4g fiber)
- Total Carbohydrate: 24g carbohydrate (10g sugars

- Cholesterol: 87mg cholesterol
- Protein: 25g protein.

489. Cheesy Beef Tetrazzini

Serving: 6 servings. | Prep: 20mins | Cook: 30mins | Ready in:

Ingredients

- 1-1/2 pounds ground beef
- 1 small onion, chopped
- 1 can (15 ounces) tomato sauce
- 1/2 to 1 teaspoon salt
- 1/4 teaspoon pepper
- 1 package (8 ounces) cream cheese, softened
- 1 cup (8 ounces) 4% cottage cheese
- 1 cup (8 ounces) sour cream
- 1/4 cup thinly sliced green onions
- 1 package (7 ounces) thin spaghetti, cooked and drained
- 1/4 cup grated Parmesan cheese

Direction

- In a large skillet, cook onion and beef over medium heat until the meat is no longer pink; then drain. Stir in pepper, salt and tomato sauce. Boil. Lower the heat and simmer, with no cover, about 5 minutes.
- Beat sour cream, cottage cheese and cream cheese in a bowl until blended. Mix in spaghetti, onions and green pepper. Put into an oiled 2-1/2-quart baking dish. Add beef mixture over top. Sprinkle Parmesan cheese over. Bake, with no cover, for 30 to 35 minutes, at 350°, until bubbly.

Nutrition Information

- Calories: 631 calories
- Cholesterol: 153mg cholesterol
- Protein: 38g protein.
- Total Fat: 37g fat (20g saturated fat)

- Sodium: 905mg sodium
- Fiber: 2g fiber)
- Total Carbohydrate: 34g carbohydrate (7g sugars

490. Cheesy Lasagna Pizza

Serving: 4-6 servings. | Prep: 50mins | Cook: 30mins | Ready in:

Ingredients

- 1 pound ground beef
- 1 can (8 ounces) tomato sauce
- 1/4 cup water
- 1 envelope spaghetti sauce mix, divided
- 1 loaf (1 pound) frozen bread dough, thawed
- 1-1/2 cups 4% cottage cheese
- 1/4 cup grated Parmesan cheese
- 1 cup shredded mozzarella cheese

Direction

- Cook beef in a skillet over medium heat until not pink anymore; drain. Mix in 3 tablespoons spaghetti sauce mix, water, and tomato sauce. Simmer for 30 minutes, with cover. In the meantime, knead the rest of the spaghetti sauce mix into the bread dough. Press onto the bottom and up the sides of a 12-inch greased pizza pan. Spread with cottage cheese. Scoop meat mixture over top. Scatter with Parmesan cheese. Bake for 25 minutes at 400 degrees. Scatter with mozzarella cheese. Bake for 5 more minutes or until the cheese melts and the crust is golden. Allow it to stand for 5 minutes before serving.

Nutrition Information

- Calories:
- Cholesterol:
- Protein:
- Total Fat:
- Sodium:

- Fiber:
- Total Carbohydrate:

491. Cincinnati Chili Dogs

Serving: 10 servings. | Prep: 20mins | Cook: 04hours00mins | Ready in:

Ingredients

- 1-1/2 pounds ground beef
- 2 small yellow onions, chopped and divided
- 2 cans (15 ounces each) tomato sauce
- 1-1/2 teaspoons baking cocoa
- 1/2 teaspoon ground cinnamon
- 1/4 teaspoon chili powder
- 1/4 teaspoon paprika
- 1/4 teaspoon garlic powder
- 2 tablespoons Worcestershire sauce
- 1 tablespoon cider vinegar
- 10 hot dogs
- 10 hot dog buns, split
- Shredded cheddar cheese

Direction

- Cook ground beef in a large skillet over medium heat setting until the beef turns brown and is starting to crumble then drain excess oil.
- Mix one chopped up onion and cooked beef together in a 3-quartz slow cooker then put in the next 8 ingredients. Cover the slow cooker and cook on low heat for about 2 hours then add in the hotdogs. Cover and continue cooking the mixture for another 2 hours on low heat until cooked through.
- Put hotdogs on bun and top off with the remaining chopped onion and grated cheese then serve.

Nutrition Information

- Calories: 419 calories

- Total Fat: 24g fat (9g saturated fat)
- Sodium: 1135mg sodium
- Fiber: 3g fiber)
- Total Carbohydrate: 29g carbohydrate (6g sugars
- Cholesterol: 67mg cholesterol
- Protein: 23g protein.

492. Cowboy Stew

Serving: 11 servings. | Prep: 10mins | Cook: 20mins | Ready in:

Ingredients

- 2 pounds ground beef
- 4 cans (16 ounces each) baked beans
- 8 hot dogs, sliced
- 1/2 cup barbecue sauce
- 1/2 cup grated Parmesan cheese

Direction

- Cook the beef in a Dutch oven over medium heat until it is not pink anymore; drain the beef. Mix in the remaining ingredients. Boil. Turn down the heat; put on a cover and simmer until the flavors are combined, 4-6 minutes.

Nutrition Information

- Calories: 457 calories
- Sodium: 1223mg sodium
- Fiber: 9g fiber)
- Total Carbohydrate: 36g carbohydrate (2g sugars
- Cholesterol: 84mg cholesterol
- Protein: 29g protein.
- Total Fat: 23g fat (9g saturated fat)

493. Creole Meat Loaf

Serving: 6 servings. | Prep: 15mins | Cook: 01hours15mins | Ready in:

Ingredients

- 1 can (5 ounces) evaporated milk
- 1 large egg, lightly beaten
- 1/2 cup chopped green pepper
- 1/4 cup chopped onion
- 1/2 cup coarsely crushed saltine crackers
- 1 teaspoon salt
- 1 teaspoon ground mustard
- 1/4 teaspoon pepper
- 1-1/2 pounds lean ground beef (90% lean)
- SAUCE:
- 1 can (10-3/4 ounces) condensed tomato soup, undiluted
- 2 tablespoons ketchup
- 1/2 teaspoon horseradish

Direction

- Combine onion, green pepper, egg, and milk in a large mixing bowl. Mix in pepper, mustard, salt, and crackers. Crumble beef over mixture and stir to combine. Press beef mixture into an unoiled 8x4-inch loaf pan.
- Bake without covering for 1 hour and 15 minutes at 350° until center is no longer pink and a thermometer registers 160°. Drain well.
- Allow meatloaf to rest for 10 minutes in the loaf pan. In the meantime, mix sauce ingredients together in a small saucepan. Heat through. Invert meatloaf on a serving platter. Spread 1/2 cup hot sauce over top of the loaf; serve meatloaf with the remainder of sauce.

Nutrition Information

- Calories: 282 calories
- Protein: 26g protein.
- Total Fat: 12g fat (5g saturated fat)
- Sodium: 899mg sodium
- Fiber: 1g fiber)

- Total Carbohydrate: 16g carbohydrate (8g sugars
- Cholesterol: 112mg cholesterol

494. Deluxe Macaroni Dinner

Serving: 4-6 servings. | Prep: 20mins | Cook: 10mins | Ready in:

Ingredients

- 1/2 pound ground beef
- 1 small onion, chopped
- 2 garlic cloves, minced
- 10 cups water
- 1 package (14 ounces) deluxe four-cheese macaroni and cheese dinner
- 2 cups chopped fresh broccoli

Direction

- Add onion and beef to a big frying pan, cook until the meat is not pink any longer. Add garlic, cook for 60 more seconds. Drain.
- Boil water in a big saucepan. Add macaroni, cook for 5 minutes. Add broccoli, cook until the broccoli and macaroni get tender, about 4 to 5 more minutes.
- Drain, save 1/4 cup of cooking liquid. Add the contents of cheese sauce mix to the saucepan. Mix in the saved liquid, beef mixture and macaroni mixture and heat through.

Nutrition Information

- Calories: 300 calories
- Cholesterol: 42mg cholesterol
- Protein: 18g protein.
- Total Fat: 11g fat (6g saturated fat)
- Sodium: 512mg sodium
- Fiber: 2g fiber)
- Total Carbohydrate: 32g carbohydrate (4g sugars

495. Double Duty Layered Enchilada Casserole

Serving: 12 servings. | Prep: 15mins | Cook: 35mins | Ready in:

Ingredients

- 5 cups reserved Double-Duty Hearty Chili without Beans or any thick chili without beans
- 1-1/2 cups frozen corn (about 8 ounces)
- 1 can (15 ounces) black beans, rinsed and drained
- 1 can (15 ounces) pinto beans, rinsed and drained
- 6 flour tortillas (10 inches)
- 3 cups shredded Mexican cheese blend, divided
- 1 can (10 ounces) enchilada sauce
- Shredded lettuce and chopped fresh tomatoes, optional

Direction

- Set oven to 375° to preheat. Stir beans, corn and reserved chili in a large bowl. Distribute a cup chili mixture evenly into a greased 13x9 inch baking pan. Put layers of 2 tortillas, 2 cups chili mixture, 1 cup cheese, and 1/2 cup enchilada sauce over the mixture in the baking pan. Repeat layering. Put leftover tortillas and chili mixture on top.
- Bake for 20-25 minutes while covered, until heated through. Scatter leftover cheese on top. Bake for 10 to 15 more minutes while uncovered, until cheese is melted. Let sit for 10 minutes before slicing. Serve together with tomatoes and lettuce (optional). Freeze option: Freeze uncooked casserole while covered. Before using, defrost partly in the fridge overnight. Take out of the fridge half an hour before baking. Set oven to 375° to preheat. Cover with foil; bake following directions, rising covered time until a thermometer inserted in the middle registers 165°, about 40 to 45 minutes. Serve following directions.

Nutrition Information

- Calories: 409 calories
- Total Fat: 17g fat (7g saturated fat)
- Sodium: 1031mg sodium
- Fiber: 6g fiber)
- Total Carbohydrate: 41g carbohydrate (5g sugars
- Cholesterol: 60mg cholesterol
- Protein: 25g protein.

496.   Easy Beef Stuffed Shells

Serving: 10 servings. | Prep: 45mins | Cook: 45mins | Ready in:

Ingredients

- 20 uncooked jumbo pasta shells
- 1 pound ground beef
- 1 large onion, chopped
- 1 carton (15 ounces) ricotta cheese
- 2 cups shredded Italian cheese blend, divided
- 1/2 cup grated Parmesan cheese
- 1/4 cup prepared pesto
- 1 large egg
- 1 jar (26 ounces) spaghetti sauce, divided

Direction

- Cook pasta shells following the package instructions to al dente; strain and put in cold water to rinse. Cook onion and beef in a big frying pan over medium heat until the meat is not pink anymore; strain. Mix 1/2 the beef mixture, egg, pesto, Parmesan cheese, 1 1/2 cups Italian cheese blend, and ricotta cheese together in a big bowl.
- In a 13x9-inch greased baking dish, spread 3/4 cup spaghetti sauce. Spoon into the pasta shells with the cheese mixture; put into the baking dish. Mix together spaghetti sauce and the rest of the beef mixture; pour over shells.

Sprinkle with leftover cheese over. Put a cover on and chill overnight.

- Take out of the fridge before baking, about 30 minutes. Put a cover on and bake for 40 minutes at 350°. Remove the cover, bake until the cheese melts, about another 5-10 minutes.

Nutrition Information

- Calories: 405 calories
- Cholesterol: 90mg cholesterol
- Protein: 25g protein.
- Total Fat: 22g fat (10g saturated fat)
- Sodium: 730mg sodium
- Fiber: 2g fiber)
- Total Carbohydrate: 26g carbohydrate (8g sugars

497.   Easy Skillet Supper

Serving: 4-6 servings. | Prep: 15mins | Cook: 45mins | Ready in:

Ingredients

- 1 pound lean ground beef (90% lean)
- 4 medium potatoes, peeled and diced
- 2 cups fresh corn or frozen corn
- 1 small onion, chopped
- Salt and pepper to taste
- 1 can (10-3/4 ounces) condensed cream of mushroom soup, undiluted

Direction

- Break the beef into crumbs in a big frying pan. Put onion, corn and tomatoes on top. Dredge the pepper and salt on top. Add the soup and spread out.
- Cook while covered over medium heat for 10 minutes. Lower the heat, simmer while covered until the potatoes get tender and the meat is not pink any longer, about 30 – 45 minutes.

Nutrition Information

- Calories:
- Fiber:
- Total Carbohydrate:
- Cholesterol:
- Protein:
- Total Fat:
- Sodium:

---

498.   Eggplant Casserole

Serving: 8 servings. | Prep: 20mins | Cook: 30mins | Ready in:

Ingredients

- 4 cups water
- 1 medium eggplant, peeled and cubed
- 1-1/2 pounds ground beef
- 1 medium onion, chopped
- 1 medium green pepper, chopped
- 3 medium tomatoes, chopped
- Salt and pepper to taste
- 1/2 cup milk
- 1 egg, beaten
- 1/2 cup dry bread crumbs
- 2 tablespoons butter, melted

Direction

- Take water to a boil in a saucepan; add eggplant. Boil until tender, about 5 to 8 minutes; drain and put aside.
- Cook green pepper, onion and beef over medium heat in a skillet until the meat is not pink anymore; drain. Put in pepper, salt and tomatoes. Cook and mix until the tomato is soft, about 5 minutes. Take away from the heat. Mix in eggplant, egg and milk; blend well.
- Shift to a greased baking dish of 13 x 9 inch. Stir in butter and bread crumbs; dust over the top. Bake, uncovered, for 30 minutes at 375°, until heated through.

Nutrition Information

- Calories: 278 calories
- Fiber: 3g fiber)
- Total Carbohydrate: 15g carbohydrate (6g sugars
- Cholesterol: 93mg cholesterol
- Protein: 21g protein.
- Total Fat: 15g fat (7g saturated fat)
- Sodium: 151mg sodium

---

499.   Enchilada Casser Ole!

Serving: 8 servings. | Prep: 25mins | Cook: 30mins | Ready in:

Ingredients

- 1 pound lean ground beef (90% lean)
- 1 large onion, chopped
- 2 cups salsa
- 1 can (15 ounces) black beans, rinsed and drained
- 1/4 cup reduced-fat Italian salad dressing
- 2 tablespoons reduced-sodium taco seasoning
- 1/4 teaspoon ground cumin
- 6 flour tortillas (8 inches)
- 3/4 cup reduced-fat sour cream
- 1 cup shredded reduced-fat Mexican cheese blend
- 1 cup shredded lettuce
- 1 medium tomato, chopped
- 1/4 cup minced fresh cilantro

Direction

- Place onion and beef in a large frying pan, cook on medium heat until beef is not pink. Drain the excess grease. Mix in cumin, dressing, beans, and taco seasoning. Line the bottom of a greased 11x7-in. baking dish with three tortillas. Place half of the meat and bean mixture, then one layer each of sour cream and cheese. Repeat the layers. Bake in a 400-degree oven covered for 25 minutes. Remove cover and return to oven until heated through about 5-10 minutes. Remove from oven and let cool for 5 minutes. Serve by topping with cilantro, lettuce and tomato.

Nutrition Information

- Calories: 357 calories
- Sodium: 864mg sodium
- Fiber: 3g fiber)
- Total Carbohydrate: 37g carbohydrate (6g sugars
- Cholesterol: 45mg cholesterol
- Protein: 23g protein. Diabetic Exchanges: 3 lean meat
- Total Fat: 12g fat (5g saturated fat)

500. Family Style Meat Loaf Dinner

Serving: 6 servings. | Prep: 35mins | Cook: 05hours00mins |Ready in:

Ingredients

- 2 eggs
- 1 cup crushed saltines
- 1 medium onion, chopped
- 1/2 cup old-fashioned oats
- 1/2 cup heavy whipping cream
- 2 tablespoons Worcestershire sauce
- 2-1/2 teaspoons Montreal steak seasoning
- 1/2 teaspoon coarse ground pepper
- 2-1/2 pounds ground beef
- 4 medium potatoes, peeled and cubed
- 2 cups fresh baby carrots
- 1/3 cup finely chopped onion
- 2 cans (10-3/4 ounces each) condensed cream of mushroom soup, undiluted
- 2 cans (4 ounces each) mushroom stems and pieces, drained
- 1 envelope pork gravy mix

Direction

- Slice three 25x3-inch strips from a heavy-duty foil; form into crisscrosses that look like spokes of a wheel. Arrange the strips up the sides and on the bottom of a 6-quart slow cooker. Grease the strips.
- Blend pepper, steak seasoning, Worcestershire sauce, cream, oats, onion, cracker crumbs, and eggs in a large bowl. Crumble the beef over the mixture, then combine thoroughly. Form into a loaf; arrange in the center of the strips. Put onion, carrots, and potatoes around the meat.
- Blend gravy mix, mushrooms, and soup in a small bowl; place the mixture over the vegetables and meat. Put a cover on and cook on low heat until no longer pink and a thermometer registers 160 degrees, 5-6 hours. Place gravy and vegetables in a serving bowl. Transfer the meatloaf to a platter with foil strips as handles; then divide the meat into 12 slices.

Nutrition Information

- Calories: 726 calories
- Fiber: 6g fiber)
- Total Carbohydrate: 52g carbohydrate (9g sugars
- Cholesterol: 219mg cholesterol
- Protein: 42g protein.
- Total Fat: 38g fat (15g saturated fat)
- Sodium: 1775mg sodium

501. Favorite Baked Spaghetti

Serving: 10 servings. | Prep: 25mins | Cook: 60mins | Ready in:

Ingredients

- 1 package (16 ounces) spaghetti
- 1 pound ground beef

- 1 medium onion, chopped
- 1 jar (24 ounces) meatless spaghetti sauce
- 1/2 teaspoon seasoned salt
- 2 large eggs
- 1/3 cup grated Parmesan cheese
- 5 tablespoons butter, melted
- 2 cups 4% cottage cheese
- 4 cups part-skim shredded mozzarella cheese

Direction

- Cook spaghetti according to the directions on the package. While it cooks, get a large skillet to cook the onion and beef on medium heat until the beef isn't pink and drain it. Mix in spaghetti sauce along with some seasoned salt and put it aside.
- Whisk up the eggs, butter, and parmesan cheese in a big bowl. Drain off the spaghetti and put it in the egg mix; mix it to coat the spaghetti.
- Put about half of the spaghetti mix into a baking dish that's 3 qt and greased. Place about half of the cottage cheese, mozzarella cheese, and meat sauce on it. Then repeat the layers.
- Cover it and let it bake for 40 minutes at 350°F. Remove the cover and let it bake for another 20-25 minutes or until the cheese melts.

Nutrition Information

- Calories: 526 calories
- Sodium: 881mg sodium
- Fiber: 3g fiber)
- Total Carbohydrate: 45g carbohydrate (9g sugars
- Cholesterol: 127mg cholesterol
- Protein: 31g protein.
- Total Fat: 24g fat (13g saturated fat)

502. Garlic Beef Enchiladas

Serving: 5 servings. | Prep: 30mins | Cook: 40mins | Ready in:

Ingredients

- 1 pound ground beef
- 1 medium onion, chopped
- 2 tablespoons all-purpose flour
- 1 tablespoon chili powder
- 1 teaspoon salt
- 1 teaspoon garlic powder
- 1/2 teaspoon ground cumin
- 1/4 teaspoon rubbed sage
- 1 can (14-1/2 ounces) stewed tomatoes, cut up
- SAUCE:
- 1/3 cup butter
- 4 to 6 garlic cloves, minced
- 1/2 cup all-purpose flour
- 1 can (14-1/2 ounces) beef broth
- 1 can (15 ounces) tomato sauce
- 1 to 2 tablespoons chili powder
- 1 to 2 teaspoons ground cumin
- 1 to 2 teaspoons rubbed sage
- 1/2 teaspoon salt
- 10 flour tortillas (6 inches), warmed
- 2 cups shredded Colby-Monterey Jack cheese, divided
- Optional toppings: halved grape tomatoes, minced fresh cilantro, sliced jalapeno peppers and medium red onion, chopped or sliced

Direction

- Set an oven to 350 degrees and start preheating. Cook the onion and beef over medium heat in a large skillet for 6-8 minutes until the beef is not pink anymore, breaking the meat into crumbles; then drain the beef. Stir in seasonings and flour. Put in tomatoes; then boil. Turn down the heat; put on a cover and simmer for 15 minutes.
- Heat the butter over medium-high heat in a saucepan. Put in garlic; stir and cook until it becomes tender, about a minute. Add flour and stir until combined; beat in the broth

gradually. Then boil; stir and cook until thick, 2 minutes. Stir in the seasonings and tomato sauce; heat through.

- Add 1 1/2 cups of sauce to an ungreased 13x9-inch baking dish. Top each tortilla with approximately 1/4 cup of the beef mixture, but not in the center. Put 1-2 tablespoons of cheese on top. Roll and place over the sauce with seam side down. Place the remaining sauce on top.
- Put on a cover and bake for 30-35 minutes until heated through. Dust with the remaining cheese. Remove the cover and bake for 10-15 more minutes until the cheese melts. If desired, serve together with toppings of your choice.

Nutrition Information

- Calories: 751 calories
- Total Carbohydrate: 56g carbohydrate (8g sugars
- Cholesterol: 128mg cholesterol
- Protein: 38g protein.
- Total Fat: 43g fat (21g saturated fat)
- Sodium: 2536mg sodium
- Fiber: 4g fiber)

503. Grandma's Cabbage Rolls

Serving: 12 servings. | Prep: 45mins | Cook: 06hours00mins | Ready in:

Ingredients

- 1 large head cabbage, cored
- 1 egg
- 1 medium onion, finely chopped
- 1/2 cup uncooked converted rice
- 1 tablespoon snipped fresh dill or 1 teaspoon dill weed
- 1 teaspoon paprika
- 1 teaspoon dried savory or thyme

- 1/2 teaspoon salt
- 1/2 teaspoon pepper
- 1-1/2 pounds lean ground beef (90% lean)
- 2 cups sauerkraut, rinsed, well drained and chopped
- 2 cups canned crushed tomatoes
- 6 bacon strips, chopped
- 1 can (14-1/2 ounces) vegetable broth

Direction

- In the boiling water, cook the cabbage just until the outer leaves can be easily pulled away from the head. Put 12 large leaves aside for the rolls. Put the remaining cabbage in the fridge for later use. Trim off the thick vein from the bottom of each leaf to have a V-shaped slice.
- Blend pepper, salt, savory, paprika, dill, rice, onion, and egg in a large bowl. Crumble the beef over the mixture, combine well. Put in a cabbage leaf the 1/3 cup of the meat mixture; overlap the cut ends of leaf. Fold the sides in. Roll up starting with the cut end. Repeat the process for the filling and remaining cabbage leaves.
- Blend bacon, tomatoes, and sauerkraut. Scoop half of them into a 6-quart slow cooker. Place 6 cabbage rolls with seam side down on the sauerkraut mixture. Put rolls and the remaining sauerkraut mixture on top. Pour the broth into the slow cooker. Put a cover on and cook on low heat until a thermometer inserted in the rolls register 160 degrees or for 6-8 hours.

Nutrition Information

- Calories: 227 calories
- Total Fat: 10g fat (4g saturated fat)
- Sodium: 620mg sodium
- Fiber: 4g fiber)
- Total Carbohydrate: 18g carbohydrate (5g sugars
- Cholesterol: 61mg cholesterol
- Protein: 16g protein.

504.　　Ground Beef Lo Mein

Serving: 6 servings. | Prep: 5mins | Cook: 20mins | Ready in:

Ingredients

- 8 ounces uncooked spaghetti
- 1/2 pound cooked lean ground beef (90% lean)
- 1 package (16 ounces) frozen stir-fry vegetable blend, thawed
- 1 jar (12 ounces) home-style beef gravy
- 1/4 teaspoon reduced-sodium soy sauce
- 1/4 teaspoon garlic powder
- 1/8 teaspoon pepper

Direction

- Following package directions to cook spaghetti. In the meantime, cook beef in a big skillet on medium heat until heated through, or about 2 to 3 minutes. Put in pepper, garlic powder, soy sauce, gravy and vegetables, then bring all to a boil. Lower the heat, then cover and simmer until vegetables are tender but still crispy, or about 8 to 10 minutes. Drain spaghetti and put into the beef mixture, stir well.

Nutrition Information

- Calories: 267 calories
- Total Carbohydrate: 42g carbohydrate (2g sugars
- Cholesterol: 21mg cholesterol
- Protein: 16g protein.
- Total Fat: 4g fat (1g saturated fat)
- Sodium: 425mg sodium
- Fiber: 4g fiber)

505.　　Ground Beef Spiral Bake

Serving: 2 casseroles (8 servings each). | Prep: 40mins | Cook: 25mins | Ready in:

Ingredients

- 1 package (16 ounces) spiral pasta
- 2 pounds ground beef
- 2/3 cup chopped onion
- 1 teaspoon minced garlic
- 2 jars (26 ounces each) spaghetti sauce
- 2 tablespoons tomato paste
- 1 teaspoon dried basil
- 1 teaspoon dried oregano
- 4 cups shredded part-skim mozzarella cheese

Direction

- Based on the instruction on package, cook the pasta; drain off. At the same time, in a Dutch oven, cook the onion and beef on medium heat till the meat is not pink anymore. Put in the garlic; cook for 60 seconds more. Drain off. Whisk in oregano, basil, tomato paste and spaghetti sauce. Boil. Lower the heat; let simmer without a cover for 5 to 10 minutes.
- Whisk the pasta into the meat mixture. Move into two greased 13x9-inch baking plates. Scatter each with 2 cups of the cheese. Put a cover on and freeze one casserole for no more than 3 months.
- Bake leftover casserole without a cover at 350 degrees till thoroughly heated, about 25 to 30 minutes.
- To use the freeze casserole: Thaw in fridge overnight. Bake without a cover at 350 degrees till thoroughly heated, about 35 to 40 minutes.

Nutrition Information

- Calories: 359 calories
- Total Fat: 15g fat (6g saturated fat)
- Sodium: 627mg sodium
- Fiber: 3g fiber)
- Total Carbohydrate: 32g carbohydrate (8g sugars

- Cholesterol: 54mg cholesterol
- Protein: 23g protein.

506. Hearty Baked Stew

Serving: 6 servings. | Prep: 15mins | Cook: 01hours30mins | Ready in:

Ingredients

- 3 medium potatoes, peeled and sliced
- 3 medium carrots, sliced
- 3/4 pound lean ground beef (90% lean)
- 1 can (14-1/2 ounces) diced tomatoes, undrained
- 1/2 cup frozen peas
- 2 medium onions, sliced
- 2 tablespoons butter
- Salt and pepper to taste

Direction

- Arrange carrots and potatoes in layers in an oiled 13x9-inch baking dish. Break beef into small pieces over carrots. Layer with onions, peas, and tomatoes. Dot butter over surface. Add pepper and salt to season.
- Bake, covered, for 1 hour and 30 minutes at 350° until vegetables are tender and meat is no longer pink.

Nutrition Information

- Calories: 284 calories
- Total Carbohydrate: 32g carbohydrate (9g sugars
- Cholesterol: 48mg cholesterol
- Protein: 16g protein.
- Total Fat: 11g fat (5g saturated fat)
- Sodium: 185mg sodium
- Fiber: 5g fiber)

507. Hearty Cheese Tortellini

Serving: 6 servings. | Prep: 30mins | Cook: 06hours15mins | Ready in:

Ingredients

- 1/2 pound Johnsonville® Ground Mild Italian sausage
- 1/2 pound lean ground beef (90% lean)
- 1 jar (24 ounces) marinara sauce
- 1 can (14-1/2 ounces) Italian diced tomatoes
- 1 cup sliced fresh mushrooms
- 1 package (9 ounces) refrigerated cheese tortellini
- 1 cup shredded part-skim mozzarella cheese

Direction

- Place a small skillet on medium heat; cook the beef and sausage till no longer pink; drain. Move to a 3-quart slow cooker. Mix in mushrooms, tomatoes and marinara sauce. Cook with a cover on low till heated through, about 6-7 hours.
- Follow the package instructions to prepare tortellini; mix into the meat mixture. Top with cheese. Cook with a cover till the cheese is melted, for 15 minutes.

Nutrition Information

- Calories: 388 calories
- Fiber: 3g fiber)
- Total Carbohydrate: 40g carbohydrate (15g sugars
- Cholesterol: 63mg cholesterol
- Protein: 24g protein.
- Total Fat: 14g fat (7g saturated fat)
- Sodium: 908mg sodium

508. Italian Cabbage Casserole

Serving: 6 | Prep: 20mins | Cook: 55mins | Ready in:

Ingredients

- 3 slices bacon, diced
- 1 pound bulk mild Italian sausage
- 1 (14 ounce) can beef broth
- 2 cups diced celery
- 1 white onion, diced
- 5 ounces shredded carrots
- 2 tablespoons Italian seasoning
- 2 teaspoons ground coriander
- 1 1/2 teaspoons garlic, minced
- 1 teaspoon ground black pepper
- 1/2 teaspoon coarse sea salt
- 1 head cabbage, shredded
- 1 sweet apple, diced

Direction

- In a Dutch oven over medium heat, cook and stir bacon until browned and crisp, about 5 - 10 minutes. Place bacon to a plate lined with paper-towel and drain grease from Dutch oven.
- In the same oven, cook and stir Italian sausage until browned and crumbly, about 5 - 10 minutes. Add beef broth into Dutch oven and let it come to a boil while using a wooden spoon to scrap the browned food bits off of the pan's bottom.
- Mix sea salt, black pepper, garlic, coriander, Italian seasoning, carrot, onion and celery into beef broth mixture; bring to a simmer and cook until liquid is lessened and vegetables are tender, about 15 - 20 minutes. Mix cooked bacon, apple and cabbage into vegetable mixture; cook for 30 - 45 minutes, until desired consistency is reached and apples and cabbage are tender.

Nutrition Information

- Calories: 302 calories;
- Total Fat: 16.9
- Sodium: 1181
- Total Carbohydrate: 23.8
- Cholesterol: 35
- Protein: 16

509.   Lori's Marzetti Bake

Serving: 2 casseroles (12 servings each). | Prep: 30mins | Cook: 35mins | Ready in:

Ingredients

- 2 pounds ground beef
- 1 cup sliced fresh mushrooms
- 1 medium onion, finely chopped
- 1/3 cup chopped green pepper
- 2 garlic cloves, minced
- 1 teaspoon salt
- 1/2 teaspoon pepper
- 3 cans (15 ounces each) plus 1 can (8 ounces) tomato sauce
- 1 can (15 ounces) diced tomatoes, undrained
- 2 tablespoons brown sugar
- 1 package (16 ounces) egg noodles
- 3 cups shredded cheddar cheese, divided

Direction

- Set the oven to 400° and start preheating. In a Dutch oven over medium heat, cook the first seven ingredients until vegetables are tender and beef is no longer pink for about 8-10 minutes, breaking beef into crumbles; drain. Stir in brown sugar, tomatoes and tomato sauce; let it come to a boil. Lower the heat; let it simmer while stirring occasionally until flavors are blended, about 10-15 minutes.
- In the meantime, cook noodles following package instructions. Drain; pour into the sauce. Mix in 2 cups of cheese. Place onto two greased 11x7-inch baking dishes.
- Use greased foil to cover and bake until heated through, about 30-35 minutes. Top with the remaining cheese; bake with no cover until cheese is melted, about 5 more minutes.

Nutrition Information

- Calories:

- Sodium:
- Fiber:
- Total Carbohydrate:
- Cholesterol:
- Protein:
- Total Fat:

---

510. Low Sodium Spaghetti Sauce

Serving: 10 servings (2-1/2 quarts). | Prep: 10mins | Cook: 02hours10mins | Ready in:

Ingredients

- 1/2 pound lean ground beef (90% lean)
- 1 pound fresh mushrooms, sliced
- 3 medium sweet red peppers, chopped
- 1 medium green pepper, chopped
- 1 large onion, chopped
- 3 garlic cloves, minced
- 1 tablespoon olive oil
- 2 cans (29 ounces each) tomato puree
- 2 cups water
- 1/2 cup red wine or additional water
- 2 bay leaves
- 2 tablespoons dried oregano
- 2 tablespoons dried basil
- 1/2 teaspoon dried rosemary, crushed
- 1/4 to 1/2 teaspoon crushed red pepper flakes
- 1/4 teaspoon dried mint
- 1/2 cup chopped fresh parsley
- 3 tablespoons sugar

Direction

- Cook beef until not pink in a large nonstick frying pan on medium heat. Drain excess grease and set beef aside. Add oil to same pan and sauté peppers, garlic, mushrooms, and onion until soft. Mix next nine ingredients in a big Dutch oven. Add veggies and beef to Dutch oven. Heat to a boil. Do not cover, decrease heat, and simmer for 2-3 hours. Mix

in sugar and parsley. Remove bay leaves before eating.

Nutrition Information

- Calories: 143 calories
- Cholesterol: 12mg cholesterol
- Protein: 9g protein. Diabetic Exchanges: 4 vegetable
- Total Fat: 3g fat (1g saturated fat)
- Sodium: 57mg sodium
- Fiber: 4g fiber)
- Total Carbohydrate: 22g carbohydrate (0 sugars

---

511. Meat Loaves With Pesto Sauce

Serving: 4 servings. | Prep: 20mins | Cook: 25mins | Ready in:

Ingredients

- PESTO SAUCE:
- 2 cups fresh spinach or parsley
- 2 garlic cloves, peeled
- 1/2 cup walnuts
- 1 cup olive oil
- 1 tablespoon dried basil
- 1/2 cup grated Parmesan cheese
- Salt and pepper to taste
- MEAT LOAVES:
- 1/2 cup seasoned bread crumbs
- 1/4 cup finely chopped onion
- 1 can (8 ounces) tomato sauce,divided
- 1 large egg, beaten
- 1/2 teaspoon salt
- 1/4 teaspoon pepper
- 1 pound lean ground beef (90% lean)
- 1 tablespoon canola oil
- 1/4 cup water

Direction

- Combine pesto ingredients in a blender. Put on the lid, and blend mixture into paste. Put to one side.
- Combine 3 tablespoons pesto sauce, pepper, salt, egg, 2 tablespoons tomato sauce, onion, and bread crumbs in a mixing bowl. Crumble beef over mixture and stir to combine. Form beef mixture into 4 loaves.
- Heat oil in a skillet. Cook meat loaves in heated oil until all sides are browned. Stir together the remaining tomato sauce, water, 1 tablespoon pesto sauce; pour over meat. Simmer, covered until meat is no longer pink inside, for 20 minutes. Spread tomato-pesto sauce over loaves to serve. Chill or freeze the remainder of pesto sauce for another use.

Nutrition Information

- Calories: 903 calories
- Fiber: 3g fiber)
- Total Carbohydrate: 17g carbohydrate (3g sugars
- Cholesterol: 117mg cholesterol
- Protein: 33g protein.
- Total Fat: 79g fat (14g saturated fat)
- Sodium: 1059mg sodium

512.   Mini Meat Loaf

Serving: 1 serving. | Prep: 10mins | Cook: 35mins | Ready in:

Ingredients

- 1/2 slice bread, crumbled
- 2 tablespoons finely shredded carrot
- 1 tablespoon each chopped onion, celery and green pepper
- 1/4 teaspoon salt
- Dash pepper
- 2 tablespoons chili sauce or ketchup, divided
- 1/4 pound ground beef

Direction

- Mix 1 tablespoon of chili sauce, pepper, salt, green pepper, celery, onion, carrot, and bread in a bowl. Put in beef and combine well. Form into a 3x2-1/2-inch loaf; put in an ungreased shallow baking dish. Use the remaining chili sauce to top the loaf. Bake without a cover at 350 degrees for 35-40 minutes.

Nutrition Information

- Calories: 299 calories
- Cholesterol: 75mg cholesterol
- Protein: 24g protein.
- Total Fat: 14g fat (6g saturated fat)
- Sodium: 1183mg sodium
- Fiber: 1g fiber)
- Total Carbohydrate: 17g carbohydrate (8g sugars

513.   Mushroom Beef Patties

Serving: 3-4 servings. | Prep: 20mins | Cook: 10mins | Ready in:

Ingredients

- 2 tablespoons milk
- 1 tablespoon Worcestershire sauce
- 1/4 cup dry bread crumbs
- 1 teaspoon salt, divided
- 1/2 teaspoon pepper
- 1/2 teaspoon garlic powder
- 1 pound ground beef
- 1/2 pound sliced fresh mushrooms
- 1 teaspoon dried basil
- 5 tablespoons butter, divided
- 2 tablespoons all-purpose flour
- 1/2 cup half-and-half cream
- 1/2 to 3/4 cup water
- 1/4 teaspoon hot pepper sauce
- 1/4 cup shredded cheddar cheese
- 2 tablespoons chopped green onions

Direction

- In a bowl, mix garlic powder, pepper, half teaspoon of the salt, breadcrumbs, Worcestershire sauce and milk. Break up the beef on top of mixture and stir them well. Form into 3-4 oval patties. In a big skillet, cook the patties on medium heat till not pink anymore.
- In a separate skillet, sauté the basil and mushrooms in 2 tablespoons butter till soften; drain off. Take the mushrooms out using the slotted spoon and put aside.
- In that skillet, melt the rest of the butter; whisk in the flour till smooth. Slowly stir in rest of the salt, pepper sauce, half cup of the water and cream. Boil; cook and stir till bubbly and thicken or for 2 minutes. Pour in enough of the rest of water to have a medium thin sauce. Put in the reserved mushrooms; heat fully. Serve on top of the beef patties; add the onions and cheese on top.

Nutrition Information

- Calories: 478 calories
- Cholesterol: 137mg cholesterol
- Protein: 28g protein.
- Total Fat: 34g fat (18g saturated fat)
- Sodium: 955mg sodium
- Fiber: 1g fiber)
- Total Carbohydrate: 13g carbohydrate (2g sugars

514.   Nacho Cheese Beef Bake

Serving: 4 servings. | Prep: 25mins | Cook: 15mins | Ready in:

Ingredients

- 2 cups uncooked egg noodles
- 1 pound ground beef
- 1 can (14-1/2 ounces) diced tomatoes, undrained
- 1 can (10-3/4 ounces) condensed nacho cheese soup, undiluted
- 1 jar (5-3/4 ounces) sliced pimiento-stuffed olives, drained
- 1 can (4 ounces) chopped green chilies
- 1-1/2 cups shredded cheddar cheese
- 2 cups crushed tortilla chips
- 1/3 cup prepared ranch salad dressing
- Shredded lettuce, sour cream and/or salsa, optional

Direction

- Following the package instructions, cook the noodles; drain. At the same time, cook the beef in a large saucepan over medium heat until it is not pink anymore; then drain the beef. Stir in chilies, olives, soup, and tomatoes. Boil. Turn down the heat; simmer without covering for 10 minutes. Add noodles and stir.
- Place into an 11x7-inch baking dish coated with cooking spray. Dust with cheese. Bake at 350 degrees until heated through, 15-20 minutes. Put tortilla chips on top; sprinkle with the salad dressing. If desired, serve alongside sour cream, lettuce, or/and salsa.

Nutrition Information

- Calories: 827 calories
- Cholesterol: 158mg cholesterol
- Protein: 42g protein.
- Total Fat: 55g fat (24g saturated fat)
- Sodium: 2131mg sodium
- Fiber: 4g fiber)
- Total Carbohydrate: 41g carbohydrate (6g sugars

515. Old Fashioned Cabbage Rolls

Serving: 6 servings. | Prep: 25mins | Cook: 01hours30mins | Ready in:

Ingredients

- 1 medium head cabbage (3 pounds)
- 1/2 pound uncooked ground beef
- 1/2 pound uncooked ground pork
- 1 can (15 ounces) tomato sauce, divided
- 1 small onion, chopped
- 1/2 cup uncooked long grain rice
- 1 tablespoon dried parsley flakes
- 1/2 teaspoon salt
- 1/2 teaspoon snipped fresh dill or dill weed
- 1/8 teaspoon cayenne pepper
- 1 can (14-1/2 ounces) diced tomatoes, undrained
- 1/2 teaspoon sugar

Direction

- Boil the water then add the cabbage, cook until the outer leaves pull away easily from the head. Save 12 big leaves for the rolls. Mix the cayenne, dill, salt, parsley, rice, onion, half a cup of tomato sauce, pork and beef well together in a small bowl.
- Cut out the thick vein from the bottom of leaves to create a V-shaped cut. Put about 1/4 cup of the meat mixture on the cabbage leaf to overlap the cut ends of the leaf. Fold in the sides, start with the cut end and roll. Do the same with the rest.
- Cut the rest of cabbage into slices, add them to an ovenproof Dutch oven. Lay the cabbage rolls on top of cabbage slices with the seam side down. Mix the rest of tomato sauce, sugar and tomatoes then pour on top of the rolls. Set oven at 350°, bake while covered until the cabbage rolls get tender, about 1 1/2 hours.

Nutrition Information

- Calories: 260 calories
- Sodium: 694mg sodium
- Fiber: 3g fiber)
- Total Carbohydrate: 23g carbohydrate (5g sugars
- Cholesterol: 50mg cholesterol
- Protein: 18g protein.
- Total Fat: 10g fat (4g saturated fat)

516. Old Fashioned Poor Man's Steak

Serving: 9 servings. | Prep: 25mins | Cook: 04hours00mins | Ready in:

Ingredients

- 1 cup crushed saltine crackers (about 30 crackers)
- 1/3 cup water
- Salt and pepper to taste
- 2 pounds ground beef
- 1/4 cup all-purpose flour
- 2 tablespoons canola oil
- 2 cans (10-3/4 ounces each) condensed cream of mushroom soup, undiluted
- Hot mashed potatoes or noodlles

Direction

- Mix pepper, salt, water, and cracker crumbs in a large bowl. Break up the beef into crumbles and add over the mixture, combine thoroughly. Press into an ungreased 9-inch square pan. Put on a cover and put in the fridge for minimum of 3 hours.
- Slice into 3-inch squares and dredge in the flour. Cook the meat squares in oil in a large skillet until both sides are browned.
- Using a slotted spoon or spatula, place into a 3-quart slow cooker. Put in the soup.
- Put on a cover and cook on high until the meat is not pink anymore, 4 hours. Serve alongside noodles or mashed potatoes.

Nutrition Information

- Calories: 292 calories
- Sodium: 372mg sodium
- Fiber: 1g fiber)
- Total Carbohydrate: 10g carbohydrate (1g sugars
- Cholesterol: 68mg cholesterol
- Protein: 22g protein.
- Total Fat: 18g fat (6g saturated fat)

---

517.   One Pot Saucy Beef Rotini

Serving: 4 servings. | Prep: 10mins | Cook: 20mins | Ready in:

Ingredients

- 3/4 pound lean ground beef (90% lean)
- 2 cups sliced fresh mushrooms
- 1 medium onion, chopped
- 3 garlic cloves, minced
- 3/4 teaspoon Italian seasoning
- 2 cups tomato basil pasta sauce
- 1/4 teaspoon salt
- 2-1/2 cups water
- 3 cups uncooked whole wheat rotini (about 8 ounces)
- 1/4 cup grated Parmesan cheese

Direction

- Cook the first 5 ingredients together in a 6-quart stock pot on medium high heat until beef is not pink anymore, or about 6 to 8 minutes. Break up cooked beef into crumbles and drain.
- Put in pasta sauce, water and salt, then bring the mixture to a boil. Stir in rotini and bring mixture back to a boil. Lower the heat and simmer with a cover until pasta is al dente while stirring sometimes, or about 8 to 10 minutes. Serve together with cheese.

Nutrition Information

- Calories: 414 calories
- Cholesterol: 57mg cholesterol
- Protein: 28g protein.
- Total Fat: 11g fat (4g saturated fat)
- Sodium: 806mg sodium
- Fiber: 8g fiber)
- Total Carbohydrate: 49g carbohydrate (12g sugars

---

518.   Pantry Skillet

Serving: 6 servings. | Prep: 10mins | Cook: 20mins | Ready in:

Ingredients

- 1 pound ground beef
- 1 can (10-3/4 ounces) condensed tomato soup, undilute
- 1-1/2 cups water
- 1 envelope onion mushroom soup mix
- 1/2 pound fresh mushrooms, sliced
- 1-1/2 cups frozen cut green beans
- 3 medium carrots, grated
- 1 cup cooked rice
- 2 slices process American cheese, cut into strips

Direction

- Cook the beef in a large skillet over medium heat until it is not pink anymore; drain. Stir in the soup mix, water, and soup. Mix in rice, carrots, beans, and mushrooms. Boil. Turn down the heat; put on a cover and simmer until the beans become tender, 5-7 minutes. Put cheese on top; put on a cover and allow to stand until the cheese melts.

Nutrition Information

- Calories:
- Sodium:

- Fiber:
- Total Carbohydrate:
- Cholesterol:
- Protein:
- Total Fat:

---

519.   Potluck Baked Spaghetti

Serving: 12 servings. | Prep: 25mins | Cook: 25mins | Ready in:

Ingredients

- 2 pounds ground beef
- 2 medium onions, chopped
- 2 cans (one 15 ounces, one 8 ounces) tomato sauce
- 1 can (8 ounces) sliced mushrooms, drained
- 1 teaspoon garlic powder
- 1 teaspoon dried oregano
- 2 packages (7 ounces each) uncooked spaghetti
- 1 package (8 ounces) cream cheese, softened
- 2 cups (16 ounces) 4% cottage cheese
- 1/2 cup sour cream
- 2 tablespoons minced chives
- 1/4 cup dry bread crumbs
- 1-1/2 teaspoons butter, melted

Direction

- Cook onions and beef over medium heat in a large skillet until no longer pink; drain. Add oregano, garlic powder, mushrooms and tomato sauce. Bring to boiling. Lower the heat; simmer without a cover while stirring occasionally for 15 minutes.
- In the meantime, cook the spaghetti as directed on the package; drain. Mix chives, sour cream, cottage cheese and cream cheese in a small bowl; whisk well. Transfer 1/2 of the spaghetti sauce in a greased 4-qt. baking dish. Scoop cream cheese mixture over the top evenly. Layer the rest of the spaghetti over and top with all beef mixture.

- Toss butter and bread crumbs; scatter over the beef mixture. Bake with a cover for 20 minutes at 350°. Bake without a cover until heated through or for 5-10 more minutes.

Nutrition Information

- Calories: 378 calories
- Total Carbohydrate: 23g carbohydrate (5g sugars
- Cholesterol: 87mg cholesterol
- Protein: 25g protein.
- Total Fat: 20g fat (10g saturated fat)
- Sodium: 586mg sodium
- Fiber: 2g fiber)

---

520.   Prairie Meat Loaf

Serving: 2 loaves (6-8 servings each). | Prep: 15mins | Cook: 01hours15mins | Ready in:

Ingredients

- 2 large eggs
- 1/2 cup ketchup
- 2 tablespoons prepared mustard
- 3 cups old-fashioned oats
- 2 teaspoons salt
- 1 teaspoon garlic powder
- 1 teaspoon dried thyme
- 1 teaspoon dried basil
- 1-1/2 cups beef broth
- 1-1/2 cups finely chopped onion
- 1-1/2 cups finely chopped celery
- 2-1/2 cups shredded cheddar cheese, divided
- 4 pounds lean ground beef (90% lean)

Direction

- Beat eggs in a large bowl; stir in basil, thyme, garlic powder, salt, oats, mustard and ketchup. Boil broth in a small saucepan; pour in oat mixture. Mix in 2 cups of cheese, celery and onion. Put crumbled beef on the mixture and mix well.

- Put into two 9x5-in. loaf pans without grease. Bake for 1-1/4 hours at 375° until no pink remains and a thermometer shows 160°; then drain. Top with a sprinkle of the rest of the cheese; allow to sit until melted.

Nutrition Information

- Calories: 316 calories
- Protein: 29g protein.
- Total Fat: 15g fat (8g saturated fat)
- Sodium: 680mg sodium
- Fiber: 2g fiber)
- Total Carbohydrate: 15g carbohydrate (2g sugars
- Cholesterol: 101mg cholesterol

---

521. Quick Hamburger Stroganoff

Serving: 2 servings. | Prep: 10mins | Cook: 20mins | Ready in:

Ingredients

- 1/2 pound ground beef
- 1/4 cup chopped onion
- 1 tablespoon all-purpose flour
- 1/2 teaspoon salt
- 1/8 teaspoon pepper
- 1 can (4-1/2 ounces) mushroom stems and pieces, undrained
- 1/2 cup condensed cream of chicken soup, undiluted
- 1/2 cup sour cream
- Hot cooked noodles

Direction

- Cook onion and beef together in a skillet on moderate heat until beef is not pink anymore, then drain. Stir in pepper, salt and flour until

combined. Put in mushrooms, then cook and stir on low heat about 5 minutes. Stir in the soup and simmer without a cover about 10 minutes. Stir in sour cream and heat through, then serve on top of the noodles.

Nutrition Information

- Calories:
- Sodium:
- Fiber:
- Total Carbohydrate:
- Cholesterol:
- Protein:
- Total Fat:

---

522. Ramona's Chilaquiles

Serving: 4 servings. | Prep: 10mins | Cook: 20mins | Ready in:

Ingredients

- 1/2 pound lean ground beef (90% lean)
- 1/2 pound fresh chorizo or bulk spicy pork sausage
- 1 medium onion, finely chopped
- 1 garlic clove, minced
- 1 can (14-1/2 ounces) diced tomatoes with mild green chilies, undrained
- 1 can (10 ounces) diced tomatoes and green chilies, undrained
- 4 cups tortilla chips (about 6 ounces)
- 1 cup shredded Monterey Jack cheese
- Chopped fresh cilantro
- Optional toppings: sour cream, diced avocado and sliced red onion

Direction

- Set the oven to 350 degrees to preheat. Cook and crumble beef and chorizo with garlic and onion in a big skillet for 5 to 7 minutes on medium heat until beef is not pink anymore, then drain. Stir in both tomatoes and bring to a boil. Layer 2 cups of chips, a half of the meat mixture with 1/2 cup of cheese in a greased 8-inch square or 1 1/2-quart baking dish, then repeat layers.

- Bake without a cover for 12 to 15 minutes, until cheese is melted, then sprinkle with cilantro. Serve together with toppings, if wished.

Nutrition Information

- Calories: 573 calories
- Protein: 33g protein.
- Total Fat: 35g fat (14g saturated fat)
- Sodium: 1509mg sodium
- Fiber: 4g fiber)
- Total Carbohydrate: 28g carbohydrate (5g sugars
- Cholesterol: 110mg cholesterol

523.   Salisbury Steak Deluxe

Serving: 6 servings. | Prep: 20mins | Cook: 10mins | Ready in:

Ingredients

- 1 can (10-3/4 ounces) condensed cream of mushroom soup, undiluted
- 1 tablespoon prepared mustard
- 2 teaspoons Worcestershire sauce
- 1 teaspoon prepared horseradish
- 1 large egg
- 1/4 cup dry bread crumbs
- 1/4 cup finely chopped onion
- 1/2 teaspoon salt
- Dash pepper
- 1-1/2 pound ground beef
- 1 to 2 tablespoons canola oil
- 1/2 cup water
- 2 tablespoons chopped fresh parsley

Direction

- Mix horseradish, Worcestershire sauce, mustard, and soup together in a small bowl. Put aside. Gently whisk the egg in a separate bowl. Add 1/4 cup of the soup mixture, pepper, salt, onion, and bread crumbs. Crumble over the mixture with beef and stir thoroughly. Form into 6 patties.
- Brown the patties with oil in a big skillet; strain. Mix water with the leftover soup mixture; add onto the patties. Put a cover on and cook on low heat until a thermometer displays 160° and the meat is not pink anymore, about 10-15 minutes. Transfer the patties to a serving platter. Enjoy the meat with sauce. Sprinkle parsley over.

Nutrition Information

- Calories: 319 calories
- Cholesterol: 113mg cholesterol
- Protein: 25g protein.
- Total Fat: 20g fat (7g saturated fat)
- Sodium: 706mg sodium
- Fiber: 1g fiber)
- Total Carbohydrate: 9g carbohydrate (1g sugars

524.   Salisbury Steak For Two

Serving: 2 servings. | Prep: 15mins | Cook: 15mins | Ready in:

Ingredients

- 1 egg
- 1 slice bread, torn into small pieces
- 1 tablespoon finely chopped onion
- 1/2 pound lean ground beef (90% lean)
- 2 teaspoons canola oil
- 1 can (10-3/4 ounces) condensed golden mushroom soup, undiluted
- 1/2 cup water
- 1 jar (4-1/2 ounces) whole mushrooms, drained

- Dash pepper

Direction

- Mix together onion, bread and egg in a small bowl, then crumble beef over the mixture and combine well. Form into 2 patties.
- Brown both sides of patties in oil, if wanted, in a big nonstick skillet on medium heat, then drain. Mix together pepper, mushrooms, water and soup, then pour over patties. Bring to a boil, then lower heat and simmer, covered, until meat is not pink anymore.

Nutrition Information

- Calories: 306 calories
- Protein: 28g protein.
- Total Fat: 17g fat (5g saturated fat)
- Sodium: 414mg sodium
- Fiber: 1g fiber)
- Total Carbohydrate: 9g carbohydrate (1g sugars
- Cholesterol: 176mg cholesterol

---

525. Salisbury Steak With Onion Gravy

Serving: 6 servings. | Prep: 10mins | Cook: 25mins | Ready in:

Ingredients

- 1 egg
- 1 can (10-1/2 ounces) condensed French onion soup, undiluted, divided
- 1/2 cup dry bread crumbs
- 1/4 teaspoon salt
- Pinch pepper
- 1-1/2 pounds ground beef
- 1 tablespoon all-purpose flour
- 1/4 cup water
- 1/4 cup ketchup
- 1 teaspoon Worcestershire sauce

- 1/2 teaspoon prepared mustard
- 6 cups hot cooked egg noodles
- Chopped fresh parsley, optional

Direction

- Beat egg in a big bowl then stir the breadcrumbs, 1/3 cup of soup, pepper and salt in. Insert the beef, mixing gently. Form into six oval patties. In a skillet on medium heat, cook the patties for 3 to4 minutes per side until browned. Move it out of the pan and set aside, throwing the drippings away. Combine water and flour in the skillet until smooth then add the Worcestershire sauce, ketchup, mustard and the leftover soup. Boil then stir and cook for 2 minutes. Transfer the patties back into the skillet and cover it up. Let it simmer until the meat is not pink, about 15 minutes. Top patties and gravy on noodles and garnish using parsley, if you want. Serve.

Nutrition Information

- Calories:
- Sodium:
- Fiber:
- Total Carbohydrate:
- Cholesterol:
- Protein:
- Total Fat:

---

526. Slow Cooked Shepherd's Pie

Serving: 5 servings. | Prep: 35mins | Cook: 05hours15mins | Ready in:

Ingredients

- 2 pounds medium Yukon Gold potatoes, peeled and quartered
- 2 tablespoons butter
- 1/4 to 1/3 cup 2% milk

- 3/4 teaspoon salt, divided
- 1/2 teaspoon pepper, divided
- 1 pound ground beef
- 1 large onion, chopped
- 2 garlic cloves, minced
- 3 tablespoons tomato paste
- 1-3/4 cups sliced fresh mushrooms
- 2 medium carrots, chopped
- 1 cup beef broth
- 1/4 cup dry white wine
- 2 teaspoons Worcestershire sauce
- 1/2 teaspoon dried thyme
- 1/3 cup frozen peas
- 1/2 cup shredded Monterey Jack cheese
- 1 tablespoon minced fresh parsley

Direction

- In a big saucepan, put potatoes and add water to cover. Boil it. Lower the heat; put a cover on and cook until soft, about 10-15 minutes. Strain, and shake potatoes on low heat to dry, about 1 minute. Mash the potatoes, slowly adding sufficient milk and butter to achieve the consistency you want. Mix in 1/4 teaspoon pepper and 1/2 teaspoon salt.
- In the meantime, cook garlic, onion, and beef in a big frying pan over medium heat until the meat is not pink anymore; strain.
- Pour in tomato paste and cook for 2 minutes. Add thyme, Worcestershire sauce, wine, broth, carrots, and mushrooms. Boil it. Lower the heat; simmer without a cover until the liquid has mostly evaporated. Mix in peas. Flavor with pepper and the leftover salt.
- Remove the beef mixture to an oiled 4-quart slow cooker. Spread over the top with the mashed potatoes. Put the lid on and cook on low until bubbling, about 5-6 hours. Sprinkle cheese over. Put the lid on and cook until the cheese melts, about 10 minutes more. Sprinkle parsley on top right before serving.

Nutrition Information

- Calories: 419 calories

- Total Carbohydrate: 35g carbohydrate (7g sugars
- Cholesterol: 79mg cholesterol
- Protein: 24g protein.
- Total Fat: 19g fat (9g saturated fat)
- Sodium: 746mg sodium
- Fiber: 4g fiber)

527.   Southwest Beef Stew

Serving: 8 servings. | Prep: 20mins | Cook: 20mins | Ready in:

Ingredients

- 2 pounds lean ground beef (90% lean)
- 1-1/2 cups chopped onions
- 1 can (28 ounces) diced tomatoes, undrained
- 1 package (16 ounces) frozen corn, thawed
- 1 can (15 ounces) black beans, rinsed and drained
- 1 cup picante sauce
- 3/4 cup water
- 1 teaspoon ground cumin
- 3/4 teaspoon salt
- 1/2 teaspoon garlic powder
- 1/2 teaspoon pepper
- 1/2 cup shredded reduced-fat cheddar cheese

Direction

- Cook onion and beef until not pink and onion in a Dutch oven set on medium heat. Drain excess grease. Mix in pepper, salt, tomatoes, water, picante sauce, pepper, garlic powder, cumin, corn, and beans. Heat to a boil. Cover, decrease heat, and gently boil until corn is done, 15 minutes. Spread cheese on top.

Nutrition Information

- Calories: 344 calories
- Cholesterol: 45mg cholesterol

- Protein: 31g protein. Diabetic Exchanges: 4 lean meat
- Total Fat: 12g fat (5g saturated fat)
- Sodium: 847mg sodium
- Fiber: 7g fiber)
- Total Carbohydrate: 28g carbohydrate (0 sugars

528.   Southwest Zucchini Boats

Serving: 4 servings. | Prep: 15mins | Cook: 10mins | Ready in:

Ingredients

- 4 medium zucchini
- 1 pound ground beef
- 3/4 cup salsa
- 1/4 cup dry bread crumbs
- 1/4 cup minced fresh cilantro
- 1 teaspoon chili powder
- 1/2 teaspoon ground cumin
- 1/4 teaspoon salt
- 1/8 teaspoon pepper
- 1 cup shredded Monterey Jack cheese, divided
- Sour cream, optional

Direction

- Cut zucchini in half lengthwise; using a sharp knife, slice a thin layer off the bottom of each so that zucchini can sit flat. Leave 1/4-in. shells by scooping out pulp.
- Put shells in a 3-qt. microwave-safe dish that is ungreased. Microwave with a cover for 3 minutes on high, until crisp-tender; then drain and put aside.
- In the meantime, cook beef in a large skillet over medium heat until no longer pink; then drain. Take away from heat; stir in the 1/2 cup cheese, pepper, salt, chili powder, cumin, cilantro, breadcrumbs and salsa. Spoon into zucchini shells.

- Microwave without a cover for 4 minutes on high. Sprinkle top with the rest of cheese. Microwave for 3 to 4 minutes more or until zucchini are softened and cheese melts. If preferred, serve along with sour cream.

Nutrition Information

- Calories: 387 calories
- Sodium: 618mg sodium
- Fiber: 3g fiber)
- Total Carbohydrate: 15g carbohydrate (6g sugars
- Cholesterol: 95mg cholesterol
- Protein: 30g protein.
- Total Fat: 23g fat (11g saturated fat)

529.   Spaghetti Squash Boats

Serving: 4-6 side-dish servings or 2 main-dish servings. | Prep: 60mins | Cook: 20mins | Ready in:

Ingredients

- 1 medium spaghetti squash (2 to 2-1/2 pounds)
- 1/4 pound ground beef (90% lean)
- 1/2 cup chopped onion
- 1/2 cup chopped green pepper
- 1/2 cup sliced fresh mushrooms
- 1 garlic clove, minced
- 1/2 teaspoon dried basil
- 1/2 teaspoon dried oregano
- 1/4 teaspoon salt
- 1/8 teaspoon pepper
- 1 can (14-1/2 ounces) diced tomatoes, drained
- 1/3 cup shredded part-skim mozzarella cheese

Direction

- Lengthwise, cut squash in half; scoop seeds out. Put squash in baking dish, cut side down. Use hot water to dill pan to 1/2-in. depth.

Bake for 30-40 minutes till tender at 375°, uncovered.

- Scoop squash out when cool to touch; use a fork to separate strands. Put squash and shells aside.
- Cook green pepper, onion and beef in skillet on medium heat till meat isn't pink; drain. Add pepper, salt, oregano, basil, garlic and mushrooms; mix and cook for 2 minutes. Add tomatoes; mix and cook for 2 minutes. Mix squash in.
- Cook for 10 minutes, uncovered, till liquid evaporates. Fill shells; put into shallow baking dish.
- Bake for 15 minutes at 350°, uncovered. Sprinkle cheese; bake till cheese melts for 5 more minutes.

Nutrition Information

- Calories: 102 calories
- Total Carbohydrate: 13g carbohydrate (4g sugars
- Cholesterol: 13mg cholesterol
- Protein: 7g protein. Diabetic Exchanges: 1 starch
- Total Fat: 3g fat (1g saturated fat)
- Sodium: 246mg sodium
- Fiber: 3g fiber)

---

530. Spoon Bread Tamale Bake

Serving: 8 servings. | Prep: 25mins | Cook: 30mins | Ready in:

Ingredients

- 1-1/2 pounds lean ground beef (90% lean)
- 1 large onion, chopped
- 1 small green pepper, chopped
- 1 garlic clove, minced
- 1 can (28 ounces) diced tomatoes, undrained
- 1-1/2 cups frozen corn

- 1 can (2-1/4 ounces) sliced ripe olives, drained
- 4-1/2 teaspoons chili powder
- 1/2 teaspoon salt
- 1/4 teaspoon pepper
- 1/2 cup cornmeal
- 1 cup water
- TOPPING:
- 1-1/2 cups fat-free milk, divided
- 1/2 cup cornmeal
- 1/2 teaspoon salt
- 1/2 cup shredded reduced-fat cheddar cheese
- 2 tablespoons butter
- 1/2 cup egg substitute

Direction

- Cook garlic, green pepper, onion and beef on medium heat in a Dutch oven coated with cooking spray till meat is not pink anymore; drain. Mix in pepper, salt, chili powder, olives, corn and tomatoes. Boil. Lower the heat; let simmer, while uncovered, for 5 minutes.
- Mix water and cornmeal till becoming smooth; slowly mix into the pan. Boil. Lower the heat; let simmer, while uncovered, for 10 minutes, mixing once in a while. Move to a 2-1/2-qt. baking dish that's coated using cooking spray.
- Boil 1 cup of milk in a small-sized saucepan. Mix the leftover milk, salt and cornmeal; gradually mix into boiling milk. Cook and stir till mixture is back to a boil. Lower the heat; cook and stir till becoming thick a bit or for 3 to 4 minutes.
- Take out of the heat; mix in butter and cheese till becoming melted. Mix in egg substitute. Add on top of meat mixture. Bake, while uncovered, at 375 degrees till topping becomes browned a bit or for 30 to 40 minutes.

Nutrition Information

- Calories: 331 calories
- Total Carbohydrate: 30g carbohydrate (7g sugars
- Cholesterol: 55mg cholesterol

- Protein: 25g protein. Diabetic Exchanges: 3 lean meat
- Total Fat: 12g fat (6g saturated fat)
- Sodium: 754mg sodium
- Fiber: 4g fiber)

---

531.   Spud Stuffed Peppers

Serving: 2 servings. | Prep: 25mins | Cook: 40mins | Ready in:

Ingredients

- 2 medium green peppers
- 1/2 pound lean ground beef (90% lean)
- 1 medium potato, peeled and grated
- 1-1/2 teaspoons chili powder
- 1/4 teaspoon salt
- Dash coarsely ground pepper
- 1/4 cup shredded reduced-fat cheddar cheese

Direction

- Cut off the tops of peppers and get rid of seeds. Cook peppers in boiling water in a big saucepan about 4 to 5 minutes. Drain and rinse under cold water, invert on paper towels.
- Cook potato and beef in a nonstick skillet over moderate heat until meat is not pink anymore, drain. Stir in pepper, salt and chili powder, scoop into peppers.
- Put in a small baking pan covered with cooking spray, then cover and bake at 350 degrees for 35 minutes. Sprinkle cheese over and bake without a cover until cheese is melted, about 5 to 10 more minutes.

Nutrition Information

- Calories: 332 calories
- Fiber: 5g fiber)
- Total Carbohydrate: 28g carbohydrate (5g sugars
- Cholesterol: 66mg cholesterol

- Protein: 29g protein. Diabetic Exchanges: 3 lean meat
- Total Fat: 12g fat (6g saturated fat)
- Sodium: 487mg sodium

---

532.   Stuffed Zucchini

Serving: 8 | Prep: 15mins | Cook: 45mins | Ready in:

Ingredients

- 4 medium zucchini
- 1 pound ground beef
- 1 pound Italian sausage
- 1 small onion, chopped
- 1/2 cup dried bread crumbs
- 1 egg, beaten
- 1 (28 ounce) can crushed tomatoes
- 1 (10.75 ounce) can condensed tomato soup
- 1 cup water

Direction

- Preheat an oven to 175°C/350°F; spray/grease 13x9-inch baking dish.
- Lengthwise halve zucchini; scoop seeds out with spoon. Chop; keep 3/4 seeds for stuffing. Mix reserved zucchini seeds, egg, breadcrumbs, chopped onion, sausage and ground beef in medium bowl. Evenly put meat mixture in all zucchini halves, piling on top; put filled zucchini halves in prepped baking dish.
- Mix water, tomato soup and crushed tomatoes in bowl; liberally scoop the tomato mixture on filled zucchini. In preheated oven, bake for 45 minutes; if you want, put foil/cookie sheet under baking sheet because it can splash and bubble over.

Nutrition Information

- Calories: 359 calories;
- Cholesterol: 80

- Protein: 21.7
- Total Fat: 20.9
- Sodium: 905
- Total Carbohydrate: 22.9

- Protein: 16g protein.
- Total Fat: 14g fat (8g saturated fat)
- Sodium: 897mg sodium
- Fiber: 2g fiber)

533.   Taco Pasta Shells

Serving: 10-15 servings. | Prep: 25mins | Cook: 25mins | Ready in:

Ingredients

- 1-1/2 pounds ground beef
- 1 medium onion, chopped
- 1 package (8 ounces) cream cheese, cubed
- 2 envelopes taco seasoning
- 1 to 2 tablespoons minced chives
- 1 package (12 ounces) jumbo pasta shells, cooked and drained
- 2 cups taco sauce
- 2 cups shredded plain or Mexican process cheese (Velveeta)
- 1 cup coarsely crushed tortilla chips

Direction

- In a big skillet, cook the onion and beef on medium heat till the meat is not pink anymore; drain. Whisk in chives, taco seasoning, and cream cheese; cook till the cream cheese melts. Stuff to the pasta shells.
- Add into the greased 4-quart baking dish. Add the taco sauce on the top. Bake, with no cover, at 350 degrees till completely heated or for 20 minutes. Scatter with the tortilla chips and cheese. Bake till cheese melts or for 5 minutes more.

Nutrition Information

- Calories: 310 calories
- Total Carbohydrate: 29g carbohydrate (5g sugars
- Cholesterol: 49mg cholesterol

534.   Taco Platter

Serving: 2 servings. | Prep: 15mins | Cook: 15mins | Ready in:

Ingredients

- 1/4 cup uncooked long grain rice
- 1/4 pound lean ground beef (90% lean)
- 1/4 cup chopped onion
- 1 garlic clove, minced
- 3/4 cup canned Mexican diced tomatoes, undrained
- 2 teaspoons tomato paste
- 3/4 cup canned Ranch Style beans (pinto beans in seasoned tomato sauce), undrained
- 1 package (1 ounce) corn chips
- 1/4 cup shredded cheddar cheese
- 1/2 cup shredded lettuce
- 1 medium tomato, diced
- 2 tablespoons sliced ripe olives
- 2 tablespoons salsa

Direction

- Following package directions to cook rice. At the same time, cook garlic, onion and beef in the small skillet on moderate heat until meat is not pink anymore, then drain.
- Put in tomato paste and tomatoes, then bring to a boil. Lower heat, then cover and simmer about 5 minutes. Put in beans and simmer without a cover until heated through, about 3 minutes more.
- Place on 2 serving plates with corn chips, then put salsa, olives, tomato, lettuce, cheese, meat mixture and rice on top.

Nutrition Information

- Calories: 464 calories
- Total Carbohydrate: 57g carbohydrate (13g sugars
- Cholesterol: 38mg cholesterol
- Protein: 24g protein.
- Total Fat: 15g fat (5g saturated fat)
- Sodium: 1139mg sodium
- Fiber: 9g fiber)

535. Taco Ramekins

Serving: 2 servings. | Prep: 15mins | Cook: 20mins | Ready in:

Ingredients

- 1/4 pound lean ground beef (90% lean)
- 1/4 teaspoon chili powder
- 1/8 teaspoon salt
- 1/8 teaspoon pepper
- 3/4 cup biscuit/baking mix
- 3 tablespoons cold water
- 1 medium tomato, sliced
- 1/4 cup chopped green pepper
- 2 tablespoons sour cream
- 2 tablespoons mayonnaise
- 2 tablespoons shredded cheddar cheese
- 1 tablespoon chopped onion

Direction

- Cook beef on medium heat in a skillet till meat is not pink anymore; drain. Mix in pepper, salt, and chili powder. Take out of the heat and put aside.
- Mix water and biscuit mix to form soft dough. Push onto the bottom and up the sides of two 10-oz. ramekins or custard cups that coated using cooking spray. Fill with meat mixture; add green pepper, and tomato on top. Mix onion, cheese, mayonnaise and sour cream; spread equally on the tops.
- Bake, while uncovered, at 375 degrees till thoroughly heated or for 20 to 25 minutes.

Nutrition Information

- Calories: 369 calories
- Fiber: 2g fiber)
- Total Carbohydrate: 40g carbohydrate (7g sugars
- Cholesterol: 43mg cholesterol
- Protein: 18g protein.
- Total Fat: 15g fat (5g saturated fat)
- Sodium: 892mg sodium

536. Taco Stir Fry

Serving: 8 servings. | Prep: 10mins | Cook: 15mins | Ready in:

Ingredients

- 1 pound lean ground beef (90% lean)
- 1/4 cup chopped onion
- 1 can (14-1/2 ounces) stewed tomatoes
- 1 cup frozen corn
- 2 tablespoons chili powder
- 1 teaspoon sugar
- 1/2 teaspoon dried oregano
- 1/4 teaspoon salt
- 1/8 teaspoon pepper
- 1 cup shredded reduced-fat cheddar cheese
- 1 medium head iceberg lettuce, shredded
- Tortilla chips
- 1 cup salsa

Direction

- Cook onion and beef over medium heat in a non-stick skillet until meat is no longer pink; drain. Mix in pepper, salt, oregano, sugar, chili powder, corn and tomatoes. Take to a boil. Lower the heat; cover and simmer, mixing occasionally for 10 minutes. Toss in cheese.
- Put 10 tortilla chips with shredded lettuce on each plate; top with 2 tablespoons salsa and taco mixture.

Nutrition Information

- Calories: 416 calories
- Protein: 20g protein.
- Total Fat: 18g fat (5g saturated fat)
- Sodium: 641mg sodium
- Fiber: 5g fiber)
- Total Carbohydrate: 44g carbohydrate (6g sugars
- Cholesterol: 38mg cholesterol

537.   Tex Mex Meat Loaf

Serving: 4 servings. | Prep: 15mins | Cook: 60mins | Ready in:

Ingredients

- 1 can (15 ounces) tomato sauce, divided
- 1/3 cup crushed tortilla chips
- 1/4 cup chopped onion
- 2 tablespoons chopped green pepper
- 1 envelope taco seasoning
- 1 pound ground beef

Direction

- Mix taco seasoning, green pepper, onion, chips, and 1 cup of tomato sauce in a big bowl. Crumble beef over the mixture and combine well. Pat into a 9x5-inch loaf pan coated with oil. Bake without a cover at 350 degrees until a thermometer reads 160 degrees and the meat is not pink anymore, 1 hour; drain. Heat the remaining tomato sauce. Slice meat loaf; drizzle tomato sauce on top.

Nutrition Information

- Calories: 292 calories
- Protein: 25g protein.
- Total Fat: 14g fat (6g saturated fat)
- Sodium: 1352mg sodium
- Fiber: 1g fiber)

- Total Carbohydrate: 15g carbohydrate (2g sugars
- Cholesterol: 75mg cholesterol

538.   Three Cheese Meatball Mostaccioli

Serving: 10 servings. | Prep: 15mins | Cook: 35mins | Ready in:

Ingredients

- 1 package (16 ounces) mostaccioli
- 2 large eggs, lightly beaten
- 1 carton (15 ounces) part-skim ricotta cheese
- 1 pound ground beef
- 1 medium onion, chopped
- 1 tablespoon brown sugar
- 1 tablespoon Italian seasoning
- 1 teaspoon garlic powder
- 1/4 teaspoon pepper
- 2 jars (24 ounces each) pasta sauce with meat
- 1/2 cup grated Romano cheese
- 1 package (12 ounces) frozen fully cooked Italian meatballs, thawed
- 3/4 cup shaved Parmesan cheese
- Minced fresh parsley or fresh baby arugula, optional

Direction

- Set oven at 350° to preheat. Follow the package instructions to cook the mostaccioli until tender but firm enough to bite then drain. In the meantime, mix the ricotta cheese with eggs in a small bowl.
- Add onion and beef to a 6-quart stockpot, cook for 6 to 8 minutes until the beef is not pink any longer, crumbling the beef and drain. Mix in seasonings and brown sugar. Add the mostaccioli and pasta sauce and mix to combine.
- Take half of the pasta mixture to a 13x9-inch baking dish coated with cooking spray. Lay the ricotta mixture and the rest of pasta

mixture over top. Scatter with Romano cheese. Add Parmesan cheese and meatballs on top.

- Bake in the preheated oven while uncovered until heated through, about 35 to 40 minutes. Add parsley on top if preferred.

Nutrition Information

- Calories: 541 calories
- Fiber: 5g fiber)
- Total Carbohydrate: 55g carbohydrate (13g sugars
- Cholesterol: 105mg cholesterol
- Protein: 34g protein.
- Total Fat: 23g fat (11g saturated fat)
- Sodium: 1335mg sodium

539.   Upside Down Meat Pie

Serving: 4 servings. | Prep: 25mins | Cook: 20mins | Ready in:

Ingredients

- 1 pound ground beef
- 1/2 cup chopped onion
- 1/2 teaspoon salt
- 1 can (15 ounces) tomato sauce
- BAKING POWDER BISCUITS:
- 1 cup all-purpose flour
- 2 teaspoons baking powder
- 1 teaspoon celery salt
- 1 teaspoon paprika
- 1/2 teaspoon salt
- 1/4 teaspoon pepper
- 3 tablespoons butter
- 1/2 cup milk

Direction

- Cook onion and ground beef in a large ovenproof skillet until the onion becomes tender and the beef is browned; then drain.

Put tomato sauce and salt; then bring to a simmer for 10-15 minutes.

- At the same time, in a bowl, mix pepper, salt, paprika, celery salt, baking powder, and flour. Slice in the butter until the mixture looks like a coarse meal. Pour in milk and stir to form a soft dough. Add in tablespoonfuls on the meat mixture.
- Remove the cover and bake at 475 degrees until the biscuits turn golden, or for 20 minutes.

Nutrition Information

- Calories: 421 calories
- Protein: 26g protein.
- Total Fat: 20g fat (11g saturated fat)
- Sodium: 1827mg sodium
- Fiber: 2g fiber)
- Total Carbohydrate: 33g carbohydrate (5g sugars
- Cholesterol: 83mg cholesterol

540.   Vegetable Meat Loaf

Serving: 2 servings. | Prep: 10mins | Cook: 45mins | Ready in:

Ingredients

- 1/2 pound ground beef
- 1 slice bread, torn into small pieces
- 1 large egg, beaten
- 1/4 cup shredded carrot
- 2 tablespoons finely chopped onion
- 2 tablespoons finely chopped green pepper
- 2 tablespoons finely chopped celery
- 1/2 teaspoon salt
- Dash each pepper and garlic powder
- 5 tablespoons chili sauce or ketchup, divided

Direction

- Mix 2 tbsp. of chili sauce, seasonings, celery, green pepper, onion, carrot, egg, bread and ground beef in a bowl
- Shape into a loaf in an ungreased 5 3/4"x3"x2" loaf pan. Scoop over loaf with leftover chili sauce. Bake at 350 degrees without a cover until meat is not pink anymore, about 45 to 50 minutes.

Nutrition Information

- Calories: 330 calories
- Protein: 25g protein.
- Total Fat: 16g fat (6g saturated fat)
- Sodium: 1349mg sodium
- Fiber: 1g fiber)
- Total Carbohydrate: 20g carbohydrate (10g sugars
- Cholesterol: 163mg cholesterol

541.   Yummy Tater Topped Casserole

Serving: 6-8 servings. | Prep: 15mins | Cook: 60mins | Ready in:

Ingredients

- 1-1/2 pounds ground beef
- 1 package (16 ounces) frozen vegetables, thawed
- 1 can (2.8 ounces) french-fried onions
- 1/4 cup butter
- 1 can (10-3/4 ounces) condensed cream of celery soup, undiluted
- 1 can (10-3/4 ounces) condensed cream of chicken soup, undiluted
- 1/2 cup milk
- 1 package (16 ounces) frozen Tater Tots, thawed

Direction

- Cook beef in a large skillet over medium heat until not pink anymore; drain. Layer the beef, vegetables and onions in a greased 13x9-inch baking dish. Dot with butter.
- Mix milk and soups in a bowl; pour over vegetables. Add Tater Tots on top. Bake without covering at 350° until golden brown, about 60 minutes.

Nutrition Information

- Calories: 482 calories
- Total Fat: 31g fat (12g saturated fat)
- Sodium: 1006mg sodium
- Fiber: 4g fiber)
- Total Carbohydrate: 32g carbohydrate (3g sugars
- Cholesterol: 78mg cholesterol
- Protein: 22g protein.

Chapter 7: Awesome Ground Beef Recipes

***

542.   "Tastee" Sandwich

Serving: 26 | Prep: 20mins | Cook: 40mins | Ready in:

Ingredients

- 4 ounces ketchup, or more to taste
- 5 teaspoons salt
- 1 tablespoon prepared mustard
- 1 tablespoon creamed horseradish
- 1 tablespoon Worcestershire sauce
- 1/4 teaspoon ground black pepper

- 5 pounds 85% lean ground beef
- 1 cup warm water
- 1 cup minced onion
- 1 teaspoon monosodium glutamate (such as Ac'cent®)

Direction

- In a 1-cup measuring cup, mix ground black pepper, Worcestershire sauce, horseradish, mustard, salt and ketchup. Add more ketchup if the combination does not fill 1 cup. Stir until well combined. In a stock pot, add ground beef; pour ketchup mixture over the top of ground beef.
- Pour warm water in the same measuring cup till full. Stir to loosen any fine seasoning left; add into stock pot. Mix onion with ground beef mixture; put in monosodium glutamate. Stir till well blended.
- Over low heat, cook and stir the ground beef mixture for about 15 minutes, until the ground beef is finely crumbled. Let it come to a boil; cook for about 25 minutes, until flavors blend.

Nutrition Information

- Calories: 182 calories;
- Sodium: 577
- Total Carbohydrate: 1.9
- Cholesterol: 53
- Protein: 15.4
- Total Fat: 12.1

---

543. 'Chinese' Pie

Serving: 6 | Prep: 10mins | Cook: 45mins | Ready in:

Ingredients

- 1 tablespoon canola oil
- 1 onion, diced
- 1 pound lean ground beef
- salt and ground black pepper to taste

- 2 (15 ounce) cans cream-style corn
- 4 cups mashed potatoes

Direction

- Set the oven to 190°C or 375°F to preheat.
- In a skillet, heat canola oil on moderate heat, then cook and stir onion for 5 minutes, until translucent. Stir into onion with ground beef and use black pepper and salt to season. Cook ground beef mixture for 10 minutes longer, until crumbly and browned, then drain excess grease.
- Spread into the bottom of the prepped casserole dish with the cooked ground beef mixture, then drizzle over beef with a layer of cream-style corn. Put a layer of mashed potatoes on top.
- In the preheated oven, bake for half an hour, until casserole is bubbly and potatoes are browned.

Nutrition Information

- Calories: 412 calories;
- Total Carbohydrate: 57.2
- Cholesterol: 52
- Protein: 20.3
- Total Fat: 13.1
- Sodium: 928

---

544. A Firefighter's Meatloaf

Serving: 4 | Prep: 15mins | Cook: 1hours15mins | Ready in:

Ingredients

- 2 slices whole wheat bread
- 2 pounds ground beef
- 1 green onion, chopped
- 2 tablespoons chopped onion
- 1 cup medium salsa
- 2 tablespoons whole grain Dijon mustard

- 1 teaspoon Worcestershire sauce
- 2 tablespoons minced garlic
- salt and pepper to taste
- 1 tablespoon barbeque sauce

Direction

- Heat the oven to 190°F or 375°F.
- In a small bowl, immerse the bread in warm water. Put beef in a big bowl. Drain the bread and move it to the bowl where the beef is, then add salt, pepper, garlic, Dijon mustard, salsa, onion, green onion and Worcestershire sauce. Use your hands to mix everything together until blended well blended. Shape this mixture into a loaf and put it into a loaf pan that's greased. Bake in the oven for 1 hour. Remove the excess fat and top with barbeque (Diana) sauce. Place it back in the oven and bake for another 15 minutes.

Nutrition Information

- Calories: 526 calories;
- Protein: 39.3
- Total Fat: 33.4
- Sodium: 796
- Total Carbohydrate: 15.3
- Cholesterol: 136

545.　　Aaron's Missouri Burger

Serving: 4 | Prep: 10mins | Cook: 15mins | Ready in:

Ingredients

- 1 pound lean ground beef
- 2 teaspoons onion powder
- 1/4 cup honey mustard
- 1 teaspoon garlic powder
- 2 teaspoons crushed red pepper
- 1/2 teaspoon salt
- 1/4 cup brown sugar
- 2 tablespoons olive oil

- 4 slices Swiss cheese (optional)
- 4 hamburger buns

Direction

- In a big bowl, mix brown sugar, salt, crushed red pepper, garlic powder, honey mustard, onion powder and ground beef. Mold to 4 patties.
- In a big skillet, heat olive oil on medium heat. Cook burgers, occasionally turning, for 15-20 minutes for well done or to desired temperature. Put a Swiss cheese slice on each patty shortly before taking out of the skillet. Serve on top of hamburgers buns.

Nutrition Information

- Calories: 529 calories;
- Sodium: 717
- Total Carbohydrate: 44.4
- Cholesterol: 82
- Protein: 27.9
- Total Fat: 27.2

546.　　Abuela's Picadillo

Serving: 8 | Prep: 15mins | Cook: 1hours7mins | Ready in:

Ingredients

- 2 pounds lean ground beef
- 1/4 cup olive oil
- 1/2 onion, chopped
- 1/2 green bell pepper, chopped
- 2 tablespoons minced garlic
- 2 (8 ounce) cans tomato sauce
- 2 cups water
- 1/2 cup red cooking wine
- 3 tablespoons hot sauce (such as Louisiana®)
- 1 (1.41 ounce) package sazon seasoning (such as Badia® Tropical®)
- 1 tablespoon chopped fresh parsley

311

- 1/2 teaspoon garlic powder
- 1/2 teaspoon onion powder
- 1/2 teaspoon ground cumin
- 1/2 teaspoon ground black pepper
- 1/4 teaspoon ground bay leaf
- 3 ounces Spanish-style olives
- 1 teaspoon salt, or to taste
- 1 small butternut squash, peeled and cut into cubes

Direction

- Stir and cook ground beef until browned for 5-10 minutes in a big stockpot. Drain the grease.
- In a small skillet on medium heat, heat olive oil and put garlic, green bell pepper and onion. Stir and cook for 2-3 minutes until fragrant. Mix beef into the stockpot.
- Place hot sauce, water, cooking wine, and tomato sauce in the stockpot. Mix in parsley, sazon seasoning, pepper, cumin, bay leaf, onion powder, and garlic powder. Bring it up to a boil then bring the heat down to low. Let the picadillo simmer for about 10 minutes or until a little thick without a cover.
- Use your fingers to cut the olives in half and mix it in the picadillo; stir in the squash. Simmer until the liquid gets reduced without drying the picadillo for 45-60 minutes. Sprinkle salt to season.

Nutrition Information

- Calories: 378 calories;
- Sodium: 1856
- Total Carbohydrate: 22
- Cholesterol: 74
- Protein: 24.1
- Total Fat: 22

---

547.   Albondigas

Serving: 6 | Prep: 20mins | Cook: 20mins | Ready in:

Ingredients

- 1 quart water
- 4 carrots, sliced
- 2 small potatoes, peeled and diced
- 1 medium onion, diced
- 1 1/2 cups salsa, medium or hot
- 2 beef bouillon cubes
- 1 1/2 pounds ground beef
- 1/3 cup seasoned dry bread crumbs
- 1/3 cup milk
- chopped fresh cilantro (optional)

Direction

- Boil a big stockpot with bouillon cubes, salsa, onion, potatoes, carrots, and water. Cut heat down to a medium simmer, occasionally stirring, roughly 10 minutes.
- Mix milk, breadcrumbs, and beef in a bowl and form the mixture into 1-inch-sized meatballs, then drop them into the boiling broth. When the soup comes back to a boil, drop the heat to medium-low.
- Cook while covered for around 20 minutes until vegetables are soft and the meatball centers are no longer pink. Serve with a sprinkling of cilantro.

Nutrition Information

- Calories: 325 calories;
- Total Fat: 17.1
- Sodium: 900
- Total Carbohydrate: 20.4
- Cholesterol: 72
- Protein: 22.6

---

548.   All Protein Meatloaf

Serving: 8 | Prep: 10mins | Cook: 40mins | Ready in:

Ingredients

- 1 1/2 pounds ground beef

- 1 tablespoon Worcestershire sauce
- 1 (4 ounce) can tomato sauce
- 1/3 cup crushed fried pork skins
- 2 eggs
- 2 1/2 tablespoons chili powder
- 1 tablespoon garlic salt
- 1 tablespoon garlic pepper seasoning

Direction

- Set the oven to 375 F (190°C) and start preheating.
- Combine together eggs, crushed pork skins, tomato sauce, Worcestershire sauce, and ground beef in a big bowl. Use garlic pepper, garlic salt, and chili powder to season. Mix until well combined. Form into a loaf and put into a loaf pan coated with oil.
- Bake without a cover for 35 to 40 minutes in the prepared oven. Allow to sit for at least 5 minutes before you slice and serve.

Nutrition Information

- Calories: 316 calories;
- Total Fat: 25.4
- Sodium: 1115
- Total Carbohydrate: 3
- Cholesterol: 122
- Protein: 18.5

549. Alysia's Basic Meat Lasagna

Serving: 10 | Prep: 50mins | Cook: 45mins | Ready in:

Ingredients

- 1 1/2 pounds ground beef
- 1 teaspoon garlic powder
- 1 (28 ounce) jar sausage flavored spaghetti sauce
- 1 (8 ounce) can tomato sauce
- 1 teaspoon dried oregano

- 1 tablespoon olive oil
- 4 cloves garlic, minced
- 1 small onion, diced
- 1 (8 ounce) package mozzarella cheese, shredded
- 8 ounces provolone cheese, shredded
- 1 (15 ounce) container ricotta cheese
- 2 eggs
- 1/4 cup milk
- 1/2 teaspoon dried oregano
- 9 lasagna noodles
- 1/4 cup grated Parmesan cheese

Direction

- Set oven to 190° C (375° F) and start preheating.
- Sprinkle oregano and garlic powder to season ground beef in a skillet, on medium heat. Brown the beef, then drain.
- Add oregano, tomato sauce and spaghetti sauce in a big saucepan; put aside. Heat olive oil in a skillet. Sauté onions and garlic for 5 mins. Stir meat with sautéed garlic and onions into the sauce, cook for 15-20 minutes.
- In a medium bowl, mix provolone and mozzarella cheeses. Combine oregano, milk, eggs, and ricotta cheese in a medium bowl.
- Layer just enough sauce to cover the bottom of a 9x13 inch baking pan. In the pan, lay 3 lasagna noodles. Layer with sauce, then cover with ricotta mixture, scatter with mozzarella/provolone mixture; repeat layering for 1 more time. Ending with 1 layer of noodles and the rest of sauce. Scatter with parmesan cheese.
- Cover and bake in the prepared oven for half an hour at 375 degrees. Then, bake without a cover for 15 minutes.

Nutrition Information

- Calories: 567 calories;
- Total Fat: 31.4
- Sodium: 943
- Total Carbohydrate: 35.6

- Cholesterol: 130
- Protein: 36.1

550.   American Chop Suey II

Serving: 5 | Prep: 5mins | Cook: 25mins | Ready in:

Ingredients

- 1 (16 ounce) package uncooked elbow macaroni
- 1 pound lean ground beef
- 1 onion, chopped
- 2 (10.75 ounce) cans condensed tomato soup
- salt and pepper to taste

Direction

- Cook macaroni based on the package directions.
- In the meantime, stir-fry the onion and ground beef in a separate big skillet over medium high heat for 5 to 10 minutes or until meat turns crumbly and brown. Strain well and keep the onion and meat in the skillet. Put two cans of tomato soup into the skillet and mix well to blend.
- Once noodles are done, strain well and put the noodles back into the pot. Stir the hamburger mixture from the skillet into the pot. Blend well and add pepper and salt to taste.

Nutrition Information

- Calories: 664 calories;
- Sodium: 745
- Total Carbohydrate: 85.1
- Cholesterol: 68
- Protein: 30
- Total Fat: 22

551.   Amish Casserole

Serving: 6 | Prep: 20mins | Cook: 35mins | Ready in:

Ingredients

- 1 pound ground beef
- 1 (10.75 ounce) can condensed tomato soup
- 1/4 cup brown sugar
- 1/8 teaspoon black pepper
- 1/4 teaspoon salt
- 1 (10.75 ounce) can condensed cream of chicken soup
- 1 (12 ounce) package wide egg noodles
- 10 slices American cheese

Direction

- Preheat an oven to 175 degrees C (350 degrees F).
- Bring lightly salted water to boil in a large pot, add egg noodles and let to cook for about 7 minutes until tender. Drain the noodles and place back into the pan. Stir in cream of chicken soup until the noodles are coated.
- Over medium-high heat, crumble ground beef into a large skillet. Then drain grease and mix in the tomato soup, salt, pepper, and brown sugar. Transfer 1/2 of the beef into the bottom of a 2 1/2 quart casserole dish that is greased. Spread five slices of cheese on top of beef. Add half of the noodles on top and then repeat the layers ending with cheese on the top.
- Bake in the preheated oven for about 35 minutes until the sauce is bubbly and cheese is browned.

Nutrition Information

- Calories: 630 calories;
- Sodium: 1472
- Total Carbohydrate: 57
- Cholesterol: 141
- Protein: 33.1
- Total Fat: 29.8

552. Amish Meatloaf

Serving: 8 | Prep: 15mins | Cook: 1hours | Ready in:

Ingredients

- 2 pounds ground beef
- 2 1/2 cups crushed butter-flavored crackers
- 1 small onion, chopped
- 2 eggs
- 3/4 cup ketchup
- 1/4 cup brown sugar
- 2 slices bacon
- 1 cup ketchup
- 2 tablespoons vinegar
- 3/4 teaspoon salt, or to taste
- 2 tablespoons prepared yellow mustard
- 1/2 cup brown sugar

Direction

- Preheat an oven to 175 degrees Celsius or 350 degrees Fahrenheit.
- Mix ground beef, eggs, onion, 3/4 cup ketchup, 1/4 cup brown sugar, and crushed crackers together in a medium-sized bowl until well blended. Press into a loaf pan that's 9x5 inches. Lay two pieces of bacon on top.
- Bake for an hour or until cooked through in the heated oven. As it bakes, mix together the leftover cup of ketchup, salt, 1/2 cup brown sugar, mustard, and vinegar. Spread it on top of the meat loaf at the final 15 minutes of baking.

Nutrition Information

- Calories: 464 calories;
- Protein: 23.8
- Total Fat: 21.1
- Sodium: 1161
- Total Carbohydrate: 45.6
- Cholesterol: 118

553. Amish Poor Man's Steak

Serving: 5 | Prep: 15mins | Cook: 1hours10mins | Ready in:

Ingredients

- 1 pound ground beef
- 1 cup milk
- 1 cup crushed saltine crackers
- 1 onion, finely chopped
- 1 teaspoon salt
- 1 teaspoon ground black pepper
- 1 (14.5 ounce) can cream of mushroom soup

Direction

- Prepare a bowl then mix in milk, onion, salt, black pepper, saltine cracker crumbs, and ground beef. Take part of the mixture and shape into a loaf; Put these on a baking sheet. Cover the sheet and keep refrigerated for 8 hours to overnight.
- Prepare oven by heating to 175 degrees C or 350 degrees F.
- Using a large skillet, heat it over medium-high temperature. Slice the loaf into 1-inch-thick portions and cook each portion for 2 to 3 minutes per side on the hot skillet until it turns brown. The insides will still appear pink. Place the portions evenly on a roasting pan. On top of each portion, evenly spread some mushroom soup.
- Let the steaks bake for an hour in the oven, or until the meat does not appear pink anymore, and the soup starts to bubble. If a meat thermometer was placed in the center of a meat portion, it should indicate a temperature of 70 degrees C or 160 degrees F at the minimum.

Nutrition Information

- Calories: 334 calories;
- Total Fat: 18.1

- Sodium: 1220
- Total Carbohydrate: 22.2
- Cholesterol: 59
- Protein: 19.9

554. Andie's Stuffed Mushrooms

Serving: 10 | Prep: 30mins | Cook: 15mins | Ready in:

Ingredients

- 1 pound lean ground beef
- 2 pounds fresh mushrooms-stems removed, chopped and reserved
- 1/4 cup margarine
- 1/2 cup chopped green bell peppers
- 2 teaspoons minced garlic
- 3 teaspoons dried parsley
- 1 teaspoon dried basil leaves, crushed
- 2/3 cup dry bread crumbs
- 1/3 cup soft bread crumbs
- 2 cups shredded sharp Cheddar cheese

Direction

- Set the oven to 400°F (200°C), and start preheating.
- In a large, deep skillet, arrange ground beef; then cook over medium high heat until evenly brown. Drain, crumble and put aside.
- In a medium saucepan, melt the margarine over medium heat; then mix in basil, parsley, garlic, green bell peppers and mushroom stems.
- In a large bowl, mix Cheddar cheese, soft bread crumbs, dry bread crumbs, mushroom stem mixture and ground beef.
- On a large baking pan, arrange the mushroom caps with the hollow sides up. Generously fill each cap with the mixture.
- Bake in the oven for 15-20 minutes, or until the filling turns golden brown.

Nutrition Information

- Calories: 317 calories;
- Cholesterol: 58
- Protein: 18.1
- Total Fat: 22.3
- Sodium: 309
- Total Carbohydrate: 11.7

555. Ann's Sister's Meatloaf Recipe

Serving: 6 | Prep: 10mins | Cook: 1hours | Ready in:

Ingredients

- 2 pounds lean ground beef
- 2 eggs
- 1 1/2 cups dry bread crumbs
- 1/4 cup ketchup
- 1 teaspoon monosodium glutamate (MSG)
- 1/2 cup warm water
- 1 (1 ounce) package dry onion soup mix
- 2 slices bacon
- 1 (8 ounce) can tomato sauce

Direction

- Set the oven to 350° F (175° C) to preheat.
- Combine the soup mix, water, MSG, ketchup, crumbs, eggs and beef in a large bowl. Mix well then transfer the mixture into loaf pan using a spoon. Place 2 strips of bacon on top, then use tomato sauce to cover.
- Bake for 1 hour in prepared oven.

Nutrition Information

- Calories: 510 calories;
- Sodium: 1164
- Total Carbohydrate: 27.1
- Cholesterol: 157
- Protein: 34.9
- Total Fat: 28.3

556. Applesauce Meatballs

Serving: 4 | Prep: 25mins | Cook: 1hours10mins | Ready in:

Ingredients

- 1 cup applesauce
- 1 egg
- 1 cup bread crumbs
- 1/2 teaspoon salt and pepper to taste
- 1 pound ground beef
- flour
- 1 tablespoon vegetable oil
- 4 carrots, peeled and thinly sliced
- 2 onions, thinly sliced
- 3 cups tomato juice

Direction

- Set the oven at 350°F (175°C) and start preheating.
- Combine ground beef together with pepper, salt, bread crumbs, egg and applesauce; blend till well mixed. (This is best done by hand.) Roll the mixture into medium-sized meatballs; roll in flour.
- Place a large skillet on medium-high or high heat; heat 1 teaspoon of oil. Cook the meatballs while turning occasionally till well browned but not cooked through. Place onto a baking dish; set aside.
- Partially cook onions and carrots in the same skillet over medium-high heat. Include in tomato juice; taste with pepper and salt; allow to boil. Lower the heat; simmer for 5 minutes; transfer over the meatballs.
- Cook with a cover in the preheated oven till the meatballs are cooked through and the carrots become tender, or for 45 minutes. Cook without a cover for 10 minutes. Take away from the oven.

Nutrition Information

- Calories: 519 calories;
- Total Fat: 20.2
- Sodium: 1086
- Total Carbohydrate: 56.9
- Cholesterol: 104
- Protein: 28.3

557. Argentine Meat Empanadas

Serving: 10 | Prep: | Cook: | Ready in:

Ingredients

- 1/2 cup shortening
- 2 onions, chopped
- 1 pound lean ground beef
- 2 teaspoons Hungarian sweet paprika
- 3/4 teaspoon hot paprika
- 1/2 teaspoon crushed red pepper flakes
- 1 teaspoon ground cumin
- 1 tablespoon distilled white vinegar
- 1/4 cup raisins
- 1/2 cup pitted green olives, chopped
- 2 hard-cooked eggs, chopped
- salt to taste
- 1 (17.5 ounce) package frozen puff pastry sheets, thawed

Direction

- Melt shortening in a sauté pan, add chopped onions. Cook the onions just until they start to turn golden. Take away from heat and mix in salt to taste, crushed red pepper flakes, hot paprika, and sweet paprika.
- To slightly cook the meat, on a sieve, spread the meat and add boiling water. Let the meat cool. In a plate, put the meat and season with vinegar, cumin, and salt to taste. Stir and put the meat into the onion mixture. Stir thoroughly and put on a flat plate to harden and cool.

- Slice puff pastry dough into 10 round shells. Put on each round with the meat mixture by 1 spoonful; add some of the hard-boiled egg, olives, and raisins. Make sure the filling not touch the edges of the pastry because its greasiness will prevent good sealing. Wet the edge of the pastry a little, fold in half and attach the edges together. The shape should look like a semicircle. There should have 2/3-1/2-in. flat edge of pastry for you to work with. To seal, twist the edges, step by step, between index finger and thumb, ensuring that you press it before releasing the pinch and proceeding on to the next curl. Other ways of sealing like using 1 fork or pinching without curling cannot avoid juice leaking when baking, and the empanadas must be juicy.
- Start preheating the oven to 350°F (180°C). On a cookie sheet lined with a parchment paper, put the empanadas. Make sure to use a fork to prick the empanada close to the curl to release steam while baking. Use egg to glaze for shine, and bake for 20-30 minutes until turning golden.

Nutrition Information

- Calories: 498 calories;
- Protein: 14.7
- Total Fat: 36.8
- Sodium: 326
- Total Carbohydrate: 27.7
- Cholesterol: 73

---

558.   Asian Lettuce Wraps

Serving: 4 | Prep: 20mins | Cook: 15mins | Ready in:

Ingredients

- 16 Boston Bibb or butter lettuce leaves
- 1 pound lean ground beef
- 1 tablespoon cooking oil
- 1 large onion, chopped
- 1/4 cup hoisin sauce
- 2 cloves fresh garlic, minced
- 1 tablespoon soy sauce
- 1 tablespoon rice wine vinegar
- 2 teaspoons minced pickled ginger
- 1 dash Asian chile pepper sauce, or to taste (optional)
- 1 (8 ounce) can water chestnuts, drained and finely chopped
- 1 bunch green onions, chopped
- 2 teaspoons Asian (dark) sesame oil

Direction

- Wash the entire lettuce leaves and pat dry, be cautious not damage them. Reserve.
- Over moderately-high heat, heat a big skillet. In hot skillet, cook and mix cooking oil and beef for 5 to 7 minutes till crumbly and browned. Let drain and throw the grease; turn beef onto a bowl. In the same skillet used for beef, cook and mix the onion for 5 to 10 minutes till slightly soft. Into the onions, mix chili pepper sauce, ginger, vinegar, soy sauce, garlic and hoisin sauce. Put cooked beef, sesame oil, green onions and water chestnuts; cook and mix for 2 minutes till onions barely start to wilt.
- Place the leaves of lettuce around outer edge of a big serving platter and stack the meat mixture in the middle.

Nutrition Information

- Calories: 388 calories;
- Total Fat: 22.3
- Sodium: 580
- Total Carbohydrate: 24.3
- Cholesterol: 69
- Protein: 23.4

559. Asian Style Meatloaf

Serving: 8 | Prep: 12mins | Cook: 1hours10mins | Ready in:

Ingredients

- 1 1/2 pounds ground beef
- 1/2 pound ground pork
- 3 slices bread, broken up into small pieces
- 2 eggs, lightly beaten
- 1 small onion, finely chopped
- 2 stalks celery, finely chopped
- 3 tablespoons soy sauce
- 1 tablespoon minced fresh ginger
- 2 tablespoons hoisin sauce
- 1/2 cup hoisin sauce
- 2 tablespoons ketchup

Direction

- Set oven to 350°F (175 degrees C) for preheating.
- Combine pork, beef, eggs, bread crumbs, celery and onion in a large bowl. Mix in 3tablespoon of soy sauce, ginger and a 2 tablespoon of hoisin sauce. Transfer and press mixture into a 2-quart shallow baking pan.
- Bake for 40 minutes in the preheated oven.
- Drain oil from the pan. Combine 2 tablespoons ketchup with half cup hoisin in a small bowl. Pour mixture over meatloaf then spread. Bake for around 20 minutes. Take out from the oven and set aside to rest for 5 minutes.

Nutrition Information

- Calories: 438 calories;
- Total Fat: 30.9
- Sodium: 864
- Total Carbohydrate: 16.2
- Cholesterol: 140
- Protein: 22.5

560. Aunt Anna's Pan Pasty

Serving: 8 | Prep: 15mins | Cook: 1hours35mins | Ready in:

Ingredients

- 1 pound lean ground beef
- 4 potatoes, diced
- 4 carrots, diced
- 1 onion, chopped
- 1/2 small rutabaga, diced
- 1/4 cup water, or more as needed
- 1 teaspoon salt
- 1/2 teaspoon freshly ground black pepper
- 4 teaspoons butter (optional)

Direction

- Set the oven to 350°F (175°C) and start preheating.
- Over medium-high heat, heat a large skillet. Cook while stirring beef in the hot skillet for 5-7 minutes until crumbly and browned; drain and get rid of grease.
- In a casserole dish, combine pepper, salt, water, rutabaga, onion, carrots, potatoes and ground beef; place butter on top. Use aluminum foil or oven-safe cover to cover the dish.
- Bake for half an hour in the prepared oven; stir and add more water if necessary. Keep baking for about an hour more until vegetables become tender.

Nutrition Information

- Calories: 231 calories;
- Total Fat: 9.2
- Sodium: 370
- Total Carbohydrate: 23.9
- Cholesterol: 43
- Protein: 13.5

561. Aunt Ro's Baked Beans

Serving: 6 | Prep: 15mins | Cook: 4hours10mins | Ready in:

Ingredients

- 8 ounces bacon
- 1 pound ground beef
- 1/2 cup chopped onion
- 2 (12 ounce) cans pinto beans, drained and rinsed
- 2 (15.5 ounce) cans canned butter beans, drained and rinsed
- 2 (15 ounce) cans canned baked beans with pork
- 1 cup barbeque sauce
- 1 cup ketchup
- 1 cup brown sugar, packed

Direction

- Cook bacon in big deep skillet over medium high heat till browned evenly. On paper towels, drain; crumble. Put aside. From the skillet, drain bacon fat.
- Cook onion and ground beef in same skillet over medium heat for 5-7 minutes, mixing till meat isn't pink anymore; drain.
- Put ground beef in slow cooker. Add brown sugar, ketchup, barbeque sauce, baked beans, pork, butter beans and pinto beans to ground beef mixture. Mix to blend well and cover. Cook on high for 4 hours. Put crumbled bacon on top of each serving.

Nutrition Information

- Calories: 809 calories;
- Total Fat: 17.3
- Sodium: 2583
- Total Carbohydrate: 128.4
- Cholesterol: 70
- Protein: 38.2

562. Authentic Cincinnati Chili

Serving: 10 | Prep: 15mins | Cook: 3hours30mins | Ready in:

Ingredients

- 2 pounds lean ground beef
- 1 quart water, or amount to cover
- 2 onions, finely chopped
- 1 (15 ounce) can tomato sauce
- 2 tablespoons vinegar
- 2 teaspoons Worcestershire sauce
- 4 cloves garlic, minced
- 1/2 (1 ounce) square unsweetened chocolate
- 1/4 cup chili powder
- 1 1/2 teaspoons salt
- 1 teaspoon ground cumin
- 1 teaspoon ground cinnamon
- 1/2 teaspoon ground cayenne pepper
- 5 whole cloves
- 5 whole allspice berries
- 1 bay leaf

Direction

- In a large pan, put the ground beef, and add about 1 quart of cold water to cover. Bring to boil while stirring and breaking up the beef using a fork to a fine texture. Boil slowly for about 30 minutes until the beef is cooked thoroughly. Remove from the heat source and chill in the pan overnight.
- The following day, skim solid fat from top of the pan and get rid of the fat. Put beef mixture atop medium heat and mix in the Worcestershire sauce, onions, cinnamon, tomato sauce, vinegar, bay leaf, garlic, cayenne pepper, chocolate, allspice berries, chili powder, salt, cumin, and cloves. Bring the contents to a boil, low the heat to a simmer and then cook while stirring time to time for 3 hours. Pour in water if need be to prevent chili from burning.

Nutrition Information

- Calories: 225 calories;
- Total Carbohydrate: 10.1
- Cholesterol: 59
- Protein: 19.1
- Total Fat: 12.6
- Sodium: 674

563. Award Winning Chili Con Carne

Serving: 8 | Prep: 15mins | Cook: 2hours20mins | Ready in:

Ingredients

- 4 tablespoons vegetable oil
- 1 green bell pepper, chopped
- 1 yellow onion, chopped
- 2 1/2 pounds lean ground beef
- 2 beef bouillon cubes
- 2/3 cup red wine
- 2 (16 ounce) cans whole peeled tomatoes, chopped, juice reserved
- garlic cloves, crushed
- 1 (12 ounce) can tomato paste
- 1 1/2 teaspoons paprika
- 2 1/2 teaspoons chili powder
- 1 teaspoon cayenne pepper
- 2 1/2 teaspoons dried basil
- 1/2 teaspoon dried oregano
- 2 tablespoons dried parsley
- 1/2 teaspoon black pepper
- 1 teaspoon salt
- 12 drops hot pepper sauce (e.g. Tabasco™)
- 1 (15 ounce) can kidney beans, drained
- 3 tablespoons flour
- 3 tablespoons corn meal
- 1/2 cup water

Direction

- Heat oil over medium heat in a large saucepan. Put in onion and green pepper until

tender. Place in the ground beef and cook until the meat is brown. Crumble over bouillon cubes, and combine in wine; keep cooking for few minutes. Mix in tomato paste, garlic, and chopped tomatoes. Flavor with parsley, oregano, basil, cayenne pepper, chili powder, and paprika. Mix in salt and pepper.
- Bring to a boil over high heat. Lower the heat to medium-low. Cover, and simmer in 90 minutes, stirring on occasion.
- Combine in hot pepper sauce and kidney beans. If more liquid is needed, add in more reserved tomato juice. Keep simmering for extra 30 minutes.
- In a small bowl, combine water, cornmeal, and flour until smooth. Transfer into chili, and cook for extra 10 minutes, or until the chili thickens.

Nutrition Information

- Calories: 495 calories;
- Cholesterol: 86
- Protein: 31.6
- Total Fat: 27.2
- Sodium: 1212
- Total Carbohydrate: 29.1

564. Baby Burgers On Baguettes

Serving: 24 | Prep: 15mins | Cook: 15mins | Ready in:

Ingredients

- 1 pound ground beef
- salt and pepper to taste
- 1 pinch mesquite seasoning
- 1 French baguette, sliced into 1/4 inch rounds
- 6 leaves romaine lettuce
- 12 cherry tomatoes, thinly sliced
- ketchup
- prepared yellow mustard

Direction

- Set the oven to 350°F (175°C), and start preheating. On a cookie sheet, place the baguette slices in a single layer. Put in the preheated oven, and bake for about 5 minutes, until lightly toasted. Take away from the oven, allow to cool.
- Add mesquite seasoning into the ground beef for seasoning, and blend lightly. Form tablespoonfuls of dough into mini burger patties. Add a bit of pepper and salt into the patties.
- Heat a skillet over the medium-high heat. Cook patties until browned and well done, about 1 - 2 minutes per side.
- On a large serving tray, arrange baguette slices, and add a piece of romaine leaf on top each one. Put a mini burger on each slice, then add tomato slices on top. Put in ketchup and mustard prior to serving, or let your guests dress their own burgers.

Nutrition Information

- Calories: 95 calories;
- Total Fat: 2.7
- Sodium: 202
- Total Carbohydrate: 11.9
- Cholesterol: 11
- Protein: 5.7

---

565.   Bacon Cheeseburger Dogs

Serving: 6 | Prep: 30mins | Cook: 40mins | Ready in:

Ingredients

- cooking spray (such as Pam®)
- 6 all-beef hot dogs
- 1 teaspoon butter
- 1 (8 ounce) package sliced fresh mushrooms
- 1 small onion, diced
- 2 1/2 pounds ground beef
- 12 slices bacon
- 6 hero rolls
- 12 slices American cheese
- 2 teaspoons hamburger seasoning

Direction

- Start preheating the oven to 230°C (450°F). Line aluminum foil on a baking sheet and coat with cooking spray.
- Boil a pot of water. Cook hot dogs in boiling water for 5-10 mins, until heated through. Drain and let the hot dog cool for 5 mins.
- In the meantime, in a skillet, melt 1 teaspoon butter; sauté onion and mushrooms in butter for 5-10 mins, until softened.
- On a work surface, spread a sheet of plastic wrap. Separate ground beef into six equal portions. Over plastic wrap, spread 1 portion of beef to about 1/4 inch thick rectangle patty; flavor with hamburger seasoning. Across the center of the beef, lay one hot dog and scoop over hot dog with 1/6 mushroom mixture.
- Roll ground beef around hot dog with plastic wrap, pulling plastic wrap away from meat as you wrap. Completely seal the ends of beef around hot dog. Wrap around beef with 2 slices bacon and put on the lined baking sheet. Repeat with the rest of bacon, hot dogs and beef.
- Bake for 15 mins in the prepared oven until beef is slightly pink in the center and bacon is crisp. Add 2 slices American cheese on top of each burger-dog and continue to bake for 5 mins more, until cheese is melted. An instant-read thermometer should read 60°C (140°F) when inserted into the center.

Nutrition Information

- Calories: 1282 calories;
- Cholesterol: 223
- Protein: 69.9
- Total Fat: 77
- Sodium: 2826
- Total Carbohydrate: 73.7

566. Bacon Cheeseburger Upside Down Pizza

Serving: 6 | Prep: 15mins | Cook: 20mins | Ready in:

Ingredients

- 8 slices bacon
- 1 pound ground beef
- 1 onion, chopped
- 1 green bell pepper, chopped
- 1 1/2 cups pizza sauce
- 3 roma (plum) tomatoes, chopped
- 4 ounces shredded Cheddar cheese
- 2 eggs
- 1 cup milk
- 1 tablespoon vegetable oil
- 1 cup all-purpose flour
- 1/4 teaspoon salt

Direction

- Put the bacon in a deep and big skillet. Fry the bacon over medium-high heat until browned on all sides then drain excess oil. Reserve 2 strips of fried bacon and break the rest into small pieces. There will be 6 bacon strips to crumble.
- Preheat the oven to 400°F (200°C).
- Cook and stir the bell pepper, beef and onion in a big saucepan over medium-high heat until the beef turns brown in color. Drain excess oil and mix in the pizza sauce and 6 crumbled bacon pieces. Put the mixture in an ungreased 13x9-inch pan. Put tomatoes and cheese on top.
- Whisk the eggs a little bit in a medium-sized bowl. Stir in the oil and milk and put in the salt and flour. Whisk the mixture on medium speed for 2 minutes. Spread it evenly on top of the meat mixture. Top with the reserved bacon.

- Place in the preheated oven and bake for 20-30 minutes until the topping has puffed a little and is golden brown in color.

Nutrition Information

- Calories: 668 calories;
- Protein: 28.8
- Total Fat: 48.2
- Sodium: 947
- Total Carbohydrate: 28
- Cholesterol: 175

567. Bacon Wrapped Hamburgers

Serving: 6 | Prep: 15mins | Cook: 10mins | Ready in:

Ingredients

- 1/2 cup shredded Cheddar cheese
- 1 tablespoon grated Parmesan cheese
- 1 small onion, chopped
- 1 egg
- 1 tablespoon ketchup
- 1 tablespoon Worcestershire sauce
- 1/2 teaspoon salt
- 1/8 teaspoon pepper
- 1 pound ground beef
- 6 slices bacon
- 6 hamburger buns, split

Direction

- Preheat grill to high heat.
- Mix pepper, salt, Worcestershire sauce, ketchup, egg, onion, parmesan cheese and cheddar cheese in big bowl; crumble ground beef in. By hand, mix; shape to 6 patties. Wrap bacon slice around each one then use toothpicks to secure bacon.
- Put patties on grill; cook till well done, 5 minutes per side. Before serving over hamburger buns, remove toothpicks.

Nutrition Information

- Calories: 378 calories;
- Total Fat: 19.8
- Sodium: 842
- Total Carbohydrate: 24.4
- Cholesterol: 100
- Protein: 24.1

---

568.   Baked Pasta

Serving: 8 | Prep: | Cook: | Ready in:

Ingredients

- 1 (16 ounce) package dry pasta
- 1 pound lean ground beef
- 3 cloves garlic, minced
- 2 (15 ounce) cans tomato sauce
- 12 ounces brown gravy
- 1/2 cup half-and-half
- 1/2 cup grated Parmesan cheese
- 1 teaspoon dried oregano
- 1 teaspoon dried basil
- 1 cup shredded mozzarella cheese

Direction

- Cook ground beef while stirring in a big frying pan or a Dutch oven until it turns brown. Put in basil, oregano, Parmesan cheese, cream, gravy, tomato sauce, and garlic. Simmer the mixture for half an hour.
- At the same time, cook pasta in a big pot with boiling water till al dente. Strain.
- Mix the sauce with the cooked ziti; grease a 9x13-inch baking dish and spread the mixture into it. Top with mozzarella cheese.
- Bake at 175°C (350°C) until bubbly for 20-30 minutes.

Nutrition Information

- Calories: 490 calories;
- Total Fat: 21.3
- Sodium: 1021
- Total Carbohydrate: 49
- Cholesterol: 132
- Protein: 25.8

---

569.   Baked Pasta Casserole

Serving: 8 | Prep: 15mins | Cook: 1hours15mins | Ready in:

Ingredients

- 12 ounces mostaccioli pasta
- cooking spray
- 1 pound lean ground beef
- 1/2 cup chopped onion
- 1 teaspoon minced garlic
- 38 ounces pasta sauce
- 1/4 teaspoon Italian seasoning
- 1/4 teaspoon ground cumin
- 1/4 teaspoon salt
- 1/4 teaspoon ground black pepper
- 1 pinch garlic salt, or to taste
- 8 ounces sour cream
- 1 (8 ounce) package cream cheese, softened
- 1 (8 ounce) container ricotta cheese
- 1 1/2 cups shredded Cheddar cheese

Direction

- Bring lightly salted water in a large pot to a boil; cook mostaccioli in boiling water until al dente, stirring sometimes, for 8 to 10 minutes. Drain pasta.
- Set oven to 350°F (175°C) to preheat. Grease the inside of a 9x13-inch baking dish with cooking spray.
- Bring a large, deep skillet to medium-high heat. Cook while stirring garlic, onion, and beef in heated skillet, for 5 to 7 minutes, until beef is crumbly and browned. Drain and pour off drippings.

- Stir garlic salt, black pepper, salt, cumin, Italian seasoning, and pasta sauce into ground beef mixture; bring mixture to a boil. Lower heat; simmer for about 20 minutes or until flavors have melded.
- Whisk ricotta cheese, cream cheese, and sour cream together in a mixing bowl until no lumps remain. Mix cheese mixture and pasta together in a mixing bowl until well coated; spread in the greased baking dish. Scoop pasta sauce over pasta mixture. Cover the dish with foil.
- Bake for 20 minutes in the preheated oven. Take off foil and scatter top with Cheddar cheese. Bake for about 20 minutes longer or until cheese is bubbly.

Nutrition Information

- Calories: 667 calories;
- Total Carbohydrate: 53.8
- Cholesterol: 111
- Protein: 29.5
- Total Fat: 37.4
- Sodium: 958

570.   Baked Penne

Serving: 6 | Prep: 5mins | Cook: |Ready in:

Ingredients

- 1/2 pound extra lean ground beef
- 1/2 cup chopped onions
- 1/2 cup chopped green peppers
- 1 (24 ounce) jar spaghetti sauce
- 1 (10 ounce) tub PHILADELPHIA Italian Cheese and Herb Cooking Creme, divided
- 1 cup KRAFT Shredded Mozzarella Cheese, divided
- 3 cups hot cooked penne pasta

Direction

- Heat oven to 350°F.
- In large nonstick frying pan, brown meat with the vegetables. Stir in half cup of mozzarella, 3/4 cup cooking crème and spaghetti sauce: cook while stirring until mozzarella melts, about 2-3 minutes. Put in pasta; then mix lightly.
- Spoon into 2 quarts casserole; add the remaining mozzarella and cooking creme over top. Cover.
- Bake until heated through, about 20 minutes; remove the cover 15 minute after.

Nutrition Information

- Calories: 397 calories;
- Total Fat: 17.3
- Sodium: 922
- Total Carbohydrate: 38.8
- Cholesterol: 64
- Protein: 21.4

571.   Baked Spaghetti Squash With Beef And Veggies

Serving: 6 | Prep: 25mins | Cook: 1hours25mins |Ready in:

Ingredients

- 1 spaghetti squash, halved and seeded
- 1 pound ground beef
- 1/2 cup diced green bell pepper
- 1/2 cup diced red bell pepper
- 1/4 cup diced red onion
- 1 clove garlic, chopped
- 1 (14.5 ounce) can Italian-style diced tomatoes, drained
- 1/2 teaspoon dried oregano
- 1/2 teaspoon dried basil
- 1/4 teaspoon salt
- 1/4 teaspoon ground black pepper
- 2 1/4 cups shredded sharp Cheddar cheese

325

Direction

- Preheat an oven to 190°C/375°F.
- Put squash on baking sheet; bake till tender for 40 minutes. Take off heat; cool. Use fork to shred pulp.
- Lower oven temperature to 175°C/375°F. Grease casserole dish lightly.
- Cook ground beef in skillet on medium heat till evenly brown; drain. Mix garlic, red onion and green and red pepper in. Mix and cook till veggies are tender.
- Mix tomatoes and shredded squash into skillet; season with pepper, salt, basil and oregano. Mix and cook till heated through. Take skillet off heat; mix 2 cups cheese in till melted. Put in prepped casserole dish.
- In preheated oven, bake for 25 minutes. Sprinkle leftover cheese; bake till cheese melts for 5 minutes.

Nutrition Information

- Calories: 399 calories;
- Sodium: 590
- Total Carbohydrate: 12.8
- Cholesterol: 100
- Protein: 27.2
- Total Fat: 26.4

572.   Baked Ziti I

Serving: 10 | Prep: 20mins | Cook: 35mins |Ready in:

Ingredients

- 1 pound dry ziti pasta
- 1 onion, chopped
- 1 pound lean ground beef
- 2 (26 ounce) jars spaghetti sauce
- 6 ounces provolone cheese, sliced
- 1 1/2 cups sour cream
- 6 ounces mozzarella cheese, shredded
- 2 tablespoons grated Parmesan cheese

Direction

- Boil big pot with lightly salted water; add ziti paste. Cook for 8 minutes till al dente; drain.
- Brown ground beef and onion in big skillet on medium heat; add spaghetti sauce. Simmer 15 minutes.
- Preheat an oven to 175°C/350°F. Butter a 9x13-inch baking dish. Layer the following: 1/2 ziti, provolone cheese, the sour cream, 1/2 of sauce mixture, leftover ziti, mozzarella cheese and leftover sauce mixture. Put grated Parmesan cheese on top.
- In the preheated oven, bake for 30 minutes till cheeses melt.

Nutrition Information

- Calories: 578 calories;
- Total Fat: 25.3
- Sodium: 914
- Total Carbohydrate: 58.4
- Cholesterol: 71
- Protein: 27.9

573.   Baked Ziti III

Serving: 8 | Prep: 20mins | Cook: 30mins |Ready in:

Ingredients

- 1 (16 ounce) package dry ziti pasta
- 1 pound lean ground beef
- 1 onion, chopped
- 2 (28 ounce) jars spaghetti sauce
- 6 ounces sliced provolone cheese
- 6 ounces sliced mozzarella cheese
- 1 1/2 cups sour cream
- 1/2 cup grated Parmesan cheese
- 1/4 cup chopped fresh basil

Direction

- In a large pot, boil the lightly salted water.

Add pasta, cook until tender yet firm to bite, 8-10 minutes; drain the pasta.

- Brown the beef in a large skillet on medium heat. Add onions and sauté until it becomes tender. Drain the fat and add spaghetti sauce; then let simmer for 15 minutes.
- Set an oven to 175°C (350°F) and start preheating.
- Put 1/2 the pasta in a 2-quart, lightly greased baking dish; layer mozzarella and provolone cheese slices on top. Smear a layer of sour cream and 1/2 the spaghetti sauce mixture.
- Cover with sauce, cheese, and the rest of pasta; scatter with a layer of fresh basil and Parmesan cheese.
- In the prepared oven, bake until the sauce and cheese are bubbling, for half an hour; then serve.

Nutrition Information

- Calories: 761 calories;
- Cholesterol: 96
- Protein: 36.2
- Total Fat: 34.4
- Sodium: 1258
- Total Carbohydrate: 74.9

574.   Banana Meatloaf

Serving: 6 | Prep: 10mins | Cook: 1hours | Ready in:

Ingredients

- 1 pound lean ground beef
- 1 cup fresh bread crumbs
- 1 tablespoon minced onion
- 3/4 cup mashed banana
- 1/2 teaspoon salt
- 1/8 teaspoon ground black pepper
- 1/4 teaspoon paprika
- 1/2 teaspoon ground mustard

Direction

- Set the oven to 350°F (175°C) and start preheating. Grease a 9x5 inch loaf pan.
- Mix dry mustard, paprika, pepper, salt, banana, onion, bread crumbs and ground beef in a large bowl until well combined. Form into a loaf and put in the prepared pan.
- Bake for 1 hour in the prepared oven until the center is no longer pink.

Nutrition Information

- Calories: 242 calories;
- Total Carbohydrate: 19.7
- Cholesterol: 56
- Protein: 18.6
- Total Fat: 9.5
- Sodium: 359

575.   Bats And Cobwebs

Serving: 6 | Prep: 10mins | Cook: 30mins | Ready in:

Ingredients

- 1 (8 ounce) package farfalle (bow tie) pasta
- 1 pound ground beef
- 1 small onion, chopped (optional)
- 1 (28 ounce) jar pasta sauce
- 8 ounces mozzarella cheese, cut into 1/2 inch cubes
- 1/4 cup grated Parmesan cheese

Direction

- Warm up an oven to 400 degrees F or 200 degrees C.
- Over high heat, allow a big pot of water mixed with some salt to come to a rolling boil, then stir in the bow tie pasta and bring back to a boil. Let the pasta boil while stirring now and again for 12 minutes until cooked through but still firm to the bite, then drain thoroughly.
- In a large skillet, cook as you stir the onion and ground beef for 5 minutes until beef has

no more pink left. Drain out the fat, then stir in the pasta sauce and let the mixture boil. Lower heat to simmer.

- Mix half the mozzarella cheese and the cooked pasta into the sauce, toss to blend, then move to a 2 quart baking dish. Top with the Parmesan cheese and leftover mozzarella.
- Bake in the warmed oven until bubbly and slightly brown, about 15-20 minutes.

Nutrition Information

- Calories: 522 calories;
- Total Carbohydrate: 47.4
- Cholesterol: 76
- Protein: 30.4
- Total Fat: 23.1
- Sodium: 867

576. Bean Free Paleo Chili

Serving: 6 | Prep: 15mins | Cook: 40mins | Ready in:

Ingredients

- 2 pounds ground beef
- 1 tablespoon ghee (clarified butter), or as needed
- 1 onion, chopped
- 1 green bell pepper, chopped
- 2 cloves garlic, chopped
- 6 tomatoes
- 1 (4 ounce) can chopped green chilies
- 1 tablespoon cumin
- 1 tablespoon chili powder
- 1/2 teaspoon salt
- 1/2 teaspoon garlic powder
- 1/4 teaspoon ground black pepper

Direction

- Set a large skillet over medium-high heat. Cook while stirring in beef for 5-7 minutes, or

till crumbly and browned. Strain; discard any grease.

- While the meat is browning, set a saucepan over medium heat and melt ghee. Include in garlic, bell pepper and onion; cook for 3-5 minutes, or till the bell pepper turns soft and the onion becomes translucent. Dice 2 tomatoes; include into the saucepan with bell pepper and onion. In a blender, put in the remaining 4 tomatoes and purée; pour the purée into the saucepan with the vegetables. Mix in black pepper, garlic powder, salt, chili powder, cumin and green chiles.
- Mix the browned beef into the saucepan with the chili. Simmer for around 30 minutes, or till heated through.

Nutrition Information

- Calories: 340 calories;
- Sodium: 523
- Total Carbohydrate: 10.1
- Cholesterol: 100
- Protein: 27.6
- Total Fat: 21.1

577. Beanless Chili

Serving: 6 | Prep: 25mins | Cook: 1hours5mins | Ready in:

Ingredients

- 1 butternut squash, halved and seeded
- 2 1/2 tablespoons extra-virgin olive oil, divided
- 1 head broccoli
- 1 pound ground beef
- 1/4 cup chopped yellow onion, or to taste
- 1 clove garlic, minced
- 1 tablespoon chili powder, or to taste
- 2 teaspoons ground cumin, or to taste
- 1/2 teaspoon cayenne pepper, or to taste

- 1/2 teaspoon ground chipotle pepper, or to taste
- 3 cups filtered water, or as needed
- 1 (24 ounce) container crushed tomatoes
- 1 red bell pepper, chopped
- 1 yellow bell pepper, chopped
- 1 teaspoon sea salt
- 1 jalapeno pepper, diced

Direction

- Set oven to 200° C (400° F) and start preheating.
- Arrange squash halves on a baking tray. Use 1 1/2 tablespoons olive oil to coat the flesh.
- Put in the preheated oven and bake 25-30 minutes until tender. Let cool till safe to handle. Scrape flesh then put in a bowl and mash.
- Split broccoli florets from stems. In a food processor, grind florets.
- In a skillet, heat the rest olive oil over medium heat. Add chipotle pepper, cayenne pepper, cumin, chili powder, garlic, onion, and ground beef. Cook and stir about 5-7 minutes until crumbly and browned.
- Move beef to a stockpot over medium heat. Add jalapeno pepper, yellow bell pepper, red bell pepper, tomatoes, water, ground broccoli, and smashed squash. Heat to a boil. Decrease heat and simmer at least 30 minutes until vegetables are tender and flavors meld.

Nutrition Information

- Calories: 357 calories;
- Total Carbohydrate: 34.6
- Cholesterol: 46
- Protein: 18.1
- Total Fat: 18.5
- Sodium: 529

578. Beef Mac Casserole

Serving: 12 | Prep: 10mins | Cook: 55mins | Ready in:

Ingredients

- 1 (16 ounce) package uncooked pasta shells
- 1 pound ground beef
- 1/4 cup chopped onions
- 1/4 cup chopped green bell pepper
- 1 (3 ounce) package pepperoni, sliced
- 2 (8 ounce) cans tomato sauce
- 2 cups tomato juice
- 3/4 teaspoon dried oregano
- 1/2 teaspoon celery salt
- 1/4 teaspoon onion powder
- 1/4 teaspoon garlic salt
- 1/4 teaspoon dried basil
- 1/8 teaspoon crushed red pepper flakes
- 2 cups shredded mozzarella cheese

Direction

- Preheat the oven to 175 °C or 350 °F. Slightly oil a 9x13 inch baking dish.
- Pour slightly salted water in a big pot and over high heat, bring to a rolling boil. When boiling, mix in shell pasta, and bring back to a boil. Cook the pasta without a cover for 13 minutes, mixing from time to time, till pasta has cooked through, yet firm to the bite. Drain thoroughly in a colander placed in sink.
- Over moderately-high heat, heat a big skillet. Cook and mix the green pepper, onion and ground beef till browned. Drain off excess grease. Mix in cooked pasta, red pepper flakes, basil, garlic salt, onion powder, celery salt, oregano, tomato juice, tomato sauce and pepperoni. Add to the prepped baking dish and cover using aluminum foil.
- In the prepped oven, bake for 20 minutes. Take casserole out of oven and scatter mozzarella cheese on top. Put back into oven and bake for 5 minutes till cheese melts.

Nutrition Information

- Calories: 315 calories;
- Total Carbohydrate: 32
- Cholesterol: 43
- Protein: 18.3
- Total Fat: 13
- Sodium: 662

579. Beef Nacho Casserole

Serving: 6 | Prep: 15mins | Cook: 20mins | Ready in:

Ingredients

- 1 pound ground beef
- 1 1/2 cups chunky salsa
- 1 (10 ounce) can whole kernel corn, drained
- 3/4 cup creamy salad dressing (e.g. Miracle Whip)
- 1 teaspoon chili powder
- 2 cups crushed tortilla chips
- 2 cups Colby cheese

Direction

- Set the oven to 350°F (175°C) and start preheating.
- Over medium-high heat, in a large skillet, place ground beef. Cook while stirring to crumble until browned evenly. Drain grease. Take out of the heat; stir in chili powder, mayonnaise, corn and salsa into beef. Layer ground beef mixture, tortilla chips and cheese twice in a 2 quart casserole dish; finish with cheese on top.
- Bake without a cover in the prepared oven for 20 minutes until cheese melts and dish is heated thoroughly.

Nutrition Information

- Calories: 497 calories;
- Sodium: 1128
- Total Carbohydrate: 23.9
- Cholesterol: 98

- Protein: 26.1
- Total Fat: 33.6

580. Beef Noodle Shepherd's Pie

Serving: 6 | Prep: 15mins | Cook: 20mins | Ready in:

Ingredients

- 1 pound ground beef
- 1 1/2 cups hot water
- 1 (1.25 ounce) package beef with onion soup mix
- 1/2 cup uncooked elbow macaroni
- 2 cups prepared mashed potatoes
- 1/2 teaspoon paprika

Direction

- Prepare the oven by preheating to 425°F (220°C).
- Brown beef in a medium skillet set on medium-high heat then strain. Then add in elbow macaroni, soup mix, and water and stir; allow it to simmer everything for 5 minutes. Transfer mixture in a 9x13-inch baking dish. Put potatoes on top then dust with paprika. Place in preheated oven and bake for 15-20 minutes and serve immediately.

Nutrition Information

- Calories: 369 calories;
- Protein: 15.8
- Total Fat: 24.1
- Sodium: 614
- Total Carbohydrate: 21.5
- Cholesterol: 66

581. Beef Potato House Pie Casserole

Serving: 8 | Prep: 20mins | Cook: 40mins | Ready in:

Ingredients

- 6 large potatoes, peeled and chopped
- 1/2 cup milk
- 2 tablespoons butter
- 2 pounds ground beef
- 1 onion, chopped
- 1 green bell pepper, chopped
- salt and pepper to taste
- 1 (8 ounce) package processed American cheese, sliced

Direction

- Set the oven to 190°C or 375°F to preheat. Bring salted water in a big pot to a boil. Add potatoes in boiling water and cook for 15 minutes, until tender yet still firm. Drain potatoes and mash them together with butter and milk until smooth.
- Mix together green pepper, onion and ground beef in a big, deep skillet on medium-high heat. Cook the beef mixture until beef is browned evenly. Drain excess fat then use pepper and salt to season.
- Scoop a layer of beef mixture into a deep casserole dish. Spread the beef with a layer of mashed potato. Keep on alternating layers until the dish is full, then place cheese on top.
- In the preheated oven, bake about 20 minutes.

Nutrition Information

- Calories: 712 calories;
- Cholesterol: 132
- Protein: 31.5
- Total Fat: 42.4
- Sodium: 538
- Total Carbohydrate: 51.5

582. Beef Soft Tacos With Mango Salsa

Serving: 4 | Prep: 30mins | Cook: 55mins | Ready in:

Ingredients

- Black Beans and Rice
- 2 tablespoons olive oil
- 1 onions, finely chopped
- 1 green bell pepper, finely chopped
- 2 cloves garlic, minced
- 4 1/2 cups water
- 2 (16 ounce) cans black beans, rinsed and drained
- 2 cups brown rice
- 1 teaspoon ground cumin
- 1/2 teaspoon salt
- 1/4 teaspoon smoked paprika
- 1 bay leaf
- ground black pepper to taste
- Mango Salsa
- 2 cups chopped fresh mango
- 1 cup chopped red bell pepper
- 2/3 cup chopped green onion
- 1/4 cup chopped cilantro
- 1 jalapeno pepper, seeded and minced
- 2 tablespoons fresh lime juice
- 1 tablespoon olive oil
- Taco Filling:
- 1 pound lean ground beef
- 1 tablespoon chili powder
- 1 1/2 teaspoons ground cumin
- 1/4 teaspoon garlic powder
- 1/4 teaspoon onion powder
- 1/4 teaspoon red pepper flakes
- 1/4 teaspoon dried oregano
- 1/4 teaspoon paprika
- 1 (8 ounce) package flour tortillas

Direction

- Heat a saucepan with olive oil on medium-low heat and cook the green bell pepper and onion in hot oil until they are soft, roughly 5 minutes. Add the garlic and cook for 3 more minutes. Stir in paprika, salt, cumin, rice, black beans, and water, then add bay leave. Allow it to come to a boil and cover pan with a tight-fitting lid. Turn the heat down to low and cook until the rice becomes tender and the moisture is absorbed, around 50-60 minutes. Take out the bay leaf and discard.

- As the rice cooks, mix together olive oil, lime juice, jalapeno pepper, cilantro, green onion, red bell pepper, and mango in a big bowl, then keep refrigerated for a minimum of 30 minutes.
- Heat a big pan on medium-high heat and in hot pan, cook while stirring the beef with paprika, oregano, red pepper flakes, onion powder, garlic powder, cumin, and chili powder until crumbly and brown, 5-7 minutes. Drain and throw away grease.
- Stir the mango salsa before you serve along with the seasoned ground beef, tortillas, black beans and rice as well as the taco fillings of your choice.

Nutrition Information

- Calories: 1154 calories;
- Total Fat: 32.8
- Sodium: 1637
- Total Carbohydrate: 167.2
- Cholesterol: 74
- Protein: 49.9

583. Beef And Bean Chimichangas

Serving: 8 | Prep: 15mins | Cook: 30mins | Ready in:

Ingredients

- 1 pound lean ground beef
- 3/4 cup chopped onion
- 3/4 cup diced green bell pepper
- 1 1/2 cups whole kernel corn
- 2 cups taco sauce
- 2 teaspoons chili powder

- 1 teaspoon garlic salt
- 1 teaspoon ground cumin
- 1 (16 ounce) can refried beans
- 8 (12 inch) flour tortillas
- 1 (16 ounce) package shredded Monterey Jack cheese
- 1 tablespoon butter, melted
- shredded lettuce
- 1 tomato, diced

Direction

- Start preheating the oven to 350°F (175°C).
- In a frying pan, brown ground beef over medium-high heat. Strain excess fat, and add corn, bell pepper, and onion. Cook until the vegetables are soft, about another 5 minutes. Mix in taco sauce, and use cumin, garlic salt, and chili powder to season, whisking until combined. Cook until fully heated, and then take away from heat and put aside.
- Open the can of beans, and spread onto each tortilla with the beans in a thin layer. Down the middle, spoon the beef mixture, and then put the amount of shredded cheese you like on top. Roll the tortillas up, and put them on a cookie sheet with the seam-side turning down. Brush melted butter over the tortillas.
- Bake in the preheated oven until turning golden brown, about 30-35 minutes. Enjoy with tomato and lettuce.

Nutrition Information

- Calories: 821 calories;
- Total Fat: 36
- Sodium: 1855
- Total Carbohydrate: 83.6
- Cholesterol: 97
- Protein: 40.1

584. Beefy Cheesy Pasta

Serving: 4 | Prep: 5mins | Cook: 20mins | Ready in:

Ingredients

- 1/2 pound lean ground beef
- 1 onion, diced
- 1/4 cup soy sauce
- 1 clove garlic, minced
- 5 cups rotelle pasta
- 1/4 cup milk
- 1 tablespoon butter
- 5 slices processed American cheese

Direction

- In a big frying pan, cook garlic, soy sauce, onion, and beef over medium heat until the juices from beef run clear and brown.
- As the beef cooks, boil lightly salted water in a big pot. Put in pasta and cook until al dente, about 8-10 minutes; strain.
- Put the cooked pasta back into its pot on low heat; mix in butter and milk. Mix in the beef mixture until blended thoroughly. Mix in cheese slices, one each time, until melted. Enjoy at once.

Nutrition Information

- Calories: 551 calories;
- Cholesterol: 76
- Protein: 29
- Total Fat: 23.7
- Sodium: 1492
- Total Carbohydrate: 56.5

585.　　Beefy Oven Packets

Serving: 5 | Prep: 10mins | Cook: 1hours | Ready in:

Ingredients

- 1 pound ground beef
- 1 (15.25 ounce) can whole kernel corn
- 1 (15 ounce) can green beans
- 2 (4 ounce) jars mushrooms, drained
- 1 (16 ounce) jar processed cheese sauce

- salt and pepper to taste

Direction

- Preheat the oven to 175 degrees C (350 degrees F).
- Chop the square pieces out of the aluminum foil. Shape the beef into small, round flat hamburgers and arrange one (that is seasoned to taste) onto each of the squares. Into each burger, put a bit of mushrooms, beans, corn and one spoonful of cheese sauce. Fold the foil over so that nothing is leaked while baking.
- Bake in preheated oven for 60 minutes.

Nutrition Information

- Calories: 522 calories;
- Total Fat: 32.9
- Sodium: 2191
- Total Carbohydrate: 29.4
- Cholesterol: 122
- Protein: 29

586.　　Beer Burgers

Serving: 4 | Prep: 15mins | Cook: 10mins | Ready in:

Ingredients

- 1 pound ground beef
- 1 small onion, finely chopped
- 3 cloves garlic, minced
- 1 tablespoon Worcestershire sauce
- 1 teaspoon salt
- 1/4 teaspoon ground black pepper
- 1/4 cup beer

Direction

- Preheat the outdoor grill for medium-high heat and grease grate lightly with oil.
- In a bowl, combine the pepper, salt, Worcestershire sauce, garlic, onion and

ground beef. Stir in the beer till sucked up by the meat mixture. Shape into patties.

- On the prepped grill, cook till the burgers reaches your wished degree of doneness, approximately 5 minutes each side for well done. An inserted instant-read thermometer into the middle should register 70 °C or 160 °F.

Nutrition Information

- Calories: 226 calories;
- Protein: 19.5
- Total Fat: 13.7
- Sodium: 690
- Total Carbohydrate: 3.8
- Cholesterol: 71

---

587. Bekki's Mexican Egg Rolls

Serving: 10 | Prep: 20mins | Cook: 30mins | Ready in:

Ingredients

- 2 tablespoons vegetable oil
- 1 pound ground beef
- 1 large onion, chopped
- 5 cloves garlic, minced
- 1 red bell pepper, chopped
- 1 (1 ounce) package taco seasoning
- 1 (8 ounce) jar taco sauce
- 4 (16 ounce) packages egg roll wrappers
- 1 (1 pound) loaf processed cheese food (i.e. Velveeta®), cut into 1/4 inch thick slices
- 2 egg whites, lightly beaten
- 2 quarts canola oil

Direction

- In a big skillet, put in the ground beef and vegetable oil then cook the beef over medium-high heat until the beef meat is no longer pink inside and browned on all sides. Lower the heat to medium. Put in the bell pepper, onion

and garlic and sauté for about 5 minutes until the vegetables are soft. Add in the taco sauce and taco seasoning. Continue to stir-fry the mixture for 5 more minutes or until the sauce has started bubbling.

- Put 1 egg roll wrapper on a clean, flat surface with a corner pointing at you. Put 1 tablespoon of meat mixture in the middle of the egg wrapper and top off with a slice of cheese. Fold the corner pointing at you over the meat mixture and roll over 1 1/2 times. Fold in the 2 opposite side corners towards the center and continue rolling the wrapper until the side corners are tucked in. Dip two of your fingers in the egg whites and brush it on the last corner to help seal the roll. Do the same steps again with 1 more egg roll wrapper. Let the egg roll sit shortly on the sealed last corner until the egg white dries and the last corner stays in place.
- If the egg rolls are not yet going to be served, preheat the oven at 325°F (165°C). Put paper towels on the bottom of a heatproof dish.
- In a big wok, put in the canola oil and heat up over medium-high heat. Once the oil is glistening, gently slide 2-3 egg rolls into the wok. Fry the egg rolls for 30 seconds to 1 minute until the wrappers turn golden brown in color and have bubbled slightly. Use a strainer or slotted spoon to remove the fried egg rolls from the wok. Put the egg rolls in the prepared heatproof dish then put it inside the preheated oven and remove after 15 minutes or lower the oven's temperature. Continue cooking the rest of the egg rolls.

Nutrition Information

- Calories: 980 calories;
- Total Carbohydrate: 113.3
- Cholesterol: 80
- Protein: 34.4
- Total Fat: 41.7
- Sodium: 1972

588. Best Burgers Yet

Serving: 8 | Prep: 15mins | Cook: 15mins | Ready in:

Ingredients

- 1 pound ground beef
- 1 pound ground pork
- 1 tablespoon lard
- 2 small shallots, minced
- 3 cloves garlic, minced
- salt and ground black pepper to taste

Direction

- Use 2 spoons to mix ground pork and ground beef in a bowl.
- Heat lard in a skillet on medium heat; mix and cook garlic and shallots for 3-5 minutes till tender and fragrant. Put shallot mixture in meat mixture; season with black pepper and salt. Shape mixture to patties; try to handle mixture as little as you can.
- Preheat the outdoor grill to medium high heat; oil the grate lightly.
- On the preheated grill, grill hamburgers, 5 minutes per side/till desired doneness is reached. An instant-read thermometer inserted in middle should read at least 70°C/160°F.

Nutrition Information

- Calories: 256 calories;
- Cholesterol: 73
- Protein: 19.6
- Total Fat: 18.6
- Sodium: 82
- Total Carbohydrate: 1.2

589. Best Damn Chili

Serving: 12 | Prep: 35mins | Cook: 2hours15mins | Ready in:

Ingredients

- 4 tablespoons olive oil
- 1 yellow onion, chopped
- 1 red bell pepper, chopped
- 1 Anaheim chile pepper, chopped
- 2 red jalapeno pepper, chopped
- 4 garlic cloves, minced
- 2 1/2 pounds lean ground beef
- 1/4 cup Worcestershire sauce
- 1 pinch garlic powder, or to taste
- 2 beef bouillon cubes
- 1 (12 fluid ounce) can or bottle light beer (such as Coors®)
- 1 (28 ounce) can crushed San Marzano tomatoes
- 1 (14.5 ounce) can fire-roasted diced tomatoes
- 1 (12 ounce) can tomato paste
- 1/2 cup white wine
- 2 tablespoons chili powder
- 2 tablespoons ground cumin
- 1 tablespoon brown sugar
- 1 tablespoon chipotle pepper sauce
- 2 1/2 teaspoons dried basil
- 1 1/2 teaspoons smoked paprika
- 1 teaspoon salt
- 1/2 teaspoon dried oregano
- 1/2 teaspoon ground black pepper
- 2 (16 ounce) cans dark red kidney beans (such as Bush's®)
- 1 cup sour cream
- 3 tablespoons chopped fresh cilantro
- 1/2 teaspoon ground cumin

Direction

- In a big pot, heat oil over medium heat; in hot oil, cook and mix the garlic, jalapeno peppers, Anaheim pepper, bell pepper and onion till softened.
- Meantime, over medium-high heat, heat a big skillet. In hot skillet, cook and mix beef for 5 to

7 minutes till crumbly and browned; put garlic powder and Worcestershire sauce. Mash bouillon cubes on top of beef and put beer. Keep cooking for 3 minutes, scratching up any browned bits from the base of skillet, till liquid is hot. Into the pepper mixture, mix the beef mixture.

- To beef mixture, mix wine, tomato paste, diced tomatoes and crushed tomatoes. Put black pepper, oregano, salt, paprika, basil, pepper sauce, brown sugar, 2 tablespoons cumin and chili powder to season. Boil and turn heat to medium-low. Put cover and let simmer for 90 minutes till vegetables and meat are very soft and flavors have established in chili, mixing from time to time.
- Into the beef and vegetables, mix kidney beans. Keep simmering for 30 minutes longer till beans are hot.
- In a food processor, process remaining 1/2 teaspoon cumin, cilantro and sour cream till smooth. Serve sour cream mixture together with chili.

Nutrition Information

- Calories: 406 calories;
- Cholesterol: 74
- Protein: 25.2
- Total Fat: 21.1
- Sodium: 1014
- Total Carbohydrate: 27.6

---

590.   Best Hamburger Ever

Serving: 4 | Prep: 10mins | Cook: 20mins | Ready in:

Ingredients

- 1 1/2 pounds lean ground beef
- 1/2 onion, finely chopped
- 1/2 cup shredded Colby Jack or Cheddar cheese
- 1 teaspoon soy sauce

- 1 teaspoon Worcestershire sauce
- 1 egg
- 1 (1 ounce) envelope dry onion soup mix
- 1 clove garlic, minced
- 1 tablespoon garlic powder
- 1 teaspoon dried parsley
- 1 teaspoon dried basil
- 1 teaspoon dried oregano
- 1/2 teaspoon crushed dried rosemary
- salt and pepper to taste

Direction

- Preheat the grill for high heat.
- Combine the pepper, salt, rosemary, oregano, basil, parsley, garlic powder, garlic, onion soup mix, egg, Worcestershire sauce, soy sauce, cheese, onion and ground beef in a big bowl. Shape into 4 patties.
- On the hot grill, grill the patties till well done, about 5 minutes each side. Serve on buns with desire condiments.

Nutrition Information

- Calories: 445 calories;
- Cholesterol: 174
- Protein: 39
- Total Fat: 27.5
- Sodium: 967
- Total Carbohydrate: 8.8

---

591.   Best Low Carb Keto Meatballs

Serving: 6 | Prep: 15mins | Cook: 35mins | Ready in:

Ingredients

- 1 1/2 pounds ground beef
- 1 egg
- 2 tablespoons grated Parmesan cheese
- 1 tablespoon flaxseed meal
- 1 teaspoon dried oregano

- salt and ground black pepper to taste
- 1 tablespoon olive oil
- 1 (14 ounce) can tomato sauce

Direction

- In a bowl, mix the pepper, salt, oregano, flaxseed, Parmesan cheese, egg and ground beef, then stir until it is well blended. Roll the mixture into golf ball size meatballs.
- In a big frypan, heat the olive oil on medium heat, then add the meatballs. Let it cook for about 5 minutes per side until it turns brown. Over the meatballs, pour the tomato sauce and let it simmer for 25-30 minutes.

Nutrition Information

- Calories: 301 calories;
- Sodium: 476
- Total Carbohydrate: 4.2
- Cholesterol: 102
- Protein: 21.5
- Total Fat: 21.8

592.   Bierox Casserole

Serving: 6 | Prep: 30mins | Cook: 15mins | Ready in:

Ingredients

- 1/2 medium head cabbage, cored and shredded
- 1 pound ground beef
- 1 onion, chopped
- 1 clove chopped fresh garlic
- 1 (10 ounce) can refrigerated crescent roll dough
- 1 (1 pound) loaf processed cheese food, cubed
- salt and pepper to taste

Direction

- Set the oven to 350°F (175°C) and start preheating.

- Place ground beef and cabbage into a large skillet over medium heat. Cook while stirring to break beef into crumbles until browned evenly and cabbage becomes tender. Drain off excess grease; stir in processes cheese, garlic and onion. Spoon into a 9x13 inch baking dish. Unroll crescent roll dough; arrange over the dish. Pinch seams together to completely cover.
- Bake in the prepared oven for 15 minutes, or until top is puffed and browned.

Nutrition Information

- Calories: 591 calories;
- Total Fat: 37.8
- Sodium: 1369
- Total Carbohydrate: 30.4
- Cholesterol: 106
- Protein: 30.9

593.   Bierrocks II

Serving: 6 | Prep: 40mins | Cook: 20mins | Ready in:

Ingredients

- 1/2 pound lean ground beef
- 1 cup onions, chopped
- 3 cups cabbage, chopped
- 1 teaspoon salt
- 1 teaspoon ground black pepper
- 1 cup sharp Cheddar cheese, shredded
- 1 (1 pound) loaf frozen bread dough, thawed

Direction

- Preheat the oven to 175 ° C or 350 ° F.
- Let meat cook in a big skillet on moderate heat till browned. Mix in cabbage and onions; put on cover and let cook for 15 minutes. Take off from heat and mix in cheese, pepper and salt; cool.

- Roll dough into approximately quarter-inch thick. Slice into six squares and on every square, place meat filling. Press dough together and put on cookie sheets, seam side facing down. Allow the dough to rise for 20 minutes, then in oven, bake till brown, for 20 minutes.

Nutrition Information

- Calories: 398 calories;
- Total Fat: 15.3
- Sodium: 981
- Total Carbohydrate: 41.5
- Cholesterol: 49
- Protein: 21.3

594. Big Bad Burgers

Serving: 4 | Prep: 20mins | Cook: 25mins | Ready in:

Ingredients

- 1 tablespoon butter
- 1/2 onion, sliced
- 4 fresh mushrooms, sliced
- 1 tablespoon brown sugar
- 1 pound ground beef
- 1 egg
- 1/2 cup dry bread crumbs
- 2 tablespoons prepared horseradish
- 2 tablespoons steak sauce
- 2 tablespoons Worcestershire sauce
- 2 cloves garlic, chopped
- 2 tablespoons dried minced onion
- salt and ground black pepper to taste
- 4 slices pepperjack cheese
- 6 slices cooked bacon, cut into halves
- 1/4 cup guacamole, or to taste

Direction

- Preheat an outdoor grill to high heat and lightly grease the grate.

- In a skillet, melt butter over medium-low heat. Sauté mushrooms and onion in melted butter for 10 to 15 minutes until onions are very soft and starting to brown. Sprinkle with brown sugar over the mixture; continue to cook for 5 to 10 minutes longer until onions caramelize. Turn off the heat and put to one side.
- In a bowl, combine black pepper, salt, dried onion, garlic, Worcestershire sauce, steak sauce, horseradish, bread crumbs, egg, and ground beef; form into 4 patties, about 1/2 inch in thickness and 6 inches wide.
- Cook burgers on the preheated grill, about 3 minutes on each side, until fully browned. Lower the heat to medium and cook the burgers on each side for 3 more minutes, adding a slice of pepper jack cheese atop each burger during the last minutes of grilling.
- Top each burger with 1/4 of the mushroom and onion mixture, 3 pieces of bacon, and 1 tablespoon guacamole. Serve

Nutrition Information

- Calories: 559 calories;
- Total Fat: 36.2
- Sodium: 844
- Total Carbohydrate: 24.2
- Cholesterol: 161
- Protein: 33.7

595. Big Mac® Clone

Serving: 2 | Prep: 15mins | Cook: 14mins | Ready in:

Ingredients

- 2/3 pound ground beef (85% lean)
- 2 cups mayonnaise
- 2 tablespoons prepared yellow mustard
- 2 tablespoons sweet pickle relish
- 1 1/2 teaspoons white wine vinegar, or more to taste
- 1 teaspoon onion powder

- 1 teaspoon garlic powder
- 1 teaspoon ground paprika
- 4 hamburger bun bottoms
- 2 hamburger bun tops
- 2 tablespoons minced onion, or to taste
- 1/2 cup shredded lettuce, or to taste
- 2 tablespoons dill pickle slices, or to taste
- 2 slices American cheese
- salt and ground black pepper to taste

Direction

- Form ground beef in four flat burger patties that will easy sit in hamburger buns. Put patties on a tray with wax paper. Put inside freezer.
- In a bowl, mix paprika, garlic powder, onion powder, white wine vinegar, pickle relish, mustard and mayonnaise to make the sauce. Put inside refrigerator 10 minutes.
- Take big skillet and heat on medium heat. Toast the buns, in batches, for 1-2 minutes until light golden.
- On two bottom buns, spread a bit of sauce, 1 tablespoon of minced onion, two tablespoons of lettuce and pickles. On the remaining bottom buns, spread a little sauce and left 1 tablespoon of minced onion, two tablespoons of lettuce and American cheese.
- Sprinkle salt and pepper on the patties to season; then cook 2 at a time in hot skillet for 3-4 minutes a side until browned. Put one cooked patty over each bottom bun and cover with top buns.

Nutrition Information

- Calories: 2395 calories;
- Total Fat: 208.6
- Sodium: 2986
- Total Carbohydrate: 82.6
- Cholesterol: 218
- Protein: 51.7

596.   Big Smokey Burgers

Serving: 6 | Prep: 25mins | Cook: 10mins | Ready in:

Ingredients

- 2 pounds ground beef sirloin
- 1/2 onion, grated
- 1 tablespoon grill seasoning
- 1 tablespoon liquid smoke flavoring
- 2 tablespoons Worcestershire sauce
- 2 tablespoons minced garlic
- 1 tablespoon adobo sauce from canned chipotle peppers
- 1 chipotle chile in adobo sauce, chopped
- salt and pepper to taste
- 6 (1 ounce) slices sharp Cheddar cheese (optional)
- 6 hamburger buns

Direction

- Preheat outdoor grill to medium high heat.
- Mix chipotle pepper, adobo sauce, garlic, Worcestershire sauce, liquid smoke, grill seasoning, onion and ground sirloin in a big bowl; shape mixture to 6 patties then season with pepper and salt.
- On preheated grill, cook burgers till not pink anymore in the middle. Put cheddar cheese slice over each burger a minute before they finish cooking. Put burgers over buns; serve.

Nutrition Information

- Calories: 537 calories;
- Total Fat: 29.7
- Sodium: 1035
- Total Carbohydrate: 26.6
- Cholesterol: 121
- Protein: 38.7

597. Biggest Bestest Burger

Serving: 6 | Prep: 20mins | Cook: 20mins | Ready in:

Ingredients

- 2 pounds ground beef
- 1 onion, chopped
- 1 teaspoon salt
- 1 teaspoon ground black pepper
- 1 teaspoon dried basil
- 1/4 cup Italian seasoned bread crumbs
- 1 tablespoon grated Parmesan cheese
- 1/3 cup teriyaki sauce
- 6 slices American cheese
- 6 onion rolls

Direction

- Preheat oven to broil.
- Combine basil, ground black pepper, salt, onion and ground beef in a large bowl; stir together to well. Add teriyaki sauce, cheese, and bread crumbs. Mix well. Divide into 4 to 6 large, round balls.
- Arrange hamburger balls on a broiler pan, evenly spaced. Press down each ball into perfectly round patty using either a spatula or your palm.
- Broil for 8 minutes; flip over each patty; broil for another 8 minutes until outside of each patty is almost burnt.
- Put off the heat; top each patty with cheese slices. Once cheese is melted, take burgers out of the oven and serve on onion rolls.

Nutrition Information

- Calories: 576 calories;
- Total Fat: 30.1
- Sodium: 1862
- Total Carbohydrate: 33.5
- Cholesterol: 122
- Protein: 40

598. Black Bean Pepperpot Soup

Serving: 16 | Prep: 20mins | Cook: 35mins | Ready in:

Ingredients

- 1 pound ground beef
- 6 cups beef stock
- 2 cups water
- 2 cups black beans, rinsed and drained
- 1 sweet potato, peeled and chopped
- 1 carrot, peeled and chopped
- 1 cup salsa
- 1/2 cup chopped onion
- 1/2 cup chopped green bell pepper
- 2 jalapeno peppers, seeded and chopped
- 1 tablespoon taco seasoning
- 1 tablespoon salt
- 1 tablespoon browning sauce (such as Kitchen Bouquet®)
- 2 teaspoons adobo seasoning
- 2 bay leaves

Direction

- Over medium-high heat, heat a large pot. In the hot skillet, cook and stir the beef for 5-7 minutes, until crumbly and browned; drain and get rid of the grease.
- In the pot with the beef, mix bay leaves, adobo seasoning, browning sauce, salt, taco seasoning, jalapeno pepper, bell pepper, onion, salsa, carrot, sweet potato, black beans, water and beef stock; bring to a boil, lower the heat to medium-low, and cook for half an hour, till the vegetables are tender.

Nutrition Information

- Calories: 122 calories;
- Protein: 8.8
- Total Fat: 3.9
- Sodium: 753
- Total Carbohydrate: 12.6
- Cholesterol: 17

599. Blue Cheese, Spinach Meat Loaf Muffins

Serving: 6 | Prep: 15mins | Cook: 30mins | Ready in:

Ingredients

- 1 1/2 pounds lean ground beef
- 3/4 cup crumbled blue cheese
- 1/2 cup diced onion
- 1/2 cup Italian bread crumbs
- 1/2 cup chopped fresh spinach
- 2 eggs
- 2 tablespoons Worcestershire sauce

Direction

- Start preheating oven to 375°F (190°C). Spray a large muffin pan with the cooking spray.
- In a large bowl, combine Worcestershire sauce, eggs, spinach, bread crumbs, onion, blue cheese and ground beef until well blended. Evenly divide meat mixture into prepared muffin pan.
- Bake in prepared oven for half an hour or until no longer pink in middle. An instant-read thermometer should register at least 160°F (70°C) when inserted into middle.

Nutrition Information

- Calories: 351 calories;
- Total Fat: 20.9
- Sodium: 564
- Total Carbohydrate: 9.9
- Cholesterol: 154
- Protein: 29.4

600. Breaded Hamburgers

Serving: 4 | Prep: 10mins | Cook: 30mins | Ready in:

Ingredients

- 1 pound ground beef
- 1/4 teaspoon salt, or to taste
- 1/2 teaspoon ground black pepper, or to taste
- 1/2 teaspoon garlic powder, or to taste
- 2 teaspoons Worcestershire sauce
- 2 eggs
- 1 1/2 cups bread crumbs
- 1/4 cup vegetable oil for frying
- 1 small onion, sliced into rings

Direction

- Set oven to 350°F (175°C) to preheat.
- Beat eggs together in a small bowl. Spread bread crumbs on a plate. Combine ground beef with Worcestershire sauce, garlic powder, pepper, and salt in a medium bowl. Shape mixture into 4 patties. Immerse patties into beaten eggs, the roll in bread crumbs until evenly coated.
- In a large skillet over medium-high heat, heat oil. Cook breaded hamburgers until evenly browned, about 2 minutes on each side.
- Arrange onion rings in the bottom of a casserole dish or baking dish. Pour in water just enough to cover the bottom, not the onion. Gently position burgers atop onions without touching water in the baking dish.
- Bake in the preheated oven for 25 to 30 minutes until burgers are well-done.

Nutrition Information

- Calories: 420 calories;
- Sodium: 571
- Total Carbohydrate: 32
- Cholesterol: 162
- Protein: 27.8
- Total Fat: 19.3

601.   Bronco Burger

Serving: 8 | Prep: 10mins | Cook: 10mins | Ready in:

Ingredients

- 5 fresh jalapeno peppers
- 4 pounds ground beef
- salt and pepper to taste
- 1 egg
- 1/4 cup steak sauce, (e.g. Heinz 57)
- 1/4 cup minced white onion
- 1 teaspoon hot pepper sauce (e.g. Tabasco™)
- 1 pinch dried oregano
- 1 tablespoon Worcestershire sauce
- 1 teaspoon garlic salt
- 1/4 cup crushed Fritos® corn chips
- 8 large potato hamburger buns
- 8 slices pepperjack cheese

Direction

- Preheat grill to high heat. When grill is hot, roast jalapeno peppers until all sides are blackened. Put in a plastic bag. Let sweat and loosen the blackened skin. Rub off skin, seed (optional), then chop.
- Mix Fritos, garlic salt, Worcestershire sauce, oregano, hot pepper sauce, onion, egg, steak sauce, pepper, salt, ground beef and chopped jalapeno with your hands in a big bowl. Distribute to 8 balls. Flatten to patties.
- Grill patties, flipping once, for 10-15 minutes until well done. I always drink with one beer. Then flip, drink another beer. Take off grill. Put on buns. Top each with a Pepper jack cheese slice. Pig out.

Nutrition Information

- Calories: 681 calories;
- Cholesterol: 196
- Protein: 49.3
- Total Fat: 40.3
- Sodium: 936
- Total Carbohydrate: 27.3

602.   Bulgogi Meatballs

Serving: 45 | Prep: 30mins | Cook: 20mins | Ready in:

Ingredients

- 1/4 cup low-sodium soy sauce
- 1/4 Asian pear, grated
- 3 tablespoons dark brown sugar
- 3 tablespoons minced green onions
- 2 tablespoons toasted sesame oil
- 2 tablespoons minced garlic
- 2 teaspoons fish sauce
- 3/4 teaspoon freshly ground black pepper
- 1 pound ground beef
- 1 pound ground pork
- 1/2 cup panko bread crumbs
- 1 large egg, lightly beaten
- 2 tablespoons toasted sesame seeds (optional)

Direction

- In a large bowl, whisk together pepper, fish sauce, garlic, sesame oil, green onions, brown sugar, Asian pear and soy sauce. Add egg, bread crumbs, beef, and pork. Combine until mixed. Avoid overmixing. Cover the bowl and chill for half an hour or up to two hours.
- Preheat an oven to 220 degrees C (425 degrees F).
- Shape the meat mixture into around 45 mini meatballs. Place into two baking sheets.
- Bake for 18 to 20 minutes in the prepared oven until cooked through but still tender and turned golden. Flip the baking sheets when halfway through cooking. Decorate with toasted sesame seeds.

Nutrition Information

- Calories: 56 calories;
- Total Carbohydrate: 1.4
- Cholesterol: 17
- Total Fat: 3.8
- Protein: 3.7

- Sodium: 75

Serving: 12 | Prep: | Cook: | Ready in:

Ingredients

- 2 (4 ounce) packages Idahoan® Bacon & Cheddar Chipotle Flavored Mashed Potatoes
- 1/4 cup olive oil
- 6 cloves garlic, minced
- 1 large yellow onion, chopped
- 2 red bell peppers, diced
- 2 green bell peppers, diced
- 4 pounds ground beef*
- 6 (19 ounce) cans diced tomatoes
- 2 (10 ounce) cans RO*TEL Diced Tomatoes & Green Chilies
- 4 (15 ounce) cans kidney beans, drained and rinsed
- 2 (15 ounce) cans black beans, drained and rinsed

Direction

- Cook peppers, onion, and garlic in olive oil until the onions are translucent.
- Stir in meat and cook until evenly browned.
- Add the tomatoes and stir until the mixture is hot. Mix in packages of tomatoes.
- Mix thoroughly, stir in beans and simmer over moderate heat for at least 60 minutes.
- Top this chili with a large dollop of Fiesta Dip and serve it to your beloved guests.

Nutrition Information

- Calories: 556 calories;
- Total Fat: 23.9
- Sodium: 1270
- Total Carbohydrate: 43.6
- Cholesterol: 95
- Protein: 38.3

Serving: 4 | Prep: 20mins | Cook: 7hours | Ready in:

Ingredients

- 1 pound lean ground beef
- 1 onion, chopped
- 1 (15 ounce) can ranch-style beans
- 1/4 teaspoon ground cumin
- 3 cloves garlic, minced
- 2 1/2 cups chopped cabbage
- 1 green bell pepper, chopped
- 1 (14.5 ounce) can stewed tomatoes, with liquid
- 2 stalks celery, chopped
- 1/4 cup picante sauce
- 1 cup water
- salt to taste
- freshly ground pepper, to taste

Direction

- Brown ground beef with onion on medium heat in the skillet. Drain off fat.
- In the crock pot, mix green pepper, cabbage, garlic, cumin, and ranch-style beans. Mix in beef mixture, water, picante sauce, celery, and stewed tomatoes. Season to taste with pepper and salt.
- Keep it covered and cook for 6 - 8 hours.

Nutrition Information

- Calories: 374 calories;
- Protein: 29.9
- Total Fat: 14.3
- Sodium: 914
- Total Carbohydrate: 31.2
- Cholesterol: 74

605.   Cabbage Rolls

Serving: 12 | Prep: 30mins | Cook: 2hours | Ready in:

Ingredients

- 2 cups uncooked long-grain rice
- 4 cups water
- 2 large heads savoy cabbage
- 1 cup water
- 2 onions, chopped
- 3 tablespoons butter
- 3/4 cup uncooked long-grain rice
- 1 pound extra-lean ground beef
- 1/2 pound pork sausage
- 4 cloves garlic, minced
- 2 teaspoons dried dill weed
- 3/4 teaspoon salt
- 1/2 teaspoon ground black pepper
- 1/2 teaspoon white sugar
- 1 (26 ounce) can condensed tomato soup
- 1 (28 ounce) can whole peeled tomatoes, with liquid
- 8 bay leaves

Direction

- Rinse the rice thoroughly. Mix together 4 cups of water and 2 cups of rice in a medium saucepan, then bring to a boil. Lower heat, then cover and simmer until water is absorbed entirely, about 20 minutes.
- In the meantime, use a thin and long knife to get rid of the core from the cabbages. Put cabbage in a microwave proof container with a lid with core side down. Add 1/2 cup of water to the container with cabbage, then cover and microwave on high setting (at full power) about 10 minutes. Turn the cabbage over carefully and cook with a cover for more 10 minutes. Once cabbage is cooked, allow it to sit until cool enough to handle. Carefully separate leaves and get rid of any tough ribs. Do the same process to cook the second cabbage.
- Split chopped onions in half, then sauté one half of onions in 3 tbsp. butter. Cook just until

translucent (without browning). Combine sugar, black pepper, salt, dill weed, garlic, pork sausage, ground beef, uncooked and cooked rice, cooked and uncooked onions together, then mix well to blend.
- Scoop approximately 2 tbsp. of the mixture onto each leaf of cabbage, then bring one end of leaf over the mixture, roll and tuck ends in to avoid falling out any filling.
- Set the oven to 175°C (350°F). Put some remaining cabbage leaves in the bottom of each two 9"x13" casserole dishes. Place cabbage rolls on the cabbage leaves in one single layer tight, against each other.
- Process tomatoes and condensed tomato soup in a blender or food processor. Pour over the cabbage rolls with tomato mixture just enough to cover. Put on top of the sauce in every dish with 4 bay leaves, then use aluminum foil to cover each dish tightly.
- In the preheated oven, bake at 175°C (350°F) for 2 hours. When cooked, take the dishes out of the oven and allow to cool about 15 minutes before taking off aluminum foil. Serve hot.

Nutrition Information

- Calories: 441 calories;
- Total Carbohydrate: 59.5
- Cholesterol: 43
- Protein: 18
- Total Fat: 16
- Sodium: 801

606.   Cajun Appetizer Meatballs

Serving: 4 | Prep: 15mins | Cook: 40mins | Ready in:

Ingredients

- 1 pound lean ground beef
- 1 1/2 teaspoons hot pepper sauce
- 2 tablespoons Cajun seasoning

- 1 tablespoon Worcestershire sauce
- 1 tablespoon dried parsley
- 1/4 cup finely chopped onion
- 1/4 cup fresh bread crumbs
- 1/4 cup milk
- 1 egg
- 1/2 cup barbeque sauce
- 1/2 cup peach preserves

Direction

- Turn the oven to 350°F (175°C) to preheat. Lightly oil a medium-sized cookie sheet.
- Well combine egg, milk, breadcrumbs, onion, parsley, Worcestershire sauce, Cajun seasoning, hot pepper sauce, and ground beef in a big bowl.
- Shape the mixture into meatballs with the size of a golf ball and put on the prepared cookie sheet. Bake for 30-40 minutes in the preheated oven until the center is not pink anymore.
- Mix peach preserves and barbeque sauce together in a small bowl.
- Once the meatballs have done, put in a serving plate and add the barbeque sauce mixture to cover. Mix to blend.

Nutrition Information

- Calories: 504 calories;
- Total Carbohydrate: 45
- Cholesterol: 133
- Protein: 22.9
- Total Fat: 25.4
- Sodium: 1272

607.   Cajun Cabbage With Rice

Serving: 6 | Prep: 20mins | Cook: 1hours15mins | Ready in:

Ingredients

- 1 tablespoon vegetable oil

- 1 pound ground beef
- 1 green bell pepper, chopped
- 1 onion, chopped
- 2 cloves garlic, minced
- 1 (10 ounce) can diced tomatoes with mild green chilies, undrained
- 1 (8 ounce) can tomato sauce
- 1/2 cup long grain rice, uncooked
- 1 teaspoon salt
- 1/2 teaspoon dried basil
- 1/2 teaspoon dried oregano
- 1/4 teaspoon ground cayenne pepper
- 1/4 teaspoon ground white pepper
- 1/4 teaspoon ground black pepper
- 1 small head cabbage, chopped
- 1 cup shredded Colby cheese

Direction

- Preheat an oven to 175°C/350°F.
- In a big skillet, heat oil on medium heat. Brown garlic, onion, green pepper and beef for 8 minutes till veggies are soft and meat isn't pink then drain the liquid from the pan.
- Mix in black and white pepper (if desired add more pepper to taste), cayenne, oregano, basil, salt, rice, tomato sauce and tomatoes in. In a 9x12-in. ungreased baking pan, spread mixture. Put Colby cheese and cabbage on top.
- In preheated oven, bake for 65-75 minutes, covered, till rice is tender.

Nutrition Information

- Calories: 384 calories;
- Total Fat: 21.6
- Sodium: 850
- Total Carbohydrate: 26.9
- Cholesterol: 67
- Protein: 21.7

608.   Calico Bean Casserole

Serving: 6 | Prep: 20mins | Cook: 30mins | Ready in:

Ingredients

- 1 (15 ounce) can kidney beans, undrained
- 1 (16 ounce) can baked beans with pork
- 1 (15 ounce) can butter beans, undrained
- 1/2 cup ketchup
- 2 teaspoons white vinegar
- 1 tablespoon dry mustard
- 3/4 cup packed brown sugar
- 1 pound lean ground beef
- 4 ounces bacon, chopped
- 1/2 cup chopped onion
- salt to taste
- ground black pepper to taste

Direction

- Preheat oven to 350 degrees F (175 degrees C).
- Fry the ground beef, bacon and onion in a large skillet over medium heat until ground beef is no longer pink. Drain fat.
- Amalgamate the pork, kidney beans, baked beans and butter beans in a large mixing bowl. Stir in cooked beef mixture, ketchup, white vinegar, dry mustard, brown sugar and mix thoroughly. Season with salt and pepper to taste.
- Place the bean and meat mixture into a 9x13 inch baking dish. Cook in preheated oven for 30 to 40 minutes.

Nutrition Information

- Calories: 617 calories;
- Sodium: 1089
- Total Carbohydrate: 69.2
- Cholesterol: 75
- Protein: 27.6
- Total Fat: 26.1

---

609. Calico Beans

Serving: 8 | Prep: 10mins | Cook: 1hours15mins | Ready in:

Ingredients

- 1/2 cup bacon, chopped
- 1 pound lean ground beef
- 1 (15 ounce) can pork and beans
- 1 (15 ounce) can kidney beans, drained
- 1 (15 ounce) can butter beans
- 1 (15 ounce) can lima beans, drained
- 1/2 cup ketchup
- 1 cup packed brown sugar
- 1 cup chopped onion
- 3 tablespoons white wine vinegar
- 1 teaspoon mustard powder
- 1/2 cup chopped celery

Direction

- Put oven to heat to 350°F or 175°C.
- In a big and deep skillet, cook ground beef and bacon. Heat on medium until equally browned. Drain grease and put aside.
- Mix in a 4-qt. dish, celery, bacon, dry mustard, ground beef, vinegar, pork and beans, onion, kidney beans, ketchup, butter beans and lima beans.
- Place the cover on and let it bake for 60 minutes.

Nutrition Information

- Calories: 434 calories;
- Total Fat: 10
- Sodium: 953
- Total Carbohydrate: 66.6
- Cholesterol: 38
- Protein: 22.3

---

610. Camp David Spaghetti With Italian Sausage

Serving: 8 | Prep: 15mins | Cook: 1hours40mins | Ready in:

Ingredients

- 2 Italian sausage links, casings removed
- 1 pound lean ground beef
- 1 tablespoon olive oil
- 1 yellow onion, chopped
- 2 cloves garlic, chopped
- 1 (14.5 ounce) can whole peeled tomatoes
- 1 (15 ounce) can tomato sauce
- 1 teaspoon salt
- 1/4 teaspoon ground black pepper
- 1 teaspoon dried basil
- 1/4 cup chopped fresh oregano
- 1 bay leaf
- 1 (16 ounce) package uncooked spaghetti
- 1/2 cup grated Parmesan cheese

Direction

- Cut the sausages lengthwise, leaving them attached along one side. Spread them flat in a big skillet. Cook for about 15 minutes over medium heat, until the sausages are browned and cooked through, only flipping once. Take away from the skillet and put aside.
- In the skillet, put the garlic, onion, olive oil, and ground beef. Cook while stirring over medium heat until the beef is crumbly and browned and the onion is translucent, about 10 minutes. Drain all but reserve 2 tbsp. of the fat. Mix in the bay leaf, oregano, basil, pepper, salt, tomato sauce and tomatoes. Simmer without covering for an hour over low heat, stirring occasionally, until the flavors are blended. Take away the bay leaf.
- Set the oven at 175°C (350°F) to preheat. Boil a big pot of lightly salted water. Put in the pasta, cook while stirring occasionally for about 8-10 minutes, or until the pasta is soft. Drain and mix into the sauce.
- On oven-safe plates, place the hot pasta with sauce and put cooked, opened sausage on top. Scatter Parmesan cheese on top. Put the plates in the preheated oven and bake until the cheese melts and start to brown, about 5-10 minutes.

Nutrition Information

- Calories: 439 calories;
- Sodium: 985
- Total Carbohydrate: 47.5
- Cholesterol: 53
- Protein: 24.5
- Total Fat: 16.5

611. Cara's Creamy Stuffed Shells

Serving: 8 | Prep: 25mins | Cook: 25mins | Ready in:

Ingredients

- 1 (12 ounce) package jumbo pasta shells
- 3 pounds ground beef
- 2 eggs, lightly beaten
- 2 tablespoons olive oil
- 2 teaspoons minced garlic
- 2 teaspoons garlic salt
- 2 teaspoons parsley
- 1 (8 ounce) package cream cheese, at room temperature
- 1 1/2 (14 ounce) jars pasta sauce
- 1/2 cup freshly grated Romano cheese

Direction

- Boil a big pot of slightly salted water. In pot, add the shell pasta, allow to cook till al dente, about 8 to 10 minutes, and drain.
- Preheat an oven to 190 °C or 375 °F. Slightly oil a medium baking dish.
- In a skillet, put beef over moderate heat, and stir in parsley, garlic salt, garlic, oil and eggs. Cook till beef is equally brown. Turn onto a big bowl, and combine with a cup pasta sauce and cream cheese.
- Fill beef mixture into the cooked pasta shells, and set in the prepped baking dish. Cover equally with the rest of the sauce.
- In the prepped oven, bake till bubbly for 15 minutes. Scatter Romano cheese on top barely prior to serving.

Nutrition Information

- Calories: 698 calories;
- Sodium: 1045
- Total Carbohydrate: 43
- Cholesterol: 190
- Protein: 41.4
- Total Fat: 39

612. Caribbean Meat Pockets

Serving: 10 | Prep: 40mins | Cook: 1hours5mins | Ready in:

Ingredients

- Dough:
- 3 cups all-purpose flour
- 1 tablespoon curry powder
- 1 teaspoon salt
- 1 cup vegetable shortening
- 1 egg, beaten
- 3 tablespoons water
- Filling:
- 1/4 cup vegetable oil
- 1 onion, chopped
- 3 green onions, chopped
- 1 clove garlic, minced
- 2 tablespoons chopped pickled jalapeno peppers
- 1 pound ground beef
- 1 teaspoon dried thyme
- 2 teaspoons curry powder
- 1 teaspoon salt
- 1/2 teaspoon ground black pepper
- 1 1/2 cups water
- 1/2 cup bread crumbs

Direction

- In the mixing bowl, stir 1 tsp. of the salt, 1tbsp. of the curry powder and flour together. Stir in vegetable shortening till mixture looks like the cornmeal. Whisk in water and egg till dough is not crumbly anymore. Wrap using the

plastic wrap, and keep in the refrigerator when doing the preparation for filling.
- Heat vegetable oil on medium heat in the big skillet. Cook and stir jalapeno peppers, garlic, green onion and onion approximately 5 minutes till onion softens and turns translucent. Mix in ground beef, and cook approximately 15 minutes till becoming crumbly and brown. Drain off the redundant fat out of the pan, and then mix in 1.5 cups of the water, black pepper, 1 tsp. of the salt, 2 tsp. of the curry powder and thyme. Simmer, keep covered, and cook till water is evaporated. Move beef mixture into the food processor, drizzle in breadcrumbs, and blend till mixture turns into a paste.
- Preheat the oven to 200 degrees C (400 degrees F). Use parchment paper to line two baking sheets.
- Roll dough out on the lightly floured surface to just lower than a quarter-in. in thickness. Chop 20 6-in. circles from dough. Distribute beef mixture to 1/2 of circles, mounding in middle. Put unfilled circles on top of filling, and with the fork, seal edges closed. Arrange onto baking sheets.
- Bake in preheated oven approximately 25 minutes till becoming hot on the inside and golden brown.

Nutrition Information

- Calories: 488 calories;
- Total Fat: 32.7
- Sodium: 582
- Total Carbohydrate: 35.1
- Cholesterol: 47
- Protein: 13.2

613. Carol's Vermont Chili

Serving: 8 | Prep: 25mins | Cook: 1hours20mins | Ready in:

Ingredients

- 2 tablespoons olive oil
- 2 cloves minced garlic
- 1 large onion, coarsely chopped
- 1 red bell pepper, coarsely chopped
- 2 jalapeno peppers, seeded and sliced
- 1 (15 ounce) can tomato sauce
- 1 (28 ounce) can crushed tomatoes
- 3/4 cup maple syrup
- 1 (40 ounce) can kidney beans, drained
- 1 tablespoon coarse ground black pepper
- 2 tablespoons chili powder
- 4 pounds ground beef chuck
- salt to taste
- 2 (12 ounce) bottles beer (such as Heineken®), or as needed

Direction

- In a big pot, pour in olive oil and heat it at moderate heat. Add jalapeno peppers, red bell pepper, onion and garlic and cook them, stirring, for around 7 minutes until the onion becomes tender. Insert the kidney beans, maple syrup, crushed tomatoes and tomato sauce, followed by chilli powder and black pepper as seasoning. Lead the mixture to a boiling point. Lower the heat down to simmering point.
- Meanwhile, at a moderately high level of heat, add ground beef into a heated big skillet then scatter salt over the meat. Proceed with stirring and cooking until the meat has no hint of pink left in it anymore and is equally brown everywhere. Drain the extra grease off and throw it away. Together with 1 beer, mix the cooked beef into the chili. Leave it cooking for the next 60 minutes. During the process, stir regularly. Add salt to season it and 1 beer to get the liquid to the preferred consistency. Serve.

Nutrition Information

- Calories: 741 calories;
- Total Fat: 32.2

- Sodium: 865
- Total Carbohydrate: 59.2
- Cholesterol: 142
- Protein: 49.3

---

614.   Chad's Slow Cooker Taco Soup

Serving: 20 | Prep: 20mins | Cook: 8hours20mins | Ready in:

Ingredients

- 1 pound ground beef
- 1 pound bulk hot pork sausage
- 1 (28 ounce) can crushed tomatoes
- 1 (15.25 ounce) can whole kernel corn with red and green bell peppers (such as Mexicorn®), drained and rinsed
- 1 (14.5 ounce) can black beans, rinsed and drained
- 1 (14 ounce) can kidney beans, rinsed and drained
- 1 (1 ounce) package ranch dressing mix
- 1 (1 ounce) package taco seasoning mix
- 1 onion, chopped
- 1 green bell pepper, chopped
- 1 red bell pepper, chopped
- 1 (14.5 ounce) can diced tomatoes with green chile peppers (such as RO*TEL®), undrained
- 1/2 cup chili sauce
- 2 fresh jalapeno peppers, diced
- 1 (12 fluid ounce) can or bottle dark beer
- ground black pepper to taste

Direction

- In a large skillet, brown the ground beef completely over medium heat; let drain. Place into a slow cooker.
- In a big skillet, brown the sausage completely over medium heat; let drain. Place the beef to a slow cooker.
- Put black pepper, beer, jalapeno peppers, chili sauce, green chile peppers, diced tomatoes,

red bell pepper, green bell pepper, onion, taco seasoning mix, ranch dressing mix, kidney beans, black beans, corn, and crushed tomatoes in the slow cooker. Turn the heat of slow cooker to low and cook for 8 to 10 hours, or if you want, set the heat to high and cook for 4 to 6 hours.

Nutrition Information

- Calories: 195 calories;
- Total Fat: 8.1
- Sodium: 839
- Total Carbohydrate: 19.4
- Cholesterol: 27
- Protein: 10.9

615. Cheapskate Stew

Serving: 6 | Prep: 15mins | Cook: 45mins | Ready in:

Ingredients

- 1 1/2 pounds lean ground beef
- 1/2 onion, chopped
- 3 stalks celery, chopped
- 2 cups frozen mixed vegetables
- 2 cups water
- 3 carrots, chopped
- 2 cups cooked elbow macaroni
- 1 (15 ounce) can tomato sauce
- 1 1/2 teaspoons Italian seasoning
- salt to taste
- ground black pepper to taste

Direction

- Brown the hamburger meat with celery and onion. If it's fatty hamburger meat, drain.
- Put in carrots and water, then cook until carrots are starting to become tender. Cook for a fairly long time or the carrots will get crunchy.

- Add in Italian spices, tomato sauce, macaroni, and the remaining vegetables. Season with pepper and salt. Bring to a simmer until all ingredients get warm thoroughly and the flavors combine.

Nutrition Information

- Calories: 448 calories;
- Total Carbohydrate: 30.6
- Cholesterol: 85
- Protein: 26.1
- Total Fat: 24.5
- Sodium: 512

616. Cheddar Bacon Hamburgers With Horseradish

Serving: 4 | Prep: 10mins | Cook: 10mins | Ready in:

Ingredients

- 1 pound ground beef
- 1/2 cup shredded Cheddar cheese
- 1/2 cup bacon bits
- 2 tablespoons prepared horseradish
- 1/2 teaspoon garlic powder
- 1/2 teaspoon salt
- 1/2 teaspoon ground black pepper
- 4 hamburger buns

Direction

- Start preheating an outdoor grill on medium-high heat. Oil the grate lightly.
- In a large bowl, combine pepper, ground beef, salt, Cheddar cheese, garlic powder, bacon bits and horseradish. Equally separate into 4 parts and shape into patties.
- On the preheated grill, grill for 5 to 7 minutes per side, until patties are no longer pink in the center, They are well-done when an instant-read thermometer inserted into the center reads at least 70 degrees C (160 degrees F).

- Best served with hamburger buns.

Nutrition Information

- Calories: 584 calories;
- Protein: 32.6
- Total Fat: 39.7
- Sodium: 1125
- Total Carbohydrate: 22.7
- Cholesterol: 121

617.　　Cheese Vegetable Soup I

Serving: 5 | Prep: 20mins | Cook: 10mins | Ready in:

Ingredients

- 1 pound ground beef
- 1 (10 ounce) package frozen corn kernels
- 1 cup cubed potatoes
- 1 cup thinly sliced celery
- 1 cup sliced carrots
- 1/2 cup chopped onion
- 2 cups water
- 2 cubes beef bouillon cube
- 3/4 teaspoon hot pepper sauce
- 1 (16 ounce) jar processed cheese sauce

Direction

- Cook ground beef until evenly browned; drain well.
- Combine all ingredients (except cheese sauce) in a crock pot. Cook, covered for 8 to 10 hours over low heat.
- Mix in cheese sauce; stir well until incorporated.

Nutrition Information

- Calories: 621 calories;
- Sodium: 1935
- Total Carbohydrate: 29.4
- Cholesterol: 144

- Protein: 28.7
- Total Fat: 43.5

618.　　Cheese And Hamburger Macaroni

Serving: 4 | Prep: 10mins | Cook: 15mins | Ready in:

Ingredients

- 1/2 pound lean ground beef, or more to taste
- 1/2 small onion, minced
- 1 teaspoon garlic powder
- 1 teaspoon onion powder
- 1 pinch salt and ground black pepper to taste
- 2 cups water
- 2 cups elbow macaroni
- 8 ounces reduced-fat processed cheese food (such as Velveeta®), cut into small pieces
- 2 tablespoons reduced-fat sour cream, or more to taste

Direction

- Heat a big skillet on moderately high heat. Cook and stir together in the hot skillet with black pepper, salt, onion powder, garlic powder, onion and ground beef for 5-7 minutes, until crumbly and browned. Drain and get rid of grease.
- Turn the skillet back to burner on high heat. Put in water, then place a cover on and bring to a boil. Stir into the boiling water-ground beef mixture with macaroni, then cover and lower heat to moderate. Cook with a cover about 5 minutes. Stir, cover, and cook, for 5 minutes longer, until macaroni is soft.
- Stir into the ground beef-macaroni mixture with processed cheese food until melted. Take away from the heat and stir in sour cream.

Nutrition Information

- Calories: 449 calories;

- Cholesterol: 61
- Protein: 28.2
- Total Fat: 15.4
- Sodium: 930
- Total Carbohydrate: 47.9

---

619. Cheeseburger Meatloaf

Serving: 8 | Prep: 20mins | Cook: 1hours | Ready in:

Ingredients

- 2 pounds ground beef
- 3/4 cup fresh bread crumbs
- 1/2 cup minced onion
- 2 eggs, beaten
- 1 1/2 teaspoons salt
- 1 1/2 teaspoons ground black pepper
- 3 cups shredded Cheddar cheese

Direction

- Set oven to 175°C (350°F) and begin preheating.
- Stir pepper, salt, eggs, onion, bread crumbs and beef together in a big bowl, thoroughly combine. On wax paper, pat the mixture into a 14x18" rectangle. Sprinkle cheese on top of the mixture, leaving a 3/4" margin around the edges. Roll up jelly roll style to seal the filling and create a pinwheel loaf. Press beef in on both end enclose cheese. Transfer the loaf to a 10x15" baking dish.
- Bake for 60 minutes in the prepared oven, or until the temperature inside the meat loaf achieves 70°C (160°F).

Nutrition Information

- Calories: 410 calories;
- Sodium: 811
- Total Carbohydrate: 4
- Cholesterol: 162
- Protein: 31.7

- Total Fat: 29.1

---

620. Cheeseburger Noodle Casserole

Serving: 4 | Prep: 20mins | Cook: 45mins | Ready in:

Ingredients

- 1 pound ground beef
- 8 ounces spaghetti
- 1 (14.5 ounce) can peeled and diced tomatoes
- 1 packet dry onion soup mix
- 1 cup sour cream
- 1/2 teaspoon dried basil
- 1/4 teaspoon garlic powder
- salt and pepper to taste
- 1 cup shredded Cheddar cheese

Direction

- Set the oven at 350°F (175°C) and start preheating.
- Place a large skillet on medium-high heat; sauté in ground beef till browned, 5 minutes; strain any excess fat.
- Following the package directions, cook spaghetti properly; strain water.
- In a 2-qt. casserole, mix pepper, salt, garlic powder, basil, sour cream, onion soup mix, tomatoes, cooked spaghetti and the browned beef together. Combine properly.
- Cover the dish; bake for 15 minutes in the preheated oven. Sprinkle cheese over the top; keep baking without a cover for 15 more minutes.

Nutrition Information

- Calories: 824 calories;
- Total Carbohydrate: 49.4
- Cholesterol: 151
- Protein: 36
- Total Fat: 52.4

- Sodium: 588

621. Cheeseburger Soup I

Serving: 8 | Prep: 20mins | Cook: 30mins | Ready in:

Ingredients

- 1/2 pound ground beef
- 3/4 cup chopped onion
- 3/4 cup shredded carrots
- 3/4 cup chopped celery
- 1 teaspoon dried basil
- 1 teaspoon dried parsley
- 4 tablespoons butter
- 3 cups chicken broth
- 4 cups cubed potatoes
- 1/4 cup all-purpose flour
- 2 cups cubed Cheddar cheese
- 1 1/2 cups milk
- 1/4 cup sour cream

Direction

- Let a tablespoon of margarine and butter melt in a large pot over medium heat: stir and cook beef and vegetables until the beef turns brown.
- Stir in parsley and basil. Add potatoes and broth. Allow to boil and then allow to simmer for around 10-12 minutes until potatoes become tender.
- Let the remaining butter melt and stir in the flour. Stir in the milk until smooth.
- Pour slowly the milk mixture into the soup, stirring continuously. Allow to boil and turn down the heat to simmer. Stir in the cheese. Add the sour cream and heat through once the cheese melts. Don't boil.

Nutrition Information

- Calories: 411 calories;
- Protein: 18.9
- Total Fat: 27.3

622. Cheeseburger Stuffed Shells

Serving: 10 | Prep: 30mins | Cook: 1hours12mins | Ready in:

Ingredients

- 1 (12 ounce) box jumbo pasta shells
- 1 pound lean ground beef
- 1 small onion, chopped
- 2 teaspoons Worcestershire sauce
- 1 clove garlic, minced
- 1 (32 ounce) container ricotta cheese
- 1/2 cup shredded Cheddar cheese
- 1 egg
- 1/4 cup Parmesan cheese
- 1 tablespoon chopped fresh parsley
- 1/2 teaspoon garlic powder
- 1/2 teaspoon onion powder
- 1/2 teaspoon salt
- 1/4 teaspoon ground black pepper
- 1 (16 ounce) jar double Cheddar pasta sauce (such as Ragu®)
- 1/4 cup water
- 1 (14.5 ounce) can Italian-style diced tomatoes, drained
- 2 tablespoons shredded Cheddar cheese

Direction

- Boil a big pot of salted water. Put in the pasta shells; cook for 12 minutes, mixing from time to time, till soft but firm to the bite. Drain.
- Over moderately-high heat, heat a big skillet. Put in the garlic, Worcestershire sauce, onion and ground beef; cook and mix for 5 to 8 minutes till browned. Drain off the excess grease.
- Preheat the oven to 175 °C or 350 °F.

- In a big bowl, mix pepper, salt, onion powder, garlic powder, parsley, Parmesan cheese, egg, 1/2 cup Cheddar cheese, ricotta cheese and ground beef mixture. Fill 1 or 2 tablespoons of mixture, into each pasta shell.
- In a bowl, combine water and pasta sauce.
- In the bottom of a big baking pan, distribute 1/3 of sauce. Put half of tomatoes on top. Set the filled shells over top. On top of the shells, put the tomatoes and leftover sauce. Cover using aluminum foil.
- In the prepped oven, bake for 40 minutes till bubbly. Remove cover and scatter 2 tablespoons Cheddar cheese over top. Keep baking for 10 minutes till cheese is melted.

Nutrition Information

- Calories: 429 calories;
- Total Fat: 18.1
- Sodium: 708
- Total Carbohydrate: 37.5
- Cholesterol: 91
- Protein: 28.2

623.   Cheesy Italian Tortellini

Serving: 6 | Prep: 15mins | Cook: 8hours15mins | Ready in:

Ingredients

- 1/2 pound ground beef
- 1/2 pound Italian sausage, casings removed
- 1 (16 ounce) jar marinara sauce
- 1 (4.5 ounce) can sliced mushrooms
- 1 (14.5 ounce) can Italian-style diced tomatoes, undrained
- 1 (9 ounce) package refrigerated or fresh cheese tortellini
- 1 cup shredded mozzarella cheese
- 1/2 cup shredded Cheddar cheese

Direction

- In a large skillet, crumble the Italian sausage and the ground beef. Cook it on medium-high heat until the mixture has browned and drain. In a slow cooker, mix the mushrooms, ground meats, tomatoes and marinara sauce. Cover and for 7 to 8 hours cook on low heat.
- Slowly stir in the tortellini, sprinkle cheddar cheese and mozzarella on the top. Cover, and for 15 more minutes cook on low, or until the tortellini turns tender.

Nutrition Information

- Calories: 468 calories;
- Total Fat: 24.1
- Sodium: 1186
- Total Carbohydrate: 35.2
- Cholesterol: 82
- Protein: 26.9

624.   Chef John's Italian Meatballs

Serving: 30 | Prep: 20mins | Cook: 35mins | Ready in:

Ingredients

- 1/3 cup plain bread crumbs
- 1/2 cup milk
- 2 tablespoons olive oil
- 1 onion, diced
- 1 pound ground beef
- 1 pound ground pork
- 2 eggs
- 1/4 bunch fresh parsley, chopped
- 3 cloves garlic, crushed
- 2 teaspoons salt
- 1 teaspoon ground black pepper
- 1/2 teaspoon red pepper flakes
- 1 teaspoon dried Italian herb seasoning
- 2 tablespoons grated Parmesan cheese

Direction

- Use foil to cover a baking sheet and lightly spray with cooking spray.
- In a small bowl, soak bread crumbs in milk for 20 minutes.
- In a skillet, heat olive oil over medium heat. Cook and stir onions in hot oil for approximately 20 minutes until translucent.
- In a large bowl, mix pork and beef together. Stir into meat mixture with bread crumb mixture, onions, parsley, eggs, salt, garlic, red pepper flakes, black pepper, Parmesan cheese and Italian herb seasoning using a rubber spatula until combined. Cover and allow to sit for about one hour for cooling in refrigerator.
- Preheat an oven to 425 °F (220 °C).
- Using wet hands, roll meat mixture into balls of 1 and a half- inch in diameter. Onto prepared baking sheet, arrange those balls.
- In the preheated oven, bake for 15 to 20 minutes until cooked through and browned in color.

Nutrition Information

- Calories: 82 calories;
- Sodium: 192
- Total Carbohydrate: 1.7
- Cholesterol: 32
- Protein: 6.2
- Total Fat: 5.5

---

625. Chef John's Ricotta Meatballs

Serving: 8 | Prep: 20mins | Cook: 40mins | Ready in:

Ingredients

- 1/2 onion, minced
- 2 tablespoons olive oil
- 3 cloves garlic, minced
- 1 pound ground beef
- 1 cup whole milk ricotta cheese
- 1/4 cup packed chopped Italian parsley

- 1 egg, beaten
- 1 1/2 teaspoons kosher salt
- 1/2 teaspoon freshly ground black pepper
- 1 pinch cayenne pepper, or to taste
- 1/3 cup dry bread crumbs
- 2 tablespoons olive oil
- 1 (28 ounce) jar marinara sauce
- 1 cup water

Direction

- In a frying pan, sauté onion in 2 tablespoons of olive oil over medium heat for about 5 minutes until onion becomes translucent. Mix garlic into onion then turn off heat. Move the onion mixture to a big mixing bowl.
- Stir onion mixture with cayenne pepper, black pepper, kosher salt, egg, parsley, ricotta cheese, and ground beef until nearly combined; mix in bread crumbs then keep mixing till thoroughly blended.
- Shape each 1-inch ball with about 2 tablespoons of mixture. In the same pan used to cook onions, add 2 tablespoons of olive oil. Set pan over medium heat then brown all sides of meatballs in hot oil for about 5 minutes. Hold with your tongs a crumpled paper towel and use it to eliminate excess grease from the pan.
- In the frying pan, put water and marinara sauce over meatballs. Mix to combine then bring to a simmer. Lower heat to medium-low then simmer while stirring sometimes for around 30 minutes until meatballs are completely cooked and has no pink left in the center.

Nutrition Information

- Calories: 331 calories;
- Total Fat: 20.9
- Sodium: 865
- Total Carbohydrate: 18.9
- Cholesterol: 75
- Protein: 16.3

626.   Chef John's Shepherd's Pie

Serving: 8 | Prep: 15mins | Cook: 55mins | Ready in:

Ingredients

- 1 1/4 pounds Yukon Gold potatoes, peeled and cubed
- 3 cloves garlic, halved
- 1 pound lean ground beef
- 2 tablespoons flour
- 3/4 cup beef broth
- 3 tablespoons ketchup
- 4 cups frozen mixed vegetables
- 1/2 teaspoon black pepper
- 1/2 cup shredded Cheddar cheese, divided
- 3/4 cup light sour cream
- 1 teaspoon salt

Direction

- In a large pot, position garlic and cubed potatoes then add enough water to cover. Boil over high heat; lower heat to medium-low, simmer while covered for about 20 minutes until softened.
- Preheat the oven to 375° F (190° C).
- In a frying pan over medium heat, brown ground beef. Fold in flour, mixing with beef drippings.
- Put in vegetables, ketchup and beef broth. Stir to incorporate. Cook for about 5 minutes until thick.
- Move the beef mixture to an oven-proof casserole dish.
- Drain potatoes then lightly smash them before pouring in sour cream and a quarter cup of grated cheese. Mash together till smooth.
- On the center of the meat mixture, place potatoes. Use a fork to spread potatoes from the middle to the edges to shape the top layer.
- Dust with the rest a quarter cup of grated cheese.

- In the preheated oven, bake for 20-25 minutes, or till cheese becomes melted and golden. Allow to cool 15 minutes before serving.

Nutrition Information

- Calories: 311 calories;
- Cholesterol: 59
- Protein: 16.2
- Total Fat: 17.2
- Sodium: 546
- Total Carbohydrate: 23.5

627.   Chef John's Stuffed Peppers

Serving: 8 | Prep: 30mins | Cook: 1hours20mins | Ready in:

Ingredients

- 1 cup uncooked long grain white rice
- 2 cups water
- Sauce:
- 1 onion, diced
- 1 tablespoon olive oil
- 2 cups marinara sauce
- 1 cup beef broth
- 1 tablespoon balsamic vinegar
- 1/4 teaspoon crushed red pepper flakes
- Peppers:
- 1 pound lean ground beef
- 1/4 pound hot Italian pork sausage, casing removed
- 1 (10 ounce) can diced tomatoes
- 1/4 cup chopped fresh Italian parsley
- 4 cloves garlic, minced
- 2 teaspoons salt
- 1 teaspoon freshly ground black pepper
- 1 pinch ground cayenne pepper
- 4 large green bell peppers, halved lengthwise and seeded

- 1 cup finely grated Parmigiano-Reggiano cheese, plus more for topping

Direction

- Preheat an oven to 190°C/375°F.
- Boil water and rice in saucepan on high heat. Lower heat to medium low then cover; simmer for 20-25 minutes till liquid is absorbed and rice is tender. Put aside cooked rice.
- Cook olive oil and onion on medium heat for 5 minutes till onion starts to soften; put 1/2 cooked onion in big bowl. Put aside.
- Mix red pepper flakes, balsamic vinegar, beef broth and marinara sauce into skillet; mix and cook for a minute.
- Put sauce mixture in 9x13-in. baking dish; put aside.
- Mix cayenne pepper, black pepper, salt, garlic, Italian parsley, diced tomatoes, Italian sausage and ground beef well in bowl with reserved onions. Mix Parmigiano Reggiano and cooked rice in; stuff green bell peppers using sausage and beef mixture.
- Put stuffed green bell pepper halves over tomato sauce in baking dish; sprinkle leftover Parmigiano-Reggiano. Use aluminum foil to cover baking dish; in preheated oven, bake for 45 minutes.
- Remove aluminum foil; bake for 20-25 minutes till cheese browns on top, green peppers are tender and meat isn't pink anymore.

Nutrition Information

- Calories: 377 calories;
- Total Carbohydrate: 35.1
- Cholesterol: 52
- Protein: 20.1
- Total Fat: 16.9
- Sodium: 1274

628.   Chili Beef Casserole

Serving: 4 | Prep: 15mins | Cook: 45mins | Ready in:

Ingredients

- 3/4 pound lean ground beef
- 2 teaspoons olive oil
- 2 onions, chopped
- 1 green bell pepper, chopped
- 1/4 cup frozen green peas
- 1/2 teaspoon chili powder
- 1/2 teaspoon red pepper flakes
- 1 (14.5 ounce) can canned tomatoes, drained and chopped
- 1/4 cup tomato paste
- 1 (15.25 ounce) can kidney beans, drained
- 1 (11 ounce) can whole kernel corn, drained
- 4 (6 inch) corn tortillas, quartered
- 1/3 cup shredded reduced-fat Cheddar cheese

Direction

- Set the oven to 350°F or 175°C for preheating. Grease the medium casserole dish lightly.
- Cook the ground beef in a skillet over moderate heat. Once the beef is completely browned, drain to remove fats and set aside.
- In a separate skillet, heat the olive oil over moderate heat. Cook the onions into the hot oil until tender. Stir in peas and green pepper, and flavor the mixture with red pepper flakes and chili powder. Add the browned beef, tomato paste, and tomatoes into the mixture. Adjust the heat to low and bring the mixture to simmer for 5 minutes. Stir in corn and kidney beans.
- Divide the mixture into halves. Spread the first half into the greased casserole dish. Arrange 1/2 of the tortilla quarters into its top. Spread the remaining half of the mixture on top of the tortilla.
- Cover the dish and place it inside the preheated oven to bake. After 25 minutes, remove the cover and top it with the remaining cheese and tortillas. Bake for 10

more minutes until the cheese is golden brown and completely melted.

Nutrition Information

- Calories: 480 calories;
- Sodium: 881
- Total Carbohydrate: 58.1
- Cholesterol: 58
- Protein: 31.1
- Total Fat: 15.9

629.   Chili II

Serving: 4 | Prep: 5mins | Cook: 15mins | Ready in:

Ingredients

- 2 pounds ground beef
- 1 onion, chopped
- 2 (16 ounce) cans chili beans
- 1 (15 ounce) can tomato sauce
- 1 (10 ounce) can diced tomatoes with green chile peppers
- 1 (14.5 ounce) can peeled and diced tomatoes
- 11 1/2 fluid ounces tomato juice
- 1 (4 ounce) can diced green chiles
- 1 (1.25 ounce) package chili seasoning mix

Direction

- Cook onion and ground beef until done.
- Put all ingredients together in a Dutch oven or a slow cooker. Allow to simmer in some hours.

Nutrition Information

- Calories: 1005 calories;
- Total Fat: 63.1
- Sodium: 3321
- Total Carbohydrate: 63.6
- Cholesterol: 194
- Protein: 55.3

630.   Chili IV

Serving: 8 | Prep: | Cook: 45mins | Ready in:

Ingredients

- 1 1/2 pounds ground beef
- 1 tablespoon vegetable oil
- 1/2 teaspoon salt
- 1 (10.5 ounce) can condensed French onion soup
- 1 tablespoon chili powder
- 2 teaspoons ground cumin
- 1/2 teaspoon ground black pepper
- 1 (6 ounce) can tomato paste
- 1 (8 ounce) can tomato sauce
- 2 (15 ounce) cans kidney beans
- 2 teaspoons unsweetened cocoa
- 1 cup cola-flavored carbonated beverage

Direction

- At moderate heat, heat the oil in a big saucepan or deep skillet. Add beef and salt then cook until the meat is browned. In the meantime, pour the French onion soup into a blender and process until it smoothens out.
- After draining the meat, whisk the soup into meat. Lower the heat and leave it simmering for 5 minutes.
- Add the beans, tomato sauce, tomato paste, pepper, cumin and chilli powder, stirring until thoroughly mixed together. Add cola and cocoa. Before serving, heat it up thoroughly.

Nutrition Information

- Calories: 348 calories;
- Total Fat: 16.4
- Sodium: 1069
- Total Carbohydrate: 29.4
- Cholesterol: 54
- Protein: 22.2

631.   Chili Mac

Serving: 6 | Prep: 20mins | Cook: 35mins | Ready in:

Ingredients

- 1 pound ground beef or turkey
- 1 medium onion, chopped
- 1 green bell pepper, chopped
- 1 (14.5 ounce) can Mexican or chili-style stewed tomatoes, undrained
- 1/2 cup water
- 1 (1.25 ounce) package taco seasoning mix
- 2 cups elbow macaroni or small shells, cooked and drained
- 2 cups Sargento ® Shredded Reduced Fat 4 Cheese Mexican Cheese, divided

Direction

- Over medium heat, in a large skillet, cook green pepper, onion and ground beef until beef is no longer pink or for 5 minutes; get rid of drippings. Add taco seasoning, water and tomatoes; simmer while stirring occasionally for 5 minutes.
- Toss pasta with meat mixture. Scoop 3 cups of mixture into an 11x7-inch baking dish. Dust with a cup of cheese; place the rest of the meat mixture on top. Use foil to cover; bake in the prepared 375°F oven for half an hour. Uncover; dust with the rest of cheese. Place back in the oven until cheese melts or for 5 minutes.

Nutrition Information

- Calories: 429 calories;
- Total Carbohydrate: 37.2
- Cholesterol: 82
- Protein: 32.1
- Total Fat: 17.1
- Sodium: 894

632.   Chili Macaroni Casserole

Serving: 12 | Prep: 15mins | Cook: 55mins | Ready in:

Ingredients

- 1 (16 ounce) package elbow macaroni
- 2 pounds lean ground beef
- 1/2 cup chopped onion
- 2 (8 ounce) cans tomato sauce
- 1 (14.5 ounce) can diced tomatoes
- 1 (14 ounce) can whole kernel corn, drained
- 1 (15 ounce) can kidney beans, rinsed and drained
- 1 (1.25 ounce) package taco seasoning mix
- 1 (1.25 ounce) package chili seasoning mix
- 1 (10.75 ounce) can condensed cheddar cheese soup
- 1 (10.75 ounce) can milk
- 1 cup shredded Cheddar cheese
- 1/2 cup sour cream
- 1 1/2 teaspoons garlic powder
- 1/2 teaspoon salt
- 1/2 teaspoon black pepper
- 1 cup shredded Cheddar cheese
- 1 cup crushed tortilla chips
- 1/2 cup sour cream (optional)

Direction

- Prepare the oven by preheating to 350°F (175°C).
- Pour lightly salted water in a large pot over high heat and allow to boil over. When the water is simmering, add the macaroni, and continue to boil. Cook the pasta for about 8 minutes, without covering, whisking occasionally, until the pasta has cooked through, yet still firm to the bite. Use a colander set in the sink to strain well.
- Stir and cook ground beef with onion in a large skillet over medium heat for about 10 minutes until the meat turns brown. Crumble the meat as it cooks; strain extra grease. Add in the chili seasoning, taco seasoning, kidney beans, corn, diced tomatoes and tomato sauce;

allow to boil, lower the heat to a simmer, and cook for about 20 minutes, stirring occasionally.

- In a saucepan, mix milk and Cheddar cheese soup until it becomes smooth, and allow to boil over medium-low heat. Mix in garlic powder, 1/2 cup sour cream and 1 cup shredded Cheddar cheese; add black pepper and salt to taste.
- At the bottom of a 10x15-inch baking dish, pile the cooked macaroni, and combine with the soup mixture. Place the ground beef chili over the macaroni, and Drizzle with 1 more cup shredded Cheddar cheese and mashed tortilla chips.
- Place in the preheated oven and bake for 20-30 minutes until the casserole is bubbling and hot and the cheese topping is dissolved. Place dollops of sour cream on top to serve.

Nutrition Information

- Calories: 539 calories;
- Total Fat: 22.8
- Sodium: 1389
- Total Carbohydrate: 53.1
- Cholesterol: 81
- Protein: 30.1

633.   Chili Noodle Casserole

Serving: 6 | Prep: 10mins | Cook: 20mins | Ready in:

Ingredients

- 12 ounces spaghetti
- 1 pound lean ground beef
- 1 onion, chopped
- salt and pepper to taste
- chili powder to taste
- 1 (15.25 ounce) can kidney beans, drained

Direction

- In a large pot, boil the lightly salted water. Add in pasta and cook until al dente, or for 8-10 minutes; drain the pasta.
- In the meantime, in a skillet, brown the meat with onion; then drain the liquids. Stir in chili powder, pepper, and salt to taste. Add in kidney beans and stir, sauté for 5-10 minutes.
- Serve the bean mixture and meat over the pasta.

Nutrition Information

- Calories: 452 calories;
- Sodium: 324
- Total Carbohydrate: 60.9
- Cholesterol: 51
- Protein: 25.7
- Total Fat: 10.6

634.   Chili With Ziti

Serving: 6 | Prep: 15mins | Cook: 30mins | Ready in:

Ingredients

- 1 1/2 pounds lean ground beef
- 1 onion, finely chopped
- 1 clove garlic, minced
- 1 (8 ounce) can tomato sauce
- 2 tablespoons chili powder
- 1/2 teaspoon dried oregano, crushed
- 1/2 teaspoon ground cinnamon
- 1 (15 ounce) can kidney beans, drained
- 1/2 cup water
- salt and pepper to taste
- 16 ounces dry ziti pasta
- 1 cup shredded Cheddar cheese

Direction

- In a medium pot, brown the ground beef, onion and garlic over medium heat until no longer pink; drain the fat.

- Stir in cinnamon, oregano, chili powder, and tomato sauce; mix well. Pour in water and kidney beans; mix well. Flavor with salt and pepper. Simmer on low in 30 minutes.
- Bring a medium pot of lightly salted water to a boil. Add the ziti pasta and cook for 8 to 10 minutes, until the pasta is al dente; let drain.
- Serve the chili over the ziti and spread cheddar cheese on the top.

Nutrition Information

- Calories: 705 calories;
- Total Fat: 23.7
- Sodium: 713
- Total Carbohydrate: 79
- Cholesterol: 100
- Protein: 41.9

635. Chiliquilla

Serving: 4 | Prep: 15mins | Cook: 20mins | Ready in:

Ingredients

- 8 ounces ground beef
- 4 tablespoons margarine, divided
- 8 (6 inch) corn tortillas, torn into strips
- 3 eggs, beaten
- 3/4 cup canned mild enchilada sauce
- 1/2 cup sliced black olives
- 1/4 cup chopped green onions
- 1/2 cup sour cream
- 1/2 cup shredded Cheddar cheese

Direction

- In a large skillet, brown the ground beef over medium-high heat. Then drain, taking out of pan. Put aside.
- In skillet, melt two tablespoons of the margarine. Put in torn tortillas. Lightly brown. Push tortillas all the way to outside edge of the pan. Put remaining 2 tablespoons of the

margarine into middle; melt. Add beaten eggs; scramble until it is soft set. Push eggs to outside edge of pan. Put browned ground beef into middle of pan. Add enchilada sauce over, then lightly mix. Lower the heat to a simmer. Sprinkle over meat mixture with green onions and black olives; simmer, covered, for 10 mins.
- Discard the cover. Spoon sour cream by several dollops over. Evenly sprinkle shredded cheese over. Continue to simmer, covered, until cheese melts, about 5 more mins.

Nutrition Information

- Calories: 651 calories;
- Sodium: 524
- Total Carbohydrate: 28.5
- Cholesterol: 236
- Protein: 23.2
- Total Fat: 50.4

636. Chipotle Beef Tostadas

Serving: 8 | Prep: 10mins | Cook: 30mins | Ready in:

Ingredients

- 1 tablespoon canola oil
- 4 small potatoes, cut into very small cubes
- 1 onion, chopped
- 4 cloves garlic, minced
- 2 pounds ground beef
- 1 teaspoon seasoned salt
- 1 teaspoon garlic salt
- 2 chipotle peppers in adobo sauce
- 1/2 cup water
- 8 crispy tostada shells
- 1/4 cup sour cream, or to taste
- 1/4 cup shredded Mexican cheese blend, or to taste

Direction

- In a big skillet, heat oil over medium heat; in hot oil, cook and mix garlic, onion and potatoes for 7 minutes till onion is softened. Put the garlic salt, seasoned salt and ground beef; cook and mix for 10 to 15 minutes till ground beef is crumbly and browned.
- In a blender, blend chipotle peppers in water and adobo sauce till sauce is velvety. Into the ground beef mixture, put the sauce; cook and mix for 10 to 15 minutes longer till potatoes are soft.
- Layer every tostada with Mexican cheese blend, sour cream and chipotle beef.

Nutrition Information

- Calories: 412 calories;
- Protein: 22.5
- Total Fat: 24.8
- Sodium: 510
- Total Carbohydrate: 24.2
- Cholesterol: 77

637.   Chipotle Taco Burger

Serving: 4 | Prep: 15mins | Cook: 15mins | Ready in:

Ingredients

- 1 pound ground beef
- 1/4 cup diced onion
- 3 chipotle peppers in adobo sauce, seeded and diced
- 1 teaspoon taco seasoning

Direction

- Preheat an outdoor grill to medium high heat; oil the grate lightly.
- Thoroughly mix taco seasoning, chipotle peppers, onion and ground beef in a bowl using your hands; form to 4 patties.
- On the preheated grill, cook burgers, 7-10 minutes per side, till grey in middle, hot and

firm. An instant-read thermometer inserted in the middle should read 70°C/160°F.

Nutrition Information

- Calories: 217 calories;
- Protein: 19.2
- Total Fat: 13.8
- Sodium: 168
- Total Carbohydrate: 2.2
- Cholesterol: 71

638.   Chow Mein Noodle Casserole

Serving: 4 | Prep: 20mins | Cook: 20mins | Ready in:

Ingredients

- 1 pound ground beef
- 1 onion, chopped
- 2 stalks celery, chopped
- 1/2 cup slivered almonds
- 1 cup cooked rice
- 1 (10.75 ounce) can condensed cream of chicken soup
- 1/2 cup water
- 3 tablespoons soy sauce
- 5 ounces chow mein noodles

Direction

- Preheat the oven to 175 degrees C (350 degrees F).
- Over medium high heat, sauté ground beef for five minutes in a large skillet. Add celery and onion and then sauté for five minutes.
- Mix the soy sauce, almonds, rice, water and soup in a separate medium bowl. Combine thoroughly and pour into the beef mixture. Transfer this mix into a 9x13 inch baking dish that is lightly greased. Add chow mein noodles on top.

- Bake for 20 minutes at 175 degrees C (350 degrees F).

Nutrition Information

- Calories: 597 calories;
- Total Carbohydrate: 41.7
- Cholesterol: 75
- Protein: 28.9
- Total Fat: 35.5
- Sodium: 1514

639.   Chris' Bay Area Burger

Serving: 4 | Prep: 10mins | Cook: 20mins | Ready in:

Ingredients

- 1 pound ground beef
- 2 cloves garlic, minced
- 2 tablespoons extra virgin olive oil
- 1 1/2 teaspoons salt
- 1 teaspoon freshly ground black pepper
- 1/2 teaspoon dried basil leaves
- 4 hamburger buns, split

Direction

- Preheat the outdoor grill for high heat. Combine the basil, pepper, salt, olive oil, garlic and ground beef. Distribute into 4 balls, and flatten to form patties.
- Let the patties cook until reaching the preferred doneness, about 3 to 5 minutes per side. The inside temperature should be at minimum of 70 °C or 160 °F. Take out of grill and put on hamburger buns. Put the condiments and preferred toppings on top.

Nutrition Information

- Calories: 393 calories;
- Total Fat: 22.6
- Sodium: 1179

- Total Carbohydrate: 22.6
- Cholesterol: 71
- Protein: 22.9

640.   Classic Meatloaf

Serving: 10 | Prep: 30mins | Cook: 45mins | Ready in:

Ingredients

- Meatloaf Ingredients:
- 1 carrot, coarsely chopped
- 1 rib celery, coarsely chopped
- 1/2 onion, coarsely chopped
- 1/2 red bell pepper, coarsely chopped
- 4 white mushrooms, coarsely chopped
- 3 cloves garlic, coarsely chopped
- 2 1/2 pounds ground chuck
- 1 tablespoon Worcestershire sauce
- 1 egg, beaten
- 1 teaspoon dried Italian herbs
- 2 teaspoons salt
- 1 teaspoon ground black pepper
- 1/2 teaspoon cayenne pepper
- 1 cup plain bread crumbs
- 1 teaspoon olive oil
- Glaze Ingredients:
- 2 tablespoons brown sugar
- 2 tablespoons ketchup
- 2 tablespoons Dijon mustard
- hot pepper sauce to taste

Direction

- Set the oven to 325°F and start preheating.
- In a food processor, place garlic, mushrooms, red bell pepper, onion, celery and carrot; pulse until very finely chopped, almost to a puree. In a large mixing bowl, place minced vegetables; combine in egg, Worcestershire sauce and ground chuck. Add cayenne pepper, black pepper, salt and Italian herb. Using a wooden spoon, combine gently to incorporate egg and vegetables into the meat. Add bread crumbs. Mix in the crumbs gently

with your fingertips for about a minute just until combined.

- Shape the meatloaf into a ball. In a baking dish, place olive oil and arrange meat balls into the dish. Form the ball into a loaf, about 4 inches in height and 6 inches across.
- Bake in the prepared oven for about 15 minutes until the meatloaf turns hot.
- At the meantime, combine hot sauce, Dijon mustard, ketchup and brown sugar in a small bowl. Stir until brown sugar dissolves.
- Take the meatloaf out of the oven. Smooth this glaze on top its top, using the back of the spoon; pull a small amount of glaze down the sides of meatloaf, using the back to the spoon.
- Transfer the meatloaf back to the oven; bake for 30-40 minutes more until the inside is no longer pink and glaze has baked onto the meatloaf. The inserted instant-read thermometer into the thickest part of the loaf should register at least 160°F (70°C). Depending on the thickness and shape of the meatloaf, cooking time will be different.

Nutrition Information

- Calories: 284 calories;
- Sodium: 755
- Total Carbohydrate: 14.8
- Cholesterol: 85
- Protein: 21.6
- Total Fat: 14.9

641.   Classic Shepherd's Pie

Serving: 6 | Prep: 25mins | Cook: 35mins | Ready in:

Ingredients

- 1 tablespoon vegetable oil
- 1 onion, chopped
- 2 cloves garlic, minced
- 1 teaspoon dried thyme
- 1 teaspoon dried rosemary

- 1 teaspoon salt
- 1 teaspoon pepper
- 1 pound lean ground beef
- 4 teaspoons all-purpose flour
- 1/4 cup Heinz Tomato Ketchup
- 3/4 cup Heinz® Tomato Juice
- 2 tablespoons Heinz Worcestershire Sauce
- 2 tablespoons Dijon mustard
- 1 cup frozen mixed vegetables (such as peas and carrots)
- 3 cups cooked, warm, mashed potatoes
- 2 tablespoons butter
- 1 clove garlic, minced
- 2/3 cup warm milk

Direction

- In a frying pan, heat oil over medium heat. Add the pepper, half of the salt, rosemary, thyme, garlic and onion. Cook while often stirring for 5 - 7 minutes. Preheat the oven to 350° F (180° C).
- Crumble meat into the pan then cook till brown all over. Dust with flour. Mix in mustard, tomato juice, Worcestershire sauce and ketchup. Simmer for 5 minutes. Whisk in mixed vegetables. Move to a 9-inch (23-cm) baking dish.
- Whip potatoes with garlic, butter, pepper, remaining salt and warm milk till very fluffy. Evenly pour potatoes over meat mixture. Bake for 35 minutes or till potatoes become golden.

Nutrition Information

- Calories: 375 calories;
- Sodium: 1603
- Total Carbohydrate: 44
- Cholesterol: 57
- Protein: 18.2
- Total Fat: 17.4

642. Classic And Simple Meat Lasagna

Serving: 8 | Prep: 25mins | Cook: 1hours | Ready in:

Ingredients

- 12 whole wheat lasagna noodles
- 1 pound lean ground beef
- 2 cloves garlic, chopped
- 1/2 teaspoon garlic powder
- 1 teaspoon dried oregano, or to taste
- salt and ground black pepper to taste
- 1 (16 ounce) package cottage cheese
- 2 eggs
- 1/2 cup shredded Parmesan cheese
- 1 1/2 (25 ounce) jars tomato-basil pasta sauce
- 2 cups shredded mozzarella cheese

Direction

- Preheat an oven to 175 °C or 350 °F.
- With slightly salted water, fill a big pot and on high heat, let it come to a rolling boil. When water is boiling, put in lasagna noodles several at a time, and bring back to a boil. Let the pasta cook without a cover for about 10 minutes, mixing from time to time, till pasta has cooked through, but remain to be firm to the bite. Transfer noodles onto a plate.
- Into a skillet, put ground beef over medium heat, to the skillet, put black pepper, salt, oregano, garlic powder and garlic. Let the meat cook for approximately 10 minutes, chopping it into small chunks as it cooks, till not pink anymore. Drain extra grease.
- Combine Parmesan cheese, eggs and cottage cheese in a bowl till well incorporated.
- Put 4 noodles next to each other into the bottom of a baking pan, 9x13-inch in size; place on top a layer of tomato-basil sauce, one layer of the ground beef mixture, and a layer of cottage cheese mixture. Redo layers two more times, finishing with one layer of the sauce; scatter mozzarella cheese on top. Put aluminum foil to cover the dish.

- In prepped oven, bake for about 30 minutes till casserole bubbles and cheese melts. Take off foil and bake for 10 minutes longer till cheese stats to brown. Let it sit for a minimum of 10 minutes prior to serving.

Nutrition Information

- Calories: 501 calories;
- Total Fat: 19.3
- Sodium: 999
- Total Carbohydrate: 47.1
- Cholesterol: 115
- Protein: 35.6

643. Clean Eating Hearty Pasta Sauce

Serving: 6 | Prep: 20mins | Cook: 40mins | Ready in:

Ingredients

- Sauce:
- 1/2 pound lean ground beef
- 2 small zucchinis, chopped
- 1 onion, chopped
- 3 cloves garlic, minced
- 1 (28 ounce) can crushed tomatoes
- 1 (15 ounce) can tomato sauce
- 2 tablespoons sucanat (crystallized sugar cane juice), or to taste
- 1 1/2 tablespoons dried basil
- 1 1/2 teaspoons sea salt
- 1 teaspoon dried oregano
- 1/4 teaspoon ground black pepper
- Pasta:
- 1 (16 ounce) package whole-wheat spaghetti
- 1 gallon water
- salt

Direction

- Over medium-high heat, heat a large skillet. When it is hot, stir in garlic, onion, zucchini and ground beef; cook for 5-7 minutes with stirs until the beef is crumbly and browned. Drain; discard grease.

- Mix the beef mixture with black pepper, oregano, sea salt, basil, sucanat, tomato sauce and crushed tomatoes. Cook until it boils, then lower the heat to low. Let it simmer for at least 30 minutes or up to 1 hour to enhance the flavor until flavors have blended.
- As the sauce simmers, boil salted water to cook spaghetti following the directions on package. Pour over hot pasta to serve.

Nutrition Information

- Calories: 436 calories;
- Total Fat: 6.3
- Sodium: 2196
- Total Carbohydrate: 80
- Cholesterol: 25
- Protein: 22.5

---

644.   Cocktail Meatballs

Serving: 10 | Prep: 20mins | Cook: 1hours25mins | Ready in:

Ingredients

- 1 pound lean ground beef
- 1 egg
- 2 tablespoons water
- 1/2 cup bread crumbs
- 3 tablespoons minced onion
- 1 (8 ounce) can jellied cranberry sauce
- 3/4 cup chili sauce
- 1 tablespoon brown sugar
- 1 1/2 teaspoons lemon juice

Direction

- Turn oven to 350°F (175°C) to preheat.

- Combine minced onion, breadcrumbs, water, egg, and ground beef in a large bowl. Shape mixture into small meatballs.
- Bake for 20 to 25 minutes in the preheated oven, flipping once.
- Blend lemon juice, brown sugar, chili sauce, and cranberry sauce over low heat in a large saucepan or slow cooker. Add in meatballs; simmer for 60 minutes or until ready to serve.

Nutrition Information

- Calories: 193 calories;
- Total Fat: 10.2
- Sodium: 85
- Total Carbohydrate: 15.2
- Cholesterol: 53
- Protein: 9.8

---

645.   Cocktail Meatballs I

Serving: 8 | Prep: 25mins | Cook: 40mins | Ready in:

Ingredients

- 1 pound ground beef
- 1/2 cup dried bread crumbs
- 1/3 cup chopped onion
- 1/4 cup milk
- 1 egg
- 1 teaspoon salt
- 1/2 teaspoon Worcestershire sauce
- 1/8 teaspoon ground black pepper
- 1/4 cup shortening
- 12 fluid ounces tomato-based chili sauce
- 1 1/4 cups grape jelly

Direction

- Blend ground black pepper, Worcestershire sauce, salt, egg, milk, onion, breadcrumbs, and ground beef in a large bowl. Combine them together and form into meatballs.

- Heat shortening in a large skillet on medium heat. Put meatballs and cook for 5-7 minutes until they are browned. Take out from the skillet and transfer to paper towels to drain.
- Place jelly and chili sauce into the skillet; heat and stir until the jelly melts. Bring the meatballs back to the skillet and stir until they are coated. Turn down the heat to low. Remove the cover and bring to a simmer for half an hour.

Nutrition Information

- Calories: 458 calories;
- Cholesterol: 72
- Protein: 12.7
- Total Fat: 22.8
- Sodium: 1038
- Total Carbohydrate: 52.5

646.   Cocktail Meatballs III

Serving: 18 | Prep: 25mins | Cook: 10mins | Ready in:

Ingredients

- 3 pounds ground beef
- 2 (1 ounce) packages dry onion soup mix
- 3 slices white bread
- 2 tablespoons half-and-half
- 1 (28 ounce) bottle ketchup
- 1 cup packed dark brown sugar
- 2 tablespoons Worcestershire sauce

Direction

- Set the oven at 350°F (175°C) to preheat.
- Remove the crusts from the white bread, and shred into small bread crumbs. Combine half-and-half cream, white bread crumbs, the soup mix, and beef in a medium-size mixing bowl. Roll into 1-inch balls and place in 9x13 inch baking dishes (bake the meatballs in batches or as many baking dishes as it takes).

- Bake until browned, around 10-15 minutes.
- Set a slow cooker to high temperature, mix Worcestershire sauce, brown sugar, and ketchup together. Cook until the mixture boils, then lower the temperature to low, continue to cook until you are ready to present the meatballs.
- Put the meatballs in the sauce and enjoy.

Nutrition Information

- Calories: 346 calories;
- Total Carbohydrate: 27.4
- Cholesterol: 65
- Protein: 13.9
- Total Fat: 20.6
- Sodium: 863

647.   Cornish Pasties III

Serving: 12 | Prep: | Cook: | Ready in:

Ingredients

- 4 cups all-purpose flour
- 1 teaspoon salt
- 2 cups lard
- 1 cup cold water
- 3 tablespoons vegetable oil
- 1 onion, finely diced
- 5 carrots, diced (optional)
- 2 rutabagas, diced
- 1 pound lean ground beef
- 1 pound ground pork
- 10 green onions, chopped
- salt and pepper to taste
- 1/2 cup butter
- 2 tablespoons milk

Direction

- Crust: Mix salt and flour in a big bowl well. Cut in lard until mixture becomes crumbly. Mix in water. Mix just until dough makes a ball. Let dough rest in the fridge while making filling.

- Filling: Heat a big skillet on medium high heat. Add vegetable oil then the onions. If you're using rutabagas and carrots, add them. Sauté for 10 minutes until veggies are soft.
- Put in green onions, ground pork and ground beef. Sauté until meat isn't pink anymore. Put pepper and salt. Preheat oven to 200 degrees C/400 degrees F.
- Distribute dough to 12 portions. Roll each portion to fit in a 9-in. pie plate.
- Put pastry circle in pie pan. Fill 1/2 of pan with the meat filling. Dot some margarine/butter. Pat water on crust edges. Fold the other crust half over. Trim edges. Crimp to seal. Create steam vents on top of the crust. Brush using milk. Repeat until all filling and dough are used.
- Bake for 45 minutes in the oven until crust is golden brown.

Nutrition Information

- Calories: 800 calories;
- Protein: 18.9
- Total Fat: 61.8
- Sodium: 330
- Total Carbohydrate: 41.4
- Cholesterol: 109

648. Country Goulash

Serving: 6 | Prep: 10mins | Cook: 30mins | Ready in:

Ingredients

- 2 pounds lean ground beef
- 1 large yellow onion, chopped
- 3 cloves garlic, chopped
- 3 tablespoons paprika, or to taste
- 2 teaspoons ground black pepper, or to taste
- 2 teaspoons seasoned salt, or to taste
- 2 (15 ounce) cans tomato sauce

- 1 (8 ounce) can tomato paste
- 1 cup water, or as desired
- 2 cups uncooked elbow macaroni

Direction

- On medium-high heat, heat a big pan; add on garlic, onion, and beef. Cook and stir for 5-7 minutes until crumbly and brown.
- Sprinkle seasoned salt, black pepper, and paprika over the beef to season. Mix in tomato sauce and tomato paste in the beef mixture until smooth. Pour on water and put in macaroni; mix.
- Boil the liquid and turn heat to medium-low. Let it simmer for 20 minutes until the macaroni is al dente. Pour in water if necessary to maintain the desired consistency. Season according to taste; serve.

Nutrition Information

- Calories: 509 calories;
- Cholesterol: 99
- Protein: 37.8
- Total Fat: 19.9
- Sodium: 1435
- Total Carbohydrate: 46.3

649. Cowboy Casserole

Serving: 5 | Prep: 5mins | Cook: 20mins | Ready in:

Ingredients

- 1/2 pound bacon
- 1 pound ground beef
- 1 small onion, chopped
- 2 (15 ounce) cans baked beans with pork
- 1/3 cup barbeque sauce
- 1 (7.5 ounce) package refrigerated biscuit dough

Direction

- Cook bacon in Dutch oven/big skillet on medium heat till browned evenly; drain. Cut to bite-sized pieces; put aside. Add onion and hamburger to skillet; cook till onion is tender and not pink. Drain.
- Mix barbeque sauce, baked beans and bacon into ground beef; boil. Lower heat to medium low; in 1 layer, put biscuits over mixture. Cover; simmer till biscuits are done for 10 minutes. Put 2 biscuits on every plate; put beans over.

Nutrition Information

- Calories: 601 calories;
- Sodium: 1580
- Total Carbohydrate: 62
- Cholesterol: 84
- Protein: 32.8
- Total Fat: 25.2

---

650.   Cowboy Lasagna

Serving: 6 | Prep: | Cook: | Ready in:

Ingredients

- 2 pounds lean ground beef
- 1 (6 ounce) can chopped black olives
- 1 (4.5 ounce) can mushrooms, drained
- 1 onion, chopped
- 1 (16 ounce) jar spaghetti sauce
- 9 lasagne noodles, cooked and drained
- 1 1/4 cups frozen corn kernels
- 1 1/4 cups frozen green peas
- 8 ounces shredded mozzarella cheese
- 1 pinch ground black pepper
- 1 pinch dried oregano
- 1 pinch Italian seasoning

Direction

- Preheat oven at 350°F (175°C). Use cooking spray to grease a 9x13-inch pan.

- In a pan, cook beef over medium heat until brown then drain excess oil. Mix in the onion, olives and mushrooms. Sauté and stir the onions until tender. Add in the oregano, Italian seasoning, pepper and spaghetti sauce; mix.
- Mix corn and peas together in small bowl.
- In the greased pan, put 3 lasagna noodles at the bottom; then layer with 1/2 the beef mixture and 1/2 of the corn-pea mixture. Do the whole layering process again. Finish the layers with the remaining lasagna noodles.
- Put in heated oven and bake 25 minutes. Put cheese on top of the lasagna then bake for 5 more minutes. Before slicing, allow the lasagna to cool down for 10 minutes then serve while still warm.

Nutrition Information

- Calories: 791 calories;
- Total Fat: 43.7
- Sodium: 1020
- Total Carbohydrate: 53.8
- Cholesterol: 139
- Protein: 45.6

---

651.   Cowboy Skillet Casserole

Serving: 6 | Prep: 15mins | Cook: 20mins | Ready in:

Ingredients

- 1 pound ground beef
- 1/2 onion, chopped
- 2 red bell peppers, cut into 2 inch pieces
- 1 (15 ounce) can baked beans
- 1 tablespoon dry fajita seasoning
- 1 (8.5 ounce) package corn bread mix
- 1 egg
- 1/3 cup milk

Direction

- Preheat oven to 175°C or 350°Fahrenheit.
- On medium-high heat, break ground beef to crumbles in a big cast-iron pan. Cook and stir often until beef is evenly brown; drain grease. Cook and stir in onion until translucent; put in fajita seasoning, beans and red peppers. Cook and stir until warmed through. Layer mixture evenly at the base of the pan.
- Prepare cornbread mix with milk and egg following the package instructions. Spread evenly on top of the ground beef mixture.
- Put the pan in the preheated oven and bake for 20mins until an inserted skewer/toothpick in the layer of cornbread comes out without residue or clean. Let it cool for several minutes. Serve.

Nutrition Information

- Calories: 391 calories;
- Sodium: 1012
- Total Carbohydrate: 46
- Cholesterol: 79
- Protein: 21.2
- Total Fat: 14.2

652.   Cream Cheese Jalapeno Hamburgers

Serving: 8 | Prep: 15mins | Cook: 20mins | Ready in:

Ingredients

- 2 cups seeded and chopped jalapeno pepper
- 2 (8 ounce) packages cream cheese, softened
- 2 pounds ground beef
- 8 hamburger buns, split

Direction

- Turn grill to medium heat to preheat. Once hot, lightly grease the grate. Combine cream cheese and jalapenos together in a medium bowl.

- Separate ground beef into 16 portions; pat out each one to a thickness of 1/4 inch. Place some of the cream cheese mixture onto the middle of 8 of the patties. Top with the remainder of patties, pinch the edges together to seal.
- Grill until well done, about 10 minutes on each side, being careful not to press down on the burgers to avoid cheese coming out as they cook. Serve on buns with the toppings of your choice.

Nutrition Information

- Calories: 526 calories;
- Total Fat: 35.2
- Sodium: 472
- Total Carbohydrate: 24.4
- Cholesterol: 130
- Protein: 27.2

653.   Creamy Keto Taco Soup With Ground Beef

Serving: 8 | Prep: 10mins | Cook: 20mins | Ready in:

Ingredients

- 1 pound ground beef
- 1/2 cup chopped onion
- 2 cloves garlic, minced
- 1 tablespoon ground cumin
- 1 teaspoon chili powder
- 1 (8 ounce) package cream cheese, softened
- 2 (14.5 ounce) cans beef broth
- 2 (10 ounce) cans diced tomatoes and green chiles (such as RO*TEL®)
- 1/2 cup heavy cream
- 2 teaspoons salt, or to taste

Direction

- In a big soup pot, mix the garlic and onion with the ground beef on medium-high heat. Cook and stir for 5-7 minutes until the beef becomes crumbly and browned; drain and get rid of the grease. Add chili powder and cumin, then cook for an additional 2 minutes.

- Into the pot, drop the cream cheese by bits. Using a big spoon, mash it into the beef for 3-5 minutes, until no white spots will remain. Stir in salt, heavy cream, diced tomatoes and broth. Let it cook for about 10 more minutes until heated through.

Nutrition Information

- Calories: 288 calories;
- Total Fat: 24
- Sodium: 1310
- Total Carbohydrate: 5.4
- Cholesterol: 85
- Protein: 13.4

654.   Creamy Pasta Casserole

Serving: 8 | Prep: 20mins | Cook: 25mins | Ready in:

Ingredients

- 1 (12 ounce) package farfalle (bow tie) pasta
- 1/2 (8 ounce) package cream cheese, softened
- 1 (24 ounce) jar pasta sauce
- 1 teaspoon Italian seasoning
- 1/2 teaspoon red pepper flakes
- 1 pound ground beef
- 1 onion, minced
- 2 cloves garlic, minced
- 1/2 cup shredded mozzarella cheese

Direction

- Set oven to 350°F (175°C) to preheat.
- Bring lightly salted water in a large pot to a boil. Cook bow-tie pasta in boiling water for about 12 minutes, stirring from time to time, until al dente; drain pasta, put back into the pot. Melt cream cheese into hot pasta. Mix red

pepper flakes, Italian seasoning and pasta sauce into the pasta mixture.

- Bring a skillet to medium heat on the stove. Crumble ground beef and put into the skillet; sauté beef for 2 to 3 minutes until some of the fat renders. Stir in garlic and onion; sauté for about 5 minutes longer until ground beef is entirely browned. Mix beef mixture into the pasta mixture.
- Pour everything into a 3-quart casserole dish. Scatter top with mozzarella cheese.
- Bake for 5 to 10 minutes in the preheated oven until cheese is melted.

Nutrition Information

- Calories: 401 calories;
- Total Carbohydrate: 44.5
- Cholesterol: 57
- Protein: 19.6
- Total Fat: 16.1
- Sodium: 465

655.   Creole Black Eyed Peas And Rice

Serving: 6 | Prep: 10mins | Cook: 45mins | Ready in:

Ingredients

- 1 pound lean ground beef
- 2 small onions, chopped
- 1 cup chopped green bell pepper
- 1 cup long grain white rice
- 2 cups water
- 1 tablespoon Creole seasoning
- 1 teaspoon ground black pepper
- 1/2 teaspoon garlic powder
- 2 (15.5 ounce) cans black-eyed peas, drained

Direction

- In a big saucepan/deep skillet, crumble ground beef on medium-high heat. Add green pepper and onions. Stir and cook until beef is browned evenly. Drain grease.

- Add water and rice to the pan. Season with garlic powder, pepper and creole seasoning. Boil, cover, then lower heat to low. Simmer until water is absorbed for 30 minutes. About halfway through cooking the rice, mix in black-eyed peas.

Nutrition Information

- Calories: 388 calories;
- Cholesterol: 50
- Protein: 24.1
- Total Fat: 10.4
- Sodium: 721
- Total Carbohydrate: 48.7

---

656. Crunchy Corn Chip Tacos

Serving: 5 | Prep: 15mins | Cook: 20mins | Ready in:

Ingredients

- 1 pound ground beef
- 3/4 cup water
- 1 envelope taco seasoning mix
- 5 taco shells
- 1/2 (12 ounce) bag nacho cheese-flavored corn chips (such as Doritos®), crushed
- 2 cups shredded Mexican cheese blend
- 1 dash hot pepper sauce (such as Frank's RedHot®), or to taste

Direction

- Set the oven at 350 degrees F (175 degrees C) to preheat.
- In a big skillet, brown the ground beef on medium heat until the meat crumbles and is no longer pink, roughly 10 minutes. Drain extra grease then stir in taco seasoning mix and water. Lower heat to low and simmer

until the mixture thickens, around 4-6 minutes.

- In the preheated oven, bake the taco shells on a baking sheet until they become crispy, 3-4 minutes. Allow the shells to cool for around 5 minutes and break them into bite-sized pieces.
- Move the seasoned ground beef into a big serving bowl and mix in hot pepper sauce, Mexican cheese blend, taco shell pieces, and nacho cheese corn chips.

Nutrition Information

- Calories: 629 calories;
- Sodium: 1256
- Total Carbohydrate: 36.2
- Cholesterol: 107
- Protein: 30.7
- Total Fat: 40.6

---

657. D's Taco Pizza

Serving: 8 | Prep: 20mins | Cook: 20mins | Ready in:

Ingredients

- 1/2 pound ground beef
- 1/2 cup chopped onion
- 1 clove garlic
- 1/2 (1 ounce) packet taco seasoning mix
- 1/3 cup water
- 1 (14.5 ounce) can diced tomatoes with garlic and onion
- 1 cup salsa
- 2 tablespoons chopped fresh cilantro
- 1 cup refried beans
- 1 12-inch prepared pizza crust
- 1 1/2 cups Mexican-style shredded four-cheese blend
- 2 cups shredded lettuce
- 2 tomatoes, chopped
- 1 (2.25 ounce) can sliced black olives, drained
- 1/4 cup chopped green onion

- 1/2 cup Mexican-style shredded four-cheese blend
- 1 cup sour cream, or as desired (optional)
- 1 cup salsa, or as desired (optional)

Direction

- In a large skillet over medium-high heat, sauté garlic, onion, and ground beef together until beef is evenly browned; drain drippings from the skillet.
- Mix water and taco seasoning mix into the beef mixture; bring to a boil. Turn heat to medium-low, and simmer for 5 minutes, stirring sometimes.
- Turn oven to 350°F (175°C) to preheat.
- Lay the prepared pizza crust on a baking sheet.
- Puree cilantro, salsa, and diced tomatoes with onion and garlic in a blender until no lumps remain. Distribute refried beans in an even layer over the prepared pizza crust, leaving a 1/2-inch border uncovered around the outside.
- Place about 1 cup of diced tomato mixture in an even layer over refried beans; save the remaining sauce.
- Crumble ground beef mixture over sauce layer.
- Cover the beef with 1 1/2 cups Mexican-style shredded cheese blend.
- Bake for 15 to 20 minutes in the preheated oven until edges of the crust turn golden brown and cheese is bubbly. Put to one side and allow to cool for 5 minutes.
- Sprinkle top of pizza with shredded lettuce, chopped tomatoes, black olives, green onions and 1/2 cup Mexican-style shredded cheese blend. Serve with 1 cup salsa, sour cream, and the reserved sauce.

Nutrition Information

- Calories: 399 calories;
- Sodium: 1394
- Total Carbohydrate: 36.2
- Cholesterol: 58

- Protein: 19.1
- Total Fat: 21.5

658. Dad's Favorite Detroit Style Roquefort Burgers

Serving: 4 | Prep: 30mins | Cook: 15mins | Ready in:

Ingredients

- 1 pound lean ground beef
- 1/2 teaspoon Worcestershire sauce
- 1 teaspoon dried parsley
- salt and black pepper to taste
- 1 cup Roquefort or other blue cheese, crumbled
- 4 kaiser rolls, split and heated
- 4 slices onion, or to taste
- 4 lettuce leaves
- 4 slices tomato

Direction

- Preheat the outdoor grill on medium heat; grease the grate lightly.
- In a bowl, combine pepper, ground beef, salt, Worcestershire sauce, and parsley; split mixture into four parts. Form each part into a ball with a pocket. Fill each pocket with a quarter cup crumbled Roquefort cheese. Press the balls gently to flatten into bun-sized patties.
- Set on the preheated grill and cook for 7-8mins on each side until the patties show good grill marks, the cheese melts, the center is not pink.
- Serve with tomato, lettuce, and onion slices on the side in hot Kaiser Rolls.

Nutrition Information

- Calories: 454 calories;
- Sodium: 809
- Total Carbohydrate: 24.7
- Cholesterol: 104

- Protein: 32.7
- Total Fat: 24.3

---

659. Dad's New Zealand Mince Stew

Serving: 8 | Prep: 45mins | Cook: 3hours | Ready in:

Ingredients

- 1 tablespoon vegetable oil
- 3 large onions, sliced
- 2 pounds ground beef
- 2 cloves garlic, chopped
- 1 cup water
- 2 cups ketchup
- 1 cup beef stock
- 2 tablespoons teriyaki sauce
- 3 tablespoons black pepper
- 1 tablespoon curry powder
- 1 teaspoon garlic powder
- 1 tablespoon onion powder
- 1 tablespoon all-purpose flour
- 1/2 cup water

Direction

- In a big pot, heat oil over medium heat. Add onions and sauté until turning brown, take away from the pot, and put aside. Put ground beef in the pot, and cook until turning brown evenly. Put in garlic, and cook for 2 minutes. Mix in the browned onions, and cook for 3-5 minutes on high heat. Mix in 1 cup of water. Lower the heat, simmer with a cover for 20 minutes.
- Mix in teriyaki sauce, beef stock, and ketchup. Use onion powder, garlic powder, curry powder, and pepper to season. Simmer with a cover for 2 hours.
- Stir 1/2 cup of water and 1 tablespoon of flour. Mix into the stew, and cook until thickened.

Nutrition Information

- Calories: 474 calories;
- Total Fat: 32.4
- Sodium: 935
- Total Carbohydrate: 25.4
- Cholesterol: 96
- Protein: 21.9

---

660. Dash's Donair

Serving: 4 | Prep: 30mins | Cook: 1hours15mins | Ready in:

Ingredients

- 1 teaspoon salt
- 1 teaspoon ground oregano
- 1 teaspoon all-purpose flour
- 1/2 teaspoon ground black pepper
- 1/2 teaspoon Italian seasoning
- 1/2 teaspoon garlic powder
- 1/2 teaspoon onion powder
- 1/4 teaspoon cayenne pepper
- 1 pound ground beef
- 1 (12 fluid ounce) can evaporated milk
- 3/4 cup white sugar
- 2 teaspoons garlic powder
- 4 teaspoons white vinegar, or as needed

Direction

- Start preheating oven to 350°F (175°C). Mix cayenne pepper, onion powder, garlic powder, Italian seasoning, black pepper, flour, oregano and salt together in a small bowl or cup.
- In large bowl, put ground beef. Blend in spice mixture with your hands. You must do this in a steel mixing bowl and on a sturdy surface if you want the smooth texture of meat like the one in a real donair shop. Pick up meat, and throw down about 20 times with force, kneading before throwing the next. It helps to hold the meat together better when slicing.
- Form the meat into a loaf, and place it on a broiler pan. If you do not have one, a baking sheet will do.

- Bake for 75 mins in the prepared oven, turning the loaf over about half way through. This will ensure even cooking. Serve, or allow the meat to chill before slicing and reheating.
- For donair sauce: in medium bowl, mix garlic powder, sugar and evaporated milk together. Whisk in white vinegar gradually, until thickened to preferred consistency; put in one teaspoon at once.

Nutrition Information

- Calories: 489 calories;
- Sodium: 748
- Total Carbohydrate: 49.5
- Cholesterol: 98
- Protein: 26
- Total Fat: 20.9

---

661.   Date Night Meatloaf

Serving: 8 | Prep: 20mins | Cook: 1hours10mins |Ready in:

Ingredients

- 5 poblano peppers
- cooking spray
- 12 pitted Medjool dates
- 20 ounces 90%-lean ground beef
- 5 ounces goat cheese
- 1/4 cup barbeque sauce (such as Jack Daniel's®)
- 1/4 cup plain bread crumbs
- 1 egg
- 2 tablespoons barbeque sauce (such as Jack Daniel's®)

Direction

- Position oven rack approximately 6-inch away from heat source and preheat an oven's broiler. On baking sheet, place the peppers.

- In the prepped oven, let peppers broil for 5 to 10 minutes each side till bubbling and skin is charred. Take off from oven and turn peppers onto an ice water bowl; reserve for 10 minutes to loosen the skin from the peppers. Take peppers off water and remove charred skin from the peppers and the seeds.
- Preheat an oven to 175 °C or 350 °F. With cooking spray, coat a loaf pan, 9x5-inch in size.
- In food processor, put dates and peppers; pulse till well blended.
- In a bowl or a stand-mixer, combine egg, bread crumbs, 1/4 cup barbeque sauce, goat cheese, ground beef and pepper-date mixture together till equally incorporated. Into the prepped loaf pan, put the beef mixture. On top of meat mixture, evenly scatter 2 tablespoons of barbeque sauce.
- In the prepped oven, let bake for an hour till not pink anymore in the middle. An instant-read thermometer pricked into the middle should register at a minimum of 70 °C or 160 °F.

Nutrition Information

- Calories: 291 calories;
- Total Carbohydrate: 19.4
- Cholesterol: 87
- Protein: 20
- Total Fat: 15.1
- Sodium: 306

---

662.   Dawn Fried Rice

Serving: 4 | Prep: 10mins | Cook: 35mins |Ready in:

Ingredients

- 2 cups water
- 1 cup uncooked white rice
- 1 pound lean ground beef
- 1/4 cup soy sauce, divided

- 3 tablespoons teriyaki sauce (such as Golden Dragon® Thick Teriyaki Sauce), divided
- 2 tablespoons curry powder, divided
- 1 (4.5 ounce) can sliced mushrooms, drained
- 1/2 cup frozen peas and carrots
- 1/2 teaspoon ground cumin

Direction

- In saucepan, boil rice and water. Lower the heat to moderately-low, put a cover on, and let simmer for 20 to 25 minutes till rice is soft and liquid has soaked in.
- On moderately-high heat, heat a big skillet. In the hot skillet, cook and mix a tablespoon curry powder, a tablespoon teriyaki sauce, a dash of soy sauce and beef for 5 to 7 minutes till crumbly and browned; let drain and throw the grease.
- Into the beef, mix frozen vegetables and mushrooms; lower the heat to moderately-low, then cook and mix for 2 minutes till heated completely. Fold in the rice; mix in the rest of curry powder, teriyaki sauce and soy sauce. Put in cumin; cook for 5 minutes till heated completely.

Nutrition Information

- Calories: 435 calories;
- Sodium: 1644
- Total Carbohydrate: 45.9
- Cholesterol: 74
- Protein: 28.3
- Total Fat: 14.8

663. Delicious Grilled Hamburgers

Serving: 3 | Prep: 5mins | Cook: 10mins | Ready in:

Ingredients

- 1 pound lean ground beef

- 1 tablespoon Worcestershire sauce
- 1 tablespoon liquid smoke flavoring
- 1 teaspoon garlic powder
- 1 tablespoon olive oil
- seasoned salt to taste

Direction

- Preheat grill to high heat.
- Mix garlic powder, liquid smoke, Worcestershire sauce and ground beef lightly in medium bowl; shape, minimally handling meat, to 3 patties. Brush some oil on both sides of every patty; use seasoned salt to season.
- Put patties on grill grate; cook till well done for 5 minutes per side.

Nutrition Information

- Calories: 396 calories;
- Sodium: 220
- Total Carbohydrate: 1.9
- Cholesterol: 99
- Protein: 28.2
- Total Fat: 30

664. Dill Pickle Meatloaf

Serving: 4 | Prep: 15mins | Cook: 1hours | Ready in:

Ingredients

- 1 egg
- 1 small onion, chopped
- 1/2 cup dill pickle juice
- 3/4 teaspoon salt
- 1/4 teaspoon ground black pepper
- 1 slice bread, torn into small pieces
- 1 pound lean ground beef
- 1/4 cup chopped dill pickles
- 1/4 cup ketchup
- 2 tablespoons water
- 1 tablespoon brown sugar
- 1/2 teaspoon Worcestershire sauce

Direction

- Set an oven to 350°F (175°C) and start preheating. Coat an 8x8-inch baking dish with oil.
- In a mixing bowl, beat the egg. Whisk in pepper, salt, pickle juice, and onion. Stir in the bread until it is soggy, then combine in the ground beef until evenly blended. Shape into a loaf and put it in the prepared pan. Stir together Worcestershire sauce, sugar, water, ketchup, and chopped pickles; drizzle over the meatloaf.
- Bake in the prepared oven for about 1 hour until no pink remains in the center. An instant-read thermometer inserted into the center should read at least 160°F (70°C).

Nutrition Information

- Calories: 300 calories;
- Total Fat: 15.9
- Sodium: 842
- Total Carbohydrate: 12.6
- Cholesterol: 124
- Protein: 25.7

---

665.   Dinner In A Pumpkin I

Serving: 9 | Prep: | Cook: |Ready in:

Ingredients

- 1 medium sugar pumpkin
- 1 1/2 pounds lean ground beef
- 1 onion, chopped
- 1 clove garlic, minced
- 1 1/2 teaspoons white sugar
- 1 1/2 teaspoons Italian seasoning
- 1 1/2 teaspoons salt
- 1/8 teaspoon ground black pepper
- 4 cups tomato juice
- 3 cups shredded cabbage

- 1/2 pound fresh green beans, washed and trimmed
- 1 cup uncooked white rice

Direction

- Start preheating the oven to 350°F (175°C).
- Wash the pumpkin and cut the top off. Scrape the seeds out, discard.
- In a large, deep pan, put hamburger. Crumble; cook until brown evenly over the medium high heat. Drain the fat. Put in garlic and onion; slightly sauté.
- Put in rice, tomato juice, pepper, salt, Italian herbs and sugar, then mix thoroughly.
- Layer one-third cabbage, the green beans then the beef and the rice mixture inside the pumpkin. Repeat these layers, close the lid; bake about 2-3 hours.

Nutrition Information

- Calories: 365 calories;
- Total Fat: 16.1
- Sodium: 459
- Total Carbohydrate: 38.5
- Cholesterol: 57
- Protein: 18.3

---

666.   Dirty Diapers

Serving: 32 | Prep: 20mins | Cook: 20mins |Ready in:

Ingredients

- 1 pound ground beef
- 1 small onion, finely chopped
- 1 (10 ounce) can refrigerated crescent roll dough
- 8 slices Cheddar cheese
- 32 slices dill pickle

Direction

- Preheat an oven to 175 °C or 350 °F.

- In a skillet over medium-high heat, put the ground beef. Allow to cook, mixing to break up, till not pink anymore. To the skillet, put the onion; cook and mix till soft. Allow the grease to drain off.
- On a clean area, roll out crescent roll dough. Part the triangles and halve every triangle diagonally to create 2 smaller triangles. Pile the cheese slices and diagonally slice into 4 triangles. Onto every triangle of dough, put a triangle of cheese. On top of the cheese, scoop approximately 1 tablespoon ground beef and then put a slice of pickle on top. Fold the corners of dough directly to the middle resembles a diaper and put on a baking sheet.
- In the prepped oven, let bake till golden brown for 10 to 15 minutes.

Nutrition Information

- Calories: 90 calories;
- Sodium: 211
- Total Carbohydrate: 4
- Cholesterol: 16
- Protein: 4.8
- Total Fat: 5.9

667.   Divine Casserole

Serving: 5 | Prep: 30mins | Cook: 40mins | Ready in:

Ingredients

- 1 (8 ounce) package egg noodles
- 1 pound ground beef
- 1 (6 ounce) can tomato paste
- 1 teaspoon Worcestershire sauce
- 2 drops hot pepper sauce
- 1 pinch dried oregano
- 2 tablespoons butter
- 1 onion, chopped
- 1 (8 ounce) container creamed cottage cheese
- 1/2 (8 ounce) package cream cheese, softened
- 1/2 cup sour cream

- salt to taste
- 1/2 cup butter, melted

Direction

- Preheat an oven to 175 °C or 350 °F. Boil a big pot with lightly salted water. Put in pasta and allow to cook till al dente, or for 8 to 10 minutes; let drain.
- Allow the ground beef to brown in a skillet over medium heat till no longer pink; drain excess fat. Mix in oregano, hot sauce, Worcestershire sauce and tomato paste; put aside.
- Melt 2 tablespoons of butter in another skillet over medium heat. Sauté chopped onion till clear. Mix together sautéed onions, sour cream, cream cheese and cottage cheese in a medium bowl.
- Put half the cooked noodles in a casserole dish bottom, 2-quart in size. Sprinkle half of the melted butter over. Top with cheese mixture to cover. Toss the rest of noodles along with leftover melted butter, and spread on top of cheese mixture. Top with meat mixture to cover.
- In prepped oven, bake till bubbly, or for 40 minutes.

Nutrition Information

- Calories: 748 calories;
- Total Fat: 50.5
- Sodium: 768
- Total Carbohydrate: 43.6
- Cholesterol: 195
- Protein: 31.5

668.   Donna's Lasagna

Serving: 12 | Prep: 15mins | Cook: 1hours30mins | Ready in:

Ingredients

- 1 pound lean ground beef
- 8 ounces Italian sausage, casings removed
- 1 (10.75 ounce) can tomato puree
- 2 (6 ounce) cans tomato paste
- 2 tablespoons white sugar
- 1 teaspoon salt
- 1 clove garlic, minced
- 1 1/2 tablespoons dried parsley
- 9 lasagna noodles
- 3 cups cottage cheese
- 2 eggs, beaten
- 1/2 teaspoon ground black pepper
- 1/2 cup grated Parmesan cheese
- 1 1/2 tablespoons dried parsley
- 1/2 teaspoon salt
- 16 ounces sliced mozzarella cheese

Direction

- Let lightly salted water boil in a big pot. Allow pasta to boil for 8-10 minutes. When pasta becomes al dente, drain the excess water.
- Now, prepare the sauce in a Dutch oven or in a big pot. Let sausage and ground beef cook on a medium fire until it becomes brown and drain. Mix one teaspoon salt, 1 and a half tablespoons parsley, tomato paste, tomato puree, and garlic. Lower heat, take off cover, and let it simmer for half an hour.
- Blend together eggs, parmesan, cottage cheese, 1 and a half tablespoons parsley, half teaspoon salt and eggs in a bowl.
- Let oven heat to 350°F or 175°C. Layer 3 noodles in a 9x13 inches baking dish and top it with cottage cheese mixture, meat sauce, and cut mozzarella. Create two more layers.
- Let lasagna bake in a heated oven for an hour until it becomes hot and it forms bubbles. Wait 15 minutes then serve.

Nutrition Information

- Calories: 406 calories;
- Protein: 31.7
- Total Fat: 19.7
- Sodium: 1318

- Total Carbohydrate: 26.4
- Cholesterol: 97

669.   Down And Dirty Garlic Chili

Serving: 4 | Prep: 10mins | Cook: 30mins | Ready in:

Ingredients

- 1 pound extra lean ground beef
- 1 tablespoon chili powder
- 2 tablespoons dried onion flakes
- 1 teaspoon ground cumin
- 1 teaspoon paprika
- 2 cloves garlic, minced
- 1/4 teaspoon red pepper flakes, or to taste
- 1 (14.5 ounce) can diced tomatoes with garlic and onion
- 1 (16 ounce) can chili beans, drained
- 1 (8 ounce) can tomato sauce
- salt and pepper to taste

Direction

- Heat a large saucepan (or Dutch oven) over medium heat. Add the ground beef, and cook until evenly browned. Stir on occasion until the meat is crumbled. Flavor with red pepper flakes, garlic, paprika, cumin, onion flakes, and chili powder, blend well.
- Whisk in the tomato sauce, chili beans, and tomatoes. Lower the heat to low, and simmer for at least 30 minutes, (if you want the chili thicker, let simmer longer). Flavor with salt and pepper.

Nutrition Information

- Calories: 321 calories;
- Sodium: 1387
- Total Carbohydrate: 33.2
- Cholesterol: 75
- Protein: 34.3

- Total Fat: 8.2

670. Dutch Leek Casserole

Serving: 8 | Prep: 25mins | Cook: 45mins | Ready in:

Ingredients

- 2 pounds potatoes, peeled and chopped
- 1/4 cup milk
- 2 pounds leeks, chopped
- 1 pound ground beef
- 1 onion, chopped
- 1 red bell pepper, chopped
- 1 green bell pepper, chopped
- 1 tablespoon finely chopped green chile peppers
- soy sauce to taste
- 1 (8 ounce) package shredded Cheddar cheese
- 6 ounces cooked ham, cut into thin strips

Direction

- Preheat an oven to 175°C/350°F.
- Boil a big pot of salted water; cook potatoes for 15 minutes till tender yet firm. Drain potatoes; put in a medium bowl. Mash with milk.
- Cover leeks with enough water in a medium saucepan; boil. Cook till tender for 10 minutes. Drain; put aside.
- Mix and cook ground beef till evenly brown in a medium skillet on medium heat; mix green and red bell pepper and onion in. Season with soy sauce and green chile peppers; mix and cook till veggies are tender.
- Mix ground beef mixture, leeks and mashed potatoes in a medium baking dish. Sprinkle with cheddar cheese; put ham on top.
- In the preheated oven, bake till lightly browned and bubbly for 25 minutes.

Nutrition Information

- Calories: 515 calories;

- Cholesterol: 90
- Protein: 25
- Total Fat: 28.9
- Sodium: 554
- Total Carbohydrate: 39.7

671. Eagles Tailgating Burgers

Serving: 8 | Prep: 15mins | Cook: 15mins | Ready in:

Ingredients

- 2 pounds ground beef
- 1/4 cup garlic and herb seasoned dry bread crumbs
- 1/4 cup grated Pecorino Romano cheese
- 1/4 cup barbeque sauce
- 1/4 cup Yuengling® lager beer
- 1 egg
- 1/2 cup chopped green onion
- 2 tablespoons chopped fresh basil leaves
- 2 tablespoons Worcestershire sauce
- 2 teaspoons minced garlic
- salt and pepper to taste

Direction

- Preheat the outdoor grill over high heat.
- In a large bowl, mix the Worcestershire sauce, ground beef, green onion, bread crumbs, beer, Romano cheese, barbeque sauce, pepper, egg, salt, basil, and garlic. Use your hands to combine lightly and then shape into 8 patties.
- Rub the grill grate lightly with oil and then put the patties on the grill. Let cook for 7 to 8 minutes on each side for well done until no pink color remains at the middle.

Nutrition Information

- Calories: 258 calories;
- Cholesterol: 96
- Protein: 21.7

- Total Fat: 15.1
- Sodium: 315
- Total Carbohydrate: 7.1

672. Easy Beef Stroganoff

Serving: 8 | Prep: 10mins | Cook: 20mins | Ready in:

Ingredients

- 1 (12 ounce) package egg noodles, cooked and drained
- 6 ounces fresh mushrooms, sliced
- 1 onion, chopped
- 1/4 cup butter
- 2 pounds lean ground beef
- 4 tablespoons all-purpose flour
- 2 cups beef broth
- 1 cup sour cream
- salt and black pepper to taste

Direction

- Get a large pot with water and bring it to a boil. Cook the egg noodles in the boiling water for 8 minutes or until it's done and then drain it.
- While it cooks, create the sauce. Cook the onions and mushrooms in a large skillet with two tablespoons of butter on medium heat until it gets soft and take it out of the pan.
- With the same pan, melt the rest of the butter. Cook the ground beef in the melted butter until it gets brown. Mix in the flour and then pour and mix in the beef broth and cook it until it gets a big thick. Add in your onion and mushroom mixture and mix in the sour cream. Use pepper and salt to season it. Keep on cooking it until the sauce gets hot but not yet boiling. Serve with the sauce on top of the egg noodles.

Nutrition Information

- Calories: 602 calories;
- Sodium: 633
- Total Carbohydrate: 36.1
- Cholesterol: 148
- Protein: 28.9
- Total Fat: 37.4

673. Easy Beef Strogonoff

Serving: 3 | Prep: 10mins | Cook: 10mins | Ready in:

Ingredients

- 1 pound ground beef
- 1/2 teaspoon garlic powder
- 1/2 teaspoon salt
- 1/2 teaspoon ground black pepper
- 1 cube beef bouillon
- 1 medium onion, chopped
- 8 ounces fresh mushrooms, sliced
- 1 pint sour cream
- 4 ounces egg noodles, cooked and drained

Direction

- Brown beef in oil in a big frying pan over medium-high heat. Once the meat is brown, drain excess grease from the frying pan. Add pepper, salt, and garlic powder and mix in.
- Add mushrooms, onion, and bouillon to the frying pan and sauté until the onions turn translucent. Take away from heat (this is a must) and put in sour cream. Mix everything together and enjoy over hot cooked egg noodles.

Nutrition Information

- Calories: 977 calories;
- Total Carbohydrate: 39.9
- Cholesterol: 228
- Protein: 38.3
- Total Fat: 74.4
- Sodium: 789

674. Easy Black Bean Taco Salad

Serving: 4 | Prep: 15mins | Cook: 20mins | Ready in:

Ingredients

- 1 pound ground beef
- 1 envelope taco seasoning mix
- 3/4 cup water
- 1 (15 ounce) can black beans, drained
- 1 head romaine lettuce, shredded
- 1 (8 ounce) jar salsa
- 2 tomatoes, diced
- 2 cups shredded Mexican cheese blend
- 8 ounces sour cream
- 1 (10 ounce) bag tortilla chips

Direction

- Cook the ground beef in a skillet over medium heat until browned, no longer pinkish, and the beef is crumbly, about 8 minutes. Mix in water and taco mix. Cook for about 10 more minutes until the mixture is thickened.
- In a saucepan, simmer the black beans over medium heat.
- Arrange 1/4 of the beef mixture on a serving plate. Top it with 1/4 of the black beans. Do the same with the remaining ingredients to complete 4 salads. Layer on top of each salad the romaine lettuce, salsa, tomatoes and cheese. Garnish liberally with tortilla chips and sour cream.

Nutrition Information

- Calories: 1039 calories;
- Total Carbohydrate: 83.7
- Cholesterol: 144
- Protein: 47.2
- Total Fat: 58.6
- Sodium: 2128

675. Easy Chili I

Serving: 6 | Prep: | Cook: | Ready in:

Ingredients

- 1 pound ground beef
- 1 cup chopped onion
- 1/2 cup chopped green bell pepper
- 2 1/2 tablespoons chili powder
- 1 clove garlic, minced
- 1 bay leaf
- 1/2 teaspoon ground cumin
- 4 teaspoons finely chopped jalapeno chile peppers
- 1 (29 ounce) can diced tomatoes
- 1 (15 ounce) can tomato sauce
- 1 (16 ounce) can chili beans, undrained
- salt and pepper to taste

Direction

- In a big saucepan, combine bell peppers, onion, and ground beef atop a medium-high heat, then sauté for roughly 5 minutes, or until beef turns brown. Get rid of the excess fat.
- Add in tomato sauce, tomatoes, chile peppers, cumin, bay leaf, garlic, and chili powder, then pepper and salt to your taste. Set the mixture to boiling and drip the heat down to low. Simmer while covered for around 1 1/2 hours, stirring once in a while. Stir the beans in and cook through.

Nutrition Information

- Calories: 368 calories;
- Total Fat: 21.4
- Sodium: 1106
- Total Carbohydrate: 26.7
- Cholesterol: 65
- Protein: 19.5

676. Easy Chili II

Serving: 4 | Prep: 15mins | Cook: 30mins | Ready in:

Ingredients

- 1 pound ground beef
- 1 (16 ounce) can chili beans, undrained
- 1 (14.5 ounce) can peeled and diced tomatoes with juice
- 1 small onion, chopped
- 1/4 cup chopped green bell pepper

Direction

- Cook beef on medium heat until browned in a medium saucepan. Mix in bell pepper, onion, tomatoes and beans; lower the heat and let simmer for half an hour.

Nutrition Information

- Calories: 366 calories;
- Total Fat: 18.6
- Sodium: 729
- Total Carbohydrate: 25.7
- Cholesterol: 70
- Protein: 26

677. Easy Enchiladas

Serving: 10 | Prep: 15mins | Cook: 30mins | Ready in:

Ingredients

- 2 (16 ounce) jars prepared salsa
- 1 pound ground beef
- 1 (15.5 ounce) jar prepared salsa con queso
- 20 (8 inch) flour tortillas
- 1 (8 ounce) package shredded Cheddar-Monterey Jack cheese blend

Direction

- Preheat an oven to 350°F (175°C). Grease a baking dish that's 9x13 inches in size, then pour the salsa into the bottom. Leave aside.
- In a frying pan, cook and stir the ground beef over medium heat for 10 minutes till meat is crumbly and browned. Drain the grease from the beef, then add the salsa con queso to the frying pan, stir to mix well. On each tortilla, place about 2 tablespoons of the beef mixture down the center, roll the tortillas; in the baking dish, place them seam side down on top of the salsa. Drizzle the shredded cheese on top of the enchiladas.
- In the preheated oven, bake for approximately 15 to 20 minutes till the enchiladas are hot and bubbling and the cheese is browned.

Nutrition Information

- Calories: 595 calories;
- Sodium: 1757
- Total Carbohydrate: 68.3
- Cholesterol: 54
- Protein: 24.3
- Total Fat: 25.8

678. Easy Lasagna I

Serving: 8 | Prep: 35mins | Cook: 1hours | Ready in:

Ingredients

- 1 pound lean ground beef
- 1 onion, chopped
- 1 (4.5 ounce) can mushrooms, drained
- 1 (28 ounce) jar spaghetti sauce
- 1 (16 ounce) package cottage cheese
- 1 pint part-skim ricotta cheese
- 1/4 cup grated Parmesan cheese
- 2 eggs
- 1 (16 ounce) package lasagna noodles
- 8 ounces shredded mozzarella cheese

Direction

- Preheat an oven to 175 °C or 350 °F.
- Cook and mix ground beef in a big skillet till brown. Put in onions and mushrooms; sauté till onions are clear. Mix in sauce of pasta, and heat through.
- Mix together eggs, grated Parmesan cheese, ricotta cheese and cottage cheese in a medium bowl.
- In the pan bottom, 13x9-inch in size, spread a thin layer of meat sauce. Layer uncooked lasagna noodles, mixture of cheese, the mozzarella cheese, and the meat sauce. Keep layering till every ingredient are used, setting aside half cup of mozzarella. Place aluminum foil on pan to cover.
- In prepped oven, bake for 45 minutes. Remove cover, and put the leftover half cup of mozzarella cheese on top. Bake for 15 minutes longer. Take out of oven, and allow to sit for 10 to 15 minutes prior to serving.

Nutrition Information

- Calories: 702 calories;
- Cholesterol: 142
- Protein: 44.2
- Total Fat: 30.3
- Sodium: 1058
- Total Carbohydrate: 62.5

679.   Easy Lasagna II

Serving: 12 | Prep: 15mins | Cook: 1hours | Ready in:

Ingredients

- 1 pound lean ground beef
- 1 (32 ounce) jar spaghetti sauce
- 32 ounces cottage cheese
- 3 cups shredded mozzarella cheese
- 2 eggs
- 1/2 cup grated Parmesan cheese
- 2 teaspoons dried parsley
- salt to taste

- ground black pepper to taste
- 9 lasagna noodles
- 1/2 cup water

Direction

- Let ground beef cook over medium fire in a big skillet until it becomes brown. Mix in spaghetti sauce and let simmer for five minutes.
- Blend in a big bowl 2 cups of mozzarella cheese, cottage cheese, dried parsley, ground black pepper, salt, eggs, and 1/2 the grated parmesan cheese.
- Even out 3/4 cup of the sauce mixture on the bottom of a 9x13-inch baking dish. On top of it, arrange 3 lasagna noodles (uncooked), 1 3/4 cup of cheese mixture, and 1/4 cup sauce. Make 2 more layers. Then top again with 3 noodles, leftover sauce, leftover mozzarella and parmesan cheese. Set half cup of water to the pan edges. Use aluminum foil to cover.
- Let it bake in a warm up oven at 350°F or 175°C, about 45 minutes. Take off cover and let it bake for 10 minutes more. Wait for another 10 minutes then serve.

Nutrition Information

- Calories: 377 calories;
- Sodium: 870
- Total Carbohydrate: 26.4
- Cholesterol: 89
- Protein: 29.4
- Total Fat: 16.7

680.   Easy Meatloaf

Serving: 8 | Prep: 10mins | Cook: 1hours | Ready in:

Ingredients

- 1 1/2 pounds ground beef
- 1 egg

- 1 onion, chopped
- 1 cup milk
- 1 cup dried bread crumbs
- salt and pepper to taste
- 2 tablespoons brown sugar
- 2 tablespoons prepared mustard
- 1/3 cup ketchup

Direction

- Preheat an oven to 175 degrees C (350 degrees F).
- Mix bread OR cracker crumbs, milk, onion, egg and beef in a large bowl. Add pepper and salt to taste and transfer into a 5x9 inch loaf pan that is lightly greased or shape into a loaf and then put in a 9x13 inch baking dish that is lightly greased.
- Mix ketchup, mustard and brown sugar in a separate small bowl. Combine thoroughly and then spread on top of the meatloaf.
- Bake for 1 hour at 175 degrees C (350 degrees F).

Nutrition Information

- Calories: 372 calories;
- Total Fat: 24.7
- Sodium: 335
- Total Carbohydrate: 18.5
- Cholesterol: 98
- Protein: 18.2

681.   Easy Mexican Casserole

Serving: 6 | Prep: 20mins | Cook: 30mins | Ready in:

Ingredients

- 1 pound lean ground beef
- 2 cups salsa
- 1 (16 ounce) can chili beans, drained
- 3 cups tortilla chips, crushed
- 2 cups sour cream

- 1 (2 ounce) can sliced black olives, drained
- 1/2 cup chopped green onion
- 1/2 cup chopped fresh tomato
- 2 cups shredded Cheddar cheese

Direction

- Set the oven to 175°C or 350°F to preheat.
- Cook ground beef in a big skillet on medium-high heat until beef is not pink anymore. Stir in salsa and lower heat to simmer until liquid has been absorbed, about 20 minutes. Stir in beans and heat through.
- Use cooking spray to coat a 13"x9" baking dish. Spread dish with crushed tortilla chips then scoop over chips the beef mixture. Spread beef with sour cream and sprinkle sour cream with green onion, tomato as well as olives. Put Cheddar cheese on top.
- In the preheated oven, bake until bubbly and hot, about a half hour.

Nutrition Information

- Calories: 632 calories;
- Cholesterol: 119
- Protein: 31.7
- Total Fat: 43.7
- Sodium: 1308
- Total Carbohydrate: 32.8

682.   Easy Mini Ale And Meat Pies

Serving: 6 | Prep: 30mins | Cook: 55mins | Ready in:

Ingredients

- 1 tablespoon all-purpose flour, or as needed
- 2 (9 inch) frozen pastry crusts, at room temperature
- 3 (3x5-inch) loaf pans
- 2 tablespoons vegetable oil
- 2 medium potatoes, diced

- 2 stalks celery, diced
- 1/2 large white onion, chopped
- 1 large carrot, diced
- 1 pound ground beef
- 1/4 cup frozen peas
- 1/4 cup frozen corn
- 1 (12 fluid ounce) can or bottle dark ale
- 2 tablespoons all-purpose flour
- 2 cups reduced-sodium beef stock
- 2 tablespoons ketchup
- 1 tablespoon Worcestershire sauce
- 1 tablespoon kosher salt
- 1 tablespoon tomato bouillon (optional)
- 1 teaspoon dried rosemary
- 1 teaspoon garlic powder
- 1 egg, beaten

Direction

- Start preheating oven to 350°F (175°C).
- Flour the work surface lightly. Form each crust out to about 1/8-inch thick. Cut the dough to fit 3 loaf pans of 3x5-inch. Push the dough, using fingertips, into the tins and up the edges. Roll out the remaining dough to use as the top crusts, then put aside.
- In a large pot, heat oil over medium heat. Put in carrot, onion, celery and potatoes. Cook for about 5 mins, until the onions become translucent, stirring occasionally. Put in the beef and cook for 5 to 7 mins or until browned. Put in ale, corn and peas; cook while stirring for about 5 mins or until reduced by a bit more than half, stirring occasionally.
- Put the flour into vegetable-ale mixture. Stir often for 1-3 mins or until almost pasty and thick. Slowly add stock, stirring constantly. Put in garlic powder, rosemary, tomato bouillon, salt, Worcestershire sauce and ketchup. Lower the heat; simmer for 7-10 mins or until the potatoes are cooked through and the filling mixture reduces to preferred thickness.
- Take the pot away from the heat and cool the filling slightly. Stuff the crusts with filling. Add on top the remaining dough, then pinch the edges to seal. Brush the beaten egg wash

over the tops of pies. Create 3 slits on top of each pie for the air to escape. Put tins on the baking sheet.
- Bake in the prepared oven for about half an hour or until golden brown.

Nutrition Information

- Calories: 647 calories;
- Protein: 21.8
- Total Fat: 37.4
- Sodium: 1502
- Total Carbohydrate: 51.6
- Cholesterol: 77

683.   Easy Skillet Spaghetti

Serving: 4 | Prep: 15mins | Cook: 1hours5mins | Ready in:

Ingredients

- 1 pound ground beef
- 3 cups water
- 18 fluid ounces tomato juice
- 1 (6 ounce) can tomato paste
- 2 tablespoons dried minced onion
- 1 1/2 teaspoons chili powder, or more to taste
- 1 teaspoon white sugar
- 1 teaspoon dried oregano, crushed
- 1 teaspoon garlic salt
- 1 teaspoon salt
- 7 ounces spaghetti

Direction

- Over medium-high heat, heat a large skillet. In the hot skillet, cook beef while stirring for 5-7 minutes or until crumbly and brown.
- Mix salt, garlic salt, oregano, sugar, chili powder, minced onion, tomato paste, tomato juice and water into the ground beef. Cover the skillet and boil. Lower the heat to medium-

low; simmer the beef mixture, for half an hour or until flavors blend, stirring occasionally.
- Put spaghetti into the beef mixture; mix to separate the strands. Cover skillet; simmer for half an hour or until the spaghetti becomes tender, stirring frequently.

Nutrition Information

- Calories: 494 calories;
- Total Fat: 18.9
- Sodium: 1814
- Total Carbohydrate: 53.7
- Cholesterol: 70
- Protein: 28.3

684.   Easy Spaghetti With Tomato Sauce

Serving: 5 | Prep: | Cook: | Ready in:

Ingredients

- 12 ounces spaghetti
- 1 pound lean ground beef
- 1 teaspoon salt
- 3/4 teaspoon white sugar
- 1 teaspoon dried oregano
- 1/4 teaspoon ground black pepper
- 1/8 teaspoon garlic powder
- 2 tablespoons dried minced onion
- 2 1/2 cups chopped tomatoes
- 1 1/3 (6 ounce) cans tomato paste
- 1 (4.5 ounce) can sliced mushrooms

Direction

- Brown beef on moderate heat and get rid of the fat.
- Mix together mushrooms, tomato paste, diced tomatoes, onion flakes, garlic powder, pepper, oregano, sugar, salt and beef in a big pot. Simmer about 2 hours at low heat while stirring sometimes.

- Following package directions, cook pasta, then drain well. Serve sauce on top of the spaghetti.

Nutrition Information

- Calories: 557 calories;
- Total Fat: 20.3
- Sodium: 1002
- Total Carbohydrate: 65.7
- Cholesterol: 68
- Protein: 28.2

685.   Easy Tater Tot Hot Dish

Serving: 4 | Prep: 10mins | Cook: 1hours | Ready in:

Ingredients

- 1 pound lean ground beef
- 1/2 cup chopped yellow onion
- 1 egg
- 1 (10 ounce) can cream of chicken soup
- 1 (32 ounce) package tater tots

Direction

- Preheat the oven to 230 degrees C (450 degrees F). Coat a 9x9-inch baking dish with grease.
- In a bowl, combine together the egg, onion and ground beef. Pour evenly into the baking dish prepared. Spread tater tots on top of the beef mixture. Add chicken soup atop tater tots.
- Bake for about an hour until beef has cooked through and the internal temperature is 71 degrees C (160 degrees F).

Nutrition Information

- Calories: 695 calories;
- Sodium: 1460
- Total Carbohydrate: 63.1
- Cholesterol: 131
- Protein: 30.9
- Total Fat: 40.5

686. Easy Vegetable Beef Soup

Serving: 16 | Prep: 20mins | Cook: 3hours | Ready in:

Ingredients

- 2 pounds lean ground beef
- 4 (15 ounce) cans mixed vegetables
- 4 (16 ounce) cans diced tomatoes
- 1 onion, chopped
- ground black pepper to taste
- salt to taste

Direction

- Cook the ground meat over medium heat in a large soup pot until browned. Let the grease drain from the pot.
- Add tomatoes, mixed vegetables, and chopped onion; stir well. Then reduce the heat; simmer for about 3-4 hours. Dust pepper and salt to taste.

Nutrition Information

- Calories: 213 calories;
- Sodium: 537
- Total Carbohydrate: 11.7
- Cholesterol: 43
- Protein: 12.5
- Total Fat: 12

687. Egg Foo Yung II

Serving: 5 | Prep: 5mins | Cook: 25mins | Ready in:

Ingredients

- 8 eggs, beaten
- 1 cup thinly sliced celery
- 1 cup finely chopped onion
- 1 cup bean sprouts
- 1/2 cup diced fresh mushrooms
- 1/3 cup chopped cooked chicken breast
- 1/3 cup cooked and crumbled ground beef
- 1/3 cup chopped cooked pork
- 1 teaspoon salt
- 1/4 teaspoon ground black pepper
- FOO YUNG SAUCE
- 2 cubes chicken bouillon
- 1 1/2 cups hot water
- 1 1/2 teaspoons white sugar
- 2 tablespoons soy sauce
- 6 tablespoons cold water
- 1 1/2 tablespoons cornstarch

Direction

- In a big bowl, beat the eggs. Put in pepper, salt, pork, beef, chicken, mushrooms, bean sprouts, onion and celery. Blend together.
- In a medium work or skillet, heat the oil and brown 1/2 cup of egg mixture at a time until done. When the entire of the mixture turns brown, put aside.
- For the sauce, in a small saucepan with hot water, dissolve the bouillon; put in soy sauce and sugar and mix well over medium heat. Put in cornstarch and cold water and blend until the mixture is smooth and thickened. Serve the sauce with Egg Foo Yung.

Nutrition Information

- Calories: 240 calories;
- Protein: 22
- Total Fat: 12.6
- Sodium: 1443
- Total Carbohydrate: 9.6
- Cholesterol: 330

688. Eggplant Lasagna

Serving: 8 | Prep: 20mins | Cook: 1hours10mins | Ready in:

Ingredients

- 1 teaspoon olive oil for brushing
- 2 eggs
- 2 tablespoons water
- 1 cup grated Parmesan cheese
- 1 cup Italian-seasoned breadcrumbs
- salt and ground black pepper to taste
- 2 large eggplants, peeled and sliced into 1/2-inch rounds
- 2 tablespoons olive oil
- 1 pound ground beef
- 48 ounces chunky tomato sauce (such as Prego®)
- 2 cups shredded mozzarella cheese

Direction

- Set oven temperature to 375 degrees F (190 degrees C) and leave aside to preheat. Coat a baking tray measuring 9x13-inch and 2 baking papers with a teaspoon of olive oil.
- In a shallow dish, beat water and eggs together. Mix bread crumbs, Parmesan cheese, grounded black pepper, and salt in another shallow dish until evenly blended.
- Gently place eggplant slices into egg mixture to coat evenly, followed with gentle presses into bread crumb mixture. Carefully tap off excessive crumbs. Place the coated slices on the prepared baking papers.
- Bake the slices until they turn golden brown for 20-25 minutes in the preheated oven. Turn over the eggplant and continue baking the other side for another 20-25 minutes.
- Take eggplants out of the oven and change oven temperature to 400 degrees F (200 degrees C).
- In a skillet, heat up 2 tablespoons of olive oil at medium-high heat settings, and mix in ground beef. Use grounded black pepper and salt as a seasoning. Cook the beef for approximately 10 minutes while stirring until texture of meat is browned and crumbly. Strain out excessive grease. Mix tomato sauce into the minced beef, let it simmer and leave the sauce to one side.
- Layer as follows; 1/3 of the eggplant slices as the bottom of the tray. Followed by 1/3 of tomato sauce with minced beef above the eggplants. Scatter 1/3 mozzarella cheese on top. Repeat layering for another 2 times, with a final layer of mozzarella cheese.
- Bake for 10-15 minutes in the preheated oven until bubbles appear in the sauce and the cheese has completely melted. Allow to cool for 5 minutes before cutting.

Nutrition Information

- Calories: 404 calories;
- Total Fat: 20.6
- Sodium: 1496
- Total Carbohydrate: 30
- Cholesterol: 108
- Protein: 27.7

689. Eggplants In Red Sauce

Serving: 6 | Prep: 30mins | Cook: 25mins | Ready in:

Ingredients

- vegetable oil for frying
- 2 eggplants, sliced into rounds
- 1 pound tomatoes, halved
- 1 tablespoon olive oil
- 1 small onion, chopped
- 2 cloves garlic, minced
- 1/2 pound ground beef
- 1 large potato, diced
- 1/3 green bell pepper, chopped
- 1 tablespoon tomato paste
- salt and ground black pepper to taste
- 1/2 lemon, juiced

Direction

- In a large saucepan, over medium-high heat, heat a half inch of vegetable oil. Fry eggplants in batches for about a minute each side until golden brown. Place on paper towels to drain.
- In a blender, puree tomatoes until smooth. Press through a strainer; getting rid of skins and seeds.
- In a large skillet, over medium heat, heat olive oil. Add garlic and onion; cook while stirring for 3-5 minutes until translucent. Add beef; cook for about 5 minutes until no longer pink. Stir in tomato paste, green bell pepper and potato. Season with pepper and salt.
- Stir tomato puree into the skillet. Simmer for about 10 minutes until sauce is thickened. Add lemon juice and fried eggplant. Simmer for about 5 more minutes until flavors combine.

Nutrition Information

- Calories: 235 calories;
- Cholesterol: 24
- Protein: 10.5
- Total Fat: 11.1
- Sodium: 81
- Total Carbohydrate: 26.4

690.   Elbows And Ground Beef

Serving: 6 | Prep: | Cook: 30mins |Ready in:

Ingredients

- 1 1/2 pounds lean ground beef
- 1 green bell pepper, chopped
- 1 onion, chopped
- 2 (29 ounce) cans tomato sauce
- 1 (16 ounce) package macaroni

Direction

- Cook pasta following the package instructions. Drain.

- Brown ground beef in a Dutch oven over medium heat. Add in chopped onion, and cook until the onion is tender. Add tomato sauce and green pepper, cook until the pepper is tender.
- Enjoy with the pasta.

Nutrition Information

- Calories: 570 calories;
- Protein: 35.2
- Total Fat: 15.5
- Sodium: 1492
- Total Carbohydrate: 72.9
- Cholesterol: 74

691.   Emily's Famous Sloppy Joes

Serving: 8 | Prep: 10mins | Cook: 20mins |Ready in:

Ingredients

- 1 1/2 pounds ground beef
- 1 onion, chopped
- 1 red bell pepper, chopped
- 1 (6 ounce) can tomato paste
- 1 cup water
- 3 cloves garlic, minced
- 1 tablespoon chili powder
- 1 teaspoon paprika
- 1 teaspoon ground cumin
- 1 teaspoon distilled white vinegar
- 3 tablespoons brown sugar
- 1 teaspoon dried oregano
- 1/2 teaspoon salt
- 1/2 teaspoon ground black pepper
- 8 hamburger buns, split

Direction

- Over medium-high heat, sauté ground beef for 5 minutes in a big skillet. Put the red bell pepper and onion in; sauté until onion is soft, 5 minutes. Remove the fat.

- Mix water and tomato paste. Stir well until paste dissolves. Add chili powder, garlic, paprika, vinegar, brown sugar, cumin, oregano, pepper, and salt. Heat for 5 to 10 minutes or until mixture becomes like a thick stew.

Nutrition Information

- Calories: 328 calories;
- Total Fat: 12.6
- Sodium: 617
- Total Carbohydrate: 34.2
- Cholesterol: 52
- Protein: 19.4

692.   Empty Wallet Casserole

Serving: 5 | Prep: 20mins | Cook: 1hours10mins | Ready in:

Ingredients

- 1 pound ground beef
- salt and pepper to taste
- 1 1/2 teaspoons ground cumin
- 2 teaspoons poultry seasoning
- 2 teaspoons minced garlic
- 2 teaspoons dried thyme
- 2 tablespoons butter
- 1 small onion, sliced into thin rings
- 2 cups sliced fresh mushrooms
- 3 large potatoes, thinly sliced
- 1 (10.75 ounce) can condensed cream of chicken soup
- 20 saltine crackers, crushed
- 1 pinch paprika, for garnish

Direction

- Set the oven to 350°F (175°C) and start preheating.

- Break ground beef into crumbles into a large skillet over medium heat. Season with thyme, poultry seasoning, garlic, cumin, pepper and salt. Cook while stirring to crumble until browned evenly. Drain; place on a 9x13 inch baking dish, or large casserole dish.
- Place 2 layers of potato slices over ground beef, season each with pepper and salt. Over medium heat, in the skillet, melt butter; sauté mushrooms and onions until tender. Spread over the top of potatoes.
- Stir just enough water into the soup so that you can pour it; scoop over the top of casserole, be sure that you spread it out evenly. Scatter cracker crumbs over top; top with paprika. Use aluminum foil to cover the dish.
- Bake in the prepared oven for about an hour until potatoes become soft. Get rid of aluminum foil; place back to the oven for about 10 minutes until top turns brown.

Nutrition Information

- Calories: 500 calories;
- Total Fat: 20.7
- Sodium: 631
- Total Carbohydrate: 55.6
- Cholesterol: 72
- Protein: 23.9

693.   Feta Cheese Stuffed Meatballs

Serving: 8 | Prep: 15mins | Cook: 20mins | Ready in:

Ingredients

- cooking spray
- 1 pound ground beef
- 1 pound ground pork
- 1/4 cup Italian-seasoned bread crumbs
- 1 (1 ounce) package onion soup mix
- 1 egg

- 1 tablespoon ground black pepper
- 1 tablespoon Italian seasoning
- 1 tablespoon minced garlic
- 1/2 cup crumbled feta cheese

Direction

- Set the oven at 220°C (425°F) to preheat. Use cooking spray to lightly spray a baking sheet.
- In a bowl, mix garlic, Italian seasoning, pepper, egg, onion soup mix, bread crumbs, ground pork, and ground beef together. Form a 2 to 3-inch meatball around 1 1/2 teaspoons feta cheese. Put the stuffed meatballs on the greased baking sheet.
- In the preheated oven, bake for 10 minutes. Flip the meatballs and continue to bake for 10-20 minutes more, until browned and cooked through. Check by inserting an instant-read thermometer into the center and it should state at least 70°C (160°F). Remove the meatballs from the oven, transfer to a separate pan and use aluminum foil to cover for 3-5 minutes.

Nutrition Information

- Calories: 309 calories;
- Total Carbohydrate: 6.7
- Cholesterol: 109
- Protein: 23.5
- Total Fat: 20.6
- Sodium: 621

694.   Feta Stuffed Hamburgers

Serving: 4 | Prep: 5mins | Cook: 15mins | Ready in:

Ingredients

- 1 pound lean ground beef
- 1/2 teaspoon Worcestershire sauce
- 1 teaspoon dried parsley
- salt and pepper to taste
- 1 cup crumbled feta cheese

Direction

- Preheat outdoor grill to medium heat; oil grate lightly.
- Knead pepper, salt, parsley, Worcestershire sauce and ground beef in a bowl; shape mixture to 8 evenly-sized balls; flatten to create thin patties. Put 1/4 cup feta cheese on each of 4 patties. Put the patties without cheese over each patty with cheese then press edges together so cheese is sealed in middle.
- On preheated grill, cook, 7-8 minutes each side for well done, to desired degree of doneness. An inserted instant-read thermometer in the middle should read 70°C/160°F.

Nutrition Information

- Calories: 386 calories;
- Sodium: 780
- Total Carbohydrate: 2.8
- Cholesterol: 135
- Protein: 31
- Total Fat: 27.2

695.   Fiesta Meatloaf

Serving: 8 | Prep: 15mins | Cook: 1hours30mins | Ready in:

Ingredients

- 1 pound lean ground beef
- 1 pound lean ground pork
- 3/4 cup warm water
- 2 slightly beaten eggs
- 1/3 cup picante sauce
- 1 (1 ounce) package dry onion soup mix
- 3/4 cup dry bread crumbs
- 1/4 cup minced green bell pepper
- 1 (10.75 ounce) can condensed nacho cheese soup (such as Campbell's® Fiesta Nacho Cheese Soup)

Direction

- Set an oven to 350° F (175° C) to preheat. Grease a 9x5 inch loaf pan.
- In a mixing bowl, combine the bell pepper, breadcrumbs, onion soup mix, picante sauce, eggs, water, pork and beef until well blended. Place into the prepared loaf pan, then using a fork, poke in the loaf nearly to the bottom of the pan to make holes. Add the undiluted cheese sauce on top of the roast and evenly spread.
- Bake for about 1 1/2 hours in the prepared oven until no pink remains in the center. An instant-read thermometer should show 160° F (72° C) when inserted into the middle.

Nutrition Information

- Calories: 379 calories;
- Sodium: 776
- Total Carbohydrate: 13.6
- Cholesterol: 130
- Protein: 24.9
- Total Fat: 24.2

696.   Fiesta Tostadas

Serving: 6 | Prep: 15mins | Cook: 15mins | Ready in:

Ingredients

- 1 pound ground beef
- 1 (5.4 ounce) package Knorr® Fiesta Sides™ - Mexican Rice
- 1/2 cup red bell pepper, diced
- 12 corn tostada shells
- 1/2 head iceberg lettuce, shredded
- 2 tomatoes, diced
- 1 cup grated queso fresco cheese
- 1/2 cup sour cream

Direction

- In a medium sized pot, brown the ground beef until no longer pink, and crumbled. Using a slotted spoon, take out browned beef. Put aside. Pour fat off.
- Prepare the Knorr(R) Fiesta Sides TM-Mexican Rice in same skillet, following package instructions. Put in diced red bell pepper and browned ground beef. Mix well.
- Portion mixture among 12 tostada shells. Stack them 2 high, creating six double-decker tostadas. Add sour cream, queso fresco, tomato and shredded lettuce on top.

Nutrition Information

- Calories: 449 calories;
- Protein: 23.1
- Total Fat: 22.1
- Sodium: 219
- Total Carbohydrate: 26.4
- Cholesterol: 69

697.   Filipino Lumpia

Serving: 6 | Prep: 1hours | Cook: 10mins | Ready in:

Ingredients

- 1 lumpia wrappers
- 1 pound ground beef
- 1/2 pound ground pork
- 1/3 cup finely chopped onion
- 1/3 cup finely chopped green bell pepper
- 1/3 cup finely chopped carrot
- 1 quart oil for frying

Direction

- Be sure that the lumpia wrappers are fully thawed. On a clean dry surface, lay several lumpia wrappers and use a damp towel to cover. The edges will dry out fast and wrappers are super thin.

- Mix carrot, green pepper, onion, ground pork, and beef in a medium bowl. Put about 2 tablespoons of the meat mixture along the middle of the wrapper. The filling should no larger around than your thumb or the wrapper will burn prior the meat is done. Then fold one edge of the wrapper over to the other. Turn the outer edges in slightly, and keep on rolling into a cylinder. Damp your finger, and wet the edge to enclose. Continue with the rest of the wrappers and filling, leaving completed lumpias covered to avoid drying. This is a nice time to ask a loved one or a friend to make the job less repetitive!
- In a 9-inch skillet set at medium to medium-high heat, add oil and heat to 365-375°F (170-175°C). Then fry 3 to 4 lumpia at a time. It should only take approximately 2 to 3 minutes for each side. It will be browned nicely once done. Transfer to paper towels to drain on.
- You can slice every lumpia into thirds for parties if you want. We pair the lumpia with banana ketchup in the Philippines, yet I've never seen it promoted in America.

Nutrition Information

- Calories: 365 calories;
- Total Fat: 30.2
- Sodium: 60
- Total Carbohydrate: 2.3
- Cholesterol: 75
- Protein: 20.4

---

698.   Flatlander Chili

Serving: 10 | Prep: 15mins | Cook: 1hours30mins |Ready in:

Ingredients

- 2 pounds lean ground beef
- 1 (46 fluid ounce) can tomato juice
- 1 (29 ounce) can tomato sauce

- 1 1/2 cups chopped onion
- 1/2 cup chopped celery
- 1/4 cup chopped green bell pepper
- 1/4 cup chili powder
- 2 teaspoons ground cumin
- 1 1/2 teaspoons garlic powder
- 1 teaspoon salt
- 1/2 teaspoon ground black pepper
- 1/2 teaspoon dried oregano
- 1/2 teaspoon white sugar
- 1/8 teaspoon ground cayenne pepper
- 2 cups canned red beans, drained and rinsed

Direction

- Place the ground beef in a big deep frying pan and cook upon a medium-high heat until they are browned evenly. Drain the cooked meat and crumble, then put to the side.
- Put all the ingredients into a big kettle and boil. Cut down the heat and simmer for 1-1 1/2 hours, occasionally stirring.

Nutrition Information

- Calories: 347 calories;
- Sodium: 1246
- Total Carbohydrate: 22.6
- Cholesterol: 68
- Protein: 21.4
- Total Fat: 19.9

---

699.   French Canadian Tourtiere

Serving: 8 | Prep: 40mins | Cook: 40mins |Ready in:

Ingredients

- 1 pound lean ground pork
- 1/2 pound lean ground beef
- 1 onion, diced
- 1 clove garlic, minced
- 1/2 cup water

- 1 1/2 teaspoons salt
- 1/2 teaspoon dried thyme, crushed
- 1/4 teaspoon ground sage
- 1/4 teaspoon ground black pepper
- 1/8 teaspoon ground cloves
- 1 recipe pastry for a 9 inch double crust pie

Direction

- Mix cloves, black pepper, sage, thyme, salt, water, garlic, onion, beef, and pork in a saucepan. Cook on medium heat until the mixture boils, stir occasionally. Lower the heat to low and simmer for about 5 minutes until the meat is cooked. Let it cool to room temperature.
- Set the oven at 220°C (425°F) to preheat.
- Scoop the meat mixture into the pie crust. Put the top crust on top of the pie and pinch its edges to seal. Slice slits on the top crust to let the steam escape. Use strips of aluminum foil to cover the pie edges.
- Bake for 20 minutes in the preheated oven; take away the foil and put it back to the oven. Bake until it is golden brown for 15-20 more minutes. Let it cool for 10 minutes before cutting.

Nutrition Information

- Calories: 405 calories;
- Sodium: 749
- Total Carbohydrate: 22.1
- Cholesterol: 55
- Protein: 18.4
- Total Fat: 26.6

700.   Fry Bread Tacos II

Serving: 4 | Prep: 20mins | Cook: 22mins | Ready in:

Ingredients

- Toppings:

- 1 (15.5 ounce) can pinto beans, with liquid
- 1/2 cup picante sauce, divided
- 1 pound ground beef
- 1 (1.25 ounce) package taco seasoning mix
- Fry Bread:
- 2 cups all-purpose flour, or more as needed
- 1 tablespoon baking powder
- 1 teaspoon salt
- 1 cup milk
- oil for frying
- 2 cups shredded iceberg lettuce
- 1 cup shredded Cheddar cheese

Direction

- In a small saucepan, combine 2 tablespoons picante sauce and bean on low heat. Cook until it heats through, 5 minutes.
- In a big pan on medium-high heat, combine taco seasoning mix and ground beef; cook until it turns brown, around 5-8 minutes. Cover and keep the meat warm as you prepare the fry bread.
- In a medium-sized bowl, stir salt, baking powder, and flour. Stir in the milk and mix until dough comes together, adding more flour if needed to be able to handle it.
- Knead the dough on a floured surface until smooth, a minimum of 5 minutes. Allow the dough to rest for around 5 minutes. Break dough off into 3/4-cup-sized pieces and shape them into round 1/4-inch-thick discs, making a thinner and depressed area in the middle.
- Heat a deep, big heavy pan with 1 1/2 inches oil to 180 degrees C or 365 degrees F. Fry the dough in hot oil until both sides are golden, 3 minutes on each side; drain on paper towels.
- Top fry bread with Cheddar cheese, lettuce, ground beef, and beans, spooning picante sauce to the top.

Nutrition Information

- Calories: 808 calories;
- Total Fat: 36.5
- Sodium: 2255

- Total Carbohydrate: 76.7
- Cholesterol: 103
- Protein: 40.4

701.　　　German Tomato Soup

Serving: 8 | Prep: 30mins | Cook: 2hours | Ready in:

Ingredients

- 2 pounds ground beef
- 4 (10.75 ounce) cans condensed tomato soup
- 2 1/2 cups milk
- 1 1/8 cups water, or as needed
- 6 white potatoes, peeled and sliced 1/4 inch thick
- 1 small head cabbage, cored and sliced
- 3 carrots, sliced
- 1 small onion, chopped

Direction

- Heat on medium high heat a soup pot or big Dutch oven. Crumble in the ground beef and cook until browned evenly while stirring often. Drain the excess grease. Stir in water, milk, tomato soup, onion, carrots, potatoes and cabbage. Bring to a boil and simmer for a half hour on medium heat. Lower the heat to low and cook for 1 1/2 hours before serving.

Nutrition Information

- Calories: 489 calories;
- Total Fat: 17.5
- Sodium: 983
- Total Carbohydrate: 57
- Cholesterol: 75
- Protein: 28.2

702.　　　Glazed Meatloaf I

Serving: 6 | Prep: 10mins | Cook: 1hours10mins | Ready in:

Ingredients

- 1/2 cup ketchup
- 1/3 cup brown sugar
- 1/4 cup lemon juice, divided
- 1 teaspoon mustard powder
- 2 pounds ground beef
- 3 slices bread, broken up into small pieces
- 1/4 cup chopped onion
- 1 egg, beaten
- 1 teaspoon beef bouillon granules

Direction

- Preheat oven to 175°C/350°F.
- Combine mustard powder, 1 tablespoon of lemon juice, brown sugar, and ketchup in a small bowl.
- Combine the 1/3 of the ketchup mixture from the small bowl, the rest of the lemon juice, bouillon, egg, onion, bread, and ground beef in another large bowl and mix until well combined. Pour into a 5 x 9-inch loaf pan.
- Bake for 1 hour at 175°C/350°F, drain excess fat out and coat with the rest of the ketchup mixture, then bake for another 10 minutes.

Nutrition Information

- Calories: 589 calories;
- Sodium: 500
- Total Carbohydrate: 25.2
- Cholesterol: 160
- Protein: 27.9
- Total Fat: 41.7

703. Golompke (Beef And Cabbage Casserole)

Serving: 8 | Prep: 15mins | Cook: 1hours15mins | Ready in:

Ingredients

- 1 pound ground beef
- 1 small onion, chopped
- 1 (16 ounce) bag coleslaw mix
- 3/4 cup uncooked white rice
- 2 (10.75 ounce) cans condensed tomato soup
- 1 (10.75 ounce) can water

Direction

- Start preheating the oven to 375°F (190°).
- Place a big frying pan on medium-high heat, and mix in onion and ground beef. Stir and cook until the beef is not pink anymore, turns brown evenly, and is crumbly. Strain and dispose any excess fat.
- In a 9x13-in. baking dish, place coleslaw mix, rice and ground beef. In a medium-sized bowl, mix together water and soup. Pour over the top of the ground beef with the soup. Use foil to cover.
- Bake until the rice is soft, about 75 minutes.

Nutrition Information

- Calories: 268 calories;
- Total Fat: 9.4
- Sodium: 470
- Total Carbohydrate: 32.6
- Cholesterol: 39
- Protein: 13

704. Good Burger

Serving: 4 | Prep: 15mins | Cook: 20mins | Ready in:

Ingredients

- 1 pound ground beef chuck
- 1/2 small yellow onion, finely chopped
- 6 tablespoons brown sugar
- 1 teaspoon Cajun seasoning
- 1 teaspoon garlic powder
- 2 tablespoons steak sauce
- 1/4 cup Italian seasoned bread crumbs

Direction

- Preheat outdoor grill to high heat; oil grate lightly.
- Mix Italian seasoned breadcrumbs, steak sauce, garlic powder, Cajun seasoning, brown sugar, onion and ground chuck in medium bowl; shape mixture to 4 burger patties.
- Cook burgers on prepped grill to desired doneness or 3-5 minutes per side.

Nutrition Information

- Calories: 383 calories;
- Total Fat: 20.8
- Sodium: 421
- Total Carbohydrate: 27.8
- Cholesterol: 81
- Protein: 21

705. Gramma's Old Fashioned Chili Mac

Serving: 6 | Prep: 15mins | Cook: 25mins | Ready in:

Ingredients

- 1 cup elbow macaroni
- 1 pound ground beef
- 1 small onion, chopped
- 1 cup chopped celery
- 1/2 large green bell pepper, chopped
- 1 (15 ounce) can kidney beans, drained
- 2 (10.75 ounce) cans condensed tomato soup
- 2 (14.5 ounce) cans diced tomatoes
- 1/8 cup brown sugar

- salt and pepper to taste

Direction

- Place a lightly salted water in a big pot and make it boil. Cook in the pasta for 8-10 minutes or until al dente; strain.
- Bring green pepper and celery with water in a small saucepan to a simmer until tender; strain.
- In a big heavy skillet over medium heat, put the ground beef. Cook until equally brown. Stir in the onion and cook until translucent and tender. Remove extra fat. Mix in the green pepper and celery. Add in the brown sugar, diced tomatoes, condensed tomato soup and kidney beans and stir. Add pepper and salt to taste and mix in the macaroni.

Nutrition Information

- Calories: 489 calories;
- Total Fat: 22.4
- Sodium: 997
- Total Carbohydrate: 49.2
- Cholesterol: 64
- Protein: 22.1

706. Grammy's Comfort Meatloaf

Serving: 6 | Prep: 15mins | Cook: 45mins | Ready in:

Ingredients

- 1 1/2 pounds lean ground beef
- 2 (10.75 ounce) cans condensed tomato soup, divided
- 1 cup uncooked instant rice
- 1 onion, chopped
- 2 cloves garlic, minced
- 1 tablespoon Italian seasoning
- 1 egg
- 1/2 green bell pepper, chopped

- 1 pinch salt and ground black pepper to taste

Direction

- Set oven to 350°F (175°C) and start preheating.
- Thoroughly mix together green bell pepper, egg, Italian seasoning, garlic, onion, instant rice, 1/2 can of tomato soup, and the ground beef in a big bowl; season with black pepper and salt. Reserve the remaining tomato soup. Shape the meat mixture into a loaf and put into a 9x13-inch baking dish.
- Bake the loaf in the prepared oven for about 30 minutes until an instant-read meat thermometer reads 160°F (70°C) and is browned. Take out of oven and cover the loaf with the remaining 1 1/2 cans of tomato soup. Put it back to the oven and bake for about 10 minutes until the soup is hot and beginning to form a glaze on the meat.

Nutrition Information

- Calories: 390 calories;
- Cholesterol: 108
- Protein: 27.7
- Total Fat: 17
- Sodium: 634
- Total Carbohydrate: 31.3

707. Grandma Flo's Shipwreck

Serving: 4 | Prep: 15mins | Cook: 30mins | Ready in:

Ingredients

- 4 potatoes, peeled and sliced
- 1 pound ground beef
- 1 teaspoon salt
- 1/4 teaspoon ground black pepper
- 1 onion, thinly sliced
- 1 (15 ounce) can kidney beans, drained
- 1 (10.75 ounce) can condensed tomato soup

Direction

- Set the oven at 375°F (190°C) and start preheating. Coat a 2-qt. casserole dish with grease.
- In the bottom of the casserole dish, arrange potatoes. Crumble ground beef over the top of the potatoes; sprinkle ground black pepper and 1/2 teaspoon of salt over. Sprinkle onions then beans over the meat. Transfer undiluted soup on top. Sprinkle the remaining 1/2 teaspoon of salt over. Cover the dish.
- Bake for 30 minutes. Take the cover away; keep baking for 1 hour.

Nutrition Information

- Calories: 668 calories;
- Total Carbohydrate: 66.1
- Cholesterol: 96
- Protein: 30.4
- Total Fat: 31.9
- Sodium: 1321

---

708. Grandma's Applesauce Meatballs

Serving: 6 | Prep: 20mins | Cook: 45mins | Ready in:

Ingredients

- 1 egg
- 1/2 cup milk
- 1 1/2 cups herb seasoned croutons
- 2/3 cup applesauce
- 3 tablespoons chopped onion
- 3 tablespoons minced garlic, or to taste
- 1/2 cup shredded Cheddar cheese (optional)
- salt and black pepper to taste
- 1 1/2 pounds ground beef
- 1 (10.75 ounce) can condensed cream of celery soup
- 1/2 cup evaporated milk
- 1/4 cup grated Parmesan cheese (optional)

Direction

- Preheat oven to 350 °F (175 °C). Use cooking spray to spray a baking dish of 9x13 inch in size.
- In a large bowl, whisk the milk and egg together, and blend in the croutons. Allow the croutons to soak up for approximately 2 mins. with the milk mixture. Stir in the onion, applesauce, Cheddar cheese, garlic, pepper and salt lightly, and mix in ground beef with your hands until combined thoroughly. Form the meat mixture into balls of 1 and a half inch in size, then place into the prepared baking dish. In the same bowl, whisk the cream of celery soup with evaporated milk together. Pour the sauce over the meatballs.
- In the preheated oven, bake without covering for around 45 minutes until the meat is not pink in the middle anymore and the sauce is thickened and bubbling. Before end of baking for 15 minutes, use Parmesan cheese to sprinkle, and bake until the cheese is beginning to brown and melted. An inserted instant-read thermometer from the meatball's center should read 160 °F (70 °C).

Nutrition Information

- Calories: 430 calories;
- Total Fat: 27.4
- Sodium: 1290
- Total Carbohydrate: 18.2
- Cholesterol: 126
- Protein: 26.9

---

709. Grandma's Best Ever Sour Cream Lasagna

Serving: 8 | Prep: 40mins | Cook: 1hours10mins | Ready in:

Ingredients

- 1 (8 ounce) package lasagna noodles
- 1/2 pound ground pork sausage

- 1/2 pound ground beef
- 1 clove garlic, minced
- 1 (28 ounce) can diced tomatoes
- 1 (8 ounce) can tomato sauce
- 1 tablespoon dried parsley
- 1/2 teaspoon dried basil
- 1/2 teaspoon dried oregano
- 1 pinch white sugar
- 1 (16 ounce) container sour cream
- 3 eggs, lightly beaten
- 3/4 cup grated Parmesan cheese
- 1/2 cup chopped pitted green olives
- 2 teaspoons salt
- 1/4 teaspoon ground black pepper
- 2 (12 ounce) packages shredded mozzarella cheese, divided

Direction

- Start preheating the oven to 375°F (190°C).
- Fill lightly salted water into a large pot over high heat, bring to a rolling boil. Mix in lasagna noodles and bring back to a boil. Cook, uncovered, for 8 mins until pasta is cooked through, but still firm to the bite, stirring occasionally. Then drain.
- Over medium-high heat, heat a large skillet; cook while stirring garlic, ground beef and sausage, until the meat is evenly browned, no longer pink, and crumbly. Drain all the excess grease. Mix in sugar, oregano, basil, parsley, tomato sauce and diced tomatoes. Boil over high heat. Lower the heat to medium-low; simmer for half an hour until sauce is thickened, stirring occasionally.
- In a bowl, stir half of mozzarella cheese, black pepper, salt, green olives, Parmesan cheese, eggs and sour cream together.
- Evenly spread over the bottom of a 9x13 in. baking pan with a thin layer of meat sauce to assemble the lasagna. Layer with 1/3 lasagna noodles, 1/3 of the remaining meat sauce, 1/3 sour cream mixture to cover. Repeat layers 2 times more. Evenly sprinkle on top of lasagna with the remaining mozzarella cheese.

- Bake in the prepared oven for half an hour or until top turns golden brown and sauce is bubbly.

Nutrition Information

- Calories: 670 calories;
- Sodium: 2106
- Total Carbohydrate: 31.2
- Cholesterol: 189
- Protein: 41.3
- Total Fat: 42

---

710. Grandma's Chili

Serving: 4 | Prep: 15mins | Cook: 1hours | Ready in:

Ingredients

- 2 pounds ground beef
- 1/2 onion, chopped
- 1/2 green bell pepper, chopped
- salt and pepper to taste
- 1 (15 ounce) can baked beans
- 1 (4.5 ounce) can mushrooms, drained
- 1 tablespoon brown sugar
- 1/4 teaspoon chili powder

Direction

- In a large saucepan placed over medium-high heat and sauté the ground beef for 5 minutes, until browned. Mix in the onion and green bell pepper, then sauté for extra 5 minutes. Flavor with salt and pepper.
- Add chili powder, brown sugar, mushrooms, and beans to taste. Blend well, lower the heat to low and simmer for 20 minutes to 1 hour (depending on your time and how thick you prefer your chili, simmer for additional time).

Nutrition Information

- Calories: 832 calories;

- Total Fat: 60.8
- Sodium: 652
- Total Carbohydrate: 29.2
- Cholesterol: 193
- Protein: 43.6

711. Grandpa's Classic Coney Sauce

Serving: 12 | Prep: 10mins | Cook: 2hours | Ready in:

Ingredients

- 2 pounds ground beef
- 1/2 cup chopped onion
- 1 1/2 cups ketchup
- 1/4 cup white sugar
- 1/4 cup white vinegar
- 1/4 cup prepared yellow mustard
- 1/2 teaspoon celery seed
- 3/4 teaspoon Worcestershire sauce
- 1/2 teaspoon ground black pepper
- 3/4 teaspoon salt

Direction

- In a large skillet, put onion and ground beef over medium-high heat. Cook while stirring to crumble, until the beef is browned. Then drain. Put onion and beef into a slow cooker. Stir in mustard, vinegar, sugar and ketchup. Add salt, pepper, Worcestershire sauce and celery seed to season. Simmer, covered, for a few hours on Low setting before enjoying.

Nutrition Information

- Calories: 186 calories;
- Total Carbohydrate: 12.8
- Cholesterol: 46
- Protein: 13.5
- Total Fat: 9.2
- Sodium: 586

712. Grands!® Unsloppy Joes

Serving: 8 | Prep: 30mins | Cook: | Ready in:

Ingredients

- 1 pound lean (at least 80%) ground beef, cooked, drained
- 1 (15 ounce) can sloppy joe sauce
- 1 teaspoon chili powder
- 1 (16.3 ounce) can Pillsbury® Grands!® refrigerated biscuits
- 1/2 cup shredded Cheddar cheese

Direction

- Set an oven to 375°F and heat. Cook the ground beef in a large skillet on medium-high heat, and stir often until the beef is cooked thoroughly; then drain the beef. Stir in chili powder and sauce; let simmer for 5 minutes.
- Press each biscuit to make a 6-inch round. Place a tablespoon of cheese and 1/3 cup of the meat mixture on the center of each round. Then fold the dough in half over the filling; press the dough to seal. Arrange onto an ungreased cookie sheet.
- Bake until golden brown, or for 9-14 minutes.

Nutrition Information

- Calories: 358 calories;
- Sodium: 967
- Total Carbohydrate: 30.8
- Cholesterol: 47
- Protein: 17.5
- Total Fat: 17.2

713. Greek Stuffed Burgers

Serving: 6 | Prep: 25mins | Cook: 14mins | Ready in:

Ingredients

- 2 pounds lean ground beef (90%)
- 2 tablespoons minced garlic
- 1 teaspoon Italian seasoning, or to taste
- 1 teaspoon dried dill, or to taste
- salt and ground black pepper to taste
- 1 (4 ounce) package feta cheese
- 1 (4 ounce) container Gorgonzola cheese

Direction

- Place plastic wrap over the baking sheet. In a bowl, combine pepper, salt, dill, Italian seasoning, garlic and beef. Mix until fully incorporated and sticky using your hand. Shape beef mixture into balls; splash with some water to tighten. Press balls into large, thin patties.
- In a bowl, combine Gorgonzola cheese and feta cheese. Spread cheese mixture over the patties. Use your wet hands to fold the edges of the patties to seal the cheese. Arrange on the baking sheet and chill for about half an hour until firmed.
- Bring a large skillet to medium heat. Cook patties, about 7 to 8 minutes on each side, until the center is no longer pink or when an instant read thermometer inserted into the middle reaches at least 160°F (70°C)

Nutrition Information

- Calories: 449 calories;
- Cholesterol: 141
- Protein: 39
- Total Fat: 30.5
- Sodium: 513
- Total Carbohydrate: 1.9

714.   Green Bean Okazu

Serving: 4 | Prep: 10mins | Cook: 30mins | Ready in:

Ingredients

- 1 pound ground beef
- 1 pound green beans, trimmed and cut into 1 inch pieces
- 1 cup water
- 1/4 cup white sugar
- 1/4 cup soy sauce

Direction

- Cook the ground beef in a large skillet on medium heat until brown evenly; then drain off the excess fat.
- Stir in about a cup of water and green beans. Put a cover and cook for 15-20 minutes until the beans become tender.
- Serve along with soy sauce and sugar, then cook for 5 minutes without a cover.

Nutrition Information

- Calories: 444 calories;
- Sodium: 986
- Total Carbohydrate: 21.8
- Cholesterol: 96
- Protein: 21.9
- Total Fat: 30.3

715.   Green Chile Stew

Serving: 8 | Prep: 15mins | Cook: 30mins | Ready in:

Ingredients

- 1 pound ground beef
- 1 small onion, chopped
- 1 clove garlic, chopped
- 1 (4 ounce) can green chiles
- 2 (14.5 ounce) cans whole peeled tomatoes, chopped
- 2 (8 ounce) cans tomato sauce
- 1 (15 ounce) can whole kernel corn
- 3 potatoes, peeled and cut into chunks
- 2 cups water
- ground cayenne pepper to taste

- salt and pepper to taste

Direction

- In a saucepan or deep skillet on medium heat, put garlic, onion, and ground beef. Cook while stirring until the onion becomes tender and the beef turns browned evenly. Drain the grease. Stir in the green chiles. Then mix in potatoes, corn, tomato sauce and tomatoes. Add water. Boil. Lower the heat to low; simmer until the potatoes become tender, about 15 mins. Season with pepper, salt, and cayenne pepper.

Nutrition Information

- Calories: 242 calories;
- Sodium: 689
- Total Carbohydrate: 32.5
- Cholesterol: 34
- Protein: 14.3
- Total Fat: 7.5

716.   Grilled BBQ Meatloaf

Serving: 6 | Prep: 15mins | Cook: 1hours | Ready in:

Ingredients

- 1 1/2 pounds ground beef
- 1 1/2 pounds ground pork
- 2 cups dry bread crumbs
- 1 cup finely chopped sweet onion (such as Vidalia®)
- 1 egg, beaten
- 1 teaspoon Worcestershire sauce
- 1 teaspoon minced garlic
- 1 teaspoon dried tarragon
- 1 teaspoon sea salt
- 1 teaspoon ground black pepper
- 1/2 cup barbeque sauce
- 1/2 cup ketchup

Direction

- Prepare an outdoor grill and set to medium heat for preheating; scrape the grates. Spritz grates with nonstick cooking spray.
- In a bowl, combine black pepper, sea salt, tarragon, garlic, Worcestershire sauce, egg, onion, bread crumbs, ground pork and ground beef. Split mixture into two and make 2 loaves, each should be 6 inches long and about 4 inches in diameter. In a small bowl, combine ketchup and barbeque sauce and mix well until blended.
- Put each meatloaf directly on the prepared grill grates. Spread about 3 tablespoons of barbeque sauce mixture on top of each meatloaf. Let it cook on the grill for about an hour until the loaves reach an internal temperature of at least 160°F or 73°C.

Nutrition Information

- Calories: 656 calories;
- Sodium: 1158
- Total Carbohydrate: 41.8
- Cholesterol: 176
- Protein: 45.8
- Total Fat: 32.8

717.   Grilled Gyro Burgers

Serving: 6 | Prep: 30mins | Cook: 14mins | Ready in:

Ingredients

- 2 (8 ounce) containers plain yogurt, divided
- 1 (1 ounce) package dry Ranch-style dressing mix
- 1 cucumber, peeled, seeded, and chopped
- 1 1/2 pounds ground beef
- 1/4 cup diced onion
- 6 pita bread rounds
- 2 cups torn lettuce leaves
- 1 tomato, seeded and diced

Direction

- Combine an envelope of ranch dressing mix with 1 container of plain yogurt in a medium bowl. Transfer 1/2 of the mixture to another bowl. Add diced cucumber and pour in the remaining container of plain yogurt into one of the bowls; stir to combine. Chill the bowl, covered. Preheat the grill and lightly grease the grate.
- Stir 1/4 cup onion and ground beef into the remaining 1/2 of the yogurt mixture. Form the mixture into 6 hamburger patties.
- Grill burgers over medium heat, flipping once, about 7 minutes per side.
- Slice of 1/4 end of the pita pockets; fill with diced tomatoes, creamy cucumber sauce, grill burger, and torn lettuce.

Nutrition Information

- Calories: 590 calories;
- Total Fat: 32.1
- Sodium: 782
- Total Carbohydrate: 44.3
- Cholesterol: 101
- Protein: 28.9

718.   Grilled Italian Burgers

Serving: 4 | Prep: 5mins | Cook: 12mins | Ready in:

Ingredients

- 1 pound ground beef
- 2 tablespoons capers, drained
- 2 eggs
- 2 tablespoons kalamata olives, pitted and chopped
- 2 tablespoons garlic powder
- 1 tablespoon dried oregano
- 1/2 cup feta cheese, crumbled
- 1 cup Italian bread crumbs

Direction

- Preheat the griller in medium-high heat and gently brush the grate with oil.
- In a bowl, combine the beef, eggs, olives, garlic powder, oregano, breadcrumbs, feta cheese and capers. Then divide the mixture into 4 patties.
- Cook the patties on the preheated griller for about 6 minutes. Turn once, at 160° F (or 70°C) internal temperature, until completely cooked.

Nutrition Information

- Calories: 615 calories;
- Sodium: 904
- Total Carbohydrate: 25.5
- Cholesterol: 218
- Protein: 31.1
- Total Fat: 42.8

719.   Ground Beef 'Wellington' With Fennel

Serving: 4 | Prep: 25mins | Cook: 35mins | Ready in:

Ingredients

- 1 tablespoon vegetable oil
- 1/2 cup diced onion
- 1/4 cup fennel, chopped
- 1 tablespoon garlic, minced
- 1/2 teaspoon fennel seed
- 1/4 teaspoon crushed red pepper flakes
- 1 eggs
- 1 pound ground beef
- 2 tablespoons dry bread crumbs
- 1 tablespoon dried parsley
- 1 teaspoon salt
- 1 (8 ounce) package refrigerated crescent rolls

Direction

- Preheat an oven to 175°C/350°F; grease baking sheet lightly.

- Heat vegetable oil in skillet on medium heat then mix in garlic, fennel and onion. Mix and cook for 5 minutes till onion is translucent and soft and fennel is tender. Mix red pepper flakes and fennel seed in; cook for 1 more minute. Meanwhile, beat egg in bowl; mix in salt, parsley, breadcrumbs and ground beef. Add cooked veggie mixture; mix till combined.
- Separate crescent roll dough into 2 squares; divide meat mixture to crescent roll squares. Seal dough around meat; put on prepped baking sheet, seam side down.
- In preheated oven, bake for 30 minutes till pastry is golden brown and middle of pastries reads 71°C/160°F on a kitchen thermometer. Slice; serve.

Nutrition Information

- Calories: 536 calories;
- Sodium: 1135
- Total Carbohydrate: 27.9
- Cholesterol: 116
- Protein: 25.3
- Total Fat: 34.6

---

720.   Ground Beef Mexican Style

Serving: 4 | Prep: 10mins | Cook: 30mins | Ready in:

Ingredients

- 1 pound ground beef
- 1 cup salsa
- 1/2 cup water
- 1 green bell pepper, chopped
- 1 bunch green onions, chopped
- 1 (8 ounce) package wide egg noodles
- 1/2 cup sour cream
- 1/2 cup shredded Cheddar cheese
- 1 tomato, chopped

Direction

- Put the ground beef in a big non-stick skillet and let it cook while stirring until the beef turns brown in color. Drain any excess oil.
- Add in the water and salsa then mix. Let it simmer for 10 minutes.
- While the mixture is simmering, let the pasta cook in boiling water until it is al dente. Drain the cooked pasta.
- Mix the onions and green pepper into the beef mixture and continue to simmer the mixture until the vegetables are tender-crisp. Add in the sour cream and cooked noodles then mix. Top it off with grated cheese then cover the skillet to let the cheese melt on top. Garnish with chopped tomatoes then serve.

Nutrition Information

- Calories: 732 calories;
- Total Fat: 43.7
- Sodium: 592
- Total Carbohydrate: 52.1
- Cholesterol: 171
- Protein: 33.8

---

721.   Ground Beef Shepherd's Pie

Serving: 4 | Prep: 25mins | Cook: 35mins | Ready in:

Ingredients

- 1 tablespoon vegetable oil
- 1 onion, chopped
- 1 pound lean ground beef
- 1 teaspoon dried basil
- 1 clove garlic, minced
- 1 cup green beans
- 1 cup tomatoes, diced
- 2 potatoes, cooked and mashed
- 1 egg, beaten
- 1/2 cup water

- 1/4 cup shredded Cheddar cheese (optional)

Direction

- Set oven to 175° C (350° F) and start preheating. Spray cooking spray on a 2-qt. casserole dish.
- In a big skillet, heat oil on medium heat. In oil, cook onion and mix often for about 5 minutes. Mix in basil and ground beef; stir and cook for 5 minutes more. Stir in tomatoes, green beans, and garlic; allow to simmer 5 minutes. Place it over the prepared dish.
- Blend water, egg, and mashed potatoes together in a mixing bowl. Evenly arrange over meat mixture.
- Put in the preheated oven and bake for 15-20 minutes or until the potatoes begin to brown on top. Sprinkle cheese over top and keep cooking 5 minutes.

Nutrition Information

- Calories: 404 calories;
- Total Fat: 21.1
- Sodium: 229
- Total Carbohydrate: 25.1
- Cholesterol: 128
- Protein: 28.2

---

722. Ground Beef And Rice With Cheese

Serving: 4 | Prep: 15mins | Cook: 40mins | Ready in:

Ingredients

- 1 cup white rice
- 1 cup water
- 1 pound ground beef
- 3 (10.75 ounce) cans condensed tomato soup
- 3 tablespoons chili powder
- 8 slices processed cheese food (such as Velveeta®)

Direction

- In a saucepan, boil rice and water. Lower heat to medium low. Simmer, covered, for 20-25 minutes till liquid is absorbed and rice is tender.
- Preheat the oven to 200°C/400°F. Grease the 1-qt. baking dish.
- As rice cooks, heat a big skillet on medium high heat. Mix ground beef in. Stir and cook till beef is not pink, evenly brown and crumbly. Drain. Throw excess grease. Mix chili powder and condensed tomato soup in. Cook till heated through.
- In prepped baking dish's bottom, spread 1/3 rice. Use 1/3 ground beef mixture to cover. Put 2 processed cheese slices on meat. Use 2 extra layers of meat and rice to cover. Put leftover 6 cheese slices on top.
- In preheated oven, bake for 20 minutes till cheese is brown and bubbly and casserole is heated through.

Nutrition Information

- Calories: 882 calories;
- Sodium: 2124
- Total Carbohydrate: 74.9
- Cholesterol: 142
- Protein: 37.1
- Total Fat: 49.2

---

723. Guacamole Cilantro Lime Cheeseburger

Serving: 6 | Prep: 30mins | Cook: 10mins | Ready in:

Ingredients

- Guacamole
- 2 avocados - halved, peeled, and pitted
- 1/2 lime, juiced
- 1 fresh jalapeno peppers, seeded and minced
- 1/2 cup diced tomatoes

- 1/4 cup minced onion
- 1 1/2 teaspoons minced garlic
- 1/4 teaspoon salt to taste
- Burger
- 2 pounds lean ground beef
- 1/2 lime, juiced
- 1 tablespoon minced garlic
- 1 teaspoon chili powder
- 1/2 cup diced onion
- 1/2 cup chopped cilantro
- 6 slices Monterey Jack cheese
- 6 hamburger buns

Direction

- Prepare an outdoor grill by preheating to medium.
- Making guacamole: In a medium bowl, mash the avocado with 1 1/2 teaspoons of minced garlic, 1/4 cup onion, tomatoes, jalapeno, and the juice of half a lime; add salt to taste, then reserve.
- Combine cilantro, 1/2 cup diced onion, chili powder, 1 tablespoon garlic, the juice of half a lime, and beef together in a large bowl. Shape the meat into 6 patties.
- Place the burgers on preheated grill and cook to doneness that you want. Then put a slice of cheese to each burger throughout the last minute of cooking. Present on toasted buns with a dollop of guacamole.

Nutrition Information

- Calories: 656 calories;
- Total Fat: 41.5
- Sodium: 587
- Total Carbohydrate: 32.5
- Cholesterol: 117
- Protein: 39

724.   Habanero Hellfire Chili

Serving: 8 | Prep: 30mins | Cook: 1hours30mins | Ready in:

Ingredients

- 1/2 pound bacon
- 1 pound ground round
- 1 pound ground pork
- 1 green bell pepper, diced
- 1 yellow onion, diced
- 6 jalapeno peppers, seeded and chopped
- 6 habanero peppers, seeded and chopped
- 8 Anaheim peppers, seeded and diced
- 2 cloves garlic, minced
- 1 1/2 tablespoons ground cumin
- 1 tablespoon crushed red pepper flakes
- 3 tablespoons chili powder
- 2 tablespoons beef bouillon granules
- 1 (28 ounce) can crushed tomatoes
- 2 (16 ounce) cans whole peeled tomatoes, drained
- 2 (16 ounce) cans chili beans, drained
- 1 (12 fluid ounce) can beer
- 3 ounces tomato paste
- 1 ounce chile paste
- 2 cups water

Direction

- In a big soup pot, cook bacon on medium high heat until the color becomes evenly brown. Drain out the extra grease and leave just enough to cover the bottom of the pot. Take out the bacon and let it drain on paper towels; chop.
- Over medium high heat, cook pork and beef until they turn brown. Mix in the chile paste, tomato paste, beer, whole tomatoes, crushed tomatoes, bouillon, chili powder, red pepper flakes, cumin, garlic, Anaheim peppers, habanero peppers, jalapeno peppers, onion, bell pepper and water.
- Adjust to low heat and let it simmer for 45 to 60 minutes while stirring from time to time.

Put in bacon and beans and let simmer continuously, about 30 minutes.

Nutrition Information

- Calories: 595 calories;
- Total Fat: 31.9
- Sodium: 1575
- Total Carbohydrate: 47.9
- Cholesterol: 91
- Protein: 34.9

725. Half Baked Taco Salad

Serving: 4 | Prep: 15mins | Cook: 35mins | Ready in:

Ingredients

- Seasoning:
- 1 tablespoon chili powder
- 1 1/2 teaspoons ground cumin
- 1 teaspoon ground black pepper
- 1/2 teaspoon garlic powder
- 1/2 teaspoon sea salt
- 1/2 teaspoon smoked paprika
- 1/2 teaspoon onion powder
- 1/2 teaspoon cayenne pepper
- 1/2 teaspoon dried oregano
- Meat:
- 1 pound 93% lean ground beef
- 1/2 cup water
- 1 (15 ounce) can no salt-added kidney beans
- Salad:
- 4 tomatoes
- 2 heads romaine lettuce, chopped
- 4 large green bell peppers, sliced
- 1 ounce finely grated Parmesan cheese
- 4 ounces coarsely grated extra-sharp Cheddar cheese
- 1 cup salsa

Direction

- In a bowl, mix together the garlic powder, onion powder, oregano, cayenne pepper, cumin, chili powder, black pepper, sea salt, and paprika.
- Set the oven at 350°F (175°C) for preheating. Use an aluminum foil or parchment paper to line the baking sheet.
- Heat the large skillet over medium-high heat. Cook and stir the beef in a hot skillet for 5-7 minutes, until crumbly and browned. Add the spice mixture into the ground beef and mix until the beef is coated evenly. Add water. Let it simmer for 10-15 minutes until the liquid has evaporated. Add the kidney beans. Simmer for about 10 minutes until the beans are heated through.
- Cut the tomatoes in half down the middle. Slice 1 of each of the tomato halves into thin and round cross-sections. Chop the remaining tomato halves.
- Arrange the romaine lettuce into the prepared baking sheet; spread. Top the romaine lettuce with the tomato slices and green bell peppers. Sprinkle the tomato layer with Parmesan cheese.
- Place it inside the preheated oven and bake for 10-20 minutes until the edges of the romaine lettuce are crisp but not that burned.
- Place the taco meat mixture, salsa, chopped tomato, and Cheddar cheese on top of the salad. Using a spatula, transfer the salad into the serving plate.

Nutrition Information

- Calories: 565 calories;
- Protein: 42.3
- Total Fat: 28.3
- Sodium: 1018
- Total Carbohydrate: 41.7
- Cholesterol: 104

726. Hamburger Goulash

Serving: 8 | Prep: 15mins | Cook: 1hours20mins | Ready in:

Ingredients

- 1 pound lean ground beef
- 4 potatoes, peeled and cubed
- 1/4 cup sliced onion
- 1 1/2 cups frozen corn kernels
- 1 (15 ounce) can cut green beans, drained
- 1 cup elbow macaroni
- 1 teaspoon salt
- 1 teaspoon ground black pepper
- 2 (8 ounce) cans tomato sauce
- 2 teaspoons Worcestershire sauce (optional)
- 1 teaspoon garlic salt
- 1/2 teaspoon dried basil

Direction

- In a large and deep skillet, add ground beef. Cook over medium-high heat until equally browned. Drain, crumble, and leave it aside.
- Add all ingredients but noodles to cooked ground meat then simmer for about 1 hour, finally add noodles.

Nutrition Information

- Calories: 333 calories;
- Total Fat: 12.4
- Sodium: 1021
- Total Carbohydrate: 40.5
- Cholesterol: 43
- Protein: 16.1

727. Hamburger Pie II

Serving: 8 | Prep: 15mins | Cook: 30mins | Ready in:

Ingredients

- 1 recipe pastry for a 9 inch double crust pie

- 1 pound lean ground beef
- 1 onion, grated
- 1 (10.75 ounce) can condensed tomato soup
- 3 tablespoons Worcestershire sauce
- 1 teaspoon seasoning salt
- 1 (4.5 ounce) can mushrooms, drained
- 4 ounces Cheddar cheese, sliced

Direction

- Preheat an oven to 175°C/350°F.
- Crumble ground beef in a big skillet; cook on medium high heat for 3 minutes. Add onion; cook till onion and meat are both browned. Drain extra fat off.
- Mix in mushrooms, seasoned salt, Worcestershire sauce and soup; put mixture into the pastry-lined pan. Use top crust to cover. Seal edges; on top, cut steam vents.
- In preheated oven, bake till crust is golden brown for 30 minutes. Put cheese slices over pie; serve the pie while hot.

Nutrition Information

- Calories: 475 calories;
- Sodium: 817
- Total Carbohydrate: 29.1
- Cholesterol: 57
- Protein: 17.4
- Total Fat: 32

728. Hamburger Potato Casserole

Serving: 6 | Prep: 20mins | Cook: 1hours | Ready in:

Ingredients

- 1 pound lean ground beef
- 3 cups peeled and thinly sliced potatoes
- 1 (10.75 ounce) can condensed cream of mushroom soup
- 1/2 cup chopped onion

- 3/4 cup milk
- salt to taste
- freshly ground pepper, to taste
- 1 cup shredded Cheddar cheese

Direction

- Preheat the oven to 175 degrees C (350 degrees F).
- In the medium-sized skillet on medium heat, brown ground beef; drain off the fat.
- In the medium-sized mixing bowl, mix the pepper, salt, milk, onion and cream of mushroom soup to taste.
- Alternately layer potatoes, the soup mixture and the meat in the 11x7-in. (2-qt.) baking plate. Bake in preheated oven till the potatoes soften or for 1-1.5 hours. Add the Cheddar cheese on top, and keep baking till the cheese melts.

Nutrition Information

- Calories: 403 calories;
- Total Carbohydrate: 17.1
- Cholesterol: 83
- Protein: 22.1
- Total Fat: 26.9
- Sodium: 538

729.   Hamburger Rice Soup

Serving: 6 | Prep: | Cook: | Ready in:

Ingredients

- 1 pound ground beef
- 2 (14.5 ounce) cans diced tomatoes
- 2 cups cubed potatoes
- 2 carrots, chopped
- 1 onion, chopped
- 4 teaspoons salt
- 1/4 cup uncooked white rice
- 1/8 teaspoon ground black pepper

- 6 cups water

Direction

- In the big sauce pan on medium heat, sauté ground beef till turning brown or for 5 minutes. Drain off the redundant fat and put in the tomatoes along with the water, black pepper, rice, salt, onion, carrots, potatoes and liquid. Boil and lower the heat to low. Let simmer for 60 minutes and serve.

Nutrition Information

- Calories: 346 calories;
- Total Fat: 20.3
- Sodium: 1928
- Total Carbohydrate: 23.4
- Cholesterol: 64
- Protein: 15.7

730.   Hamburger Soup II

Serving: 6 | Prep: 15mins | Cook: 10mins | Ready in:

Ingredients

- 1 1/2 pounds lean ground beef
- 2 large potatoes, sliced
- 2 stalks celery, sliced
- salt and pepper to taste
- 2 onions, thinly sliced
- 1 (15 ounce) can peas
- 3 small carrots, sliced
- 1 (10.75 ounce) can condensed tomato soup
- 1 1/4 cups water

Direction

- In a big, deep frying pan, put ground beef. Cook on medium-high heat until turning brown evenly. Strain, break apart and put aside.
- Cover the bottom of a slow cooker with a layer of potatoes. Sprinkle over the potatoes with

celery, and place ground beef in 1 layer. Use pepper and salt to season each layer. Add peas, onions, and carrots. Stir together water and tomato soup, and put on top. Put a cover on and cook for 6-8 hours on low.

Nutrition Information

- Calories: 492 calories;
- Sodium: 530
- Total Carbohydrate: 41
- Cholesterol: 85
- Protein: 26.4
- Total Fat: 24.7

731. Hamburger Soup III

Serving: 5 | Prep: | Cook: | Ready in:

Ingredients

- 1 pound ground beef
- 1 onion, chopped
- 3 (14 ounce) cans beef broth
- 2 (14.5 ounce) cans stewed tomatoes
- 1 (16 ounce) package frozen peas and carrots
- 1 teaspoon ground black pepper
- 1 teaspoon garlic salt
- 1 cup uncooked elbow macaroni

Direction

- Sear chopped onion and ground beef in a big stock pot. Strain the grease from the pot.
- Put water in a medium-sized saucepan and make it boil. Stir in the pasta and cook until soft then strain.
- Mix in the cooked pasta, garlic salt, pepper, frozen peas and carrots, tomatoes and beef broth. Cook for 15 minutes over medium heat or until the carrots and peas are cooked. Let it simmer until ready to serve.

Nutrition Information

- Calories: 479 calories;
- Total Fat: 25.9
- Sodium: 1633
- Total Carbohydrate: 38.9
- Cholesterol: 77
- Protein: 25.6

732. Hamburger Steak With Onions And Gravy

Serving: 4 | Prep: 15mins | Cook: 25mins | Ready in:

Ingredients

- 1 pound ground beef
- 1 egg
- 1/4 cup bread crumbs
- 1/8 teaspoon ground black pepper
- 1/2 teaspoon seasoned salt
- 1/2 teaspoon onion powder
- 1/2 teaspoon garlic powder
- 1 teaspoon Worcestershire sauce
- 1 tablespoon vegetable oil
- 1 cup thinly sliced onion
- 2 tablespoons all-purpose flour
- 1 cup beef broth
- 1 tablespoon cooking sherry
- 1/2 teaspoon seasoned salt

Direction

- Combine Worcestershire sauce, garlic powder, onion powder, salt, pepper, bread crumbs, egg, and ground beef in a big bowl. Roll into 8 balls, then flatten to form patties.
- In a big skillet, heat oil on medium heat. Fry the patties and onion, for 4 minutes each side, in the oil until patties are well-browned. Transfer the fried patties to a plate; keep warm. In the skillet, dust flour onto the onions and drippings. Using a fork, whisk in the flour, while scraping bits of beef off of skillet's bottom. Slowly pour in sherry and beef broth. Add seasoned salt to taste. Reduce heat to medium-low, then simmer and whisk for

about 5 minutes until the gravy is thickened. Switch to low heat, placing patties into the gravy and cover, then simmer for an additional 15 minutes.

Nutrition Information

- Calories: 319 calories;
- Total Fat: 18.5
- Sodium: 597
- Total Carbohydrate: 13.5
- Cholesterol: 115
- Protein: 23.1

733.   Hamburger Stew

Serving: 7 | Prep: | Cook: |Ready in:

Ingredients

- 1 pound ground beef
- 1 (1.25 ounce) package taco seasoning mix
- 1 (10.75 ounce) can condensed tomato soup
- 3 3/4 cups water
- 1 cup chopped onion
- 4 carrots, chopped
- 3 potatoes, peeled and cubed
- 1 stalk celery, chopped
- 1 (15 ounce) can pork and beans

Direction

- Sauté ground beef in a big pot over medium-high heat. Add beans, celery, potatoes, carrots, onions, water, soup, and taco seasoning. Lower the heat to low. Simmer with a cover until the vegetables are soft, about 30 minutes.

Nutrition Information

- Calories: 409 calories;
- Total Fat: 19
- Sodium: 943
- Total Carbohydrate: 43.4

- Cholesterol: 59
- Protein: 17.1

734.   Hamburger Vegetable Soup

Serving: 4 | Prep: 5mins | Cook: 25mins |Ready in:

Ingredients

- 1 pound ground beef
- 4 cups chicken broth
- 4 cups water
- 2 (1 ounce) packages dry onion soup mix
- 1 (15 ounce) can tomato sauce
- 2 stalks celery, chopped
- 1 onion, chopped
- 1 (16 ounce) package frozen mixed vegetables
- 3/4 cup elbow macaroni

Direction

- Brown ground beef in a sauté pan over medium heat.
- Mix macaroni, frozen vegetables, onion, celery, tomato sauce, onion soup mix, water, and broth together in a big stockpot. Boil and then simmer until the macaroni is cooked.
- Add the browned ground beef, stir and enjoy.

Nutrition Information

- Calories: 466 calories;
- Sodium: 2687
- Total Carbohydrate: 48.9
- Cholesterol: 69
- Protein: 33.2
- Total Fat: 16.2

735.   Hamburgers And Ketchup Gravy

Serving: 4 | Prep: 10mins | Cook: 45mins | Ready in:

Ingredients

- 1 pound ground beef
- 1/2 cup ketchup
- 1/2 cup bread crumbs
- 1 teaspoon onion powder
- 1/2 teaspoon steak seasoning, or to taste
- salt and pepper to taste
- 2 teaspoons vegetable oil
- 1 large onion, cut into chunks
- 1 cup ketchup
- 1/2 cup water, or as needed

Direction

- Combine pepper, salt, steak seasoning, onion powder, bread crumbs, 1/2 cup of ketchup and ground beef in a medium bowl. Shape the mixture into small fat hamburger meatballs or patties.
- In a big heavy skillet, heat oil over moderately high heat. In the skillet, put patties and cook both sides until browned. Transfer the patties to a plate and drain the grease from skillet.
- Stir together water and leftover ketchup gradually in the same pan. If the mixture seems thick, put in more water, conversely, put in more ketchup if the mixture seems thin. Put in onion and bring to a boil. Lower heat to moderately low then bring patties back to pan and simmer, covered, about a half hour. Stir after a half hour and keep on simmering without a lid in case the gravy is still thin, until you get thickened gravy.

Nutrition Information

- Calories: 378 calories;
- Sodium: 1323
- Total Carbohydrate: 36.1
- Cholesterol: 69
- Protein: 22.8

- Total Fat: 16.6

736.   Hawaiian Stew

Serving: 8 | Prep: 20mins | Cook: 1hours | Ready in:

Ingredients

- 2 pounds ground beef
- 2 pounds fresh green beans, cut into 1 inch pieces
- 2 large Spanish onions, sliced
- 2 green bell peppers, chopped
- 2 large tomatoes, sliced
- 2 medium heads cabbage, quartered
- soy sauce
- 1 cup white rice

Direction

- Layer green beans, ground beef, bell peppers, onions, and tomatoes in a big stockpot. Complete with a cabbage layer, and equally dot soy sauce on top. Then cook for 1 hour on medium, covered, or until meat becomes well done and cabbage is softened. Lower heat as necessary to avoid burning.
- In the meantime, in a fine mesh strainer, place the rice and wash under cold running water until not cloudy. Then place in a medium saucepan and pour 2 cups of water to cover. Make it boil, cover, and lower heat. Boil for 15 minutes, separate from heat and allow it to rest for 10 minutes, or until liquid has completely evaporated. Then serve on rice.

Nutrition Information

- Calories: 415 calories;
- Protein: 28.1
- Total Fat: 13.9
- Sodium: 1447
- Total Carbohydrate: 47.4
- Cholesterol: 69

- Total Fat: 12.8

737. Healthier Brown Sugar Meatloaf

Serving: 8 | Prep: 20mins | Cook: 1hours | Ready in:

Ingredients

- 3 tablespoons packed brown sugar
- 1/2 cup ketchup
- 1 1/2 pounds lean ground beef
- 3/4 cup low-fat (1%) milk
- 2 eggs
- 1 1/2 teaspoons salt
- 1/4 teaspoon ground black pepper
- 1 small onion, chopped
- 1/4 teaspoon ground ginger
- 3/4 cup whole wheat bread crumbs
- 1/4 cup chopped parsley

Direction

- Set an oven to preheat to 175°C (350°F), then grease a 9x5-inch loaf pan lightly.
- Press brown sugar in the bottom of the prepped loaf pan, then spread the ketchup on top of the sugar.
- In a mixing bowl, mix the parsley, breadcrumbs, ginger, onion, ground pepper, salt, eggs, milk and ground beef well together. Form it into a loaf and put it on top of the ketchup.
- Let it bake in the preheated oven for about an hour until the center is not pink anymore. An inserted instant-read thermometer in the middle should register at least 70°C (160°F).

Nutrition Information

- Calories: 265 calories;
- Sodium: 735
- Total Carbohydrate: 16.3
- Cholesterol: 106
- Protein: 21.2

738. Hearty Hamburger Soup

Serving: 10 | Prep: 30mins | Cook: 2hours | Ready in:

Ingredients

- 1 1/2 pounds ground beef
- 1 onion, minced
- 4 carrots, minced
- 3 celery ribs, thinly sliced
- 1/2 cup barley
- 1 (28 ounce) can diced tomatoes
- 2 cups water
- 3 (10 ounce) cans beef broth
- 1 (10.75 ounce) can condensed tomato soup
- 1 bay leaf
- 1 tablespoon parsley
- 1 teaspoon minced garlic
- 1/2 teaspoon dried thyme
- ground black pepper, to taste

Direction

- Heat a big stockpot upon a medium-high heat and crumble in ground beef. Cook, stirring, until the meet is no longer pink and browned evenly. Dry and throw out any of the extra grease.
- Stir in barley, celery, carrots, and onions, then pour in tomato soup, broth, water, and diced tomatoes. Season the soup with pepper, thyme, garlic, parsley, and bay leaf, then set to boiling. Drop down the heat and simmer while covering for 2 hours, stirring often. Take out the bay leaf before you serve.

Nutrition Information

- Calories: 223 calories;
- Cholesterol: 41
- Protein: 14.7
- Total Fat: 8.9

- Sodium: 621
- Total Carbohydrate: 20.2

- Cholesterol: 149
- Protein: 22.1
- Total Fat: 29
- Sodium: 554

739.   Herald's Impossibly Easy Cheeseburger Pie

Serving: 6 | Prep: 20mins | Cook: 25mins | Ready in:

Ingredients

- 1 pound ground beef
- 1 onion, chopped
- 2 cloves garlic, minced
- 1 tomato, sliced
- 1/2 teaspoon garlic salt
- 1 teaspoon ground black pepper
- 1 teaspoon dried oregano
- 1 cup shredded Cheddar cheese
- 1/2 cup buttermilk baking mix
- 1 cup milk
- 2 eggs

Direction

- Start preheating the oven to 200°C (400°F). Grease a 10-inch deep dish pie plate.
- Heat a big skillet on medium heat. Put in garlic, onion, and ground beef; cook while stirring until the beef becomes brown. Strain off the fat. Spread into the prepared pie plate.
- Add the oregano, black pepper, and salt on top of the meat. Place tomatoes slices over the meat and sprinkle with shredded cheese.
- Combine together the eggs, milk, and the baking mix in a small bowl. Pour over the cheese.
- Bake until the knife inserted in the middle comes out clean for about 25 minutes. Let it cool for 5 minutes, then serve.

Nutrition Information

- Calories: 403 calories;
- Total Carbohydrate: 13

740.   Hidden Cheeseburger

Serving: 4 | Prep: 20mins | Cook: 35mins | Ready in:

Ingredients

- 2 pounds ground beef
- 2 small dill pickles, minced
- 1 small onion, minced
- 2 tablespoons grated Parmesan cheese
- 1 tablespoon mayonnaise
- 1 tablespoon ketchup
- 1 teaspoon minced garlic
- salt and pepper to taste
- 2 tablespoons olive oil
- 2 tablespoons all-purpose flour
- 1 pound frozen bread dough, thawed
- 8 slices American cheese
- 1 tablespoon melted butter

Direction

- In a bowl, combine pepper, salt, garlic, ketchup, mayonnaise, Parmesan cheese, onion, pickles and ground beef. Shape the mixture into 4 patties.
- In a skillet, heat olive oil over medium heat. Cook hamburger patties in heated oil until burgers reach your desired doneness, about 8 to 10 minutes for well-done.
- Line parchment paper over a baking sheet; put to one side. Sprinkle flour over a flat work surface. Cut the bread dough into even quarters; roll each piece on the floured work surface into a flattened rectangle at least twice the size of the American cheese slices. Arrange 1 slice of American cheese on each piece of dough. Place one cooked patty over each; top each with another American cheese slice. Fold the dough over the top of cheese and meat.

Pinch around the edges to seal the dough completely. Place seam side facing down, on the prepared baking sheet. Brush melted butter all over the tops; allow to rise for 20 minutes in a warm place.

- Turn the oven to 425°F (220°C) to preheat.
- Bake for about 20 minutes in the preheated oven until the bread has browned.

Nutrition Information

- Calories: 1037 calories;
- Total Fat: 55.5
- Sodium: 1958
- Total Carbohydrate: 62.2
- Cholesterol: 202
- Protein: 67

741.   Hobo Dinner

Serving: 4 | Prep: 15mins | Cook: 1hours | Ready in:

Ingredients

- 1 pound ground beef
- 5 potatoes, peeled and cut into steak fries
- 4 large carrots, peeled and sliced lengthwise
- 1 onion, peeled and sliced into rings
- salt to taste
- ground black pepper to taste
- garlic salt to taste

Direction

- Set oven to 400°F (200°C) to preheat. Use aluminum foil to line the inside of a 9x13 inch baking pan.
- Shape patties out of the ground beef and place in pan. Top the beef patties with layers of vegetables, beginning with the potatoes, then carrots, and onion rings at last. Flavor with garlic salt, pepper and salt to taste.

- Cover the top with aluminum foil and seal edges. Bake for 1 hour in preheated oven, to preferred doneness.

Nutrition Information

- Calories: 451 calories;
- Total Fat: 14.1
- Sodium: 132
- Total Carbohydrate: 56
- Cholesterol: 71
- Protein: 25.5

742.   Hodie's Sloppy Joes

Serving: 6 | Prep: 10mins | Cook: 25mins | Ready in:

Ingredients

- 1 pound ground beef
- 1/2 cup chopped onion
- 1 (8 ounce) can tomato sauce
- 1/3 cup ketchup
- 2 tablespoons brown sugar
- 1 tablespoon apple cider vinegar

Direction

- In a skillet, cook and stir chopped onion and ground beef on medium heat until onions are translucent and beef is browned thoroughly. Drain the grease off the skillet and put back the skillet on medium heat. Whisk in vinegar, brown sugar, ketchup and tomato sauce. Lower heat to medium-low and let simmer for 20 minutes.

Nutrition Information

- Calories: 280 calories;
- Total Fat: 20.2
- Sodium: 398
- Total Carbohydrate: 11.1
- Cholesterol: 64

- Protein: 13.5

743. Homemade Albondigas Soup

Serving: 6 | Prep: 30mins | Cook: 1hours | Ready in:

Ingredients

- 1 pound ground beef
- 1 bunch cilantro, finely chopped
- 1 small onion, chopped
- 4 cloves garlic, minced
- 1 pinch garlic salt
- 1 pinch onion powder
- salt and ground black pepper to taste
- 4 (14.5 ounce) cans chicken broth
- 4 large carrots, cut into 1/2 inch pieces
- 3 stalks celery, cut into 1 inch pieces
- 3 potatoes, cubed

Direction

- In a bowl, arrange the onion powder, garlic salt, garlic, half of the chopped onion, half of the cilantro, and ground beef. Use black pepper and salt to sprinkle and lightly blend until mixed. Shape the mixture into meatballs with the size of a golf ball.
- Use non-stick spray to grease a large skillet, then gently brown the meatballs on medium-high heat; take the meatballs out and put aside (cooking the meatballs thoroughly is not necessary, they will get completely cooked in the soup). In the same skillet, stir and cook the remainder of onion on medium-low heat for around 10 minutes until translucent.
- In a large pot, add the chicken broth and stir the onion in; put in the potatoes, celery, and carrots. Start boiling on high heat; turn down the heat and allow to simmer for around 15 minutes until potatoes nearly become tender. Add in the remaining cilantro and the meatballs; allow to simmer for 30 minutes. Use black pepper and salt to season to taste.

Nutrition Information

- Calories: 275 calories;
- Protein: 15.7
- Total Fat: 12.1
- Sodium: 159
- Total Carbohydrate: 26
- Cholesterol: 46

744. Homemade BBQ Meatballs

Serving: 30 | Prep: 45mins | Cook: 1hours | Ready in:

Ingredients

- 4 eggs, beaten
- 1/2 cup vodka
- 1/2 cup water
- 1 tablespoon Worcestershire sauce
- 2 tablespoons dried minced onion flakes
- 1 teaspoon garlic powder, or to taste
- 1/2 teaspoon salt, or to taste
- 1/2 teaspoon ground black pepper, or to taste
- 3 pounds ground beef
- 2 pounds ground turkey
- 1 (15 ounce) package Italian seasoned bread crumbs
- 2 (28 ounce) cans crushed tomatoes
- 2 (14.25 ounce) cans tomato puree
- 1 (18 ounce) bottle hickory smoke flavored barbeque sauce
- 1 (8 ounce) can crushed pineapple
- 1 cup brown sugar
- 1 (14 ounce) bottle ketchup
- 1/2 cup vodka
- 2 tablespoons dried minced onion flakes
- 1 teaspoon garlic powder, or to taste
- 1/2 teaspoon salt, or to taste
- 1/2 teaspoon ground black pepper, or to taste

Direction

- In a large bowl, combine Worcestershire sauce, half a cup of vodka and eggs. Put in garlic powder, 2 tablespoons onion flakes, pepper and salt to taste. Mix in bread crumbs, ground turkey and ground beef. Form into meatballs, and put aside.
- In a very large pot over medium heat, combine tomato puree, crushed tomatoes, pineapple, barbeque sauce, ketchup, brown sugar, and half a cup of vodka. Add garlic powder, onion flakes, pepper and salt for seasoning. Let it boil, lower the heat and let it simmer.
- Heat a large heavy skillet over medium heat. Cook meatballs until brown evenly on all sides. Carefully arrange into sauce, and simmer for at least one hour.

Nutrition Information

- Calories: 369 calories;
- Total Carbohydrate: 34.9
- Cholesterol: 87
- Protein: 17.3
- Total Fat: 16.3
- Sodium: 885

---

745. Homemade Beef Breakfast Sausage Patties

Serving: 8 | Prep: 5mins | Cook: 10mins | Ready in:

Ingredients

- 1 tablespoon brown sugar
- 2 teaspoons dried sage
- 2 teaspoons salt
- 2 teaspoons dried basil
- 1 teaspoon ground black pepper
- 1 teaspoon onion powder
- 1/4 teaspoon dried marjoram
- 1/8 teaspoon crushed red pepper flakes
- 2 pounds ground beef (75% to 80% lean)

Direction

- In a small bowl, stir red pepper flakes, marjoram, onion powder, black pepper, basil, salt, sage and the brown sugar together. In a large bowl, put ground beef and mix the spice blend into the ground beef until evenly integrated with your hands. Refrigerate for a day to let the flavors blend.
- Portion ground beef mixture into eight patties.
- Heat the large pan over medium heat. Cook the patties in the pan for 5-7 mins per side, until hot, firm, and cooked in the middle. An instant-read thermometer reads 160°F (70 °C) when inserted into the center.

Nutrition Information

- Calories: 215 calories;
- Total Fat: 13.7
- Sodium: 648
- Total Carbohydrate: 2.4
- Cholesterol: 71
- Protein: 19.2

---

746. Homemade Lasagna

Serving: 8 | Prep: 1hours | Cook: 45mins | Ready in:

Ingredients

- 1 (16 ounce) package lasagna noodles
- 1/2 pound ground pork
- 1/2 pound lean ground beef
- 1 (8 ounce) can tomato sauce
- 1 (28 ounce) can crushed tomatoes
- 1 tablespoon chopped fresh parsley
- 1 clove garlic, crushed
- 1/2 teaspoon dried oregano
- 1/2 cup minced onion
- 1/8 teaspoon white sugar
- 1 1/2 teaspoons dried basil
- 1 1/2 teaspoons salt
- 1 pound small curd cottage cheese
- 3 eggs
- 3/4 cup grated Parmesan cheese

- 2 teaspoons salt
- 1/4 teaspoon ground black pepper
- 1 pound shredded mozzarella cheese

Direction

- Let oven heat up to 375°F or to 195°C. Boil a big pot of lightly salted water. Allow noodles to cook until al dente for 8 -10 minutes. Discard excess water and put aside.
- In a big, deep skillet, cook beef and pork on medium fire until it becomes brown. Mix in crushed tomato, tomato sauce, oregano, garlic, parsley, salt, and onion. Let it simmer on medium to low fire for half an hour with occasional stirring.
- Mix in egg, cottage cheese, parsley, pepper, salt and parmesan cheese in a big bowl.
- On the bottom of a 9x13 inch baking dish, arrange 2 layers of noodles then even out half of the sauce, half of the cheese mixture, and half of the mozzarella cheese. Duplicate layers.
- Use aluminum foil to cover and let it bake in a heated oven for 30-40 minutes. Take off the foil and let it bake for 5 to 10 minutes more. Wait for 10 minutes to cut and then serve.

Nutrition Information

- Calories: 638 calories;
- Total Fat: 27.2
- Sodium: 2053
- Total Carbohydrate: 54.1
- Cholesterol: 161
- Protein: 45.7

747.   Husband's Delight

Serving: 6 | Prep: 20mins | Cook: 25mins | Ready in:

Ingredients

- 10 ounces egg noodles
- 1 1/2 pounds ground beef

- 1 (14.5 ounce) can peeled and diced tomatoes with juice
- 1 teaspoon salt
- 1 tablespoon white sugar
- 1 1/2 cups sour cream
- 3 ounces cream cheese
- 1/2 onion, chopped
- 1 cup shredded Cheddar cheese

Direction

- Turn the oven to 350°F (175°C) to preheat.
- Boil lightly salted water in a big pot. Add pasta and cook until al dente or 8-10 minutes; drain.
- In a big frying pan, brown ground beef over medium heat. Add sugar, salt, and tomatoes with juice and simmer for 15 minutes.
- Mix onion, cream cheese, and sour cream together in another medium-sized bowl and thoroughly combine. Put 1/2 of the egg noodles, and then the whole meat mixture, and then the cream mixture in a 9x13-in. baking dish. Put the leftover noodles on top and sprinkle the cheese over.
- Bake for 25 minutes at 350°F (175°C).

Nutrition Information

- Calories: 667 calories;
- Total Fat: 39.7
- Sodium: 778
- Total Carbohydrate: 41.5
- Cholesterol: 172
- Protein: 34.6

748.   Inside Out Ravioli I

Serving: 8 | Prep: | Cook: | Ready in:

Ingredients

- 16 ounces pasta
- 1 (10 ounce) package frozen chopped spinach

- 1/2 cup bread crumbs
- 2 eggs, beaten
- 1/4 cup olive oil
- 1 cup shredded mozzarella cheese
- 1 pound lean ground beef
- 1/2 cup chopped onion
- 1 clove garlic, minced
- 1 (8 ounce) can tomato sauce
- 1 (6 ounce) can tomato paste
- 1 (16 ounce) jar spaghetti sauce

Direction

- Cook pasta in boiling salted water in a medium pot till al dente. Drain thoroughly.
- Cook spinach following package instruction.
- In the meantime, in a big skillet, brown minced garlic, chopped onion and ground beef over medium heat. Mix in pasta sauce, tomato paste and tomato sauce. Let simmer for 10 minutes.
- Mix olive oil, beaten eggs, shredded cheese, bread crumbs, cooked pasta and cooked spinach.
- Scatter spinach mixture equally into the base of a 9x13-inch baking dish. Put meat mixture on top.
- In a 175 °C or 350 °F preheated oven, bake for half an hour.

Nutrition Information

- Calories: 545 calories;
- Cholesterol: 142
- Protein: 25.7
- Total Fat: 26.4
- Sodium: 779
- Total Carbohydrate: 51.7

749.   Instant Pot® Shepherd's Pie With Potatoes And Yams

Serving: 10 | Prep: 20mins | Cook: 45mins | Ready in:

Ingredients

- Topping:
- 1 cup low-sodium chicken broth
- 1 large yam, chopped
- 1 large russet potato, chopped
- 1 teaspoon Himalayan pink salt
- 1/2 cup milk
- 3 tablespoons butter
- Meat Filling:
- 1 tablespoon vegetable oil
- 1/2 onion, chopped
- 2 cloves garlic, mashed
- 1 1/8 pounds ground beef
- salt and ground black pepper to taste
- 6 mushrooms, sliced
- 1 cup frozen corn
- 1 cup frozen green peas
- 1 crown broccoli, diced
- 1 carrot, chopped
- 1 stalk celery, chopped
- 1 (.87 ounce) package low-sodium gravy mix
- 1 tablespoon water, or as needed
- 1/2 cup shredded Cheddar cheese

Direction

- Prepare a multi-functional electric pressure cooker and place the chicken broth. Set a steamer rack in the pot, and arrange the potato and yam over it. Sprinkle pink salt on top; close and lock the lid of the cooker. Turn the valve to "Seal." Following the manufacturer's instructions, set the cooker on high, and set the timer for 8 minutes. Let the pressure build for about 10 to 15 minutes.
- Refer to the manufacturer's instructions in carefully releasing the pressure with the quick-release method for about 5 minutes. Unlock and uncover. Take off the rack, and the potato and yam. Strain the liquid into a glass measuring cap and reserve. Place the potato and yam back to the pot. Add in butter and milk and mash with masher the potatountil smooth, and scrape the mashed potato topping using a silicone spatula into a bowl.
- Preheat the oven to 350°F or 175°C.

- Set the pressure cooker in its "Sauté" function. Heat up the oil on high mode then cook garlic and onion, sauté for about 1 to 2 minutes or until they are slightly tender. Mix in pepper, ground beef, and salt. Cook and stir for about 2 to 3 minutes or until filling is well combined. Add in the mushrooms and stir for about a minute or until they begin to soften.
- Add in the celery, corn, broccoli, carrot, and peas into the pot with the filling. Mix in the reserved potato liquid. Close and seal the lid, and set pot into "Manual" Function.
- Set on low pressure, following the manufacturer's instructions. Set the timer for 3 minutes. Let the pressure build for about 5 to 10 minutes.
- Refer to the manufacturer's instructions and carefully release the pressure with the quick-release method for about 5 minutes. Unlock and uncover. Strain and discard the excess liquid then return filling to the pot. Select the "Sauté" mode.
- Mix enough water and gravy mix to dissolve the powder, then add to the filling in the pot. Cook for about 2 minutes, while stirring, or until the gravy thickens. Place the filling on a baking dish and cover with the mashed topping. Place cheddar cheese on top. Bake in the preheated oven for about 10 minutes or until the cheese is melted.
- Place the oven rack about 6 inches from the heat source and preheat the oven's broiler. Broil the shepherd's pie for about 3 to 5 minutes or until the top turns brown. Leave for 5 minutes to sit before serving.

Nutrition Information

- Calories: 309 calories;
- Total Fat: 15
- Sodium: 467
- Total Carbohydrate: 29.8
- Cholesterol: 47
- Protein: 14

---

750. Instant Pot® Spaghetti And Meatballs

Serving: 6 | Prep: 15mins | Cook: 40mins | Ready in:

Ingredients

- 1 onion, halved, divided
- 1 (16 ounce) package ground beef
- 1 egg
- 1 tablespoon minced fresh parsley
- 1 tablespoon dry bread crumbs
- 1 teaspoon Dijon mustard
- 1 teaspoon salt
- cracked black pepper to taste
- 1 1/2 tablespoons olive oil, divided, or as needed
- 1 (28 ounce) can tomato puree
- 1 tablespoon butter, or more to taste
- 1 teaspoon salt
- 1 (16 ounce) package spaghetti

Direction

- In a bowl, grate 1/2 of the onion and mix it together with pepper, ground beef, a teaspoon salt, egg, mustard, parsley, and bread crumbs. Form the mixture into meatballs.
- Set a multi-functional cooker like Instant Pot® on and select Sauté mode; cover the base of the pot with 1 tablespoon olive oil. Cook meatballs for 5-7 minutes until browned. Flip and cook the other side for another 5-7 minutes until browned.
- In the pot, add a teaspoon salt, butter, tomato puree and the remaining half of the onion. Secure lid and set the cooker on Meat/Stew mode, set timer at 20 minutes. Let the pressure build for 10-15 minutes.
- Boil a big pot of lightly salted water; add the spaghetti in the boiling water. Cook for 12 minutes until al dente yet firm to the bite, stir regularly. Drain and pour 1 1/2 teaspoon olive oil to prevent the spaghetti from sticking together.

- Use the quick-release method in relieving pressure carefully for 5 minutes, following the cooker's manual. Unlock and remove lid, remove and dispose the onion. Ladle meatball sauce over the spaghetti.

Nutrition Information

- Calories: 566 calories;
- Protein: 26
- Total Fat: 19.4
- Sodium: 1401
- Total Carbohydrate: 72.2
- Cholesterol: 82

751.   Iowa Maid Rites

Serving: 15 | Prep: 30mins | Cook: 2hours |Ready in:

Ingredients

- 4 pounds ground beef
- 1 (1 ounce) envelope dry onion soup mix
- 1 1/2 (10.5 ounce) cans condensed French onion soup
- 16 hamburger buns, split

Direction

- Crush ground beef into small pieces into a large skillet over medium-high heat. Cook beef until browned, stirring to crumble beef more while cooking. Drain off drippings. Mix in French onion soup and onion soup mix. Simmer, covered, about 2 hours over low heat. (You can cook mixture in a slow cooker at this step).
- Spoon mixture on hamburger buns like a sloppy Joe to serve.

Nutrition Information

- Calories: 367 calories;
- Total Carbohydrate: 26.8

- Cholesterol: 75
- Protein: 25
- Total Fat: 17
- Sodium: 748

752.   It's Chili By George!!

Serving: 10 | Prep: 10mins | Cook: 1hours45mins |Ready in:

Ingredients

- 2 pounds lean ground beef
- 1 (46 fluid ounce) can tomato juice
- 1 (29 ounce) can tomato sauce
- 1 (15 ounce) can kidney beans, drained and rinsed
- 1 (15 ounce) can pinto beans, drained and rinsed
- 1 1/2 cups chopped onion
- 1/4 cup chopped green bell pepper
- 1/8 teaspoon ground cayenne pepper
- 1/2 teaspoon white sugar
- 1/2 teaspoon dried oregano
- 1/2 teaspoon ground black pepper
- 1 teaspoon salt
- 1 1/2 teaspoons ground cumin
- 1/4 cup chili powder

Direction

- In a large deep skillet add ground beef. Cook over medium-high heat until evenly brown. Drain and break up the beef.
- Add to a large pot over high heat, combine the ground beef, onions, bell pepper, tomato juice, tomato sauce, kidney beans, pinto beans, cayenne pepper, sugar, cumin, chili powder, oregano, ground black pepper and salt, bring to a boil then turn heat to low. Simmer for 1 1/2 hours. (Note: If using a slow cooker, add all the ingredients and cook on low for 8 to 10 hours.)

Nutrition Information

- Calories: 305 calories;
- Total Fat: 13.7
- Sodium: 1267
- Total Carbohydrate: 25.5
- Cholesterol: 55
- Protein: 22.3

753. Italian Baked Cannelloni

Serving: 6 | Prep: 45mins | Cook: 25mins | Ready in:

Ingredients

- 1/2 cup olive oil, or as needed
- 1 pound lean ground beef
- 1 onion, thinly sliced
- 1/4 teaspoon dried sage
- 1/4 teaspoon dried rosemary
- salt to taste
- 1/2 cup white wine
- 4 tablespoons butter
- 4 tablespoons all-purpose flour
- 2 cups milk
- 2 egg yolks, lightly beaten
- 12 ounces mozzarella cheese, cubed
- For the Tomato Sauce:
- 2 tablespoons butter
- 1 onion, thinly sliced
- 1/2 cup white wine
- 2 (14.5 ounce) cans stewed tomatoes
- salt and pepper to taste
- 12 cannelloni pasta shells

Direction

- Heat the oil in a big skillet over moderate heat and sauté ground beef with rosemary, sage and onion; cook till meat is crumbly and equally browned. Drain off the grease. Put in 1/2 cup white wine and salt; cook till wine is vaporized. Reserve the mixture.
- For Bechamel sauce: in a medium saucepan, liquify 4 tablespoons of butter over moderate heat. Put the flour and mix till well combined. Mix in milk and bring to a gentle boil till mixture thickens. Take sauce away from heat. Add bechamel in a steady stream to beaten egg yolks, mixing continuously. Mix the sauce into the meat mixture. Mix in the diced mozzarella.
- Liquify 2 tablespoons butter in a medium saucepan over moderately-low heat and sauté the onion till translucent and tender. Put in half cup of white wine and cook down to evaporate; put in the salt and stewed tomatoes. Combine thoroughly; simmer for 15 minutes.
- Boil a big pot of slightly salted water. Put the pasta, a few at a time, and cook till al dente, about 8 to 10 minutes; quickly transfer to a pot filled with cold water using a slotted spoon. Remove pasta using a slotted spoon and set on a flat area.
- Preheat an oven to 200 °C or 400 °F. Slightly oil a 9x13-inch baking dish.
- In each shell, place a line of filling, beginning from an end and use finger to press filling inside of each shell. In prepped baking dish, put the cannelloni and cover with the tomato sauce mixture.
- In prepped oven, bake for 15 minutes or till heated through; once completed baking, let sit for 5 minutes, serve.

Nutrition Information

- Calories: 890 calories;
- Total Fat: 58.1
- Sodium: 826
- Total Carbohydrate: 47.4
- Cholesterol: 198
- Protein: 37.4

754. Italian Meatloaf

Serving: 6 | Prep: 15mins | Cook: 1hours | Ready in:

Ingredients

- 1/2 cup sun-dried tomatoes
- 1 cup hot water
- cooking spray
- 1 pound ground beef
- 1 cup seasoned bread crumbs
- 3/4 cup finely chopped onion
- 3/4 cup chopped fresh basil
- 1/2 cup ketchup
- 2 ounces shredded sharp provolone cheese
- 2 egg whites
- 2 cloves garlic, chopped

Direction

- Place tomatoes in a bowl. Add hot water into the bowl and let the tomatoes soak for about half an hour, until they become soft, then strain.
- Start preheating the oven to 175°C (or 350°F). Use a cooking spray to grease a loaf pan.
- In a bowl, combine garlic, egg whites, provolone cheese, ketchup, basil, onion, bread crumbs, ground beef, and drained tomatoes, and arrange in the greased loaf pan.
- Bake for about 60 minutes in the prepared oven, until it is no longer pink in the middle of the loaf. The temperature should register at least 70°C (or 160°F) when inserting an instant-read thermometer in the middle of the meat loaf.

Nutrition Information

- Calories: 294 calories;
- Protein: 20.6
- Total Fat: 13
- Sodium: 816
- Total Carbohydrate: 23.9
- Cholesterol: 54

755.   Italian Mini Meat Loaves

Serving: 4 | Prep: 10mins | Cook: 45mins | Ready in:

Ingredients

- 2 tablespoons olive oil
- 1 pound lean ground beef
- 8 ounces bulk mild Italian sausage
- 1/2 cup diced white onion
- 1 (24 ounce) jar Classico® Fresh Four Cheese Sauce, divided
- 1 egg, lightly beaten
- 1/3 cup Italian seasoned bread crumbs
- 1/4 cup shredded Parmesan cheese
- 1/4 teaspoon garlic powder
- 1/2 teaspoon salt
- 1/8 teaspoon black pepper
- 1 tablespoon chopped fresh parsley
- 1 cup shredded mozzarella cheese

Direction

- Heat the oven to 350°F. Oil the base of a 9x13-inch baking dish generously.
- In a big bowl, put the Italian sausage and ground beef together then mix the parsley, pepper, salt, garlic powder, Parmesan cheese, bread crumbs, egg, half a jar of four cheese red sauce and onion until thoroughly blended.
- Split the mixture into 4 oval mini loaves and set them in the prepped baking dish. Pour the remaining red sauce over the top of all meat loaves.
- Use a non-stick cooking spray to coat the bottom of a big piece of foil and cover the dish securely/tightly. Bake for 45 minutes before opening it up to sprinkle shredded mozzarella cheese over the loaves.
- Turn the oven temperature up to 400°F and bake the unsealed loaves for about 10 minutes more. It is done when the cheese melts and the internal temperature reaches 165°F.

Nutrition Information

- Calories: 675 calories;

- Total Carbohydrate: 27.8
- Cholesterol: 172
- Protein: 43.6
- Total Fat: 42.9
- Sodium: 1863

┌─────────────────────────────────────┐
│ 756.   Italian Portuguese Meat   │
│   Loaf Fusion   │
└─────────────────────────────────────┘

Serving: 6 | Prep: 10mins | Cook: 1hours | Ready in:

Ingredients

- 1 pound ground beef
- 2 links chorizo sausage, casings removed
- 1 cup plain bread crumbs
- 1/2 cup prepared pasta sauce
- 1 egg, beaten
- 2 teaspoons jarred minced garlic
- 1 teaspoon Italian seasoning
- salt and ground black pepper to taste
- 1 tablespoon prepared pasta sauce

Direction

- Preheat an oven to 175°C/350°F.
- Mix pepper, salt, Italian seasoning, garlic, egg, 1/2 cup of pasta sauce, breadcrumbs, chorizo sausage and ground beef till well combined in a bowl; shape the meat mixture into the loaf pan. On top of the loaf, spread 1 tbsp. prepped pasta sauce.
- In preheated oven, bake for 1 hour till not pink in the middle anymore; an inserted instant-read thermometer in the middle should read no less than 70°C/160°F.

Nutrition Information

- Calories: 346 calories;
- Cholesterol: 94
- Protein: 20.8
- Total Fat: 21
- Sodium: 544

- Total Carbohydrate: 17.1

┌─────────────────────────────────────┐
│ 757.   Italian Spaghetti Sauce   │
│   With Meatballs   │
└─────────────────────────────────────┘

Serving: 6 | Prep: 20mins | Cook: 2hours | Ready in:

Ingredients

- MEATBALLS
- 1 pound lean ground beef
- 1 cup fresh bread crumbs
- 1 tablespoon dried parsley
- 1 tablespoon grated Parmesan cheese
- 1/4 teaspoon ground black pepper
- 1/8 teaspoon garlic powder
- 1 egg, beaten
- SAUCE
- 3/4 cup chopped onion
- 5 cloves garlic, minced
- 1/4 cup olive oil
- 2 (28 ounce) cans whole peeled tomatoes
- 2 teaspoons salt
- 1 teaspoon white sugar
- 1 bay leaf
- 1 (6 ounce) can tomato paste
- 3/4 teaspoon dried basil
- 1/2 teaspoon ground black pepper

Direction

- Mix beaten egg, garlic powder, 1/4 teaspoon black pepper, Parmesan, parsley, bread crumbs and ground beef in a big bowl; stir well. Shape into 12 balls then cover and keep in the refrigerator until needed.
- Sauté the garlic and onion in olive oil until onion becomes translucent in a big saucepan over medium heat. Mix in bay leaf, sugar, salt and tomatoes. Cover and turn the heat to low. Allow it to simmer for 1 1/2 hours. Mix in the meatballs, half a teaspoon of pepper, basil and tomato paste. Simmer for another 30 minutes then serve.

Nutrition Information

- Calories: 349 calories;
- Cholesterol: 77
- Protein: 18.9
- Total Fat: 21.2
- Sodium: 1492
- Total Carbohydrate: 23.7

758. Italian Style Meatloaf I

Serving: 6 | Prep: 15mins | Cook: 1hours |Ready in:

Ingredients

- 1 1/2 pounds ground beef
- 2 eggs, beaten
- 3/4 cup dry bread crumbs
- 1/4 cup ketchup
- 1 teaspoon Italian-style seasoning
- 1 teaspoon dried oregano
- 1 teaspoon dried basil
- 1 teaspoon garlic salt
- 1 (14.5 ounce) can diced tomatoes, drained
- 1 1/2 cups shredded mozzarella cheese

Direction

- Start preheating the oven at 350°F (175°C).
- Combine ketchup, bread crumbs, eggs and ground beef in a large bowl. Flavor with cheese, diced tomatoes, garlic salt, basil, oregano and Italian-style seasoning. Press into a 9x5-inch loaf pan, and use foil to cover loosely.
- Bake in the prepared oven for about 1 hour until internal temperature achieves 160°F (70°C).

Nutrition Information

- Calories: 538 calories;
- Sodium: 941
- Total Carbohydrate: 15.6
- Cholesterol: 181

- Protein: 29.8
- Total Fat: 38.9

759. Italian Taco Salad

Serving: 6 | Prep: 15mins | Cook: 10mins |Ready in:

Ingredients

- 1 pound ground beef
- 3 cups crushed tortilla chips
- 2 cups shredded mozzarella cheese
- 2 cups shredded Cheddar cheese
- 1 (10 ounce) package mixed salad greens
- 1 (8 ounce) bottle zesty Italian dressing

Direction

- Cook the ground beef in a medium skillet over medium heat until browned evenly. Remove the mixture from the heat and let it drain.
- Combine mozzarella cheese, salad greens, ground beef, Cheddar cheese and tortilla chips in a large bowl. Toss the mixture with the Italian dressing to coat well. Serve.

Nutrition Information

- Calories: 610 calories;
- Total Carbohydrate: 13.6
- Cholesterol: 110
- Protein: 32.9
- Total Fat: 46.8
- Sodium: 1186

760. Italian Wedding Soup With Orzo

Serving: 4 | Prep: 25mins | Cook: 29mins |Ready in:

Ingredients

- 1/4 pound ground pork
- 1/4 pound ground beef
- 1 egg white
- 3 tablespoons panko bread crumbs, or more as needed
- 1 teaspoon Italian seasoning
- 1 tablespoon olive oil
- 2 carrots, diced
- 2 stalks celery, diced
- 1 parsnip, diced
- 1/2 cup minced onion
- 1 tablespoon herbes de Provence
- 1 teaspoon red pepper flakes
- salt and ground black pepper to taste
- 4 cups chicken broth
- 1 cup orzo pasta
- 2 cups chopped fresh spinach
- 1/4 cup grated Parmesan cheese

Direction

- In a bowl, combine Italian seasoning, bread crumbs, egg white, beef and pork; shape into very little pea-sized meatballs.
- Heat oil in a Dutch oven or soup pot on medium heat. Add the pepper, salt, red pepper flakes, herbes de Provence, onion, parsnip, celery and carrots. Let it cook and stir for 7-10 minutes, until the veggies are soft.
- Pour the chicken broth into the pot; boil. Add the orzo pasta and mini meatballs. Lower the heat to low and let it simmer for 15-20 minutes to combine the flavors; add spinach. Cook for 2-3 minutes, until it wilts. Add Parmesan cheese on top to garnish.

Nutrition Information

- Calories: 413 calories;
- Total Fat: 14.7
- Sodium: 1400
- Total Carbohydrate: 48.8
- Cholesterol: 46
- Protein: 22.3

761. Japanese Wafu Burger

Serving: 6 | Prep: 25mins | Cook: 20mins | Ready in:

Ingredients

- 1 (14 ounce) package firm tofu
- 1 pound ground beef
- 1/2 cup sliced shiitake mushrooms
- 2 tablespoons miso paste
- 1 egg, lightly beaten
- 1 teaspoon salt
- 1 teaspoon ground black pepper
- 1/4 teaspoon ground nutmeg
- 1/4 cup mirin (Japanese sweet wine)
- 2 tablespoons soy sauce
- 1 teaspoon garlic paste
- 1/4 teaspoon minced fresh ginger root
- 1 tablespoon vegetable oil

Direction

- On a plate, put a tofu block then top with another plate; put a 3-5 pound weight or a container with water on top, press the tofu for 10-15 mins. Drain and remove the collected liquid. Slice the tofu into half-inch cubes.
- In a big bowl, mix nutmeg, tofu, pepper, ground beef, salt, shiitake mushrooms, egg, and miso paste. Split into six balls then flatten each ball into patty.
- In a small bowl, mix ginger, mirin, garlic paste, and soy sauce; set aside.
- On medium-high heat, heat vegetable oil in a big pan. Cook burgers for 2 mins on each side, or until brown. Turn to low heat; cook for 5 mins while covered, or until the juices are clear. Drain and get rid of the surplus grease.
- Add the soy sauce mixture to the pan. Move the pan constantly to avoid burning the sauce, turn the burgers from time to time to coat each side in sauce. The sauce will be thick and a shiny glaze will form on the burgers. The burgers are ready once the sauce is completely used.

Nutrition Information

- Calories: 307 calories;
- Protein: 25.5
- Total Fat: 18.1
- Sodium: 999
- Total Carbohydrate: 8.9
- Cholesterol: 77

---

762.   Jeannie's Famous Potato Hamburger Casserole

Serving: 8 | Prep: 30mins | Cook: 1hours45mins | Ready in:

Ingredients

- 1 tablespoon olive oil
- 1 yellow onion, thinly sliced
- 1 pound ground beef
- 1/4 cup butter
- 1/4 cup all-purpose flour
- 3 cups milk
- 1 pint heavy cream
- salt and pepper to taste
- 5 potatoes, sliced
- 2 cups shredded Cheddar cheese
- 2 cups shredded Monterey Jack cheese
- 1 cup milk

Direction

- Preheat the oven to 175 degrees C (350 degrees F).
- Heat the oil on medium heat in the big heavy skillet. Cook and whisk onions till translucent; put aside. Cook the ground beef till equally browned. Drain off surplus fat, and put the beef aside. Melt the butter in skillet. Put in the flour, and whisk using the whisk for 5 minutes. Slowly stir in 3 cups of the milk, then cream. Let simmer, whisk often, on medium-low heat till sauce becomes thick and smooth or for 10 minutes. Use the pepper and salt to season, and take out of the heat.

- Spread a little bit of the sauce in bottom of the 9x13-in. casserole plate. Alternate layers of the potatoes, onions, ground beef, the cheese and sauce, with 2 - 3 layers per each. Save some of the cheese to drizzle over the top. If you lack of sauce, push down on all of the layers, and pour in the milk as necessary. Drizzle the leftover cheese over the top.
- Bake in the preheated oven till the potatoes soften or for 45 - 55 minutes.

Nutrition Information

- Calories: 849 calories;
- Total Carbohydrate: 35.4
- Cholesterol: 210
- Protein: 31.9
- Total Fat: 65
- Sodium: 488

---

763.   Jen's Hearty Three Meat Chili

Serving: 8 | Prep: 20mins | Cook: 2hours | Ready in:

Ingredients

- 1 pound hot or sweet Italian sausage
- 1 pound ground beef
- 1/2 onion, chopped
- 1 1/2 pounds beef stew meat, cut into 1/2 inch pieces
- 1 (28 ounce) can diced tomatoes
- 1 (12 fluid ounce) bottle dark beer
- 2 cups water
- 1/4 cup chili powder, or to taste
- 1/4 teaspoon red pepper
- 1/4 teaspoon white pepper
- 1/4 cup white sugar
- 1/2 teaspoon ground cinnamon
- salt and black pepper to taste
- 3 tablespoons tomato paste (optional)
- 1 (15 ounce) can kidney beans, rinsed and drained (optional)

Direction

- In a large skillet, cook and stir the sausage over medium heat until brown. Drain; transfer the sausage in a large pot that can hold all ingredients. In the same skillet, cook and stir onion and ground beef over medium heat, until onions are softened and meat is browned; drain and place to the large pot.
- In the same skillet, cook and stir stew beef over medium heat until brown. Place the stew beef into the large pot without draining.
- Pour water, beer, and tomatoes into the pot with meats. Blend in cinnamon, sugar, white pepper, red pepper, and chili powder. Flavor with salt and black pepper. Simmer until stew beef is very tender, for at least 2 hours, stirring from time to time and adding extra water if needed. If you want a thicker chili, use the tomato paste to thicken as preferred. If putting in kidney beans, put in 10 minutes before enjoying, just in the right time to thoroughly heat.

Nutrition Information

- Calories: 620 calories;
- Total Fat: 36.1
- Sodium: 804
- Total Carbohydrate: 24.7
- Cholesterol: 141
- Protein: 44.2

764.   Jen's Nachos

Serving: 4 | Prep: 5mins | Cook: 10mins | Ready in:

Ingredients

- 1 pound ground beef
- 8 ounces shredded Cheddar cheese
- 3/4 (18 ounce) bottle barbecue sauce
- 1 (14.5 ounce) can stewed tomatoes, drained
- 1 (15 ounce) can whole kernel corn, drained

- 1 (14.5 ounce) package nacho-flavor tortilla chips

Direction

- In a large skillet, brown beef over a medium-high heat. When the meat turns browned, strain the fat from the pan.
- Mix into the meat with barbecue sauce, corn, tomatoes, and Cheddar cheese. Heating this mixture, occasionally stirring.
- During the time the mixture is heating, on each of 4 plates, create bed of chips. Cover the chips with hot mixture. Enjoy!

Nutrition Information

- Calories: 1355 calories;
- Cholesterol: 159
- Protein: 44.9
- Total Fat: 76.8
- Sodium: 2648
- Total Carbohydrate: 123.7

765.   Jimmy's Mexican Pizza

Serving: 8 | Prep: 20mins | Cook: 25mins | Ready in:

Ingredients

- 1/2 pound ground beef
- 1 medium onion, diced
- 1 clove garlic, minced
- 1 tablespoon chili powder
- 1 teaspoon ground cumin
- 1/2 teaspoon paprika
- 1/2 teaspoon black pepper
- 1/2 teaspoon salt
- 1 (16 ounce) can refried beans
- 4 (10 inch) flour tortillas
- 1/2 cup salsa
- 1 cup shredded Cheddar cheese
- 1 cup shredded Monterey Jack cheese
- 2 green onions, chopped

- 2 roma (plum) tomatoes, diced
- 1/4 cup thinly sliced jalapeno pepper
- 1/4 cup sour cream (optional)

Direction

- Start preheating oven to 350°F (175°C). Coat non-stick cooking spray over two pie plates.
- In a skillet, put garlic, onion and beef over medium heat. Then cook until the beef is browned evenly. Drain the grease off. Add pepper, salt, paprika, cumin and chili powder to season the meat.
- In each pie plate, lay 1 tortilla. Cover with 1 refried beans layer. Spread over each one with 1/2 seasoned ground beef. Cover with the second tortilla. Bake in prepared oven for 10 mins.
- Take plates out of the oven. Allow to cool slightly. Spread onto each top of tortilla with 1/2 salsa. Add 1/2 Cheddar and Monterey Jack cheeses to cover each pizza. Top each one with 1/2 tomatoes, 1/2 green onions and 1/2 jalapeno slices.
- Put pizzas back to oven. Bake until cheese melts, about 5-10 mins more. Take out of the oven. Allow to cool slightly. Then slice each one into four pieces.

Nutrition Information

- Calories: 370 calories;
- Cholesterol: 55
- Protein: 19.6
- Total Fat: 18.6
- Sodium: 848
- Total Carbohydrate: 31.6

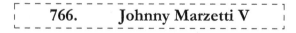

766.   Johnny Marzetti V

Serving: 10 | Prep: 25mins | Cook: 30mins | Ready in:

Ingredients

- 1 (8 ounce) package dry egg noodles

- 2 pounds ground beef
- 1 small onion, chopped
- 2 strips celery, chopped
- 1 small green bell pepper, chopped
- 1 clove garlic, minced
- 1 (4.5 ounce) can sliced mushrooms, drained
- 1 (10.75 ounce) can condensed tomato soup
- 1 (10.75 ounce) can condensed cream of mushroom soup
- 1/2 cup shredded Cheddar cheese
- 1/2 cup shredded mozzarella cheese
- salt and pepper to taste

Direction

- Preheat oven to 350°F (175°C). Grease a baking dish of 9x13 inch lightly.
- In a large pot, boil lightly salted water. Add egg noodles and cook for 8 to 10 minutes or till al dente; drain and leave aside.
- In a medium sized saucepan, stir the mushrooms, garlic, green bell pepper, celery, onion and ground beef together over medium high heat. Cook till beef is browned evenly and vegetables are tender. Drain the fat. Stir in cream of mushroom soup and the tomato soup.
- In the prepared baking dish, place half of the cooked egg noodles. Layer with half of the meat mixture and half of both cheddar and mozzarella cheeses. Add pepper and salt to taste, then repeat the layers with the rest of cheese being the top layer; season again with pepper and salt to taste, if you want.
- In the preheated oven, bake for 30 minutes or till the surface is hot and bubbly and the cheese is melted completely.

Nutrition Information

- Calories: 335 calories;
- Total Fat: 17.3
- Sodium: 553
- Total Carbohydrate: 22.3
- Cholesterol: 82
- Protein: 22.2

767. Juicy Gourmet Burger Sliders

Serving: 4 | Prep: 20mins | Cook: 20mins | Ready in:

Ingredients

- 1 1/2 cups chopped cremini mushrooms
- 1/4 cup minced shallots
- 3 cloves garlic, minced
- 3/4 tablespoon chopped fresh thyme
- 1/2 teaspoon sea salt, or to taste
- 1/2 teaspoon ground black pepper
- 1 1/2 tablespoons olive oil
- 1/4 cup full-bodied dry red wine, or as needed
- 1 pound lean ground chuck
- 1 3/4 tablespoons white truffle oil
- 1 baguette, cut into 1-inch slices
- 12 thin slices Parmesan cheese
- 1 1/2 cups arugula

Direction

- Preheat outdoor grill to medium high heat. Oil the grate lightly.
- In a bowl, mix pepper, salt, thyme, garlic, shallots and mushrooms. In a skillet, heat olive oil on medium heat. Stir and cook mushroom mixture for 8 minutes until golden. Pour red wine into skillet. Simmer for 2 minutes, slowly stirring, until liquid evaporates. On a plate, spread mushroom mixture. Cool for 5 minutes to room temperature.
- In a bowl, crumble ground chuck. Put truffle oil on beef. Gently massage oil into beef until distributed evenly. Fold mushroom mixture into the beef mixture until it's combined. Shape 6 patties to baguette slices size.
- Grill patties, 3 minutes per side, until it's not pink in the middle. An instant-read thermometer inserted in the middle should register a minimum of 70°C/160°F.
- Toast baguette slices until golden and crisp. Put a patty on each baguette slice. Top with

1/4 cup arugula, 2 shaved parmesan cheese slices then a 2nd baguette slices. Use a toothpick to secure every slider.

Nutrition Information

- Calories: 632 calories;
- Sodium: 992
- Total Carbohydrate: 52.5
- Cholesterol: 85
- Protein: 36.7
- Total Fat: 29

768. Kay's Spaghetti And Lasagna Sauce

Serving: 8 | Prep: 20mins | Cook: 40mins | Ready in:

Ingredients

- 1 (28 ounce) can stewed tomatoes
- 1 (28 ounce) can crushed tomatoes
- 1 pound lean ground beef
- 2 yellow onions, chopped
- 2 green bell peppers, chopped
- 5 cloves garlic, chopped
- 2 tablespoons white sugar
- 1 tablespoon dried basil
- 1/2 teaspoon dried oregano
- salt and pepper to taste

Direction

- In a blender, blend the crushed tomatoes and stewed tomatoes. Brown the ground beef with garlic, peppers, and onions in a big kettle or stockpot. Put in the tomatoes then reduce the heat. Put in oregano, basil and sugar then simmer for about 40 minutes. Use pepper and salt to season. Serve.

Nutrition Information

- Calories: 206 calories;

- Total Fat: 8.4
- Sodium: 379
- Total Carbohydrate: 22
- Cholesterol: 34
- Protein: 13.2

769.   Keftedes Greek Meatballs

Serving: 6 | Prep: 20mins | Cook: 30mins | Ready in:

Ingredients

- oil for frying
- 1/4 cup fresh lemon juice
- 5 white potatoes, peeled
- 2 pounds ground beef
- 1 large onion, grated
- 3/4 cup dry bread crumbs
- 1 cup chopped fresh parsley
- 1/3 cup dried mint, crushed
- 1/2 teaspoon ground cinnamon
- zest from 1 lemon
- 2 eggs, beaten
- 1 1/2 tablespoons salt
- 1 teaspoon ground black pepper
- lemon wedges

Direction

- Heat oil to 165°C/325°F in big saucepan/deep fryer.
- Put lemon juice in big bowl. Grate potations coarsely into lemon juice; mix well to avoid browning. Mix pepper, salt, eggs, lemon zest, cinnamon, mint, parsley, breadcrumbs, onion and ground beef in; combine well. Form to 2-inch wide, 1-inch thick oblong balls.
- Working in batches, put meatballs in hot oil; don't crowd. Fry for 6-7 minutes per batch till cooked through and golden brown; serve with lemon wedges.

Nutrition Information

- Calories: 627 calories;
- Total Fat: 35.3
- Sodium: 1977
- Total Carbohydrate: 46.9
- Cholesterol: 154
- Protein: 33.6

770.   Kellie's Kavatini

Serving: 6 | Prep: 15mins | Cook: 45mins | Ready in:

Ingredients

- 1 cup ziti pasta
- 1 cup rotelle pasta
- 1 cup seashell pasta
- 1 1/2 pounds lean ground beef
- 8 ounces shredded Cheddar cheese
- 8 ounces shredded mozzarella cheese
- 1 (8 ounce) package sliced pepperoni sausage
- 3 (14 ounce) cans pizza sauce
- 1/4 cup grated Parmesan cheese

Direction

- Preheat the oven to 175 °C or 350 °F. Boil a big pot of slightly salted water. Put in seashell pasta, rotelle and ziti, and cook till al dente, about 8 to 10 minutes; allow to drain.
- Cook the ground beef in big skillet over moderately-high heat till brown. Drain.
- Mix pizza sauce, pepperoni, mozzarella, cheddar, ground beef and pasta in big Dutch oven, mix thoroughly. Scatter Parmesan all over top and bake for 45 minutes, or till surface is bubbly and golden.

Nutrition Information

- Calories: 908 calories;
- Protein: 56.6
- Total Fat: 52.4
- Sodium: 2260
- Total Carbohydrate: 49.4

432

- Cholesterol: 175

771. Kelsey's Favorite Stuffed Green Peppers

Serving: 6 | Prep: 30mins | Cook: 45mins | Ready in:

Ingredients

- 2 cups water
- 1 cup uncooked white rice
- 3 large green bell peppers, halved and seeded
- 1 1/2 pounds lean ground beef
- 1 onion, diced
- garlic powder to taste
- salt to taste
- ground black pepper to taste
- 1 (15 ounce) can tomato sauce
- 2 cups finely shredded mozzarella cheese

Direction

- Bring water to boiling in a medium saucepan. Add rice; stir. Lower the heat; simmer with a cover for 20 minutes.
- Set the oven to 350°F (175°C) and start preheating.
- In a medium saucepan, place green bell peppers; pour water into the saucepan to cover. Bring to boiling; cook 10 minutes. Take the peppers out of the water; put aside in a 9x13 inch baking dish.
- Brown ground beef over medium heat in a large saucepan; drain. Bring back to the heat; mix in pepper, salt, garlic powder, cooked rice and onion. Pour tomato sauce into the saucepan; combine thoroughly. Allow to simmer for about 10 minutes. Take out of the heat.
- Scoop meat mixture onto each half of green peppers. Bake in the prepared oven until mixture starts turning golden brown or for 45 minutes.
- Top over each stuffed pepper with mozzarella cheese. Transfer back to the oven; bake for

about 5-10 minutes until cheese turns light brown.

Nutrition Information

- Calories: 465 calories;
- Sodium: 675
- Total Carbohydrate: 35
- Cholesterol: 98
- Protein: 34.7
- Total Fat: 20.3

772. Keto Beef Egg Roll Slaw

Serving: 6 | Prep: 15mins | Cook: 15mins | Ready in:

Ingredients

- 2 tablespoons sesame oil
- 1/2 cup diced onion
- 5 green onions, chopped, white and green parts separated
- 3 cloves garlic, minced
- 1 1/2 pounds ground beef
- 1 tablespoon chili-garlic sauce (such as sriracha)
- 1/2 teaspoon ground ginger
- sea salt to taste
- ground black pepper to taste
- 1 (14 ounce) package coleslaw mix
- 3 tablespoons soy sauce
- 1 tablespoon apple cider vinegar

Direction

- In a big frying pan, heat the oil in medium-high heat, then add garlic, green onion's white parts and diced onion, then sauté for about 5 minutes, until the onions become translucent and the garlic is aromatic. Add black pepper, salt, ginger, sriracha and ground beef. Sauté for about 5 minutes, until the beef becomes crumbly and brown.

- In the beef mixture, stir the cider vinegar, soy sauce and coleslaw mix, then sauté for about 4 minutes more, until the coleslaw becomes soft. Put the rest of the green onions on top.

Nutrition Information

- Calories: 350 calories;
- Total Carbohydrate: 12
- Cholesterol: 75
- Protein: 20.6
- Total Fat: 24
- Sodium: 694

773.   Kibby (Kibby Bel Saneeya)

Serving: 4 | Prep: 10mins | Cook: 30mins | Ready in:

Ingredients

- 1 cup cracked wheat
- 1 pound ground beef
- 1 small onion, chopped
- 1 tablespoon lemon juice
- 2 teaspoons ground cinnamon
- salt and ground black pepper to taste
- 1 tablespoon butter, cut into small pieces (optional)
- 1/2 cup pine nuts

Direction

- In a bowl, put in the wheat and fill it up with warm water; let it soak for about 25 minutes until the wheat has soaked up the water a bit. Drain off the water and squeeze the wheat to remove any excess moisture.
- Preheat the oven to 350°F (175°C). Coat a 10x14-inch baking dish with oil.
- In a bowl, combine the onion, salt, lemon juice, black pepper, soaked wheat, cinnamon and ground beef together. Put the beef mixture

into the greased baking dish and spread it evenly; top it with pine nuts and butter.
- Put it in the preheated oven and let it bake for about 25 minutes until the ground beef is not pink inside anymore. Switch on the oven broiler and let the mixture cook in the broiler for 5 minutes until the top turns brown in color.

Nutrition Information

- Calories: 439 calories;
- Protein: 27.6
- Total Fat: 25.8
- Sodium: 89
- Total Carbohydrate: 27.1
- Cholesterol: 79

774.   Kicked Up Goulash

Serving: 4 | Prep: 10mins | Cook: 25mins | Ready in:

Ingredients

- 2 1/2 cups elbow macaroni
- 3/4 pound ground beef
- 1 cup frozen pearl onions
- 1 cup canned corn kernels, drained
- 1 1/2 teaspoons Italian seasoning, or more to taste
- 1 (26 ounce) jar chunky spaghetti sauce (such as Del Monte®)
- salt to taste
- 1/3 cup shredded Cheddar-Monterey Jack cheese blend

Direction

- Boil lightly salted water in a large pot. In the boiling water, cook elbow macaroni for nearly 8 minutes till cooked through but still firm to the bite, stirring occasionally. Drain. Place drained macaroni back into pot.

- Heat a large skillet over medium-high heat. In the hot skillet, cook and stir beef for around 3 to 5 minutes till brown partially; add Italian seasoning, corn, and pearl onions. Continue to cook and stir for approximately 2 minutes till the beef is no longer pink. Cover the skillet and cook for around 3 to 5 minutes till the onions are heated through. Drain and eliminate excess fat. Add beef mixture to the macaroni.
- Pour over the beef and pasta with spaghetti sauce; mix to coat. Heat over medium-low heat for nearly 5 minutes, stirring occasionally, till hot.
- If you want, add more Italian seasoning and salt to season the pasta mixture; put Cheddar-Monterey Jack cheese blend on top and serve.

Nutrition Information

- Calories: 659 calories;
- Sodium: 982
- Total Carbohydrate: 88
- Cholesterol: 65
- Protein: 30.2
- Total Fat: 19.8

---

775. Kid's Favorite Pizza Casserole

Serving: 6 | Prep: 15mins | Cook: 35mins | Ready in:

Ingredients

- 2 cups elbow macaroni
- 1 pound ground beef
- 1 (14 ounce) jar pizza sauce
- 1 (4 ounce) can tomato sauce
- 1 (4.5 ounce) can sliced mushrooms, drained
- 1 pound shredded mozzarella cheese

Direction

- Set the oven to 350°F (175°C) and start preheating.
- Pour water into a large pot, lightly salt and bring to a boil. In boiling water, cook elbow macaroni, stirring occasionally for 8 minutes until cooked through but firm to bite. Drain.
- Cook while stirring ground beef over medium heat in a skillet for about 10 minutes until meat is browned and crumbly; drain excess grease.
- In a bowl, mix mushrooms, tomato sauce, pizza sauce, macaroni and cooked ground beef. Place 1/2 macaroni mixture into a 9x12-inch baking dish; sprinkle with half mozzarella cheese. Layer the remaining macaroni mixture on top; top with the rest of mozzarella cheese. Use aluminum foil to cover.
- Bake in the prepared oven for about 35 minutes until cheese melts and casserole is bubbling. Allow to cool for 3-5 minutes; serve.

Nutrition Information

- Calories: 497 calories;
- Total Fat: 21.5
- Sodium: 1054
- Total Carbohydrate: 36.5
- Cholesterol: 94
- Protein: 37.2

---

776. Kim's Lasagna

Serving: 10 | Prep: 30mins | Cook: 1hours10mins | Ready in:

Ingredients

- 1 pound bulk Italian sausage
- 1 pound ground beef
- 1 cup chopped onion
- 4 cloves garlic, minced
- 2 (8 ounce) cans tomato sauce
- 1 (14 ounce) can crushed tomatoes

- 1 (14 ounce) can Italian-style crushed tomatoes
- 2 (6 ounce) cans tomato paste
- 3 tablespoons chopped fresh basil
- 2 tablespoons chopped fresh parsley
- 2 teaspoons brown sugar
- 1 teaspoon salt
- 1 teaspoon Italian seasoning
- 1/4 teaspoon ground black pepper
- 1/2 teaspoon fennel seeds (optional)
- 1/2 cup grated Parmesan cheese
- 12 lasagna noodles
- 1 egg
- 1 (15 ounce) container ricotta cheese
- 2 tablespoons chopped fresh parsley
- 1/2 teaspoon salt
- 1 pinch ground nutmeg
- 1 (16 ounce) package shredded mozzarella cheese, divided
- 3/4 cup grated Parmesan cheese, divided

Direction

- Sauté the onion, beef, sausage, and garlic over medium heat in a large pot or Dutch oven. Thoroughly cook and stir for 10-15 minutes until the meat is heated through. Drain grease and discard. Pour the tomato sauce, tomato paste, Italian-style crushed tomatoes, crushed tomatoes, Italian seasoning, basil, fennel seeds, brown sugar, salt, black pepper, 1/2 cup of Parmesan cheese, and 2 tablespoons of parsley in meat mixture. Let it boil. Set the heat on low and let it simmer for at least an hour. Stir from time to time. To bring out more flavor, simmer for up to 6 hours.
- Prepare the lasagna noodles by soaking them for 30 minutes in very hot water in a covered deep bowl.
- Beat the egg in a separate bowl. Add 1/2 teaspoon salt, 2 tablespoons parsley, ricotta cheese and nutmeg. Mix well.
- Preheat the oven to 190°C (375°F).
- Pour a cup of sauce into the 13x 9-inch baking dish. Layer four soaked lasagna noodles, 1/3 of ricotta cheese mixture, 1/3 of mozzarella shredded, and 1/4 cup of Parmesan on top. Repeat the process for another 2 layers. Finish

with the mozzarella and Parmesan before covering the baking dish with some aluminum foil.
- Place it in the preheated oven and bake for about 50 minutes or until the lasagna noodles are soft and the dish is bubbly. Uncover and bake for another 15 to 20 minutes or until the cheese on top is light brown. Remove from the oven and cool for 15 minutes. Serve.

Nutrition Information

- Calories: 594 calories;
- Sodium: 1898
- Total Carbohydrate: 43.4
- Cholesterol: 115
- Protein: 41.2
- Total Fat: 29.1

```
777.        Kimchi Bokeumbab
            (Kimchi Fried Rice)
```

Serving: 4 | Prep: 10mins | Cook: 25mins | Ready in:

Ingredients

- 2 teaspoons sesame oil
- 1/2 pound ground beef
- 1 cup chopped kimchi
- 4 cups cooked rice
- 4 eggs

Direction

- Heat a big skillet or wok on medium-high heat. Add sesame oil. Sauté ground beef for 5-7 minutes until crumbly and brown. Add kimchi; stir and cook for 10 minutes. Add rice, stir and cook for 5 minutes until heated through.
- Move fried rice to a side of the wok. Crack eggs in wok, cooking for 2-3 minutes until bottoms are set. Flip eggs then cook for 2-3

minutes until set. Serve an egg on top of each portion of fried rice.

Nutrition Information

- Calories: 482 calories;
- Cholesterol: 234
- Protein: 20.6
- Total Fat: 23
- Sodium: 359
- Total Carbohydrate: 46.4

---

778.   Klupskies (Polish Burgers)

Serving: 4 | Prep: 15mins | Cook: 20mins | Ready in:

Ingredients

- 1 pound ground beef
- 1 small onion, diced
- 1/2 green pepper, diced
- 1 egg
- 2 tablespoons ketchup
- 1/4 teaspoon sea salt
- 2 slices white bread, torn into small pieces
- 1 serving cooking spray with olive oil

Direction

- In a bowl, mix together sea salt, ketchup, green pepper, egg, onion and ground beef. Then mix in white bread pieces until they are evenly distributed. Shape mixture into four patties.
- Spray olive oil cooking spray over a large skillet, then set over the medium heat. Cook burgers for 10 mins or until well-browned on bottoms, turn the burgers over, cook for 8-10 more mins. until juices run clear and meat is no longer pink.

Nutrition Information

- Calories: 270 calories;

- Sodium: 363
- Total Carbohydrate: 10.6
- Cholesterol: 115
- Protein: 21.9
- Total Fat: 15.1

---

779.   Kubbe

Serving: 25 | Prep: 45mins | Cook: 45mins | Ready in:

Ingredients

- Shell:
- 3 cups fine bulgur
- 2 cups all-purpose flour
- 6 tablespoons vegetable oil
- 1 tablespoon crushed red pepper flakes, or to taste
- 2 tablespoons coarse kosher salt, or to taste
- 1 tablespoon ground cumin, or to taste
- 1 cup water, or as needed
- Filling:
- 3 tablespoons vegetable oil
- 2 large onions, finely chopped
- 1 1/2 pounds ground beef
- 1/2 teaspoon ground allspice
- 1/2 teaspoon coarse salt
- 1/2 teaspoon ground cinnamon
- 1/2 cup pine nuts (optional)
- 3 cups oil for frying, or as needed

Direction

- In a large bowl, put bulgur. Stir in cumin, salt, red pepper flakes, 6 tablespoons vegetable oil and flour. Mix in the cup of water gradually to form the stiff dough (but not crumbly). Knead to bind ingredients fully for a few mins. Allow it to sit for a while if it gets too mushy; bulgur will absorb some water.
- To make filling: in a large skillet, heat 3 tablespoons of oil over medium-high heat. Put in onions; cook until they are browned. Discard from skillet. Then crumble ground beef into skillet; cook, stirring frequently, until

browned evenly. Drain any excess grease. Add cinnamon, salt, and allspice to season. Stir in pine nuts and cooked onions. Let cool enough to handle.

- Shape dough into the walnut-sized balls. Using your thumb, press into the ball while it's enclosed in the other hand to make a tube. The cylinder should be 2-in. long; the thinner the walls are, the better they will cook. Stuff as much of meat mixture as possible into the cavity, then make torpedo shape by sealing the end. Do the same with the remaining filling and dough. Kubbe may be frozen at this point. Place on baking sheets to freeze. Once solid, move to the freezer bags.
- In a heavy saucepan or deep fryer, heat oil to 375°F (190°C). Kubbe will fall apart if oil is not hot enough. Put kubbe carefully into hot oil, and fry for one min, until browned nicely. Using tongs, transfer to the paper towels to drain. Enjoy with tahini.

Nutrition Information

- Calories: 231 calories;
- Protein: 8.5
- Total Fat: 12.6
- Sodium: 519
- Total Carbohydrate: 22.3
- Cholesterol: 17

---

780. LaDonna's Spaghetti With Sauce

Serving: 11 | Prep: | Cook: |Ready in:

Ingredients

- 2 pounds lean ground beef
- 1 onion, chopped
- 1 (46 fluid ounce) can tomato juice
- 1 (29 ounce) can tomato sauce
- 2 (6 ounce) cans tomato paste
- 1 cup finely grated carrots

- 4 tablespoons Italian seasoning
- 1 pound fresh mushrooms, quartered
- 5 cloves garlic, minced
- salt to taste
- ground black pepper to taste
- 2 pounds spaghetti

Direction

- Cook onion and ground beef over medium heat until done. Drain off the grease.
- In a large pot, combine pepper and salt, garlic, mushrooms, seasoning, grated carrots, tomato sauce, tomato paste, tomato juice and onion and beef. Simmer on very low heat for 2-3 hours.
- Cook pasta following the package instructions. Drain. Add sauce over the pasta. Serve.

Nutrition Information

- Calories: 611 calories;
- Total Fat: 19
- Sodium: 1018
- Total Carbohydrate: 81.2
- Cholesterol: 62
- Protein: 30.3

---

781. Layered Casserole

Serving: 9 | Prep: 10mins | Cook: 50mins |Ready in:

Ingredients

- 1 1/2 pounds lean ground beef
- 8 ounces fresh pasta
- 1 (8 ounce) container sour cream
- 1 (8 ounce) package cream cheese, softened
- 1/2 cup shredded Cheddar cheese
- 6 green onions, thinly sliced
- 2 (8 ounce) cans tomato sauce
- 1 tablespoon white sugar
- 2 tablespoons shredded Cheddar cheese

Direction

- Cook ground beef over medium-high heat in a large, deep skillet until evenly brown. Drain grease, crumble beef, and put to one side.
- Cook pasta in boiling salted water in a large pot until al dente. Drain thoroughly.
- Arrange the cooked and drained pasta over the bottom of an oiled 13x9-inch casserole dish.
- Combine chopped green onions, shredded Cheddar cheese, cream cheese, and sour cream in a medium mixing bowl. Distribute sour cream mixture over pasta in the baking dish.
- Combine cooked ground beef with tomato sauce and sugar in a small mixing bowl; spread over sour cream mixture. Scatter top with more shredded Cheddar cheese, if desired.
- Chill casserole in the fridge overnight. Take out of the fridge 60 minutes before baking.
- Bake for 30 to 40 minutes at 350°F (175°C). Let sit for 10 to 15 minutes before serving.
- For frozen casserole, let it cool to room temperature for 60 minutes before baking.

Nutrition Information

- Calories: 466 calories;
- Sodium: 459
- Total Carbohydrate: 20.3
- Cholesterol: 122
- Protein: 21.7
- Total Fat: 33

782. Lea's Hamburgers

Serving: 4 | Prep: 15mins | Cook: 10mins | Ready in:

Ingredients

- 1 1/2 pounds ground beef
- 1 small onion, finely chopped
- 1 egg
- 1/2 cup bread crumbs
- 1/4 cup bacon bits
- garlic salt to taste
- 4 hamburger buns, split and toasted

Direction

- Preheat the outdoor grill to high heat.
- Mix bacon bits, breadcrumbs, egg, onion and ground beef in a medium bowl. Season using garlic salt. Divide to 4 balls; pat to patties.
- Oil grate lightly; put patties on grill. Cook till not pink in middle and firm for 5 minutes per side. Serve over toasted buns with preferred hamburger toppings.

Nutrition Information

- Calories: 528 calories;
- Total Fat: 25.6
- Sodium: 758
- Total Carbohydrate: 33.1
- Cholesterol: 155
- Protein: 38.7

783. Lemon Barbeque Meatloaf

Serving: 6 | Prep: 10mins | Cook: 45mins | Ready in:

Ingredients

- 1 1/2 pounds ground beef
- 1/4 cup lemon juice
- 1/2 cup water
- 1 egg, beaten
- 4 slices day-old bread, torn into small pieces
- 1/4 cup chopped onion
- 2 teaspoons seasoning salt
- 1/2 cup ketchup
- 1/3 cup brown sugar
- 1 teaspoon mustard powder
- 1/4 teaspoon ground allspice
- 1/4 teaspoon ground cloves

- 6 slices lemon

Direction

- Set the oven to 350°F (175°C) and start preheating. Coat a 9x13-inch baking dish or a dish of the same size with oil.
- Combine together seasoning salt, onion, bread, egg, water, lemon juice, and ground beef in a big bowl until well combined. Form into 6 separate loaves - I like to make big balls. Put them in the baking dish.
- Bake in the prepared oven for 15 minutes while preparing the topping. Stir together cloves, allspice, mustard powder, brown sugar, and ketchup in a small bowl. Drizzle the loaves with the sauce, then use a slice of lemon to top each one. Put them back to the oven and bake until cooked through, about half an hour more.

Nutrition Information

- Calories: 336 calories;
- Total Fat: 15
- Sodium: 724
- Total Carbohydrate: 29
- Cholesterol: 100
- Protein: 22.1

784. Linda's Lasagna

Serving: 8 | Prep: 45mins | Cook: 1hours45mins | Ready in:

Ingredients

- 1 pound lean ground beef
- 1 onion, chopped
- 2 (6 ounce) cans tomato paste
- 1 (14.5 ounce) can crushed tomatoes
- 2 cups water
- 1 tablespoon dried oregano
- 2 teaspoons garlic powder
- 2 teaspoons salt
- 1/4 teaspoon ground black pepper
- 1 tablespoon white sugar
- 12 ounces cottage cheese
- 1/2 cup grated Parmesan cheese
- 1 egg
- 9 lasagna noodles
- 1 pound shredded mozzarella cheese

Direction

- Let beef cook in a big skillet on medium fire. Drain. Let onion cook in another skillet on medium fire until it becomes transparent. In a big saucepan, cook onion and beef then add water, garlic powder, pepper, salt, sugar, and crushed tomatoes. Let it boil on medium fire. Lower heat to low and allow it to simmer for an hour.
- Blend parmesan, cottage cheese, and egg until it smoothens while sauce is simmering. Put it aside.
- Boil lightly salted water place in a big pot. Allow pasta to cook until it becomes al dente for 8-10 minutes. Discard excess water.
- Let oven heat up to 350°F or to 175°C.
- At the bottom of a 9x13 inches baking dish, level out one cup of sauce. Assemble 3 noodles on top of the sauce. Then flatten noodles with 1/3 of the leftover sauce. Use half the mozzarella and place on top. On top of the mozzarella, make another layer of noodles and sauce then top it with cottage cheese mixture. Create another layer with leftover 3 noodles and sauce.
- Let it bake in the heated oven for half an hour. Dash with extra mozzarella and bake for another 15 minutes until it becomes golden brown and form bubbles.

Nutrition Information

- Calories: 494 calories;
- Total Fat: 21.8
- Sodium: 1626
- Total Carbohydrate: 38.2
- Cholesterol: 104
- Protein: 38.2

785. Loose Meat On A Bun, Restaurant Style

Serving: 12 | Prep: 10mins | Cook: 50mins | Ready in:

Ingredients

- 3 pounds ground beef
- 1/4 cup minced onion
- 3 tablespoons Worcestershire sauce
- 4 cups beef broth
- 1 teaspoon salt
- 1 teaspoon ground black pepper
- 2 teaspoons butter
- 12 hamburger buns, split

Direction

- Crumble onion and ground beef into a big skillet over moderately high heat. Cook the mixture until beef is not pink anymore while stirring to break up lumps. Drain off grease and bring skillet back to the stove. Put in butter, pepper, salt, beef broth and Worcestershire sauce. Bring the mixture to a boil then set the heat to low and simmer without a cover for 40 minutes, until liquid is nearly completely gone. Take away from the heat, place on a cover and allow to rest about 15 minutes prior to serving on buns.

Nutrition Information

- Calories: 341 calories;
- Total Fat: 16.4
- Sodium: 810
- Total Carbohydrate: 22.9
- Cholesterol: 71
- Protein: 23.6

786. Lori's Spicy Chipotle Lasagna

Serving: 12 | Prep: 35mins | Cook: 1hours25mins | Ready in:

Ingredients

- 1 pound lean ground beef
- 1 pound bulk hot Italian sausage
- 1 onion, chopped
- 1 pint sliced fresh mushrooms
- 3 cloves garlic, minced
- 1 chipotle chile in adobo sauce, chopped
- 1 (6 ounce) can tomato paste
- 2 (15 ounce) cans stewed tomatoes
- sea salt and ground black pepper to taste
- 1/2 cup chopped fresh basil
- 1/4 cup chopped fresh oregano
- 2 (8 ounce) packages cream cheese, at room temperature
- 1 pound frozen chopped spinach, thawed
- 9 lasagna noodles
- 2 (8 ounce) balls of fresh mozzarella, sliced
- 2 zucchini, thinly sliced lengthwise
- 1 cup grated Asiago cheese
- 1 cup grated Parmesan cheese

Direction

- In a Dutch oven or big saucepan set on medium-high heat, cook Italian sausage and ground beef until light brown in color. Drain off excess oil. Cook garlic, onions, and mushroom for 5 minutes or until the onions become clear and tender. Add in tomato paste, chipotle chili, and stewed tomatoes. Let the mixture boil; lower the heat to medium-low and leave to simmer for 15 minutes. Add pepper and salt to taste. Mix in oregano and basil and simmer for 5 more minutes, then take off from heat.
- Meanwhile, combine chopped spinach and cream cheese. The water released by the soggy spinach will thin out the mixture, making it more sour cream-like.
- Preheat the oven to 400°F or 200°C.

- Grease the bottom of a 9x13-inch baking tray or layer with aluminum foil. At the bottom of the pan, layer 3 pieces of lasagna noodles and top with a third of the made spinach mixture. Pour in a third of the chipotle meat sauce and spread evenly. Top the layer with a third of the mozzarella cheese and a third of the zucchini. Sprinkle a third of the Parmesan cheese and a third of the Asiago cheese at the top. Repeat these layers twice, topping everything off with the cheeses.
- Cover the pan with aluminum foil; bake in the preheated oven for 40 minutes. Remove the foil and return to oven to bake for 15 to 20 minutes or until the top becomes bubbly.

Nutrition Information

- Calories: 581 calories;
- Total Fat: 38.5
- Sodium: 969
- Total Carbohydrate: 27.5
- Cholesterol: 128
- Protein: 32.6

787.   Low Carb Taco Soup

Serving: 6 | Prep: 10mins | Cook: 44mins | Ready in:

Ingredients

- 3 cups chicken broth, divided
- 1 small head cauliflower, finely chopped
- 1 tablespoon olive oil, or as needed
- 1 onion, finely chopped
- 1 (4 ounce) can diced jalapeno peppers
- 1 pound ground beef
- 1 (8 ounce) package cream cheese, cubed
- 1 (26 ounce) container diced tomatoes
- 1 teaspoon ground paprika
- salt and ground black pepper to taste

Direction

- In a pot, mix the cauliflower and 2 cups of broth on medium-high heat, then boil. Lower the heat to medium-low and let it cook for about 20 minutes until it becomes soft.
- In a frying pan, heat the oil on medium-high heat. Sauté the jalapenos and onion for about 5 minutes, until the onion becomes translucent. Add the beef and let it cook and stir for about 6 minutes, until it becomes crumbly and brown.
- In a blender, place the cooked cauliflower then puree. Put it back into the pot, then add leftover 1 cup of broth and cream cheese. Let it cook and stir for about 3 minutes on medium heat, until the cheese melts. Add the paprika, tomatoes and beef mixture, then sprinkle pepper and salt to season. Let it cook and stir for about 5 minutes, until the flavors combined.

Nutrition Information

- Calories: 377 calories;
- Sodium: 1281
- Total Carbohydrate: 12.6
- Cholesterol: 91
- Protein: 18.4
- Total Fat: 27.6

788.   Luma's Beef And Veg Lasagna With Eggplant Sauce

Serving: 12 | Prep: 20mins | Cook: 2hours40mins | Ready in:

Ingredients

- 1 onion, crushed
- 2 (16 ounce) packages ground beef
- 3 tomatoes, chopped
- 1 small eggplant, chopped
- 8 white mushrooms, sliced, or more to taste
- 1 green bell pepper, chopped
- 1 zucchini, chopped, or more to taste

- 2 cloves garlic, minced
- 1 (16 ounce) can tomato sauce
- 1 pinch dried oregano, or to taste
- salt and ground black pepper to taste
- 1 tablespoon butter, or as needed
- 3 tablespoons all-purpose flour
- 1 gallon milk
- 1 (8 ounce) package no-boil lasagna (such as Skinner® Oven Ready Lasagne), or to taste
- 4 cups shredded mozzarella cheese

Direction

- Put a saucepan over medium-high heat. Sauté onion for 5 minutes or until soft. Put in the beef and cook for 5-7 minutes or until brown and crumbling. Mix in the tomatoes and cook for about 10 minutes or until soft. Stir in the mushrooms, green bell pepper, garlic, mushrooms, eggplant and zucchini. Continue to cook for 15-20 minutes or until the vegetables are soft. Add in salt, pepper, tomato sauce and oregano.
- In a separate saucepan, melt butter over medium heat. Put the flour into the melted butter and slowly add in the milk. Put pepper and salt to taste. Let the béchamel sauce boil. Stir for 5-7 minutes or until the consistency of the sauce is thick.
- Preheat the oven at 350°F (175°C). Brush a baking pan with melted butter.
- In the greased baking pan, put some béchamel sauce evenly on the bottom. Put in a layer of lasagna noodles and beef sauce then top with some mozzarella cheese. Do the whole layering process again for the remaining ingredients until pan is fully filled then top off with a sprinkle of the remaining mozzarella cheese.
- Put in the preheated oven and bake for about 2 hours until the lasagna is cooked through and the top is brown.

Nutrition Information

- Calories: 479 calories;
- Total Carbohydrate: 31.5
- Cholesterol: 101
- Protein: 35.8
- Total Fat: 23.2
- Sodium: 633

789.   Lumpia (Shanghai Version)

Serving: 20 | Prep: 1hours | Cook: 20mins | Ready in:

Ingredients

- 1 pound ground pork
- 1 pound ground beef
- 1 medium onion, finely chopped
- 1 carrot, grated
- 1/4 cup soy sauce
- 2 1/2 teaspoons black pepper
- 1 1/2 tablespoons garlic powder
- 2 tablespoons salt
- 1 (16 ounce) package spring roll wrappers
- 1 1/2 quarts oil for frying

Direction

- Mix carrot, onion, and ground beef and pork in a large bowl. Make sure to fully blend everything. I recommend using your hands, getting down and dirty. Massage the meat in the bowl if you must. Slowly mix in the salt, garlic powder, black pepper, and soy sauce until everything are equally distributed.
- On a flat surface, lay out a few wrappers at a time, and put about 2 tablespoons of the filling in a line down the middle of the wrapper. Be sure the filling is not thicken than your thumb, or the wrapper will cook faster than the meat. Fold the bottom and top edges of the wrapper towards the center Grab the right and left sides, then fold them towards the middle. Dampen the last edge of the wrapper to enclose. Now continue with the rest of the wrappers, and have the children or hubby to help you out.

- In a heavy skillet or deep fryer, add oil to heat to 375°F (190°C). Cook lumpia, 3 or 4 at a time. Then fry for approximately 3 or 4 minutes, flipping once. Once the lumpia floats, they are cooked, and the wrapper turns golden brown. Slice in half, or serve as is paired with dipping sauce. We like banana ketchup, soy sauce with lemon, or sweet and sour sauce.

Nutrition Information

- Calories: 261 calories;
- Total Fat: 17.8
- Sodium: 1037
- Total Carbohydrate: 14.6
- Cholesterol: 38
- Protein: 10.2

---

790.   Lumpia Rolls

Serving: 40 | Prep: 1hours | Cook: 20mins | Ready in:

Ingredients

- 2 pounds ground beef
- 2 pounds ground pork
- vegetable oil
- 1 1/2 cups carrots, finely chopped
- soy sauce to taste
- 3 cups bean sprouts
- 1 cup sugar snap peas, chopped
- 1 cup fresh mushrooms, finely chopped
- 1 cup green onions, finely chopped
- salt to taste
- garlic powder to taste
- black pepper to taste
- 1 (14 ounce) package Lumpia Wrappers
- 1 egg white, beaten
- canola oil for frying

Direction

- In a large frying pan, pour a small amount of oil on medium heat and cook beef and pork until brown. Remove from pan, drain, and set aside in a large mixing bowl. Pour soy sauce in pan and cook the carrots in it until tender. Stir in snap peas, mushrooms, green onions and bean sprouts with a drizzle of each soy sauce, garlic powder, black pepper, and salt; stir and cook for 5 minutes, or until vegetables soften. Add to pork and beef and toss to mix.
- Cover spring roll wrappers with damp cloth to avoid drying them out and work in batches of about 5 or so at a time. On a clean work surface, position the wrapper in a way that one corner is facing you; put small amount of filling mixture on the closest corner to you. Fold over and fold the two outside corners inward. Roll it with the top corner open like a burrito. Using a brush, apply a small amount of egg white on top corner, roll it up and then seal. Do the same with the rest of the wrappers and filling.
- Fry rolls until golden brown, about 5 minutes in a deep skillet or a deep-fryer with vegetable oil heated to 190 degrees C or 375 degrees F, and then rest on paper towels to drain.

Nutrition Information

- Calories: 313 calories;
- Sodium: 170
- Total Carbohydrate: 7.2
- Cholesterol: 37
- Protein: 9.1
- Total Fat: 27.6

---

791.   Macaroni Gratinee

Serving: 10 | Prep: 20mins | Cook: 1hours15mins | Ready in:

Ingredients

- 1 tablespoon olive oil
- 2 pounds ground beef
- 1 small onion, finely chopped

- 3 cloves garlic, chopped
- 1/2 teaspoon Italian seasoning
- 1/2 teaspoon cayenne pepper
- 1/2 teaspoon salt
- 1 (6 ounce) can tomato paste
- 1 (16 ounce) can crushed tomatoes
- 1 1/3 (16 ounce) packages elbow macaroni
- 1 pound sharp Cheddar cheese, shredded
- 1/2 cup grated Parmesan cheese

Direction

- In a large skillet over medium-high heat, put olive oil to heat, and add in the ground beef and cook for about 5 minutes until not pink and crumbly. Mix in the salt, cayenne pepper, Italian seasoning, garlic and onion; keep on cooking for about 5 more minutes until the onion has turned glassy and softened. Remove the extra grease, and stir in the crushed tomatoes and tomato paste. Make it simmer, then minimize heat to medium-low, and simmer for an hour, covered.
- Place an oven rack at about 6 inches from the heat source and prepare the oven's broiler by preheating.
- Place a lightly salted water in a large pot and make it boil. Put in the pasta and cook for 8-10 minutes or until al dente; strain. Add the cooked macaroni into the meat sauce and stir until well combined, then transfer into a 9x13-inch baking dish and spread. Dust with Parmesan and Cheddar cheeses.
- Place in the preheated oven and bake for about 5 minutes until the cheese is golden in color and bubbly.

Nutrition Information

- Calories: 736 calories;
- Total Fat: 36.6
- Sodium: 755
- Total Carbohydrate: 52.9
- Cholesterol: 144
- Protein: 47.3

792.   Man Vs. Meat Stromboli

Serving: 32 | Prep: 20mins | Cook: 35mins | Ready in:

Ingredients

- 4 (1 pound) loaves frozen bread dough, thawed
- 1/2 pound ground beef
- 1 tablespoon garlic powder
- 1 tablespoon dried oregano
- 1 teaspoon dried parsley
- 1 teaspoon salt
- 1 teaspoon ground black pepper
- 2 cups shredded mozzarella cheese
- 1 (8 ounce) can tomato sauce (such as Goya®)
- 1/2 pound thinly sliced provolone cheese
- 1/2 pound thinly sliced salami
- 1/2 pound thinly sliced pepperoni
- 1/2 pound thinly sliced coppa ham
- 2 cups shredded sharp Cheddar cheese
- 1/2 cup grated Romano cheese
- 1 egg yolk, beaten

Direction

- In a large, lightly oiled bowl, put bread dough and allow to rise in a warm place for 2 - 3 hours, until doubled in size. Punch dough down and roll each loaf into a rectangle of 12x15-inch.
- Set the oven to 375°F (190°C), and start preheating. Coat 2 baking sheets with oil.
- Over medium-high heat, heat a large skillet; cook and stir black pepper, salt, parsley, oregano, garlic powder and ground beef until the beef is crumbly, browned evenly, and no pink color. Drain and remove any grease left.
- Sprinkle evenly mozzarella cheese over the bread dough. Spread about 1/2 the tomato sauce atop the mozzarella cheese.
- Layer in order the seasoned ground beef, provolone cheese, salami, pepperoni, and then coppa ham on top; spread the rest of the tomato sauce over the meat. Sprinkle Romano

cheese and Cheddar cheese on top of the tomato sauce.

- Roll each portion into a log, starting with the longer side. Press and seal the ends and seam of each roll. On the prepped baking sheets, place rolls with seam-side down. Brush the rolls with egg yolk.
- Bake in the preheated oven for 25 - 30 minutes, until golden brown. Allow to rest for 5 minutes then slice. Serve warm.

Nutrition Information

- Calories: 349 calories;
- Total Carbohydrate: 28.8
- Cholesterol: 51
- Protein: 18.7
- Total Fat: 16.7
- Sodium: 1002

793.   Marianne's Hot Dish

Serving: 4 | Prep: 20mins | Cook: 1hours10mins | Ready in:

Ingredients

- 1 pound ground beef
- 1/2 onion, minced
- 3 large cloves garlic, minced
- 1 (10.75 ounce) can condensed cream of mushroom soup
- 1 (8 ounce) package sliced fresh mushrooms
- 1 (8 ounce) package fresh sugar snap peas
- 5 slices American cheese, or more to taste
- 1 1/2 cups frozen diced southern-style hash brown potatoes, or more to taste

Direction

- Preheat the oven to 175 degrees C (350 degrees F).
- Over medium-high heat, heat a large skillet and add garlic, onion and beef. Cook while stirring in the hot skillet for 5 to 7 minutes

until crumbly and browned. Use a slotted spoon to pour the ground beef mixture into a 2-quart casserole dish. Leave the drippings in skillet.

- Pour cream of mushroom soup atop the ground beef mixture.
- Over medium heat, cook while stirring the mushrooms in the beef drippings for 5 to 10 minutes until browned and tender. Pour atop the soup layer in the casserole dish.
- Spread snap peas on top of mushroom layer and then cover with slices of American cheese. Spread a layer of potatoes on top of cheese.
- Bake for about an hour in oven until the cheese has melted and the potatoes are crisp and browned.

Nutrition Information

- Calories: 501 calories;
- Sodium: 1075
- Total Carbohydrate: 21.1
- Cholesterol: 101
- Protein: 31.5
- Total Fat: 32.2

794.   Mariu's Spaghetti With Meat Sauce

Serving: 6 | Prep: 45mins | Cook: 2hours | Ready in:

Ingredients

- 2 tablespoons olive oil
- 1/2 cup minced onion
- 1 clove garlic, minced
- 1/2 cup minced celery
- 2 tablespoons butter
- 1 pound lean ground beef
- 1/2 teaspoon white sugar
- 1 teaspoon salt
- 1/2 teaspoon dried mint
- 6 ounces fresh chopped mushrooms
- 1 (6 ounce) can tomato paste

- 2 (10.5 ounce) cans beef broth
- 2 teaspoons dried basil
- 1 pound spaghetti
- 1 teaspoon olive oil
- 3 tablespoons salt
- 1 tablespoon chopped fresh parsley, for garnish
- 1/4 cup grated Romano cheese

Direction

- Heat olive oil in a big skillet over low heat; sauté celery, garlic and onion until onion turns clear.
- Mix in butter then turn up the heat to medium; cook beef until it has lost all the pink color. Stir in sugar, one teaspoon of salt, mushrooms and mint; reduce the heat and stir for three minutes.
- Mix together broth and tomato paste in a big bowl then transfer into a pot including basil. Over very low heat, simmer for two hours, stirring once in a while.
- Bring a big pot with water, one teaspoon of olive oil and three tablespoons of salt to a rolling boil. Put in spaghetti, grabbing the ends until spaghetti slightly soften. Cook just for 7-8 minutes on high heat. Spaghetti is cooked properly when it no longer tastes raw yet remains firm.
- Before serving, stir meat sauce with pasta; place on a warmed bowl or platter and put Romano cheese and parsley over to serve.

Nutrition Information

- Calories: 627 calories;
- Protein: 28.1
- Total Fat: 27.8
- Sodium: 4578
- Total Carbohydrate: 65.7
- Cholesterol: 72

795.   Marmite Mince

Serving: 4 | Prep: | Cook: |Ready in:

Ingredients

- 1 tablespoon butter
- 2 small onion, diced
- 1 pound lean ground beef
- 4 teaspoons yeast extract spread, e.g. Marmite/Vegemite
- 2 1/2 cups sliced fresh mushrooms
- 1 teaspoon paprika
- 2 cubes beef bouillon
- 2 tablespoons brown gravy mix
- 1 cup water

Direction

- In a wok, melt the butter over medium heat. Put in onions and fry until it becomes soft. Crumble the ground beef into the wok and cook while stirring, until it becomes equally brown. Push all of the onion and the beef out to the sides and leave a pool of butter in the middle. Put the yeast spread into the pool, then stir until it dissolves. Mix it into the ground beef.
- Stir in bouillon cubes and paprika. The mixture will bind together and get sticky. Stir in gravy mix and water. At first, it will get sticky. Just mix and bring to a simmer, then serve.

Nutrition Information

- Calories: 293 calories;
- Sodium: 850
- Total Carbohydrate: 8.2
- Cholesterol: 82
- Protein: 26
- Total Fat: 17.4

796. Mary's Meatloaf

Serving: 6 | Prep: 20mins | Cook: 2hours | Ready in:

Ingredients

- 1 1/2 pounds lean ground beef
- 1 large onion, chopped
- salt to taste
- ground black pepper to taste
- garlic powder to taste
- 6 slices white bread, cut into cubes
- 1/2 cup milk
- 1 egg
- 3 tablespoons yellow mustard, divided
- 1/2 cup ketchup, divided
- 3 tablespoons brown sugar

Direction

- Set oven to 350°F (175°C) to preheat.
- Mix well the ground beef, garlic powder, salt, pepper and onion in a large bowl. Fold in 1/4 cup of ketchup, 2 tablespoons of mustard, egg, milk and bread.
- Put the mixture in a 9x5-inch loaf pan and press. Stir together brown sugar, ketchup and the rest of mustard in a small bowl; pour over the meat loaf.
- Bake for about 2 hours in the prepared oven until an instant-read thermometer shows 165°F (74°C) when inserted into the center.

Nutrition Information

- Calories: 450 calories;
- Sodium: 582
- Total Carbohydrate: 28.3
- Cholesterol: 118
- Protein: 24.7
- Total Fat: 25.9

797. Massachusetts Straub Chili

Serving: 8 | Prep: 30mins | Cook: 2hours20mins | Ready in:

Ingredients

- 3 tablespoons vegetable oil
- 2 large onions, chopped
- 1 green bell pepper, chopped
- 4 cloves garlic, minced
- 1/2 pound lean ground beef
- 1/2 pound beef stew meat, diced into 1 inch pieces
- 1 (28 ounce) can crushed tomatoes
- 1 (14 ounce) can beef broth
- 1/2 pound dry kidney beans
- 2 1/2 tablespoons chili powder
- 1 teaspoon Italian seasoning
- 1 teaspoon salt
- 2 tablespoons brown sugar

Direction

- Warm the oil in a huge stockpot over medium heat. Cook bell pepper and onions until both are tender. Stir in ground beef, garlic, and stew meat. Let it cook for 10 minutes until the meat is no longer pink.
- Mix in beef broth, kidney beans, and tomatoes to the stockpot. Cover the stockpot and bring it to boil for 4-5 minutes. Season the mixture with Italian seasoning, brown sugar, salt, and chili powder. Bring it to simmer for 2 hours while uncovered, until the beans are tender and the chili already thickened.

Nutrition Information

- Calories: 311 calories;
- Total Fat: 12.8
- Sodium: 641
- Total Carbohydrate: 32.2
- Cholesterol: 32
- Protein: 19.7

798. Meal In One

Serving: 8 | Prep: 5mins | Cook: 1hours | Ready in:

Ingredients

- 1 1/2 pounds lean ground beef
- 2 cloves garlic, minced
- salt and pepper to taste
- 1 (10.5 ounce) can condensed French onion soup
- 1 tablespoon Worcestershire sauce
- 2 teaspoons prepared yellow mustard
- 2 tablespoons cold water
- 1 tablespoon all-purpose flour
- 3 cups peeled and thinly sliced potatoes
- 2 (10 ounce) packages frozen mixed vegetables, thawed
- 1 cup shredded Cheddar cheese

Direction

- Preheat an oven to 190 ° C or 375 ° F.
- In skillet on moderately-high heat, let ground beef cook till equally browned. Drain extra grease. Add pepper, salt and garlic to season. Mix in mustard, Worcestershire sauce and onion soup and boil. Combine flour and cold water together, and mix into sauce. Simmer for several minutes on low heat, then reserve.
- Meantime, in saucepan, put potatoes and pour in sufficient water to submerge. Boil, and cook not till soft for 3 minutes. Let drain.
- Scatter 1/2 mixture of beef in a baking dish base, 9x13-inch in size. Place 1/2 of potatoes on top of beef. Top with a layer of mixed vegetables to cover. Redo the layers.
- Put on dish cover, and bake in prepped oven for 50 minutes. Remove cover, and scatter shredded cheese on the surface. Bake till cheese melts for 10 minutes more.

Nutrition Information

- Calories: 349 calories;
- Sodium: 537
- Total Carbohydrate: 24.5
- Cholesterol: 75
- Protein: 25
- Total Fat: 17.1

799. Meat Filled Manicotti

Serving: 6 | Prep: 20mins | Cook: 50mins | Ready in:

Ingredients

- 1 (8 ounce) package manicotti pasta
- 1 pound lean ground beef
- 1 1/2 cups cottage cheese
- 2 cups shredded mozzarella cheese
- 1/2 cup grated Parmesan cheese
- 2 egg whites
- 1/2 teaspoon dried oregano
- 1 (32 ounce) jar spaghetti sauce

Direction

- In a large pot, boil lightly salted water. Put in pasta and cook for approximately 8 to 10 minutes till al dente. Drain and cool. Reserve.
- In the meantime, in a large skillet, brown beef over medium heat. Drain and cool.
- Preheat oven to 350 °F (175 °C).
- Combine cottage cheese, beef, Parmesan cheese, egg whites, oregano and 1 cup mozzarella cheese. Well mix. Stuff the mixture into shells.
- Grease a baking dish of 9x13 inches lightly. Cover the bottom of the prepared dish with enough spaghetti sauce. Place stuffed noodles into the dish. Cover with spaghetti sauce and add the rest 1 cup mozzarella cheese on top. In preheated oven, bake for nearly 50 minutes.

Nutrition Information

- Calories: 668 calories;
- Total Carbohydrate: 50.5

449

- Cholesterol: 104
- Protein: 40.1
- Total Fat: 33.3
- Sodium: 1249

---

800. Meat Lover's Burger

Serving: 2 | Prep: 30mins | Cook: 25mins | Ready in:

Ingredients

- 8 slices bacon
- 1/2 white onion, diced
- 1 clove garlic, minced
- 1 tablespoon balsamic vinegar, or to taste
- 5 fresh mushrooms, chopped
- 1/2 pound ground beef
- 1/2 cup dry bread crumbs
- 1 teaspoon Italian seasoning
- 1 1/2 tablespoons grated Parmesan cheese
- 1 egg
- salt and pepper to taste
- 1 malted wheat hamburger bun, split in half
- 2 slices tomato
- 2 slices Swiss cheese

Direction

- Preheat an oven to 190°C/375°F.
- Cook bacon till crisp and brown in a skillet on medium heat. Put bacon from skillet onto paper towels; drain.
- Put skillet back on the heat; put temperature on medium high. Add garlic and onion; stir-fry till garlic starts to brown and onion is soft. Add balsamic vinegar; cook for 1 minute while mixing. Add chopped mushrooms; cook for another 3 minutes. Take off the heat; put aside.
- Chop 4 bacon slices finely; put aside the leftover 4. Mix egg, mushroom mixture, Parmesan cheese, Italian seasoning, bread crumbs, ground beef and chopped bacon in a medium bowl, stir well using hands. Use pepper and salt to season; shape into 2 patties.

- Open 2 hamburger bun halves on an ungreased cookie sheet. On each half, put 1 beef patty; cover each with 1 Swiss cheese slice, 2 reserved bacon slices and 1 tomato slice.
- In preheated oven, bake till meat cooks through or for 25 minutes.

Nutrition Information

- Calories: 778 calories;
- Total Carbohydrate: 41.1
- Cholesterol: 232
- Protein: 53.7
- Total Fat: 43.5
- Sodium: 1386

---

801. Meatball Sub Casserole

Serving: 8 | Prep: 10mins | Cook: 50mins | Ready in:

Ingredients

- 1 (16 ounce) package frozen garlic bread
- 2 (24 ounce) jars spaghetti sauce
- 40 Italian-style frozen meatballs
- 2 cups shredded mozzarella cheese
- 1/4 cup grated Parmesan cheese

Direction

- Set the oven to 220°C or 425°F.
- In the preheated oven, heat garlic bread on a baking sheet, spread side up, for 10-12 minutes, until warm and turn golden brown. Set aside to let it cool.
- Lower the heat of the oven to 175°C or 350°F.
- In a big pot, bring spaghetti sauce to a boil, put into sauce frozen meatballs. Lower heat to low and simmer for 20 minutes, until meatballs are heated through.
- Separate garlic bread into bite-size pieces and scatter into the bottom of a 9"x13" baking dish. Pour over garlic bread with meatballs and

spaghetti sauce, distributing meatballs evenly and coating bread well with sauce. Spread over top with mozzarella cheese, in one layer, followed by a layer of Parmesan cheese.

- Bake casserole for 20-25 minutes, until cheese is melted.

Nutrition Information

- Calories: 733 calories;
- Protein: 39.1
- Total Fat: 37.2
- Sodium: 1386
- Total Carbohydrate: 58
- Cholesterol: 140

802.   Meatball Sub Sandwich

Serving: 4 | Prep: 30mins | Cook: 30mins | Ready in:

Ingredients

- 5 Ball Park® Tailgaters Brat Buns
- 1 pound lean ground beef
- 1/4 cup milk
- 1 egg
- 2 tablespoons grated Parmesan cheese
- 1 teaspoon Italian seasoning
- 1/2 teaspoon onion powder
- 1/2 teaspoon garlic powder
- salt and pepper to taste
- 1 (24 ounce) jar marinara sauce
- 1 cup arugula
- 4 tablespoons shredded mozzarella cheese
- Chopped fresh basil or crushed red pepper for garnish

Direction

- Set oven to 425°F to preheat.
- Toast 1 bun until it turns golden brown; put into a blender and chop until finely crumbly.
- Transfer bread crumbs to a large bowl and pour in milk. Allow to soak for 5 minutes.

- Mix pepper, salt, garlic powder, onion powder, Italian seasoning, Parmesan, eggs and ground beef into the bread crumb mixture until thoroughly incorporated.
- Distribute mixture into 16 golf ball-sized meatballs, and arrange on a greased baking pan.
- Bake meatballs in the preheated oven for 10 minutes.
- While baking meatballs, heat marinara sauce over medium-high heat in a large pot. Put in cooked meatballs and simmer for 15 minutes.
- In the meantime, toast the rest of buns; divide over the top of each bun with spinach or arugula, meatballs and mozzarella.
- Garnish on top with crushed red pepper (optional) and chopped basil. Enjoy!

Nutrition Information

- Calories: 768 calories;
- Protein: 35.7
- Total Fat: 34
- Sodium: 1363
- Total Carbohydrate: 75.2
- Cholesterol: 143

803.   Meatloaf Cordon Bleu

Serving: 8 | Prep: 15mins | Cook: 1hours15mins | Ready in:

Ingredients

- 2 pounds extra-lean ground beef
- 1 cup Italian seasoned bread crumbs
- 1 small onion, chopped
- 2 eggs, beaten
- 1/8 teaspoon garlic powder
- 1 teaspoon salt
- 1 teaspoon pepper
- 4 ounces thinly sliced cooked ham
- 4 ounces provolone cheese, sliced

Direction

- Turn the oven to 350°F (175°C) to preheat.
- Combine onion, eggs, bread crumbs, and ground beef in a medium-sized bowl. Use pepper, salt, and garlic powder to season. On a waxed paper piece, pat the meat mixture out, and flatten until the thickness is 1/2-inch. On the flattened meat, place ham slices, and put cheese slices on top. Lift the edge of the waxed paper and roll the flattened meat up to form a log. Discard the waxed paper, seal the seam and ends, and put the loaf into a 9x5-in. loaf pan.
- Bake in the preheated oven for 75 minutes until the inside of the loaf is not pink anymore.

Nutrition Information

- Calories: 376 calories;
- Total Fat: 20.9
- Sodium: 878
- Total Carbohydrate: 11.4
- Cholesterol: 148
- Protein: 33.6

804.   Meatloaf That Doesn't Crumble

Serving: 10 | Prep: 30mins | Cook: 2hours | Ready in:

Ingredients

- 1 green bell pepper, seeded and cubed
- 1 medium onion, roughly chopped
- 3 small stalks celery
- 1 1/4 pounds ground beef
- 1 pound mild pork sausage
- 1 1/2 cups cracker crumbs
- 1 (1 ounce) envelope dry onion soup mix
- 1/4 teaspoon salt
- 1/4 teaspoon ground black pepper
- 1/2 teaspoon dried sage
- 1 1/2 cups milk

- 1/2 cup ketchup

Direction

- Preheat an oven to 175°C/350°F.
- Process celery, onion and bell pepper till finely chopped yet not liquid in a food processor/blender; put into big bowl. Add milk, sage, pepper, salt, onion soup mix, cracker crumbs, ground pork and ground beef; use your hands to mix well or mix using a paddle attachment of a stand mixer. Put into 9x5-in. loaf pan; shape to a loaf, mounding in middle. Use a generous ketchup layer to cover.
- In preheated oven, bake for 1 1/2 hours; serve hot. Refrigerate the leftovers. Slice; serve cold in sandwiches.

Nutrition Information

- Calories: 413 calories;
- Total Fat: 27.6
- Sodium: 790
- Total Carbohydrate: 22.7
- Cholesterol: 68
- Protein: 17.8

805.   Meatloaf With Fried Onions And Ranch Seasoning

Serving: 6 | Prep: 10mins | Cook: 1hours | Ready in:

Ingredients

- 1 1/2 pounds ground beef
- 2 eggs, beaten
- 1/4 cup ketchup
- 3/4 cup herb-seasoned dry bread stuffing mix
- 1/2 (1 ounce) package dry Ranch-style dressing mix
- 1 (6 ounce) can French-fried onions

Direction

- Preheat the oven to 350°F (175°C).

- Mix fried onions, ketchup, eggs, meat, ranch dressing mix and stuffing mix together in a big bowl and form it into loaf shape. Place it into a 9-inch by 5-inch loaf pan and cover it up loosely with foil. Bake until meat is cooked all the way through for 50 to 60 minutes.

Nutrition Information

- Calories: 668 calories;
- Total Fat: 46.7
- Sodium: 1013
- Total Carbohydrate: 34.9
- Cholesterol: 159
- Protein: 23.9

---
806.   Meaty Stuffed Pepper Casserole

Serving: 8 | Prep: 25mins | Cook: 50mins | Ready in:

Ingredients

- 2 tablespoons butter
- 6 small green bell peppers, chopped
- 1 large onion, chopped
- 2 cloves garlic, chopped
- 1 pound ground Italian sausage
- 1 pound ground beef
- salt and ground black pepper to taste
- 1 pinch dried oregano, or to taste
- 1 pinch garlic powder, or to taste
- 2 (14.5 ounce) cans diced tomatoes
- 1 cup cooked white rice
- 1 (6 ounce) can tomato paste
- 2 teaspoons Worcestershire sauce
- 2 (10.75 ounce) cans condensed tomato soup
- 1/4 (10.75 ounce) can water
- 2 cups shredded Cheddar cheese

Direction

- Set oven to 175°C (or 350°F) and start preheating.

- In a large pot, melt butter on medium heat; cook and stir garlic, onion and green bell peppers in hot butter for 2 minutes until vegetables start to soften slightly. Stir in ground beef and sausage; cook and stir frequently for 10-12 minutes until meat is browned and crumbly. Drain off grease. Add garlic powder, oregano, black pepper and salt into the mixture to season.
- Combine Worcestershire sauce, tomato paste, rice and diced tomatoes into the meat mixture and simmer; cook and stir from time to time in about 5 minutes until heated through. Transfer mixture into a big baking dish.
- In a bowl, stir water and tomato soup together until smooth; add soup onto meat mixture. Spread over the casserole with Cheddar cheese.
- Bake for approximately half an hour in prepared oven until Cheddar cheese is bubbly and browned and casserole is thoroughly heated.

Nutrition Information

- Calories: 512 calories;
- Total Fat: 31
- Sodium: 1467
- Total Carbohydrate: 30.1
- Cholesterol: 94
- Protein: 28.3

---
807.   Melanie's Chili

Serving: 6 | Prep: 10mins | Cook: 20mins | Ready in:

Ingredients

- 1 pound ground beef
- 1 onion, chopped
- 1 (14.5 ounce) can diced tomatoes
- 1 (15 ounce) can tomato sauce
- 1 (16 ounce) can pinto beans
- 1 teaspoon chili powder

- 1 teaspoon ground cumin
- 1/2 teaspoon ground cayenne pepper
- 1 teaspoon minced garlic

Direction

- Cook onion and beef in a big saucepan over medium -high heat till meat is not pink anymore. Mix in garlic, cayenne, cumin, chili powder, beans, tomato sauce and tomatoes. Put cover, lower the heat and allow to simmer for 20 minutes.

Nutrition Information

- Calories: 452 calories;
- Total Fat: 13.3
- Sodium: 524
- Total Carbohydrate: 54.2
- Cholesterol: 46
- Protein: 30.1

---

808.   Melt In Your Mouth Meat Loaf

Serving: 6 | Prep: 15mins | Cook: 5hours15mins | Ready in:

Ingredients

- 2 eggs
- 3/4 cup milk
- 2/3 cup seasoned bread crumbs
- 2 teaspoons dried minced onion
- 1 teaspoon salt
- 1/2 teaspoon rubbed sage
- 1/2 cup sliced fresh mushrooms
- 1 1/2 pounds ground beef
- 1/4 cup ketchup
- 2 tablespoons brown sugar
- 1 teaspoon ground mustard
- 1/2 teaspoon Worcestershire sauce

Direction

- In a big bowl, mix mushrooms, sage, salt, onion, breadcrumbs, milk and eggs then crush ground beef on the mixture and stir it well until combined. Use the mixture to form a round loaf and put it on a 5-quart slow cooker. Cover it then adjust the setting to low and cook for 5-6 hours. It is ready when a meat thermometer registers at 71°F or 160°F.
- In a small bowl, whisk Worcestershire sauce, mustard, brown sugar and ketchup together. Ladle this on the meat loaf and place it back in the slow cooker. Adjust the setting to low and cook until thoroughly heated, around 15 minutes. Leave it rest for 10 minutes before slicing.

Nutrition Information

- Calories: 328 calories;
- Sodium: 841
- Total Carbohydrate: 18.4
- Cholesterol: 136
- Protein: 24.7
- Total Fat: 16.9

---

809.   Mexican Egg Rolls

Serving: 14 | Prep: 15mins | Cook: 15mins | Ready in:

Ingredients

- 1 (14 ounce) package egg roll wrappers
- 1 pound lean ground beef
- 1 (1.25 ounce) package taco seasoning mix
- 1 (4 ounce) can diced green chilies, drained
- 2 cups shredded pepperjack cheese
- 4 cups oil for frying, or as needed

Direction

- Into a big skillet, break ground beef up over medium-high heat. Let cook till equally browned, and drain off oil. Put the taco seasoning, and allow to cook following packaging instructions. Reserve.

- In a big skillet, heat an-inch of oil, or preheat the deep-fryer to 190 °C or 375 °F.
- Spread out an egg roll wrapper at a time, and in the middle, put a bit more than 1 tablespoon ground beef. Place a small spoonful of green chilies on top, and a small amount of shredded cheese. Roll up following packaging directions, and enclose edges, moistening with water if needed. Redo with the rest of filling and wrappers.
- In hot oil, fry rolls for 5 minutes till golden brown on every side. Take off from oil to drain on paper towels. Serve while hot and fresh.

Nutrition Information

- Calories: 286 calories;
- Total Fat: 17.2
- Sodium: 571
- Total Carbohydrate: 19
- Cholesterol: 42
- Protein: 12.5

810.   Mexican Lasagna I

Serving: 6 | Prep: 10mins | Cook: 1hours40mins | Ready in:

Ingredients

- 1 pound lean ground beef
- 1 (16 ounce) can refried beans
- 2 teaspoons dried oregano
- 1 teaspoon ground cumin
- 1 teaspoon garlic powder
- 12 uncooked lasagna noodles
- 2 cups water
- 2 1/2 cups picante sauce
- 2 cups sour cream
- 2 (2 ounce) cans sliced black olives
- 1 1/2 cups shredded Monterey Jack cheese
- 1/2 cup shredded Cheddar cheese

Direction

- Preheat oven to 350 degrees F (175 degrees C).
- In a large bowl, combine beef, beans, oregano, cumin and garlic powder.
- Place 4 uncooked noodles in bottom of a 9x13 inch pan. Spread half of beef mixure over noodles. Top with 4 noodles. Spread with remaining mixure, and top with remaining noodles.
- In a medium bowl, mix water and picante sauce. Pour evenly over layers. Cover tightly with foil.
- Bake 1 1/2 hours in the preheated oven, or until noodles are tender.
- Blend sour cream and olives in a medium bowl. Spoon over lasagna, and top with Jack and Cheddar cheese. Bake uncovered until cheese melts, about 5 to 10 minutes.

Nutrition Information

- Calories: 804 calories;
- Total Fat: 47.7
- Sodium: 1340
- Total Carbohydrate: 58.9
- Cholesterol: 131
- Protein: 37.6

811.   Mexican Meatloaf

Serving: 8 | Prep: 25mins | Cook: 45mins | Ready in:

Ingredients

- 2 pounds lean ground beef
- 1 (1.25 ounce) package taco seasoning mix
- 1 (16 ounce) can refried beans
- 4 (8 inch) flour tortillas
- 3/4 cup fresh salsa
- 1/2 cup shredded Cheddar cheese

Direction

- Set oven to 350°F (175°C) to preheat.

- Thoroughly mix together the taco seasoning and ground beef in a medium bowl; put aside. Cook the refried beans in a medium saucepan on medium-low heat until they are heated through completely.
- Put the ground beef mixture on a large sheet of foil. Pat the mixture into a closely 1-inch thick square shape. Top the flattened beef with the refried beans by spreading evenly. Put a layer of the flour tortillas over the top of the refried beans, cutting the excess to fit the square. Layer salsa and Cheddar cheese over tortillas, leaving 1/2 to 1 inch away from edges.
- Roll gently the layered beef to form a Swiss roll shape, patting while compacting the loaf as you roll. Pinch then seal the edges. Use the foil to wrap and seal.
- Bake for 40 to 45 minutes in prepared oven, until no pink remains in the center. If necessary, slice loaf in half to check for doneness.

Nutrition Information

- Calories: 488 calories;
- Cholesterol: 99
- Protein: 27.8
- Total Fat: 28.8
- Sodium: 886
- Total Carbohydrate: 27

812.   Mexican Mostaccioli

Serving: 8 | Prep: 5mins | Cook: 20mins | Ready in:

Ingredients

- 1 (16 ounce) package mostaccioli pasta
- 1 pound ground beef
- 1 (24 ounce) jar picante sauce
- 1 (15 ounce) can stewed tomatoes with juice
- 1 1/2 cups shredded Mexican-style cheese

Direction

- Bring lightly salted water in a big pot to a boil. Cook mostaccioli at a boil for 11 minutes, until cooked through but still firm to the bite, then drain mostaccioli.
- In a big pot, cook and stir ground beef for 5-7 minutes over medium-high heat until beef is not pink anymore, browned evenly and crumbly. Drain and get rid of any excess grease.
- Add into the ground beef the stewed tomatoes and picante sauce. Cook the mixture for 10 minutes while stirring sometimes, until tomatoes are totally soft. Stir ground beef mixture gently with cooked mostaccioli. Add in Mexican-style cheese, then cook and stir for 5 minutes, until cheese has melted.

Nutrition Information

- Calories: 439 calories;
- Total Fat: 16.6
- Sodium: 890
- Total Carbohydrate: 49.2
- Cholesterol: 60
- Protein: 24.2

813.   Mexican Pizza I

Serving: 4 | Prep: 17mins | Cook: 30mins | Ready in:

Ingredients

- 1 (16 ounce) can refried beans
- 1 pound ground beef
- 1 (1.25 ounce) package taco seasoning mix
- 1 tablespoon vegetable oil
- 4 (6 inch) corn tortillas
- 8 ounces shredded Cheddar cheese
- 8 tablespoons sour cream
- 2 roma (plum) tomatoes, chopped
- 2 green onion, chopped
- 1 (4 ounce) can diced green chiles, drained

- 1/2 avocado, diced
- 1 tablespoon black olives, sliced

Direction

- Warm the refried beans.
- Place the ground beef into a large skillet and brown. Mix in the seasoning packet.
- Prepare the oven by preheating to 350°F (175°C).
- In large skillet, put a small amount of vegetable oil. Allow the oil to heat, then put one corn tortilla in the skillet. Then turn the tortilla over after 15 seconds and allow to fry for another 15 seconds. Continue this process with the remaining tortillas, allowing them to drain on paper towels when they have been warmed. Once the tortillas have drained, lay them on a cookie sheet.
- On the tortillas, spread a thin layer of beans, next layer the beef and cheese.
- Place the tortillas in the preheated oven and bake for 20 to 30 minutes. Cut the tortillas into wedges and lay them on plates or a serving platter and decorate them with olives, avocado, chiles, green onions, tomatoes and sour cream.

Nutrition Information

- Calories: 770 calories;
- Total Fat: 48.1
- Sodium: 1542
- Total Carbohydrate: 42.3
- Cholesterol: 150
- Protein: 42.1

---

814.   Mexican Rice & Beef Tacos

Serving: 4 | Prep: 19mins | Cook: 20mins | Ready in:

Ingredients

- 2 tablespoons I Can't Believe It's Not Butter!® Spread, divided
- 1 pound lean ground beef
- 1 green or red bell pepper, chopped
- 1 medium red onion, chopped
- 2 cups water
- 1 (5.4 ounce) package Knorr® Fiesta Sides™ - Mexican Rice
- 1 medium tomato, chopped
- 8 taco shells

Direction

- In a big non-stick skillet on moderately-high heat, liquify a tablespoon of Spread and browned ground beef, add pepper and salt to season, if wished; take off and reserve.
- In the same skillet, on moderately-high heat, liquify leftover 1 tablespoon of Spread and cook onions and peppers for 5 minutes, mixing from time to time, till crisp-tender. Mix in tomato, Knorr(R) Fiesta Sides (TM) - Mexican Rice and water and boil on high heat. Lower the heat and let simmer with cover for 7 minutes or till rice is soft.
- Mix in the beef; heat completely. Scoop into the taco shells and serve along with wedges of lime, if wished. Put your favorite taco toppings over like shredded lettuce, chopped red onion and sour cream, if wished.

Nutrition Information

- Calories: 613 calories;
- Total Fat: 27.8
- Sodium: 307
- Total Carbohydrate: 41.1
- Cholesterol: 79
- Protein: 29.8

---

815.   Mexican Stuffed Peppers

Serving: 4 | Prep: 30mins | Cook: 1hours | Ready in:

Ingredients

- 2 cups water
- 1 (8 ounce) package yellow rice mix
- 2 tablespoons olive oil
- 4 large green bell peppers, tops and seeds removed
- 1 (16 ounce) can refried beans, or as needed
- 1 (11 ounce) can whole kernel corn, drained
- 1 (4 ounce) can sliced black olives, drained
- 1/4 (8 ounce) jar salsa
- 1 (8 ounce) package shredded Mexican blend cheese, divided

Direction

- Preheat oven to 165 degrees Celsius or 325 degrees Fahrenheit.
- Boil water in a saucepan and mix in olive oil and yellow rice mix. Boil for a minute.
- Cover it and bring the heat down to low and simmer it until the rice gets tender and the water gets absorbed, around 25 minutes.
- Scoop 3 tablespoons of yellow rice onto the bottom of every pepper. Cover the rice in layers of corn, black olives, and refried beans, filling the peppers nearly to the top. Put salsa on the peppers. Place the stuffed peppers upright on a baking dish.
- Bake it in the heated oven until the filling is hot and the peppers are tender for around 30 minutes. Split the Mexican cheese blend on the peppers, put them back in the oven, and bake until the cheese melts for about 5 minutes more.

Nutrition Information

- Calories: 703 calories;
- Cholesterol: 64
- Protein: 26.7
- Total Fat: 30.7
- Sodium: 2230
- Total Carbohydrate: 87.1

---

816.   Mexican Taco Ring

Serving: 8 | Prep: 10mins | Cook: 30mins | Ready in:

Ingredients

- 1 pound ground beef
- 1 small onion, chopped
- 3/4 cup water
- 1 (1.25 ounce) package taco seasoning
- 2 (8 ounce) cans refrigerated crescent rolls
- 1 (8 ounce) package shredded Mexican cheese blend

Direction

- On moderately high heat, heat a big skillet, then cook and stir in the hot skillet with onion and beef for 5-7 minutes, until crumbly and browned. Drain and get rid of grease, then put into beef mixture with taco seasoning and water. Bring mixture to a boil, then lower heat to on moderately low and simmer while stirring sometimes for 10-15 minutes, until water has evaporated.
- Set the oven to 190°C or 375°F to preheat. Remove crescent roll dough from packaging and split into individual pieces.
- Place on a pizza stone or pan with crescent roll triangles, points facing outward. Scoop into the center of each dough piece with ground beef mixture, making a ring shape. Sprinkle over ground beef mixture with Mexican cheese blend, then fold crescent roll points toward the middle and seal dough together.
- In the preheated oven, bake for 11-13 minutes, until dough is browned slightly.

Nutrition Information

- Calories: 468 calories;
- Total Fat: 30
- Sodium: 1017
- Total Carbohydrate: 26.7
- Cholesterol: 62
- Protein: 19.9

817. Michelle's Marvelous Mini Meat Loaves

Serving: 8 | Prep: 15mins | Cook: 40mins | Ready in:

Ingredients

- cooking spray
- 1 pound ground beef
- 1/2 cup chopped onion
- 1/2 cup rolled oats
- 1 cup shredded Cheddar cheese
- 3/4 cup milk
- 1 egg
- 1 teaspoon salt
- 2/3 cup ketchup
- 1/2 cup brown sugar
- 1 1/2 teaspoons dry mustard

Direction

- Preheat the oven to 350°F (175°C). Use cooking spray to grease a 9x13-inch baking dish lightly.
- In a bowl, mix salt, egg, milk, Cheddar cheese, oats, onion and ground beef together; stir well. Split the meat mixture equally into 8 portions and shape each into a loaf. Set the loaves in the prepped baking dish.
- In a bowl, stir mustard, brown sugar and ketchup together until smooth, then spread this mixture over the meat loaves.
- Place the baking dish into the preheated oven. Bake for around 40 minutes until the center is not pink anymore. When an instant-read thermometer is inserted into the center, it should register at a minimum of 160°F (70°C).

Nutrition Information

- Calories: 278 calories;
- Protein: 15.9
- Total Fat: 13.2
- Sodium: 657
- Total Carbohydrate: 24.3
- Cholesterol: 75

818. Middle Eastern Cumin Meatballs

Serving: 4 | Prep: 15mins | Cook: 20mins | Ready in:

Ingredients

- Meatballs:
- 1 1/2 pounds lean ground beef
- 1 egg
- 2 tablespoons minced garlic
- 1/4 cup bread crumbs
- 1/2 teaspoon cumin
- salt and pepper to taste
- 3 tablespoons vegetable oil
- Tomato Sauce:
- 1 1/2 cups water
- 3 tablespoons tomato paste
- 2 tablespoons lemon juice
- 1/4 teaspoon garlic powder
- salt and pepper to taste

Direction

- In a large bowl, mix together pepper, salt, cumin, bread crumbs, garlic, egg and ground beef till well combined. Form into egg-sized balls; set aside.
- Place a large skillet on medium-high heat; heat vegetable oil. Include in the meatballs; cook on all sides for around 10 minutes, till firm and well browned. Take the meatballs away from the skillet; skim fat.
- Pour water into the same skillet; allow to boil over medium-high heat. Mix in pepper, salt, garlic powder, lemon juice and tomato paste. Allow to boil; then turn the heat down to medium. Include in the cooked meatballs; simmer in the tomato sauce till completely cooked, 5-10 minutes.

Nutrition Information

- Calories: 483 calories;
- Cholesterol: 165
- Protein: 36.5
- Total Fat: 32.7
- Sodium: 632
- Total Carbohydrate: 9.5

819. Military S.O.S. Feasty Style

Serving: 6 | Prep: 10mins | Cook: 20mins | Ready in:

Ingredients

- 2 teaspoons butter
- 1 (12 ounce) package maple flavored sausage
- 1 pound extra-lean ground beef
- 1 cup sifted all-purpose flour
- 4 cups milk
- 2 teaspoons beef bouillon
- 6 slices white bread
- 3 sprigs fresh parsley (optional)

Direction

- In a large skillet, melt butter over medium-high heat. Add maple sausage and ground beef, and cook until no pink remains. Slowly stir in flour, while whisking continually, until the mixture is pasty and thick. You may have some flour left. With a fork, gradually stir in milk to prevent forming lumps. Mix in bouillon. Keep stirring and cooking until the mixture has the consistency you want. The longer you cook the mixture, the thicker it will get.
- Toast white bread slices, and put the meat gravy on top. Use a small amount of fresh parsley to garnish, and enjoy.

Nutrition Information

- Calories: 582 calories;
- Total Fat: 34.6

- Sodium: 912
- Total Carbohydrate: 39.3
- Cholesterol: 97
- Protein: 32.8

820. Minced Collops

Serving: 5 | Prep: 5mins | Cook: 40mins | Ready in:

Ingredients

- 1 pound lean ground beef
- 1/2 onion, minced
- 1 teaspoon salt, to taste
- 1/2 teaspoon ground black pepper
- 2/3 cup steel-cut oats
- 1 1/2 cups beef stock
- 2 tablespoons Worcestershire sauce

Direction

- In a skillet, crumble ground beef over medium heat, add pepper, salt and onion. Cook while stirring for 7-10 minutes, until the beef is no longer pink.
- Blend in oats until coated. Put the beef stock in the beef mixture, boil, put the cover on skillet, lower the heat to low. Cook at a simmer for 30 mins, until oats are totally cooked.
- Stir in the Worcestershire sauce and serve.

Nutrition Information

- Calories: 281 calories;
- Sodium: 613
- Total Carbohydrate: 19
- Cholesterol: 59
- Protein: 21.4
- Total Fat: 12.7

821.　Mini Cheeseburgers

Serving: 4 | Prep: 10mins | Cook: 25mins | Ready in:

Ingredients

- 1 pound lean ground beef
- 1/2 cup ketchup
- 1/2 cup shredded Cheddar cheese
- 1 egg
- 1 pinch garlic powder
- 1/4 cup shredded Cheddar cheese
- 1/4 cup ketchup

Direction

- Preheat an oven to 350°F (175°C). Line aluminum foil on a baking sheet.
- In a large bowl, combine together garlic powder, egg, 1/2 cup shredded cheese, 1/2 cup ketchup and ground beef. Shape the mixture into balls of 1 inch, and slightly press onto the prepped baking sheet to create the mini-burgers.
- Bake in prepped oven for 20 minutes. Spread remaining ketchup onto burgers, and sprinkle the rest of cheese on top. Put burgers back to the oven, and bake for about 5 minutes, till cheese is melted and bubbling.

Nutrition Information

- Calories: 389 calories;
- Total Carbohydrate: 11.9
- Cholesterol: 149
- Protein: 31.6
- Total Fat: 23.8
- Sodium: 725

822.　Mini Meatball Subs

Serving: 8 | Prep: 20mins | Cook: 50mins | Ready in:

Ingredients

- 1 pound ground beef
- 1/2 cup chopped onion
- 1/2 cup chopped green pepper
- 1/2 cup crushed butter-flavored crackers
- 1 egg
- 1 teaspoon Worcestershire sauce
- 1 teaspoon chopped garlic
- 1 teaspoon seasoned salt
- 1 teaspoon ground black pepper
- 1 (26.5 ounce) can spaghetti sauce
- 1/2 cup shredded mozzarella cheese
- 1/3 cup grated Parmesan cheese
- 8 dinner rolls, split

Direction

- Preheat the oven to 175 degrees C/350 degrees F.
- In a big bowl, mix egg, crackers, green pepper, onion and ground beef. Season with pepper, seasoned salt, garlic and Worcestershire sauce. Mix well. Form mixture to 8 meatballs. Put meatballs in a 9x13-in. baking dish.
- Bake meatballs for 20 minutes in preheated oven. Put spaghetti sauce into a big saucepan. Simmer on low heat. Mix baked meatballs into simmering sauce. Don't turn off the oven. Simmer sauce for about 20 minutes until meatballs cook fully.
- Between each roll, put 1 meatball, a bit of sauce, and a sprinkle of parmesan and mozzarella. Put sandwiches in the hot oven. Bake for about 7 minutes until cheeses melt.

Nutrition Information

- Calories: 351 calories;
- Protein: 18
- Total Fat: 16.4
- Sodium: 821
- Total Carbohydrate: 32.2
- Cholesterol: 68

823.   Mini Meatloaves

Serving: 8 | Prep: 15mins | Cook: 45mins | Ready in:

Ingredients

- 1 egg
- 3/4 cup milk
- 1 cup shredded Cheddar cheese
- 1/2 cup quick cooking oats
- 1 teaspoon salt
- 1 pound ground beef
- 2/3 cup ketchup
- 1/4 cup packed brown sugar
- 1 1/2 teaspoons prepared mustard

Direction

- Set oven to 350°F (175°C) and start preheating.
- Mix salt, oats, cheese, milk, and egg in a big bowl. Put in ground beef, combine well, then shape the mixture into 8 small meatloaves. Put them in a 9x13-inch baking dish coated lightly with oil.
- Mix mustard, brown sugar, and ketchup in another small bowl. Stir thoroughly and drizzle over each meat loaf.
- Bake without a cover for 45 minutes at 350°F (175°C).

Nutrition Information

- Calories: 255 calories;
- Cholesterol: 74
- Protein: 15.1
- Total Fat: 14.4
- Sodium: 656
- Total Carbohydrate: 16.6

824.   Mini Shepherd's Pies

Serving: 6 | Prep: 15mins | Cook: 35mins | Ready in:

Ingredients

- 12 jumbo-size (3 1/2-inch) foil baking cups
- 1 pound ground beef
- 2 cloves garlic, minced
- 1 (10.75 ounce) can Campbell's® Condensed Cream of Mushroom Soup (Regular or 98% Fat Free)
- 1 cup frozen mixed vegetables
- 1 tablespoon Worcestershire sauce
- 3 cups hot prepared mashed potatoes
- 3/4 cup shredded Cheddar cheese

Direction

- Set the oven at 350°F to preheat. Use baking cups to line 12 muffin-pan cups (2 1/2 -inch each).
- In a 10-inch skillet, cook the beef over medium-high heat until entirely brown, stirring frequently to prevent the meat from sticking together. Discard the fat.
- Put garlic into the skillet and cook while stirring for 1 minute. Take the skillet away from the heat. Stir in Worcestershire sauce, veggies and soup. Fill each baking cup with 1/4 cup of beef mixture. Top each by piping or spreading 1/4 cup of potatoes.
- Bake them for 20 minutes or until the minis become hot. Put 1 tablespoon of cheese on top of each.
- Bake for 5 more minutes or until the cheese melts.

Nutrition Information

- Calories: 340 calories;
- Total Fat: 16.7
- Sodium: 845
- Total Carbohydrate: 26.8
- Cholesterol: 65
- Protein: 19.6

825. Mock Chicken Fried Steak

Serving: 6 | Prep: 45mins | Cook: 15mins | Ready in:

Ingredients

- 1 pound ground beef
- 2 teaspoons chopped fresh parsley
- 1 tablespoon chili powder
- 1 teaspoon salt
- 1 egg
- 2 cups crushed saltine crackers, divided
- 1/2 cup oil for frying

Direction

- Combine a cup of crushed saltine crackers, egg, salt, chili powder, parsley, and ground beef together in a medium bowl. Shape into 6 balls and flatten them into patties. Coat the patties in the rest of cracker crumbs, then arrange onto a plate. Put into the refrigerator for half an hour or more.
- In a large skillet, heat the oil over medium heat. Fry the patties until the outside turns golden brown and the centers are well done, 7 minutes on each side.

Nutrition Information

- Calories: 412 calories;
- Total Fat: 30.9
- Sodium: 707
- Total Carbohydrate: 17.4
- Cholesterol: 77
- Protein: 16

826. Mom's 'Best Ever' Meatloaf

Serving: 6 | Prep: 10mins | Cook: 1hours15mins | Ready in:

Ingredients

- 2 pounds ground beef
- 3/4 cup bread crumbs
- 2 (10.75 ounce) cans golden mushroom soup, divided
- 1 egg, beaten
- 1 tablespoon dried minced onion
- 1 teaspoon salt
- 1/3 cup water

Direction

- Set oven to 190°C (or 375°F) and start preheating.
- In a bowl, combine salt, dried minced onion, egg, half a can of golden mushroom soup, bread crumbs and ground beef and blend until smooth. Pat the mixture into an 8x4" loaf and transfer to a baking dish.
- Bake for about 75 minutes in the prepared oven until no remaining pink meat left in the middle of the loaf. The temperature should reach at least 70°C (or 160°F) when putting an instant-read thermometer into the center of the loaf.
- In a saucepan, whisk together the leftover soup and hot water, then let it simmer. Pour the soup mixture onto the meatloaf.

Nutrition Information

- Calories: 406 calories;
- Sodium: 1306
- Total Carbohydrate: 18.4
- Cholesterol: 130
- Protein: 30
- Total Fat: 22.6

827. Mom's Basic Vegetable Beef Stew

Serving: 8 | Prep: 15mins | Cook: 40mins | Ready in:

Ingredients

- 1 tablespoon olive oil, or as needed
- 2 onions, roughly chopped, divided
- 4 carrots, cut into 1/2-inch rounds
- 1 clove garlic, minced
- 1/4 teaspoon red pepper flakes
- 1/4 teaspoon Greek seasoning (such as Cavender's®) (optional)
- 1 pinch dried rosemary
- 1 pinch ground thyme
- 1 pinch dried basil
- 1 pinch Italian seasoning
- 1 bay leaf
- salt and ground black pepper to taste
- 1 (32 ounce) can diced tomatoes with juice
- 1 pound ground beef
- 4 potatoes, peeled and cut into chunks
- 1 stalk celery, chopped

Direction

- Add enough of the olive oil to a big stock pot to coat bottom; put in pepper, salt, bay leaf, Italian seasoning, basil, thyme, rosemary, Greek seasoning, red pepper flakes, garlic, carrots and 1 onion. Cook and whisk the onion mixture on medium heat for roughly 15 minutes till the onion softens and turns brown slightly.
- Add the diced tomatoes on top of the onion mixture; put in the ground beef, crumble using a wooden spoon and whisk. Boil the liquid and cook for roughly 10 minutes till the carrots soften and the ground beef becomes thoroughly cooked.
- Whisk the celery, the rest of the onion and potatoes to the tomato mixture and cook for 15-20 minutes till the potatoes soften. Take the stockpot out of the heat and allow it to sit for 20-30 minutes.

Nutrition Information

- Calories: 279 calories;
- Total Fat: 10.8
- Sodium: 279

- Total Carbohydrate: 31.3
- Cholesterol: 35
- Protein: 13.5

828.   Mom's Best Meatloaf

Serving: 7 | Prep: 15mins | Cook: 1hours | Ready in:

Ingredients

- 1 1/2 pounds ground beef
- 1/4 cup chopped onion
- 1/4 cup quick-cooking oats
- 1/8 cup cornmeal
- 1 cup dried bread crumbs
- 1 1/2 teaspoons salt
- 1 tablespoon white sugar
- 1 egg, beaten
- 1/2 cup tomato juice
- 1/2 cup water
- 1 tablespoon barbecue sauce
- 1 dash liquid smoke flavoring
- 1 tablespoon distilled white vinegar
- 1/4 cup ketchup
- 1 tablespoon brown sugar
- 2 teaspoons prepared mustard
- 2 dashes liquid smoke flavoring

Direction

- Set the oven to 175 degrees C or 350 degrees F.
- In a big bowl, combine vinegar, 1/8 teaspoon of liquid smoke, barbecue sauce, water, tomato juice, egg, sugar, salt, breadcrumbs, cornmeal, oatmeal, onion, and beef. Mix thoroughly and place onto a 9x5-inch loaf pan that has been greased lightly.
- In another bowl, combine 2 drops liquid smoke, mustard, brown sugar, and ketchup and mix well, then pour over the meatloaf top.
- Bake at 350 degrees F (175 degrees C) for around 1 hour.

Nutrition Information

- Calories: 428 calories;
- Total Fat: 28.1
- Sodium: 856
- Total Carbohydrate: 23
- Cholesterol: 109
- Protein: 20

- Calories: 617 calories;
- Sodium: 1630
- Total Carbohydrate: 50.4
- Cholesterol: 80
- Protein: 32.6
- Total Fat: 32.7

829. Mom's Hot Mexican Salad

Serving: 8 | Prep: 10mins | Cook: 20mins | Ready in:

Ingredients

- 1 1/2 pounds lean ground beef
- 1 onion, diced
- 1 green bell pepper, diced
- 1 tablespoon garlic powder
- 1 tablespoon ground cumin
- 1 pound processed cheese food (e.g. Velveeta), cubed
- 1 (4 ounce) can diced green chiles
- 1 cup tomato sauce
- 3/4 head iceberg lettuce - rinsed, dried, and shredded
- 2 tomatoes, chopped
- 1 (16 ounce) package corn chips

Direction

- In a large and deep skillet, combine the bell pepper, cumin, garlic, onion, and beef. Cook it over medium-high heat until the hamburger is browned all over. Let it drain, discarding any excess fat.
- Mix tomato sauce, cheese, and green chilies into the beef mixture. Allow it to cook for 5 minutes or until the cheese melted.
- Distribute the lettuce among salad plates evenly. Top each lettuce with the meat and cheese mixture. Garnish each with corn chips and chopped tomato.

Nutrition Information

830. Mom's Meatloaf

Serving: 6 | Prep: 20mins | Cook: 1hours15mins | Ready in:

Ingredients

- 2 pounds lean ground beef
- 1/2 cup crushed saltine crackers
- 1 (8 ounce) can tomato sauce
- 2 eggs, beaten
- 1/4 cup finely chopped onion
- 2 tablespoons finely chopped green bell pepper
- 1 teaspoon salt
- 1/4 teaspoon ground thyme
- 1/4 teaspoon ground marjoram
- 1/4 cup ketchup
- 2 tablespoons light corn syrup

Direction

- Preheat the oven to 175 ° C or 350 ° F.
- In a big bowl, mix marjoram, thyme, salt, bell pepper, onion, eggs, tomato sauce, cracker crumbs and ground beef and combine thoroughly. Form mixture of beef into 2 evenly-sized loaves. Put both loaves in one baking dish, 9x13-inch in size. Cover in foil and in prepped oven, bake for an hour. Meantime, in small bowl, combine corn syrup and ketchup to create glaze.
- Take baking dish out of oven and take off foil. Brush loaves with glaze. Put baking dish with no cover back to oven, and keep baking for 15 to 20 minutes till loaves are not pink anymore in the middle. An inserted instant-read

thermometer into the middle must register at minimum of 70 ° C or 160 ° F.

Nutrition Information

- Calories: 395 calories;
- Total Fat: 21.6
- Sodium: 859
- Total Carbohydrate: 14.9
- Cholesterol: 165
- Protein: 34.3

831. Mozechilli Casserole

Serving: 4 | Prep: | Cook: | Ready in:

Ingredients

- 1 pound lean ground beef
- 1 (28 ounce) jar spaghetti sauce
- 1 (16 ounce) package rotini pasta
- 2 cups mozzarella cheese, shredded

Direction

- Boil a large pot of lightly salted water. Include in pasta; cook for 8 to 10 minutes till al dente; strain. Set the oven at 350°F (175°C) and start preheating.
- Place a skillet on medium heat; cook in beef till browned. Strain any excess fat from the meat.
- Include rotini pasta and spaghetti sauce to the browned beef. Layer the meat mixture into a 3-qt. casserole dish; then layer mozzarella cheese and repeat.
- Bake for 25 minutes in the preheated oven.

Nutrition Information

- Calories: 1040 calories;
- Total Fat: 43.8
- Sodium: 1239
- Total Carbohydrate: 109.7
- Cholesterol: 133

- Protein: 50.9

832. My Chili

Serving: 8 | Prep: | Cook: | Ready in:

Ingredients

- 2 pounds ground beef
- 2 onions, chopped
- 4 cloves garlic, minced
- 2 tablespoons chili powder
- 2 teaspoons salt
- 2 teaspoons dried oregano
- 4 (14.5 ounce) cans stewed tomatoes
- 1 (15 ounce) can tomato sauce
- 1 (15 ounce) can kidney beans with liquid

Direction

- In a big stockpot, mix onion, garlic and ground beef. Stir and cook on medium until it becomes brown. Discard grease.
- Mix tomato sauce, chili powder, oregano, salt and tomatoes; stir until tomatoes break up. Bring to a boil, lower the heat, cover, and let simmer. Let it cook with occasional stirring for 60 minutes.
- Mix in beans. Let it simmer without cover 20 minutes with occasional stirring.

Nutrition Information

- Calories: 482 calories;
- Total Fat: 31.2
- Sodium: 1517
- Total Carbohydrate: 27.9
- Cholesterol: 96
- Protein: 24.9

833. My Man's Cheesy Smoked Meatloaf

Serving: 8 | Prep: 30mins | Cook: 1hours14mins | Ready in:

Ingredients

- 2 pounds lean ground beef
- 1 red onion, coarsely chopped
- 3/4 cup Italian-seasoned bread crumbs
- 2 eggs
- 1 pinch salt and ground black pepper to taste (optional)
- 1 (8 ounce) package shredded smoked mozzarella cheese
- 1 teaspoon vegetable oil, or as needed
- 4 slices hardwood smoked bacon
- 1 1/2 teaspoons Dijon mustard, divided
- 1 1/2 teaspoons Worcestershire sauce, divided
- 1 red bell pepper, sliced into strips
- 1/2 cup sliced fresh mushrooms
- 1 (8 ounce) package crumbled aged feta cheese

Direction

- Start preheating the oven at 350°F (175°C).
- Combine pepper, salt, eggs, bread crumbs, red onion, and ground beef in a large bowl. Separate the mixture into 2 parts. Press 1/2 of the mixture in the base of a loaf pan.
- Slide 2 fingers lengthwise down the center of the beef mixture. Stuff the space with mozzarella cheese. Mold the beef mixture left around cheese, pressing down firmly.
- In a large skillet, on medium-high heat, heat oil. Cook bacon slices for about 5 minutes until lightly browned. Place bacon slices over beef mixture.
- In the skillet, cook and stir 3/4 teaspoon of Worcestershire sauce and 3/4 teaspoon of mustard and in the bacon grease for 1 minute. Put in bell pepper; cook for 3 to 4 minutes until tender. Spread over bacon with bell pepper.
- Put mushrooms, Worcestershire sauce, and the leftover mustard in the skillet; cook and stir

for about 5 minutes until soft. Evenly spread over bell pepper. Sprinkle feta cheese over mushrooms.
- Use aluminum foil to cover loaf pan; arrange on top of a baking sheet.
- Bake in the prepared oven for 60 to 90 minutes until an instant-read thermometer shows at least 160°F (71°C) when inserted into the beef.

Nutrition Information

- Calories: 486 calories;
- Protein: 34.7
- Total Fat: 32
- Sodium: 843
- Total Carbohydrate: 12.8
- Cholesterol: 158

834. My Mom's Baja Burger

Serving: 8 | Prep: 20mins | Cook: 30mins | Ready in:

Ingredients

- 2 pounds ground beef
- 1 cup corn chips (such as Fritos®, crushed
- salt and ground black pepper to taste
- 1 (28 ounce) can tomato sauce
- 1/2 onion, chopped
- 1/2 teaspoon garlic salt
- 1/2 teaspoon chili powder
- 1/2 cup shredded Cheddar cheese
- 8 (6 inch) French bread rolls, split in half lengthwise

Direction

- Combine ground beef with crushed corn chips; shape mixture into 8 oblong patties; sprinkle with pepper and salt to taste. Combine chili powder, garlic salt, onion, and tomato sauce in a small bowl. On medium high heat, heat a large skillet.

Cook patties for 4 to 5 minutes in the heated skillet; turn over; cook the other side for 4 more minutes. Add tomato sauce into the skillet when burgers finish cooking; allow to simmer for 4 to 5 minutes longer. Place Cheddar cheese on top of each burger and heat until cheese is melted. Top bread with burgers; spoon sauce onto the patties before sandwiching them.

Nutrition Information

- Calories: 863 calories;
- Protein: 38.7
- Total Fat: 38.6
- Sodium: 1701
- Total Carbohydrate: 90.6
- Cholesterol: 104

---

835. Nacho Pizza

Serving: 4 | Prep: 20mins | Cook: 15mins | Ready in:

Ingredients

- 1 pound lean ground beef
- 1 (1.25 ounce) package taco seasoning mix
- 1 (12 inch) parbaked thin pizza crust
- 5 tablespoons queso dip
- 1 cup shredded aged Cheddar cheese
- 1 jalapeno pepper, seeded and minced
- 4 green onions, diced
- 4 tablespoons salsa
- 1/2 cup crushed tortilla chips
- 2 tablespoons sour cream, or to taste

Direction

- Start preheating the oven to 450°F (230°C).
- In a big frying pan, cook beef for 5 minutes until not pink anymore. Strain. Mix in seasoning mix until evenly blended.
- On a work surface, put pizza crust. Evenly spread over the crust with queso dip. Put

green onions, jalapeno, cooked beef mixture, and Cheddar cheese on top. Put on the pizza with salsa in random places, ensuring you don't mix the salsa with the other toppings. Sprinkle over the top with crushed tortilla chips.

- Put directly on the center oven rack in the preheated oven and bake for 8 minutes until cheese melts and is hot. Serve with sour cream.

Nutrition Information

- Calories: 747 calories;
- Total Fat: 36.4
- Sodium: 1751
- Total Carbohydrate: 62.4
- Cholesterol: 121
- Protein: 43.1

---

836. Nanny's Goulash

Serving: 6 | Prep: 25mins | Cook: 35mins | Ready in:

Ingredients

- 1 pound lean ground beef
- 1 (8 ounce) package fresh mushrooms, sliced
- 1 green bell pepper, cut into 1/2 inch pieces
- 1 red bell pepper, cut into 1/2 inch pieces
- 1 zucchini, thickly sliced
- 1 small red onion, sliced
- 4 tablespoons olive oil
- 1/2 tablespoon paprika
- 1/2 tablespoon dried basil
- 1 teaspoon garlic salt
- 1/2 teaspoon white pepper
- 1 (14.5 ounce) can whole peeled tomatoes with liquid, chopped

Direction

- Brown ground beef in a big frying pan. Take the beef out using a slotted spoon and remove the fat.

- Put the frying pan into the stove again. Add in olive oil and heat over medium-high heat. Mix in pepper, garlic salt, basil, paprika, onion, squash, red and green peppers, and mushrooms. Cook for 5 minutes, you can stir it occasionally.
- Lower the heat to medium. Mix in tomatoes and beef; simmer for 20 minutes, you stir it occasionally.

Nutrition Information

- Calories: 273 calories;
- Sodium: 448
- Total Carbohydrate: 8.9
- Cholesterol: 46
- Protein: 16
- Total Fat: 19.8

837.   New Mexico Green Chile Meatloaf

Serving: 8 | Prep: 15mins | Cook: 1hours10mins |Ready in:

Ingredients

- 1 1/2 pounds hamburger
- 1 (14.5 ounce) can diced tomatoes
- 1 (6 ounce) can diced green chiles
- 3/4 cup chopped onion
- 1/2 cup milk, or as needed
- 2 eggs
- 15 crushed crackers
- 1/2 teaspoon salt, or more to taste
- 1/2 teaspoon ground black pepper

Direction

- Set the oven to 350°F (175°C) for preheating. Lightly grease a loaf pan.
- In a bowl, mix green chiles, eggs, salt, pepper, crackers, milk, tomatoes, hamburger, and

onion. Pour the mixture into the prepared loaf pan.
- Let it bake inside the preheated oven for 1 hour and 10 minutes until it's no longer pink in the center. To check, see if an instant-read thermometer that is inserted into its center registers at least 160°F (70°C).
- Allow it to cool in the pan for 10 minutes. Transfer it into a serving dish.

Nutrition Information

- Calories: 260 calories;
- Sodium: 608
- Total Carbohydrate: 8.9
- Cholesterol: 100
- Protein: 17.3
- Total Fat: 16.6

838.   New York System Hot Wiener Sauce I

Serving: 12 | Prep: 20mins | Cook: 1hours |Ready in:

Ingredients

- 3 pounds ground beef
- 2 teaspoons chili powder
- 2 teaspoons dry mustard
- 1/2 teaspoon ground allspice
- 1/2 teaspoon ground nutmeg
- 1/2 teaspoon onion salt
- 1/2 teaspoon garlic salt
- 1/2 teaspoon celery salt
- 1/4 teaspoon minced fresh ginger root
- 1 teaspoon ground cumin
- 1/2 teaspoon Worcestershire sauce
- 1 teaspoon soy sauce
- 10 ounces ketchup

Direction

- In a deep, big pan, put the ground beef and

cook on medium-high heat until it becomes brown evenly, then drain.

- In the frypan, mix the ketchup, soy sauce, Worcestershire sauce, cumin, ginger root, celery salt, garlic salt, onion salt, nutmeg, allspice, dry mustard and chili powder. Let it simmer for a minimum of 1 hour until it reaches the preferred consistency. Serve it hot.

Nutrition Information

- Calories: 381 calories;
- Cholesterol: 96
- Protein: 19.6
- Total Fat: 30.6
- Sodium: 582
- Total Carbohydrate: 6.6

839.   No Sour Cream Beef Stroganoff

Serving: 4 | Prep: 20mins | Cook: 15mins | Ready in:

Ingredients

- 1 1/2 pounds ground beef
- salt to taste
- 1 tablespoon butter
- 1 (8 ounce) can mushrooms, drained
- 1 onion, chopped
- 1 clove garlic, minced
- 4 tablespoons flour
- 1/2 cup white wine
- 1 (10.5 ounce) can cream of mushroom soup
- 1/2 (10.5 ounce) can beef broth
- Worcestershire sauce to taste

Direction

- In large skillet, brown ground beef over medium heat. Season with salt. Add in butter, onion, mushrooms and garlic; cook until the onions are soft.

- Mix together flour and white wine in a small bowl. Add this mixture along with the beef broth and mushroom soup into the meat. Simmer for 10 to 15 minutes until thick. Add more broth if necessary. Season with a dash of Worcestershire sauce and serve.

Nutrition Information

- Calories: 473 calories;
- Protein: 32.4
- Total Fat: 27.6
- Sodium: 962
- Total Carbohydrate: 17.3
- Cholesterol: 111

840.   Noodles Mexicana

Serving: 8 | Prep: 15mins | Cook: 30mins | Ready in:

Ingredients

- 1 pound ground beef
- 1 onion, chopped
- 2 cloves garlic, minced
- 1 (11 ounce) can whole kernel corn, with liquid
- 1 (2.25 ounce) can sliced black olives, with liquid
- 1 (14.5 ounce) can tomatoes with juice, chopped
- 1 (15 ounce) can chili beans, drained
- 1/2 cup chopped green onions
- 1 (1.25 ounce) package taco seasoning mix
- 1/2 teaspoon salt
- 1 (16 ounce) package uncooked egg noodles
- 1/2 cup sour cream, for topping

Direction

- In a big skillet, cook garlic, onion and ground beef over medium heat until meat is brown evenly. Drain.
- Stir in the skillet the green onions, chili beans, tomatoes, olives and corn. Add salt and taco

seasoning to season. Cook with cover for 15 minutes.

- Stir in egg noodles. Keep cooking with cover until egg noodles soften, or about 12 minutes. Add sour cream dollop on top of each serving.

Nutrition Information

- Calories: 443 calories;
- Total Fat: 14.3
- Sodium: 1013
- Total Carbohydrate: 60.1
- Cholesterol: 82
- Protein: 21

---

841. Noodles Riviera

Serving: 9 | Prep: 15mins | Cook: 1hours10mins | Ready in:

Ingredients

- 1 tablespoon olive oil
- 1 pound extra lean ground beef
- 1/2 teaspoon ground dried thyme
- 1 (1.5 ounce) envelope spaghetti sauce seasoning mix
- 1 (6 ounce) can tomato paste
- 3 cups water
- salt and black pepper to taste
- 1 (8 ounce) package egg noodles
- 1 (3 ounce) package cream cheese, softened
- 1 tablespoon chopped fresh parsley
- 1/4 cup grated Parmesan cheese
- 1 (8 ounce) container sour cream
- 1 cup shredded mozzarella cheese, divided

Direction

- On medium-high heat, heat olive oil in a big pan. Cook and stir in ground beef for 5-7mins until the meat is evenly brown, crumbly, and not pink anymore; drain excess grease. Mix in water, thyme, tomato paste, and spaghetti

sauce mix; sprinkle pepper and salt to season. Let it simmer then turn to medium-low heat. Let it simmer for 25mins, covered, while stirring from time to time.

- Preheat oven to 175°C or 350°Fahrenheit. Oil a 9-in x 13-in baking dish.
- As the meat simmers, boil a big pot of lightly salted water on high heat and bring to a rolling boil. Add egg noodles then boil. Cook pasta for about 5mins, without cover, until firm to chew and cooked through; stir from time to time. Drain pasta in a colander over the sink.
- In a bowl, combine Parmesan cheese with parsley and cream cheese until the cream cheese is not lumpy. Mix in three-fourths of shredded mozzarella and sour cream until well blended. Transfer 1/2 of the egg noodles then 1/2 of the meat sauce respectively, in the oiled baking dish. Slather 1/2 of sour cream mixture on top of the meat sauce. Use the leftover sour cream mixture, egg noodles, and meat sauce to repeat the layering process. Add the remaining mozzarella cheese on top.
- Bake for about 35mins in the preheated oven until the mozzarella is golden brown and bubbly.

Nutrition Information

- Calories: 336 calories;
- Total Fat: 16.5
- Sodium: 744
- Total Carbohydrate: 26.2
- Cholesterol: 84
- Protein: 20.9

---

842. Not Your Mom's Mac And Cheese

Serving: 8 | Prep: 25mins | Cook: 30mins | Ready in:

Ingredients

- 1 (16 ounce) package gemelli (small twisted pasta)
- 1 tablespoon olive oil
- 1 pound lean ground beef
- salt and ground black pepper to taste
- 3 tablespoons butter
- 3 tablespoons all-purpose flour
- 3 cups milk
- 1 cup shredded fontina cheese
- 1 cup shredded sharp Cheddar cheese
- 1 cup shredded white Cheddar cheese
- 1/4 cup grated Parmesan cheese
- 1/8 teaspoon paprika
- 1/8 teaspoon ground nutmeg
- 1/8 teaspoon garlic powder
- 1 pinch ground cinnamon
- 1 pinch chili powder
- 2 tablespoons butter
- 1/2 cup Italian-seasoned breadcrumbs
- 2 tablespoons grated Parmesan cheese

Direction

- Pour lightly salted water in a large pot till full and let come to a rolling boil over high heat. Stir in the gemelli when the water is boiling, and return to a boil. Cook for nearly 8 minutes, with no cover, stirring occasionally, till the pasta has cooked through but still firm to the bite. Place in a colander set in the sink to drain thoroughly. Add olive oil, and toss pasta till coated; leave aside.
- Heat a large skillet over medium-high heat and mix in the ground beef. Add black pepper and salt to season. Cook and stir for around 10 minutes till the beef is crumbly, brown evenly, and no longer pink. Drain and get rid of any excess grease. Leave aside.
- Preheat an oven to 350 °F (175 °C).
- In a large skillet, heat the flour and 3 tablespoons butter over low heat. Cook and stir till the flour is incorporated and the butter melts, then whisk in the milk slowly. Mix in the sharp Cheddar cheese, fontina cheese, 1/4 cup Parmesan cheese, and white Cheddar cheese; cook for approximately 5 minutes, whisking constantly, till sauce thickens and

cheese melts. Add nutmeg, paprika, garlic powder, chili powder, and cinnamon to season. Season with black pepper and salt to taste. Blend in the pasta and beef, and place mixture to a large baking dish.
- In a bowl, combine the leftover 2 tablespoons Parmesan cheese, bread crumbs, and 2 tablespoons butter. Sprinkle over the pasta in baking dish with mixture.
- In the preheated oven, bake for around 12 minutes till bubbly then set the oven on broil. Broil for an addition of 3 minutes till brown lightly.

Nutrition Information

- Calories: 660 calories;
- Total Fat: 34
- Sodium: 600
- Total Carbohydrate: 53.9
- Cholesterol: 115
- Protein: 35

843.   One Pot Chili Mac And Cheese

Serving: 6 | Prep: 10mins | Cook: 20mins | Ready in:

Ingredients

- 1 tablespoon extra virgin olive oil
- 1 medium sweet onion, diced small
- 3 cloves garlic, minced
- 1 pound lean ground beef
- 2 cups low-sodium chicken broth
- 2 cups Ragu® Old World Style® Traditional Pasta Sauce
- 1 (10 ounce) can diced tomatoes with green chile peppers
- 1 (16 ounce) can mild chili beans, undrained
- 1 teaspoon chili powder
- 1 teaspoon cumin
- salt and ground black pepper to taste
- 1 1/2 cups uncooked elbow macaroni

- 3/4 cup shredded Cheddar cheese
- 1/4 cup chopped fresh parsley

Direction

- Over medium-high heat, heat olive oil in a pot or a large Dutch oven. Add beef, garlic and onion. Cook while stirring frequently for about 3 minutes until meat is crumbly and browned. Drain excess fat.
- Stir in cumin, chili powder, beans, mild green chilies with diced tomatoes, Ragu(R) sauce and chicken broth. Sprinkle with pepper and salt to taste. Bring to a boil; stir in pasta; cover and lower the heat to simmer; cook for about 14 minutes until pasta is al dente.
- Take out of the heat. Stir in parsley and cheese. Immediately serve, decorated with more parsley and cheese if preferred.

Nutrition Information

- Calories: 463 calories;
- Total Fat: 19.2
- Sodium: 1233
- Total Carbohydrate: 45.9
- Cholesterol: 66
- Protein: 28.5

844.   Oven Meatballs

Serving: 5 | Prep: 10mins | Cook: 45mins | Ready in:

Ingredients

- 1 1/2 pounds ground beef
- 1/2 cup ketchup
- 1 tablespoon cornstarch
- 3/4 cup water
- 1/2 cup white sugar
- 1 teaspoon vinegar
- 1 teaspoon dry mustard powder
- 3/4 teaspoon salt
- 3 tablespoons soy sauce

Direction

- Set the oven to 350°F (175°C) and start preheating. Grease a 9x9 inch baking dish; put aside.
- Shape ground beef into 20 meatballs. In a large skillet, over medium heat, brown them on all sides, about 15 minutes.
- In a bowl, beat together soy sauce, salt, dry mustard, vinegar, sugar, water, cornstarch and ketchup until sugar dissolves and cornstarch becomes smooth.
- Transfer browned meatballs in the greased baking dish; top over with sauce. Bake in the prepared oven for 30-40 minutes until meatballs are cooked through and sauce becomes thickened.

Nutrition Information

- Calories: 402 calories;
- Total Fat: 21.5
- Sodium: 1237
- Total Carbohydrate: 28.3
- Cholesterol: 83
- Protein: 23.6

845.   Over The Top Nachos

Serving: 6 | Prep: 5mins | Cook: 5mins | Ready in:

Ingredients

- 1 pound ground beef
- 1 onion, finely diced
- salt and pepper to taste
- 2 cups shredded Cheddar cheese
- 1 (16 ounce) can refried beans
- 1 (14.5 ounce) package tortilla chips
- 1 fresh jalapeno pepper, sliced

Direction

- Place a large skillet on medium heat; cook in ground beef, pepper, salt and onion till browned. Crumble the meat while cooking. Strain off the grease once the meat is cooked thoroughly.

- On a microwavable platter, spread the chips. Sprinkle beans over. Add a layer of 1/2 of the cheese, then a layer of the ground beef mixture, and a final layer of the remaining cheese. Spread jalapeno peppers over the top.
- Microwave on medium-high till the cheese is melted. Serve immediately.

Nutrition Information

- Calories: 829 calories;
- Sodium: 846
- Total Carbohydrate: 58.4
- Cholesterol: 119
- Protein: 33.6
- Total Fat: 52.1

846.   Pakistani Meatballs With Gravy (Koftay)

Serving: 3 | Prep: 20mins | Cook: 40mins | Ready in:

Ingredients

- 1 1/4 pounds lean ground beef
- 2 onions, thinly sliced, divided
- 1 teaspoon chili powder
- 1/2 teaspoon ground black pepper
- 1/2 teaspoon ground cloves
- 1/2 teaspoon ground cumin
- 1/2 teaspoon ground cardamom
- 1 tablespoon vegetable oil
- 1 cup yogurt
- 1/2 cup dry lentils
- 1 teaspoon ginger paste
- 1 teaspoon garlic paste
- 1 teaspoon crushed coriander seed
- 2 1/2 cups water
- crushed red pepper to taste
- salt to taste

Direction

- Combine cardamom, cumin, cloves, black pepper, chili powder, half of the onions and lean ground beef in a medium bowl. Form into around six 2-in. meatballs.
- Place a big heavy saucepan on medium heat; cook while stirring the remaining onion in vegetable oil till tender. Combine in salt, red pepper, water, coriander seed, garlic paste, ginger paste, lentils and yogurt. Transfer the meatballs into the mixture. Turn the heat down to low; cook till the lentils become tender and the meatballs are well browned, 30 minutes.

Nutrition Information

- Calories: 606 calories;
- Cholesterol: 119
- Protein: 45.8
- Total Fat: 32.6
- Sodium: 235
- Total Carbohydrate: 31.6

847.   Papa Funk's Campfire Chili

Serving: 12 | Prep: 25mins | Cook: 8hours | Ready in:

Ingredients

- 3 pounds lean ground beef (80% lean)
- 1 pound bulk sweet sausage
- 2 (29 ounce) cans tomato sauce (such as Hunt's®)
- 1 (40 ounce) can dark red kidney beans, drained and rinsed
- 4 Roma (plum) tomatoes, chopped
- 4 stalks celery, chopped
- 2 green bell peppers, chopped
- 1 (15.5 ounce) can light red kidney beans, drained and mashed

- 1 (15.5 ounce) can white kidney beans, drained and rinsed
- 1 (12 fluid ounce) can or bottle lager-style beer (such as Yuengling®)
- 1 sweet onion (such as Vidalia®), chopped
- 1 red bell pepper, chopped
- 2 (6 ounce) cans tomato paste (such as Hunt's®)
- 2 (4 ounce) cans diced green chile peppers (such as Old El Paso®)
- 1/4 cup chili powder, or more to taste
- 4 chipotle chile peppers in adobo sauce (such as Goya®), chopped
- 3 tablespoons adobo sauce from chipotle peppers (such as Goya®)
- 3 tablespoons ground cumin
- 2 tablespoons barbeque sauce (such as KC Masterpiece®)

Direction

- Break sausage and ground beef into small pieces, then add to the crock of a large slow cooker; add barbeque sauce, cumin, adobo sauce, chipotle peppers, chili powder, green chile peppers, tomato paste, red bell pepper, sweet onion, beer, white kidney beans, light red kidney beans, green bell pepper, celery, roma tomatoes, dark red kidney beans and tomato sauce.
- Cook for 8 hours on Low.

Nutrition Information

- Calories: 570 calories;
- Protein: 40.8
- Total Fat: 24
- Sodium: 2032
- Total Carbohydrate: 48.3
- Cholesterol: 101

---

848.   Party Italian Wedding Soup

Serving: 12 | Prep: 15mins | Cook: 1hours | Ready in:

Ingredients

- 1 (48 fluid ounce) can chicken broth
- 1 (10 ounce) package frozen chopped spinach, thawed and drained
- 2 onions, chopped
- 2 cups chopped carrot
- 2 stalks celery, chopped
- 1 pound ground beef
- 1 cup dry bread crumbs
- 1 egg
- 1 pound skinless, boneless chicken breast halves - cut into chunks
- 3 ounces dry pasta
- salt and pepper to taste

Direction

- In a big pot, combine celery, carrots, onions, spinach, and chicken broth over medium heat. Mix thoroughly and let simmer.
- Place egg, bread crumbs, and ground beef in a separate big bowl, combine thoroughly. Shape the mixture into 1/2-in diameter meatballs; drop meatballs into the soup deliberately.
- Add chunks of chicken breast to the soup; decrease to low heat. Let simmer 1 hour. About 30 minutes before serving, add pasta; season with pepper and salt to taste.

Nutrition Information

- Calories: 260 calories;
- Total Carbohydrate: 17
- Cholesterol: 81
- Protein: 19.7
- Total Fat: 12.2
- Sodium: 733

849. Pasta Lasagna

Serving: 5 | Prep: 10mins | Cook: 50mins | Ready in:

Ingredients

- 1/2 pound penne pasta
- 1/2 pound lean ground beef
- 1 (26 ounce) jar pasta sauce
- 1 (15 ounce) container ricotta cheese
- 8 ounces shredded mozzarella cheese, divided
- 1/4 cup grated Parmesan cheese
- 1 egg, beaten

Direction

- Heat oven beforehand up to 350°F (175°C) and prepare a greased 2 1/2-quart baking pan.
- Get a big pot of lightly salted water and boil. Put pasta and let it cook for 8-10 mins until firm to bite. Let it drain.
- In a huge pan, cook the beef over a medium heat until it turns brown, then drain. Mix it with pasta sauce before removing from the heat.
- Put together Parmesan, beaten egg, 1 cup of mozzarella and ricotta in a bowl. Mix until it is well blended.
- Layer half of the pasta, half of the sauce, and half the cheese mixture in the prepared pan. Repeat the layers and top it with the remaining mozzarella.
- Let it bake on the preheated oven until it's bubbly and hot for about 34-40 mins.

Nutrition Information

- Calories: 644 calories;
- Cholesterol: 127
- Protein: 40.1
- Total Fat: 27.3
- Sodium: 1087
- Total Carbohydrate: 59

850. Pastitsio II

Serving: 10 | Prep: 45mins | Cook: 1hours30mins | Ready in:

Ingredients

- Pasta:
- 1 pound dry ziti pasta
- 4 tablespoons butter
- 1/4 cup grated Parmesan cheese
- 1 dash ground nutmeg
- 1 pinch salt and pepper to taste
- 3 eggs, lightly beaten
- Meat Sauce:
- 2 tablespoons butter
- 1 large onion, chopped
- 1 clove garlic, crushed
- 1 1/2 pounds lean ground beef
- 1/4 cup tomato paste
- 1/2 cup dry red wine
- 1/2 cup vegetable broth
- 2 tablespoons chopped fresh parsley
- salt and pepper to taste
- Cream Sauce:
- 1/2 cup butter
- 1/2 cup all-purpose flour
- 3 cups milk
- 1/4 teaspoon ground nutmeg
- 1 egg, lightly beaten
- salt and pepper to taste
- cooking spray
- 1/4 cup grated Parmesan cheese

Direction

- Set oven to 175°C (350°F) and start preheating.
- Boil a big pot of slightly salted water. Put in ziti; cook for 8-10 minutes until soften yet still firm to bite.
- Heat butter until melted and golden brown; transfer on top of ziti; put in pepper, salt, nutmeg and Parmesan cheese. Stir thoroughly. Allow to cool a little. Put in eggs and stir again; put aside.
- For the meat sauce: In a skillet, fry garlic and onion gently in butter for 3-5 minutes until

onion is tender. Turn up the heat and put in ground beef; stir thoroughly. Cook for 5 minutes until the beef begins to turn brown. Put in pepper, salt, parsley, broth, wine and tomato paste. Over low heat, simmer with cover for 20 minutes.

- For the cream sauce: In a saucepan, heat butter to melt; mix in flour and gently cook for 2 minutes. Put in all of the milk and boil the mixture, stirring continuously. Gently boil for a minute. Put in pepper, salt and nutmeg. Allow to cool a little, then mix in beaten egg. Pour half a cup of this sauce into the meat sauce.
- For pastitsio assembly: Coat a 9x13-inch baking dish with grease. Evenly scoop 1/2 amount of prepared ziti into the pan's bottom; add meat sauce over. Add the rest of ziti on top. Add on cream sauce and scatter out to entirely coat ziti. Scatter Parmesan cheese over.
- Bake at 175°C (350°F) until golden brown, or about 50 minutes. Allow to sit for 10 minutes then slice into square pieces.

Nutrition Information

- Calories: 576 calories;
- Total Carbohydrate: 45.9
- Cholesterol: 168
- Protein: 25.7
- Total Fat: 31
- Sodium: 432

---

851.   Pepperoni Meatza

Serving: 6 | Prep: 30mins | Cook: 15mins | Ready in:

Ingredients

- 1 tablespoon salt
- 1 teaspoon caraway seeds (optional)
- 1 teaspoon dried oregano
- 1 teaspoon garlic salt

- 1 teaspoon ground black pepper
- 1 teaspoon red pepper flakes, or to taste (optional)
- 2 pounds extra lean ground beef
- 2 eggs
- 1/2 cup grated Parmesan cheese
- 1 (12 ounce) package shredded mozzarella cheese
- 1 cup tomato sauce
- 1 (3.5 ounce) package sliced pepperoni, or to taste

Direction

- Start preheating the oven at 450°F (230°C).
- Combine crushed red pepper flakes, ground black pepper, garlic salt, oregano, caraway seeds, and salt in a small bowl.
- In a mixing bowl, mix eggs and ground beef until well incorporated. Add seasoning mixture and Parmesan cheese to beef; blend. In a 12x17-inch pan, press the ground beef mixture and spread out evenly.
- Bake in the prepared oven for about 10 minutes until meat is not pink anymore. Drain the grease.
- Place the oven rack about 6 inches from the heat source and start to heat the oven's broiler.
- Scatter 1/3 of the mozzarella cheese over the baked meat, followed by tomato sauce in a level layer. Scatter again 1/3 of the mozzarella cheese over the sauce and place slices of pepperoni on top. Sprinkle pizza with the leftover mozzarella cheese.
- Broil for 3 to 5 minutes until cheese melts, bubbles, and turns to lightly brown.

Nutrition Information

- Calories: 506 calories;
- Total Fat: 27.8
- Sodium: 2521
- Total Carbohydrate: 5.1
- Cholesterol: 220
- Protein: 56.5

852.   Personal Shepherd's Pies

Serving: 4 | Prep: 20mins | Cook: 25mins |Ready in:

Ingredients

- 1 pound ground beef
- 1 onion, chopped
- 1 (10.75 ounce) can condensed cream of mushroom soup
- 1 cup frozen corn
- 1 tablespoon ketchup
- 1/4 teaspoon black pepper
- 2 cups prepared instant mashed potatoes
- 3/4 cup shredded Cheddar cheese (optional)

Direction

- In a frying pan, cook and stir onion and beef over medium-high heat for around 5 minutes, until beef is crumbly and browned; drain and eliminate grease.
- Decrease heat to low. Stir pepper, ketchup, corn, and mushroom soup into beef mixture; cook for around 2 minutes until heated through. Distribute beef mixture into four 4-inch round baking pans; pour the prepared mashed potatoes over beef mixture.
- In the preheated oven, bake for around 15 minutes until potatoes become lightly browned.
- Place oven rack about 6 inches away from the heat source then preheat the oven's broiler.
- Evenly sprinkle Cheddar cheese over pies. On a baking sheet, position the pies.
- Broil for approximately 2 minutes, until cheese becomes melted. Before serving, let cool for 5 minutes.

Nutrition Information

- Calories: 574 calories;
- Total Fat: 34.6
- Sodium: 914
- Total Carbohydrate: 37.1

- Cholesterol: 94
- Protein: 29.5

853.   Philly Cheesesteak Casserole

Serving: 10 | Prep: 20mins | Cook: 35mins |Ready in:

Ingredients

- 1 (16 ounce) package bow tie pasta
- 2 tablespoons vegetable oil
- 2 onions, chopped
- 1 1/2 pounds lean ground beef
- 2 (10.75 ounce) cans condensed cream of mushroom soup
- 1 (10.75 ounce) can milk
- 1 (4 ounce) can sliced mushrooms
- 1/2 teaspoon dried thyme
- 3 cups shredded sharp Cheddar cheese
- salt and pepper to taste
- 1 cup dry bread crumbs
- 3 tablespoons butter or margarine, melted
- 1 cup shredded sharp Cheddar cheese

Direction

- Set an oven to preheat at 190°C (375°F). Grease a 9x13-inch baking dish lightly. Boil a big pot of lightly salted water then add the pasta. Let it cook for about 8 minutes until al dente, drain, put in a big bowl then put aside.
- In a pan, heat the vegetable oil on medium heat. Sauté the onions until it starts to soften. Stir in ground beef then cook, mixing, until it browns evenly. Drain the grease and transfer it into the bowl with pasta. Mix in the condensed soup, then using a soup can, measure the milk. Stir in thyme and mushrooms until well combined. Stir in 3 cups of cheese and sprinkle pepper and salt to season. Put it in the baking dish, then spread.
- Mix the melted butter and bread crumbs together in a small bowl, then stir in leftover a

cup of cheese. On top of the baking dish, sprinkle this mixture evenly.

- Bake in the oven until the topping turns golden and crispy, or for 30-35 minutes

Nutrition Information

- Calories: 648 calories;
- Total Fat: 35.3
- Sodium: 882
- Total Carbohydrate: 49
- Cholesterol: 104
- Protein: 34.1

854. Picadillo De Platano

Serving: 8 | Prep: 20mins | Cook: 30mins | Ready in:

Ingredients

- 4 plantains, peeled and cut into 3 pieces
- 1/2 pound ground beef
- 2 cloves garlic, minced
- 2 tablespoons minced onion
- 2 teaspoons salt
- 1/2 teaspoon pepper
- 1 1/2 tablespoons chopped cilantro
- 1/2 cup tomato, chopped
- 2 teaspoons Worcestershire sauce
- 1 dash hot pepper sauce

Direction

- Simmer plantain pieces in salted water over medium-high heat till tender. Once tender, drain; allow to cool; finely chop.
- In a skillet over medium-high heat, heat oil. Mix in onion, garlic and beef; spice with pepper and salt. Cook till the onion is soft and the beef is crumbly. Mix in tomato, cilantro and chopped plantain. Spice with hot pepper sauce and Worcestershire sauce; cook till everything is hot, around 10 minutes.

Nutrition Information

- Calories: 203 calories;
- Total Fat: 7.9
- Sodium: 623
- Total Carbohydrate: 29.8
- Cholesterol: 24
- Protein: 6.1

855. Pineapple Teriyaki Burgers

Serving: 2 | Prep: 25mins | Cook: 20mins | Ready in:

Ingredients

- cooking spray
- 2 slices canned pineapple, drained
- 3/4 pound ground beef
- 1/2 cup plain bread crumbs
- 1/2 (8 ounce) can sliced water chestnuts, drained and chopped
- 1/4 cup teriyaki sauce
- 1 egg
- 1 (1 inch) piece fresh ginger, minced
- 1 1/2 teaspoons Asian seasoning blend
- 1/2 teaspoon onion powder
- 1/4 teaspoon garlic powder
- 1/2 cup shredded lettuce, divided
- 2 hamburger buns, split

Direction

- Preheat the broiler of the oven and place the oven rack about 6 inches away from the heat. Use a cooking spray to grease a broiling rack.
- On a baking sheet, put in the sliced pineapples then place it in the preheated broiler and let it broil for about 1 minute on every side until it turns light brown in color. Put the broiled pineapple slices aside.
- In a bowl, combine the water chestnuts, minced ginger, ground beef, Asian seasoning blend, garlic powder, bread crumbs, egg, teriyaki sauce and onion powder together and

mix well; Divide the mixture into 2 equal portions and shape each portion into 2 big patties. Put the patties on the greased broiling rack.

- Let the patties cook in the broiler for 5-8 minutes on every side until the patties turn brown in color and are not anymore pink inside. A poked instant-read meat thermometer at the center of the patties must indicate a temperature of not less than 160°F (70°C).
- Put a layer of half of the lettuce, broiled patty and broiled sliced pineapple on top of each of the bottom half of the buns. Finish off each sandwich with the top half of the buns on top then serve.

Nutrition Information

- Calories: 675 calories;
- Total Carbohydrate: 65.3
- Cholesterol: 196
- Protein: 41.9
- Total Fat: 26.3
- Sodium: 2650

856.   Pizza Casserole

Serving: 7 | Prep: 30mins | Cook: 30mins | Ready in:

Ingredients

- 2 cups uncooked egg noodles
- 1/2 pound lean ground beef
- 1 onion, chopped
- 2 cloves garlic, minced
- 1 green bell pepper, chopped
- 1 cup sliced pepperoni sausage
- 16 ounces pizza sauce
- 4 tablespoons milk
- 1 cup shredded mozzarella cheese

Direction

- Following package directions to cook noodles.
- Set the oven to 175°C or 350°F to preheat.
- Brown the ground beef together with green bell pepper, garlic and onion in a medium skillet on moderately high heat, then drain the excess fat. Stir in milk, pizza sauce, pepperoni and noodles, then blend well. Transfer this mixture into a 2-qt. casserole dish.
- Bake at 175°C or 350°F about 20 minutes then put cheese on top. Bake for another 5-10 minutes.

Nutrition Information

- Calories: 386 calories;
- Cholesterol: 79
- Protein: 20.2
- Total Fat: 25.3
- Sodium: 903
- Total Carbohydrate: 17.7

857.   Poor Man's Stroganoff

Serving: 4 | Prep: 10mins | Cook: 20mins | Ready in:

Ingredients

- 1 (12 ounce) package egg noodles
- 1 pound ground beef
- 1 teaspoon Greek seasoning (such as Cavender's®)
- salt and ground black pepper to taste
- 1 teaspoon vegetable oil
- 1 (16 ounce) package sliced fresh mushrooms
- 1 pint sour cream

Direction

- Bring lightly salted water in a big pot to a boil. In the boiling water, cook egg noodles for 5 minutes while stirring sometimes, until cooked through yet still firm to the bite. Drain noodles.

- Heat a big skillet on moderately high heat. Cook and stir in the hot skillet with beef for 5-7 minutes, until crumbly and browned. Drain and get rid of grease. Use pepper, salt and Greek seasoning to season the beef.
- In a separate skillet, heat vegetable oil on moderate heat. Cook and stir in the hot oil with mushrooms for 5 minutes, until soft, then put cooked mushrooms into the ground beef.
- Stir into the ground beef mixture with sour cream, then cook and stir for 5 minutes, until the mixture is hot. Serve on top of egg noodles.

Nutrition Information

- Calories: 810 calories;
- Cholesterol: 192
- Protein: 38.2
- Total Fat: 43.1
- Sodium: 268
- Total Carbohydrate: 68.8

pepper, garlic powder, celery salt and salt, then stir well. Form into 1 1/2-inch balls.
- Set an oven to 175°C (350°F) to preheat. Brown the meatballs in a big skillet on medium heat, then drain the fat.
- Mix together the 1 cup of water and tomato sauce in an 11x7-inch baking dish. Put the brown meatballs into the tomato sauce, flipping to coat well.
- Put cover on and bake for 45 minutes in a preheated oven. Take off the cover and cook for another 15 minutes.

Nutrition Information

- Calories: 275 calories;
- Protein: 18.5
- Total Fat: 12.8
- Sodium: 1107
- Total Carbohydrate: 21.1
- Cholesterol: 55

---

858. Porcupines

Serving: 5 | Prep: 30mins | Cook: 1hours | Ready in:

Ingredients

- 1 pound lean ground beef
- 1/2 cup uncooked white rice
- 1/2 cup water
- 1/2 cup chopped onion
- 1 teaspoon salt
- 1/2 teaspoon celery salt
- 1/8 teaspoon garlic powder
- 1/8 teaspoon ground black pepper
- 1 (15 ounce) can tomato sauce
- 1 cup water

Direction

- Mix together the onion, 1/2 cup of water, rice and ground beef in a big bowl. Blend in

---

859. Pork Pie

Serving: 8 | Prep: | Cook: | Ready in:

Ingredients

- 2 (9 inch) unbaked pie shells
- 2 pounds lean ground pork
- 1 pound lean ground beef
- 1 1/2 cups mashed potatoes
- salt to taste
- ground black pepper to taste
- 1 teaspoon ground nutmeg
- 1 egg white

Direction

- Cook ground pork and beef over medium heat until browned and well cooked. Drain off excess oil.
- Take a 9" pie dish and line it with pastry. Turn the cooked meat mixture into the pie crust.

Top this with another pie crust and brush the top with egg white. Wrap alumium foil around the crust edges to prevent them from burning.

- Bake for 45 minutes at 375-degrees F (190-degrees C). Remove foil after 30 minutes and continue baking until the edges brown.

Nutrition Information

- Calories: 712 calories;
- Total Fat: 51.1
- Sodium: 462
- Total Carbohydrate: 27.6
- Cholesterol: 125
- Protein: 33.2

---

860. Potpourri Soup

Serving: 4 | Prep: 15mins | Cook: 1hours | Ready in:

Ingredients

- 1 pound ground beef
- 2 onions, chopped
- 6 cups water
- 1 (28 ounce) can whole peeled tomatoes, with liquid
- 1/3 cup barley
- 3 carrots, chopped
- 3 stalks celery, chopped
- 1 (16 ounce) can chili beans, drained
- 1 tablespoon salt
- 1/2 teaspoon ground black pepper
- 1 teaspoon Worcestershire sauce
- 1 teaspoon steak sauce
- 1 dash hot pepper sauce

Direction

- Mix together onions and ground beef in a large pot over medium heat; sauté until the onions are softened and the beef is browned, 10 minutes.

- Put in hot pepper sauce, steak sauce, Worcestershire sauce, ground black pepper, salt, beans, celery, carrots, barley, tomatoes and water. Bring to a boil. Lower the heat to low; simmer until barley and vegetables are softened, about 1 hour.

Nutrition Information

- Calories: 586 calories;
- Sodium: 2705
- Total Carbohydrate: 50.9
- Cholesterol: 97
- Protein: 29.7
- Total Fat: 31.9

---

861. Presidential Debate Chili

Serving: 8 | Prep: 20mins | Cook: 1hours10mins | Ready in:

Ingredients

- 1 pound ground beef
- 1 cup chopped onion
- 2 cloves garlic, minced
- 2 (16 ounce) cans diced tomatoes
- 1 cup beef broth
- 1 (4 ounce) can diced green chiles
- 3/4 tablespoon chili powder
- 1 tablespoon brown sugar
- 2 teaspoons dried oregano
- 1 teaspoon ground cumin
- 1/2 teaspoon salt
- 2 (15 ounce) cans ranch-style beans

Direction

- In a big pot, crumble beef over medium-high heat; add garlic and onion. Stir and cook beef for 7-10 minutes until fully turning brown. Strain and dispose the extra fat. Reheat the pot to medium-high heat.

- Mix salt, cumin, oregano, brown sugar, chili powder, diced green chilies, beef broth, and diced tomatoes into the beef mixture. Add beans and boil.
- Lower the heat to medium-low, cover the pot and simmer for 1 hour.

Nutrition Information

- Calories: 240 calories;
- Cholesterol: 35
- Protein: 17.1
- Total Fat: 7.2
- Sodium: 1137
- Total Carbohydrate: 24.4

---

862. Proper English Cottage Pie

Serving: 6 | Prep: | Cook: | Ready in:

Ingredients

- 1 pound lean ground beef
- 1 onion, diced
- 3 carrots, diced
- 2 tablespoons all-purpose flour
- 1/2 teaspoon ground cinnamon
- 1 tablespoon Italian seasoning
- 2 tablespoons chopped fresh parsley
- 1 1/2 cups beef broth
- 1 tablespoon tomato paste
- salt and pepper to taste
- 4 potatoes, peeled and diced
- 1/4 cup butter, softened
- 1 cup milk
- salt and pepper to taste
- 1/4 pound shredded Cheddar cheese

Direction

- Start preheating the oven to 200°C (400°F).
- For meat filling: Heat a big skillet over medium heat. Crumble in ground beef, and

then sauté for about one minute. Put in carrot and onion and keep on cooking for about 5 minutes, or until the onion turns brown and the meat is not pink anymore. Stir in parsley, mixed herbs, cinnamon, and flour.
- Mix together tomato paste and beef broth in a small bowl. Stir together and then pour into the beef mixture. Season the mixture with pepper and salt. Reduce the heat and simmer until almost all of the liquid has been absorbed, stirring occasionally, about 15 minutes. Scoop the mixture into a 9-inch pie plate.
- For potato topping: Add diced tomatoes to a medium saucepan. Pour in water to cover the potatoes and put over high heat. Bring it to a boil and boil until the potatoes become soft, about 15 minutes. Drain.
- Mash the potatoes till smooth, then put in margarine or butter before putting in the milk. Whisk until fluffy and season with pepper and salt. Spread the potato mixture over beef filling and scatter with grated Cheddar cheese.
- Bake in the preheated oven until the cheese is bubbly and the top turns brown, about 25 minutes.

Nutrition Information

- Calories: 512 calories;
- Cholesterol: 100
- Protein: 24.1
- Total Fat: 30.9
- Sodium: 491
- Total Carbohydrate: 34.8

---

863. Pumpkin Chili

Serving: 8 | Prep: 20mins | Cook: 1hours | Ready in:

Ingredients

- 2 pounds ground beef
- 1 large onion, diced

- 1 green bell pepper, diced
- 2 (15 ounce) cans kidney beans, drained
- 1 (46 fluid ounce) can tomato juice
- 1 (28 ounce) can peeled and diced tomatoes with juice
- 1/2 cup canned pumpkin puree
- 1 tablespoon pumpkin pie spice
- 1 tablespoon chili powder
- 1/4 cup white sugar

Direction

- Add beef into a big pot. At moderate heat, cook until the beef is browned then drain it. Mix in bell pepper and onion then continue cooking for 5 minutes. Add pumpkin puree, diced tomatoes, tomato juice and beans, stirring throughout. Put in sugar, chili powder and pumpkin pie spice to season the dish. Leave it simmering for 60 minutes.

Nutrition Information

- Calories: 409 calories;
- Total Fat: 16.4
- Sodium: 924
- Total Carbohydrate: 37.6
- Cholesterol: 69
- Protein: 28.2

864.   Quick Chili I

Serving: 8 | Prep: | Cook: |Ready in:

Ingredients

- 2 pounds ground beef
- 1 onion, finely diced
- 3 cloves garlic, minced
- 1 (14.5 ounce) can diced tomatoes
- 2 (14.5 ounce) cans diced tomatoes with green chile peppers
- 1 (8 ounce) can tomato sauce
- 1 cup water

- 1 (15 ounce) can kidney beans
- 1 (15 ounce) can pinto beans
- 2 tablespoons chili powder
- 1 tablespoon ground cumin
- 2 tablespoons white sugar
- 1 tablespoon salt
- 1 teaspoon ground black pepper
- 1 tablespoon hot pepper sauce

Direction

- Cook ground beef in a big stock pot until it is lightly brown and then discard grease.
- Mix in garlic and onion until it becomes transparent.
- Mix in water, hot sauce, pinto beans, tomatoes, kidney beans, cumin, salt, pepper, pinto beans, sugar, chili powder, tomato sauce and diced tomatoes with chile peppers. Let it simmer for half an hour before serving.

Nutrition Information

- Calories: 489 calories;
- Total Fat: 31.3
- Sodium: 1909
- Total Carbohydrate: 26.9
- Cholesterol: 96
- Protein: 25.6

865.   Quick Crescent Taco Pie

Serving: 6 | Prep: | Cook: |Ready in:

Ingredients

- 1 (1.25 ounce) package taco seasoning mix
- 1 pound lean ground beef
- 1/2 cup water
- 1/3 cup black olives, pitted and sliced
- 1 (8 ounce) package refrigerated crescent rolls
- 2 cups crushed tortilla chips
- 1 cup sour cream
- 1 cup shredded Cheddar cheese

Direction

- Brown ground chuck in a fry pan. Strain the oil. Mix in olives, water, and seasoning mix. Let simmer for 5 minutes.
- Divide crescent dough into 8 triangles. In a non-oiled 10-in. pie pan, put the triangles, pressing to make a crust. Sprinkle over the bottom of the crust with 1 cup corn chips. Spoon over the corn chips and crust with the meat mixture. Spread over the meat mixture with sour cream, and put on cheese to cover. Sprinkle over the top with the leftover corn chips.
- Bake at 375°F (190°C) until the crust turns golden brown, about 20-25 minutes.

Nutrition Information

- Calories: 521 calories;
- Sodium: 1013
- Total Carbohydrate: 26.7
- Cholesterol: 86
- Protein: 23.7
- Total Fat: 34.4

866. Quick And Easy Sicilian Meatloaf

Serving: 6 | Prep: 20mins | Cook: 1hours | Ready in:

Ingredients

- 1 1/2 pounds lean ground beef
- 1/2 cup dry bread crumbs
- 1 (1 ounce) package dry onion soup mix
- 1/4 cup barbecue sauce
- 1 clove garlic, minced
- 1 egg
- 1 tablespoon all-purpose flour
- ground black pepper to taste
- 8 thin slices deli ham, or as needed
- 1 cup shredded Swiss cheese, or as needed
- 1/4 cup ketchup

- 1 teaspoon mustard
- 1 tablespoon brown sugar
- 1 dash soy sauce

Direction

- Preheat oven to 175 degrees Celsius or 350 degrees Fahrenheit. Place a sheet of parchment paper that's 24 inches long on a work surface.
- Stir bread crumbs, ground beef, barbecue sauce, egg, flour, black pepper, garlic and onion soup mix until well combined in a bowl. Put the meat mixture on the parchment paper and pat and shape it to a rectangle that's about 10x16 inches. Place deli ham slices on the meat and keep a 1-inch margin of space on the rectangle on all sides. Sprinkle Swiss cheese on the ham. Gently lift up the short edge of the meat square using the parchment paper and carefully roll and nudge the meat. Seal the ends and edges well. Put the meat roll in a baking dish that's 9x13 inches.
- Bake for 45 minutes in the heated oven.
- While it's cooking, mix mustard, soy sauce, brown sugar, and ketchup together and mix it until the sugar dissolves. Take the roll out of the oven and place the ketchup mixture on the roll. Place it back in the oven for another 15 minutes.

Nutrition Information

- Calories: 427 calories;
- Total Fat: 22.4
- Sodium: 1064
- Total Carbohydrate: 20.9
- Cholesterol: 136
- Protein: 34.1

867. Quick And Spicy Chili

Serving: 16 | Prep: 20mins | Cook: 1hours | Ready in:

Ingredients

- 2 pounds lean ground beef
- 2 (15 ounce) cans kidney beans, drained and rinsed
- 1 (11 ounce) can whole kernel corn, drained
- 1 (15 ounce) can tomato sauce
- 1 (6 ounce) can tomato paste
- 2 cups water
- 2 jalapeno peppers
- 1 habanero pepper (optional)
- 1/2 red onion
- 2 large cloves garlic
- 3 tablespoons masa harina flour
- 1 tablespoon ground cayenne pepper
- 4 tablespoons chili powder
- 1 1/2 teaspoons salt
- 1 teaspoon ground black pepper
- 2 teaspoons white sugar (optional)

Direction

- At moderate heat, cook the beef in a skillet until equally browned everywhere then drain the grease off.
- Bring the combination of water, tomato paste, tomato sauce, corn and beans in a big pot to a boil. Adjust the heat to low. Insert garlic, onion, habanero and finely chopped jalapenos into a food processor. Stir this into the pot, followed by the cooked beef and masa flour. Add sugar, black pepper, salt, chilli powder and cayenne pepper to season it. Cook for 45 minutes to 60 minutes. During the process, stir from time to time.

Nutrition Information

- Calories: 201 calories;
- Sodium: 665
- Total Carbohydrate: 18.7
- Cholesterol: 37
- Protein: 15.5
- Total Fat: 7.9

868. Quinoa Chili

Serving: 8 | Prep: 30mins | Cook: 35mins | Ready in:

Ingredients

- 1 cup uncooked quinoa, rinsed
- 2 cups water
- 1 pound extra lean ground beef
- 1 tablespoon olive oil
- 1 onion, chopped
- 4 cloves garlic, minced
- 1 jalapeno pepper, seeded and minced
- 1 tablespoon chili powder
- 1 tablespoon ground cumin
- 1 (28 ounce) can crushed tomatoes
- 2 (19 ounce) cans black beans, rinsed and drained
- 1 green bell pepper, chopped
- 1 red bell pepper, chopped
- 1 zucchini, chopped (optional)
- 1 teaspoon dried oregano leaves
- 1 teaspoon dried parsley
- salt and ground black pepper to taste
- 1 cup frozen corn kernels, thawed
- 1/4 cup chopped fresh cilantro

Direction

- Add the quinoa and water in a saucepan and boil over high heat. Lower the heat to medium-low, cover, and simmer until the quinoa softens, and the water is absorbed about 15 to 20 minutes.
- Over medium-high heat, heat a large skillet and stir in the ground beef. Cook and stir until crumbly and evenly browned, and no longer pink. Drain and discard the excess grease; put the beef aside.
- In a large pot, heat the olive oil over medium heat. Blend in jalapeno pepper, garlic, and onion; cook and stir until the onion is tender and translucent about 5 minutes. Flavor with chili powder and cumin; cook for extra 1 minute to release the flavor of the spices. Mix in parsley, oregano, zucchini, red bell pepper, green bell pepper, black beans, and tomatoes.

Season with salt and black pepper. Simmer until the bell peppers are soft, about 20 minutes.

- When the red and green peppers are tender, mix in corn kernels, beef, and quinoa. Get back to a simmer, and cook in 5 minutes to reheat. Blend in the cilantro to serve.

Nutrition Information

- Calories: 412 calories;
- Total Carbohydrate: 52.8
- Cholesterol: 45
- Protein: 27.5
- Total Fat: 11.5
- Sodium: 705

869.   Ragu Bolognese

Serving: 6 | Prep: 10mins | Cook: 3hours | Ready in:

Ingredients

- 1/2 cup extra virgin olive oil
- 1/2 cup butter
- 1 cup minced onion
- 1/2 cup minced celery
- 1/4 cup minced carrot
- 1 pound ground veal
- 1 pound ground pork
- 1/2 pound ground beef
- 1/4 cup finely chopped pancetta bacon
- 1/2 cup milk
- 2 cups tomato sauce
- 2 cups beef broth

Direction

- On medium heat, heat butter and olive oil in big saucepan; sauté carrots, celery and onion till soft. Add pancetta, beef, pork and veal; cook for 15-20 minutes till evenly brown. Add milk; cook for 15 minutes till liquid

evaporates. Mix beef broth and tomato sauce in; cover. Simmer for 2 1/2 hours.

Nutrition Information

- Calories: 750 calories;
- Sodium: 991
- Total Carbohydrate: 8.8
- Cholesterol: 182
- Protein: 36.6
- Total Fat: 63

870.   Ranch Burger

Serving: 4 | Prep: | Cook: | Ready in:

Ingredients

- 1 pound ground beef (93% lean or leaner)
- 1/4 cup soft bread crumbs
- 1 egg white
- 1 teaspoon seasoned salt
- 1 medium red onion, cut crosswise into 1/2-inch thick slices
- 1 tablespoon vegetable oil, divided
- 4 whole-wheat buns, split and toasted
- Romaine lettuce
- Tomato slices
- 1/4 cup reduced-fat creamy ranch dressing

Direction

- In medium bowl, mix together seasoned salt, egg white, bread crumbs and Ground Beef, stirring lightly but well. Lightly form into 4 half-inch thick patties. Use a half tablespoon of oil to brush onion slices.
- On grid over medium, ash-covered coals, put onion slices and patties. With cover, grill patties for 8 to 10 minutes (on preheated gas grill, grill for 7 to 9 minutes over medium heat), till an instant-read thermometer inserted horizontally into the middle reads 160 °F, flipping from time to time. Grill the onions for

11 to 13 minutes till soft, brushing with leftover a half tablespoon of oil and flipping from time to time.

- Line lettuce on the bottom of every bun. Top lettuce with tomatoes and burgers. Spoon dressing on top of burgers; put onions atop. Close sandwiches.

Nutrition Information

- Calories: 732 calories;
- Protein: 38.1
- Total Fat: 26.8
- Sodium: 1275
- Total Carbohydrate: 86.9
- Cholesterol: 66

---

871.   Ranch Burgers

Serving: 8 | Prep: 15mins | Cook: 10mins |Ready in:

Ingredients

- 2 pounds lean ground beef
- 1 (1 ounce) package ranch dressing mix
- 1 egg, lightly beaten
- 3/4 cup crushed saltine crackers
- 1 onion, chopped

Direction

- Preheat a grill to high heat.
- Mix onion, crushed crackers, egg, ranch dressing mix and ground beef in bowl; shape to hamburger patties.
- Oil grill grate lightly; put patties on grill. Cook till well done, 5 minutes per side.

Nutrition Information

- Calories: 268 calories;
- Total Carbohydrate: 7.7
- Cholesterol: 98
- Protein: 23.1

- Total Fat: 15.2
- Sodium: 393

---

872.   Ranch Burgers From Hidden Valley®

Serving: 6 | Prep: 10mins | Cook: 15mins |Ready in:

Ingredients

- 1 (1 ounce) packet Hidden Valley® Original Ranch® Salad Dressing & Seasoning Mix
- 2 pounds lean ground beef
- 1 small yellow onion, peeled and minced
- 1 teaspoon freshly ground black pepper
- 1/2 cup seasoned dry bread crumbs (optional)
- 6 hamburger buns, lightly toasted
- 6 leaves butter lettuce, or more as needed
- 1 medium tomato, sliced

Direction

- Preheat the broiler or grill.
- Mix pepper, beef, onion, and seasoning mix together thoroughly in a big bowl. Mix in bread crumbs if desired.
- Form the mixture into six 1-in. patties using your wet hands. Grill burgers for 5-7mins on each side until the juices are clear and the internal temperature reaches 165°Fahrenheit.
- Serve burgers with tomato and lettuce on top.

Nutrition Information

- Calories: 469 calories;
- Sodium: 415
- Total Carbohydrate: 30.6
- Cholesterol: 91
- Protein: 31.7
- Total Fat: 23.5

873. Rancho Baked Beans

Serving: 10 | Prep: 15mins | Cook: 55mins | Ready in:

Ingredients

- cooking spray
- 1 pound ground beef
- 2 cups chopped onion
- 2 (16 ounce) cans pork and beans
- 1 (16 ounce) can kidney beans, drained
- 1 cup ketchup
- 3/4 cup brown sugar
- 2 tablespoons mustard
- 1 tablespoon white vinegar
- 1 teaspoon salt

Direction

- Preheat the oven to 350°F (175°C). Use cooking spray to spray casserole dish. Add onion and ground beef into a skillet. At moderate heat, start cooking and stirring for 10 to 15 minutes until the onions become semitransparent and the meat browns then drain it thoroughly.
- In a big bowl, combine salt, vinegar, mustard, brown sugar, ketchup, kidney beans, beans and pork. Add the hamburger mixture to the bean mixture, stirring to mix. Transfer the combined mixture to the prepped casserole dish and put it into the preheated oven. Bake for around 45 minutes until it starts to bubble.

Nutrition Information

- Calories: 298 calories;
- Sodium: 961
- Total Carbohydrate: 45.7
- Cholesterol: 34
- Protein: 15.7
- Total Fat: 7

874. Randy's Slow Cooker Ravioli Lasagna

Serving: 8 | Prep: 15mins | Cook: 4hours5mins | Ready in:

Ingredients

- 1 pound ground beef
- 1 tablespoon chopped garlic
- 1 teaspoon garlic powder
- 1 teaspoon salt
- 1/2 teaspoon ground black pepper
- 2 (24 ounce) jars prepared pasta sauce
- 1 teaspoon Italian seasoning
- 1 teaspoon dried basil
- 1 teaspoon dried oregano
- 1 (25 ounce) package frozen cheese ravioli
- 2 cups shredded mozzarella cheese

Direction

- Over medium-high heat, heat a big skillet. In the hot skillet cook and mix pepper, salt, garlic powder, garlic and beef till meat is crumbly and browned for 5 to 7 minutes. Drain and throw grease. Into ground beef mixture, mix oregano, basil, Italian seasoning and pasta sauce.
- Into the bottom of a slow cooker, ladle a generous layer of meat sauce; put 1 layer of ravioli. Ladle one more layer of meat sauce on top of ravioli layer; alternate with leftover ravioli and meat sauce till every ingredients are used.
- Allow to cook on Low for 3 to 5 hours. Scatter ravioli mixture with mozzarella cheese over and keep cooking till cheese is melted for 45 minutes to an hour longer.

Nutrition Information

- Calories: 544 calories;
- Total Fat: 23.6
- Sodium: 1334
- Total Carbohydrate: 52.9
- Cholesterol: 91

- Protein: 29.4

875. Rotini Pasta Bake

Serving: 8 | Prep: | Cook: | Ready in:

Ingredients

- 1 (16 ounce) package rotini pasta
- 1/2 pound lean ground beef
- 1 teaspoon diced onion
- 1 teaspoon salt
- 1/4 teaspoon ground black pepper
- 1 (28 ounce) jar spaghetti sauce
- 3 cups shredded mozzarella cheese

Direction

- In a big pot of boiling salted water, cook rotini pasta until al dente. Drain pasta.
- In a medium skillet, cook ground beef or turkey until brown. Put in pepper, salt and diced onion. Stir in 1/2 jar of spaghetti sauce.
- In a big bowl, put cooked beef mixture to the drained pasta; mix in the rest of spaghetti sauce. Transfer to a 2-quart baking dish. Use aluminum foil to cover.
- Bake in a prepped 230°C (425°F) oven for 20 minutes. Take off foil and scatter shredded mozzarella cheese over; continue baking for 5-10 minutes. Serve while still warm.

Nutrition Information

- Calories: 487 calories;
- Total Fat: 19.2
- Sodium: 978
- Total Carbohydrate: 55.2
- Cholesterol: 56
- Protein: 23.5

876. Ruby Drive Sloppy Joes

Serving: 6 | Prep: 5mins | Cook: 30mins | Ready in:

Ingredients

- 1 pound ground beef
- 1 1/2 cups ketchup
- 1 cup chunky salsa
- 2 tablespoons brown sugar
- 1 tablespoon Worcestershire sauce
- 2 tablespoons white vinegar
- 2 tablespoons Dijon mustard
- 1 teaspoon hot sauce
- 6 potato rolls

Direction

- Place a big frying pan on medium-high heat and mix in ground beef. Stir and cook until the beef is not pink anymore, evenly brown, and crumbly. Strain and dispose any excess fat.
- Mix in hot sauce, Dijon mustard, white vinegar, Worcestershire sauce, brown sugar, salsa, and ketchup. Simmer and cook over low heat, whisking sometimes, about 20-30 minutes. Enjoy on potato rolls.

Nutrition Information

- Calories: 382 calories;
- Total Fat: 15.2
- Sodium: 1338
- Total Carbohydrate: 46.2
- Cholesterol: 46
- Protein: 17.4

877. Runza Burgers

Serving: 10 | Prep: 10mins | Cook: 30mins | Ready in:

Ingredients

- 1 1/2 pounds lean ground beef
- 3 cloves garlic, minced

- 1 onion, chopped
- 1 small head cabbage, shredded
- 1 (14 ounce) can beef broth
- 2 tablespoons Worcestershire sauce
- 2 tablespoons yellow mustard
- salt and pepper to taste
- 10 hamburger buns, split

Direction

- In a big skillet, brown ground beef on high heat, then drain fat. Stir in cabbage, onion and garlic, then cook until vegetables are soft and wilted. Stir in mustard, Worcestershire sauce and beef broth. Cook on medium heat without a cover until it is reduced to the consistency of a sloppy joe. Use pepper and salt to season.
- Put on top of meat mixture with hamburger buns, then cover the skillet and steam for a minute. To serve, fill beef and cabbage mixture into steamed buns.

Nutrition Information

- Calories: 284 calories;
- Total Fat: 10.8
- Sodium: 493
- Total Carbohydrate: 27.9
- Cholesterol: 45
- Protein: 18.3

---

878.   Runza Burritos International

Serving: 8 | Prep: 20mins | Cook: 25mins | Ready in:

Ingredients

- 1 1/2 pounds ground round
- 1/2 medium head cabbage, chopped
- 1 1/2 onion, chopped
- 1 tablespoon minced garlic
- 1 teaspoon crushed red pepper flakes
- 1 teaspoon ground black pepper

- 1 cup water
- 8 (10 inch) flour tortillas
- 2 cups shredded Cheddar cheese

Direction

- Over medium high heat, stir in the ground beef in a heated big skillet. Cook while stirring until the beef is not pink anymore, browned evenly and crumbly. Drain out and remove extra fat. Mix in the water, black pepper, red pepper flakes, garlic, onion, and cabbage. Cook while stirring for 10 minutes until the water has cooked away and the veggies become tender. Over medium heat, warm the tortillas one at a time in a big skillet until they become bendable.
- On a work surface, put in tortilla and spread the filling halfway between the base edge and the middle. Using the back of a spoon, flat the filling into a rectangle. Drizzle quarter cup of Cheddar cheese on top of the filling. Gently fold the base on to the filling and then fold in opposite sides of the tortilla. Roll the burrito up towards the top edge. This will make a tight cylinder. Repeat process with the rest of the ingredients.

Nutrition Information

- Calories: 448 calories;
- Sodium: 647
- Total Carbohydrate: 44.3
- Cholesterol: 58
- Protein: 24
- Total Fat: 19.3

---

879.   Runzas

Serving: 16 | Prep: 45mins | Cook: 45mins | Ready in:

Ingredients

- 4 cups ground beef
- 1 onion, chopped

- 4 cups shredded cabbage
- 1 teaspoon salt, or to taste
- 2 cups warm water (100 to 110 degrees F/40 to 45 degrees C)
- 1/3 cup butter, melted
- 2/3 cup instant dry milk powder
- 1/4 cup white sugar
- 1 1/2 teaspoons salt
- 1 teaspoon active dry yeast
- 1 egg, beaten
- 4 cups all-purpose flour

Direction

- Place a large skillet over medium-high heat. Stir and cook onion and ground beef in the hot skillet until the meat crumbles, is not pink anymore, and browned evenly. Drain excess grease out of the skillet. Stir cabbage in and add 1 teaspoon of salt to season. Stir and cook for another 20 minutes, or until the cabbage is tender. Set aside and allow the mixture to cool.
- In a large bowl, mix butter with warm water. In a separate bowl, combine yeast, 1 1/2 teaspoons of salt, sugar, and dry milk powder, then stir into the bowl with the butter mixture. Add egg. Stir in 1/2 cup of flour at a time, gradually, until the dough smoothens.
- Lightly dust a work surface with flour and roll out the dough to 1/4-inch thick. Cut 4-inch squares out of the dough. Fill each square with the beef mixture. Pinch the dough's corners together at the top to seal. Transfer, seam side down, to a baking sheet. Repeat process with the rest of the dough and filling. Use a damp cloth to cover the rolls and wait for 20 minutes, or until the dough has risen.
- Preheat oven to 190°C/375°F.
- Bake for 20 minutes, or until golden brown.

Nutrition Information

- Calories: 243 calories;
- Cholesterol: 41
- Protein: 10.9
- Total Fat: 8
- Sodium: 444

- Total Carbohydrate: 31.3

880. Salisbury Steak Slow Cooker Style

Serving: 10 | Prep: 20mins | Cook: 3hours45mins | Ready in:

Ingredients

- 2 1/2 pounds extra lean ground beef
- 3/4 cup finely chopped onion
- 3/4 cup finely chopped celery
- 1/2 cup milk
- 1/2 cup finely chopped mushrooms
- 1/2 cup Italian-seasoned panko (Japanese bread crumbs)
- 2 tablespoons all-purpose flour
- 2 tablespoons whole wheat flour
- 3 tablespoons vegetable oil, divided
- 1 (4 ounce) package sliced fresh mushrooms
- 1/2 onion, thinly sliced
- 2 (10.75 ounce) cans reduced-fat, reduced-sodium cream of mushroom soup (such as Campbell's® Healthy Request)
- 3/4 cup low-sodium beef broth
- 2 tablespoons low-sodium Worcestershire sauce
- 1 (1 ounce) packet dry onion gravy mix
- 1 teaspoon ground black pepper

Direction

- In a big bowl, mix together panko, chopped mushrooms, milk, celery, chopped onion and ground beef. Form mixture into 10 patties.
- In a wide and shallow bowl, mix whole wheat flour and all-purpose flour. Put patties in the flour mixture and coat. Transfer coated patties on a platter but do not stack them.
- Use a big skillet to heat 2 tablespoons of oil on medium high heat. Put in patties and cook for 3-5 minutes per side until browned. Transfer browned patties in a slow cooker crock.

- In a small skillet, heat the remaining oil on medium heat and cook while stirring sliced mushrooms and sliced onion for about 5 minutes until they are tender.
- In a bowl, mix together cream of mushroom soup with cooked mushroom and onion mixture, black pepper, onion gravy mix, Worcestershire sauce and beef broth until smooth. Pour the mixture on top of beef patties in the slow cooker.
- Let it cook for 3-3 1/2 hours on High until patties are very firm, hot and grey in the middle. You may also cook for 4-5 hours on Low. An instant-read thermometer should read 160°F or 70°C when inserted in the middle.

Nutrition Information

- Calories: 369 calories;
- Sodium: 472
- Total Carbohydrate: 16.7
- Cholesterol: 93
- Protein: 29.7
- Total Fat: 20.2

---

881. Salisbury Steak With Mushrooms

Serving: 4 | Prep: 15mins | Cook: 25mins | Ready in:

Ingredients

- 1 pound lean ground beef
- 1/3 cup dry bread crumbs
- 1/4 cup chopped onions
- 1 egg, beaten
- 1 teaspoon salt
- 1/4 teaspoon ground black pepper
- 2 cups beef broth
- 1 large onion, thinly sliced
- 1 cup sliced mushrooms
- 3 tablespoons cornstarch
- 3 tablespoons water

Direction

- In a bowl, mix black pepper, salt, egg, chopped onion, breadcrumbs and ground beef together until evenly combined. Form the beef mixture into 4 patties about 3/4-inch thick.
- In a big skillet over medium heat, fry the patties for about 10 minutes until both sides are browned. Mix in the mushrooms, onion and beef broth and bring it to a boil. Adjust the heat to low and cover it up. Let it simmer for about 10 minutes more until there is no hint of pink in the center of the patties. Move the patties onto a platter and keep warm.
- Bring the onion mixture to a boil. In a small bowl, stir water and cornstarch together then mix it into the onion mixture. Cook and stir for about 1 minute until the onion gravy thickens. Pour the gravy over the patties. Serve.

Nutrition Information

- Calories: 323 calories;
- Protein: 26.6
- Total Fat: 15.8
- Sodium: 1129
- Total Carbohydrate: 17.2
- Cholesterol: 115

---

882. San Antonio Salad

Serving: 6 | Prep: 15mins | Cook: 10mins | Ready in:

Ingredients

- 1 pound lean ground beef
- 2 tablespoons chili powder
- 1/2 teaspoon ground cumin
- salt and pepper to taste
- 1 head iceberg lettuce, shredded
- 1 (15.5 ounce) can pinto beans
- 2 tomatoes, cubed
- 1 cup shredded Cheddar cheese
- 1/4 cup chopped fresh cilantro

- 1 (12 ounce) package corn tortilla chips, broken
- 1 jalapeno pepper, seeded and chopped (optional)
- 1/2 cup chopped green onion (optional)
- 1 cup salsa (optional)

Direction

- Cook ground beef in a large skillet over medium-high heat until browned. Season the beef with cumin, pepper, salt, and chili powder. Once the beef is cooked through, remove the mixture from the heat.
- Combine pinto beans with its juice, Cheddar cheese, lettuce, tomato, and cilantro in a large salad bowl. Stir in corn chips and ground beef. If desired, you can toss in salsa, jalapeno, and green onion.

Nutrition Information

- Calories: 674 calories;
- Total Carbohydrate: 57.5
- Cholesterol: 81
- Protein: 29.5
- Total Fat: 37.7
- Sodium: 1043

883.   Sandy's Summer Sausage

Serving: 16 | Prep: 15mins | Cook: 2hours | Ready in:

Ingredients

- 2 pounds ground beef
- 2 tablespoons mustard seed
- 1 tablespoon garlic powder
- 2 tablespoons liquid smoke flavoring
- 2 tablespoons sugar-based curing mixture (such as Morton® Tender Quick®)
- 1 teaspoon coarse ground black pepper

Direction

- Mix together the ground beef, garlic powder, mustard seeds, curing salt, liquid smoke, and pepper in a large bowl. Mix well using your hands. Form mixture into two even logs, wrap each in aluminum foil, shiny side facing the meat. Chill for 24 hours.
- Preheat the oven to 165 degrees C (325 degrees F). Poke small holes in the aluminum foil on the bottom of the meat rolls using a toothpick.
- Fill the broiler pan with 1/2 inch of water and place the meat rolls on a broiler rack
- Bake in a 325° F preheated oven for 90 minutes. Let it cool for a bit then chill for 12 hours before unwrapping then serve.

Nutrition Information

- Calories: 136 calories;
- Sodium: 896
- Total Carbohydrate: 1
- Cholesterol: 34
- Protein: 9.5
- Total Fat: 10.3

884.   Savory Feta Pies

Serving: 4 | Prep: 25mins | Cook: 25mins | Ready in:

Ingredients

- 1 tablespoon olive oil
- 1 small onion, sliced
- 1 pound lean ground beef
- 1 small tomato, diced
- 1 teaspoon garlic powder
- 1/2 teaspoon ground coriander
- 1 teaspoon dried oregano
- 1/4 teaspoon cayenne pepper
- salt and pepper to taste
- 1 egg, beaten
- 1 cup feta cheese
- 2 (9 inch) frozen pie crusts, thawed

Direction

- In a big skillet, heat the oil on moderately high heat. Sauté onion for 2 minutes, till tender. Put in the beef and slightly brown; let extra fat drain. Mix in pepper, salt, cayenne pepper, oregano, coriander, garlic powder and tomato and cook for 10 to 15 minutes, till meat is equally browned. Take off from heat and reserve.
- Preheat the oven to 200 ° C or 400 ° F.
- Take a pie crust off pan and unroll on a slightly floured area. Slice pastry making 4 6-inch rounds; on lined cookie sheet, put rounds and slightly brush with the egg beat. Onto every round, put quarter cup feta cheese and put some mixture of beef on top, leaving sufficient room to enclose the dough 'pockets'.
- Take another pie crust off pan and unroll on a slightly floured area. Slice pastry making 4 6-inch rounds, as the initial pie crust. Brush egg beat on one side of every round and put over of prepped pie rounds, egg-side facing down. Press crusts together around edges to enclose. Fill any tears or holes in pie 'pockets' with dough scraps. Brush egg beat on tops and create one small slash in top of every pie to vent the steam.
- In the prepped oven, bake till golden brown and cooked completely, for 15 to 25 minutes.

Nutrition Information

- Calories: 998 calories;
- Sodium: 1371
- Total Carbohydrate: 49.1
- Cholesterol: 188
- Protein: 37
- Total Fat: 72.1

---

885.   Savory Hamburger Supper

Serving: 6 | Prep: 10mins | Cook: 20mins | Ready in:

Ingredients

- 1 pound ground beef
- 1/4 cup chopped onion
- 2 teaspoons chili powder
- 2 1/4 cups hot water
- 17 ounces whole kernel corn
- 1 (14.5 ounce) can diced tomatoes
- 1 (7.25 ounce) package macaroni and cheese mix

Direction

- Heat a saucepan of 3-quart over medium-high heat. In the hot skillet, cook and stir onion and beef for around 5 to 7 minutes till crumbly and brown; drain and eliminate grease.
- Return pan to heat and add chili powder to season ground beef mixture. In the saucepan, pour water and let come to a boil. Stir macaroni, tomatoes, and corn into the mixture; simmer and cook for nearly 10 minutes till the macaroni is tender.
- Sprinkle over the mixture with contents of cheese packet from macaroni and cheese package; stir.

Nutrition Information

- Calories: 350 calories;
- Sodium: 445
- Total Carbohydrate: 41.4
- Cholesterol: 52
- Protein: 21.5
- Total Fat: 11.5

---

886.   Seahawk Burger

Serving: 4 | Prep: 15mins | Cook: 25mins | Ready in:

Ingredients

- 1 teaspoon vegetable oil
- 1 sweet onion (such as Walla Walla), sliced
- 8 ounces mushrooms, sliced

- salt and ground black pepper to taste
- 1/2 cup Washington state red wine (such as a Merlot or Syrah)
- 4 (6 ounce) grass-fed ground beef patties
- Seattle Aioli:
- 1/2 cup mayonnaise
- 1/2 teaspoon Sriracha sauce
- 1/2 shot brewed espresso (such as Starbucks®)
- 4 whole grain or artisan hamburger buns (such as Macrina Bakery®)
- 4 slices Monterey Jack cheese (such as Beecher's® Just Jack®)
- 1 cup farmer's market arugula, or more to taste

Direction

- Over medium-high temperature, heat oil in a big skillet. Sauté mushrooms and onion in hot oil for 5 minutes or until onion starts to soften. Season vegetable mixture with pepper and salt. Sauté until onions and mushrooms turn brown, 5 more minutes.
- Add the red wine to the pan and heat to a boil. With a wooden spoon, scrape the browned bits of food from the bottom of pan. Stir and cook 2 minutes until wine is evaporated. Take off heat.
- Set an outdoor grill on medium-high temperature and lightly grease grate.
- Cook burgers until they are hot in the center, firm, and just starting to turn from pink to gray (for medium well, it takes 8-10 minutes). A thermometer inserted in the middle should say 150 deg F or 65 deg C.
- In a bowl, mix Sriracha sauce, espresso, and mayonnaise together until aioli becomes smooth.
- On each hamburger bun, spread aioli. Put a beef patty on the bottom bun, garnish with a slice of Monterey Jack cheese, 1/4 cup arugula, 1/4 the onion-mushroom mixture, and put top bun on. Repeat procedure with the rest of the burgers.

Nutrition Information

- Calories: 833 calories;
- Sodium: 654
- Total Carbohydrate: 29.4
- Cholesterol: 134
- Protein: 40.5
- Total Fat: 58.9

887. Serbian Cevapcici

Serving: 4 | Prep: 10mins | Cook: 30mins | Ready in:

Ingredients

- 1 1/2 pounds ground pork
- 1 pound lean ground beef
- 1/2 pound ground lamb
- 1 egg white
- 4 cloves garlic, minced
- 1 teaspoon salt
- 1 teaspoon baking soda
- 2 teaspoons ground black pepper
- 1 teaspoon cayenne pepper
- 1/2 teaspoon paprika

Direction

- Prepare the grill by preheating at medium-low heat.
- Mix the ground beef, egg white, ground pork, and the ground lamb in a big bowl. Toss in salt, baking soda, cayenne pepper, paprika, garlic, and black pepper. Use your hands to blend mixture well. Mold mixture into a sausage shapes the length of a finger and 3/4 inch thick.
- On grilling surface, lightly oil. For 30 minutes, grill sausages while flipping as necessary until cooked completely.

Nutrition Information

- Calories: 690 calories;
- Total Fat: 46.1
- Sodium: 1097

- Total Carbohydrate: 2.1
- Cholesterol: 223
- Protein: 62.8

888. Serbian Ground Beef, Veggie, And Potato Bake

Serving: 4 | Prep: 25mins | Cook: 1hours | Ready in:

Ingredients

- 1 pound ground beef
- 1 tablespoon olive oil
- 1 green bell pepper, chopped
- 1 onion, chopped
- 1 carrot, shredded
- 2 celery stalks, chopped
- 1/2 tablespoon paprika
- 1/2 teaspoon salt
- 3/4 teaspoon black pepper
- 1/4 teaspoon crushed red pepper
- 1 pinch ground cinnamon
- 1 pinch ground cloves
- 1/4 cup water
- 1/8 cup red wine
- 1 cube beef bouillon
- 2 tablespoons half-and-half
- 2 potatoes, peeled and sliced

Direction

- Set the oven to 400°F or 200°C for preheating. Grease a casserole dish lightly.
- Cook the beef in a skillet that is set over medium heat until browned evenly. Remove the beef from the skillet and reserve its juices. Put the beef aside. Stir in olive oil. Sauté the carrot, celery, green pepper, and onion until tender.
- Place the beef back into the skillet. Season it with black pepper, cinnamon, cloves, paprika, red pepper, and salt. Pour in red wine and water and stir until heated through. Add the beef bouillon and dissolve it into the mixture.

Take the skillet away from the heat. Stir in half-and-half.

- Layer the bottom of the prepared casserole dish with enough slices of potato. Top the potatoes with the beef and vegetable mixture. Place the remaining potatoes on top of the mixture.
- Place it inside the preheated oven and cook it while covered for 45 minutes until the potatoes are tender.

Nutrition Information

- Calories: 367 calories;
- Sodium: 567
- Total Carbohydrate: 27.2
- Cholesterol: 72
- Protein: 22.7
- Total Fat: 18.1

889. Shay's Irish Chili

Serving: 6 | Prep: 15mins | Cook: 1hours10mins | Ready in:

Ingredients

- 2 tablespoons vegetable oil
- 1 pound ground beef chuck
- 1 clove garlic, minced
- 1 large onion, chopped
- salt and pepper to taste
- 1 pinch ground nutmeg
- 2 teaspoons beef bouillon
- 1 tablespoon chili powder
- 1 tablespoon white sugar
- 1 (28 ounce) can diced tomatoes
- 1/2 (19 ounce) can light red kidney beans, drained and mashed
- 1 (15.5 ounce) can dark red kidney beans, drained and rinsed
- 1 (15 ounce) can sliced potatoes, drained

Direction

- In a soup pot, heat the oil on medium heat. Add onion, garlic, and ground beef. Cook and stir to break the ground beef into crumbles until the beef is not pink anymore. Drain all the excess grease. Flavor with chili powder, beef bouillon, nutmeg, pepper, and salt. Add potatoes, dark and light kidney beans, tomatoes, and sugar. Put a cover on and let simmer, stirring from time to time, for an hour on medium-low heat.

Nutrition Information

- Calories: 388 calories;
- Sodium: 703
- Total Carbohydrate: 28.8
- Cholesterol: 55
- Protein: 21
- Total Fat: 20.6

---

890. Shepherd's Pie

Serving: 8 | Prep: 25mins | Cook: 45mins | Ready in:

Ingredients

- 5 potatoes, peeled and quartered
- 1 pound lean ground beef
- 1 (4 ounce) can sliced mushrooms
- 1 (15 ounce) can mixed vegetables
- 1 (10.75 ounce) can condensed cream of mushroom soup
- 1 (10.75 ounce) can condensed cream of celery soup
- salt and pepper to taste
- 3 tablespoons butter

Direction

- Start preheating oven to 350 degrees F or 175 degrees C. Grease a 9x13 pan.
- Boil a big saucepan of salted water. Add potatoes to the boiling water and cook for 15 minutes or until tender. Drain liquid, reserve

the liquid. Use some of the cooking liquid to mash potatoes. Set them aside.
- Cook beef until brown in a big frying pan on medium-high heat. Drain the grease. Stir in pepper, mixed veggies, celery soup, mushrooms, salt, and mushroom soup; cook through. Dump into the greased pan, put mashed potatoes on top, and put little chunks of butter on.
- Put in preheated oven and bake until meat and vegetable mixture are bubbling and hot and potatoes are golden, 30 minutes.

Nutrition Information

- Calories: 336 calories;
- Total Fat: 16.3
- Sodium: 1064
- Total Carbohydrate: 33.7
- Cholesterol: 50
- Protein: 14.1

---

891. Shepherd's Pie V

Serving: 12 | Prep: 1hours | Cook: 20mins | Ready in:

Ingredients

- 7 potatoes, peeled and cubed
- 1 pound ground round
- 1 cup water
- 2 cubes beef bouillon
- 1 cube chicken bouillon
- 1 teaspoon dried rosemary
- 1/2 teaspoon salt
- 1 teaspoon ground black pepper
- 1 teaspoon steak seasoning
- 1 tablespoon dried minced onion flakes
- 1 1/2 cups frozen mixed vegetables

Direction

- Bring salted water in a big pot to a boil. Put in

potatoes and cook for 15 minutes, until soft. Drain potatoes, then cool and mash them.

- Set the oven to 175°C or 350°F to preheat. Coat a 2-qt. casserole dish lightly with grease.
- Sauté meat in a big heavy skillet until all sides are browned, while stirring sometimes. Drain excess fat and turn the meat back to pan on moderate heat. Add in water and use onion flakes, steak seasoning, pepper, salt, rosemary, and chicken bouillon to season beef. Stir in frozen vegetables and cook until water has mostly evaporated while stirring sometimes.
- Add to a 2-qt. casserole dish with the meat mixture. Use mashed potatoes to cover the top. In the preheated oven, bake until top starts to brown, about 20-30 minutes.

Nutrition Information

- Calories: 189 calories;
- Protein: 11.1
- Total Fat: 5.1
- Sodium: 417
- Total Carbohydrate: 25.1
- Cholesterol: 24

892.   Shepherd's Pie VI

Serving: 6 | Prep: 30mins | Cook: 20mins | Ready in:

Ingredients

- 4 large potatoes, peeled and cubed
- 1 tablespoon butter
- 1 tablespoon finely chopped onion
- 1/4 cup shredded Cheddar cheese
- salt and pepper to taste
- 5 carrots, chopped
- 1 tablespoon vegetable oil
- 1 onion, chopped
- 1 pound lean ground beef
- 2 tablespoons all-purpose flour
- 1 tablespoon ketchup
- 3/4 cup beef broth

- 1/4 cup shredded Cheddar cheese

Direction

- In a large pot, boil salted water. Put in the potatoes, cook for 15 minutes until they are tender but still firm. Drain them then mash. Stir in a quarter cup of shredded cheese, finely chopped onion and butter. Add pepper and salt to taste; put aside.
- In a large pot, boil the salted water. Put in the carrots, cook for 15 minutes until they are tender but still firm. Drain them then mash. Put aside. Start preheating the oven to 375°F (190°C.)
- In a large frying pan, heat oil. Put in onion, cook until it becomes clear. Put in the ground beef; cook until well browned. Pour off the excess fat, mix in the flour and cook for one minute. Put in beef broth and ketchup. Bring to a boil, lower the heat and simmer for 5 minutes.
- Spread on bottom of the 2 quart casserole dish with ground beef in an even layer. Then, spread mashed carrots in a layer. Add mashed potato mixture on top and scatter with the remaining shredded cheese.
- Bake in prepared oven until it turns golden brown, or about 20 minutes.

Nutrition Information

- Calories: 452 calories;
- Sodium: 295
- Total Carbohydrate: 52.5
- Cholesterol: 65
- Protein: 23.1
- Total Fat: 17

893.   Shipwreck Dinner

Serving: 4 | Prep: 10mins | Cook: 20mins | Ready in:

Ingredients

- 1 pound lean ground beef
- 1 (7.25 ounce) package macaroni and cheese mix
- 1 (14.5 ounce) can diced tomatoes
- 1 cup milk
- 1 cup frozen peas
- 1 cup frozen corn
- 1 teaspoon seasoned salt (such as LAWRY'S®), or to taste
- 1 cup shredded Cheddar cheese, divided

Direction

- Preheat a large skillet on medium-high. Stir and cook beef in the hot skillet for 5-7 minutes until crumbly and browned.
- Add cheese and pasta mixture from the macaroni and cheese box into the beef. Add corn, peas, milk and tomatoes to the beef mixture; mix. Let the mixture boil, minimize heat to medium-low, cover the skillet and cook at a simmer for about 12 minutes until the noodles are tender.
- Add seasoned salt to taste. Add about half of the cheddar cheese into the dish to melt. Put remaining cheese on top.

Nutrition Information

- Calories: 636 calories;
- Cholesterol: 116
- Protein: 42.9
- Total Fat: 26.7
- Sodium: 1108
- Total Carbohydrate: 55

894.   Shipwreck Stew

Serving: 10 | Prep: 20mins | Cook: 5hours | Ready in:

Ingredients

- 2 pounds ground beef
- 2 (10.75 ounce) cans condensed tomato soup

- 2 medium onions, chopped
- 5 large potatoes, cubed
- 2 (15.25 ounce) cans kidney beans, undrained

Direction

- Break up the ground beef into the big skillet on medium high heat. Cook and stir till browned. Drain off the grease and move the beef into the slow cooker. Stir in beans, potatoes, onions and the tomato soups (which are undiluted).
- Keep it covered and cooked on Low setting for 4 - 5 hours or till stew thickens and potatoes become soft.

Nutrition Information

- Calories: 425 calories;
- Total Fat: 12.1
- Sodium: 586
- Total Carbohydrate: 55.3
- Cholesterol: 55
- Protein: 24.8

895.   Sicilian Meat Roll

Serving: 8 | Prep: 20mins | Cook: 1hours15mins | Ready in:

Ingredients

- 2 eggs, beaten
- 1/2 cup tomato juice
- 3/4 cup soft bread crumbs
- 2 tablespoons snipped fresh parsley
- 1/2 teaspoon dried oregano, crushed
- 1/4 teaspoon sea salt
- 1/4 teaspoon ground black pepper
- 1 clove garlic, minced
- 2 pounds lean ground beef
- 1 (6 ounce) package thinly sliced ham
- 1 (6 ounce) package sliced mozzarella cheese

Direction

- Combine tomato juice and eggs in a large bowl. Stir in the ground beef, garlic, salt, pepper, oregano, parsley and breadcrumbs. Mix well. Set oven to 350° F (175° C) to preheat.
- Pat and form the meat into a 10x8 inch rectangle on a sheet of waxed paper or foil. Top the meat with ham slices, keeping a small space around edges. Rip the cheese slices, keeping 1 whole slice, and drizzle over the ham.
- Beginning at the short end, roll up the meat carefully, using the waxed paper or foil to lift. Seal the ends and edges of the meat. Put roll in a 9x13 inch baking dish with seam side down.
- Bake for about 75 minutes in a prepared oven. Slice the remaining slice of cheese into 4 triangles. Cover the top of the loaf with overlapped triangles. Bake for 2 minutes more, until cheese is melted.

Nutrition Information

- Calories: 449 calories;
- Total Fat: 30.4
- Sodium: 670
- Total Carbohydrate: 9.7
- Cholesterol: 157
- Protein: 31.8

896.   Silver Dollars

Serving: 4 | Prep: 15mins | Cook: 45mins | Ready in:

Ingredients

- 8 leaves cabbage
- 1 pound lean ground beef
- 1 onion, sliced into rings
- 2 carrots, chopped
- 1 potato, peeled and diced
- 1 to taste salt and pepper

Direction

- Set an outdoor grill to medium-high heat and start preheating.
- On a piece of tin foil, arrange a leaf of cabbage. Shape the ground beef into 4 equal patties and arrange a patty onto the leaf of cabbage. Arrange potato, carrot, and onion on top and flavor to taste with pepper and salt. Arrange over the potatoes with a second cabbage leaf. Place another sheet of foil on top and seal all edges. Repeat using the 3 remaining patties.
- Grill on medium-high heat until reaching the desired doneness, or for 25-35 minutes.

Nutrition Information

- Calories: 374 calories;
- Sodium: 250
- Total Carbohydrate: 16.6
- Cholesterol: 85
- Protein: 22.4
- Total Fat: 23.7

897.   Simple Beef Stroganoff

Serving: 4 | Prep: 20mins | Cook: 10mins | Ready in:

Ingredients

- 1 (8 ounce) package egg noodles
- 1 pound ground beef
- 1 (10.75 ounce) can fat free condensed cream of mushroom soup
- 1 tablespoon garlic powder
- 1/2 cup sour cream
- salt and pepper to taste

Direction

- Following the package instructions, prep the egg noodles and set it aside.
- Sauté the ground beef in a different big skillet over medium heat until browned, or about 5-10 minutes. Get rid of the fat then mix in the

garlic powder and soup. Let it simmer for 10 minutes, stirring every now and then.

- Move it away from the heat. Stir the egg noodles together with the meat mixture and add sour cream. Stir well and sprinkle with salt and pepper to taste.

Nutrition Information

- Calories: 679 calories;
- Total Carbohydrate: 48.2
- Cholesterol: 159
- Protein: 28.7
- Total Fat: 40.5
- Sodium: 660

898. Simple Hamburger Stroganoff

Serving: 6 | Prep: 20mins | Cook: 10mins | Ready in:

Ingredients

- 1 (16 ounce) package egg noodles
- 1 pound lean ground beef
- 1 (.75 ounce) packet dry brown gravy mix
- 1 (8 ounce) package cream cheese
- 1 (6 ounce) can chopped mushrooms, with liquid
- 1/2 cup milk
- 1 (8 ounce) container sour cream
- 2 (10.75 ounce) cans condensed cream of mushroom soup

Direction

- Boil a big pot of lightly salted water. Mix in the egg noodles. Cook until al dente, or for 8-10 minutes. Drain.
- In a skillet over medium heat, cook the ground beef for about 5 minutes until browned with no hint of pink left. Drain the fat. Stir in the mushrooms with hamburger, brown gravy and cream cheese until the cream cheese melts.

Combine mushroom soup, sour cream and milk into the cooked pasta. Combine hamburger mixture with pasta.

Nutrition Information

- Calories: 735 calories;
- Total Fat: 42
- Sodium: 1134
- Total Carbohydrate: 60.9
- Cholesterol: 159
- Protein: 28.9

899. Simply Traditional Lasagna

Serving: 8 | Prep: 20mins | Cook: 40mins | Ready in:

Ingredients

- 1 pound ground beef
- 1 pound bulk Italian sausage
- 1/2 cup warm water
- 1 cup sliced black olives
- 1 pinch basil
- 2 teaspoons garlic powder
- 1 tablespoon dried oregano
- 1 1/2 teaspoons dried sage
- 2 teaspoons ground black pepper
- 2 tablespoons minced garlic
- 1 tablespoon dried onion flakes
- 2 (14 ounce) jars marinara sauce
- 1 (16 ounce) package lasagna noodles
- 8 ounces ricotta cheese
- 1 pound mozzarella cheese, shredded

Direction

- In a large pan, cook over medium-high heat the ground beef and Italian sausage until they turn brown. Drain the fats and mix in the minced garlic, sage, water, black olives, garlic powder, basil, onion flakes, pepper and oregano for the seasoning. Let it simmer while you constantly stir it for 15 minutes. Mix in the marinara sauce before taking it out from the heat.

- Set your oven to 375°F (190°C) for preheating.
- On a 9x13-inch baking pan, layer the meat and sauce and cover it with dry noodles. Put on top a thin layer of ricotta cheese and drizzle some mozzarella cheese. Spread another layer of sauce and continue making a layer with the same steps and ingredients. It should end with a meat and sauce on its top. Save half cup of mozzarella cheese and set aside.
- Bake it inside the preheated oven for 45 minutes. Be sure to check it after 30 minutes of baking in the oven to observe the thickness of the lasagna. It is done when a knife can be easily inserted into it. Use the reserved half cup of mozzarella cheese to drizzle on its top and then put it back in the oven for another 10 minutes until the cheese completely melted.

Nutrition Information

- Calories: 736 calories;
- Sodium: 1452
- Total Carbohydrate: 62.5
- Cholesterol: 104
- Protein: 43.8
- Total Fat: 34.6

900.   Skillet Burrito Bowl

Serving: 4 | Prep: 10mins | Cook: 5mins |Ready in:

Ingredients

- 1 tablespoon vegetable oil
- 1 pound ground beef
- 1 tablespoon fajita seasoning
- 1 (15 ounce) can pinto beans, drained and rinsed
- 1 (8 ounce) jar salsa
- 1 cup cooked brown rice
- 1/2 cup shredded Mexican cheese blend

Direction

- In a big skillet, heat oil over medium-high heat. In hot skillet, cook and mix beef for 5 to 10 minutes till crumbly and browned; let drain and throw the grease. Into the ground beef, mix fajita seasoning till equally coated.
- Into the ground beef mixture, put brown rice, salsa and pinto beans; place Mexican cheese blend on top.

Nutrition Information

- Calories: 472 calories;
- Total Fat: 27.5
- Sodium: 856
- Total Carbohydrate: 28
- Cholesterol: 86
- Protein: 28.1

901.   Skillet Chili

Serving: 6 | Prep: 5mins | Cook: 1hours10mins |Ready in:

Ingredients

- 1 1/2 pounds lean ground beef
- 1 onion, finely diced
- 1/4 cup chopped green bell pepper
- 1 (15 ounce) can tomato sauce
- 6 ounces tomato paste
- 1 (16 ounce) can chili beans, drained
- 1 tablespoon chili powder
- 1 teaspoon hot pepper sauce
- 1/2 teaspoon seasoning salt
- 1/2 teaspoon ground cayenne pepper
- 1/4 teaspoon garlic powder

Direction

- In a deep and big skillet, put ground beef. Cook until evenly brown over medium-high heat. Drain unwanted fat then crumble. Mix in chili beans, tomato paste, tomato sauce, green pepper, and onion. Put in garlic powder, cayenne pepper, seasoning salt, hot sauce, and chili powder to season.

- Cook over low heat, mixing from time to time, until wanted consistency (cook for minimum of 1 hour for best flavor).

Nutrition Information

- Calories: 417 calories;
- Sodium: 1098
- Total Carbohydrate: 25.4
- Cholesterol: 85
- Protein: 26.7
- Total Fat: 24.6

902.   Slider Style Mini Burgers

Serving: 24 | Prep: 10mins | Cook: 40mins | Ready in:

Ingredients

- 2 pounds ground beef
- 1 (1.25 ounce) envelope onion soup mix
- 1/2 cup mayonnaise
- 2 cups shredded Cheddar cheese
- 24 dinner rolls, split
- 1/2 cup sliced pickles (optional)

Direction

- Preheat the oven to 175 degrees C (350 degrees F). Use aluminum foil to cover a baking sheet and then spritz with cooking spray.
- In a large skillet, combine together the onion soup mix and ground beef. Cook while stirring on medium-high heat until beef has browned evenly, crumbly and no pink color remains. Drain and get rid of the excess grease. Take out from the heat source. Mix the Cheddar cheese and mayonnaise into ground beef mixture.
- Spread the bottoms of dinner rolls in the baking sheet prepared. Then spread cheese

and beef mixture onto the bottom half of every roll. Replace the tops and then cover with another sheet of aluminum foil that is sprayed with cooking spray.

- Bake for about half an hour in the preheated oven until the cheese has melted and the burgers have heated through. You can serve together with sliced pickles.

Nutrition Information

- Calories: 232 calories;
- Protein: 12
- Total Fat: 13.2
- Sodium: 428
- Total Carbohydrate: 16.1
- Cholesterol: 36

903.   Sloppy Joe Fries

Serving: 6 | Prep: 15mins | Cook: 1hours | Ready in:

Ingredients

- 1 (28 ounce) package frozen French fries
- 1 pound ground beef
- 1 (15.5 ounce) can sloppy joe sauce (such as Hunt's® Manwich®)
- 1 (18 ounce) bottle barbeque sauce
- 1 (12 ounce) bag shredded Mexican cheese blend

Direction

- Set the oven to 350°F (175°C) and start preheating.
- In an 11x13-inch glass baking dish, place frozen French fries; bake in the prepared oven for about 25 minutes until golden brown.
- Over medium-high heat, heat a large skillet. Cook while stirring beef in the hot skillet for 5-7 minutes until crumbly and browned; drain and get rid of grease. Lower the heat to medium; add barbecue sauce and sloppy joe

sauce to ground beef; cook for about 15 minutes until heated through.

- Pour ground beef mixture over French fries; top with shredded Mexican cheese blend; place back in the oven; bake for about 10 minutes until cheese is bubbling.

Nutrition Information

- Calories: 522 calories;
- Total Carbohydrate: 41.7
- Cholesterol: 101
- Protein: 26.4
- Total Fat: 27.4
- Sodium: 1826

904.   Sloppy Joes II

Serving: 6 | Prep: 10mins | Cook: 30mins | Ready in:

Ingredients

- 1 pound lean ground beef
- 1/4 cup chopped onion
- 1/4 cup chopped green bell pepper
- 1/2 teaspoon garlic powder
- 1 teaspoon prepared yellow mustard
- 3/4 cup ketchup
- 3 teaspoons brown sugar
- salt to taste
- ground black pepper to taste

Direction

- Put the onion, green pepper and ground beef in a medium-sized skillet and let the mixture cook over medium heat setting until it turns brown in color; drain the cooking liquid off the mixture.
- Add in the ketchup, garlic powder, brown sugar and mustard and thoroughly mix everything together. Lower the heat setting and let the mixture simmer for 30 minutes. Add in pepper and salt to season.

Nutrition Information

- Calories: 189 calories;
- Protein: 15.1
- Total Fat: 9.4
- Sodium: 416
- Total Carbohydrate: 11.2
- Cholesterol: 50

905.   Slovak Stuffed Cabbage

Serving: 8 | Prep: 30mins | Cook: 1hours30mins | Ready in:

Ingredients

- 1 pound ground beef
- 1 pound ground pork
- 1 onion, chopped
- 1 teaspoon salt
- black pepper to taste
- 1 teaspoon chopped fresh parsley
- 1/2 cup cooked brown rice
- 1 1/4 teaspoons garlic salt
- 2 (10.75 ounce) cans condensed tomato soup
- 27 ounces sauerkraut, drained
- 1 (29 ounce) can diced tomatoes
- 1 medium head cabbage
- 5 slices bacon
- 2 tablespoons white sugar
- 3 cups water

Direction

- Turn the oven to 350°F (175°C) to preheat. Boil water in a pot.
- Combine pork and beef. Mix in 1/2 can of tomato soup, garlic salt, pepper, salt, parsley, cooked rice, and onion. Thoroughly combine.
- Remove the core from the cabbage head, put in the boiling water and boil until slightly cooked. Remove the leaves and trim the stems. Keep approximately 24-32 whole leaves. Slice

the leftover leaves and line onto a big roasting pan's bottom.

- Gently pack the meat mixture by a small handful and put in the middle of a cabbage leaf. Fold over the mixture with the top part of the leaves, and then fold the sides in and roll to fully enclose the mixture. In the pan, top the shred cabbage leaves with the rolls. Evenly put over the rolls with sauerkraut. Top the sauerkraut with bacon. Sprinkle 1-2 tablespoons of sugar over. Combine water, soup, and chopped tomatoes and add to the rolls. Add more water until coming to the top of cabbage rolls.
- Bake at 350°F (175°C) until fully cooked, about 1 1/2 hours.

Nutrition Information

- Calories: 556 calories;
- Total Fat: 36.5
- Sodium: 2096
- Total Carbohydrate: 31.6
- Cholesterol: 101
- Protein: 25.9

---

906.   Slow Cooker Barbecue Beans

Serving: 8 | Prep: 15mins | Cook: 6hours | Ready in:

Ingredients

- 1 pound lean ground beef
- 3/4 cup chopped raw bacon
- 1 small onion, finely chopped
- 2 (16 ounce) cans baked beans with pork
- 1 (15.25 ounce) can red kidney beans, with liquid
- 1 (15 ounce) can lima beans, partially drained
- 1 cup ketchup
- 1 tablespoon liquid smoke flavoring
- 1 tablespoon salt
- 1 tablespoon hot sauce

- 1/4 tablespoon garlic powder

Direction

- In a big and deep skillet, cook beef over medium-high heat until completely brown. Discard then put aside. In a big and deep skillet, cook bacon over medium-high heat until completely brown, Discard then put aside. Mix onion, salt, ketchup, kidney beans, lima beans, baked beans, hot sauce, liquid smoke, garlic powder, bacon and ground beef. Let it cook in low fire for 4 to 6 hours,

Nutrition Information

- Calories: 472 calories;
- Total Fat: 18.4
- Sodium: 2150
- Total Carbohydrate: 53.2
- Cholesterol: 60
- Protein: 25

---

907.   Slow Cooker Chili II

Serving: 8 | Prep: 15mins | Cook: 8hours | Ready in:

Ingredients

- 1 pound ground beef
- 3/4 cup diced onion
- 3/4 cup diced celery
- 3/4 cup diced green bell pepper
- 2 cloves garlic, minced
- 2 (10.75 ounce) cans tomato puree
- 1 (15 ounce) can kidney beans with liquid
- 1 (15 ounce) can kidney beans, drained
- 1 (15 ounce) can cannellini beans with liquid
- 1/2 tablespoon chili powder
- 1/2 teaspoon dried parsley
- 1 teaspoon salt
- 3/4 teaspoon dried basil
- 3/4 teaspoon dried oregano
- 1/4 teaspoon ground black pepper

- 1/8 teaspoon hot pepper sauce

Direction

- Cook and evenly brown beef in a skillet over medium heat. Drain excess grease.
- Put the beef into a slow cooker, mix in celery, green pepper, onion, garlic, tomato puree, kidney beans, and cannellini beans. Season with oregano, parsley, salt, basil, black pepper, hot pepper sauce and chili powder.
- Cover and cook on low for 8 hours.

Nutrition Information

- Calories: 273 calories;
- Total Fat: 7.6
- Sodium: 975
- Total Carbohydrate: 33.4
- Cholesterol: 34
- Protein: 18.9

908.   Slow Cooker Lasagna

Serving: 10 | Prep: 20mins | Cook: 4hours20mins | Ready in:

Ingredients

- 1 pound lean ground beef
- 1 onion, chopped
- 2 teaspoons minced garlic
- 1 (29 ounce) can tomato sauce
- 1 (6 ounce) can tomato paste
- 1 1/2 teaspoons salt
- 1 teaspoon dried oregano
- 1 (12 ounce) package lasagna noodles
- 12 ounces cottage cheese
- 1/2 cup grated Parmesan cheese
- 16 ounces shredded mozzarella cheese

Direction

- Cook garlic, ground beef, and onion until brown in a big skillet with heat on medium.

Mix in tomato paste, oregano, tomato sauce, and salt make sure to stir well. Cook mixture until entirely heated.
- Mix grated Parmesan, shredded mozzarella, and cottage cheese in a big bowl.
- Put a layer of the beef mixture on the bottom of slow cooker. Take the uncooked lasagna noodles and put a double layer on beef mixture. Noodles should be broken to fit in the slow cooker. Put some of the cheese mixture on the noodles. Repeat the layers, sauce, noodles, and cheese, until everything is used.
- Place cover; set to low and cook for 4-6 hours.

Nutrition Information

- Calories: 446 calories;
- Total Carbohydrate: 35.7
- Cholesterol: 72
- Protein: 31.2
- Total Fat: 20.3
- Sodium: 1420

909.   Slow Cooker Pizza

Serving: 6 | Prep: 20mins | Cook: 4hours | Ready in:

Ingredients

- 1 1/2 pounds ground beef
- 1 (8 ounce) package rigatoni pasta
- 1 (16 ounce) package shredded mozzarella cheese
- 1 (10.75 ounce) can condensed cream of tomato soup
- 2 (14 ounce) jars pizza sauce
- 1 (8 ounce) package sliced pepperoni sausage

Direction

- Pour lightly salted water in a big pot and boil. Add pasta, cook until it gets tender but firm enough to bite, about 8 to 10 minutes. Drain and set aside. Add the ground beef to a frying pan, brown over medium high heat. Drain to remove the fat.

- Layer the ground beef, noodles, cheese, soup, sauce and pepperoni alternately in the slow cooker.
- Set the cooker on low setting and cook for 4 hours.

Nutrition Information

- Calories: 820 calories;
- Total Carbohydrate: 50.9
- Cholesterol: 154
- Protein: 53.8
- Total Fat: 43.3
- Sodium: 2181

---

910. Slow Cooker Salisbury Steak

Serving: 8 | Prep: 15mins | Cook: 5hours | Ready in:

Ingredients

- 2 pounds lean ground beef
- 1 (1 ounce) envelope dry onion soup mix
- 1/2 cup Italian seasoned bread crumbs
- 1/4 cup milk
- 1/4 cup all-purpose flour
- 2 tablespoons vegetable oil
- 2 (10.75 ounce) cans condensed cream of chicken soup
- 1 (1 ounce) packet dry au jus mix
- 3/4 cup water

Direction

- Use your hands to mix milk, breadcrumbs, onion soup mix and ground beef in a big bowl; form to 8 patties.
- Heat oil on medium high heat in a big skillet. Dredge patties into flour to just coat; brown quickly on both sides in hot skillet. Put browned patties into slow cooker, alternately

stacking like a pyramid. Mix water, au jus mix and cream of chicken soup in a medium bowl; put on meat. Cook for 4-5 hours on low setting till ground beef gets well done.

Nutrition Information

- Calories: 388 calories;
- Sodium: 1378
- Total Carbohydrate: 18
- Cholesterol: 75
- Protein: 23.5
- Total Fat: 24

---

911. Slow Cooker Taco Soup

Serving: 8 | Prep: 10mins | Cook: 8hours | Ready in:

Ingredients

- 1 pound ground beef
- 1 onion, chopped
- 1 (16 ounce) can chili beans, with liquid
- 1 (15 ounce) can kidney beans with liquid
- 1 (15 ounce) can whole kernel corn, with liquid
- 1 (8 ounce) can tomato sauce
- 2 cups water
- 2 (14.5 ounce) cans peeled and diced tomatoes
- 1 (4 ounce) can diced green chile peppers
- 1 (1.25 ounce) package taco seasoning mix

Direction

- Let ground beef cook in a medium skillet over medium heat until it becomes brown. Discard then put aside.
- In a slow cooker, mix onion, green chile peppers, chili beans, corn, water, kidney beans, diced tomatoes, tomato sauce, taco seasoning and ground beef. Blend together and let it cook on low for 8 hours.

Nutrition Information

- Calories: 362 calories;
- Total Fat: 16.3
- Sodium: 1356
- Total Carbohydrate: 37.8
- Cholesterol: 48
- Protein: 18.2

912. Slow Cooker Vegetable Beef Soup

Serving: 8 | Prep: 15mins | Cook: 7hours10mins |Ready in:

Ingredients

- 1 pound ground beef
- 2 cloves garlic, minced
- 1 small onion, diced
- 1 green bell pepper, diced
- 3 stalks celery, diced
- 1 (29 ounce) can Italian-style stewed tomatoes, drained
- 1 (15 ounce) can mixed vegetables, drained
- 2 quarts beef broth
- 3 tablespoons soy sauce
- 2 tablespoons Worcestershire sauce
- 3/4 teaspoon paprika
- salt and pepper to taste
- 6 ounces dry fusilli pasta

Direction

- In a skillet over medium heat, put the beef. Add in green bell pepper, onion, and garlic. Cook and stir till the vegetables are soft and the beef is evenly browned. Drain fat, remove to a slow cooker.
- Into the slow cooker, combine Italian-style stewed tomatoes, celery, and mixed vegetables. Pour in beef broth, Worcestershire sauce, and soy sauce. Use pepper, salt, and paprika to season.
- Cover the lid, cook on high heat for about 7 hours. During the last 15 minutes of the cooking time, mix in pasta.

Nutrition Information

- Calories: 264 calories;
- Cholesterol: 34
- Protein: 18
- Total Fat: 7.9
- Sodium: 1504
- Total Carbohydrate: 30.5

913. Slow Cooker Beef And Potato Stew

Serving: 4 | Prep: 20mins | Cook: 3hours35mins |Ready in:

Ingredients

- 1 pound lean ground beef
- 1 pinch garlic salt, or to taste
- 1 pinch cayenne pepper, or to taste (optional)
- 2 1/2 cups water
- 1 (14.25 ounce) can low-sodium beef broth
- 1 (15.25 ounce) can yellow sweet corn
- 10 small red potatoes, peeled and cut into cubes
- 6 fresh jalapeno peppers, sliced into rings
- 1 small white onion, chopped
- 1 pinch onion powder, or to taste
- ground black pepper to taste

Direction

- Break up the ground beef into the skillet on medium heat; use cayenne pepper and garlic salt to season. Cook and stir ground beef for 5-7 minutes or till browned totally, crumble into small pieces as you mix. Drain as much grease out of the beef as you can.
- In the slow cooker, mix black pepper, onion powder, onion, sliced jalapeno peppers, potatoes, corn, beef broth and water; put in the drained ground beef. Cook over High heat for

3.5-4 hours or till potatoes become soft, mixing once in a while.

Nutrition Information

- Calories: 632 calories;
- Total Fat: 16.2
- Sodium: 530
- Total Carbohydrate: 91.3
- Cholesterol: 74
- Protein: 35

914. Smokey Chipotle Meatloaf

Serving: 8 | Prep: 15mins | Cook: 1hours | Ready in:

Ingredients

- 2 eggs
- 1/3 cup hickory flavored barbeque sauce
- 2 cloves garlic, minced, or to taste
- 2 chipotle chilies in adobo sauce, minced, or to taste
- 2 tablespoons adobo sauce from chipotle peppers
- 1 teaspoon kosher salt
- 1 teaspoon coarse ground black pepper
- 1/2 teaspoon celery salt
- 1/2 teaspoon ground cumin
- 1 tablespoon Worcestershire sauce
- 1 onion, chopped
- 1/2 cup dry oatmeal
- 2 pounds lean ground beef
- 2 tablespoons hickory flavored barbeque sauce

Direction

- Preheat the oven to 175 °C or 350 °F. With cooking spray, coat a loaf pan, 9x5-inch in size.
- In a big mixing bowl, whisk the eggs till smooth, then beat in Worcestershire sauce, cumin, celery salt, black pepper, kosher salt, adobo sauce, chipotle chiles, garlic and 1/3

cup of barbeque sauce till smooth evenly. Using your hands, add in ground beef, oatmeal and onion till equally combined. Into the prepared pan, put the mixture. With additional of 2 tablespoons of barbeque sauce, brush top of meatloaf.

- In the prepped oven, bake for an hour till not pink anymore in the middle. An instant-read thermometer pricked into the middle should register at a minimum of 70 °C or 160 °F.

Nutrition Information

- Calories: 306 calories;
- Total Carbohydrate: 12.7
- Cholesterol: 124
- Protein: 25.8
- Total Fat: 16.2
- Sodium: 635

915. Sour Cream Noodle Bake

Serving: 6 | Prep: | Cook: | Ready in:

Ingredients

- 1 (8 ounce) package wide egg noodles
- 1 pound lean ground beef
- 1 tablespoon butter
- 1 teaspoon salt
- 1/8 teaspoon ground black pepper
- 1/4 teaspoon garlic salt
- 1 cup tomato sauce
- 1 cup cottage cheese, creamed
- 1 cup sour cream
- 1 cup chopped green onions
- 1 cup shredded sharp Cheddar cheese

Direction

- In boiling salted water, let noodles cook. Wash with cold water and allow to drain.
- Preheat an oven to 175 °C or 350 °F.

- In butter, brown the meat; put in tomato sauce, garlic salt, pepper and salt. Let it simmer for 5 minutes. Combine noodles, meat sauce, onions, sour cream and cottage cheese. Put in a casserole dish and scatter cheddar cheese over.
- Bake without a cover, for 20 to 25 minutes at 175 °C or 350 °F.

Nutrition Information

- Calories: 589 calories;
- Sodium: 1068
- Total Carbohydrate: 33
- Cholesterol: 140
- Protein: 31.2
- Total Fat: 36.7

916.   Southwestern Black Bean Stew

Serving: 6 | Prep: | Cook: | Ready in:

Ingredients

- 1 pound ground beef
- 1 (1.25 ounce) package taco seasoning mix
- 1 (15 ounce) can whole kernel corn, drained
- 1 (15 ounce) can black beans, undrained
- 1 (6 ounce) can tomato paste
- 1 1/2 cups water
- 1/2 cup sour cream
- 2 (8 ounce) packages shredded Cheddar cheese

Direction

- Sauté ground beef in a big frying pan over medium-high heat and strain the extra fat. Add taco seasoning and mix. Lower the heat, simmer with a cover for 10 minutes.
- Mix water, tomato paste, beans, and corn together over low heat in a slow cooker. Stir thoroughly. Add sour cream and seasoned

meat. Increase the heat to high setting and simmer for 20 minutes. Add to separate bowls and use shredded cheddar cheese to garnish.

Nutrition Information

- Calories: 635 calories;
- Total Fat: 38.9
- Sodium: 1596
- Total Carbohydrate: 33.5
- Cholesterol: 133
- Protein: 38.7

917.   Southwestern Haystacks

Serving: 6 | Prep: 10mins | Cook: 10mins | Ready in:

Ingredients

- 1 pound ground beef
- 1 (16 ounce) can diced tomatoes
- 1 (15 ounce) can whole kernel corn
- 1 (15 ounce) can kidney beans, drained
- 1 teaspoon garlic powder
- salt to taste
- ground black pepper to taste
- 1 (16 ounce) package macaroni
- 1 (8 ounce) container sour cream
- 2 cups shredded Cheddar cheese

Direction

- Brown hamburger in a big skillet over medium high heat. Strain fat then mix in beans, corn and tomatoes and heat through. Add pepper, salt, and garlic powder to taste.
- In a big pot of boiling water, cook elbow macaroni until tender. Separate the pot from heat and strain.
- Place meat mixture, grated cheddar and a dollop of sour cream on top of macaroni.

Nutrition Information

- Calories: 877 calories;
- Sodium: 844
- Total Carbohydrate: 84.5
- Cholesterol: 121
- Protein: 39.2
- Total Fat: 42.6

918. Spaghetti Bake

Serving: 6 | Prep: 15mins | Cook: 1hours5mins | Ready in:

Ingredients

- 1 (16 ounce) package spaghetti
- 1 cup chopped onion
- 1 cup chopped green bell pepper
- 1 pound ground beef
- 2 (24 ounce) jars spaghetti sauce
- 2 cups shredded Cheddar cheese
- 1 (10.75 ounce) can condensed cream of mushroom soup
- 1/2 cup sliced fresh mushrooms
- 1 (4 ounce) can sliced black olives
- 2 teaspoons dried oregano
- 1 tablespoon white sugar
- 1 cup shredded mozzarella cheese
- 1/2 cup grated Parmesan cheese

Direction

- Set the oven at 350°F (175°C) and start preheating. Coat a 9x13-in. baking sheet with grease.
- Boil a large pot of lightly salted water. Cook in spaghetti for around 12 minutes, stirring occasionally, till cooked through but still firm to bite. Strain.
- Place a large skillet on medium heat; cook while stirring in bell pepper and onion for around 5 minutes, or till tender. Remove the vegetables into a large bowl. Turn the skillet back to the stove top; turn the heat up to medium-high. Cook while stirring in ground beef for 5-7 minutes, or till crumbly and

browned; strain and discard the grease. Remove the beef into the bowl with the vegetables.
- Combine sugar, oregano, olives, mushrooms, cream of mushroom soup, Cheddar cheese, spaghetti sauce and spaghetti into the beef mixture. Transfer the spaghetti mixture into the prepared baking sheet; sprinkle Parmesan and mozzarella cheeses on top.
- Bake for around 45 minutes in the preheated oven, or till hot and bubbly.

Nutrition Information

- Calories: 928 calories;
- Total Carbohydrate: 98.7
- Cholesterol: 109
- Protein: 44.7
- Total Fat: 38.8
- Sodium: 1912

919. Spaghetti Pie II

Serving: 6 | Prep: | Cook: | Ready in:

Ingredients

- 1 (6 ounce) package spaghetti
- 2 tablespoons butter
- 1/3 cup grated Parmesan cheese
- 2 eggs, beaten
- 1 pound lean ground beef
- 1/2 cup chopped onion
- 1/4 cup chopped green bell pepper
- 1 clove garlic, minced
- 1 (14.5 ounce) can diced tomatoes
- 1 (6 ounce) can tomato paste
- 1 teaspoon white sugar
- 1 teaspoon dried oregano
- 1 cup cottage cheese
- 1/2 cup shredded mozzarella cheese

Direction

- Let spaghetti cook and drain. While spaghetti is still hot, mix in eggs, parmesan cheese and margarine. In a 10-inch buttered pie plate, shape the spaghetti mixture into a crust.
- Preheat an oven to 175 °C or 350 °F.
- Cook garlic, green pepper, onion and beef in a skillet. Drain off the fat and mix in oregano, sugar, tomato paste and undrained tomatoes. Heat through.
- On top of spaghetti crust, spread the cottage cheese then add tomato and beef mixture.
- Bake for 20 minutes at 175 °C or 350 °F. On pie surface, scatter mozzarella cheese then bake it till cheese melts for an additional of 5 minutes.

Nutrition Information

- Calories: 488 calories;
- Sodium: 750
- Total Carbohydrate: 32.4
- Cholesterol: 144
- Protein: 29.5
- Total Fat: 26.1

920.   Spaghetti Pie III

Serving: 7 | Prep: 35mins | Cook: 30mins | Ready in:

Ingredients

- 1 pound spaghetti
- 1 pound lean ground beef
- 1/4 teaspoon salt
- 1/4 teaspoon ground black pepper
- garlic powder to taste
- 1/2 cup chopped green bell pepper
- 1 (26 ounce) jar pasta sauce
- 3/4 cup sour cream
- 1/2 cup chopped green onions
- 1/2 (8 ounce) package cream cheese
- 1 1/2 cups shredded Cheddar cheese

Direction

- Heat a large pot of lightly salted water until boiling. Put in pasta and cook until al dente, 8 to 10 minutes; let it drain.
- Set oven to 3500F (1750 C) and preheat.
- Stir the ground beef until brown in a skillet over medium heat. Drain and crumble. In the skillet, add crumbled beef. Mix in pasta sauce, bell pepper, garlic powder, pepper and salt. Bring to a boil; reduce the heat to a simmer for 20 minutes.
- Mix together cream cheese, green onions and sour cream in a small bowl and put aside. Use cooking spray to grease a 9x13-inch baking dish and add the cooked spaghetti. Pour the cream cheese mixture over it, add the meat mixture and top with Cheddar Cheese.
- Put in the prepared oven, bake, covered, for 25 minutes. Bake without a cover until the cheese is bubbly, about 5 more minutes.

Nutrition Information

- Calories: 671 calories;
- Total Fat: 31.5
- Sodium: 787
- Total Carbohydrate: 65.8
- Cholesterol: 95
- Protein: 29.9

921.   Spaghetti Pizza Lasagna

Serving: 12 | Prep: | Cook: 50mins | Ready in:

Ingredients

- 1 pound spaghetti
- 1 pound lean ground beef
- 1 cup milk
- 2 eggs, beaten
- salt and pepper to taste
- 1 (32 ounce) jar pasta sauce
- 1 teaspoon dried oregano
- 1 teaspoon garlic powder
- 1 tablespoon dried minced onion

- 1 (8 ounce) package sliced pepperoni sausage
- 3 cups shredded Cheddar cheese

Direction

- Set oven to 175°C (350°F) and start preheating.
- Boil lightly salted water in a big pot. Put in pasta; cook until al dente, about 8-10 minutes; drain pasta.
- In a big skillet, cook beef over medium heat until brown and drain.
- Whisk eggs and milk until thoroughly blended; add pepper and salt to season. In a 9x13-inch baking dish, add the pasta. Evenly pour milk mixture ono pasta. Pour pasta sauce onto the milk.
- Evenly spread beef over the sauce; scatter pepperoni slices, minced onion, garlic powder and oregano over. Add shredded cheese over the top.
- Bake for half an hour at 175°C (350°F) oven until it bubbles and becomes hot.

Nutrition Information

- Calories: 511 calories;
- Total Fat: 26.6
- Sodium: 834
- Total Carbohydrate: 40.4
- Cholesterol: 106
- Protein: 25.9

---

922.   Spanish Rice Bake

Serving: 6 | Prep: 15mins | Cook: 45mins | Ready in:

Ingredients

- 1 pound lean ground beef
- 1/2 cup finely chopped onion
- 1/4 cup chopped green bell pepper
- 1 (14.5 ounce) can canned tomatoes
- 1 cup water
- 3/4 cup uncooked long grain rice

- 1/2 cup chile sauce
- 1 teaspoon salt
- 1 teaspoon brown sugar
- 1/2 teaspoon ground cumin
- 1/2 teaspoon Worcestershire sauce
- 1 pinch ground black pepper
- 1/2 cup shredded Cheddar cheese
- 2 tablespoons chopped fresh cilantro

Direction

- Preheat an oven to 190°C/375°F.
- In a big skillet, brown ground beef on medium high heat. Drain extra fat. Put beef into a big pot on medium low heat. Mix in ground black pepper, Worcestershire sauce, cumin, brown sugar, salt, chile sauce, rice, water, tomatoes, green bell pepper and onion.
- Simmer for about 30 minutes, occasionally mixing. Put into a 2-qt. casserole dish. Firmly press down. Sprinkle shredded cheddar cheese on top.
- Bake for 10-15 minutes till cheese is bubbly and melted at 190°C/375°F. Put chopped fresh cilantro on top.

Nutrition Information

- Calories: 350 calories;
- Protein: 18.5
- Total Fat: 19.1
- Sodium: 604
- Total Carbohydrate: 24.9
- Cholesterol: 67

---

923.   Spanish Style Albondigas In A Sunny Mediterranean Sauce

Serving: 4 | Prep: 20mins | Cook: 1hours20mins | Ready in:

Ingredients

- 2/3 pound ground beef
- 1/3 pound ground pork
- 2 tablespoons minced green onion
- 2 tablespoons minced fresh oregano
- 1 tablespoon minced fresh flat-leaf parsley
- 1 clove garlic, minced
- 2 dashes Worcestershire sauce, or to taste
- salt and ground black pepper to taste
- 3 1/2 ounces fresh white bread crumbs
- 2 tablespoons extra-virgin olive oil
- 3 1/2 ounces pancetta, chopped
- 3 tablespoons minced onion
- 1 clove garlic, minced
- 2 tablespoons minced carrot
- 2 tablespoons minced celery
- 2 tablespoons minced red bell pepper
- 1 1/2 teaspoons dried basil
- 1 1/2 teaspoons dried oregano
- 1/4 teaspoon ground coriander
- 2 grinds ground black pepper
- 1 cup white wine
- 2 tablespoons tomato puree
- 1 (28 ounce) can Italian plum tomatoes, chopped
- 2 tablespoons extra-virgin olive oil, or as needed

Direction

- In a bowl, mix ground pork, ground beef, oregano, green onion, garlic, parsley, Worcestershire sauce, black pepper, and salt together. Slowly pour in the meat mixture with the breadcrumbs mixture to reach the desired consistency. Shape mixture into balls, coat them by rolling in the leftover bread crumbs, and place onto a shallow tray. Use plastic wrap to cover meatballs and allow to sit at least 30 minutes in the refrigerator.
- In a large pot over medium heat, heat 2 tablespoons of olive oil. Cook and mix pancetta in the hot oil for around 4 minutes until browned. Add garlic and onion to the pancetta; continue to cook and stir for another 1 minute until fragrant. Stir into the pancetta mixture with red bell pepper, celery, and carrot; cook for approximately 3 minutes until

the carrot slightly soften. Sprinkle oregano, basil, black pepper, and coriander over pancetta mixture; season evenly by stirring.
- Pour wine over the pancetta mixture. Raise to medium-high heat and cook until the liquid decreases by about half.
- Into the pancetta mixture, mix quickly tomato puree; then put in chopped tomatoes. Cook and stir the mixture for approximately 5 minutes till the tomatoes start to break down into a sauce. Lower to low heat and simmer for 60 to 90 minutes until the sauce thickens.
- In a large skillet over low heat, heat 2 tablespoons oil. Cook and mix batches of meatballs in hot oil for 5 to 7 minutes until cooked through and browned evenly; place on a plate lined with paper towel for draining.
- Drop meatballs gently into the simmering sauce; then cook together for approximately 10 minutes until meatballs are heated through.

Nutrition Information

- Calories: 615 calories;
- Total Carbohydrate: 26.4
- Cholesterol: 87
- Protein: 26.4
- Total Fat: 40.1
- Sodium: 760

924.   Spanish Style Beef & Rice

Serving: 6 | Prep: 10mins | Cook: 17mins | Ready in:

Ingredients

- 1 tablespoon olive oil
- 1 pound lean ground beef
- 1 onion, diced
- 1 green bell pepper, diced
- 1 (15.5 ounce) can pinto beans, drained
- 1 cup UNCLE BEN'S® Flavor Infusions Spanish Style Rice
- 2 cups water

- 2 tablespoons chopped fresh cilantro

Direction

- Put oil and ground beef in a skillet and fry on medium high heat till browned, occasionally mixing.
- Mix in green bell pepper and onions; fry till lightly brown for 2-3 minutes more.
- Mix in water, UNCLE BEN'S® Flavor Infusions Spanish Style Rice and pinto beans. Keep stirring to mix.
- Boil; lower to medium heat and simmer till water is absorbed for 15 minutes, covered.
- Garnish using fresh cilantro.

Nutrition Information

- Calories: 346 calories;
- Sodium: 625
- Total Carbohydrate: 35.8
- Cholesterol: 50
- Protein: 21
- Total Fat: 12.8

---
925.   Spiced Ham Loaf

Serving: 12 | Prep: | Cook: | Ready in:

Ingredients

- 1 pound ground ham
- 1 1/2 pounds lean ground beef
- 1 egg
- 1 cup milk
- 1 cup bread crumbs
- 1/2 teaspoon salt
- ground black pepper to taste
- 1/2 cup packed brown sugar
- 1/2 cup water
- 1 teaspoon ground mustard
- 1/4 cup distilled white vinegar

Direction

- Combine pepper, salt, bread crumbs, milk, egg, beef, and ham. Shape into a loaf and put in a casserole dish.
- In a small saucepan, combine vinegar, mustard, water, and brown sugar over medium-high heat. Bring to a boil. Boil for 10 minutes. Then pour over the loaf.
- Bake at 175°C (350°F) for about 1 hour, or until done, basting occasionally.

Nutrition Information

- Calories: 341 calories;
- Total Carbohydrate: 16.5
- Cholesterol: 95
- Protein: 22.7
- Total Fat: 19.8
- Sodium: 241

---
926.   Spicy Beef And Bean Enchilada Pie

Serving: 8 | Prep: 25mins | Cook: 50mins | Ready in:

Ingredients

- 1 pound ground beef
- 1/2 cup diced onion
- 2 cloves garlic, minced
- 1 (15 ounce) can Tex Mex-style diced tomatoes
- 1 (4 ounce) can chopped green chilies
- 2 tablespoons chopped fresh cilantro
- 1 (1 ounce) packet taco seasoning mix
- 1 (20 ounce) can refried black beans
- 2 (10 ounce) cans red enchilada sauce (such as Old El Paso®)
- 2 cups shredded pepperjack cheese
- 2 cups shredded Monterey Jack cheese
- 6 (8 inch) flour tortillas
- 1/2 cup sour cream, or to taste (optional)

Direction

- Set oven to 400°F (200°C) to preheat.

- In a large skillet over medium-high heat, cook and stir onions and ground beef for 7 to 10 minutes until the meat is crumbly and browned. Add in garlic; sauté for about half a minute until aromatic. Mix in taco seasoning mix, cilantro, green chiles, and diced tomatoes. Turn off the heat. In a bowl, combine 1 can red enchilada sauce and black beans until creamy.
- In another bowl, mix together Monterey Jack cheese and Pepper Jack cheese.
- Bring a cast-iron skillet over medium heat on the stove. Cook 1 tortilla at a time, about 15 seconds on each side, until a little crispy.
- Lay 1 tortilla on the bottom of an 8-inch springform pan. Generously spread black bean mixture in a layer on top of tortilla, then top with 1 layer of ground beef mixture. Top meat mixture with 1 cup of cheese mixture and pour 1/4 cup red enchilada sauce over the top. Repeat layering process with tortilla, bean, meat, cheese, and sauce, finishing with enchilada sauce and cheese on top.
- Use aluminum foil to cover the pan. Bake for about 40 minutes in the preheated oven until enchiladas are thoroughly cooked and cheese is bubbly. Allow to cool for 15 minutes. Serve enchilada with sour cream.

Nutrition Information

- Calories: 642 calories;
- Total Carbohydrate: 45.5
- Cholesterol: 102
- Protein: 32.7
- Total Fat: 36.2
- Sodium: 1684

927.　　Spicy Cheesy Mini Meatloaves

Serving: 6 | Prep: 10mins | Cook: | Ready in:

Ingredients

- 1 pound lean ground beef
- 1/2 pound VELVEETA®, cut into 1/2-inch cubes
- 1/2 cup crushed tortilla chips
- 1 (10 ounce) can RO*TEL Diced Tomatoes and Green Chilies, undrained
- 1 egg

Direction

- Set the oven to 400°F to preheat.
- Mix ingredients just until combined.
- Press into 12 muffin pan cups greased with cooking spray. Create indentation in middle of each using back of spoon. Put muffin pan on rimmed baking sheet covered with foil.
- Bake for 20 to 25 minutes until meatloaves are cooked (160°F).

Nutrition Information

- Calories: 289 calories;
- Sodium: 824
- Total Carbohydrate: 6.7
- Cholesterol: 114
- Protein: 22.4
- Total Fat: 18.8

928.　　Spicy Melted Cheese Dip

Serving: 48 | Prep: 5mins | Cook: 15mins | Ready in:

Ingredients

- 1/2 pound ground beef
- 1/2 pound ground pork sausage
- 2 pounds processed cheese food, cubed
- 1 (10 ounce) can diced tomatoes with green chile peppers, with liquid

Direction

- In a large deep skillet, arrange ground pork sausage and ground beef. Cook to brown evenly over medium high heat.

- Let the processed cheese food melt over low heat in a medium saucepan. Meanwhile, add green chilie peppers and diced tomatoes, stir while processed cheese food is melting.
- Drain ground sausage and ground beef. Add into the processed cheese food mixture and mix. Place into a medium dish. Serve warm.

Nutrition Information

- Calories: 98 calories;
- Sodium: 241
- Total Carbohydrate: 1.8
- Cholesterol: 19
- Protein: 5.1
- Total Fat: 7.8

929. Spicy Rye Rounds

Serving: 8 | Prep: 10mins | Cook: 7mins | Ready in:

Ingredients

- 1 pound lean ground beef
- 1 pound spicy Italian sausage
- 1 pound processed cheese food, cubed
- 1 (1 pound) loaf cocktail rye bread

Direction

- Set oven to 325°F (165°C) and start preheating.
- Cook sausage and ground beef in a big skillet until browned. After sausage and beef are browned, add cheese and mix frequently. When all ingredients are well combined, spoon on each piece of rye bread with 1 tablespoon of the beef and sausage mixture. Place bread with toppings on a baking sheet.
- Bake for 5 to 7 minutes.

Nutrition Information

- Calories: 676 calories;
- Cholesterol: 122

- Protein: 34.6
- Total Fat: 45.2
- Sodium: 1375
- Total Carbohydrate: 31.7

930. Spicy Serrano Burgers

Serving: 4 | Prep: 15mins | Cook: 10mins | Ready in:

Ingredients

- 1 pound lean ground beef (90% lean)
- 1/4 cup dark beer (such as Guinness®)
- 1 (6 inch) serrano pepper, diced
- 2 tablespoons butter, softened
- 4 slices Monterey Jack cheese with jalapeno peppers

Direction

- Preheat an outdoor grill for high heat; grease grate lightly.
- In a bowl, combine butter, serrano pepper, beer and ground beef together; Shape into 4 patties.
- On the prepped grill, cook the burgers for 5 minutes. Turn, keep cooking for 3 minutes. Atop each burger with a slice of Monterey Jack cheese then cook for 2 minutes additional, till burger juices run clear and no longer pink in the middle. An inserted instant-read thermometer in the middle should register minimum 74°C or 165°F.

Nutrition Information

- Calories: 382 calories;
- Protein: 28.7
- Total Fat: 28.2
- Sodium: 262
- Total Carbohydrate: 1.1
- Cholesterol: 115

931. Spicy Slow Cooked Beanless Chili

Serving: 6 | Prep: 10mins | Cook: 6hours35mins | Ready in:

Ingredients

- 2 pounds ground beef
- 2 (8 ounce) cans tomato sauce
- 1 (14.5 ounce) can diced tomatoes
- 1 onion, chopped
- 2 jalapeno peppers, chopped
- 3 tablespoons chili powder
- 1 tablespoon cayenne pepper
- 2 teaspoons salt
- 2 teaspoons minced garlic
- 1 teaspoon ground black pepper

Direction

- Heat on moderate high heat a big skillet. Cook and stir beef for 5-7 minutes in the hot skillet until crumbly and browned; drain and get rid of the grease.
- Stir black pepper, garlic, salt, cayenne, chili powder, jalapeno peppers, onion, diced tomatoes and tomato sauce in the crock of a slow cooker, then put in ground beef and stir.
- Cook on low setting for about 10 hours or on high setting for about 6 hours and a half.

Nutrition Information

- Calories: 340 calories;
- Total Fat: 19.3
- Sodium: 1402
- Total Carbohydrate: 13.3
- Cholesterol: 95
- Protein: 28.2

932. Spicy Slow Cooked Chili

Serving: 10 | Prep: 30mins | Cook: 4hours | Ready in:

Ingredients

- 2 pounds ground beef
- 2 (16 ounce) cans kidney beans, rinsed and drained
- 2 (14.5 ounce) cans diced tomatoes, drained
- 1 (8 ounce) can tomato sauce
- 2 onions, chopped
- 1 green bell pepper, chopped
- 2 cloves garlic, minced
- 3 tablespoons chili powder
- 1 tablespoon cayenne pepper
- 2 teaspoons salt
- 1 teaspoon ground black pepper
- 1/2 cup shredded Cheddar cheese

Direction

- Place a large skillet over medium-high heat. Cook and stir the ground beef for 7 minutes until the beef is no longer pink and when the beef is now crumbly and evenly browned. Drain the beef and discard any excess grease.
- In a slow cooker, combine diced tomatoes, ground beef, onions, kidney beans, chili powder, black pepper, cayenne pepper, salt, garlic, tomato sauce, and bell pepper. Cover and set the cooker to Low and cook for 10 hours. You can also cook it on High setting for 4 hours.
- Distribute it into the bowls and top each with Cheddar cheese.

Nutrition Information

- Calories: 308 calories;
- Total Fat: 13.8
- Sodium: 1024
- Total Carbohydrate: 22.3
- Cholesterol: 62
- Protein: 23.4

933. Squash Stuff

Serving: 8 | Prep: 15mins | Cook: 1hours | Ready in:

Ingredients

- 1 pound ground beef
- 1 (28 ounce) can crushed tomatoes, undrained
- 1 (28 ounce) can diced tomatoes, undrained
- 1 (15.25 ounce) can whole kernel corn, undrained
- 1 yellow squash, sliced
- 1 zucchini, sliced
- 2 potatoes, peeled and cubed
- 1 tablespoon seasoning salt
- 1 tablespoon ground black pepper

Direction

- Cook ground beef over medium heat in a big pan until equally browned; drain the fat.
- Combine the corn with liquid, yellow squash, mashed tomatoes with liquid, cubed tomatoes with liquid, potatoes and zucchini into the pan with the beef. Sprinkle with pepper and salt. Let it boil; add water as needed to cover the ingredients. Turn down the heat to low and let it simmer until the potatoes are tender for 20 minutes. Drain. Serve.

Nutrition Information

- Calories: 248 calories;
- Sodium: 901
- Total Carbohydrate: 32.4
- Cholesterol: 34
- Protein: 15
- Total Fat: 7.6

934. Stromboli

Serving: 4 | Prep: 20mins | Cook: 30mins | Ready in:

Ingredients

- 1 (10 ounce) package pizza crust dough
- 1/2 pound lean ground beef
- 1 cup cooked ham, diced
- 1 green bell pepper, chopped
- 1 red onion, finely chopped
- 1 (14 ounce) jar pizza sauce
- 1 (4.5 ounce) can mushrooms, drained
- 1/4 cup butter, melted
- 1 (8 ounce) package sliced pepperoni sausage
- 1 cup shredded mozzarella cheese

Direction

- Set an oven to preheat at 200°C (400°F).
- Brown the ground beef in a pan on medium heat, until no longer pink, then drain. Stir in the mushrooms, pizza sauce, onions, bell pepper and ham.
- On a cookie sheet, place the pizza dough laying flat. Scatter pepperoni slices on top of the dough. Put a mound of sauce mixture on one side of the dough (some may be left out). Sprinkle mozzarella cheese on top, then fold the dough over, pinching the sides and ends together. Poke holes on top and use melted butter to brush on it.
- Cook in the preheated oven until it turns golden brown, or for 30 minutes. Cut into individual sections then serve.

Nutrition Information

- Calories: 907 calories;
- Total Fat: 57.3
- Sodium: 2785
- Total Carbohydrate: 50.2
- Cholesterol: 161
- Protein: 44.8

935. Stuffed Bell Pepper Rings

Serving: 6 | Prep: 25mins | Cook: 50mins | Ready in:

Ingredients

- 2 pounds ground beef sirloin
- 1 cup cooked rice
- 1 onion, diced
- 2 eggs
- 1/2 cup cooked corn
- 1 carrot, shredded
- 3 tablespoons olive oil, divided
- 2 tablespoons Italian-seasoned bread crumbs
- 1 tablespoon sun-dried tomato pesto
- 1 tablespoon minced fresh parsley
- 2 tablespoons chopped fresh dill, divided
- 1 clove garlic, minced
- salt and ground black pepper to taste
- 4 large yellow bell peppers - tops removed, sliced into 2-inch rings, seeded, or to taste
- 2 tomatoes, sliced, or to taste
- 1/2 cup pasta sauce
- 1/2 cup chicken broth
- 3 green onions, thinly sliced, or to taste

Direction

- Start preheating the oven to 350°F (175°C).
- In a big bowl, mix together black pepper, salt, garlic, 1 tablespoon dill, parsley, pesto, bread crumbs, 1 tablespoon olive oil, carrot, corn, eggs, onion, rice, and ground beef.
- Cut any left pieces of yellow bell pepper and put them in a baking plate's bottom. Add the left dill, green onions, chicken broth, pasta sauce, tomatoes, and the left olive oil.
- In the baking plate, put the yellow bell pepper rings and use the beef-rice mixture to fill. Cover with the pasta sauce mixture on top. Use aluminum foil to cover the baking plate.
- Put in the preheated oven and bake for 30 minutes. Take away the aluminum foil and keep baking for another 20 minutes until the peppers are still tender-crisp and the beef turns brown.

Nutrition Information

- Calories: 408 calories;
- Total Fat: 18.8

- Sodium: 361
- Total Carbohydrate: 27.9
- Cholesterol: 128
- Protein: 32.4

---

936.   Stuffed Mexican Peppers

Serving: 6 | Prep: 15mins | Cook: 1hours | Ready in:

Ingredients

- 1 pound ground beef
- 1 (1 ounce) package taco seasoning mix
- 3/4 cup water
- 2 teaspoons chili powder
- 1/2 cup cooked rice
- 1/4 teaspoon salt
- 1/4 teaspoon garlic salt
- 1/8 teaspoon ground black pepper
- 2 (8 ounce) cans tomato sauce, divided
- 3 large red bell peppers
- 6 (1 inch) cubes Colby-Jack cheese

Direction

- Turn on the oven to 350°F (175°C) to preheat. Prepare a 9x13-inch baking dish and grease it. In a skillet over medium heat, add ground beef; brown the meat for 8 minutes while breaking it into crumbles. Drain to remove excess fat. Mix in 1 can of tomato sauce, black pepper, garlic salt, salt, cooked rice, chili powder, water and taco seasoning; mix until well-combined. Bring to a boil; lower the heat to low and simmer for 20 minutes.
- At the same time, cut each bell pepper into 2 pieces lengthwise; discard seeds, cores, membranes and stems. In a large saucepan, place a steamer insert; pour in water so that it fills just below the steamer's bottom. Bring to a boil with a cover over high heat. Arranger peppers in the steamer insert; steam with cover for 3-5 minutes until softened.
- In the baking dish, arrange steamed peppers; add meat filling to fill lightly. Into the center of

the filling in each pepper, insert 1 cube of Colby-Jack cheese; spread the remaining can of tomato sauce onto the peppers. Use aluminum foil to cover the dish.

- Put into the oven to bake for 25-30 minutes until the filling is hot and the peppers are softened.

Nutrition Information

- Calories: 322 calories;
- Sodium: 1182
- Total Carbohydrate: 17.3
- Cholesterol: 73
- Protein: 21.2
- Total Fat: 18.5

937.   Stuffed Peppers

Serving: 6 | Prep: 20mins | Cook: 1hours | Ready in:

Ingredients

- 1 pound ground beef
- 1/2 cup uncooked long grain white rice
- 1 cup water
- 6 green bell peppers
- 2 (8 ounce) cans tomato sauce
- 1 tablespoon Worcestershire sauce
- 1/4 teaspoon garlic powder
- 1/4 teaspoon onion powder
- salt and pepper to taste
- 1 teaspoon Italian seasoning

Direction

- Preheat the oven to 175°C or 350°Fahrenheit.
- Boil water and rice together in a saucepan. Lower heat and cook rice for 20mins while covered. On medium heat, cook beef in a pan until evenly brown.
- Remove the membranes, seeds, and tops of the bell pepper; place with the pepper's hollowed

side up in a baking dish. If needed, cut the base of the peppers to help them stay upright.

- Stir pepper, browned beef, salt, cooked rice, onion powder, a can of tomato sauce, garlic powder, and Worcestershire sauce together. Evenly scoop in mixture into each pepper. In a bowl, combine Italian seasoning and remaining tomato sauce together; drizzle on top of the stuffed peppers.
- Bake peppers in the 350°Fahrenheit oven for an hour until tender. Every 15mins, baste peppers with sauce.

Nutrition Information

- Calories: 248 calories;
- Total Fat: 9.4
- Sodium: 564
- Total Carbohydrate: 25.6
- Cholesterol: 46
- Protein: 16

938.   Summer Feta Burger With Gourmet Cheese Spread

Serving: 8 | Prep: 20mins | Cook: 20mins | Ready in:

Ingredients

- 1 (8 ounce) package cream cheese, softened
- 1 clove garlic, minced
- 2 tablespoons chopped fresh basil
- 1 tablespoon chopped fresh dill
- 2 tablespoons extra virgin olive oil
- 1 clove garlic, minced
- 1 red onion, minced
- 1 3/4 pounds ground beef
- 1/4 pound ground pork sausage
- 1 1/2 cups crumbled feta
- 1/4 cup red wine
- 1 egg
- 1 teaspoon salt
- 1 teaspoon fresh-ground black pepper
- 1 large heirloom tomato, sliced

- 1 medium red onion, sliced
- 8 leaves green leaf lettuce leaves
- 8 Kaiser rolls, split

Direction

- Mix dill, basil, 1 minced garlic clove and cream cheese in medium bowl. Cover; put aside.
- Heat olive oil in medium skillet on medium heat; cook onion and 1 minced garlic clove till translucent for 4-6 minutes. Take off heat; cool.
- Preheat outdoor grill to high heat; oil grate lightly.
- As grill heats, mix pepper, salt, egg, red wine, feta cheese, pork sausage, ground beef, cooked onion and garlic gently in a big bowl; don't overwork the mixture. Divide to 8 even parts; shape to patties.
- On preheated grill, grill patties till well done, 5-10 minutes per side. Toast split buns for 1-2 minutes on grill. Make burgers by spreading 1 1/2 tbsp. herb and cheese spread to both bottom and top of every roll. Put patties on bottom roll halves; stack a lettuce leaf, sliced red onion and tomato slice on each burger then add roll tops. Serve.

Nutrition Information

- Calories: 566 calories;
- Total Fat: 36.3
- Sodium: 1104
- Total Carbohydrate: 27.5
- Cholesterol: 148
- Protein: 30.2

939.   Summer Lasagna

Serving: 8 | Prep: 15mins | Cook: 1hours | Ready in:

Ingredients

- 1 pound ground beef
- 1/2 cup chopped onion
- 1/2 cup chopped green bell pepper
- 1/4 cup finely chopped carrots
- 2 cloves garlic, minced
- 1 (15 ounce) can tomato sauce
- 1/2 teaspoon dried oregano
- 1/2 teaspoon dried basil
- salt and pepper to taste
- 5 medium zucchini, sliced lengthwise into 1/4-inch thick strips.
- 1 cup cottage cheese
- 1 egg, beaten
- 3/4 cup shredded mozzarella cheese
- 1/4 cup grated Parmesan cheese

Direction

- Set your oven to 350°F (175°C) for preheating. Prepare a medium sized baking pan that is lightly greased.
- Cook the ground beef in a skillet with a medium heat until the color turns evenly to brown. Drain its juices before mixing the green bell pepper, tomato sauce, garlic, onion and carrots. Sprinkle salt, oregano, pepper and basil for the seasoning. Let it boil before decreasing the heat to low and let it simmer for about 10 minutes. Be sure that after cooking, the vegetables are all tender.
- Layer into the bottom of the prepared baking pan half of the zucchini strips. Get a bowl and whisk together the egg and cottage cheese before spreading it on top of the strips. Spread 1/2 of the beef mixture on its top and drizzle half of the mozzarella cheese over it. Repeat layers using the remaining strips, beef mixture, and the mozzarella cheese. Sprinkle Parmesan cheese on top.
- Let it bake for 45 minutes in the preheated oven. Before serving, let it rest first for 10 minutes and then slice.

Nutrition Information

- Calories: 237 calories;
- Sodium: 570
- Total Carbohydrate: 10.3
- Cholesterol: 71

- Protein: 19.7
- Total Fat: 13.5

Serving: 8 | Prep: 15mins | Cook: 45mins | Ready in:

Ingredients

- 2 pounds ground beef
- 1/2 onion, chopped
- 2 eggs, beaten
- 3/4 cup small chunks of bread
- 1/2 cup milk
- 1/2 cup chopped green bell pepper
- 1 1/2 teaspoons salt
- 1/4 teaspoon sage
- 1/4 teaspoon ground black pepper
- 1/2 cup ketchup, or to taste

Direction

- Set oven to 350°F (175 degrees C) for preheating.
- In a bowl, combine well the ground beef, eggs, milk, onion, bread, salt, sage, green bell pepper, and black pepper. Press down into the loaf pan. Put ketchup on top of the loaf, then spread.
- In the preheated oven, bake for about 45 minutes until center is no longer pink. Using an instant-read thermometer, check current temperature by inserting it in the center; the temperature should not be less than 160°F (70 degrees C).

Nutrition Information

- Calories: 262 calories;
- Cholesterol: 119
- Protein: 21.9
- Total Fat: 15.4
- Sodium: 715
- Total Carbohydrate: 8.1

940.   Supa Dupa Egg Sandwich

Serving: 1 | Prep: 5mins | Cook: 10mins | Ready in:

Ingredients

- 1/4 pound extra lean ground beef
- 2 (1 ounce) slices bread
- ketchup
- mayonnaise
- 1 egg
- 2 slices mozzarella cheese
- 2 slices ham
- 1 slice fresh tomato

Direction

- Position a frying pan on medium heat. Shape the ground beef into a patty and cook till it reaches the preferred doneness. Fry egg in a slightly oiled small-sized pan on medium heat. Turn the egg over and cover using cheese. Cook till cheese melts and the yolk hardens.
- Spread mayonnaise and ketchup on the slices of bread. Add the egg onto one of the bread slices. Heat the ham in the pan, and add over the egg. Add slices of tomato and hamburger on top. Position the other slice of bread on top, and then halve it.

Nutrition Information

- Calories: 643 calories;
- Sodium: 1120
- Total Carbohydrate: 35.9
- Cholesterol: 301
- Protein: 50
- Total Fat: 32.6

942.   Super Nachos

Serving: 12 | Prep: 30mins | Cook: 20mins | Ready in:

Ingredients

- 1 pound ground beef
- 1 (1.25 ounce) package taco seasoning mix
- 3/4 cup water
- 1 (18 ounce) package restaurant-style tortilla chips
- 1 cup shredded sharp Cheddar cheese, or more to taste
- 1 (15.5 ounce) can refried beans
- 1 cup salsa
- 1 cup sour cream, or more to taste
- 1 (10 ounce) can pitted black olives, drained and chopped
- 4 green onions, diced
- 1 (4 ounce) can sliced jalapeno peppers, drained

Direction

- In a frying pan, stir and cook ground beef over medium heat for 5-10 minutes until the meat is not pink anymore and is crumbly. Strain the extra grease. Mix in water and taco seasoning mix, simmer for 8-10 minutes until the beef mixture is thick.
- Put the oven rack approximately 6-inches from the heat source and start preheating the broiler. Use an aluminum foil to line a cookie sheet.
- On the prepared cookie sheet, spread tortilla chips; use Cheddar cheese to put on top, dot with ground beef mixture and refried beans.
- Put in the preheated oven and broil for 3-5 minutes until the cheese melts, watching closely to avoid burning.
- Put jalapeno peppers, green onions, black olives, sour cream, and salsa on top of the nachos.

Nutrition Information

- Calories: 432 calories;

- Total Fat: 24.5
- Sodium: 1081
- Total Carbohydrate: 39.7
- Cholesterol: 44
- Protein: 15.2

943.   Super Stuffed Meatloaf

Serving: 8 | Prep: 30mins | Cook: 1hours5mins | Ready in:

Ingredients

- Meatloaf:
- 1 1/2 pounds ground beef
- 1 1/3 cups dry bread crumbs
- 1 egg, slightly beaten
- 1/2 onion, finely chopped
- 1/4 cup milk
- 1 tablespoon Worcestershire sauce
- 1 tablespoon chopped fresh garlic
- 1 1/2 teaspoons Italian seasoning
- 1 teaspoon dry mustard
- 1 teaspoon salt
- 1/2 teaspoon ground black pepper
- Filling:
- 1 tablespoon butter
- 1 yellow onion, chopped
- 1 (6 ounce) package portobello mushroom caps, chopped
- 1 cup shredded Cheddar cheese

Direction

- Set oven to 350° F (175° C) to preheat.
- In a bowl, combine ground beef, Worcestershire sauce, milk, 1/2 a chopped onion, egg and breadcrumbs; flavor with black pepper, salt, dry mustard, Italian seasoning and garlic. Move the meat mixture to a sheet of aluminum foil or waxed paper and flatten to shape a 1/2-inch thick rectangle.
- In a skillet, melt butter over medium heat. Cook while stirring mushrooms and yellow onion in melted butter for about 5 minutes

until the mushrooms are tender and onion is translucent. Take away from heat, allowing to cool.

- Spread filling mixture into the middle of meat rectangle. Top the filling with a sprinkle of Cheddar cheese, keeping a little space at one end to roll and seal easier. Hold up the edge of the foil or waxed paper to roll the well-flattened meat around the filling into a log. Seal the seam and ends, then put the loaf into a 9x5-inch loaf pan.
- Bake in the prepared oven for about 30 minutes until oil from the cheese starts to pool. Drain off the oil and keep baking for about 30 to 60 minutes more until no pink remains in the middle. An instant-read thermometer should reach at least 160° F (70° C) when inserted into the middle.

Nutrition Information

- Calories: 396 calories;
- Total Fat: 23.7
- Sodium: 705
- Total Carbohydrate: 18.5
- Cholesterol: 110
- Protein: 26.4

----
944.   Swedish Meatballs (Svenska Kottbullar)

Serving: 6 | Prep: 25mins | Cook: 1hours | Ready in:

Ingredients

- 2 slices day-old white bread, crumbled
- 1/2 cup heavy cream
- 1 teaspoon butter
- 1 small onion, minced
- 2/3 pound ground beef
- 1/3 pound finely ground pork
- 1 egg
- 1 tablespoon brown sugar (optional)
- 1 teaspoon salt

- 1/4 teaspoon ground black pepper
- 1/4 teaspoon ground nutmeg
- 1/4 teaspoon ground allspice
- 1/8 teaspoon ground ginger (optional)
- 1 tablespoon butter
- 1/4 cup chicken broth
- 3 tablespoons all-purpose flour, or as needed
- 2 cups beef broth, or as needed
- 1/2 (8 ounce) container sour cream

Direction

- Turn on the oven. Preheat it to 350 degr. F (175 degr. C).
- In a small bowl mix the bread crumbs and the cream. Allow 10 minutes for the crumbs to absorb the cream. While the breadcrumbs are soaking, in a skillet melt a teaspoon of the butter over medium heat. Stir in the onion and cook about 10 minutes until it becomes light brown. Transfer the onion into a big bowl; mix the onion with the ground pork, ground beef, brown sugar, egg, salt, nutmeg, ginger, black pepper, and allspice. Add the soaked bread crumbs into the meat mixture.
- In a large skillet, melt a tablespoon of butter over medium heat. Take about 1,5 tablespoon of the meat mixture and form the meatball. Arrange meatballs into the skillet, and cook about 5 minutes, until making the meatballs just brown outside. The center of the meatballs will still be pink. Turn the meatballs often. Transfer the meatballs from the skillet into a baking dish, cover with the chicken broth; cover with a foil.
- Bake about 40 minutes in the preheated oven, until the meatballs are soft. Place the meatballs to a serving dish.
- Make a brown gravy by pouring pan drippings into a saucepan. Place the saucepan over medium heat, whisking in the flour until smooth. Continue cooking while gradually adding enough beef broth, total 2,5 cups of liquid. Simmer the gravy and whisk it constantly about 5 minutes, until thick. Just before serving, whisk in the sour cream.

Season with salt and black pepper to taste. Serve with the meatballs.

Nutrition Information

- Calories: 309 calories;
- Total Fat: 21.3
- Sodium: 794
- Total Carbohydrate: 11.9
- Cholesterol: 108
- Protein: 16.9

---

945.   Swedish Meatballs I

Serving: 4 | Prep: 25mins | Cook: 1hours | Ready in:

Ingredients

- 1 egg
- 1/4 cup milk
- 1 pound ground beef
- 1/4 cup dry cream of wheat cereal
- 1/4 cup minced onion
- 1 (10.75 ounce) can condensed cream of chicken soup
- 1 (10.75 ounce) can condensed cream of mushroom soup
- 1 (12 fluid ounce) can evaporated milk
- 1 tablespoon chopped fresh parsley

Direction

- Heat oven to 175 degrees C (350 degrees F).
- Beat the egg and the milk in a large bowl. Mix in the wheat cream, onion and beef. Mould into balls of 1 inch. Lightly lubricate a baking sheet and place the balls on it.
- Bake balls on the greased baking sheet at 175 deg C (350 deg F) for about 20 minutes. If needed, drain meatballs on paper towels. Transfer meatballs into a lightly greased 2 quart casserole dish. Mix the soups with the evaporated milk, stir until it becomes smooth

in a separate medium bowl. Pour over the meatballs.

- Bake uncovered for another 40 minutes at 175 degrees C (350 degrees F). Serve sprinkled with parsley.

Nutrition Information

- Calories: 662 calories;
- Total Fat: 47.8
- Sodium: 1193
- Total Carbohydrate: 26.3
- Cholesterol: 178
- Protein: 31.2

---

946.   Sweet Garlic Tomato Beef Pasta

Serving: 8 | Prep: 15mins | Cook: 20mins | Ready in:

Ingredients

- 1 (16 ounce) package medium seashell pasta
- 1 1/2 pounds ground beef
- 1 small onion, chopped
- 2 cloves garlic, minced
- 3 (14.5 ounce) cans Italian stewed tomatoes
- 3 beef bouillon cubes
- 1 1/2 tablespoons white sugar
- 1 teaspoon garlic salt
- 1/8 teaspoon ground black pepper

Direction

- Boil a big pot of slightly salted water. In the pot, put the pasta, allow to cook till al dente, about 8 to 10 minutes, and drain.
- Combine garlic, onion and beef in a big skillet over moderate heat and cook till beef is equally brown.
- Liquify tomatoes in a food processor or blender. Put into skillet together with beef. Stir in pepper, garlic salt, sugar and beef bouillon. Place a cover on skillet, and simmer for 10

minutes, mixing from time to time, till bouillon has dissolved. Mix in pasta till equally coated in sauce, serve.

Nutrition Information

- Calories: 432 calories;
- Total Carbohydrate: 56.9
- Cholesterol: 52
- Protein: 24
- Total Fat: 11.4
- Sodium: 926

947. Sweet Potato Cauliflower Shepherd's Pie

Serving: 8 | Prep: 20mins | Cook: 1hours | Ready in:

Ingredients

- Sweet Potato Cauliflower Layer:
- 1 pound sweet potatoes, peeled and chopped
- 1/2 pound cauliflower florets, chopped
- 1/4 cup chicken broth
- 3 tablespoons butter
- 1 teaspoon salt
- 1/2 teaspoon ground black pepper
- Ground Beef Layer:
- 2 tablespoons light olive oil
- 2 carrots, diced
- 1/2 onion, diced
- 2 cloves garlic, minced
- 1 teaspoon salt
- 1/2 teaspoon ground black pepper
- 1 1/2 pounds ground beef
- 2 tablespoons tapioca starch
- 1 cup chicken broth
- 1/2 cup peas
- 1/2 cup corn
- 3 tablespoons tomato paste
- Topping:
- 1/2 cup freshly grated Parmesan cheese

Direction

- Set an oven to 200°C (400°F) and start preheating.
- In a pot, put the sweet potatoes and cover with water. Boil and cook for 15 minutes. Pour in additional water if necessary and cauliflower; cook for 15 more minutes until all vegetables become tender. Then drain. Mash 1/2 teaspoon of black pepper, a teaspoon of salt, butter, and 1/4 cup of the broth with cauliflower and sweet potatoes.
- In a large skillet, heat the olive oil on medium-high. Put in onion and carrots; sauté for 5 minutes until soften. Put in 1/2 teaspoon of black pepper, a teaspoon of salt, and garlic; then cook for 5 more minutes. Put in the beef; stir and cook for 5-10 minutes until crumble and brown.
- Dust the beef mixture in the skillet with tapioca starch. Pour in tomato paste, corn, peas, and a cup of broth. Boil. Turn down the heat and allow to simmer for 10-15 minutes. In baking dish, scatter mixture of beef evenly. Put mixture of mashed sweet potato on top. Dust the top with Parmesan cheese.
- In the prepared oven, bake for 25 minutes until the top is brown lightly. Before serving, allow to stand for 15 minutes.

Nutrition Information

- Calories: 366 calories;
- Protein: 19
- Total Fat: 22.7
- Sodium: 1047
- Total Carbohydrate: 21.9
- Cholesterol: 69

948. Sweet And Sour Meatballs

Serving: 12 | Prep: 20mins | Cook: 1hours30mins | Ready in:

Ingredients

- 1 (12 fluid ounce) can or bottle chile sauce
- 2 teaspoons lemon juice
- 9 ounces grape jelly
- 1 pound lean ground beef
- 1 egg, beaten
- 1 large onion, grated
- salt to taste

Direction

- Mix grape jelly, lemon juice, and chili sauce. Pour into the slow cooker and simmer on low heat until warm.
- Mix salt, onion, egg, and ground beef. Stir well and roll into 1 inch balls. Put into the sauce and simmer for 1 1/2 hours.

Nutrition Information

- Calories: 152 calories;
- Total Carbohydrate: 17.4
- Cholesterol: 38
- Protein: 8.3
- Total Fat: 5.6
- Sodium: 22

949.   Sweet And Sour Meatballs I

Serving: 7 | Prep: 10mins | Cook: 5hours | Ready in:

Ingredients

- 2 pounds ground beef
- 1 egg
- 1 onion, chopped
- 1 pinch salt
- 1 (12 fluid ounce) can or bottle chili sauce
- 2 teaspoons lemon juice
- 1 cup grape jelly

Direction

- Place the salt, onion, egg, and beef in a large bowl. Combine them together, form into little balls.
- Blend the grape jelly, lemon juice, and chili sauce in a slow cooker. Add in the meatballs and stir, cook for 4-5 hours on high.

Nutrition Information

- Calories: 562 calories;
- Sodium: 99
- Total Carbohydrate: 37.5
- Cholesterol: 137
- Protein: 24
- Total Fat: 35.2

950.   Sweet And Sour Meatballs II

Serving: 5 | Prep: 5mins | Cook: 15mins | Ready in:

Ingredients

- 1 pound ground beef
- 1 egg
- 1 onion, chopped
- 1 cup dry bread crumbs
- salt and pepper to taste
- 1 cup water
- 1/2 cup cider vinegar
- 1/2 cup ketchup
- 2 tablespoons cornstarch
- 1 cup brown sugar
- 2 tablespoons soy sauce

Direction

- In a big bowl, mix together pepper, salt, bread crumbs, onion, egg, and beef. Shape into 1 – 1 1/2 -inch meatballs.
- In a big skillet, sauté meatballs over medium heat till all sides are browned.
- In another medium bowl, combine soy sauce, sugar, cornstarch, ketchup, vinegar, and

water. Spread over meatballs, let sauce thicken. Keep heating till the sauce has just begun to bubble.

Nutrition Information

- Calories: 601 calories;
- Total Fat: 26.3
- Sodium: 878
- Total Carbohydrate: 70.5
- Cholesterol: 114
- Protein: 20.4

| 951. | Sweet And Sour Meatballs V |

Serving: 7 | Prep: 15mins | Cook: 1hours | Ready in:

Ingredients

- 1 cup milk
- 1 cup fresh bread crumbs
- 2 pounds ground beef
- 1/3 cup finely chopped onion
- 1 egg
- 1 teaspoon salt
- ground black pepper to taste
- 2 (12 ounce) bottles chile sauce
- 1 cup grape jelly
- 1/2 cup water
- 1 cup sour cream

Direction

- Blend the breadcrumbs with milk in a mixing bowl. Put in pepper, salt, egg, onion, and ground beef. Combine through and shape into 1-inch balls.
- Blend water, grape jelly, and chili sauce in a large saucepan; allow to simmer. Put the meatballs into the chili sauce mixture gently and bring to a simmer for an hour. As needed, remove excess fat from time to time.

- Just before serving, add in sour cream and stir. Before the sour cream starts boiling, take away from the heat.

Nutrition Information

- Calories: 544 calories;
- Total Carbohydrate: 47.2
- Cholesterol: 132
- Protein: 33
- Total Fat: 24.9
- Sodium: 481

| 952. | Sweet And Sour Stuffed Cabbage |

Serving: 10 | Prep: 1hours | Cook: 3hours50mins | Ready in:

Ingredients

- 2/3 cup uncooked white rice
- 1 cup water
- 2 heads cabbage, cored
- 3 pounds ground beef chuck
- 2 eggs
- 1 1/2 teaspoons garlic powder
- salt and pepper to taste
- 1/2 cup ketchup
- 1 onion, sliced
- 3 (28 ounce) cans crushed tomatoes
- 1/2 cup raisins
- 1 teaspoon citric acid powder
- 1 1/2 teaspoons garlic powder
- salt and pepper to taste
- 1/2 cup ketchup
- 1/2 cup white sugar
- 1 cup ketchup
- 1/2 cup white sugar, or to taste (optional)

Direction

- In a saucepan over high heat, boil water and rice. Turn heat to medium-low, put cover, and allow to simmer for 20 to 25 minutes till liquid has been soaked in and rice is soft.

- Fill big pot with water and boil. Let the heads of cabbage boil for 5 minutes, one by one, till softened yet remain firm. Take off and allow to cool for 15 minutes.
- In a bowl, mix half cup ketchup, salt and pepper, 1 1/2 teaspoons of garlic powder, cooked rice, eggs and ground beef. Combine using hands till well incorporated.
- Have cabbage leaves ready by shaving off 1 slice of big vein in the middle of leaves so that it can be rolled easily. In the middle of leaf, put a heaping spoonful of filling. Fold in right and left edges and roll leaf up from bottom, creating a firm cylinder. Seal using toothpicks if needed. Keep filling and rolling the leaves; get the smaller leaves of cabbage and reserve.
- Slice the reserved leaves of cabbage. In a big pot, put sliced cabbage. Put remaining 1 1/2 teaspoons garlic powder, 1/2 cup ketchup, salt and pepper, sour salt or citric acid powder, raisins, crushed tomatoes and chopped onion. Mix in half cup white sugar and boil the mixture.
- Taste and adjust the sauce sweetness, if wished, by putting half cup more of sugar. Into the sauce, put cabbage rolls. Add the leftover 1 cup ketchup over the rolls. Cover pot, and lower heat to simmer.
- Allow the rolls to cook for 3 hours, basting after every 30 minutes.

Nutrition Information

- Calories: 599 calories;
- Protein: 33.4
- Total Fat: 18.2
- Sodium: 1216
- Total Carbohydrate: 82.9
- Cholesterol: 120

953.   Swiss Cheese Noodle Bake

Serving: 8 | Prep: 20mins | Cook: 50mins | Ready in:

Ingredients

- 1 pound ground beef
- 1 pound bulk Italian sausage
- 2 (26 ounce) jars chunky style pasta sauce (such as Prego®)
- 1 (16 ounce) package broad egg noodles
- 3 (8 ounce) packages sliced Swiss cheese (such as Sargento®)

Direction

- Set the oven to 350°F (175°C) for preheating. Grease a 9x13-inches baking dish.
- In a large and deep skillet, cook the sausage and ground beef for 5 minutes, or until well browned. Drain the fat. Mix in pasta sauce. Simmer the mixture.
- While the sauce simmers, boil a large pot of salted water over high heat. Mix in egg noodles and boil it for 5 minutes, or until cooked through yet still al dente. Drain the noodles well.
- Scoop 1/2 of the meat mixture into the greased baking dish. Pour half of the cooked noodles on top. Sprinkle it with 1 1/2 packages of the cheese slices. Do the same layer with the remaining sauce, cheese, and noodles.
- Let it bake uncovered inside the preheated oven for 40 minutes, or until the cheese is browned and melted. Allow it to stand for 5 minutes. Serve.

Nutrition Information

- Calories: 951 calories;
- Sodium: 1427
- Total Carbohydrate: 71.2
- Cholesterol: 186
- Protein: 50.9
- Total Fat: 50.6

954. Taco Dinner

Serving: 4 | Prep: 10mins | Cook: 15mins | Ready in:

Ingredients

- 1 pound ground beef
- 1 (12 ounce) bag Birds Eye® Recipe Ready Southwest Blend
- 1 (11.04 ounce) box taco dinner kit
- 1/4 cup water
- Sour cream
- Shredded lettuce

Direction

- Use a big nonstick pan to brown the ground beef, then drain the fat.
- Add in water, taco seasoning, and Recipe Ready Southwest Blend. Cook the mixture atop a medium-high heat, occasionally stirring, until the vegetables become tender, 5 minutes.
- Serve in taco shells and tortillas topped with sour cream, shredded lettuce, and taco sauce.

Nutrition Information

- Calories: 519 calories;
- Total Carbohydrate: 43.5
- Cholesterol: 77
- Protein: 26.5
- Total Fat: 25.1
- Sodium: 1272

955. Taco Mix With Black Beans

Serving: 8 | Prep: 5mins | Cook: 10mins | Ready in:

Ingredients

- 1 pound lean ground beef

- 1 (19 ounce) can black beans, rinsed and drained
- 1/2 cup salsa
- 1/4 cup water
- 2 tablespoons taco seasoning mix

Direction

- On moderate heat, heat a big skillet. In hot skillet, cook and mix the beef for 5 to 7 minutes till crumbly and browned.
- Mix ground beef and black beans; put in taco seasoning mix, water and salsa. Cook for 5 to 7 minutes, mixing often, till mixture is heated completely.

Nutrition Information

- Calories: 182 calories;
- Total Fat: 7.1
- Sodium: 554
- Total Carbohydrate: 13.7
- Cholesterol: 37
- Protein: 15.1

956. Taco Pasta Salad

Serving: 6 | Prep: 10mins | Cook: 20mins | Ready in:

Ingredients

- 2 cups spiral pasta
- 1 pound ground beef
- 1 (1.25 ounce) package taco seasoning
- 3 cups shredded lettuce
- 2 cups halved cherry tomatoes
- 1 cup shredded Cheddar cheese
- 1/2 cup chopped onion
- 1/2 cup French salad dressing
- 1 (7 ounce) bag corn chips
- 2 tablespoons sour cream

Direction

- Boil a large pot of lightly salted water. Cook the spiral pasta into the boiling water for about 12 minutes, stirring from time to time, until cooked through but firm to the bite. Let it drain.
- Heat a large skillet over medium-high heat. Stir in ground beef and cook and stir for about 10 minutes until the beef is browned all over, crumbly and no longer pink. Allow it to drain, discarding any excess grease. Mix taco seasoning into the beef mixture; set aside to cool.
- Mix the beef mixture into the pasta. Toss in Cheddar cheese, corn chips, French dressing, lettuce, onion, and tomatoes. Top the mixture with sour cream.

Nutrition Information

- Calories: 618 calories;
- Total Fat: 38.4
- Sodium: 980
- Total Carbohydrate: 46.4
- Cholesterol: 68
- Protein: 22.8

957.   Taco Queso Dip

Serving: 10 | Prep: 5mins | Cook: 20mins | Ready in:

Ingredients

- 1 pound ground beef
- 1 package taco seasoning
- 1 (12 fluid ounce) can or bottle beer
- 1 1/2 tablespoons butter
- 1 1/2 tablespoons all-purpose flour
- 2 cups shredded Mexican cheese blend
- 1 cup shredded white Cheddar cheese

Direction

- Over medium-high heat, heat a large skillet. In the hot skillet, cook while stirring beef for 5-7

mins until crumbly and browned. Then drain and remove the grease. Stir the taco seasoning into ground beef to coat.
- Boil beer in small saucepan.
- In a large saucepan, melt butter. Mix the flour into the melted butter; cook for 5 mins until starting to brown, stirring continually. Stir beer slowly into butter mixture. Put in white Cheddar cheese and Mexican cheese blend in small amounts, letting each addition melt into beer mixture between each addition, stirring continually. Stir the beef into cheesy mixture.

Nutrition Information

- Calories: 278 calories;
- Total Carbohydrate: 5.5
- Cholesterol: 71
- Protein: 16.8
- Total Fat: 19.6
- Sodium: 572

958.   Taco Salad II

Serving: 7 | Prep: 15mins | Cook: 20mins | Ready in:

Ingredients

- 1 pound lean ground beef
- 1 (1.25 ounce) package taco seasoning mix
- 1 head iceberg lettuce - rinsed, dried, and shredded
- 1 onion, chopped
- 1 green bell pepper, chopped
- 3 cups shredded Cheddar-Monterey Jack cheese blend
- 2 tomatoes, chopped
- 4 ounces crushed tortilla chips
- 1/4 cup French dressing

Direction

- In a large and deep skillet, cook the hamburger over medium-high heat until browned evenly, and then drain. Add the taco seasoning mix. Follow the package directions on how to prepare it; put aside to cool.

- Mix beef, tortilla chips, lettuce, tomatoes, cheese, onions, and bell pepper in a large bowl. Coat the salad with enough dressing, tossing it well until evenly coated. Refrigerate the salad overnight.

Nutrition Information

- Calories: 467 calories;
- Sodium: 859
- Total Carbohydrate: 23.4
- Cholesterol: 85
- Protein: 25.3
- Total Fat: 30

959.   Taco Salad III

Serving: 8 | Prep: 15mins | Cook: 15mins | Ready in:

Ingredients

- 16 ounces lean ground beef
- 1 (1.25 ounce) package taco seasoning mix
- 1 head iceberg lettuce, shredded
- 1 red onion, sliced
- 1 bunch green onions, chopped
- 1 (15 ounce) can pinto beans, drained
- 1 (15 ounce) can kidney beans, drained
- 2 large tomatoes, chopped
- 1 avocados - peeled, pitted, and cubed
- 8 ounces shredded Cheddar cheese
- 1 (16 ounce) package corn chips
- 1 (16 ounce) bottle Catalina salad dressing

Direction

- Follow the direction of taco seasoning package to prepare the ground beef and reserve.
- Mix in a large bowl the cheese, avocado, tomatoes, kidney beans, pinto beans, green

and red onion, lettuce and beef mixture. Combine well.

- Prior to serving, put the corn chips and enough dressing to coat. Combine well and serve right away.

Nutrition Information

- Calories: 945 calories;
- Total Fat: 60.7
- Sodium: 1682
- Total Carbohydrate: 75.7
- Cholesterol: 72
- Protein: 27.3

960.   Taco Soup II

Serving: 6 | Prep: 5mins | Cook: 45mins | Ready in:

Ingredients

- 2 pounds lean ground beef
- 1 onion, chopped
- 1 (4 ounce) can diced green chiles
- 1 teaspoon salt
- 1 teaspoon ground black pepper
- 1 (15 ounce) can pinto beans, drained
- 1 (15 ounce) can lima beans, drained
- 1 (1.25 ounce) package taco seasoning mix
- 1 1/2 cups water
- 1 (1 ounce) package ranch dressing mix
- 1 (15 ounce) can white hominy, drained
- 1 (14.5 ounce) can stewed tomatoes
- 1 (15 ounce) can kidney beans, drained and rinsed

Direction

- Brown beef and chopped onion over medium heat in a large Dutch oven. Drain off excess fat.
- Add beans, chilies, stewed tomatoes, salt, pepper, water, hominy and seasoning mixes to

the beef and onion. Bring to the boil. Turn down heat and simmer for 30 minutes.
- Serve with chips and top with shredded cheese.

Nutrition Information

- Calories: 669 calories;
- Sodium: 2300
- Total Carbohydrate: 52.2
- Cholesterol: 114
- Protein: 38.5
- Total Fat: 32.9

---

961. Taco Taters

Serving: 6 | Prep: 15mins | Cook: 35mins | Ready in:

Ingredients

- 1 pound ground beef
- 1 (15.25 ounce) can corn
- 1 (8 ounce) jar salsa
- 1 ounce processed cheese (such as Velveeta®)
- 1 ounce cream cheese
- 1 package taco seasoning mix
- 1 (16 ounce) package frozen bite-size potato nuggets (such as Tater Tots®)
- 1 (4 ounce) can sliced black olives
- 1 (4 ounce) can diced jalapeno peppers
- 4 ounces shredded Cheddar cheese
- 1 (8 ounce) container sour cream

Direction

- Start preheating the oven at 400°F (200°C).
- Heat over medium-high heat a large skillet. In the hot skillet, cook and stir beef for 5 to 7 minutes until crumbled and browned; drain and discard the fat. Add taco seasoning, cream cheese, processed cheese, salsa, and corn to ground beef and stir until blended.
- Pour the beef mixture over the base of a 9x13-inch baking dish. Place potato nuggets on the

beef mixture, sprinkle Cheddar cheese, jalapenos, and black olives on top.
- Bake in the prepared oven for about 25 minutes until potato nuggets seem crisp and cheese is bubbling. Top with sour cream.

Nutrition Information

- Calories: 565 calories;
- Cholesterol: 91
- Protein: 24.3
- Total Fat: 35.9
- Sodium: 1892
- Total Carbohydrate: 42.7

---

962. Tacos In Pasta Shells

Serving: 6 | Prep: 30mins | Cook: 30mins | Ready in:

Ingredients

- 1 1/4 pounds lean ground beef
- 1 (3 ounce) package cream cheese
- 1 teaspoon salt
- 1 teaspoon chili powder
- 18 jumbo pasta shells
- 2 tablespoons butter, melted
- 1 cup taco sauce
- 1 cup shredded Cheddar cheese
- 1 cup shredded Monterey Jack cheese
- 1 1/2 cups crushed tortilla chips
- 1 cup sour cream

Direction

- Brown beef in a big skillet over moderate heat till not pink anymore; drain. Put in the chili powder, salt and cream cheese; stir and simmer for 5 minutes.
- In the meantime, boil a big pot of slightly salted water. Put in the pasta and cook until al dente, about 8 to 10 minutes; drain. Toss butter and cooked shells.
- Preheat the oven to 175 °C or 350 °F.

- Stuff the shells with beef mixture, and set in a9x13 inch baking dish; on top of the shells, put the taco sauce. Cover using foil; and in prepped oven, bake for 15 minutes.
- Take dish out of oven and put tortilla chips, Monterey Jack cheese and Cheddar cheese on top; put dish back into oven to cook for an additional of 15 minutes.
- Place onions and sour cream over top; serve.

Nutrition Information

- Calories: 735 calories;
- Total Carbohydrate: 47.6
- Cholesterol: 136
- Protein: 35.7
- Total Fat: 44.2
- Sodium: 1054

---

963.   Talerini

Serving: 6 | Prep: 20mins | Cook: 20mins | Ready in:

Ingredients

- 1 (8 ounce) package wide egg noodles
- 1 pound ground beef
- 1 (8 ounce) can tomato sauce
- 1 (11 ounce) can whole kernel corn, drained
- 1 (4 ounce) can sliced black olives, drained
- 2 cups shredded Cheddar cheese
- 1 teaspoon chili powder, or to taste

Direction

- Turn the oven to 375°F (190°C) to preheat. Boil lightly salted water in a big pot. Add noodles and cook for about 7 minutes until tender. Drain and put back into the pot.
- In a big frying pan, crumble ground beef over medium-high heat. Stir and cook until it turns brown evenly. Drain off the fat. Mix in olives, corn, and tomato sauce. Use chili powder to season. Mix the noodles with the beef mixture.

Pour to a 9x13-in. baking dish. Put Cheddar cheese on top.
- Bake in the preheated oven for 20 minutes until the cheese melts.

Nutrition Information

- Calories: 503 calories;
- Total Fat: 25.6
- Sodium: 801
- Total Carbohydrate: 40.2
- Cholesterol: 117
- Protein: 29.4

---

964.   Tasty Baked Meatballs

Serving: 6 | Prep: 15mins | Cook: 30mins | Ready in:

Ingredients

- 3 pounds ground beef
- 1 1/2 cups Italian-seasoned dry bread crumbs
- 1 (10.5 ounce) can cream of mushroom soup
- 3 eggs, lightly beaten
- 1/4 cup grated Parmesan cheese
- 1 (1 ounce) package dry onion soup mix

Direction

- Preheat an oven to 350°F (175°C). Use aluminum foil to line two baking sheets then lightly grease them.
- Combine the onion soup mix, Parmesan cheese, eggs, cream of mushroom soup, bread crumbs, and ground beef. Form the mixture into balls with a golf ball's size. Position on the prepped baking sheets.
- In the preheated oven, bake for about 30 minutes until the center is not pink anymore. An instant-read thermometer pinned into the center should reach no less than 160°F (70°C).

Nutrition Information

- Calories: 614 calories;
- Total Carbohydrate: 26
- Cholesterol: 234
- Protein: 47.1
- Total Fat: 34.5
- Sodium: 1147

- Calories: 360 calories;
- Protein: 11
- Total Fat: 21.8
- Sodium: 599
- Total Carbohydrate: 30.7
- Cholesterol: 33

965.   Tasty Meat Pie

Serving: 12 | Prep: | Cook: 45mins | Ready in:

Ingredients

- 1 pound ground beef
- 1 onion, chopped
- 1 (10.75 ounce) can condensed vegetable beef soup, undiluted
- 1 (10.75 ounce) can condensed cream of mushroom soup
- 3 potatoes, peeled and cubed
- 4 carrots, sliced
- 1/4 teaspoon salt
- 1/8 teaspoon black pepper
- 1 recipe pastry for a 9 inch double crust pie

Direction

- Start preheating the oven to 175°C (350°F).
- Cook the chopped onion and the ground beef in a big skillet until the meat is not pink anymore. Take away from heat and remove the excess fat. Mix in the cream of mushroom soups and the vegetable beef, the carrots and potatoes. Add pepper and salt to taste. Divide the mixture between two 9-in. pie plates.
- Fit the top of each pie with pastry. Cover each pie and cut slits in the top to let the steam escape.
- Bake for about 45-50 minutes in the preheated oven, until the pies become golden brown. Let it sit on for 15 minutes on a wire rack, then serve.

Nutrition Information

966.   Tater Tot Casserole

Serving: 5 | Prep: 10mins | Cook: 25mins | Ready in:

Ingredients

- 1 pound ground beef
- 1 medium onion, chopped
- 1 (10.75 ounce) can Campbell's® Condensed Cream of Mushroom Soup (Regular or 98% Fat Free)
- 1 tablespoon ketchup
- 1 tablespoon Worcestershire sauce
- 3 cups frozen Tater Tots

Direction

- Cook the onion and beef in the 10-in. skillet on medium-high heat till the beef becomes browned well, whisking to crumble the meat. Pour off the fat.
- Whisk the Worcestershire sauce, ketchup and soup to the skillet. Scoop the beef mixture into the 12x8-in. shallow baking plate. Arrange the potatoes round the edge of the casserole.
- Bake at 425°F till the potatoes are done or for 25 minutes.

Nutrition Information

- Calories: 356 calories;
- Total Fat: 21
- Sodium: 849
- Total Carbohydrate: 26.5
- Cholesterol: 59
- Protein: 17.8

967.   Tater Tot Casserole II

Serving: 6 | Prep: 10mins | Cook: 1hours | Ready in:

Ingredients

- 1 (32 ounce) package frozen potato rounds
- 1 (16 ounce) container sour cream
- 1 cup shredded Cheddar cheese
- 1 (10.75 ounce) can condensed cream of mushroom soup
- 1 (6 ounce) can French-fried onions

Direction

- Preheat the oven to 175 degrees C (350 degrees F). Grease the 9x13-in. baking plate.
- Arrange the tater tots in prepped baking plate.
- In the mixing bowl, mix the mushroom soup, cheese and sour cream. Add this mixture on top of tater tots. Drizzle the onions on top of casserole.
- Bake in 175 degrees C (350 degrees F) oven for 45-60 minutes.

Nutrition Information

- Calories: 718 calories;
- Cholesterol: 53
- Protein: 11.5
- Total Fat: 53.3
- Sodium: 1330
- Total Carbohydrate: 56.2

968.   Tater Tot Casserole III

Serving: 8 | Prep: 15mins | Cook: 1hours | Ready in:

Ingredients

- 2 pounds tater tots, thawed
- 1 (10.5 ounce) can condensed cream of chicken soup

- 1 cup finely chopped onion
- 1 (16 ounce) container sour cream
- 1 (8 ounce) package sharp Cheddar cheese, shredded
- 1 dash garlic powder
- 1/2 teaspoon seasoning salt
- 1/2 cup butter, softened
- 3 cups cornflakes cereal
- 1/2 cup butter, melted
- 2 tablespoons grated Parmesan cheese
- paprika to taste

Direction

- Preheat the oven to 175 degrees C (350 degrees F). Grease the 9x13-in. casserole plate.
- In the big mixing bowl, mix the softened butter, seasoning salt, garlic powder, cheese, sour cream, and onion, soup, and tater tots; stir them well. Move into the casserole plate. In the medium-sized bowl, mix the melted butter and cereal; spread on the casserole. Drizzle top with the parmesan cheese (adjust to taste) and paprika.
- Bake in the preheated oven till brown or for 45-60 minutes. Note: You should place one cookie sheet under casserole plate, in case it becomes bubbly over when cooking.

Nutrition Information

- Calories: 707 calories;
- Sodium: 1267
- Total Carbohydrate: 44.9
- Cholesterol: 119
- Protein: 14.2
- Total Fat: 56.3

969.   Tater Tot Hot Dish II

Serving: 6 | Prep: 10mins | Cook: 1hours | Ready in:

Ingredients

- 1 1/2 pounds lean ground beef
- 1 onion, chopped
- 3/4 teaspoon salt
- 1 pinch ground black pepper
- 1 (32 ounce) package tater tots, thawed
- 1 (10.75 ounce) can condensed cream of mushroom soup
- 1 (10.75 ounce) can condensed cream of celery soup
- 1 (6 ounce) can French-fried onion rings

Direction

- Preheat the oven to 175 degrees C (350 degrees F).
- Cook the ground beef together with pepper, onion, and salt in a large skillet. Drain off grease and then transfer into a 9x13 inch baking dish. Add in tater tots. Combine cream of celery soup and cream of mushroom together and then spread the mixture atop the dish. If using, add onion rings on top.
- Bake for an hour in the oven.

Nutrition Information

- Calories: 744 calories;
- Sodium: 1706
- Total Carbohydrate: 59.6
- Cholesterol: 68
- Protein: 25.4
- Total Fat: 47.7

970.   Taylor's Piroshki

Serving: 11 | Prep: 1hours30mins | Cook: 20mins | Ready in:

Ingredients

- 1 1/2 pounds ground beef
- 1 onion, finely chopped
- 1 teaspoon salt
- ground black pepper to taste
- dried dill weed to taste
- 1 (.25 ounce) package active dry yeast
- 1/4 cup warm water
- 1 cup milk
- 3 eggs
- 1/2 cup vegetable oil
- 2 tablespoons granulated sugar
- 1 teaspoon salt
- 4 cups all-purpose flour
- 3 cups oil for frying

Direction

- Put the ground beef in a medium-sized skillet and let it cook on medium heat until all of the ground beef turned brown in color; drain off any excess oil. Add in the onion and sauté it with the cooked ground beef until the onion becomes translucent. Put in the pepper, dill and salt to taste. Let it cool down first before using it.
- Mix the yeast and 1/4 cup of warm water until the yeast has fully dissolved then put it in a warm place for 10-15 minutes until it is foamy. Put the milk in a medium-sized saucepan and let it heat up on low heat until it is warm; lightly mix the sugar, eggs, salt and oil in the warm milk. Take the pan away from the heat.
- In a big mixing bowl, put in 1/2 of the flour and slowly mix in the milk mixture. Put in the yeast solution and alternate it with the leftover flour; mix the mixture after every addition. Mix it thoroughly. Knead the dough until it forms into a ball and is no longer sticky. (Note: Use 4 cups of flour first. Just add a little more flour at a time as the dough is being kneaded.) Use a clean cloth to cover the bowl. Place it in a warm spot and let it rise in volume until it has doubled in size.
- Take the risen dough from the bowl and put it on a clean surface covered with a little bit of flour. Divide the dough into even pieces in the size of a golf ball. Flatten out each piece into a 3 1/2 to 4-inch disk.
- Put a tablespoonful of the cooled ground beef mixture in the middle of each of the dough disks. Fold the dough over the beef filling and

secure the edges by pinching it together firmly. Place it on a clean, flat surface and let it rest for 10 minutes.

- Put the oil in a deep fryer or a big and heavy skillet and let it heat up to 375°F (190°C) temperature. Place the piroshki into the hot oil and let it cook in batches until one side turns golden brown in color, then slowly flip the piroshki over onto the other side and let the other side cook as well. Place the cooked piroshki on a paper towel-lined plate to drain any excess oil.

Nutrition Information

- Calories: 447 calories;
- Total Fat: 24.7
- Sodium: 478
- Total Carbohydrate: 42.4
- Cholesterol: 67
- Protein: 13.5

971.   Tennessee Meatloaf

Serving: 10 | Prep: 40mins | Cook: 1hours | Ready in:

Ingredients

- Brown Sugar Glaze:
- 1/2 cup ketchup
- 1/4 cup brown sugar
- 2 tablespoons cider vinegar
- Meatloaf:
- cooking spray
- 1 onion, chopped
- 1/2 green bell pepper, chopped
- 2 cloves garlic, minced
- 2 large eggs, lightly beaten
- 1 teaspoon dried thyme
- 1 teaspoon seasoned salt
- 1/2 teaspoon ground black pepper
- 2 teaspoons prepared mustard
- 2 teaspoons Worcestershire sauce

- 1/2 teaspoon hot pepper sauce (such as Tabasco®)
- 1/2 cup milk
- 2/3 cup quick cooking oats
- 1 pound ground beef
- 1/2 pound ground pork
- 1/2 pound ground veal

Direction

- In a mixing bowl, combine cider vinegar, brown sugar, and ketchup until well mixed.
- Set oven to 350°F (175°C) to preheat. Line two 9x5-inch loaf pans with aluminum foil or coat with cooking spray.
- Put green pepper and onion in a microwave container; cook, covered for 1 to 2 minutes until tender; put to one side and allow to cool.
- Combine oats, milk, hot sauce, Worcestershire sauce, mustard, black pepper, seasoned salt, thyme, eggs, and garlic in a large mixing bowl; stir well. Mix in cooked green pepper and onion. Add veal, pork, and ground beef. Mix all ingredients in the mixing bowl with your gloved hands until well incorporated and uniform.
- Separate meat mixture into 2 equal portions; press each portion into a loaf pan. Brush half of the glaze over loaves; set aside the remaining glaze.
- Bake for 50 minutes in the preheated oven. Take loaf pans out of the oven; drain fat carefully. Brush the remainder of glaze over loaves. Put the pans back into the oven; bake for 10 minutes longer. Take the loaf pans out of the oven; allow meatloaf to rest for 15 minutes before cutting.

Nutrition Information

- Calories: 233 calories;
- Total Fat: 11.2
- Sodium: 324
- Total Carbohydrate: 15.9
- Cholesterol: 92
- Protein: 17.1

972.   Tequila Chili

Serving: 4 | Prep: 15mins | Cook: 30mins |Ready in:

Ingredients

- 1 pound ground beef
- 1 (14.5 ounce) can Italian-style stewed tomatoes
- 1 (15 ounce) can light red kidney beans, drained
- 1 onion, chopped
- 1 clove garlic, minced
- 1 (8 ounce) can tomato sauce
- 1 1/2 fluid ounces tequila
- 1 tablespoon chili powder
- 1 1/2 teaspoons ground cumin
- 1 teaspoon salt
- 1/2 teaspoon cayenne pepper

Direction

- In a big pot over medium heat, brown ground beef; use a spoon to break it up while cooking. Drain. Mix in cayenne pepper, salt, cumin, chili powder, tequila, tomato sauce, garlic, onion, kidney beans, and tomatoes; let simmer for 20 minutes.

Nutrition Information

- Calories: 379 calories;
- Total Fat: 14.4
- Sodium: 1405
- Total Carbohydrate: 30.2
- Cholesterol: 69
- Protein: 27

973.   Tex Mex Patty Melts

Serving: 3 | Prep: 15mins | Cook: 10mins |Ready in:

Ingredients

- 1 pound ground beef
- 3 tablespoons chili seasoning mix
- 2 chipotle peppers in adobo sauce, minced
- 1/2 fluid ounce beer
- 1/4 cup mayonnaise
- 1 chipotle pepper in adobo sauce, minced
- 6 (1 ounce) slices white bread
- 6 (1/2 ounce) slices pepperjack cheese

Direction

- In a bowl, combine beer, adobo sauce, 2 minced chipotle peppers, chili seasoning mix, and ground beef. Separate beef mixture into 3 patties.
- In a small bowl, mix together adobo sauce, 1 minced chipotle pepper, and mayonnaise. Divide the mayonnaise mixture among the bread slices and distribute evenly. Top mayonnaise mixture on each slice of bread with a slice of pepper jack cheese.
- Heat a large skillet on medium-high heat. Cook patties in the heated skillet until center is no longer pink, about 5 to 7 minutes per side for well-done. Place cooked burgers onto a slice of bread; sandwich with the remaining bread slices.
- Drain the skillet, retaining 2 tablespoons of drippings. Heat the reserved dripping over medium-high heat in the skillet. Grill sandwiches, about 1 to 2 minutes on each side, until cheese is melted and bread turns golden brown.

Nutrition Information

- Calories: 691 calories;
- Total Fat: 44.2
- Sodium: 1574
- Total Carbohydrate: 35.4
- Cholesterol: 129
- Protein: 37.3

974.   Texas Cowboy Stew

Serving: 10 | Prep: 30mins | Cook: 1hours | Ready in:

Ingredients

- 2 pounds ground beef
- 2 (16 ounce) packages kielbasa sausage, sliced into 1/2 inch pieces
- 2 cloves garlic, chopped
- 1 onion, chopped
- 2 (14.5 ounce) cans peeled and diced tomatoes, drained
- 4 medium baking potatoes, peeled and diced
- 2 (15 ounce) cans pinto beans, with liquid
- 2 (15.2 ounce) cans whole kernel corn, with liquid
- 1 (14.5 ounce) can diced tomatoes with green chile peppers, with liquid
- 1 (10 ounce) package frozen mixed vegetables
- 4 cups water
- 2 teaspoons ground cumin
- 2 teaspoons chili powder
- salt and pepper to taste

Direction

- Into a big skillet, break up the ground beef over medium-high heat. Put onion, garlic and sausage; cook and mix till meat is not pink anymore. Allow the grease to drain off, and to a big pot, put the substance of the skillet.
- Into the pot the meat, put the tomatoes, and mix in diced tomatoes, corn, pinto beans, potatoes with water, mixed vegetables and chilies. Add pepper, salt, chili powder and cumin to season. Place the cover, and allow to simmer for a minimum of 1 hour over medium-low heat. Mix from time to time. The more this stew cooks, the better it tastes.

Nutrition Information

- Calories: 677 calories;
- Total Fat: 37.1
- Sodium: 1620
- Total Carbohydrate: 52.2
- Cholesterol: 115
- Protein: 35.3

975.   Texas Taco Soup

Serving: 10 | Prep: 5mins | Cook: 1hours | Ready in:

Ingredients

- 3 pounds ground beef
- 2 onions, chopped
- 2 (15 ounce) cans pinto beans
- 2 (16 ounce) packages frozen corn kernels
- 3 (10 ounce) cans diced tomatoes with green chile peppers
- 6 serrano peppers, crushed
- 1 (1.25 ounce) package taco seasoning mix
- 1 (1 ounce) package ranch dressing mix

Direction

- Cook beef in a big pot over medium heat till brown. Mix in onion and allow to cook for several minutes longer. Let drain.
- Mix in ranch dressing mix, taco seasoning, serrano peppers, diced tomatoes with green chilies, corn and pinto beans. With water, fill the pot to reach within 2 inches of the surface. Boil for 30 minutes, mixing from time to time, then lower the heat and allow to simmer for 30 minutes longer.

Nutrition Information

- Calories: 605 calories;
- Total Fat: 20.9
- Sodium: 885
- Total Carbohydrate: 67.8
- Cholesterol: 82
- Protein: 40

976. The Best Meatballs

Serving: 8 | Prep: 30mins | Cook: 20mins | Ready in:

Ingredients

- 1 pound ground beef
- 1/2 pound ground veal
- 1/2 pound ground pork
- 2 cloves garlic, minced
- 2 eggs
- 1 cup freshly grated Romano cheese
- 1 1/2 tablespoons chopped Italian flat leaf parsley
- salt and ground black pepper to taste
- 2 cups stale Italian bread, crumbled
- 1 1/2 cups lukewarm water
- 1 cup olive oil

Direction

- Mix pork, veal, and beef together in a big bowl. Add in cheese, salt, pepper, eggs, parsley, and garlic.
- Blend the bread crumbs into the meat mixture. Gradually add 1/2 a cup of water at a time. The mixture will be very moist, but it can still hold its shape when you roll it into meatballs. (I typically use about 1 1/4 cups of water). Form into meatballs.
- In a big skillet, heat up olive oil. Fry the meatballs in batches. Once the meatball becomes very brown and slightly crisp, take it off the heat and let it drain on paper towels. (If the mixture is very wet, cover the meatballs as they cook to keep their shape better).

Nutrition Information

- Calories: 613 calories;
- Total Carbohydrate: 6.6
- Cholesterol: 149
- Protein: 26.6
- Total Fat: 53.2
- Sodium: 333

977. The Best Meatballs You'll Ever Have

Serving: 4 | Prep: 15mins | Cook: 20mins | Ready in:

Ingredients

- 1 pound lean ground beef
- 3/4 cup crushed seasoned croutons
- 1/4 cup chopped sweet onion
- 1 egg, lightly beaten
- 2 cloves garlic, chopped
- 3 tablespoons Worcestershire sauce
- 1 tablespoon prepared yellow mustard
- 1 teaspoon red pepper flakes
- 1 teaspoon Cajun seasoning
- 1 teaspoon extra virgin olive oil
- 1 tablespoon butter

Direction

- In a large bowl, combine Cajun seasoning, red pepper flakes, mustard, Worcestershire sauce, garlic, egg, sweet onion, croutons and ground beef together. Shape the mixture into meatballs by hand.
- Place a skillet on medium heat; melt the butter and heat the olive oil. Arrange the meatballs in the skillet; cook while turning continually for 20 minutes or to desired doneness.

Nutrition Information

- Calories: 336 calories;
- Sodium: 482
- Total Carbohydrate: 9.7
- Cholesterol: 123
- Protein: 22.7
- Total Fat: 22.6

978.   The Best Meatloaf

Serving: 6 | Prep: 15mins | Cook: 1hours | Ready in:

Ingredients

- 1/2 cup milk
- 1 cup soft bread crumbs
- 1 1/2 pounds ground beef
- 1 1/4 teaspoons salt
- ground black pepper to taste
- 1 egg, slightly beaten
- 3 tablespoons steak sauce, (e.g. Heinz 57)
- 1 onion, chopped
- 1/2 cup diced green bell pepper
- 1/4 cup steak sauce, or more to taste

Direction

- Set oven to 350°F (175°C) and start preheating. Lightly coat an 8 1/2 x 4 1/2-inch loaf pan with oil.
- In a small bowl, mix soft breadcrumbs and milk and let it soften, about 5 minutes.
- Mix green bell pepper, chopped onion, 3 tablespoons of steak sauce, egg, pepper, salt, and ground beef in a mixing bowl. Put in breadcrumb mixture and mix with your hands until all ingredients are blended.
- Pat the mixture in the prepared loaf pan. Brush the extra steak sauce over the top.
- Bake in the prepared oven until done, 1 hour. Let it rest for 5 minutes before you slice.

Nutrition Information

- Calories: 288 calories;
- Total Fat: 17.9
- Sodium: 867
- Total Carbohydrate: 10.1
- Cholesterol: 101
- Protein: 20.9

979.   The Best Meatloaf I've Ever Made

Serving: 12 | Prep: 15mins | Cook: 1hours10mins | Ready in:

Ingredients

- 1 tablespoon butter
- 1/4 cup minced onion
- 2 cloves garlic, minced
- 1 1/2 teaspoons salt
- 1 1/2 teaspoons freshly ground black pepper
- 2 pounds extra-lean ground beef
- 3 slices bread, toasted and crumbled
- 7 buttery round crackers, crushed
- 1 egg, lightly beaten
- 3 1/2 tablespoons sour cream
- 1 1/2 tablespoons Worcestershire sauce
- 1 (15 ounce) can tomato sauce, divided
- 1/4 cup milk (optional)
- 3 tablespoons ketchup

Direction

- Set oven to 350°F (175°C) to preheat.
- In a skillet over medium heat, heat butter until melted; cook garlic and onion in melted butter until onion is tender, for 5 minutes. Turn off the heat, and sprinkle with pepper and salt to season.
- Combine 1/2 can tomato sauce, Worcestershire sauce, sour cream, egg, crushed crackers, crumbled bread, garlic and onion, and beef in a large mixing bowl. Slowly whisk in milk, 1 teaspoon at a time until mixture is moist, but not mushy. Pour mixture into a 5x9-inch loaf pan.
- Bake without covering for 40 minutes in the preheated oven. Raise temperature to 400°F (200°C), and keep baking until internal temperature of meatloaf reaches 160°F (70°C), about 15 minutes.
- Combine ketchup and leftover tomato sauce in a small mixing bowl. Stream over top of the meatloaf, and keep baking for 10 minutes longer.

Nutrition Information

- Calories: 213 calories;
- Protein: 17.9
- Total Fat: 11.6
- Sodium: 649
- Total Carbohydrate: 8.7
- Cholesterol: 76

Nutrition Information

- Calories: 285 calories;
- Total Fat: 13.9
- Sodium: 809
- Total Carbohydrate: 18.3
- Cholesterol: 69
- Protein: 20.9

980. The Burger Your Mama Warned You About!

Serving: 8 | Prep: 15mins | Cook: 12mins | Ready in:

Ingredients

- 2 pounds ground beef
- 1 red onion, finely chopped
- 1 green bell pepper, finely chopped
- 1/3 cup minced garlic
- 1 (1 ounce) envelope dry onion soup mix
- 1/2 cup barbeque sauce
- 1/2 cup bread crumbs
- 3 tablespoons Worcestershire sauce
- 1/2 teaspoon salt
- 1 tablespoon ground black pepper

Direction

- In a big mixing bowl, combine the black pepper, salt, Worcestershire sauce, bread crumbs, barbeque sauce, onion soup mix, garlic, green pepper, red onion and ground beef. Split the ground beef mixture into 8 even balls and shape each one to create a patty. On a baking sheet, put the patties, cover and chill for a minimum of an hour to let all of the flavors incorporate.
- Preheat the outdoor grill for high heat and grease grate lightly with oil.
- Cook the patties for 6 minutes each side till an inside temperature of 71 °C or 160 °F for well-done burgers.

981. The Original Donair From The East Coast Of Canada

Serving: 6 | Prep: 10mins | Cook: 1hours10mins | Ready in:

Ingredients

- 1 pound ground beef
- 1 teaspoon ground black pepper
- 1 teaspoon onion powder
- 1 teaspoon garlic powder
- 1 teaspoon salt
- 1 teaspoon paprika
- 2 teaspoons cayenne pepper
- 1 teaspoon dried oregano
- 1 (12 ounce) can evaporated milk
- 1/2 cup white sugar
- 1/4 cup white vinegar, or to taste
- 6 large pita bread rounds

Direction

- Mix oregano, cayenne pepper, salt, paprika, garlic powder, onion powder, black pepper and ground beef thoroughly in bowl; pack spiced meat to thick loaf shape then cover. Rest overnight in the fridge.
- Preheat an oven to 175°C/350°F.
- Put meatloaf on baking sheet; bake for 1 hour. Halfway through cooking, flip loaf; cool meatloaf so it holds together while being sliced.

- Mix white sugar and evaporated milk till sugar dissolves in bowl; by teaspoons, add vinegar to taste, mixing after each. Refrigerate sauce till serving.
- Cut meatloaf to 1/4-in. thick slices; brown slices in skillet for 5 minutes per side on medium heat till both sides are crisp and brown.
- Sprinkle little water on pita bread rounds; to warm up, press each on heated skillet.
- Serve: put several meat slices on warmed pita bread; put 2 tbsp. sauce on meat. Roll pita bread to cone shape; use aluminum foil to wrap sauce from dipping out then serve.

Nutrition Information

- Calories: 450 calories;
- Sodium: 814
- Total Carbohydrate: 57.3
- Cholesterol: 64
- Protein: 22.4
- Total Fat: 14.3

982.   The Sarge's Goetta German Breakfast Treat

Serving: 20 | Prep: 5hours | Cook: 10mins | Ready in:

Ingredients

- 3 quarts water
- 2 tablespoons salt
- 2 teaspoons ground black pepper
- 5 cups steel cut oats
- 2 pounds ground beef
- 2 pounds ground pork sausage
- 2 large onions, finely chopped
- 1/4 cup cooking oil

Direction

- Bring to boil water, pepper, and salt in a slow cooker that is set to High. Mix in the steel cut

oats, cover the cooker and let to cook for 90 minutes.
- Combine onions, mix beef, and pork in a large bowl. Mix into the oat mixture and decrease the heat to Low. Cover and continue to cook while stirring time to time for 3 hours.
- Pour the mixture into a medium baking pan and let to cool until semi-solid. Roll out on top of a wax paper and then refrigerate for 1 hour or until firm.
- Over medium high heat, heat oil in a large, heavy skillet. Chop the chilled mixture into thin slices and then cook the slices one by one in the hot oil until brown evenly.

Nutrition Information

- Calories: 511 calories;
- Total Fat: 35.6
- Sodium: 1036
- Total Carbohydrate: 29
- Cholesterol: 69
- Protein: 18

983.   The Shorba Freekeh Of Algeria

Serving: 8 | Prep: 30mins | Cook: 3hours | Ready in:

Ingredients

- 2 large tomatoes, cut into chunks
- 2 onions, cut into chunks
- 1 serrano pepper, cut into chunks
- 1 Anaheim pepper, cut into chunks
- 1/2 zucchini, cut into chunks
- 3 cloves garlic
- 1/4 cup olive oil
- 1 pound lamb stew meat, cut into 1-inch cubes
- 3/4 pound ground beef
- 2 teaspoons salt
- 2 cubes vegetable bouillon, or more to taste
- 2 teaspoons ground cumin
- 1 teaspoon ground black pepper

- 1 teaspoon paprika
- 1/2 teaspoon ground coriander
- 1/4 teaspoon ground turmeric
- 1/4 teaspoon cayenne pepper
- 2 1/2 quarts water
- 1 (6 ounce) can tomato paste
- 1/2 cup finely ground freekeh
- 2 cups green peas
- 2 tablespoons butter
- 1 bunch cilantro, coarsely chopped
- 1 lemon, cut into wedges, or more to taste

Direction

- In a blender, process together garlic, zucchini, Anaheim pepper, serrano pepper, onions and tomatoes until vegetables are pureed totally.
- In a big pot, heat olive oil on moderate heat. Cook beef and lamb on hot oil together with a pinch of salt while stirring sometimes, for 25 minutes, until all sides of lamb is browned and cooked through.
- Stir into lamb mixture with cayenne pepper, turmeric, coriander, paprika, black pepper, cumin, vegetable bouillon and vegetable puree. Bring mixture to a simmer and lower heat to moderately low. Cook and stir sometimes for 35 minutes, until flavors start to combine.
- Pour into lamb mixture with water and tomato paste, then bring to a simmer. Lower heat to moderately low and cook for 1 1/2 hours, until lamb begins to tenderize. Put in freekeh and simmer for a half hour, until freekeh is blended into soup.
- Stir into soup with butter and peas. Take pot away from the heat and stir into soup with cilantro. Scoop into bowls with soup and squeeze lemon juice into bowls.

Nutrition Information

- Calories: 375 calories;
- Total Fat: 22.5
- Sodium: 835
- Total Carbohydrate: 24.3

- Cholesterol: 62
- Protein: 20.9

984.　　The Very Best Burgers!

Serving: 10 | Prep: 15mins | Cook: 10mins | Ready in:

Ingredients

- 3 pounds lean ground beef
- 1/2 medium potato, shredded
- 1 tablespoon minced garlic
- 12 ounces crumbled blue cheese
- 2 teaspoons seasoned salt, or to taste
- freshly ground black pepper to taste
- 1/2 medium onion, chopped
- 1/4 cup Worcestershire sauce
- 2 eggs, beaten
- 1/2 cup dry bread crumbs

Direction

- Preheat the grill for high heat. Once hot, grease the grate lightly with oil.
- Combine the bread crumbs, eggs, Worcestershire sauce, onion, pepper, seasoned salt, blue cheese, garlic, potato and ground beef in a big bowl. Shape into 10 balls, and pat into patties.
- Allow to grill till well done, about 5 minutes each side. Serve on buns with your desire condiments.

Nutrition Information

- Calories: 437 calories;
- Sodium: 863
- Total Carbohydrate: 9
- Cholesterol: 158
- Protein: 36.1
- Total Fat: 27.7

985.   Thirty Minute Meal

Serving: 6 | Prep: 10mins | Cook: 20mins | Ready in:

Ingredients

- 1 pound ground beef
- 1 onion, chopped
- 1 medium head cabbage, shredded
- 1 (10.75 ounce) can condensed tomato soup
- 1 3/4 cups water
- salt and pepper to taste

Direction

- On medium high heat, mix onion and ground beef together in a big pot. Sauté until the onion is tender and the beef is brown, about 10 minutes.
- Pour the water, soup and cabbage in. Add pepper and salt to taste. Stir well until mixed together. Adjust the heat to low and cover. Let it simmer until the cabbage reaches desired tenderness, about 20 minutes.

Nutrition Information

- Calories: 314 calories;
- Total Fat: 21
- Sodium: 361
- Total Carbohydrate: 17.2
- Cholesterol: 64
- Protein: 15.5

986.   Three Animal Italian Meatballs

Serving: 8 | Prep: 30mins | Cook: 30mins | Ready in:

Ingredients

- 1 pound ground beef
- 1 pound ground turkey
- 1 pound ground Italian sausage
- 1 large onion, diced

- 2 eggs
- 1/2 cup Italian-style seasoned bread crumbs
- 1/2 cup quick cooking oats
- 2 tablespoons Italian-style seasoning
- 1 cup vegetable oil, or as needed

Direction

- Set oven to 175° C (350° F) and start preheating.
- In a big bowl, mix together seasoning, oats, bread crumbs, eggs, onion, and ground meat. Form into 2-in. balls in diameter.
- In a big sauté pan, heat sufficient vegetable oil to be 1/2-in. deep. In the hot oil, brown meatballs for approximately 5 minutes. Remove to a glass baking dish.
- Put into the preheated oven and bake 25 minutes.

Nutrition Information

- Calories: 635 calories;
- Sodium: 663
- Total Carbohydrate: 12.8
- Cholesterol: 145
- Protein: 31.8
- Total Fat: 50.9

987.   Three Meat Loaf

Serving: 16 | Prep: 20mins | Cook: 1hours | Ready in:

Ingredients

- Sauce:
- 1/4 cup tomato sauce
- 2 tablespoons Worcestershire sauce
- 1 tablespoon spicy mustard
- 1 tablespoon honey
- Meat loaves:
- 1/2 pound ground beef
- 1/2 pound ground turkey
- 1/2 pound ground lamb

- 2 1/4 cups tomato sauce
- 1 1/2 cups rolled oats
- 1 egg
- 1/2 sweet onion, chopped
- 1 teaspoon salt
- 1/2 teaspoon ground black pepper

Direction

- Set oven to 350°F (175°C) to preheat.
- In a bowl, mix together honey, spicy mustard, Worcestershire sauce and 1/4 cup of tomato sauce; put aside.
- In a large bowl, thoroughly mix ground lamb, ground turkey, ground beef, salt, pepper, sweet onion, egg, oats and 2 1/4 cup of tomato sauce; separate into halves and shape 2 loaves. Place loaves into loaf pans.
- Bake for 45 minutes in the prepared oven, top with sauce using a brush, and keep baking for about 15 minutes more until no pink remains in the center. An instant-read thermometer should show at least 160°F (70°C) when inserted into the center. Allow to cool lightly in pans before serving.

Nutrition Information

- Calories: 125 calories;
- Total Carbohydrate: 9.2
- Cholesterol: 40
- Protein: 9.6
- Total Fat: 5.6
- Sodium: 408

988.   Traditional Gyros

Serving: 12 | Prep: 15mins | Cook: 45mins | Ready in:

Ingredients

- 1 small onion, cut into chunks
- 1 pound ground lamb
- 1 pound ground beef
- 1 tablespoon minced garlic
- 1 teaspoon dried oregano
- 1 teaspoon ground cumin
- 1 teaspoon dried marjoram
- 1 teaspoon dried thyme
- 1 teaspoon dried rosemary
- 1 teaspoon freshly ground black pepper
- 1/4 teaspoon sea salt
- boiling water as needed
- 12 tablespoons hummus
- 12 pita bread rounds
- 1 small head lettuce, shredded
- 1 large tomato, sliced
- 1 large red onion, sliced
- 6 ounces crumbled feta cheese
- 24 tablespoons tzatziki sauce

Direction

- In food processor, put onion; blend until chopped finely. Place onion onto a piece of cheese cloth; then squeeze liquid out. Put onion into a large bowl.
- Using hands, mix onion with salt, black pepper, rosemary, thyme, marjoram, cumin, oregano, garlic, beef and lamb until mixed well. Wrap the bowl in plastic wrap. Place in the refrigerator for 120 minutes until the flavors blend.
- Start preheating the oven to 325°F (165°C).
- In food processor, put meat mixture; pulse for one minute, until they are tacky and chopped finely. Pack the meat mixture into a loaf pan (about 7x4 inches), making sure there have no air pockets. Position loaf pan into the roasting pan. Pour around loaf pan with enough of boiling water to reach halfway up sides.
- Bake in prepared oven for 45-60 minutes until middle is no longer pink. The instant-read thermometer should register at least 165°F (74°C) when inserted into middle. Pour off all the accumulated fat. Let cool slightly.
- Slice gyro meat mixture thinly.
- Spread on every pita bread with one tablespoon of the hummus; add tzatziki sauce, feta cheese, red onion, tomato, lettuce and gyro meat mixture over top of each.

Nutrition Information

- Calories: 425 calories;
- Total Carbohydrate: 42.8
- Cholesterol: 61
- Protein: 22.4
- Total Fat: 40.8
- Sodium: 620

---

989. Triple Bypasses

Serving: 6 | Prep: 25mins | Cook: 10mins | Ready in:

Ingredients

- 1 1/2 pounds ground beef
- 1 egg, beaten
- 1/2 cup chopped onion
- salt and pepper to taste
- 1 tablespoon red pepper flakes, or to taste
- 6 hot dogs
- 1 pound sliced bacon
- toothpicks
- 2 cups barbecue sauce, your choice
- 6 hoagie rolls, split lengthwise

Direction

- Preheat outdoor grill to medium heat; put barbeque sauce in square baking dish. Put aside.
- Use your hands to mix red pepper flakes, pepper, salt, onion, egg and ground beef in medium bowl; pack enough meat around every hot dog to cover it completely, but not too thick. Around each beef covered hot dog, wrap bacon slices; use toothpicks to secure.
- Oil the grilling surface lightly; put bacon-wrapped hamburger covered hot dogs on grill. Cook, occasionally but carefully turning, for 10 minutes till bacon is browned nicely and beef is cooked through. Remove from grill; roll to

coat in dish with barbeque sauce. Remove toothpicks; serve over hoagie rolls.

Nutrition Information

- Calories: 998 calories;
- Sodium: 2792
- Total Carbohydrate: 101.1
- Cholesterol: 149
- Protein: 44.2
- Total Fat: 44.8

---

990. Turkish Rissoles

Serving: 6 | Prep: 30mins | Cook: 10mins | Ready in:

Ingredients

- 1 pound ground lamb
- 1 pound ground beef
- 1 teaspoon salt
- 1 teaspoon ground black pepper
- 1 tablespoon ground cumin
- 2 teaspoons ground sweet paprika
- 3 tablespoons tomato paste
- 2 onions, peeled and cut into chunks
- 4 cloves garlic, peeled
- 1 tablespoon olive oil
- 1/4 bunch fresh parsley, chopped
- 3 tablespoons all-purpose flour
- 2 small eggs

Direction

- In a large bowl, place cumin, paprika, salt, pepper, tomato paste, lamb and beef (Do not mix, put aside only).
- Blend onions and garlic then slowly add in olive oil until paste-like mixture. Add in chopped parsley and then blend for 5 seconds. Transfer the blended mixture to the meat. Add flour and eggs then gently knead with clean hands. Let it stand for 5 minutes to develop

flavor and lightly knead again to well combine all the ingredients.

- Shape the meat mixture into small balls and press gently between palms to flatten and form patty. Take a small handful of the meat each time. Put on a big plate. Repeat to all remaining meat mixture. Separate patty layers and cover it using plastic wrap then chill on the fridge for at least an hour.
- Preheat broiler and put rack 3 inches away from source of heat. Position rissoles 1/2 inch apart on lined pan with aluminum foil. Broil the rissoles until it changed to golden brown and do the same for the other side.

Nutrition Information

- Calories: 381 calories;
- Total Fat: 25.1
- Sodium: 548
- Total Carbohydrate: 9.9
- Cholesterol: 142
- Protein: 28.2

991. Unstuffed Cabbage Dinner

Serving: 4 | Prep: 30mins | Cook: 30mins | Ready in:

Ingredients

- 1 pound ground beef
- 3/4 teaspoon garlic powder
- 1 teaspoon ground black pepper
- 1 (14.5 ounce) can low-sodium beef broth
- 1 (1 ounce) envelope dry onion soup mix
- 1/2 small onion, chopped
- 1 cup instant white rice
- 2 cups coarsely shredded green cabbage
- 1 1/2 cups tomato-vegetable juice cocktail

Direction

- In a skillet over medium-high heat, crumble the ground beef. Put in the onion, then flavor with garlic powder and pepper; cook and stir till the beef becomes evenly browned. Strain off the excess grease.
- In the skillet, pour the onion soup mix and beef broth along with the beef, stir to combine. Set to a boil, then add the vegetable juice cocktail, cabbage and rice. Mix together, simmer while covering for 30 minutes over low heat, or till the rice becomes softened and the liquid is absorbed.

Nutrition Information

- Calories: 361 calories;
- Total Carbohydrate: 32.6
- Cholesterol: 69
- Protein: 24.7
- Total Fat: 14.4
- Sodium: 970

992. Unstuffed Cabbage Roll

Serving: 6 | Prep: 20mins | Cook: 35mins | Ready in:

Ingredients

- 2 pounds ground beef
- 1 large onion, chopped
- 1 small head cabbage, chopped
- 2 (14.5 ounce) cans diced tomatoes
- 1 (8 ounce) can tomato sauce
- 1/2 cup water
- 2 cloves garlic, minced
- 2 teaspoons salt
- 1 teaspoon ground black pepper

Direction

- Heat a big skillet or Dutch oven on moderately high heat. Cook and stir together in the hot Dutch oven with onion and beef for 5-7 minutes, until beef is crumbly and browned.

Drain and get rid of grease. Put in pepper, salt, garlic, water, tomato sauce, tomatoes and cabbage, then bring mixture to a boil. Place a cover on the Dutch oven and lower heat; simmer for half an hour, until cabbage is softened.

Nutrition Information

- Calories: 398 calories;
- Protein: 28.5
- Total Fat: 23.8
- Sodium: 1294
- Total Carbohydrate: 16.3
- Cholesterol: 93

---

993. Vegetable Beef Minestrone

Serving: 6 | Prep: 15mins | Cook: 1hours | Ready in:

Ingredients

- 2 slices bacon, chopped
- 1/2 pound lean ground beef
- 2 carrots, chopped
- 2 cloves garlic, minced
- 1 large onion, chopped
- 1 stalk celery, chopped
- 1 bay leaf
- 1 teaspoon dried basil
- 1 teaspoon dried rosemary, crushed
- 1/4 teaspoon crushed red pepper flakes
- 1 (14.5 ounce) can stewed tomatoes
- 1 (10.5 ounce) can beef broth
- 1 (15 ounce) can chickpeas (garbanzo beans), drained
- 2 ounces spaghetti, broken into pieces

Direction

- Cook ground beef and bacon in a big saucepan until well done; breaking up beef when cooking. Drain to remove grease; add celery,

onion, garlic, and carrots. Season with red pepper flakes, rosemary, basil, and bay leaf. Cook until onions become translucent, about 5 minutes. Mix in beef stock and tomatoes.
- Allow to simmer for 20 minutes; add broken spaghetti and chickpeas. Cook with cover till spaghetti is al dente, about 10 minutes. Take out bay leaf then serve.

Nutrition Information

- Calories: 273 calories;
- Sodium: 570
- Total Carbohydrate: 26.3
- Cholesterol: 35
- Protein: 13
- Total Fat: 13.1

---

994. Vegetarian Meatloaf With Vegetables

Serving: 9 | Prep: 20mins | Cook: 1hours30mins | Ready in:

Ingredients

- 1/2 (14 ounce) package vegetarian ground beef (e.g., Gimme Lean TM)
- 1 (12 ounce) package vegetarian burger crumbles
- 1 onion, chopped
- 2 eggs, beaten
- 2 tablespoons vegetarian Worcestershire sauce
- 1 teaspoon salt
- 1/3 teaspoon pepper
- 1 teaspoon ground sage
- 1/2 teaspoon garlic powder
- 2 teaspoons prepared mustard
- 1 tablespoon vegetable oil
- 3 1/2 slices bread, cubed
- 1/3 cup milk
- 1 (8 ounce) can tomato sauce
- 4 carrots, cut into 1 inch pieces
- 4 potatoes, cubed

- 1 cooking spray

Direction

- Preheat oven to 350° F (175° C).
- In a big bowl, combine milk, bread cubes, oil, mustard, sage, pepper, salt, Worcestershire sauce, garlic powder, eggs, onion, vegetarian ground beef crumbles and vegetarian ground beef. Move into a 9x13-inch baking dish and shape into a loaf. Spread tomato sauce on top.
- Set potatoes and carrots around loaf, then use cooking spray to spray vegetables.
- Bake for 30 - 45 minutes; toss the vegetables. Bake for another 30 - 45 minutes. Allow to stand for 15 minutes before slicing.

Nutrition Information

- Calories: 225 calories;
- Sodium: 814
- Total Carbohydrate: 30.6
- Cholesterol: 42
- Protein: 15.1
- Total Fat: 4.9

---

995. Venus De Milo Soup

Serving: 8 | Prep: 15mins | Cook: 20mins | Ready in:

Ingredients

- 1 pound ground beef
- 1 small onion, minced
- 1 teaspoon minced garlic
- 1/2 (6 ounce) can tomato paste
- 1 (28 ounce) can crushed tomatoes
- 1 envelope onion soup mix
- 2 beef bouillon cubes
- 1 bay leaf
- 1 (16 ounce) package frozen mixed vegetables
- 2 quarts water
- 2/3 cup orzo pasta
- salt and ground black pepper to taste

Direction

- Over medium heat, cook ground beef in a large pot for about 7 to 10 minutes until browned completely. Then drain as much grease from the beef as you can. Add garlic and onion to beef. Cook while stirring for about 5 minutes until onion becomes softened.
- Add beef bouillon cubes, tomato paste, onion soup mix, water, bay leaf, crushed tomatoes and mixed vegetables to ground beef mixture. Increase the heat to medium-high and then heat the mixture to boil. Mix orzo pasta into the boiling liquid and let it cook for about ten minutes until orzo becomes tender. Add black pepper and salt to taste and serve.

Nutrition Information

- Calories: 254 calories;
- Total Fat: 7.8
- Sodium: 805
- Total Carbohydrate: 32.5
- Cholesterol: 36
- Protein: 16.3

---

996. Waikiki Style Meatballs

Serving: 6 | Prep: 15mins | Cook: 3hours30mins | Ready in:

Ingredients

- 1 1/2 pounds ground beef
- 2/3 cup plain breadcrumbs
- 1/3 cup minced onion
- 1/4 cup milk
- 1 egg
- 1 1/2 teaspoons salt
- 2 tablespoons cornstarch
- 1/2 cup brown sugar
- 1 (15 ounce) can pineapple chunks, juice reserved
- 1/3 cup vinegar

- 1/3 cup chopped green bell pepper

Direction

- Turn the oven to 350°F (175°C) to preheat.
- In a bowl, well combine together salt, egg, milk, onion, bread crumbs, and ground beef. Form the mixture into balls and place onto a cookie sheet.
- In the preheated oven, bake for 25 minutes, or until the bottoms of the meatballs turn brown. Remove to a slow cooker.
- In the bottom of a saucepan, mix together brown sugar and cornstarch and heat on low heat. Add vinegar and the reserved pineapple juice; whisk until smooth. Boil the mixture for exactly 1 minute, and then take away from heat. In the slow cooker, pour the mixture over the meatballs.
- Add green bell pepper and pineapple chunks to the slow cooker.
- In the slow cooker, cook the mixture on Low for 3-4 hours, or until the flavors are fully blended.

Nutrition Information

- Calories: 393 calories;
- Total Fat: 15.1
- Sodium: 757
- Total Carbohydrate: 41.8
- Cholesterol: 101
- Protein: 22.5

997.   Wedding Gift Spaghetti Sauce

Serving: 30 | Prep: 10mins | Cook: 2hours30mins | Ready in:

Ingredients

- 1/2 cup butter
- 3 tablespoons olive oil

- 1 large onion, chopped
- 3 cloves garlic, chopped
- 1 pound ground beef
- 1 pound mild sausage
- 4 teaspoons Italian seasoning
- 2 teaspoons salt (optional)
- 2 teaspoons dried rosemary
- 1 1/2 teaspoons dried oregano
- 1/2 teaspoon ground black pepper
- 76 fluid ounces water
- 1 (29 ounce) can tomato puree
- 3 (6 ounce) cans tomato paste

Direction

- In a big pot, heat olive oil and butter along with garlic and onion over a medium heat. Cook and stir in the sausage and ground beef for 10-15 minutes until crumbly and brown. Stir in black pepper, oregano, rosemary, salt, and Italian seasoning, and then simmer the mixture for 20 minutes.
- Pour in the tomato paste, tomato puree, and water. Simmer, occasionally stirring, over low heat for a minimum of 2 hours until flavors combine.

Nutrition Information

- Calories: 137 calories;
- Cholesterol: 26
- Protein: 5.9
- Total Fat: 10.2
- Sodium: 564
- Total Carbohydrate: 6.5

998.   Wedding Soup

Serving: 24 | Prep: 20mins | Cook: 2hours | Ready in:

Ingredients

- 1 (4 pound) whole chicken
- 1 large onion

- 6 stalks celery with leaves, chopped
- 9 carrots, sliced
- 1 sweet potato, cubed
- 1/2 medium head cabbage, coarsely chopped
- 2 (14.5 ounce) cans chicken broth
- 2 (6 ounce) cans roasted garlic tomato paste
- 1 1/2 pounds lean ground beef
- 2 eggs
- 1/2 cup dry bread crumbs
- 1/2 cup grated Romano cheese
- 1 (16 ounce) package acini di pepe pasta
- 1 cup grated Parmesan cheese for topping

Direction

- Arrange cans of broth, whole onion, and the chicken in a large stockpot. Cover the chicken with enough water. Allow to boil and cook until the chicken falls off the bones.
- Take the chicken out of the pot and separate the meat from the bones. Make the chicken into bite-sized pieces by tearing and bring them back to the soup pot. Take the onion out from the broth, chop and bring it back to the pot. Put in the cabbage, sweet potato, carrots, and celery. Add in the tomato paste and stir.
- Add the Romano cheese, breadcrumbs, eggs, and ground beef in a medium bowl. Use your hands to mix thoroughly then shape into walnut-sized balls. Put the balls into the soup. Keep on cooking the soup until the vegetables become tender for 1 more hour.
- Allow to boil a large pot of lightly salted water. Add in the pasta and cook until firm to the bite, 8-10 minutes; let drain. Pour the soup over pasta to serve and put a generous pinch of grated Parmesan cheese on top of each bowl.

Nutrition Information

- Calories: 297 calories;
- Sodium: 311
- Total Carbohydrate: 23.5
- Cholesterol: 71
- Protein: 21.5

- Total Fat: 12.4

999. Wild Rice Meatballs In Mushroom Sauce

Serving: 6 | Prep: 10mins | Cook: 45mins | Ready in:

Ingredients

- 1 1/2 pounds ground beef
- 1 small onion, finely chopped
- 1/2 cup cooked wild rice
- 1/2 teaspoon seasoned salt
- 1/2 teaspoon garlic salt
- 1/3 cup bread crumbs
- 1/2 cup evaporated milk
- Sauce:
- 1 tablespoon butter
- 8 ounces sliced fresh mushrooms
- 1/2 teaspoon salt
- 2/3 cup dry white wine
- 2/3 cup water
- 1 (10.75 ounce) can low-sodium cream of mushroom soup
- 1/4 teaspoon dried sage
- 1 (9.74 ounce) package Idahoan Signature™ Russets Mashed Potatoes

Direction

- Prepare the oven by preheating to 375°F (190°C).
- Mix evaporated milk, bread crumbs, garlic salt, seasoned salt, rice, onion, and beef. Form into 1-inch meatballs. Transfer meatballs into a rimmed baking sheet.
- Place in the preheated oven and bake for approximately 15 minutes until brown.
- In a skillet set on medium heat, dissolve butter. Put in mushrooms and dust with salt; stir-fry for approximately 10 minutes until mushrooms give out their moisture and soften. Add the sage, salt, soup, water, and wine into the saucepan; whisk to mix.

- Place meatballs to the sauce and simmer for 30 minutes until cooked well and hot.
- Ready Idahoan Signature Russets Mashed Potatoes based on the package directions. Pair with meatballs and the mushroom sauce to serve.

Nutrition Information

- Calories: 353 calories;
- Total Carbohydrate: 16.6
- Cholesterol: 84
- Protein: 24.1
- Total Fat: 18.5
- Sodium: 764

1000.   World's Best Lasagna

Serving: 12 | Prep: 30mins | Cook: 2hours30mins | Ready in:

Ingredients

- 1 pound sweet Italian sausage
- 3/4 pound lean ground beef
- 1/2 cup minced onion
- 2 cloves garlic, crushed
- 1 (28 ounce) can crushed tomatoes
- 2 (6 ounce) cans tomato paste
- 2 (6.5 ounce) cans canned tomato sauce
- 1/2 cup water
- 2 tablespoons white sugar
- 1 1/2 teaspoons dried basil leaves
- 1/2 teaspoon fennel seeds
- 1 teaspoon Italian seasoning
- 1 tablespoon salt
- 1/4 teaspoon ground black pepper
- 4 tablespoons chopped fresh parsley
- 12 lasagna noodles
- 16 ounces ricotta cheese
- 1 egg
- 1/2 teaspoon salt
- 3/4 pound mozzarella cheese, sliced
- 3/4 cup grated Parmesan cheese

Direction

- Put onion, garlic, ground beef and sausage in a Dutch oven and cook over medium heat until brown in color. Add in water, tomato paste, tomato sauce and crushed tomatoes then mix well. Mix in basil, sugar, 1 tablespoon of salt, pepper, 2 tablespoons of parsley, Italian seasoning and fennel seeds. Cover the Dutch oven and let it simmer for 1 1/2 hours occasionally stirring.
- Let a big pot of water with a little bit of salt boil. Put the lasagna noodles in the boiling water and cook for 8-10 minutes. Drain the lasagna noodles and with cold water rinse in cold water. Mix ricotta cheese, 1/2 teaspoon of salt, the remaining parsley and egg together in a mixing bowl.
- Preheat the oven at 375°F (190°C).
- In a 9x13-inch pan, put 1 1/2 cups meat sauce evenly on bottom. Lengthwise lay 6 lasagna noodles on top of the meat sauce. Put 1/2 of the ricotta cheese mixture evenly on top of the noodles. Put on 1/3 of the mozzarella cheese slices. Put 1 1/2 cups of meat sauce on top of the mozzarella slices; then sprinkle on 1/4 cup of Parmesan cheese. Do the whole layering process again finishing with left mozzarella and Parmesan. Use a greased aluminum foil to cover the baking dish to keep it from sticking in the cheese, you may also use an ungreased foil but make sure it won't touch the cheese on top.
- Put in the heated oven and bake 25 minutes. Remove the foil cover and bake for another 25 minutes. Let it cool down for 15 minutes then serve while still warm.

Nutrition Information

- Calories: 448 calories;
- Total Carbohydrate: 36.5
- Cholesterol: 82
- Protein: 29.7
- Total Fat: 21.3
- Sodium: 1788

1001.   Zucchini Stew

Serving: 10 | Prep: 10mins | Cook: 35mins | Ready in:

Ingredients

- 2 zucchini, diced
- 1 onion, chopped
- 2 (14.5 ounce) cans peeled and diced tomatoes
- 2 cups uncooked white rice
- 3 pounds ground beef
- salt and pepper to taste

Direction

- Combine onion, and zucchini in a large pot. Pour 3 inches of water to cover vegetables. Bring everything to a boil over medium heat. Mix in rice and tomatoes; lower heat and simmer.
- Cook beef in a large skillet over medium heat until browned. Mix into the soup, add more water if needed. Add pepper and salt to taste, and simmer until rice is tender, for 20 more minutes.

Nutrition Information

- Calories: 442 calories;
- Sodium: 206
- Total Carbohydrate: 36.6
- Cholesterol: 82
- Protein: 27.8
- Total Fat: 19

Index

Yam 11,420

Z

Zest 3,7,33,250

L

lasagna
52,117,118,119,120,121,123,124,125,126,127,128,129,130,
131,132,133,135,136,137,138,140,141,142,143,144,145,14
6,147,148,149,150,151,152,153,155,156,157,158,159,160,1
61,162,163,164,165,166,167,168,170,172,173,174,175,313,
365,369,379,383,384,399,400,418,436,440,441,442,443,45
5,502,503,507,556

Conclusion

Thank you again for downloading this book!

I hope you enjoyed reading about my book!

If you enjoyed this book, please take the time to share your thoughts and post a review on Amazon. It'd be greatly appreciated!

Write me an honest review about the book – I truly value your opinion and thoughts and I will incorporate them into my next book, which is already underway.

Thank you!

If you have any questions, **feel free to contact at:** *author@persimmonrecipes.com*

Susan Morris

persimmonrecipes.com

CPSIA information can be obtained
at www.ICGtesting.com
Printed in the USA
LVHW050143140423
744367LV00012B/356